Kenya

Joseph Bindloss
Tom Parkinson
Matt Fletcher

D0262860

LONELY PLANET PUBLICATIONS
Melbourne • Oakland • London • Paris

KENYA

LAKE TURKANA
Impossibly vast soda
lake in the
semidesert north

KAKAMEGA FOREST
RESERVE
Beautiful but
shrinking rainforest
with wonderful birdlife

LAKE NAKURU
An old favourite, back in
favour since the return
of the flamingos

MT KENYA
Trekkers' paradise and
Kikuyu sacred land

MERU NATIONAL PARK
The next Masai Mara?
Watch this space

KENYA

LAMU
An ancient Swahili city-state with a centuries old way of life

GEDE
Fascinating ruins of a 17th-century Arab-Swahili town

FORT JESUS
An imposing 16th-century Portuguese fort, focal point of the battle for the East African coast

TIWI BEACH
A dazzling white beach and the most relaxed and low-key resort area in Kenya

KISITE-MPUNGUTI MARINE NATIONAL PARK
Fantastic snorkelling, diving and dhow tours around this pristine coral reef

TSAVO NATIONAL PARK
Kenya's largest national park, famous for its rhinos and elephants

MASAI MARA NATIONAL RESERVE
Providing the classic image of African Savanna Country

ELEVATION
3000m
2000m
1000m
500m
250m
0

Kenya
5th edition – April 2003
First published – February 1991

Published by
Lonely Planet Publications Pty Ltd ABN 36 005 607 983
90 Maribyrnong St, Footscray, Victoria 3011, Australia

Lonely Planet Offices
Australia Locked Bag 1, Footscray, Victoria 3011
USA 150 Linden St, Oakland, CA 94607
UK 10a Spring Place, London NW5 3BH
France 1 rue du Dahomey, 75011 Paris

Photographs
Many of the images in this guide are available for licensing from
Lonely Planet Images.
w www.lonelyplanetimages.com

Front cover photograph
Masai giraffes and sunset, Kenya, Africa (Jeff Hunter, The Image Bank)

ISBN 1 86450 303 3

text & maps © Lonely Planet Publications Pty Ltd 2003
photos © photographers as indicated 2003

Printed by SNP SPrint (M) Sdn Bhd
Printed in Malaysia

Contents – Text

WESTERN KENYA
278

NORTHERN KENYA
309

LANGUAGE
333

GLOSSARY
337

THANKS
339

INDEX
347

MAP LEGEND
back page

METRIC CONVERSION
inside back cover

Contents – Maps

MAP INDEX

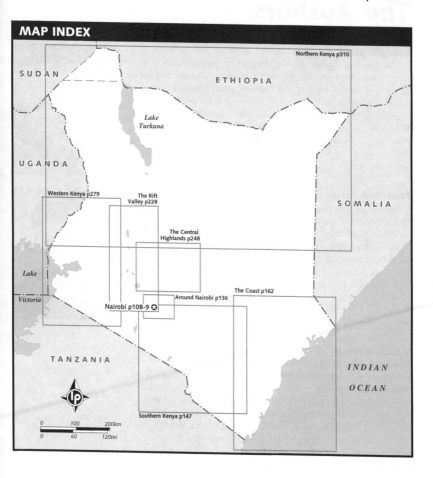

SUDAN

ETHIOPIA

Northern Kenya p310

Lake
Turkana

UGANDA

SOMALIA

Western Kenya p279

The Rift
Valley p228

The Central
Highlands p248

Lake

Victoria

Nairobi p108-9

Around Nairobi p136

The Coast p162

TANZANIA

INDIAN

OCEAN

Southern Kenya p147

0   100   200km
0   60   120mi

The Authors

Joseph Bindloss

Joe was born in Cyprus, grew up in England and has since lived and worked in the US, Australia and several other places, though he still calls London home. He first developed an incurable case of wanderlust on family trips through Europe in the old VW Kombi. After a degree in Biology eliminated science from his future choice of careers, Joe moved through a string of occupations, including mural painting and sculpting, before finally settling on journalism. Joe has previously written for LP in *India, Mauritius, Réunion & Seychelles*, the *Philippines, Australia* and *Britain*.

Tom Parkinson

A modern languages graduate, Tom drifted into freelancing as a logical continuation of the student lifestyle. His previous travel experiences have taken him round Europe from Amsterdam to Zagreb, including a year in Berlin, as well as luring him further afield to Tanzania and Bali; professionally, he has contributed to the Music section of LP *Britain* and updated Morocco for the *Mediterranean Europe* guide. He now also holds an unofficial record for driving in the wrong direction (an impressive 220km). As well as paying the rent, Kenya left him with a slight tan, a new sense of perspective, and a lingering distrust of salad.

Matt Fletcher

As a child Matt spent his holidays in small, rain-soaked English beach resorts, usually in the off season. A teenage, shoestring tour of Europe cemented an incurable wanderlust, but it was trips to Kenya and Mozambique that inspired a career in travel writing. Matt has contributed to Lonely Planet's *Walking in Spain, Walking in Australia, Morocco, Kenya, East Africa, West Africa* and *Tonga* guides, and has yet to be found out. For Lonely Planet's *Unpacked* and *Unpacked Again* he got stranded in a Madagascan swamp and had a dingo steal his breakfast.

FROM THE AUTHORS
Joseph Bindloss

Firstly my thanks to the staff of the many KWS offices and national parks throughout Kenya for their valuable assistance. Thanks also to the many travellers who wrote in or passed on useful tips while I was on the road. In Tsavo East National Park, many thanks to Trevor Jennings at Tarhi Fly Camp for helping out after my 4WD incident, and also to Veronicah at Budget Car Hire for all her help in Nairobi. Credit is also due to the many Kenyans who passed on their wisdoms about the political scene in the run up to the elections.

Tom Parkinson

Asante sana rafiki to Sammy Kamau, driver and unofficial co-worker (three vehicles, 8000km and 22 punctures in five weeks!). Thanks to: Kenneth at Treetops, Charles and Absalom at ACC, KWS Mweiga, Patrick at Elsamere, Tom Albright at USGS and Tom Moorhouse at Clean Lakes for their assistance; Josphat and Peter for Mt Kenya; Abdulla Ismaily, the Barnleys, John Perret, Guy Grant, Chris Field, and especially Pop and Grev Gunson for unwarranted hospitality; and David Else for colleaguely advice. Shout-outs to everyone I met and interrogated: Heather, Cameron and Michael; Emma, Georgie and Kim; Emma and Charlotte; Pencoed World Challenge Team; Cambridge/UEA OTC camel racers (cheers Dave for Suswa info); and K Nina Kupenda, just because.

This Book

Hugh Findlay and Geoff Crowther researched and wrote the first three editions of *Kenya* and the fourth edition was updated by Matt Fletcher. For this edition, Joseph Bindloss revised the introductory chapters as well as the Nairobi, Around Nairobi, Southern Kenya and The Coast chapters, while Tom Parkinson revised the Rift Valley, Central Highlands, Western Kenya and Northern Kenya chapters. The Wildlife Guide was prepared by Sean Pywell.

From the Publisher

This fifth edition of *Kenya* was produced in Lonely Planet's Melbourne office under the project management of Ray Thomson. Hilary Rogers commissioned the title. Evan Jones coordinated the editing with assistance from Tom Smallman, Nancy Ianni, Nina Rousseau, Melanie Dankel, Darren O'Connell and Nick Tapp. Mandy Sierp coordinated the mapping with assistance from Katie Cason, Daniel Fennessy, Corinne Waddell and Chris Thomas. Hunor Csutoros prepared the climate charts, while the images were supplied by Lonely Planet Images. Nick Stebbing and David Burnett provided timely technical advice. Quentin Frayne compiled the Language chapter, while the cover was designed by Maria Vallianos. Pablo Gastar and Sonya Brooke laid the book out, and Birgit Jordan and Sonya Brooke designed the colour pages. Kate McDonald and Adriana Mammarella checked the laid-out pages and Shahara Ahmed checked the mapping.

Foreword

ABOUT LONELY PLANET GUIDEBOOKS

The story begins with a classic travel adventure: Tony and Maureen Wheeler's 1972 journey across Europe and Asia to Australia. There was no useful information about the overland trail then, so Tony and Maureen published the first Lonely Planet guidebook to meet a growing need.

From a kitchen table, Lonely Planet has grown to become the largest independent travel publisher in the world, with offices in Melbourne (Australia), Oakland (USA), London (UK) and Paris (France).

Today Lonely Planet guidebooks cover the globe. There is an ever-growing list of books and information in a variety of media. Some things haven't changed. The main aim is still to make it possible for adventurous travellers to get out there – to explore and better understand the world.

At Lonely Planet we believe travellers can make a positive contribution to the countries they visit – if they respect their host communities and spend their money wisely. Since 1986 a percentage of the income from each book has been donated to aid projects and human rights campaigns, and, more recently, to wildlife conservation.

Although inclusion in a guidebook usually implies a recommendation we cannot list every good place. Exclusion does not necessarily imply criticism. In fact there are a number of reasons why we might exclude a place – sometimes it is simply inappropriate to encourage an influx of travellers.

UPDATES & READER FEEDBACK

Things change – prices go up, schedules change, good places go bad and bad places go bankrupt. Nothing stays the same. So, if you find things better or worse, recently opened or long-since closed, please tell us and help make the next edition even more accurate and useful.

Lonely Planet thoroughly updates each guidebook as often as possible – usually every two years, although for some destinations the gap can be longer. Between editions, up-to-date information is available in our free, monthly email bulletin *Comet* (W www.lonelyplanet.com/newsletters). You can also check out the *Thorn Tree* bulletin board and *Postcards* section of our website, which carry unverified, but fascinating, reports from travellers.

Tell us about it! We genuinely value your feedback. A well-travelled team at Lonely Planet reads and acknowledges every email and letter we receive and ensures that every morsel of information finds its way to the relevant authors, editors and cartographers.

Everyone who writes to us will find their name listed in the next edition of the appropriate guidebook. The very best contributions will be rewarded with a free guidebook.

We may edit, reproduce and incorporate your comments in Lonely Planet products such as guidebooks, websites and digital products, so let us know if you don't want your comments reproduced or your name acknowledged.

How to contact Lonely Planet:
Online: e talk2us@lonelyplanet.com.au, W www.lonelyplanet.com
Australia: Locked Bag 1, Footscray, Victoria 3011
UK: 10a Spring Place, London NW5 3BH
USA: 150 Linden St, Oakland, CA 94607

Introduction

If you've ever fantasised about Africa – sleeping in the bush surrounded by wildlife beneath the broad African sky or walking with tribespeople through the cradle of humanity – then Kenya is for you. Kenya's incredible natural environment and cultural heritage is almost unmatched in Africa, and travel is easy and inexpensive.

For many people Kenya means wildlife, and there are some incredible natural phenomena to look out for. Every July and October, up to a million wildebeest and zebra pass through southern Kenya on their annual migration, attracting an entourage of cheetahs, lions and other predators. For sheer majesty it's hard to beat the sight of wild elephants in front of Africa's most famous mountain, Kilimanjaro, while bird-watchers flock to the spectacle of millions of pink flamingos fringing the Rift Valley soda lakes. Kenya is a fantastic place to take a safari, and with the incredible variety of national parks and reserves and plenty of competition between operators, it needn't cost the earth. It's also possible to visit some reserves on foot with native guides, providing a far more intimate experience than driving through the parks.

Kenya's other famous drawcard is its coast, a historic region coloured by Arabic

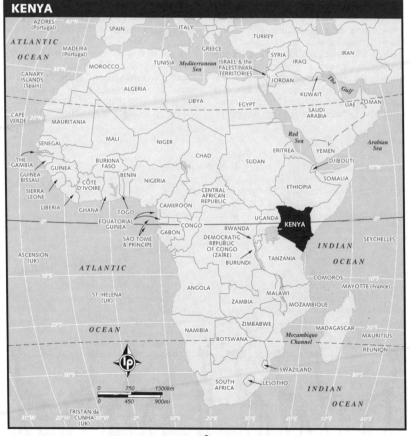

KENYA

influences, with kilometre after kilometre of fine, white-sand beaches. Mombasa is the hub of the beach resort scene, but there are many smaller and more peaceful coves where you can kick back and unwind without the crowds. If you tire of the beaches, the Swahili villages and mangrove islands off the coast provide an unique opportunity to step back in time. In Lamu, the Swahili way of life has changed little in centuries and there are endless secluded beaches and remote Swahili outposts nearby that can only be reached by traditional Arab dhows. For a languorous break, away from the pressures of life, it's hard to beat.

Those people seeking more energetic pursuits will find no shortage of challenges – Kenya has some excellent mountains to climb, especially rugged Mt Kenya. This jagged peak has captivated the popular imagination since prehistoric times – for many Kenyan tribes it was the logical home of the gods, while early European explorers and adventurers saw a snowcapped peak this close to the equator as an anomaly that had to be explored and conquered. Another epic climb is Mt Elgon, on the Ugandan border, with its famous salt-mining elephants.

Organised camel treks through Kenya's arid north also attract a steady stream of hardy souls who want to get back to basics in the place where human beings first evolved.

The heart of this relatively prosperous country is the bustling capital, Nairobi. Love it or loathe it, it's a modern place where you can take care of business and get hold of the goods you may have expected only to see in the shops of Europe or North America – quite a pleasant shock if you've come from many of the surrounding nations.

Although Kenya has its fair share of problems, including soaring crime in the cities, disease and political violence, you can avoid most of these with a little care and common sense. Tourism took a nose dive after the tragic bombing of the US embassy in 1998, and its recovery received a jolt with the car bombing of the Paradise Hotel in Kikambala in 2002, but this place is simply too good to ignore for long.

Excellent air connections with Europe and elsewhere in Africa make Kenya the ideal place for an African break, or the starting or finishing point for a longer sojourn in the continent. Either way, the African fantasy is unlikely to go unfulfilled!

Facts about Kenya

HISTORY
The Birthplace of Humanity
Thanks to some inquisitive poking around in the dirt by the Leakey family at Olduvai Gorge (Tanzania) and around Lake Turkana (Kenya), the Rift Valley that runs through the centre of Kenya has been established as the 'cradle of humanity'. The Leakeys' discoveries of several hominoid skulls, one of which is estimated to be 2½ million years old, radically altered the accepted theories on the origin of humans.

Before the East African digs, the generally accepted theory was that there were two species of proto-humans: the 'robust' hominids, and the 'gracile' hominids, which eventually gave rise to modern humans. However, the Leakey discoveries suggested that there was a third species, *Homo habilis*, and that it was this group that gave rise to modern humans.

Since then, the human family tree has gained several more branches with the discovery of several new species in central Africa, including *Kenyanthropus platyops*, discovered in 2002 at Lake Turkana by another of the Leakey clan. Another recent discovery was of bones belonging to a six-million year old hominid, nicknamed 'Millennium Man', a strong contender for man's oldest ancestor.

Early Settlement
Over the millennia, this part of East Africa has been populated by peoples from the whole of the continent: from the Galla of northern Somalia to the San (formerly Bushmen) and Khoikhoi (formerly Hottentots) of South Africa. The first to arrive were the tall, nomadic, Cushitic-speaking people from Ethiopia who began to move south around 2000 BC, basing themselves first at Lake Turkana and then moving south as their livestock outstripped the vegetation. A second group of pastoralists, the Eastern Cushitics, followed them in around 1000 BC and occupied much of central Kenya.

The ancestors of most of the tribes that occupy Kenya today arrived from all over Africa from around AD 1000. The first immigrants were Bantu-speaking people from West Africa (who gave rise to the Gusii, Kikuyu, Akamba and Meru amongst other tribes), who came to occupy much of southern and western Kenya by the end of the 15th century. The Nilotic speakers, who gave rise to the Maasai, Luo, Samburu and Turkana, came from the Nile valley in southern Sudan at the end of the 16th century. Although these were the biggest migrations, tribes continued to move into and out of Kenya right up to the beginning of the 20th century.

Arab & Persian Traders
While tribal migrations were going on in the interior, a non-African force was massing on the coast. Muslims from the Arabian Peninsula and Persia (now Iran) began to visit the coast from the 8th century AD onwards, as part of their annual trade migration around the Indian Ocean. Many set up trading posts on the coast, intermarrying with Africans and creating the culture that later became known as Swahili. Slaves and ivory were the primary African commodities, but along with their human cargo, the Arab dhows exported tortoiseshell, rhino horn and gold.

Before long there were Arab-Swahili city-states all along the coast from Somalia to Mozambique, acting as entrepots for the trans-Indian Ocean trade. The communities were almost continually at war with each other for supremacy in the region, but these internecine squabbles were generally short-lived. Arab-Swahili domination on the coast received its first serious challenge with the arrival of the Portuguese in the 16th century.

Portuguese Invaders
While the Spanish crown was busy backing expeditions to the Americas, the Portuguese were determined to break the Ottoman Turks' grip on trade with the Far East, particularly the trade in spices – worth more than their weight in gold in Europe. In 1498 Vasco da Gama stopped in at current-day Malindi on his way to India, preparing the way for a full-scale invasion in 1505. In that year, Dom Francisco de Almeida's armada of 23 ships made short work of the city-states of Sofala, Kilwa (in Tanzania) and Mombasa before sailing on to India. The Portuguese sacked Mombasa again in 1528.

Although they came to dominate the coast, the Portuguese experiment was never a great success. Collecting 'tributes' from the Swahili usually required brute force and all attempts to convert the Muslims to Catholicism were a dismal failure. Some city-states underwent an annual conversion when the Portuguese ships arrived, reverting to Islam as soon as the ships departed for Goa.

In 1593 the Portuguese constructed Fort Jesus at Mombasa to give them a permanent presence in the region, but the fort changed hands dozens of times during the rebellions of the 17th century. As long as the armada was in town things were generally fine, but as soon as the battleships sailed on for India, the fort was besieged and the occupants massacred. In response to this, the Portuguese mounted 'punitive expeditions', which normally involved sailing up the coast and bombarding the least defended city-state with heavy artillery.

Although the Portuguese are widely blamed for the decline of the Arab-Swahili states, evidence from abandoned cities along the coast suggests that ultimately, it was a combination of failing water supplies and attacks by African tribes that eventually put paid to the Swahili hegemony. Both the Zimba, a cannibalistic tribe from Malawi, and the Galla, who swept down from Somalia, ransacked the coast throughout the 17th and 18th centuries.

The Portuguese's grip over the East African coast was always tenuous and the end came in 1698 when Fort Jesus fell to Baluchi Arabs from Oman after a 33-month siege. A few token attempts were made to regain power but, by 1729, the Portuguese had left the Kenyan coast for good.

Omani Dynasties

The Omani Arabs remained in control of the East African coast until the arrival of the British and Germans in the late 19th century (and, nominally, right up until independence), and established their main base on Zanzibar, off the Tanzanian coast. Although they shared the same faith, the Swahili regarded them as just as much of a colonising force as the Portuguese, and there were numerous rebellions, most famously by the powerful Mazrui rulers of Mombasa.

Eventually, Sultan Seyyid Said of Oman decided enough was enough and dispatched the Omani navy to bring the Mazrui-ruled states of Mombasa, Paté and Pemba into line in 1822. The Mazrui clan appealed for help to the commander of a British warship, who declared Mombasa a British Protectorate, but this was repealed three years later and Seyyid Said reasserted his control the following year.

Seyyid Said established huge clove plantations on Zanzibar and the spice business soon became so profitable that he moved his entire court there in 1832. Simultaneously, the slave trade went into overdrive to supply workers for the spice plantations and the French coffee and sugar plantations on Mauritius and Reunion. By 1800, more than 8000 slaves were passing through the slave markets of Zanzibar every year. Perhaps four times as many were killed before ever reaching the markets.

Although native Africans stood little chance against the firearms of the Arabs, a handful of tribes waged a resistance war against the slavers. These included Manwa Sera, who besieged the Swahili stronghold of Kaze in modern-day Tanzania in the 1860s, and chief Mirambo, who accumulated a massive arsenal of guns and caused so much trouble at Kaze during the 1870s that, at one point, the Sultan ceded all claim to the area.

British East Africa

While all this was happening, thousands of miles away in Britain, a growing voice of public opinion was calling for an end to the East African slave trade. The report by explorer Dr Livingstone of a massacre of 400 Bagenya people by slavers at Nyangwe, near Lake Tanganyika, finally forced the British government to play its hand. By using a mixture of knife-edge diplomacy and strong-arm tactics, Sultan Barghash of Zanzibar was forced to sign a treaty banning the slave trade in 1873.

With German expansion into Tanganyika, an agreement was reached between the British and the Germans, granting the sultan to a 16km-wide strip of the Kenyan coastline, which would remain under a British Protectorate. The agreement remained in place right up until independence, when the last Sultan of Zanzibar, Seyyid Khalifa, ceded the territory to the new government.

Although the coast was largely sewn up, the interior, particularly the Rift Valley and the Aberdare highlands, were largely impregnable to outsiders due the fearsome Maasai and other warlike tribes. A handful of explorers braved the Maasai heartland, including Gustav Fischer, a German whose party was virtually annihilated at Hell's Gate on Lake Naivasha in 1882, but most attempts to enter the Rift Valley were doomed to failure.

The united front of the Maasai began to crack in the late 19th century, following a brutal civil war between the Ilmaasai and Iloikop groups and the simultaneous arrival of rinderpest (a cattle disease), cholera, smallpox and famine. Because of this, the British were able to negotiate a treaty with Olonana (known today as Lenana), the *laibon* (chief or spiritual leader) of the Maasai, allowing them to march the Mombasa–Uganda railway line right through the heart of the Maasai grazing lands. On one level, the Maasai were just accepting the inevitable – their end-of-the-world myth spoke of an 'iron snake' that would one day crawl across their land.

White Settlement

With the completion of the railway, the headquarters of the colonial administration was moved from Mombasa to the cooler, small settlement of Nairobi, and white settlers began to occupy the fertile highlands north of Nairobi. Their interests clashed with those of the Maasai, prompting the colonial authorities to pressure Olonana into restricting the Maasai to two reserves, one on either side of the new railway. However, the white settlers soon wanted the northern reserve as well, and in 1910 and 1911, the Maasai who lived there were forced to trek south, despite Olonana's objections.

Although the Maasai suffered the worst annexations of land, the Kikuyu, a Bantu tribe from the highlands around Mt Kenya and the Aberdares, came to nurse a particular grievance about their alienation from the land. Tribes who lived on poor agricultural land, such as the Luo and Luyha and the tribes of the northeast were hardly affected at all by British settlement.

White settlement in the early years of the 20th century was led by Lord Delamere, a pugnacious gentleman-farmer from Cheshire, England. Since he was not familiar with the land, its pests and its wildlife, his first ventures – into sheep farming and, later, wheat growing – were disastrous. By 1912, however, Delamere and his followers shifted to the highlands near Nairobi and establish mixed agricultural farms, turning a profit for the colony for the first time. Other Europeans established coffee plantations in the area at around the same time, including Karen Blixen (aka Isak Dinesen) and her hunter husband, Bror.

The white settlement of Kenya was interrupted by WWI – when two-thirds of the 3000 white settlers formed impromptu cavalry units and went off in search of Germans in neighbouring Tanganyika (Tanzania) – but it resumed after the war under a scheme where veterans of the European campaign were offered subsidised land in the highlands around Nairobi. The net effect was a huge upsurge in the white Kenyan population, from 9000 in 1920 to 80,000 in the 1950s.

Kenyan Nationalism

Meanwhile, the sense of grievance among Africans was growing stronger. Led by the charismatic Harry Thuku, the Kikuyu people spearheaded the movement to reclaim Kenya. In March 1922, the colonial authorities promptly arrested Thuku, and a large crowd of Africans gathered outside the Nairobi Central police station where he was being held. In the subsequent 'restoration of order', between 21 and 100 Africans were killed and Thuku was exiled to Kisimayo in Somalia. He was only released in 1930 after agreeing to cooperate with the authorities.

With his reputation tarnished, Thuku was quickly replaced by another Kikuyu, Johnstone Kamau, later Jomo Kenyatta, who went become Kenya's first president. Born in 1892 in the highlands north of Nairobi to a peasant farming family, Kenyatta famously ran away to a Church of Scotland mission school to gain an education and worked in Nairobi as a court interpreter and water-meter reader, before joining the East Africa Association, which was campaigning for land reform, better wages, education and medical facilities for Africans.

Although it was official British government policy to favour African interests over those of the settlers in the event of conflicts, it was hard for black African interests to be heard in the whites-only legislative council. Kenyatta soon joined the more outspoken Kikuyu Central Association, which was subsequently banned for campaigning against white rule.

In 1929, with money supplied by Indian communists, Kenyatta sailed for London to plead the Kikuyu case with the British colonial secretary, who, predictably, declined his invitation to a meeting. While in London, Kenyatta hooked up with a group called the League Against Imperialism, which took him to Moscow and Berlin, back to Nairobi and then back to London, where he stayed for the next 15 years. During this time, he perfected his oratory on the crowds in Trafalgar Square, studied revolutionary tactics in Moscow and built up the Pan-African Federation with Hastings Banda (who later became the president of Malawi) and Kwame Nkrumah (who later became the president of Ghana).

By the time he returned to Kenya in 1946, he was the leader of a bona fide Kenyan liberation movement. Kenyatta quickly assumed the top spot of the Kenya African Union (KAU), a pro-independence group that had considerable support from African war veterans who had been pressured into fighting for the British in WWII.

Mau Mau Rebellion

Although the colonial authorities made some concessions to the KAU, the main agitation for independence was going on underground. Tribal groups of Kikuyu, Maasai and Luo took secret oaths, which bound participants to kill Europeans and their African collaborators. The most famous of these was Mau Mau, formed in 1952 by disenchanted Kikuyu people, which aimed to drive the white settlers from Kenya forever.

The first blow was struck early in 1953 with the killing of a white farmer's entire herd of cattle followed a few weeks later, by the massacre of 21 Kikuyu loyal to the colonial government. The Mau Mau rebellion had started. The government declared a state of emergency and began to gather the tribespeople into 'protected villages', surrounded by barbed wire and booby-trapped trenches, primarily to keep the villagers from being recruited to the ranks of the Mau Mau revolutionaries.

Within a month of the rebellion, Kenyatta and several other KAU leaders were put on trial as the alleged leaders of the Mau Mau, and Kenyatta was convicted on spurious evidence and sentenced to seven years jail. The various Mau Mau sects came together under the umbrella of the Kenya Land Freedom Army led by Dedan Kimathi, and staged frequent attacks against white farms and government outposts, including Treetops Lodge, where Britain's Queen Elizabeth II spent her last night before becoming queen.

By the time the rebellion ended in 1956 with the Mau Mau's defeat, the death toll stood at over 13,500 Africans (guerrillas, civilians and troops) and just over 100 Europeans (including 37 settlers) – fairly predicable numbers for the British Empire! Following the end of the rebellion, Dedan Kimathi was publicly hanged by a British colonel named Henderson, who was later deported from Kenya for crimes against humanity.

Upon his release in 1959, Kenyatta resumed his campaign for independence while under house arrest in Lodwar. Soon even white Kenyans began to hear the wind of change. Some left voluntarily for Rhodesia (now Zimbabwe), South Africa and Australia, while others slowly fell in line with the idea of transfer of power to a democratically elected African government. This became the official policy of the British Government at the Lancaster House Conference in London in 1960. Independence was scheduled for December 1963, accompanied by grants and loans of US$100 million to enable the Kenyan assembly to buy out European farmers in the highlands and restore the land to the tribes.

In the meantime, a division occurred in the ranks of KAU between those who wanted a unitary form of government with centralised control in Nairobi, and those who favoured *majimbo*, a federal setup, in order to avoid Kikuyu domination. The centralists renamed their party the Kenya African National Union (KANU), while the federalists split off under the leadership of Ronald Ngala to become the Kenya African Democratic Union (KADU). Kenyatta was released from house arrest in mid-1961 and assumed the presidency of KANU.

Although some resistance by white settlers was inevitable, the run-up to independence was surprisingly smooth. Over subsequent years, a few farms owned by white settlers were bought out by the government, and the land divided up into small subsistence plots supporting 15 to 20 people. The experiment wasn't a great success; Kenyans regarded it as too little, too late, while white farmers feared that the trickle would soon turn into a flood. As Zimbabwe was to discover nearly 40 years later, the immediate effect of land redistribution was to cause a significant decline in agricultural production, from which Kenya never quite recovered.

Independence

With independence scheduled for 1963, the political handover began in earnest in 1962. KANU and KADU formed a coalition government, but the coalition was abandoned after the first Kenyan elections in May 1963. Jomo Kenyatta became Kenya's first president on 12 December 1963, ruling until his death in 1978. Under Kenyatta's presidency, Kenya developed into one of Africa's most stable and prosperous nations. The opposition KADU party was voluntarily dissolved in 1964.

While Kenyatta is still seen as one of the few success stories of Britain's withdrawal from empire, he wasn't without his faults. Biggest among these was his excessive bias in favour of his own tribe. Opponents of his regime who became too vocal for comfort frequently 'disappeared', and corruption soon became endemic at all levels of the power structure.

At the same time, the British kept a toehold in Kenya in order to provide a training ground for the British Army. Over the next 50 years, huge amounts of ordnance were lobbed around, much of it ending up unexploded in rural areas. In July 2002, the British government finally agreed to pay nearly UK£7 million in compensation to the hundreds of Maasai and Samburu tribespeople injured or killed after accidentally detonating the unexploded bombs.

The 1980's

Kenyatta was succeeded in 1978 by his vice president, Daniel arap Moi. A Kalenjin, Moi was regarded by establishment power brokers as a suitable front man for their interests as his tribe was relatively small and in thrall to the Kikuyu. Moi went on to become one the most enduring 'Big Men' in Africa, ruling in virtual autocracy for nearly 25 years. In the process, he accrued an incredible personal fortune; today many believe him to be the richest man in Africa.

Although Moi's regime was stable compared to the desperate situation in many surrounding countries, it has also been characterised by nepotism, corruption, arrests of dissidents, censorship, the disbanding of tribal societies and the closure of universities, as well as the nefarious activities of KANU Youth, the party's student body.

In 1982 KANU publicly banned opposition parties, leading to a military coup by the airforce, which was promptly quashed by pro-government forces. The 12 ringleaders were executed and 900 other participants were jailed indefinitely. In the run-up to the 1987 election, Moi introduced a new voting system and jailed the opposition leaders without trial, ensuring that the sole candidate from the sole political party in the country won the election – no prizes for guessing who that was!

After his 'win', Moi expanded the cabinet to fit in more of his cronies and rushed through constitutional reforms allowing him to dismiss senior judges and public servants without any redress. When dissenting politicians were arrested, Christian church leaders took up the call for change, turning their sermons into political speeches, supported by an outspoken critic of government nepotism, Professor Wangari Maathai, leader of the Green Belt Movement (see the boxed text for more details).

Sooner or later something had to give.

The 1990s

With the collapse of communism and the break-up of the Soviet Union it was no longer necessary for Western powers to prop up corrupt noncommunist regimes in Africa. Donors who previously turned a blind eye to civil rights misdemeanours began calling for multiparty elections if economic aid was to be maintained. The multiparty movement gained huge grassroots support in Kenya.

In response, KANU Youth was mobilised to disrupt pro-democracy rallies and harass opposition politicians. The vocal former foreign affairs minister, Dr Robert Ouko, was murdered in 1990, seemingly with collusion from very some powerful people, although nothing was ever proved. Things came to a head on 7 July 1990 when the military and police raided an opposition demonstration in Nairobi, killing 20 and arresting politicians, human-rights activists and journalists.

The rally, known thereafter as Saba Saba ('seven seven' in Swahili), was a pivotal

The Green Belt Movement

On Earth Day in 1977 Professor Wangari Maathai planted seven trees in her back yard, setting in motion the grass-roots environmental campaign that came to be known as the Green Belt Movement. Since then, more than 20 million trees have been planted in Kenya and the movement has expanded to more than 30 African countries. The core aim of the movement is to educate women – who make up some 70% of farmers in Africa – about the link between soil erosion, undernourishment and poor health, and encouraging individuals to protect their immediate environment by planting 'green belts' of trees to prevent erosion and establishing tree nurseries. Seedlings are then distributed free to groups and individuals wanting to improve their environment.

Even with these successes, the movement has a huge amount of work ahead. Less than 3% of Kenya's original forest cover remains and conservation efforts have been hampered by government apathy and active collusion in forest clearing by officials. The Kenyan parliament recently passed a bill allowing previously restricted groups to gather firewood, including hospitals, prisons, army barracks and schools, as well as several less deserving causes such as Pan African Paper-Mills and the Del Monte fruit corporation! Hot on the heels of this new law, it was announced in August 2002 that 14% of protected Kenyan forests were to lose their protected status.

Maathai has worked extensively with international organizations to exert leverage on the Kenyan government and, in December 1984, she was awarded Sweden's Right Livelihood Award (the alternative Nobel prize). She has also been a recipient of the UN's Africa Prize for Leadership, and the Golden Ark Award. However, the Kenyan government has consistently vilified her as a 'threat to the order and security of the country' for her activism and she has suffered repeated violence at the hands of government agents, most recently in 1999, while protesting against the clearance of the Karura forest near Nairobi (part of a highly controversial real-estate deal). Maathai's book *The Green Belt Movement* has recently been published worldwide and is well worth tracking down.

event in the push for a multiparty Kenya. The following year, the Forum for the Restoration of Democracy (FORD) party was formed, led by Jamagori Oginga Odinga, a powerful Luo politician who was vice-president under Jomo Kenyatta. FORD was initially banned and Odinga was arrested, but the resulting outcry led to his release and, finally, a change in the constitution that allowed opposition parties to register for the first time.

Faced with a foreign debt of nearly US$9 billion and blanket suspension of foreign aid, Moi was pressured into holding multiparty elections in early 1992, but independent observers reported a litany of electoral inconsistencies, including widespread vote-buying. Just as worrying, about 2000 people were killed during ethnic clashes in the Rift Valley, widely believed to have been triggered by KANU agitation. Nonetheless, Moi was overwhelmingly re-elected.

Following the elections, KANU bowed to some Western demands for economic reforms, but agitation and harassment of opposition politicians continued unabated. After the death of Odinga in 1994, the op-position coalition fell victim to damaging internal disputes, leading to the creation of a new opposition party, Safina, headed by the white Kenyan palaeontologist Richard Leakey. A resilient figure, Leakey, had lost both his legs in a plane crash in 1993, widely alleged to be a result of sabotage, and endured widespread vilification and even public beatings by hired thugs in his quest to shake up Kenyan politics.

The 1997 election was accompanied by violence and rioting, particularly during the Saba Saba anniversary rally. Again, mysterious provocateurs stirred up ethnic violence, this time on the coast around Likoni. European and North American tour companies cancelled their bookings and around 60,000 Kenyans lost their jobs. Moi was able to set himself up as peacemaker, calming the warring factions and gaining 50.4% of the seats for KANU, compared to the 49.6% won by the divided opposition parties.

The scene was set for a confrontational parliament, but in a trademark Moi man-oeuvre, KANU immediately entered into a cooperative arrangement with the two biggest opposition parties, the Democratic Party (DP; Kikuyu) and the National Development Party (NDP; Luo). Despite its reformist agenda, Safina was unable to allay the nation's unease about white men in politics and polled just six seats. Other seats were taken by FORD-Kenya and it's various splinter groups.

After the failure of Safina, Leakey returned to his job as head of the Kenya Wildlife Service (KWS), where he managed to gain IMF and World Bank backing for many proposed national park projects. At the same time, Kenya was lashed first by torrential 'El Nino' rains and then by a desperate drought that continued right up to 2000, causing terrible hardship in rural areas.

Preoccupied with internal problems, Kenya was quite unprepared for the events of 7 August 1998. Early in the morning, massive blasts simultaneously ripped apart the American embassies in Nairobi and Dar es Salaam in Tanzania, killing more than 200 people. Almost all the victims in Nairobi were Kenyans with no links to the embassy (see the boxed text 'Embassy Bombings' in the Nairobi chapter for more details). The effect on Kenyan tourism, and the economy as a whole, was devastating. Tourist numbers dropped by 50% and have never fully recovered. During the next four years, though, coastal businesses slowly moved to rebuild the tourist industry, helped in part by Italian tour operators, who filled the gap left by American, British and German companies. The car bombing of the Paradise Hotel in Kikambala, near Mombasa, on 28 November 2002 is likely to set the recovery back and keep tourist numbers down in the near future.

End of an Era?

In an unexpected act of apparent reconciliation, Moi appointed Leakey – a man he once described as the 'anti-Christ' and an 'atheistic colonial' – to the Head of the Civil Service and Governor of the Central Bank in 1999. The appointment was probably a sweetener for the IMF, who refused to lend the government money unless it adopted widespread reforms, but it did allow Leakey to weed out some of the corrupt old guard, including the head of the Kenya Tourism Board, and hire some young, capable technocrats.

Simultaneously, the government embarked on a constitutional review with the aim of creating a new less corruptible political system, which is due to be completed in 2003. Among the proposals is a return to *majimbo*, or federalism.

The anti-corruption purge, though, was only able to go so far before it hit an impassable wall. The most prominent corruption case, the Goldenberg Scandal – an incredible scam involving KSh20 billion in fraudulent compensation claims for nonexistent exports of diamonds and gold – has implicated the upper echelons of the government, and the nation's duty-free shops! Whatever the truth, the anti-corruption unit was wound down in 2001, and Leakey stepped down in March of that year, without giving his reasons. The IMF promptly re-imposed its moratorium on aid to Kenya.

In June 2001, KANU entered into a formal coalition government with the NDP and DP, creating a formidable power-base for the ruling party. However, with Moi's presidency due to end in 2002, many felt that Moi would alter the constitution again. This time, though, he announced his intention to retire – on an absurdly generous benefits package – with elections to be held in December 2002.

As his successor, Moi put his weight firmly behind Uhuru Kenyatta, the son of Jomo Kenyatta, even going as far as to fire vice-president George Saitoti for refusing to support Kenyatta's nomination. Meanwhile, 12 opposition parties – including the DP, FORD-Kenya, FORD-Asili, the National Party of Kenya and Saba Saba-Asili – and several religious groups united under the umbrella of the National Alliance Party of Kenya (NAK), later known as the National Rainbow Coalition (Narc), and presidential candidate Mwai Kibaki, the former head of the Democratic party.

Although initially dogged by infighting, within weeks the opposition transformed itself into a dynamic and unified political party. International observers were braced for violence and electoral irregularities, but when the election came on 27 December 2002, it was peaceful and fair and the result was dramatic – a landslide two-thirds majority for Mwai Kibaki and Narc.

Despite being injured in a car accident while campaigning, Kibaki was inaugurated as Kenya's third president on 30 December 2002. At the same time, Moi was pelted with mud during his final presidential

Suicide Attack in Kenya

On 28th November 2002, the 55th anniversary of the partition of Palestine, suicide bombers slammed an explosives-laden car into the lobby of the Paradise Hotel at Kikambala, near Mombasa. Ten Kenyans and three Israelis were killed in the explosion, as well as the three suicide bombers. Moments before the Israeli-owned hotel was attacked, missiles were fired at an Israeli passenger plane taking off from Mombasa's airport. The missiles, fired from a shoulder-launcher, only narrowly missed the Boeing 757 headed for Tel Aviv.

Although the missile attack failed, this was a sophisticated operation. The synchronised nature of the attacks is characteristic of al-Qaeda, who has since claimed responsibility for the bombing. This is the first time Israelis have been directly targeted by the terrorist organisation that has been linked to September 11 attacks in the USA and the bombing in Bali in October 2002. Early indications are that a local group worked in conjunction with al-Qaeda to carry out the attack.

speech! Kibaki has a proven track record in both the Kenyatta and Moi governments, when he made efforts to tackle corruption, and with a Narc majority in parliament, many are enthusistically expecting great things of the new government. However, the constitutional review is still incomplete, a couple of Kibaki's ministers have been accused of corruption when serving under Moi and there are concerns that departing KANU politicians may plunder the national coffers before leaving office. Whatever happens, the first priority of the new president will be to get the IMF and World Bank back on side.

GEOGRAPHY & GEOLOGY

Kenya straddles the equator and covers an area of some 583,000 sq km, which includes around 13,600 sq km of Lake Victoria. It is bordered to the north by the arid bushlands and deserts of Ethiopia and Sudan, to the east by the Indian Ocean and the wastes of Somalia, to the west by Uganda and Lake Victoria, and to the south by Tanzania.

Kenya is dominated by the Rift Valley, a vast range of valleys, rather than a single valley that follows a 5000km-long crack in the earth's crust. Within the Rift Valley are numerous 'swells' (raised escarpments) and 'troughs' (deep valleys, often containing lakes), and there are some huge volcanoes, including Mt Kenya, Mt Elgon and Mt Kilimanjaro (across the border in Tanzania). The floor of the Rift Valley is still dropping, although – at the rate of a few millimetres per year – you are hardly likely to notice!

The Rift Valley divides the flat plains of the coast from the gentle hills along the lakeshore. Nairobi, the capital, sits in the Central Highlands, which are on the eastern edge of the Rift Valley. The other main population centres are Mombasa, on the coast, and Kisumu, on the shores of Lake Victoria. Kenya can roughly be divided into four zones: the coastal plains; the Rift Valley and Central Highlands; the lakeshore; and the arid wastelands of northern Kenya.

The main rivers in Kenya are the Athi/Galana River, which empties into the Indian Ocean near Malindi, and the Tana River, which hits the coast midway between Malindi and Lamu. Aside from Lake Victoria, Kenya has numerous small volcanic lakes and mighty Lake Turkana, known as the Jade Sea, which straddles the Ethiopian border.

Within volcanic craters, and on the Rift Valley floor, are several soda lakes, rich in sodium bicarbonate, created by the filtering of water through mineral-rich volcanic rock and subsequent evaporation.

CLIMATE

Kenya's diverse geography means that temperature, rainfall and humidity patterns vary widely, but there are effectively four zones about which generalisations can be made.

The undulating plateau of western Kenya is generally hot and fairly humid with rainfall spread throughout the year. The greatest precipitation is usually during April when a maximum of 200mm may be recorded, while the lowest falls are in January with an average of 40mm. Temperatures range from a minimum of 14°C to 18°C to a maximum of 30°C to 36°C over the year.

The Central Highlands and Rift Valley enjoy perhaps the most agreeable climate in the country. Average temperatures vary from a minimum of 10°C to 14°C to a maximum of 22°C to 28°C. Rainfall varies from a minimum of 20mm in July to 200mm in April

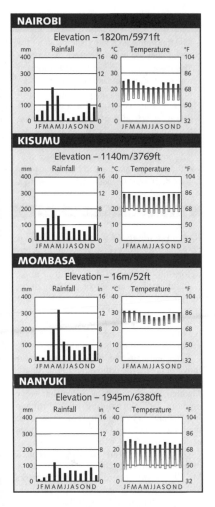

NAIROBI
Elevation – 1820m/5971ft

KISUMU
Elevation – 1140m/3769ft

MOMBASA
Elevation – 16m/52ft

NANYUKI
Elevation – 1945m/6380ft

and falls essentially in two seasons – March to the beginning of June (the 'long rains') and October to the end of November (the 'short rains'). Mt Kenya and the Aberdare mountains are the country's main water-catchment areas, and falls of up to 3000mm per year are recorded in these two places.

In the vast semiarid bushlands, deserts and lava flows of northern and eastern Kenya, the temperature can vary from highs of up to 40°C during the day to less than 20°C at night. Rainfall in this area is sparse and, when it does fall, it often comes in the form of violent storms. July is generally the driest month and November the wettest. The average annual rainfall varies between 250mm and 500mm.

The fourth climatic zone is the coastal belt, which is hot and humid year-round, though tempered by coastal sea breezes. Rainfall ranges from a minimum of 20mm in February to a maximum of 300mm in May, and is dependent on the monsoon, which blows from the northeast from October to April and from the southwest for the rest of the year. The annual average rainfall is between 1000mm and 1250mm (less in drought years). Average temperatures vary little throughout the year, ranging from 22°C to around 30°C.

For weather forecasts online, visit the website of the Kenya Meteorological Office (www.meteo.go.ke).

ECOLOGY & ENVIRONMENT
Wildlife Conservation
Kenya Wildlife Service (KWS) With the total ban on hunting in 1977, the KWS was free to concentrate solely on conserving Kenya's wildlife, which came just in time, as the 1970s and '80s were marred by a shockingly high degree poaching linked to the drought in Somalia, which drove hordes of poachers across the border into Kenya. A staggering number of Kenya's rhinos and elephants were slaughtered and many KWS officers worked in league with poachers until famous palaeontologist Dr Richard Leakey cleaned up the organisation in the 1980s and '90s. A core part of his policy was arming KWS rangers with modern weapons and high-speed vehicles and allowing them to shoot poachers on sight, which seems to have dramatically reduced the poaching problem. However, there were several new attacks on elephants and rhinos by poachers in 2001 and 2002.

To concentrate their efforts where they can achieve the best results, there is now open talk of abandoning some of the more remote parks (such as those close to the Ethiopian or Somali borders) and concentrating on the parks that actually receive visitors. At the same time, community conservation projects are being encouraged, and many community-owned ranches are now being opened up as private wildlife reserves, with the backing of the KWS and international donors. Good examples are the Lumo Community Wildlife Sanctuary and the Kimana Wildlife Sanctuary, which border Tsavo West National Park.

Private Conservation It has been claimed that more than 75% of Kenya's wildlife lies outside the national parks and reserves, and an increasing number of important wildlife conservation areas now exist on private land. Lewa Downs, near Isiolo, is a prime example. Private wildlife reserves often have the resources to work intensively on specific conservation issues and it is no accident that some of the largest concentrations of rhinos are within these areas.

In recent years, there has been a shift in thinking by ranchers, who now tend to regard wildlife as something to be protected rather than a menace to be eradicated. There are even attempts to farm 'game meat' animals as a way of funding conservation, although this is a contentious issue. The target market currently consists of the upmarket restaurants prepared to pay top dollar for game meat, but there has also been an upsurge in poaching to supply illegal *nyama choma* (barbecued meat) restaurants. Game ranching is not possible on a large scale, so it's likely to continue as just a lucrative sideline for ranch owners.

The **Laikipia Wildlife Forum** (☎ 0176-31600; Ⓦ www.laikipia.org) is an umbrella organisation representing many lodges and conservation areas in Laikipia, the large slab of ranch land northwest of Mt Kenya. Ranches in this area are particularly active in wildlife conservation, and the forum is a good source of up-to-date information about projects and accommodation in the area. Other private game ranches and conservation areas can be found around Tsavo and Amboseli National Parks.

The East African Wildlife Society based in Nairobi is at the forefront of conservation efforts in the region (see Clubs & Societies in the Nairobi chapter).

Deforestation
More than half of Africa's forests have been destroyed over the last century, and forest destruction continues on a large scale in parts of Kenya. Illegal logging, charcoal burning and agricultural encroachment all take their toll, and it seems that little is being done to stop it. However, millions of

Jiko

One innovative idea to try and minimise the use of firewood is the *jiko* stove, based on a Thai design and modified to suit the Kenyan way of cooking. Easy and cheap to manufacture, the *jiko* consists of an hourglass-shaped metal casing and a ceramic insulator that delivers 25% to 40% of the heat from the fire to the pot. Traditional open fires transfer less than a quarter of that. After some uncertainty, Kenyans have embraced the *jiko* with enthusiasm and hundreds of open-air *jua kali* workshops now provide stoves for nearly a million households.

Kenyans still rely on wood and charcoal for cooking fuel, so every traveller to Kenya will almost certainly contribute to this deforestation whether they like it or not.

Land grabbing and the degazetting of protected forests are also hot issues. Until recently, the cause celebre was the Karura Forest just outside Nairobi, but all that went out of the window when the Moi government effectively lifted the ban on logging.

Spearheading the forest conservation movement and the opposition to the logging of the Karura Forest is Professor Wangari Maathai, who founded the Green Belt Movement in 1977, promoting the planting of 'green belts' of trees to limit soil erosion (see the boxed text 'The Green Belt Movement' earlier in this chapter for more details).

Despite these problems, some large areas of protected forest remain. The Mt Kenya, Mt Elgon and Aberdare National Parks, Kakamega Forest Reserve and Arabuko Sokoke Forest are all tremendous places to visit, packed with thousands of species of fauna and flora. There are also some large areas of coastal forest, although another swathe of these will go when Tiomin Resources Inc builds its titanium-ore port at Shimoni (for more details see the boxed text 'Mining, Multinationals and Marine Life' in The Coast chapter).

Tourism
The tourist industry is the cause of some of Kenya's environmental problems, most notably the erosion caused by safari minibuses, which cut across and between trails and fol-

low wildlife into the bush, creating a virtual dustbowl in parks such as Amboseli, Samburu and Masai Mara. The problem is particularly bad in the Masai Mara, where minibuses pretty much go where they please. A number of operators were recently banned from the reserve for misdemeanours ranging from nonpayment of rent for tented camps to harassment of wildlife, but there are few signs that the ban is being enforced.

The lodges within the parks consume considerable amounts of firewood – just those in Masai Mara get through upwards of 100 tonnes of firewood a year. For its part, the KWS insists that every new lodge and camp must be designed in an ecofriendly manner, which is usually enforced. As a result, there are growing numbers of 'ecolodges' in Kenya, which keep their impact on the environment to a minimum through recycling, use of renewable energy resources and strict controls on dumping of refuse and the types of fuel that is used. (For more ideas on how travellers can minimise their impact on the environment, see Responsible Tourism in the Facts for the Visitor chapter.)

FLORA & FAUNA
Flora
Kenya's flora is notably diverse because of the country's wide range of physiographic regions. The vast plains of the south are characterised by distinctive flat-topped acacia trees, interspersed with the equally distinctive baobab trees (with their pendulous edible fruit), and savage whistling thorn bushes, which made early exploration of the continent such a tortuous process.

The savanna grassland of the Masai Mara supports a huge variety of animal life. The grass grows tremendously fast after the rains, and provides food for a huge range and number of herbivores and insects that in turn are food for a variety of predators. The trampling and grazing of herbivores promotes the growth of grasses, rather than broadleaf plants, which are more vulnerable to damage from grazing, drought and fire.

On the slopes of Mt Elgon and Mt Kenya the flora changes with altitude. Thick evergreen temperate forest grows between 1000m and 2000m, giving way to a belt of bamboo forest up to about 3000m. Above this height is mountain moorland, charac-

terised by the amazing groundsel tree and giant lobelias (see the boxed text 'Mt Kenya's Flora' in the Central Highlands chapter for more details). In the semidesert plains of the north and northeast, the vegetation cover is thorn bush, which seem to go on forever. In the northern coastal areas mangroves are prolific and there are still a few small pockets of coastal rainforest.

Fauna
There's such a dazzling array of animals in Kenya that viewing them in the national parks is one of the main reasons for visiting. The 'Big Five' – lion, buffalo, elephant, leopard and rhino – can be seen in at least two of the major parks, plus a huge variety of other less famous but equally impressive animals. Some of the most interesting are described in the Wildlife Guide in this book, or in much more detail in Lonely Planet's *Watching Wildlife East Africa*.

The birdlife here is equally varied and includes such interesting species as the ostrich, vulture and marabou stork, whose spooky bill-clacking can be heard in thorn trees across the country. Around bodies of water, you may see flamingos, exotic cranes and storks, and pelicans, while the forests are home to huge hornbills and rare species such as the yellow weaver bird, sunbird and turaco. Superb starlings are a beautiful bronze and turquoise and you'll see them everywhere. There are also dozens of species of weaver birds, which make the distinctive bag-like nests seen hanging from acacia trees.

Endangered Species
Many of Kenya's major predators and herbivores have become endangered because of the continuous destruction of their natural habitat by people in search of agricultural and grazing land and by merciless poaching for ivory, skins, horn and bush meat.

The black rhino is probably Kenya's most endangered species, due to poaching for its horn, which is used to make Yemeni and Omani dagger-handles, and to a lesser extent, aphrodisiacs in Asia. Faced by relentless poaching by heavily armed poachers in the 1980s, the wild rhino population plummeted from 20,000 in 1969 to between 400 and 900 today. **Rhino Ark** (☎ 020-8944 6688; e *rhinoark@globalnet.co.uk;* w *www.rhino*

ark.org), in London, raises funds to create rhino sanctuaries in the parks, complete with electric fencing, and donations are always appreciated. There are currently sanctuaries in Tsavo and Lake Nakuru National Parks, while Aberdare National Park is also due to be fenced. Despite these efforts, Somali poachers managed to kill four rhinos in Tsavo East National Park in November 2001, triggering fears of a resurgence in the rhino-horn trade.

While the elephant is not technically endangered, it is still the target of poachers, and a number are killed every year. Ten elephants were killed in March 2002, again in Tsavo East. The international trade in ivory was banned by the UN Convention on International Trade in Endangered Species (Cites) in 1989, but the ban has been repeatedly challenged by South Africa, Botswana, Namibia and Zimbabwe, who gained approval for a one-off sale of ivory from culled elephants at the 2002 Cites meeting in Santiago, under the belief that revenue from sales would be used for conservation. The sale was strongly opposed by Kenya and India – which, coincidentally, have the largest elephant populations – as previous sales have led to steep rises in ille-

gal poaching. When the UN authorised a trial auction of ivory to Japan in 1999, poachers went on the rampage in Kenya (over 350kg of illegal ivory was seized by KWS officials in just one raid in Maralal) and conservationists are predicting more trouble ahead for Kenya's elephants.

NATIONAL PARKS & RESERVES

Kenya's national parks and reserves rate among the best in Africa and, despite the ravages of human land exploitation and poaching, there are still an incredible variety of birds and mammals in the parks.

Going on safari (from the Swahili for 'journey') is an integral part of the Kenyan experience, and more popular parks such as Masai Mara National Reserve and Amboseli National Park can become so overcrowded in the high season (January to February) that you'll struggle to get a wildlife photo without a crowd of nonendemic Nissan Urvans in the background.

Fortunately, the smaller and more remote parks, such as Saiwa Swamp National Park, only see a handful of visitors at any time of year. In addition to protecting wildlife, some parks have been created to preserve the landscape itself – Mt Kenya, Mt Elgon, Hell's

National Park Entry Fees

Park entry fees in Kenya are slowly being converted to a 'smartcard' system, which covers the cost of entry for vehicles and passengers, and camping fees. The cards must be charged with credit in advance and can only be topped-up at certain locations. The main purpose of the system is to enable the park wardens to keep track of who is in the parks and make sure that everyone has paid the entry fee. The cards remain the property of the KWS and must be surrendered once they run out of credit. Any credit left on the card once you finish your trip cannot be refunded.

At the time of writing the smartcard system was in use at Nairobi, Lake Nakuru, Aberdare, Amboseli, Tsavo East and Tsavo West National Parks. The other parks still work on a cash system. You can purchase and charge smartcards at the KWS headquarters in Nairobi and Mombasa, at Aberdare National Park headquarters, at the main gate at Lake Nakuru, at Voi Gate in Tsavo East, and at the Malindi Marine National Park office.

There are five categories of parks In Kenya. These are:

rating	park
A	Aberdare, Amboseli, Lake Nakuru
B	Tsavo East & West
C	Nairobi, Shimba Hills, Meru
D	All other land-based parks, except Arabuko Sokoke and Kakamega
Marine	Kisite-Mpunguti, Diani-Chale, Mombasa, Watamu, Malindi

Gate, Mt Longonot and Kakamega Forest are all worth investigating.

A number of marine national parks have also been established, providing excellent diving and snorkelling (see The Coast chapter for further information). Although all the parks provide the chance to get 'up close and personal' with wildlife, remember that these are wild animals and their actions can be unpredictable.

Heed the warnings of guides and rangers while on safari and seek local advice before venturing off alone into the wilds – swimming in waterholes, lakes and rivers is particularly hazardous.

Probably the most important national parks and reserves are:

Aberdare National Park It offers dramatic highlands with majestic Chania and Karura waterfalls tumbling into the rainforest below.
Amboseli National Park Amboseli's dry plains and scrub forest is famous for large elephant herds, backed by looming Mt Kilimanjaro.
Arabuko Sokoke Forest Reserve This coastal forest area has plentiful birdlife and excellent walking opportunities.
Hell's Gate National Park Hell's Gate has dramatic rocky outcrops and gorges – making it a great place for cyclists and walkers.

Kakamega Forest Reserve Here you'll find virgin tropical rainforest, with red-tailed monkeys, flying squirrels and 330 species of exotic birds.
Lake Bogoria National Park The highlight here is a scenic soda lake with over one million lesser flamingos.
Lake Nakuru National Park This national park is an ornithological paradise with more than 400 recorded bird species, including huge numbers of flamingos and many rhinos.
Masai Mara National Reserve Kenya's most famous park, it has an astonishing amount of wildlife; the highlight is the annual wildebeest migration in July and October.
Meru National Park Meru has rainforests, swamplands and grasslands, with plentiful wildlife, including zebras, giraffes and buffaloes.
Mt Elgon National Park Its famous salt-digging elephants and ancient caves are at the base of a vast extinct volcano, which can be explored by foot.
Mt Kenya National Park The trek to the summit of Africa's second highest mountain (5199m) is one of the great African hikes.
Nairobi National Park Easily accessible from Nairobi, this is a great place to spot black rhinos, birdlife and the less-common antelopes.
Saiwa Swamp National Park Its swamplands and riverine forest are home to the rare sitatunga antelope, crown crane, otter and black-and-white colobus.

National Park Entry Fees

The Masai Mara, Samburu, Buffalo Springs & Shaba National Reserves have the same entry fees as class A national parks. Arabuko Sokoke and Kakamega Forest Reserves are joint KWS and Forestry Department projects and, since January 2003, they have incurred an entry fee of US$10/5 for an adult/child. Entry and camping fees to the parks per person per day are as follows:

category	nonresident (US$) adult/child	resident (KSh) adult/child	camping nonresident (US$)/resident (KSh)
A	30/10	500/200	10/300
B	27/10	500/200	10/300
C	23/10	500/200	10/300
D	15/5	500/200	8/200
Marine	8/5	500/200	-

The land-based parks and reserves charge KSh 200 for vehicles with under six seats and KSh 500 for vehicles seating six to 12. Trekkers and mountaineers pay US$15/8 for nonresident adult/child, or KSh 500/200 per resident, per day for entry to parks that allow these activities. In addition to the public camping areas, there are special camp sites, which change location every year, but these cost more and there's a KSh 5000 setup fee. Guides are available in most parks for KSh 500 per day.

All fees cover visitors for a 24-hour period. So if you enter a park at 3pm, you're allowed to be inside the park until 3pm the following day, even if you leave to stay outside the park.

Samburu, Buffalo Springs & Shaba National Reserves These reserves encompass semiarid open savanna, with easily spotted wildlife and all of the 'Big Five' except rhino.

Shimba Hills National Reserve Shimba Hills has densely forested hills overlooking the coast, with numerous elephants and the rare sable antelope (seen only here).

Tsavo East & West National Parks The largest of Kenya's national parks, Tsavo has sweeping plains, ancient volcanic cones and the 'Big Five'.

Smaller parks and reserves include: **Longonot National Park**, with another volcano trek; **Marsabit National Park & Reserve**, with large herbivores and dense forest; and remote **Sibiloi National Park** and **Central Island National Park** on Lake Turkana. **Chyulu Hills National Park** and **Tana River Primate Reserve** are, to some extent, unknown quantities, as the infrastructure for tourism in these parks is not yet really in place.

Entry fees to national parks are controlled by the KWS, while national reserves, such as Masai Mara, are administered by the local council. See the boxed text 'National Park Entry Fees' for park categories and prices.

GOVERNMENT & POLITICS

Kenya is officially a multiparty state, although the previous long-serving ruling party, KANU, until recently led by Daniel Arap Moi, issued repeated warnings to opposition parties to stay out of politics except during elections. In the last election in 2002, though, KANU was routed and the newly formed coalition of parties, the National Rainbow Coalition, won over two-thirds of the seats. Until then, KANU had ruled the country since independence.

The system of government consists of the president, who holds executive power, and a single legislative assembly consisting of 210 members, the attorney general, the speaker, and 12 members who are nominated by the major parties in parliament in proportion to the number of seats won. Before the 1992 election, it was agreed that subsequent presidents could only serve two five-year terms. In 1987 Moi assumed the right to dismiss judges without recourse to a tribunal, effectively silencing them as a source of opposition. This meant that laws were interpreted according to the KANU party line. With a constitutional review nearly complete, its aim being to make

Kenyan politics less corrupt, there is a high expectation in Kenya that new president, Mwai Kibaki, will institute long-waited reforms.

ECONOMY

The cornerstone of Kenya's capitalist economy is agriculture, which employs around 80% of the population. Agriculture accounts for over 50% of the country's export earnings, but contributes only 25% of the GDP. The principal food crops are maize, sorghum, cassava, beans and fruit, while the main cash crops are coffee, tea, cotton, sisal (agave), pyrethrum (a natural insecticide) and tobacco. Food crops are mostly grown by subsistence farmers on small plots of land, whereas cash crops are produced on large, privately owned plantations employing contract labour. All were hit very hard during the drought of 1997 to 2000.

Coffee and tea are the largest agricultural export earners, with large markets in Asia and the Middle East. However, both have suffered recently due to the global fall in tea prices and the after-effects of the recent drought. Quotas, internationally imposed in order to help European and American interests, exacerbate the situation by limiting Kenya's ability to dispose of its stockpile.

Tourism has slipped back from its previous position as the country's biggest export earner, due to recent violence in Kenya. Unfortunately, events such as the hawker riots in Mombasa in December 2001 and the bombing of the US embassy in 1998 have seen tourists cancelling their holidays in droves. Since that bombing, over 500,000 people have visited annually, contributing more than US$350 million to the economy. It's widely anticipated that tourist numbers will drop further in response to the November 2002 suicide bombing of the Paradise Hotel near Mombasa, and fears of political instability and possible ethnic violence after the December 2002 elections.

Kenya has a relatively well-developed industrial base that accounts for some 13% of GDP. However, poor infrastructure (including power, water and roads), high taxation and rampant corruption are strangling this vital industrial base, which is concentrated around Nairobi and Mombasa. The principal products include processed food, beer, vehicles and their accessories, construction materials (including cement), engineering, textiles, glass and chemicals. If the controversial Tiomin Resources Inc mine near Kwale (southwest of Mombasa) goes ahead, titanium could soon join that list.

A uniquely African economic sector is the *jua kali* industry (literally, 'under the fierce sun'). Under one of Moi's more enlightened policies, open-air and covered workshops were allowed to proliferate across Kenya, producing pots, ironware, weaving, furniture, crafts and basketry. You'll see *jua kali* workshops on the roadside wherever you go.

Kenya's external debt of around US$6.2 billion (in 2000) is still considered to be low by African standards, but a huge proportion of the country's foreign-exchange earnings go into servicing foreign debt. Aid to Kenya from the IMF was suspended in 1997 after Kenya failed to meet anticorruption and good governance requirements, and again in 2001, after a brief resumption. As the Kenyan budget relies on receiving at least US$300 million a year in foreign aid, the most important task facing Moi's successor will be to get the international donors back on side, but how quickly that can be done without radical changes to the status quo remains to be seen.

With the resumption of the Comesa free-trade agreement with Tanzania and Uganda, East Africa has become the biggest market for Kenyan exports, overtaking the EU.

Inflation is currently running at under 5%, GDP per capita is US$360 and Kenya is the 17th poorest country in the world. Kenya also has the third-largest gap between rich and poor, with a staggering 42% of the population subsisting on less than KSh60 per day. Perversely, as the economy gets worse and worse, more shopping centres seem to be built and more *wa benzi* (people who drive Mercedes Benz cars on, it's implied, the proceeds of corruption) are seen on the roads.

POPULATION & PEOPLE

Kenya's population in 2001 was estimated at 30,765,900 and is made up almost entirely of Africans, with small (although influential) minorities of Asians (about 80,000), Arabs (about 30,000) and Europeans (about 30,000). The population growth rate, currently at around 2.8%, has slowed in the last few years due to the soaring incidence of HIV/AIDS, which now infects 15% of adults.

According to 2001 UN figures, life expectancy in Kenya is 52 years, although some sources place it as low as 47, due to the effects of HIV/AIDS. Only 42% of the population has access to clean drinking water but 87% are now thought to have access to adequate sanitation. The infant-mortality rate is 65 per 1000 births (a marked increase on the 1997 figure) and 51% of the population is aged under 18. A sign of growing poverty in rural regions is migration to urban areas where 33% of all Kenyans now live, mostly in squalor.

Africans

Kenya is home to more than 70 tribal groups. The most important distinguishing feature between the tribes is language. The majority of Kenya's Africans fall into two major language groups: the Bantu and the Nilotic. The Bantu people arrived in East Africa in waves from West Africa after 500 BC, and include the Kikuyu, Meru, Gusii, Embu, Akamba and Luyha, as well as the Mijikenda, who preceded the Swahili in many parts of the coast.

Nilotic speakers migrated into the area from the Nile Valley some time later. This group includes the Maasai, Turkana, Samburu, Pokot, Luo and Kalenjin, which, together with the Bantu speakers, account for more than 90% of Kenya's African population. The Kikuyu and the Luo are by far the most numerous groups, and between them hold practically all the positions of power and influence in the country.

A third language grouping, and in fact the first migrants into the country, are the Cushitic speakers. They occupy the northeast of the country and include such tribes as the El-Molo, Somali, Rendille and Galla.

On the coast, Swahili is the name given to the local people who, although they have various tribal ancestries, have intermarried with Arab settlers over the centuries and now have a predominantly Arabic culture.

See the special section 'Tribes of Kenya' for more details on the major groups and their diverse cultures.

Asians

India's connections with East Africa go back to the days of the spice trade, but the first permanent settlers from the Indian subcontinent were indentured workers, brought here from Gujarat and the Punjab by the British to build the Uganda Railway. After the railway was finished, the British allowed many workers to stay and start up businesses, and hundreds of *dukas* (small shops) were set up across the country.

Asian numbers were augmented after WWII and the Indian community came to control large sectors of the East African economy. However, few gave their active support to the black nationalist movements in the run-up to independence, despite being urged to do so by India's prime minister, and were hesitant to accept local citizenship after independence. This earned the distrust of the African community, who felt the Indians were simply there to exploit African labour.

Although Kenya escaped the anti-Asian pogroms that plagued Uganda during the rule of Idi Amin, thousands of shops owned by Asians were confiscated and Asians were forbidden to trade in rural areas. Fortunately, Kenya has learned from the lessons of the economic collapse in Uganda and calls for Asians to 'go home' have faded from the political agenda.

EDUCATION

Literacy rates in Kenya are around 79%, which is markedly higher than any of Kenya's neighbours. Among 15- to 24-year-olds, this shoots up to 95%. This figure is remarkable considering that everyone has to pay for school education in Kenya. The fees at secondary schools are expensive and competition for places is fierce. Although education isn't compulsory, the motivation to get an education is huge, and you'll see children in school uniform everywhere in Kenya, even in the most impoverished rural communities.

Around 65% of all the eligible children attend the 15,000 or so primary schools but only 26% of boys and 22% of girls go on to secondary education at the country's 2500 secondary schools. The rate of university attendance is much lower, mainly for financial reasons, with less than 8% of Kenyans going on to further education. The nation's universities are the University of Nairobi (established in 1956), Kenyatta University (1972) and Kenyatta University of Agricul-

ture and Technology (1981), all in Nairobi; Egerton University (1939) in Nakuru; and Moi University (1984) in Eldoret. Together, they account for around 38,000 students.

ARTS
Music

Although there is an indigenous Kenyan music scene, the overriding musical influence in the country comes from nearby Congo (Zaïre). The Congolese styles of *rumba* and *soukous*, known collectively as *lingala*, were first introduced into Kenya by artists such as Samba Mapangalal (who is still playing) in the 1960s and have come to dominate most of East Africa. This upbeat, party music is characterised by clean guitar licks and a driving *cavacha* drum rhythm.

Kenyan bands were also active during the 1960s, producing some of the most popular songs in Africa, including Fadhili William's famous *Malaika* (Angel), and *Jambo Bwana*, Kenya's unofficial anthem, written and recorded by the hugely influential Them Mushrooms.

Music from Tanzania was influential in the early 1970s, when the band Simba Wanyika helped create Swahili *rumba*, which was taken up by bands such as the Maroon Commandos and Les Wanyika.

Benga is the contemporary dance music of Kenya. It originated among Luo people in western Kenya and became very popular from the 1950s onwards. Since then it has spread throughout the country and been taken up by Akamba and Kikuyu musicians. The music is characterised by clear electric guitar licks and a bounding bass rhythm. Some well-known exponents of *benga* include DO Misiani (a Luo) and his group Shirati Jazz, who have been around since the 1960s and are still churning out the hits. You should also look out for Globestyle, Victoria Kings and Ambira Boys.

Contemporary Kikuyu music often borrows from *benga*. Stars include Sam Chege, Francis Rugwati and Daniel 'Councillor' Kamau who was popular in the 1970s and is still going strong. Joseph Kamaru, the popular musician and notorious nightclub owner of the late 1960s, converted to Christianity in 1993 and now dominates the gospel music scene.

Taarab, the music of the East African coast, originally only played at Swahili weddings and other special occasions, has been given a new lease of life by coastal pop singer Malika.

Popular bands today are heavily influenced by *benga*, *soukous* and also Western music, with lyrics generally in Swahili. These include bands such as Them Mushrooms (now reinvented as Uyoya) and Safari Sound. American-influenced gangster rap and hip hop are also on the rise, including such acts as Necessary Noize, Poxi Presha and Hardstone. For upbeat dance tunes, Ogopa DJs, Nameless, Redsan and Deux Vultures are recommended acts.

The live-music scene in Nairobi is quite fluid, but always vibrant, and a variety of clubs cater for traditional and contemporary musical tastes. A good reference is the *Daily Nation*, which publishes weekly top 10 African, international and gospel charts and countrywide gig listings on Saturday. Live-music venues are listed throughout this book.

Sigana

This is a traditional African performance form. It contains elements of all the major traditional African cultural forms – narration, song, music, dance, chant, ritual, mask, movement, banter and poetry – blending into one long, wonderful storytelling performance. This is not something you'll find very often on the tourist trail, but you have a chance of seeing a show at the Mzizi Arts Centre in Nairobi, which puts on monthly Sigana performances (for more details see the Nairobi chapter).

Literature

There are plenty of novels, plays and biographies by contemporary Kenyan authors, but they can be hard to find outside Africa, despite being published by the African branches of major Western publishing companies. The Heinemann's African Writers Series offers a major collection of such works but they are generally only available in Nairobi and Mombasa.

Two of Kenya's best authors are Ngugi wa Thiong'o and Meja Mwangi. Ngugi is uncompromisingly radical, and his harrowing criticism of the neocolonialist politics of the Kenyan establishment landed him in jail for a year (described in his *Detained – A Prison Writer's Diary)*, lost him his job at Nairobi University and forced him into exile. Meja Mwangi sticks more to social issues and urban dislocation, but has a brilliant sense of humour that threads its way right through his books.

Some titles worth reading by Ngugi wa Thiong'o include *Petals of Blood*, *Matigari*, *The River Between*, *A Grain of Wheat* and *Devil on the Cross*. He has also written extensively in his native language, Gikuyu. Recent titles by Meja Mwangi include *The Return of Shaka*, *Weapon for Hunger* and *The Cockroach Dance*. Most of these titles are published by Heinemann, although some have since been reissued.

Kenya's latest rising star is Binyavanga Wainaina, currently a writer for the South African *Sunday Times* newspaper, who won the Caine Prize for African Writing in July 2002. The award-winning piece was the short story *Discovering Home*, about a young Kenyan working in Cape Town who returns to his parents' village in Kenya for a year. *The Man from Pretoria* is an interesting novel by Kenyan conservationist and journalist Hilary Ngweno.

For writing by women in Africa try *Unwinding Threads*, a collection of short stories by many authors from all over the continent. An interesting female writer working in Kenya is Marjorie Oludhe Magoye, who's *The Present Moment* follows the life stories of a group of elderly women in a Christian refuge in Kenya.

SOCIETY & CONDUCT
Traditional Culture

Kenya's myriad tribal groups each have their own set of traditions and customs. See Population & People earlier in this chapter and the special section 'Tribes of Kenya' for details.

The Dispossessed The break-up of many traditional communities as a result of colonial policies designed to bring people into the money economy has led to the large-scale movement of people to urban areas. Most arrive with nothing and are forced to live in overcrowded shanty towns (some 60% of Nairobi's population lives in just one of these slums, Kibera) with little hope of any reasonable quality of life. All the symptoms of urban alienation can be found in these places, and both alcohol and drug addiction, theft and rape are fairly commonplace. The problem is exacerbated by the incidence of HIV and the government's relocation programme, where hawker slums are bulldozed and the occupants removed to equally squalid camps further from any urban areas. Much of the recent violence in Nairobi and on the coast has been linked to forced evictions and destruction of hawker stalls.

Refugees Conflicts in southern Sudan, southern Ethiopia and Somalia have led to a massive influx of refugees into Kenya. There are many big camps in northern Kenya, especially around Lokichoggio, and many refugees have moved further south setting up home in the Central Highlands, Nairobi, Mombasa and to a lesser degree, the coastal resort towns. In African terms, Kenya is a relatively stable country, with opportunities to make a living or at least receive hand-outs from tourists. Although most refugees are fleeing genuine persecution or hardship, a significant proportion of Kenya's bandits and poachers are Sudanese and Somalis who slip across the porous border to carry out mischief. The civil wars in these countries have led to a huge proliferation of guns, and armed cattle raids that extend into Kenya kill many tribespeople every year.

RELIGION

It's probably true to say that most Kenyans outside the coastal and eastern provinces are Christians of one sort or another, while most of those on the coast and in the east of the country are Muslim. Muslims make up some 30% of the population. In the more remote tribal areas you'll find a mixture of Muslims, Christians and those who follow their ancestral tribal beliefs, although these are definitely a minority.

Christianity

As a result of intense missionary activity from colonial times to the present, just about every Christian denomination is represented in Kenya, from Lutherans and Catholics to Seventh Day Adventists and Wesleyans. The success enjoyed by all these groups is largely due to their combination of Jesus with education and medicine – getting to the soul through the body, if you will.

As in Central and South America, African Christianity is frequently a combination of traditional and Christian beliefs. There are also many pure, home-grown African Christian groups that do not owe allegiance to any of the major Western groups. Street preachers are common throughout the country, and their fire and brimstone sermons normally attract a large crowd.

It's also worth checking out a few churches while you're in Kenya. Even if you can't understand the words, you'll certainly be captivated by what only Africans can do with such beauty and precision – unaccompanied choral singing.

Islam

Most Muslims in Kenya belong to the Sunni branch of the faith and generally practise a moderate version of Islam, although Wahabi fundamentalism is on the rise due to the numerous *madrassas* (religious schools) built here by Saudi Arabia. Religious demonstrations – usually against America or Israel – are on the increase, and hardline beliefs such as *purdah* (requiring women to cover everything but their eyes) are becoming more and more common along the coast.

Only a small minority of Kenyans belong to the Shiah branch of Islam, and most are found among people from the Indian subcontinent. Within the Asian community are representatives of virtually all Shiite sects, but the most influential are the Ismailis – followers of the Aga Khan. As with all Ismailis, they represent a very liberal version of Islam and are perhaps the only branch of the faith strongly committed to the education of women at all levels as well as their participation in commerce and business.

Hinduism

There are a considerable number of Hindu temples in larger urban areas where people from the Indian subcontinent settled after the completion of the Uganda Railway. Both Mombasa and Nairobi have some grand and ornate temples, most of them used by part of the Swaminarayan sect, who are firm devotees of Vishnu. There are scores of other Hindu sects in Kenya – too numerous to mention here – and many are economically quite influential. Westlands in Nairobi has probably the most influential Hindu population.

Female Genital Mutilation

The controversial practice of female genital mutilation (FGM), often euphemistically termed 'female circumcision', is still widespread across Africa, including throughout Kenya. In some parts of tribal Kenya more than 90% of women and girls are subjected to FGM in some form.

The term FGM covers a wide range of procedures from a small, mainly symbolic, cut to the total removal of the clitoris and external genitalia (known as infibulation); the open wound is then stitched up.

The effects of FGM can be fatal. Other side effects, including chronic infections, the spread of HIV, infertility, severe bleeding and lifelong pain during sex, are not uncommon.

Thanks to decades of work by international and local human rights' groups, FGM is now banned in Kenya for girls under 17, but the ritual still has widespread support in parts of the community and continues clandestinely. Despite backing from the World Health Organisation, attempts to stamp out FGM are widely perceived as part of a Western conspiracy to undermine African cultural identity. Many local women's groups, such as the community project Ntanira na Mugambo (Circumcision Through Words), are working towards preserving the rite of passage aspect of FGM without any surgery. It seems likely that it will be African initiatives such as Ntanira na Mugambo, rather than Western criticism, that will finally put an end to FGM.

Traditional Beliefs

Most people leading a tribal existence in Kenya are animists, and their beliefs and rituals are closely linked to the coming of the rains. God is most commonly manifested in the sun, moon, stars, thunder, lightning and trees, particularly the wild fig tree. Colours are also associated with the manifestations of god – black is considered a 'cool', and therefore good, colour, while red and white are bad, 'hot' colours. Another common belief is in spirit beings, who dwell in powerful places and can be violent and unpredictable. Witchdoctors and soothsayers are employed to act as intermediaries with the spirit world.

Most tribes employ rites of passage for both men and women, marking the boundary between childhood and adulthood. Circumcision is still an important ritual for boys, and groups such as the Bukusu, from near Bungoma, stage mass circumcisions every August. Although female circumcision – or more correctly female genital mutilation – is illegal in Kenya, tribal cults such as the Mungiki sect, whose members have carried out forced circumcisions and massacres, have issued frequent edicts that all Kenyan women should be circumcised. See the boxed text 'Female Genital Mutilation' for more details on this contentious issue. Scarification of men and women is still widely practised and most *morani* (warriors) have distinctive scars on their cheeks.

Facts for the Visitor

HIGHLIGHTS

Without doubt it is the wildlife parks that attract most people to Kenya – the wildlife viewing here is still arguably the best and most easily accessible in Africa. The Masai Mara National Reserve may be the best known, but other parks such as Amboseli and Samburu also provide great viewing. There are plenty of less commonly visited parks, which combine plentiful wildlife with wonderful scenery such as Tsavo. Bird-watchers will be well satisfied with a visit to Kakamega Forest Reserve, Saiwa Swamp National Park, or the Rift Valley lakes. Nairobi National Park also has a stunningly varied bird population.

Although wildlife is a major drawcard, Kenya also has an incredibly rich tribal heritage. The cultures here are straight from the pages of *National Geographic* and the way of life for many has changed little in the last few thousand years. You'll see tribal people everywhere, but you'll need to make a bit off effort and get off the established tourist routes to really experience these fascinating cultures. Many tribally owned ranches are being transformed into wildlife sanctuaries, providing the great experience of walking through the bush with a native guide.

Kenya's other big selling point is the beaches, although tourism on the coast is very developed. Offshore are numerous marine parks that offer excellent snorkelling and scuba diving. For an antidote to mass tourism, there are small Swahili communities tucked in among the mangroves, where the pace of life is slow and languorous and the influence of Arabia is still strong. Lamu in particular has a rich and vibrant Swahili culture that has changed little since the days of the Omani sultans.

For the really adventurous, climbing the snowy heights of Mt Kenya, the second-highest peak in Africa, is a superb experience and it doesn't require specialised equipment. Other options include rock climbing, camel safaris, white-water rafting, hiking safaris, windsurfing, sailing trips, gliding, and ballooning over the savanna. The Central Highlands has some excellent trout fishing, while offshore is some of the best deep-sea fishing in the world.

SUGGESTED ITINERARIES
One Week

Rather than trying to cram as much as possible into seven days, you're better off making a choice between the coast or wildlife parks. If you're desperate to see the 'Big Five' (lion, buffalo, elephant, leopard and rhino), join an organised tour to the Masai Mara and Lake Nakuru parks. Those wanting less crowded wildlife viewing should head to Tsavo, Aberdare or Meru National Parks.

On the coast, Tiwi Beach, Watamu and Lamu are the most laid-back places. Malindi is geared up for mass tourism but it's still very pleasant and the beach is fabulous. History buffs may want to check out Fort Jesus in Mombasa or the Gede ruins near Watamu. If you must see a wildlife park as well as the sea, a day trip to the Shimba Hills, near Mombasa, offers almost-certain elephant sightings. Organised coast and Masai Mara packages are widely available but tend to be a little rushed (see the Safaris chapter for further details).

Two Weeks

Having two weeks allows you to explore at a more leisurely pace. There's time for a week-long safari, including two or more of the southern national parks, and you could also fit in some of the Rift Valley lakes or some time on the coast. A more exotic option is to take a Lake Turkana truck safari, which will cover a huge area of the country in around seven to 10 days, taking in many of the parks in the centre of Kenya. Climbing Mt Kenya is also a great experience and will take around five days. In any remaining time you could take a dhow trip to one of the islands off the coast, or kick back for a while in Lamu, which has some of the finest beaches in Kenya. There may also be time to work in a few adventure activities, such as trekking, horse riding, ballooning or scuba diving into your itinerary (see Activities later in this chapter).

One Month

With a month at your disposal, there's time to explore the coast, including a multi-day dhow trip from Lamu, and follow the route of the early explorers right across to Lake Victoria.

A longer safari, to Lake Turkana or several of the less-visited parks in the centre of Kenya is also recommended, and there'll still be time to climb Mt Kenya and visit Masai Mara. Several smaller parks allow trekking, including Kakamega Forest Reserve and Saiwa Swamp National Park, and you can get close to tribal culture by taking a trek in the Cherangani Hills, west of Lake Turkana.

Three Months

A stay of three months allows time for serious exploration of all the obvious attractions and many marvellous places well off the beaten track: the Kerio Valley National Reserve and Sibiloi, Meru and Kora National Parks all await. Getting to the more-remote parks will take you through some fascinating and little-visited tribal areas. Think about trekking opportunities in the more-remote quarters of Kenya, Loroghi Plateau and Suguta Valley. If you don't have a vehicle you still have the time to explore some of the lesser-known national parks and reserves on foot, including the Aberdare, Mt Elgon and Ruma National Parks, but you'll need to make arrangements with the wardens well in advance. Also allow for at least one stay in a luxury lodge or tented camp if you can. After all that backpacking, it's worth it.

PLANNING

If this is your first trip to Africa you might want to check out Lonely Planet's *Read This First: Africa* guide. It's full of useful predeparture information on planning, buying tickets, visa applications, health issues and what to expect from the continent. It also includes a country-profile section with full colour maps.

When to Go

There are a number of factors to take into account when considering what time of year to visit Kenya. The main tourist season (high season) is January and February when the weather is generally considered to be the best – hot and dry. It's also when you'll find the largest concentrations of birdlife on the Rift Valley lakes. At this time, the animals in the wildlife parks tend to congregate more around the watercourses as other sources dry up, making them easier to spot. However, the parks can get crowded and rates for accommodation go through the roof.

June to October, could be called the 'shoulder season' as the weather is still dry. During this period occurs that visual extravaganza – the annual wildebeest migration into the Masai Mara National Reserve from the Serengeti in July and October.

During the long rains (from March to the end of May, the low season) things are much quieter, and you can get some great deals; this is also true during the short rains from October to December. The rains generally don't affect your ability to get around and see things unless you are right out in the sticks (although Amboseli National Park can be flooded out); it's just that you may get rained on, especially in the late afternoon in the Central Highlands and western Kenya.

If you're planning to visit Lamu, you might want to time your visit to coincide with the centuries-old Maulid Festival, which falls on the Prophet Mohammed's birthday (see Lamu in The Coast chapter for more information).

Maps

The *Tourist Map of Kenya*, printed and published in Kenya, gives good detail, as does the *Kenya Route Map*; both cost around KSh250. Marco Polo's 1:1,000,000 *Shell Euro Karte Kenya* and Geocenter's *Kenya* (1:1,000,000) are useful overview maps that are widely available in Europe. The scale and clarity are very good, but the location of some minor features are inaccurate. For those planning a longer trip in Southern and East Africa, Michelin's 1:4,000,000 map 955 (Africa Central and South) is very useful.

Macmillan publishes a series of maps to the wildlife parks and these are not bad value at around KSh250 each (three are available in Europe – Amboseli, Masai Mara and Tsavo East and West). Tourist Maps also publishes a national park series for roughly the same price. They might look a bit flimsy on detail, but they include the numbered junctions in the national parks.

The most detailed and thorough maps are published by the Survey of Kenya, but the majority are out of date and many are out of print. Better bookshops in Nairobi have copies of the most important maps including *Amboseli National Park* (SK 87), *Masai Mara Game Reserve* (SK 86), *Meru National Park* (SK 65), *Tsavo East National Park* (SK 82) and *Tsavo West National Park* (SK 78). It may be worth a visit to the office of the **Kenya Institute of Surveying & Mapping** (☎ 02-861486; e *kism@iconnect.co.ke; Thika Rd, Nairobi)*, but it can take all day and there's no guarantee they'll have any more stock than the bookshops. To get there, take matatu No 44 or 145 from the KBS bus station and ask to be dropped at the Survey of Kenya (opposite the Kenya School of Monetary Studies). Note that some sheets are restricted for security reasons. Getting authorisation requires approval from the Ministry of Defence, which can take weeks.

What to Bring

Bring the minimum. Unless it's absolutely essential, *leave it at home!* A rucksack (backpack) is far more practical than an overnight bag. For security, bags need to be ones that zip shut.

A sleeping bag is handy but not really necessary. If you're going on safari or climbing Mt Kenya, you can hire bags from the safari company.

A tent is a bulky item, and plenty of travellers bring them only to discover they never use them. There are plenty of places you can camp around the country, but if you visit on a safari, they'll provide the tents. If you're only intending to use a tent for a short period, say to climb Mt Kenya, you might be better hiring one from **Atul's** *(Biashara St, Nairobi)* or from the hotels around Mt Kenya.

Clothes need to be both practical and take into account local sensibilities. T-shirts and shorts are frowned on but tolerated. A loose-fitting cotton shirt and long trousers are far better received. The coast is hot and steamy year-round, while Nairobi and the surrounding highlands get decidedly cool in the evening in July and August, so you need to carry one decent warm pullover or fleece. A windproof and waterproof jacket also comes in handy during the rainy seasons.

A good pair of sunglasses is indispensable as is a hat that shades your face and neck, particularly if you're trekking. Also useful is a good, unbreakable water bottle of at least one litre – the collapsible bottles produced by Platypus are very practical.

Other useful items are a Swiss Army knife, a small sewing kit (including a few metres of fishing line and a large needle for emergency rucksack surgery), a roll of insulation or gaffer tape, a length of light nylon cord for a

washing line and half a tennis ball (which makes a good fits-all washbasin plug). A *kikoi*, a striped coloured sarong worn around the waist by men on the coast, can serve as just about anything from a scarf to a towel.

Most toiletries – soap, shaving cream, shampoo, toothpaste, toilet paper, tampons, sanitary towels – are available throughout the country. Disposable nappies are very expensive.

Bring a pair of binoculars. When out in the wildlife parks they're essential for identifying the dozens of species of mammals and birds that you'll come across.

RESPONSIBLE TOURISM

The thousands of people who pass through the Kenyan safari industry each year have had a marked sociological and environmental impact. Thankfully, an increasing number of tourist-orientated companies are aware of this and have chosen to develop 'ecofriendly' packages, using local guides and camp sites owned by the community or by sponsoring a school or similar project. Even the big hotels are wising up to the fact that visitors expect them to make some contribution to the local community. Tourist facilities operated directly by the local community are also springing up all over Kenya with encouragement from development organisations, although most are affiliated with more upmarket places to stay, which guarantee them a reliable income.

Even if you aren't able to choose an obviously 'ecofriendly' company, there are steps you can take to reduce your impact on the environments and societies you come into contact with. Question your own actions and those of companies providing the services and facilities you use and look at the actions of governments, both local and global.

Being a responsible tourist doesn't mean you have to get depressed and spoil your holiday. In fact, by asking a few questions and getting a deeper insight, it can make your trip even more rewarding.

Guidelines

A British organisation called **Tourism Concern** (☎ 020-7753 3330, fax 7753 3331; w *www .tourismconcern.org.uk; Stapleton House, 277-281 Holloway Rd, London N7 8HN)* has come

[Continued on page 41]

Tribes of Kenya

Pokot tribesmen, northern Kenya

Kenyan runner in training

Maasai girls wearing traditional dress and jewellry

El-Molo woman fetching water

Kikuyu witchdoctor with feather headdress

Maasai *morani* (warriors) perform the *numba*

TRIBES OF KENYA

There are more than 70 tribal groups in Kenya, although distinctions between many of the groups are becoming increasingly blurred, largely as a result of migration to the cities and encroaching Western cultural values. Many smaller tribes have come under the umbrella of larger tribal groups to gain protection in intertribal disputes.

Even though many Africans have outwardly drifted away from tribal traditions, the tribe is still the most important aspect of a Kenyan's identity: upon meeting a fellow Kenyan, the first question on anyone's lips is 'What tribe do you come from?'

Although most Kenyans are nominally Christian, there's a surprising number who still practice traditional religious customs.

Akamba

The region east of Nairobi towards Tsavo National Park is the traditional homeland of the Akamba people, which they call Ukambani. Their ancestors were Bantu-speaking, and the Akamba migrated from areas further south several centuries ago.

The Akamba became great traders in ivory, beer honey, iron weapons and ornaments, covering the region all the way from the coast to Lake Victoria and up to Lake Turkana. They traded for food stocks from the neighbouring Maasai and Kikuyu, as their own low-altitude land was relatively poor and couldn't sustain their increasing population.

During colonial times, the Akamba were highly regarded by the British for their intelligence and fighting ability, and were drafted in large numbers into the British Army. Thousands lost their lives in WWI. The British returned the favour by trying to limit the number of cattle the Akamba could own (by confiscating them) and also settled more Europeans in Ukambani. In the 1930s the Akamba responded by marching en masse to Nairobi to squat peacefully at Kariokor Market in protest. After three weeks, the administration gave way and the cattle were eventually returned to the people.

All adolescents go through initiation rites to adulthood at about the age of 12. Young parents are known as 'junior elders' (*mwanake* for men, *mwiitu* for women) and are responsible for the maintenance and upkeep of the village, later becoming 'medium elders' *(nthele)* and 'full elders' *(atumia ma kivalo)*, when they take on the responsibility for death ceremonies and administering the law. The last stage of a person's life is that of 'senior elder' *(atumia ma kisuka)*, who is charged with responsibility for maintaining holy places.

The Akamba are famous for their *makonde*-style (ebony) carvings. Subgroups of the Akamba include the Kitui, Masaku and Mumoni.

El-Molo

This tiny tribal group has strong links with the Rendille, their close neighbours on the shores of Lake Turkana. Both tribes worship the same god, Wak, and bury their dead under stone cairns. The El-Molo rely on Lake Turkana for their existence, living mainly on a diet of fish and occasionally crocodile, turtle and other wildlife. Hippos are hunted from doum-palm rafts with harpoons, and great social status is given to the warrior who kills a hippo.

Inset: Pokot girl (photo by Eric L Wheater)

33

An ill-balanced protein-rich diet and the effects of too much fluoride have taken their toll on the tribe which, over the centuries, has become increasingly vulnerable to disease and attacks from stronger tribes. At one stage there were just 500 El-Molo, living in two small villages on islands on the lake.

Intermarriage with other tribes and abandonment of the nomadic lifestyle has helped to raise their numbers to about 4000, who now live on the mainland near Loyangalani. Traditional costume is now uncommon and the traditional dome-shaped huts of the El-Molo are slowly being replaced by permanent concrete homes.

Gabbra

This small pastoral tribe of striking Arabic-looking people lives in the far north of Kenya, from the eastern shore of Lake Turkana up into Ethiopia. Many Gabbra, who are Cushitic speakers, converted to Islam during the time of slavery. Traditional beliefs include the appointment of an *abbra-olla* (father of the village), who oversees the moral and physical wellbeing of the tribe. Fathers and sons form strong relationships, and marriage provides a lasting bond between clans. Polygamy is still practised by the Gabbra, although the practice is becoming less common as old attitudes to women – as status symbols and unpaid workers – are being eroded.

Gabbra men usually wear turbans and white cotton robes, while women wear *kangas*, thin pieces of brightly coloured cotton. Although *nagaya* (peace) is a core value of the Gabbra, tribal wars with the Samburu were once common.

The Gabbra are famous for their bravery, hunting lions, rhinos and elephants in preference to 'weak' animals such as antelopes.

The Gabbra lost many of their cattle herds to drought and rinderpest epidemics in the 19th century and were decimated by malaria and smallpox before being driven into the Chalbi Desert from their lands in Ethiopia by the army of Emperor Menelik. Somehow the Gabbra survived this and today continue to live in the harshest environment in Kenya. Cattle-rustling is still commonplace among the Gabbra, and these days is carried out with automatic weapons.

ARIADNE VAN ZANDBERGEN

Left: Gabbra woman in front of her desert home

Gusii

The Gusii inhabit an area in the western highlands, east of Lake Victoria, forming a small Bantu-speaking island in a mostly Nilotic-speaking area. They were driven from their original territory near Mt Elgon to the Kisii highlands about 200 years ago, as the Luo, Maasai and Kipsigis advanced into their lands. The Gusii strongly resisted the British advance and were later conscripted in large numbers into the British Army.

The Gusii family typically consists of a man, his wives and their married sons, all of whom live together in a single compound. Initiation ceremonies are performed for both boys and girls, and rituals accompany all important events. Death is considered to be the work of 'witchcraft' rather than a natural occurrence.

Traditionally, the Gusii are primarily both cattle keepers and crop cultivators, and some also brew millet beer.

As is the case with many of Kenya's tribal groups, medicine men (abanyamorigo) have a highly privileged and respected position. They are responsible for maintaining the physical and mental wellbeing of the group – performing the combined role of doctor and social worker.

One bizarre practice was (and still is) the removal of sections of the skull or spine to alleviate maladies such as backache or concussion.

Kalenjin

The term Kalenjin was formulated in the 1950s to describe the group of Nilotic-speaking peoples previously called the Nandi by the British. The Kalenjin comprise the Nandi, Kipsigis, Eleyo, Marakwet, Pokot and Tugen (former President Moi's people) and occupy the western edge of the central Rift Valley area. They first migrated to the area west of Lake Turkana from southern Sudan about 2000 years ago, but then gradually filtered south as the climate became harsher.

Although originally pastoralists, most Kalenjin groups took up agriculture. Beekeeping is still a common activity and the honey is used in trade and for brewing beer. The Kipsigis, on the other hand, have a passionate love for cattle and cattle-rustling continues to cause friction between them and neighbouring tribes.

The Nandi, the second largest of the Kalenjin communities, settled in the Nandi Hills between the 16th and 17th centuries. They had a formidable military reputation and, in the late 19th century, managed to delay the construction of the Uganda railway for more than a decade until Koitalel, their chief, was killed.

As with most tribes, Kalenjin have age-sets into which a man is initiated after circumcision. Polygamy was widely practised in the past. Administration of the law is carried out at the kok (an informal court led by the clan's elders). The Kalenjin doctors, who are mostly (and unusually) women, still use herbal remedies in their work. Other specialist doctors still practise trepanning (taking out pieces of the skull to cure certain ailments from mental illness to headaches).

Many Kenyan athletes are Nandi or Kipsigis.

Kikuyu

The Kikuyu are of Bantu origin and make up the country's largest tribal group and their heartland surrounds Mt Kenya. The original Kikuyu are thought to have migrated to the area from the east and northeast from the 16th century onwards. Famously warlike, the Kikuyu overran the lands of the Athi and Gumba tribes, becoming hugely populous in the process. Today, 20% of Kenyans are Kikuyu. The Kikuyu also fiercely resisted the British, spearheading the Mau Mau rebellion in the 1950s that was a major catalyst for the end of British rule.

The Kikuyu territory borders that of the Maasai, and intertribal raids on property and cattle were once common. Despite this, intermarriage between the two tribes occurred, and there are many cultural similarities between the tribes today. The Kikuyu are the best politically represented tribe in Kenya due the influence of Jomo Kenyatta, the first president of Kenya.

The administration of the clans *(mwaki)*, made up of many family groups *(nyumba)*, was originally taken care of by a council of elders, with a good deal of importance being placed on the role of the witchdoctor, the medicine man and the blacksmith. An important tool of the witchdoctor is the *mwano*, a gourd filled with bones and pebbles, used for divination.

The Kikuyu god, Ngai, is believed to reside on Mt Kenya (Kirinyaga – which means either the 'mountain of brightness' or 'black-and-white peak spotted like ostrich feathers'), which accounts for the practice of orientating Kikuyu homes with the door facing Mt Kenya.

Initiation rites for both boys and girls are very important ceremonies and consist of ritual circumcision for boys and female genital mutilation for girls (although the latter is slowly becoming less common). Each group of youths of the same age belongs to a *riikaan* (age-set) and passes through stages of life, and their associated rituals, together.

Subgroups of the Kikuyu include the Embu, Ndia and Mbeere.

Luo

The Nilotic-speaking Luo people are Kenya's third-largest tribal group, making up about 12% of the population. They live in the west of the country on the shores of Lake Victoria. Along with the Maasai, they migrated from the Nile region of Sudan in about the 15th century.

The Luo's cattle herds suffered terribly from the rinderpest outbreak in the 1890s and most Luo moved to fishing and subsistence agriculture.

During the struggle for *uhuru* (Swahili for 'national independence'), many of the country's leading Kenyan politicians and trade unionists were Luo, including Tom Mboya (assassinated in 1969) and the former vice president Oginga Odinga, who later spearheaded the opposition to former President Moi's one-party state.

The Luo are unusual among Kenya's tribal groups in that circumcision is not practised for either sex. The Luo traditionally extract four or six teeth from the bottom jaw, although this is uncommon today.

The family group consists of the husband, wife (or wives) and their sons and daughters-in-law. The house compound is enclosed by a fence and includes separate huts for the man and for each wife and son.

The family unit is part of a larger grouping of *dhoot* (families), several of which in turn make up an *ogandi* (group of geographically related people), each led by a *ruoth* (chief). As is the case with many tribes, great importance is placed on the role of the medicine man and the spirits.

The Luo, like the Luyha, have two major recreational passions, soccer and music. There are many distinctive Luo instruments made from gourds, gut or wire strings. Few Luo today wear traditional costume.

Luyha

The Luyha are of Bantu origin and are made up of 17 groups. They are the second-largest group after the Kikuyu, but occupy a relatively small area in western Kenya centred on Kakamega, where they settled around the 14th century. Population densities here are incredibly high.

In times past, the Luyha were skilled metal workers, forging knives and tools that were traded with other groups, but today most Luyha are agriculturists, farming groundnuts, sesame and maize. Smallholders also grow large amounts of cash crops such as cotton and sugar cane.

Many Luyha still have a strong and powerful belief in witchcraft and superstition, although, to the passing traveller, this is rarely obvious. Traditional costume and rituals are becoming less common, due mostly to the pressures of the soaring Luyha population.

Maasai

For many, the Maasai are the definitive symbol of 'tribal' Kenya. With a reputation (often exaggerated) as fierce warriors and a proud demeanour, this tribe of Nilotic origin has largely managed to stay outside the mainstream of development in Kenya and still maintains large cattle herds along the Tanzanian border.

The Maasai first migrated to central Kenya from current-day Sudan, but in the late 19th century they were decimated by famine and disease,

Top: Maasai woman and child

ALEX DISSANAYAKE

and their cattle herds were routed by rinderpest. The British gazetted the Masai Mara National Reserve in the early 1960s, displacing the Maasai, and they slowly continued to annexe more and more Maasai land. Resettlement programmes have met with limited success as the Maasai scorn agriculture and land ownership. There is a strong taboo against 'piercing' the soil, and the dead are traditionally left to be consumed by wild animals.

Maasai women are famous for their vast plate-like bead necklaces, while men typically wear a red checked *shuka* (Maasai blanket) and carry a distinctive ball-ended club. Blood and milk are the mainstay of the Maasai diet, supplemented by a drink called *mursik*, made from milk fermented with cow's urine and ashes, which is shown to lower cholesterol.

At around the age of 14, males become *el-moran* (warriors) and build a small livestock camp *(manyatta)* after their circumcision ceremony, where they live alone for up to eight years, before returning to the village to marry. *Morans* traditionally dye their hair red with ochre and fat. Female genital mutilation is common among the Maasai, despite the best efforts of various human rights' groups.

Tourism provides an income to some, either through being guides and camp guards *(askaris)*, selling everyday items (gourds, necklaces, clubs and spears), dancing or simply posing for photographs. However, the benefits are not widespread. In recent years, many Maasai have moved to the cities or coastal resorts, becoming doormen for hotels and restaurants.

Meru

The Meru arrived in the area northeast of Mt Kenya from the coast around the 14th century, following invasions by Somalis from the north. The group was led by a chief *(mogwe)* up until 1974, when the last incumbent converted to Christianity. Justice was administered by a group of tribal elders *(njuuri)*, along with the *mogwe* and witch-doctor, and would often carry out summary executions by giving poison-laced beer to an accused person. Other curious practices included holding a newly born child to face Mt Kenya and then blessing it by spitting on it. Circumcision is also still common. The Meru now live on some of the most fertile farmland in Kenya and grow numerous cash crops including *miraa* plants, the stems of which contain an amphetamine-like stimulant. Subgroups of the Meru include the Chuka, Igembe, Igoji, Tharaka, Muthambi, Tigania and Imenti.

Pokot

The Pokot are Kalenjin by language and tradition, but their diet is dominated by meat, supplemented with blood drawn from cattle, milk and honey. Pokot warriors wear distinctive headdresses of painted clay and feathers similar to those of the Turkana. Flat, aluminium nose ornaments shaped like leaves and lower-lip plugs are common among men. Circumcision is part of the initiation of men and many Pokot women undergo female genital mutilation at around 12 years old. The pastoral Pokot herd their cattle and goats across the waterless scrub north of Lake Baringo and the Cherangani Hills. Cattle raiding (these days with AK-47s), and the search for water and grazing, has often brought them into conflict with the Turkana, Samburu and the Ugandan Karamojong.

Pokot hill farmers are a separate and distinct group who grow tobacco and keep cattle, sheep and goats in the hills north of Kitale, on the approaches to Marich Pass. These hill farmers have a strong craft tradition, producing pottery and metalwork and snuff boxes from calabashes or horns.

Rendille

The Rendille, who are of Cushitic origin, are pastoralists who live in small nomadic communities in the rocky Kaisut Desert in Kenya's northeast. They have strong economic and kinship links with the Samburu and rely heavily on camels for many of their daily needs, including food, milk, clothing, trade and transport. The camels are bled by opening a vein in the neck with a blunt arrow or knife. The blood is then drunk on its own or mixed with milk. The regional colonial administration found the Rendille to be a thorn in its side, as the Rendille avoided taxation and forced labour through both indifference and outright hostility.

Rendille society is strongly bound by family ties, and these centre around monogamous couples. Mothers have a high status and the eldest son inherits the family wealth. It is dishonourable for a Rendille to refuse a loan, so even the poorest Rendille often has claims to at least a few camels and goats.

Rendille warriors often sport a distinctive visor-like hairstyle, dyed with red ochre, while women may wear several kilos of beads. After giving birth to their first child, Rendille women adopt a clay head decoration known as a *doko*, which resembles a rooster's comb.

Samburu

Closely related to the Maasai, and speaking the same language, the Samburu occupy an arid area directly north of Mt Kenya. It seems that when the Maasai migrated to the area from Sudan, some headed east and became the Samburu. As with the Rendille, Samburu warriors often paste their hair with red ochre to create a visor to shield their eyes from the sun. Age is an important factor in assigning social status and a man passes through various stages before becoming a powerful elder in his 30s.

Circumcision heralds a boy's transition to a *moran*, while female genital mutilation is performed on the day of marriage for girls (usually at around 16 years old). After marriage, women traditionally leave their clan, so their social status is much lower than that of men. Samburu women wear similar colourful bead necklaces to the Maasai.

Samburu families live in a group of huts made of branches, mud and dung, surrounded by a fence made of thorn bushes. Livestock, which are kept inside the fence perimeter at night, are used for their milk rather than for meat.

Swahili People

Although the people along the coast do not have a common heritage, they do have a linguistic link – Kiswahili (commonly referred to as Swahili), a Bantu-based language that evolved as a means of communication between Africans and the Arabs, Persians and Portuguese who colonised the East African coast. The word *swahili* is a derivative of the Arabic word for coast – *sahel*.

JANE SWEENEY

The cultural origins of the Swahili come from intermarriage between the Arabs and Persians with African slaves from the 7th century onwards. The Swahili were to become one of the principal slaving forces in Africa. Islam is practised by almost all Swahili, although it usually takes a more liberal form than that practised in the Middle East.

Swahili subgroups include Bajun, Siyu, Pate, Mvita, Fundi, Shela, Ozi, Vumba and Amu (residents of Lamu).

Turkana

The Turkana are one of Kenya's more colourful (and warlike) people. Originally from Karamojong in northeastern Uganda, the Turkana number around 250,000, living in the virtual desert country of Kenya's northwest.

Like the Samburu and the Maasai (with whom they are linguistically linked), the Turkana are primarily cattle herders, although, recently, fishing on the waters of Lake Turkana and small-scale farming is on the increase. The Turkana are one of the few tribes to have voluntarily given up the practice of circumcision.

Traditional costume is still commonplace and Turkana men cover part of their hair with mud, which is then painted blue and decorated with ostrich and other feathers. Despite the intense heat of the region, the main garment is a woollen blanket, often with garish checks. Turkana accessories include a pillow-come-stool carved out of a single piece of wood, a wooden fighting staff and a wrist knife. A woman's attire is dictated by her marital and maternal status; the marriage ritual itself is quite unusual and involves the kidnapping of the bride.

Tattooing is also common. Men were traditionally tattooed on the shoulders for killing an enemy – the right shoulder for killing a man, the left for a woman. A surprising number of men still wear these markings. Witchdoctors and prophets are held in high regard and scars on someone's lower stomach are usually a sign of a witchdoctor's attempt to cast out an undesirable spirit using incisions.

Top: Samburu man in front of an overland truck

[Continued from page 32]

up with a number of guidelines for travellers who wish to minimise negative impacts on the countries they visit. These include:

Save precious natural resources. Try not to waste water. Switch off lights and air-conditioning when you go out. Avoid establishments that clearly consume limited resources at the expense of local residents and the environment.

Support local enterprise. Use locally owned hotels and restaurants and support local traders and craft workers, particularly handicraft cooperatives. Avoid buying souvenirs made from local wildlife such as fur and skins, especially endangered species. The buying and exporting/importing of ivory products is banned in most parts of the world.

Recognise land rights. Indigenous people's ownership of land they use and occupy is recognised by international law. This should be acknowledged irrespective of whether the national government applies the law or not. When in tribal lands, tourists should behave as they would on private lands at home.

Ask before taking any close-up photographs of people. You may have to negotiate a fee in some cases, and if you promise to send them a photograph stick to it.

Don't give money, sweets, pens etc to children. This encourages begging and demeans the child. A donation to a recognised project – a health centre or school – is a more constructive and meaningful way to help.

Respect local etiquette earns *you* respect. Politeness is a virtue in most parts of the world, but remember that different people have different ideas about what is polite. Be aware that public displays of affection are uncommon in Kenya, so act with discretion.

Learn something about the history and current affairs of the country. This will help you understand the idiosyncrasies of its people and also help prevent misunderstandings and frustrations.

Be patient, friendly and sensitive. Remember that you are a guest in the country.

Child Prostitution

Child prostitution is prevalent in Kenya, particularly in Nairobi, and in the tourist areas of the coast where so-called 'sex tourism' is big business, mainly servicing European clients. The streets of downtown Nairobi, in particular, turn into an informal red-light district at night. Although the government is signatory to at least one UN convention aimed at protecting children, it has been less than vigorous in tackling the problem. It is illegal to engage in sexual activity with children under the age of 14; people caught doing so may be liable to legal action in their own country.

TOURIST OFFICES
Local Tourist Offices

Considering the extent to which the country relies on tourism, it's incredible to think that, at the time of writing, there is no tourist office in Nairobi. However, there are a number of **tourist offices** around the country (☎ 011-225428; e mcta@ikenya.com; Moi Ave, Mombasa; ☎ 0123-70747; Malindi Centre, Lamu Rd, Malindi; ☎ 0127-2234; e diani@technosoft kenya.com; Barclays Centre, Diani Beach).

Good Wood

A growing issue in Kenya is the consumption of native hard woods by its woodcarvers. An incredible 80,000 trees are chopped down every year just to provide wood for the carving industry, and trees such as mahogany and ebony (from which the popular black *makonde*-style carvings are made), are increasingly threatened.

In partnership with Kew Gardens in London, the World Wildlife Foundation (WWF; aka World Wide Fund for Nature) and Unesco have started a 'Good Wood' campaign to promote the use in carving of common fast-growing trees such as neem, jacaranda, mango and olive. These woods need to be cured before carving, but the end results are almost indistinguishable from carvings made from hard woods. Many handicraft cooperatives now exclusively use wood that is approved by the Forest Stewardship Council, an international body which certifies wood from managed forests.

By applying consumer pressure to the industry, it is hoped that the carvers in Kenya can be persuaded to switch over to 'good woods', which will protect the livelihoods of 60,000 carvers as well as Kenya's dwindling hardwood forests. For more information, visit the website W www.kew.org/peopleplants/regions/kenya.

Tourist Offices Abroad

The Ministry of Tourism maintains a number of overseas offices including the following. Most only provide information by telephone, post or email.

Canada (☎ 905-891 3909; ℮ contact@kenya tourism.ca) 1599 Hurontario St, Suite 100, Mississauga, Ontario, L5G 4S1

Germany (☎ 089-2366 2194; ℮ think@magnum .de) c/o The Magnum Group, Herzogspital-strade 5, D-80331 Munich

Italy (☎ 02-481 023 61, fax 433 183 85; ℮ kenya@adams.it) c/o Adam & Partner Italia, Via Salaino 12, 20144 Milano

Netherlands (☎ 020-421 2668, fax 670 5357; ℮ kenia@travelmc.com) Leliegracht 20, 1015 DG Amersterdam

Spain (☎ 93 292 0655, fax 93 415 4577; ℮ kenya@ketal.com) c/Tuset 10, 3o4a, 08006 Barcelona

UK (☎ 020-7836 7738, fax 7240 1024; ℮ kenya@iiuk.co.uk) 69 Monmouth St, London WC2H 9JW

USA (☎ 1-866-44-KENYA, fax 763 212 2533; ℮ inforusa@magicalkenya.com) Carlson Destination Marketing Services, PO Box 59159 Minneapolis, MN 55459-8257

VISAS & DOCUMENTS

Visas

Visas are now required by almost all visitors to Kenya, including Europeans, Australians, New Zealanders, Americans and Canadians, although citizens from a few smaller Commonwealth countries are exempt. Visas are valid for three months from the date of entry and can be obtained upon arrival at Jomo Kenyatta International Airport in Nairobi. The visa fee is UK£35 or US$50 for a single-entry visa, and UK£70 or US$100 for multiple entries. If you have any other currencies, you'll have to change them into shillings and then back into dollars. Tourist visas can be extended for a further three-month period – see Visa Extensions later – but seven-day transit visas (US$20) cannot.

It's also possible to get visas from Kenyan diplomatic missions overseas, but you should apply well in advance, especially if you're doing it by mail. Visas are usually valid for entry within three months of the date of issue. Applications for Kenyan visas are simple and straightforward in Tanzania and Uganda, and payment is accepted in local currency. Visas can also be issued on arrival at the land borders with Uganda and Tanzania, although a single-entry Kenyan visa allows you to visit Tanzania and Uganda and return without requiring a new visa.

It's always best to smarten up a bit if you're arriving by air; requests for evidence of 'sufficient funds' are usually linked to snap judgements about your appearance. If it's fairly obvious that you aren't intending to stay and work, you'll generally be given the benefit of the doubt.

(For information on having longer-term stays, see Courses and also Work later in this chapter.)

Visa Extensions Visas can be renewed at immigration offices: in Nairobi *(☎ 02-332110; ground floor, Nyayo House, cnr Kenyatta Ave & Uhuru Hwy)*; in Mombasa *(☎ 011-311745; Uhuru ni Kari building, Mama Ngina Dr)*; in Malindi *(☎ 0123-30876; Vasco da Gama Rd)*; in Lamu *(☎ 0121-33032; back from the waterfront, south of the main jetty)*; or in Kisumu *(Reinsurance Plaza, 1st floor, cnr Jomo Kenyatta Hwy & Oginga Odinga Rd)* during normal office hours. Staff at the immigration offices are generally friendly and helpful, but the process takes a while. You'll need two passport photos and KSh2200 for a three-month extension. Visas are issued the same day. You also need to fill out a form registering as an alien if you're going to be staying more than 90 days. Immigration offices are only open Monday to Friday.

Visas for Onward Travel Since Nairobi is a common gateway city to East Africa and the city centre is easy to get around, many travellers spend some time here picking up visas for other countries that they intend to visit. If you are going to do this you need to plan ahead of time and call the embassy to confirm the hours that visa applications are received (these change frequently in Nairobi). Most embassies will want you to pay visa fees in US dollars (see Embassies & Consulates later in this chapter for contact details).

Just because a country has an embassy or consulate here, it doesn't necessarily mean you can get that country's visa. The borders between Kenya and Somalia, and Kenya and Sudan, are closed, so you'll have to go to Addis Ababa in Ethiopia if you want a Sudanese visa. Somali visas are unlikely to be available for the foreseeable future.

For Ethiopia, Tanzania and Uganda, three-month visas are readily available in Nairobi and cost US$50 for most nationalities. Two passport photos are required for applications and visas can usually be issued the same day. Note that under the East African partnership system, a single-entry Kenyan visa will also allow you to enter Tanzania or Uganda and re-enter Kenya. Always check the latest entry requirements with embassies before travel.

Travel Insurance

Get some! A travel-insurance policy to cover theft, loss and medical problems is a very sensible precaution. The policies handled by STA Travel and other student travel organisations are usually good value. Some policies offer lower and higher medical-expense options, but the higher ones are chiefly for countries such as the USA that have extremely high medical costs. Medical cover is the most vital element of any policy, but make sure you check the small print:

- Some policies specifically exclude 'dangerous activities', which can include motorcycling, scuba diving, even trekking. If such activities are on your agenda you don't want that sort of policy. Using a locally acquired motorcycle licence may not be valid under your policy.
- You may prefer a policy that pays doctors or hospitals direct rather than you having to pay on the spot and claim later. If you have to claim later, make sure you keep all documentation.
- Some policies ask you to call back (reverse charges) to a centre in your home country where an immediate assessment of your problem is made. Be aware that reverse-charge calls are not always possible to a number of countries from Kenya (see Post & Communications later in this chapter).
- Check that the policy covers ambulances or an emergency flight home. If you have to stretch out on public transport you will need two seats and somebody has to pay for them!
- If you are travelling in remote areas, check with your insurance company that you can contact the Flying Doctor Services or AAR Health Services, (see following) direct in the event of a serious emergency without having to confirm it with your company at home first.

If you are travelling through Africa for some time or heading to the more remote corners of Kenya, it may be worth signing up with either the Flying Doctor Services or AAR Health Services. These two organisa-tions can come and get you should you become ill in a *lugga* (dry river bed) west of North Horr or in another remote area.

The **Flying Doctor's Society of Africa** (☎/fax 02-501300-3, 604651, fax 601594, emergency ☎ 02-501280, 602492; W www .amref.org) is part of the African Medical & Research Foundation (Amref) and operates a 24-hour air-ambulance service out of Nairobi's Wilson Airport. It will get you from wherever you are to the nearest decent hospital (often Nairobi). 'Tourist cover' costs US$25 for two months within 500km of Nairobi and US$50 within 1000km.

The private **AAR Health Services** (☎ 02-715319, emergency ☎ 717376; e info@aar .co.ke; Fourth Ngong Rd) is a comprehensive medical network that covers Kenya, Tanzania and Uganda and offers a road and local service as well as emergency air evacuation. Tourist cover is US$1 per day and an extra US$85 a year pays for a 'white card' that will get you back to the hospital of your choice anywhere in the world.

Driving Licence & Permits

An international driving licence is not necessary in Kenya, but can be useful. If you have a British credit-card–type licence, be sure to bring the counterfoil, as the date you passed your driving test – something car-hire companies here will want to know – isn't printed on the card itself.

Carnets If you're bringing a foreign-registered vehicle into Kenya, it must be covered by a *carnet de passage*. The purpose of a carnet is to exempt you from import duties, on the understanding that you'll be taking the vehicle out with you when you leave. Carnets can only be issued by national motoring organisations and they have to be absolutely sure that if the need to pay duties ever arises, you will pay these in full. Import duty can vary considerably, but, generally speaking, it's between the value of and 1½ times the value of a new vehicle.

To get a carnet you need to make an application to a national motoring organisation in the country where your vehicle is registered. It will issue you with an indemnity form for completion either by a bank or an insurance company. Once this is completed and a bond deposited with a bank or a premium paid to an insurance company, the motoring organisation issues a carnet. The cost of the carnet itself is minimal. The whole process generally takes about a week to complete. (For more information about bringing a vehicle into Kenya and driving, see Car & 4WD in the Getting Around chapter.)

Vaccination Certificates

Travellers to Kenya need not have proof of a yellow fever vaccination unless coming from a country where the disease is endemic. However, as yellow fever is endemic to Kenya, you will need it to enter another country after leaving Kenya; so have it before you arrive – and be protected from the disease at the same time. See Health later in this chapter for more details.

Copies

Important documents (passport data page and visa page, credit cards, travel insurance policy, air/bus/train tickets, driving licence etc) should be photocopied before you leave home. Leave one copy with someone at home and keep another with you, separate from the originals.

It's also a good idea to store details of your vital travel documents in Lonely Planet's free online Travel Vault in case you lose the photocopies or can't be bothered making them. Your password-protected Travel Vault is accessible online anywhere in the world – create it at Ⓦ www.ekno.lonelyplanet.com.

EMBASSIES & CONSULATES

Kenya has diplomatic representation in many countries. Where there is no Kenyan embassy or high commission, visas can be obtained from the British embassy or high commission.

It's important to realise what your own embassy – the embassy of the country of which you are a citizen – can and can't do to help you if you get into trouble. Generally speaking, it won't be much help in emergencies if the trouble you're in is remotely your own fault. Remember that you are bound by the laws of the country you are in. Your embassy will not be sympathetic if you end up in jail after committing a crime locally, even if such actions are legal in your own country.

In genuine emergencies you might get some assistance, but only if other channels have been exhausted. For example, if you

need to get home urgently, a free ticket home is exceedingly unlikely – the embassy would expect you to have insurance. If you have all your money and documents stolen, it might assist with getting a new passport, but a loan for onward travel is out of the question.

Kenyan Embassies & Consulates

Kenya maintains embassies and consulates abroad, including the following:

Austria (☎ 01-712 39 19, fax 712 39 22) Neulinggasse 29/8, 1030 Vienna
Australia (☎ 02-6247 4788, fax 6257 6613) QBE Bldg, 33-35 Ainslie Ave, Canberra, ACT 2601
Canada (☎ 613-563 1773, fax 233 6599) 415 Laurier Ave, East Ottawa, Ontario, KIN 6R4
Congo (Zaïre) (☎ 012-372 3641) 4002 Ave de l'Ouganda, BP 9667, Zone Degombe, Kinshasa
Ethiopia (☎ 01-610033, fax 611433) Fikre Miriam Rd (PO Box 3301), Addis Ababa
France (☎ 01 56 62 25 25, fax 01 47 20 44 41) 3 Rue Freycinet, 75116 Paris
Germany (☎ 030-2592 2660, 2592 6650) Markgrafenstr 63, 10969 Berlin
India (☎ 011-614 6538, fax 614 6550) E-66 Vasant Marg, Vasant Vihar, 10057 New Delhi
Israel (☎ 03-575 4633, fax 575 4788) 3rd floor, 15 Rehov Abba Hillel Silver, Ramat Gan 52522 (PO Box 52136), Tel Aviv
Italy (☎ 396-808 2714, fax 808 2707) Via Archmede 165, 00197, Rome
Japan (☎ 03-3723 4006, fax 3723 4488) No 2, 24-3 Yakumo, 3 Chome, Meguro-Ku, Tokyo 152
Netherlands (☎ 070-350 4215, fax 355 3594) Niewe Parklaan 21, 2597, The Hague
Rwanda (☎ 070-82774, fax 86234) PO Box 1215, Kigali
South Africa (☎ 012-362 2249, fax 362 2252) 302 Brooks St, Menlo Park, 0081, Pretoria
Sudan (☎ 011-460386, fax 472264) Street 3 Amarat (PO Box 8242), Khartoum
Tanzania (☎ 051-112955/7, fax 113098) NIC Investment House, Samora Ave (PO Box 5231), Dar es Salaam
Uganda (☎ 041-258235, fax 258239) Plot No 41, Nakasero Rd (PO Box 5220), Kampala
UK (☎ 020-7636 2371/5, fax 323 6717) 45 Portland Place, London W1N 4AS
USA (☎ 202-387 6101, fax 462 3829) 2249 R Street NW, Washington DC 20008

Embassies & Consulates in Kenya

A selection of countries that maintain diplomatic missions in Kenya are listed below. Missions are in Nairobi (area code ☎ 02) unless stated otherwise.

Austria (☎ 228281, fax 331792; e austria@
africaonline.co.ke) 2nd floor, City House,
Wabera St
Australia (☎ 445034, fax 444718) Riverside Dr
Canada (☎ 214804, fax 226987) Comcraft
House, Haile Selassie Ave
Congo (Zaïre) (☎ 229771, fax 334539) 12th
floor, Electricity House, Harambee Ave
Eritrea (☎ 443163, fax 443165) New Rehema
House, Westlands
Ethiopia (☎ 723027, fax 723401) State House Ave
France (☎ 339783, fax 217013; w ambafr.icon
nect.co.ke) 9th floor, Barclays Plaza, Loita St
Germany (☎ 719386, fax 714886; e ger-emb@
form-net.com) Williamson House, Fourth
Ngong Ave
India (☎ 222566, fax 334167) Jeevan Bharati
Bldg, 2nd floor, Harambee Ave
Israel (☎ 722182, fax 715966) Bishops Rd
Italy Embassy: (☎ 337320) International House,
Mama Ngina St;
Consulate (☎ 011-314705, fax 316654)
Jubilee Bldg, Moi Ave, Mombasa
Japan (☎ 332955, fax 216530) ICEA Bldg, 15th
floor, Kenyatta Ave
Mauritius (☎ 229167, 221006) International
House, Mama Ngina St,
Netherlands (☎ 4447412, fax 4447416)
Riverside Lane
Rwanda (☎ 317400, fax 317403) 2nd floor,
International House, Mama Ngina St
South Africa (☎ 215616, fax 223687) Lonrho
House, 1st floor, Standard St
Spain (☎ 335711, fax 332858) 3rd floor,
International House, Mama Ngina St
Sudan (☎ 2720883, fax 710612) AON-Minet
Bldg, Mamlaka Rd (at the time of writing, the
embassy did not issue visas)
Switzerland (☎ 228735, fax 217388) 7th floor,
International House, Mama Ngina St
Tanzania (☎ 331056, fax 218269) Reinsurance
Plaza, 9th floor, Aga Khan Walk
Uganda (☎ 330899, fax 330970; e ugahinrb@
users.africaonline.co.ke) 1st floor, Uganda
House, Baring Arcade, Kenyatta Ave
UK (☎ 714699, fax 719082; e bhcinfo@africaon
line.co.ke) Visa & Immigration Section, Upper
Hill Rd
USA (☎ 537800, fax 537810) Mombasa Rd; visa
section (☎ 240290, fax 216511) 3rd floor,
Barclays Plaza, Loita St

CUSTOMS

There are strict laws about taking wildlife
products out of Kenya. The export of products made from elephant, rhino and sea turtle
are prohibited. The collection of coral is also
not allowed. Ostrich eggs will also be confiscated unless you can prove you brought the

egg from a certified ostrich farm. Always
check to see what permits are required, especially for the export of any plants, insects and
shells.

The usual regulations apply to items you
can bring into the country – 50 cigars, 200
cigarettes, 250g of pipe tobacco, 1L of alcohol, 250ml of perfume and other personal
items such as cameras, laptop computers and
binoculars. Obscene publications are banned,
which may extend to some lad's magazines.

You are allowed to take up to KSh100,000
out of the country.

MONEY
Currency

The unit of currency is the Kenyan shilling
(KSh), which is made up of 100 cents. Notes
in circulation are KSh1000, 500, 200, 100, 50
and 20, and there are also new ('copper')
coins of KSh20, 10, 5 and 1 in circulation.
Old ('silver') coins are much bigger and
heavier, and come in the denominations of
KSh5 (seven-sided) and KSh1. The old 50,
10 and 5 cent coins are now rare. Note that
most public telephones in Nairobi and other
major towns have been modified to accept
only 'copper' coins. Locally, the shilling is
commonly known as a 'bob', after the old
English term for a one shilling coin.

Exchange Rates

After a period of instability in the early
1990s, the Kenyan shilling stabilised for a
while, but has gone through all sorts of fluc-
tuations with the recent suspensions of IMF
aid. Currents rates are:

country	unit		shilling
Australia	A$1	=	KSh44.0
Canada	C$1	=	KSh49.4
Ethiopia	Birr10	=	KSh97.1
Euro Zone	€1	=	KSh81.6
Japan	¥100	=	KSh65.7
New Zealand	NZ$1	=	KSh40.9
Switzerland	SWF1	=	KSh56.1
Tanzania	TSh1000	=	KSh83.3
UK	UK£1	=	KSh124.9
Uganda	USh1000	=	KSh45.0
USA	US$1	=	KSh77.8

Exchanging Money

While most major currencies are accepted in
Nairobi and Mombasa, once away from
these two centres you'll run into problems

with currencies other than US dollars, pounds sterling and euros. Away from the coast, you may even struggle to change euros. Play it safe and carry US dollars – it makes life much simpler. Travellers cheques are also more widely accepted if they're in US dollars, British pounds, or, increasingly, in euros.

With deregulation, the black market has almost vanished and the handful of money-changers who still wander the streets offering 'good rates' are usually involved in scams of one kind or another. The exception is at land border crossings, where moneychangers are often the only option. Most offer reasonable rates, although you should be careful not to get short changed or scammed during the transaction.

The best places to change money are foreign exchange or 'forex' bureaus, which can be found everywhere and usually don't charge commission. The rates for the main bureaus in Nairobi are published in the *Daily Nation* newspaper. Watch out for differing small bill (US$10) and large bill (US$100) rates; the larger bills usually get the better rates.

Banks also change money, but they charge large commissions and there's a fee per travellers cheque, so you're better off carrying larger denominations. The rates for travellers cheques may be better than at the bureaus, and you'll have the added bonus of being able to put your money away in the secure setting of the bank foyer. American Express (AmEx) has offices in Mombasa and Nairobi, where you can buy and sell AmEx travellers cheques.

Credit & ATM Cards Barclays Bank now has a large network of ATMs covering most major Kenyan towns. They support Master-Card, Visa, Plus and Cirrus international networks. Standard Bank ATMs are not so widespread, but now take Visa cards. The only problem is that the data link with the outside world often goes down, so don't rely on being able to withdraw money whenever you need it.

Credit cards are becoming increasingly popular, with old fraud-friendly, fully manual swipe machines slowly being replaced by electronic systems that dial up for every transaction. While there's less chance of someone making extra copies of chits this way, the connections fail with tedious regularity. Visa and MasterCard are now widely accepted, but it would be prudent to stick to upmarket hotels and restaurants and shopping centres to use them.

Be aware that credit-card companies will not post cards to Kenya, so you'll have to arrange a courier.

International Transfers Postbank, a branch of the Kenyan Post Office, is now the agent for Western Money Union, the global money-transfer company. Using their service is an easy way (if the phones are working) of receiving money in Kenya. Handily, the sender pays all the charges and there's a branch of Post Bank in most towns, often within the post office itself or close by. Senders should call **Western Money Union** *(in USA ☎ 1800 325 6000; in Australia ☎ 1800 501 500; in New Zealand ☎ 0800 270 000; in UK ☎ 0800 833 833)* or visit the website (w www.westernunion.com) to find out the location of the nearest agent.

Security

With street crime a way of life in Nairobi, you should be doubly careful with your money. The safest policy is to leave all your valuables in the hotel safe and just carry enough cash for that day. If you do need to carry larger sums around, a money belt worn under your clothes is the safest option. However, be aware that muggers will usually be expecting some kind of moneybelt. See Dangers and Annoyances later in this chapter for a complete rundown on matters of personal security.

Costs

The price of budget accommodation in Kenya is very reasonable if you're happy with communal showers and toilets. Clean sheets are provided in the better places and sometimes you'll also get soap, a towel, a pair of thongs (rubber sandals) and a sink. Camping costs around KSh200 to KSh250 per person but hostels aren't a cheap option at around KSh400 per person. For a hotel room, at the bottom end you're looking at KSh150 to KSh200 a single per night and KSh200 to KSh400 a double. If you want your own bathroom, prices rise to around KSh300 a single and KSh500 a double. The first really comfortable rooms kick in about the KSh600/1000 (per single/double) mark but you can easily pay twice this in Nairobi. For safari lodges, tented camps and beach resorts, the sky is the limit – you can pay as little as US$30 per person or as much as US$500.

For cheap eats, there are plenty of small cafés in every town that cater to local people. You can get an African meal for KSh100 to KSh200. For just a little bit more, the Indian restaurants are great value. Some offer all-you-can-eat lunches for around KSh300. There are plenty of upmarket restaurants serving cuisine from around the world, and a few truly world-class choices in Nairobi or on the coast, but you can expect to pay between KSh500 and KSh1500, and have 17% VAT added to your bill.

Tipping is often expected in Kenya's more-expensive hotels and restaurants and a 10% tip is the norm. Bills at posher places will often include a service charge.

The price of beer and soft drinks depends entirely on where you buy them. They're obviously cheapest when bought from a supermarket (around KSh50 for a beer), but cost twice this or more at many bars and restaurants. Top-end hotels charge upwards of KSh180 a bottle!

Public transport is very reasonable and the Nairobi–Mombasa train is fun and good value. To travel this route on the train in 1st/2nd class costs KSh2100/1302. The same journey by bus costs about KSh500.

The biggest expense in Kenya is safaris, although it's usually a cheaper way to see the wildlife than if you rented a 4WD and organised everything yourself. Basic camping safaris (which can also be the most fun) cost from US$65 per day per person, including transport, food, hire of tents, park fees, camping fees and the wages of the guides and cooks. For a safari with lodge or tented camp accommodation, you'll be looking at US$120 upwards per day.

If you do want to hire a car, bank on paying at least KSh7000 per day for a small 4WD or saloon, once you've factored in the insurance and kilometres (see Car & 4WD in the Getting Around chapter).

The prices used in this book are as provided by the organisation concerned, and may be quoted in US dollars, euros, British pounds or in Kenyan shillings, but payment can always be in local currency.

POST & COMMUNICATIONS
The Kenyan postal system is run by the government Postal Corporation of Kenya, now rebranded as the dynamic-sounding 'Posta'. Letters sent from Kenya rarely go astray but do take up to two weeks to reach Australia or the USA. Incoming letters to Kenya take anywhere from four days to a week to reach the post-restante service in Nairobi.

Postal Rates
The airmail rates (in KSh) for items posted from Kenya are:

item	Africa	Europe	USA & Australia
letter	55	60	80
small postcard	30	35	45
large postcard	55	60	80
aerogram	40	40	40

Note that there are different prices for large and small postcards – if in doubt, go with the large postcard price.

Parcels
If sent by surface mail, parcels take three to six months to reach Europe, while airmail parcels take around a week. As a rough guide, a 1kg parcel sent by air/surface mail would cost KSh1160/940 to Africa, KSh1270/1030 to Europe and KSh1330/1070 to the rest of the world.

Most things arrive eventually, although there *is* a problem with theft within the system. Curios, clothes and textiles will be OK, but if your parcel contains anything of obvious value, send it by courier. Posta has it's own courier service, EMS, which is considerably cheaper than the big international courier companies. The best place to send parcels from is the main post office in Nairobi (see Post & Communications in the Nairobi chapter).

Receiving Mail
Letters can be sent care of poste restante in any town. Make sure your correspondents write your name in block capitals and also underline the surname.

Some travellers use the **American Express clients mail service** *(Nairobi office ☎ 02-222906; Hilton Hotel, Mama Ngina St; Mombasa office ☎ 011-312461; Nkrumah Rd)* and this can be a useful, and more reliable, alternative. You'll need to have an AmEx card or be using their travellers cheques to avail yourself of this service. The postal addresses in Nairobi and Mombasa are:

American Express Clients Mail Service:
  Express Kenya Ltd, PO Box 40433, Nairobi
  Express Kenya Ltd, PO Box 90631, Mombasa

Telephone

The phone system is just about functional, except on the coast, where many people have to rely on prepaid mobile phones. With the new Telkom Kenya phone cards, any phone can now be used for prepaid calls – you just have to dial the access number (☎ 0844) and enter in the number and passcode on the card. There are booths selling the cards all over the country, but make sure that any cards you buy are within their expiry date. Cards come in denominations of KSh200, KSh500, KSh1000 and KSh2000.

If you want to call Kenya from another country, the country code is ☎ 254. Do not dial the first zero in the area code.

International Calls International calls from Kenya are expensive. To Europe, Australia or the USA the peak/off-peak rate is US$1.46/1.06 per minute; to the rest of the world it's US$1.82/1.45 per minute. A three-minute minimum call charge applies to these calls. It's more expensive to call through the operator. You can always dial direct using a phone card. All phones receive incoming calls (the number is usually scrawled in the booth somewhere).

Reverse-charge (collect) calls are possible, but only to countries who have set up free direct-dial numbers that allow you to reach the international operator in the country you are calling. Currently these include: the UK (☎ 0800 220441), the USA (☎ 0800 111/2), Canada (☎ 0800 220114/5), New Zealand (☎ 0800 220641) and Switzerland (☎ 0800 220411).

Calls put through a hotel operator from your room will cost an extra 25% to 50% so check before making a call.

Local & Long-Distance Calls The minimum charge for a local call from a payphone is KSh6 for three minutes, while long-distance rates vary depending on the distance. When making a local call from a public phone, make sure you put a coin into the slot first. Calls to Tanzania and Uganda are priced as long-distance calls, not international.

Mobile Phones Kenya uses the GSM 900 system, which is compatible with Europe and Australia but not with the North American GSM 1900. If you have a GSM phone, check with your service provider about using it in Kenya, and beware of calls being routed internationally (very expensive for a 'local' call).

Alternatively, if your phone isn't locked into a network, you can pick up a prepaid mobile starter pack from one of the Kenyan mobile-phone companies – the main players are Safaricom and Kencell. The start-up packages include a SIM card and KSh500 of free calls and cost KSh1200 to KSh2400, depending on where you buy them. You can buy top-up cards from shops and booths across the country.

Mobile phones can be hired from the office of **Bon Voyage** (☎ 822700) at Nairobi's Wilson Airport. Handsets cost KSh150 per day, plus KSh2000 talktime and a KSh5000 deposit.

Email & Internet Access

Email is firmly established in Kenya, although the speed fluctuates wildly, even in Nairobi. Many towns have email bureaus and computer training centres where you can surf the Internet and access Hotmail, Yahoo! and other Internet-based email accounts. In Nairobi or Mombasa, you can pay as little as KSh1 per minute, but in rural areas, the rate can be as high as KSh50 per minute!

If you haven't got one already, web-based email accounts are available from Lonely Planet's **eKno** (ⓦ www.ekno.lonelyplanet.com), or from **HotMail** (ⓦ www.hotmail.com) or **Yahoo! Mail** (ⓦ mail.yahoo.com) and others. You can then access your mail from anywhere in the world using any Internet-connected computer. Places that offer Internet access are listed throughout this book.

DIGITAL RESOURCES

With so many people booking hotels, safaris and activities from overseas, anyone who is anyone in Kenya has some kind of website. Most feature online booking or reservation services, which are pretty handy. You can book domestic flights on the websites of several regional airlines serving Kenya (see the Getting Around chapter for some of these). As well as individual companies, there are numerous websites that provide general information on things to see and do in Kenya.

A good place to start is the website of Lonely Planet (W www.lonelyplanet.com). Here you'll find information on travelling to Kenya and most other places on earth, the latest travel news, postcards from other travellers and the Thorn Tree bulletin board, where you can ask questions before you go or dispense advice when you get back. The subwwway section links you to probably the most useful travel resources elsewhere on the Web.

Other useful websites include:

Africaonline You can get excellent up-to-date information on music, events, current affairs and lots more from this site; however, their server is unpredictable.
W www.africaonline.com

Jambo Kenya Its a broad-based Kenya information website with lots of tourist information.
W www.jambokenya.com

Kenya Association of Tour Operators This site contains the names of approved members.
W www.katokenya.org

Kenyaweb It is an excellent and varied source of information on everything to do with Kenya.
W www.kenyaweb.com

Kenya Wildlife Service The KWS site contains up-to-date information on national parks and reserves.
W www.kenya-wildlife-service.org

Kenya WWW Newsgroup This popular discussion forum covers many Kenyan issues and has numerous Kenyan subscribers.
W kenya.rcbowen.com/talk

Magical Kenya This is the official website of the Kenya Tourism Board and it has some good information on things to see and do.
W www.magicalkenya.com

National Museums of Kenya This is a website for information on museums and projects across Kenya.
W www.museums.or.ke

Nation Newspaper The best Kenyan newspaper has a very good website with news, information and regular features on tourist issues.
W www.nationaudio.com

BOOKS

Large-format, hardback, photo-essay books on Africa are becoming easier to find in Western bookshops, but other books about the region can be hard to find. Many titles are published in different editions by different publishers in different countries, so a book might be a hardback rarity in one country while it's readily available in paperback in another. Fortunately, bookshops and libraries search by title or author, so your local bookshop or library is well placed to advise you on the availability of any of the following recommendations.

Lonely Planet

East Africa covers the region, with information on Kenya, Tanzania, Uganda, Rwanda and Burundi. *Africa on a shoestring* covers about 50 African countries, concentrating on practical information for budget travellers.

Trekking in East Africa, by David Else, covers a selection of treks and expeditions in the mountains and wilderness areas of Kenya, Tanzania, Uganda and Malawi, and has plenty of advice and general information about trekking in this part of the world.

The *Swahili phrasebook* will help you solve most of your basic language problems in Kenya while *Watching Wildlife East Africa* will help you identify the fauna and flora found in each major park.

Guidebooks

Insight Kenya, edited by Mohammed Amin & John Eames, offers excellent photographs and lively text. It concentrates more on the country's history, people, culture, sights and wildlife rather than on practical information and is a good book to read before you go.

Kilimanjaro & Mount Kenya: A Climbing and Trekking Guide, by Cameron M Burns, is a decent guide to these two peaks and is available outside Africa.

Travel

Journey to the Jade Sea, by John Hillaby, recounts this prolific travel writer's epic trek to Lake Turkana in northern Kenya in the days before the safari trucks began pounding up the dirt. Other seminal titles to look for include *Initiation,* by JS Fontaine, and *A Bend in the River* by VS Naipaul.

Although he only came here primarily to shoot the wildlife, Ernest Hemingway wrote some famous books about Kenya, including *The Snows of Kilimanjaro* and *Green Hills of Africa.* Also interesting are

The Life of My Choice and *My Kenya Days* by Wilfred Thesiger.

Two women's accounts of life in East Africa early the 20th century are long-term bestsellers. *Out of Africa,* by Karen Blixen (Isak Dinesen), is one of the most famous African tales and has also been made into a hugely popular movie. *West with the Night,* by the famous aviator Beryl Markham, the first person to fly east to west across the Atlantic, has also been a major bestseller.

The Flame Trees of Thika is a famous childhood memoir by Elspeth Huxley, while *African Nights* and *I Dreamed of Africa* are two chapters in the incredible life of Italian expat Kuki Gallman. *No Picnic on Mt Kenya* by Felice Benuzzi is a personal account of escaping from a British prisoner-of-war camp in World War II to climb Mt Kenya, rather than achieve freedom – fascinating stuff.

Bill Bryson's *African Diary* is about to published. It concentrates on a seven-day trip to Kenya.

History, Politics & Economics

There are numerous books on the history of Africa including *The Penguin Atlas of African History,* by Colin McEvedy, *A Short History of Africa,* by Roland Oliver & JD Fage, and *Africa: A biography of the Continent* by John Reader. Also excellent reading is *Rogue Ambassador,* by Smith Hempstone, the former American ambassador who was a little more outspoken than his bosses in Washington thought appropriate.

A fantastic local history, published in Kenya is *The Lunatic Express,* by Charles Miller, an epic tome that covers the story of the Uganda railway, and in the process touches on most of Kenya's history.

For European colonial history from an African perspective, hunt down *Mau Mau and Kenya,* by Wunyabari Maloba, and *How Europe Underdeveloped Africa* by Walter Rodney. Other challenging books covering the same topic include *The Africans,* by David Lamb, *The Making of Contemporary Africa,* by Bill Freund, and *A Year in the Death of Africa* by Peter Gill.

For opinions on Kenyan politics since independence, read *Facing Mount Kenya,* by Jomo Kenyatta, *The Challenge of Nationhood,* by Tom Mboya, a charismatic Luo politician who was killed by Kikuyu rivals in 1969, and Oginga Odinga's *Not Yet Uhuru.*

There isn't space here to cover all the books written by Dr Richard Leakey but *Wildlife Wars* is a challenging account of his radical approach to conservation during his time at the KWS. If you want a background on the famous Leakey dynasty, read *Ancestral Passions: The Leakey Family and the Quest for Humankind's Beginnings* by Virginia Morell.

Ghosts of Tsavo, by Phillip Caputo, is the latest book to look at Tsavo's famous man-eating lions, although Colonel John Patterson's *The Man Eaters of Tsavo* is still the definitive text – after all, he finally shot the man-eaters.

Soon to be published, *The Green Belt Movement,* by Wangari Maathai promises to be a fascinating account of the Kenyan Green Belt Movement. *This Our Exile,* by James Martin & Robert Coles, is an interesting exploration of the plight of Rwandan, Somali and Sudanese refugees in Kenya, seen through the eyes of a young Jesuit priest.

General

There are some excellent, but quite expensive, photo-essay hardbacks on sale in Kenya and worldwide. Many feature the excellent photographs of Kenyan photojournalist Mohammed Amin, who was tragically killed in 1996. Titles to look out for include *Journey Through Kenya,* by Mohammed Amin, Duncan Willets & Brian Tetley. You can also see Mo's work in his book *Cradle of Mankind* and *Ivory Crisis* co-written with Ian Parker.

Other good, glossy, coffee-table books covering varied aspects of Kenya include *Africa Adorned,* by Angela Fisher, *Maasai,* by Tepilit Ole Saitoti & Carol Beckwith, and *Isak Dinesen's Africa* by various authors. More challenging is *Shootback*, a collection of photos taken with disposable cameras by Nairobi's street children, edited by Lana Wong.

Various other large-format, glossy hardbacks cover various tribal societies of Kenya, especially the Maasai and Samburu; they are available in most bookshops in Nairobi and Mombasa.

Flora & Fauna Guides

The Kingdon Field Guide to African Mammals, by Jonathan Kingdon, is hard to beat for details on specific mammals. *Birds of Kenya and Northern Tanzania,* by Dale

Zimmerman & Don Turner (hardback), and *Birds of Eastern Africa,* by Ber van Perlo (paperback), are both very good references that are widely available in Kenya. The *Field Guide to Flowers of East Africa,* by Michael Blundell, is comprehensive.

NEWSPAPERS & MAGAZINES

Tabloid newspapers are printed in both English and Swahili. Of the three English-language papers, the best is the *Daily Nation* (KSh35; w www.nationaudio.com), which has local and overseas coverage, and a good no-nonsense attitude. It's very brave in its political coverage. The others are the KANU-mouthpiece *Kenya Times* (KSh35, daily; w www.kentimes.com) and the reliable *East-African Standard* (KSh35, daily; w www.eastandard.net). The *East African* is a decent weekly paper covering important stories in depth and is published by the Nation group.

There is also a good range of locally produced magazines in both English and Swahili. Principal among these is the *Weekly Review,* which is the Kenyan equivalent of *Time* and *Newsweek*. Radicals berate this magazine as being a tool of government propaganda, but it's still a good read.

Foreign newspapers (up to a week old) in English, French, Italian and German are readily available in Nairobi and Mombasa, but vary greatly in price depending on where you buy them. Current-affairs magazines such as *Time, Newsweek* and *New African* are also widely available at a controlled price that's printed on the front cover. *New African* is the best of the bunch if you're looking for detailed coverage of African affairs and events. It's published monthly.

Note that some magazines sold by street vendors can be very out of date.

RADIO & TV
Radio
The Kenyan Broadcasting Corporation (KBC) has radio transmissions in English, Swahili and African languages. The frequency for the English-language service varies depending on where you are in the country, but you can pick up the FM services in Nairobi (95.6 MHz), Mombasa (104.4 MHz), Malindi (93.6 MHz), Kisumu (96.6 MHz) and Meru (103.5 MHz). For the best in African music, tune into KBC's Metro FM

(101.9 MHz in Nairobi). Programme listings are published in the *Daily Nation*.

The **BBC World Service** (☎ 020-7557 1165; w www.bbc.co.uk/worldservice) broadcasts in English and Swahili on shifting short-wave frequencies throughout the day. The FM stations are easier to find; in Nairobi the World Service is on 93.7 MHz and in Mombasa it's on 93.9 MHz. **Voice of America** (w www.voa.gov) and **Deutsche Welle** (w dw-world.de) also transmit in Kenya; see their websites for transmission frequencies.

TV
There are currently four Kenyan TV channels – KBC1, KBC2, KTN and STV. All have a broadly similar output of imported American daytime TV shows such as *Days of Our Lives* and occasional African news and current-affairs programmes. All the channels show CNN or Sky news at least once a day, and KTN and KBC both show Kenyan and African news in the evenings. Most evenings there are also late-night action movies and lots of material from Channel O, South Africa's answer to MTV.

Cable TV from South Africa is the most recent addition to the scene in Kenya. Most mid-range and better hotels subscribe to the service, so you can watch CNN, BBC and a handful of movie and sports channels. Unfortunately, one of the most popular channels is the painfully heart-warming Hallmark Channel.

PHOTOGRAPHY & VIDEO
Photographing people remains a sensitive issue in Kenya. Some tribal groups request money for you to take their photo. See Social Graces later in this chapter for more information about photographic etiquette.

You should never get your camera out at border crossings or near government or army buildings.

Film & Equipment
You'll find Kodak and Fuji 100, 200 and 400 ASA (ISO) print and slide film widely available in Nairobi, but even 100 ISO slide film is hard to find in Mombasa. If you plan to use 64 or 800 ASA film, bring it from home. As an indication of price, 36-exposure slide film in Nairobi costs about KSh320; 36-exposure colour print film is cheaper at KSh250 to KSh350 but again, only 100, 200 and (less

frequently) 400 ASA are available. Watch out for out-of-date film on sale.

Both VHS and Hi-8 video film is available in Nairobi and Mombasa, but it's expensive.

If you don't have the inclination or the resources to buy expensive equipment but you know a bit about photography, it is possible to hire SLR cameras and lenses in Nairobi (see Photography in the Nairobi chapter).

Film Processing

Shops and booths offering film processing are popping up in small towns and villages all over Kenya. In addition, there are plenty of one-hour film-processing labs in Nairobi, and at least one in all other major towns. They can handle any film speeds, but results can vary. Depending on the print size, processing and printing costs about KSh480 to KSh650 for a 36-exposure film.

E6 slide processing can only be done in Nairobi and costs around KSh450 for a 36-exposure film.

Wildlife Photography

For serious wildlife photography an SLR (single lens reflex) camera that can take long focal length lenses is necessary.

Zoom lenses are best for wildlife photography as you can more easily frame your shot to get the best composition. This is important as the animals are almost constantly on the move. The 70mm to 210mm zoom lenses are popular and the 200mm is really the absolute minimum you need to get good close-up shots. The only problem with zoom lenses is that with all the glass (lenses) inside them they absorb about 1½ 'f' stops of light, which is where 200 and 400 ASA film starts to become useful.

Telephoto (fixed focal length) lenses give better results than zoom lenses, but you're limited by having to carry a separate lens for every focal length. A 400mm or 500mm lens brings the action right up close, but again you need fast film to make the most of it.

Another option is to carry a 2 x teleconverter, which is a small adaptor that fits between the lens and the camera body, and doubles the focal length of your lens, so a 200mm lens becomes 400mm.

When using long lenses a tripod can be extremely useful, and with anything greater than about 300mm it's a necessity. Within the confined space of the hatch of a safari minibus, you may be better off with a folding, miniature tripod, which you can rest on the roof. Remember to ask your driver to switch off the engine to stop vibrations. If you've got a large lens but no tripod, lying your camera on a small bean bag or cushion can help reduce camera shake.

A decent bag is essential to protect your gear from the elements and the rough roads. It's also vital to make sure that your travel insurance policy covers your camera gear should it get stolen.

TIME

Time in Kenya is GMT/UTC plus three hours year-round. You should also be aware of the concept of 'Swahili time', which perversely is six hours out of kilter with the rest of the world. Noon and midnight are 6 o'clock *(saa sitta)* Swahili time, and 7am and 7pm are 1 o'clock *(saa moja)*. Just add or subtract six hours from whatever time you are told; unfortunately Swahili doesn't distinguish between am and pm. You don't come across this often unless you speak Swahili, but you still need to be prepared for it.

ELECTRICITY

Kenya uses the 240V system. The power supply is usually reliable and uninterrupted in most places, although there are occasional failures. Power sockets are of the three-square-pin variety as used in the UK, although some older buildings have double round-pin sockets. Bring a universal adaptor if you need to charge your phone or run other appliances.

WEIGHTS & MEASURES

The old imperial system has gone the same way as the empire and Kenya is now a metric country. Distances are in kilometres and most things are weighed out in kilograms, though fruit and vegetables are often sold in small pyramid-shaped piles – the prices given will refer to a single stack of fruit.

LAUNDRY

There are very few laundrettes in Kenya (Nairobi is where you'll find most of them) so most people have their clothes washed by hand at the hotel where they're staying. This is a pricey business and you'll generally end up paying around KSh30 per item, or around KSh400 for a week's worth of washing.

TOILETS

These vary from pits (quite literally) to full-flush, luxury conveniences that can spring up in the most unlikely places. Nearly all hotels sport flushable sit-down types, but toilet seats are a rare commodity. You'll be riding bareback most of the time.

In the more-upmarket bush camps you'll be confronted with a long drop covered with some sort of seating arrangement. The best of these is in Tusk Camp high in the Aberdare National Park – you'll have a view across the forest to Mt Kenya. Things are less pleasant when camping in the wildlife parks. Squatting on crumbling concrete is common. When trekking it's good practice to burn your soiled toilet paper before burying it.

HEALTH

Travel health depends on your predeparture preparations, your daily health care while travelling and how you handle any medical problem that arises. While the potential dangers can seem quite frightening, in reality few travellers experience anything more than an upset stomach.

Rural clinics are common in Kenya and there are small hospitals across the country, but most are not recommended as the risks of picking up something worse than you came in with are high. Private hospitals are invariably better than government hospitals and there are some good Saudi Arabian–built hospitals on the coast. English is usually spoken. Pharmacies are very common in Kenya, and most sell antimalarial drugs and many generic medicines. Be careful of the expiry dates on medicines sold in Kenya.

If you stick to bottled water (widely available, but make sure the seal is intact), are careful with what you eat and wash your hands before eating, you should be able to avoid most of the orally transmitted diseases. Always wash fruit and vegetables with bottled water before eating and avoid salads, except in upmarket restaurants.

Predeparture Planning

Immunisations Plan at least six weeks ahead for getting your vaccinations: some of them require more than one injection, while some vaccinations should not be given together. Note that some vaccinations should not be given during pregnancy or to people with allergies – discuss this with your doctor.

Currently, yellow fever is the only vaccine that is subject to international health regulations. You'll need a yellow fever certificate if you're coming to Kenya from countries where the disease is endemic, or heading elsewhere after Kenya, which has yellow fever as well; so it makes a lot of sense to get one before leaving your home country.

Occasionally, travellers face bureaucratic problems at Kenya's land borders regarding the need for a cholera vaccination, even though all countries have dropped it as a health requirement for travel. If you're planning a cross-Africa trip it's wise to get a cholera vaccination exemption certificate from a doctor. This is not necessary if you are flying into Kenya.

Vaccinations you should consider for this trip include the following. Carry proof of your vaccinations.

Diphtheria & Tetanus Vaccinations for these two diseases are usually combined and are recommended for everyone. After an initial course of three injections (usually given in childhood), boosters are necessary every 10 years.

Polio Everyone should keep up to date with this vaccination, which is normally given in childhood. A booster every 10 years maintains immunity.

Hepatitis A Vaccine (eg, Avaxim, Havrix 1440 or VAQTA) for Hepatitis A provides long-term immunity (possibly more than 10 years) after an initial injection and a booster at six to 12 months. Alternatively, an injection of gamma globulin can provide short-term protection against hepatitis A – two to six months, depending on the dose given. It is not a vaccine, but is ready-made antibody collected from blood donations. It is reasonably effective and, unlike the vaccine, it is protective immediately, but because it is a blood product, there are current concerns about its long-term safety. Hepatitis A vaccine is also available in a combined form, Twinrix, with hepatitis B vaccine. Three injections over a six-month period are required, the first two providing substantial protection against hepatitis A.

Hepatitis B Travellers who should consider vaccination against hepatitis B include those on a long trip, or where sexual contact or needle sharing is a possibility. Vaccination involves three injections, with a booster at 12 months. More rapid courses are available if necessary.

Typhoid Vaccination against typhoid is recommended if you are travelling for more than a couple of weeks. It is now available either as an injection or as capsules to be taken orally.

Cholera The current injectable vaccine against cholera is poorly protective and has many side effects, so it is not generally recommended for travellers.

Meningococcal Meningitis Immunisation is recommended if going to Kenya for several months, especially if working among the local population in schools or hospitals or spending time in the far north of Kenya. A single injection gives good protection against the major epidemic forms of the disease for three years. Protection may be less effective in children under two years.

Yellow Fever A yellow fever vaccine is now the only vaccine that is a legal requirement for entry into certain countries, usually only enforced when coming from an infected area. Vaccination is recommended for travel in areas where the disease is endemic, which includes Kenya and most of its neighbours. You may have to go to a special yellow fever vaccination centre.

Rabies Vaccination should be considered by those who will spend a month or longer in Kenya, especially if cycling, handling animals, caving or travelling to remote areas, and for children (who may not report a bite). Pretravel rabies vaccination involves having three injections over 21 to 28 days. If someone who has been vaccinated is bitten or scratched by an animal, they will require two booster injections of vaccine; those not vaccinated require more.

Tuberculosis The risk of TB to travellers is usually very low, unless you will be living with or closely associated with local people. Vaccination against TB (BCG) is recommended for children and young adults living in these areas for three months or more.

Malaria Medication Malaria is now present across Kenya, even in Nairobi, and epidemics are common. Antimalarial drugs do not prevent you from being infected but kill the malaria parasites during a stage in their development and significantly reduce the risk of becoming very ill or dying. Expert advice on medication should be sought, as there are many factors to consider, including the risk of exposure to malaria-carrying mosquitoes, the side effects of medication, your medical history and whether you are a child or an adult or pregnant. You may like to carry a treatment dose of medication for use if symptoms occur (see Malaria under Insect-Borne Diseases for more details).

Health Insurance Make sure that you have adequate health insurance. It's important to be covered for emergency medical air evacuation with an organisation such as Amref (see Travel Insurance under Visas & Documents earlier in this chapter).

Travel Health Guides Lonely Planet's *Healthy Travel Africa* is a handy pocket size and packed with useful information including pretrip planning, emergency first aid, immunisation and disease information, and what to do if you get sick on the road. *Travel with Children* from Lonely Planet also includes advice on travel health for younger children.

There are also a number of excellent travel health sites on the Internet. From the Lonely Planet home page there are links at Ⓦ www.lonelyplanet.com/weblinks/wlheal .htm to the World Health Organization (WHO) and the US Centers for Disease Control & Prevention.

Other Preparations Make sure you're healthy before you start travelling. If you are going on a long trip, make sure your teeth are OK; if you wear glasses take a spare pair and your prescription.

If you require a particular medication, take an adequate supply, as it may not be available locally. Take part of the packaging showing the generic name rather than the brand, which will make getting replacements easier. It's a good idea to have a legible prescription or letter from your doctor to show that you legally use the medication to avoid any problems.

Basic Rules

Food There is an old colonial adage that says: 'If you can cook it, boil it or peel it you can eat it...otherwise forget it'. Vegetables and fruit should be washed with purified water or peeled where possible. Beware of ice cream that is sold in the street or anywhere it might have been melted and then refrozen; if there's any doubt (eg, a power cut in the last two days), steer clear. Shellfish such as mussels, oysters and clams should be avoided as well as undercooked meat, particularly in the form of mince. Steaming does not make shellfish safe for eating.

If a place looks clean and well run and the vendor also looks clean and healthy, then the food is probably safe. In general, places that are packed with travellers or locals will be fine, while empty restaurants are questionable. The food in busy restaurants is cooked and eaten quite quickly, with little standing around, and is probably not reheated.

Water The number one rule is *be careful of the water* and especially ice. If you don't know for certain that the water is safe, assume the worst. Reputable brands of bottled water or soft drinks are generally fine, although in some places bottles may be refilled with tap water. Only use water from containers with a serrated seal – not tops or corks. Take care with fruit juice, particularly if water may have been added. Milk should be treated with suspicion as it is often unpasteurised, although boiled milk is fine if it is kept hygienically. Tea or coffee should also be OK, since the water should have been boiled.

Water Purification The simplest way of purifying water is to boil it thoroughly. Vigorous boiling should be enough; however, at high altitude water boils at a lower temperature, so germs are less likely to be killed. Boil it for longer in these environments.

Consider purchasing a water filter for a long trip. There are two main kinds of filter. Total filters take out all parasites, bacteria and viruses and make water safe to drink. They are often expensive, but they can be more cost effective (and far more environmentally friendly) than buying bottled water. Simple filters (which can even be a nylon mesh bag) take out dirt and larger foreign bodies from the water so that chemical solutions work much more effectively; if water is dirty, chemical solutions may not work at all. It's very important when buying a filter to read the specifications, so that you know exactly what it removes from the water and what it doesn't. Simple filtering will not remove all dangerous organisms, so if you cannot boil water it should be treated chemically. Chlorine tablets or purifying tablets that include silver will kill many pathogens, but not some parasites such as giardia and amoebic cysts. Iodine is more effective in purifying water and is available in tablet form. Follow the directions carefully and remember that too much iodine can be harmful.

Medical Problems & Treatment

Self-diagnosis and treatment can be risky, so you should always seek medical help. An embassy, consulate or five-star hotel can usually recommend a local doctor or clinic. Although

we do give drug dosages in this section, they are for emergency use only. Correct diagnosis is vital. In this section we have used the generic names for medications – check with a pharmacist for brands available locally.

Note that antibiotics should ideally be administered only under medical supervision. Take only the recommended dose at the prescribed intervals and use the whole course, even if the illness seems to be cured earlier. Stop immediately if there are any serious reactions and don't use the antibiotic at all if you are unsure that you have the correct one. Some people are allergic to commonly prescribed antibiotics such as penicillin; carry this information (eg on a bracelet) when travelling.

Environmental Hazards
Altitude Sickness Lack of oxygen at high altitudes (over 2500m) affects most people to some extent. The effect may be mild or severe and occurs because less oxygen reaches the muscles and the brain at high altitude, requiring the heart and lungs to compensate by working harder. Symptoms of Acute Mountain Sickness (AMS) usually develop during the first 24 hours at altitude but may be delayed up to three weeks. Mild symptoms include headache, lethargy, dizziness, difficulty sleeping and loss of appetite. AMS may become more severe without warning and can be fatal. Severe symptoms include breathlessness, a dry, irritative cough (which may progress to the production of pink, frothy sputum), severe headache, lack of coordination and balance, confusion, irrational behaviour, vomiting, drowsiness and unconsciousness.

Treat mild symptoms by resting at the same altitude until recovery, usually a day or two. Paracetamol or aspirin can be taken for headaches. If symptoms persist or become worse, however, *immediate descent is necessary*; even 500m can help. Drug treatments should never be used to avoid descent or to enable further ascent.

The drugs, acetazolamide and dexamethasone, are recommended by some doctors for the prevention of AMS. However, their use is controversial. They can reduce the symptoms, but they may also mask warning signs; severe and fatal AMS has occurred in people taking these drugs. In general, we do not recommend them for travellers.

To help prevent acute mountain sickness:

- Ascend slowly – have frequent rest days, spending two to three nights at each rise of 1000m. If you reach a high altitude by trekking, acclimatisation takes place gradually and you are less likely to be affected than if you fly directly to high altitude. It is always wise to sleep at a lower altitude than the greatest height reached during the day if possible. Also, once above 3000m, care should be taken not to increase the sleeping altitude by more than 300m per day.
- Drink extra fluids. The mountain air is dry and cold and moisture is lost as you breathe. Evaporation of sweat may occur unnoticed and result in dehydration.
- Eat light, high-carbohydrate meals for more energy.
- Avoid alcohol as it may increase the risk of dehydration.
- Avoid sedatives.

Heat Exhaustion Dehydration and salt deficiency can cause heat exhaustion. Take time to acclimatise to high temperatures, drink sufficient liquids and do not do anything too physically demanding.

Salt deficiency is characterised by fatigue, lethargy, headaches, giddiness and muscle cramps; salt tablets may help, but adding extra salt to your food is better.

Anhidrotic heat exhaustion is a rare form of heat exhaustion that is caused by an inability to sweat. It tends to affect people who have been in a hot climate for some time, rather than newcomers. It can progress to heatstroke. Treatment involves removal to a cooler climate.

Heatstroke This serious, occasionally fatal, condition can occur if the body's heat-regulating mechanism breaks down and the body temperature rises to dangerous levels. Long, continuous periods of exposure to high temperatures and insufficient fluids can leave you vulnerable to heatstroke.

The symptoms are feeling unwell, not sweating very much (or at all) and a high body temperature (39°C to 41°C or 102°F to 106°F). Where sweating has ceased, the skin becomes flushed and red. Severe, throbbing headaches and lack of coordination will also occur, and the sufferer may be confused or aggressive. Eventually the victim will become delirious or convulse. Hospitalisation is essential, but in the interim get victims out of the sun, remove their clothing, cover them with a wet sheet or towel and then fan continually. Give fluids if they are conscious.

Hypothermia Too much cold can be just as dangerous as too much heat. If you are trekking at high altitudes or simply taking a long bus trip over mountains, particularly at night, be prepared. On Mt Kenya, Mt Elgon or when walking anywhere in the Central Highlands, you should always be prepared for cold, wet or windy conditions even if you're just out walking or hitching.

Hypothermia occurs when the body loses heat faster than it can produce it and the core temperature of the body falls. It is best to dress in layers; silk, wool and some of the new artificial fibres are all good insulating materials. A hat is important, as a lot of heat is lost through the head. A strong, waterproof outer layer (and a 'space' blanket for emergencies when on treks in exposed areas) is essential. Carry basic supplies, including food containing simple sugars to generate heat quickly and fluid to drink.

Symptoms of hypothermia are exhaustion, numb skin (particularly fingers and toes), shivering, slurred speech, irrational or violent behaviour, lethargy, stumbling, dizzy spells, muscle cramps and violent bursts of energy. Irrationality may take the form of sufferers claiming they are warm and trying to take off their clothes.

To treat mild hypothermia, get the person out of the wind and/or rain, remove their clothing if it's wet and change with dry, warm clothes. Give them hot liquids – not alcohol – and some high-kilojoule, easily digestible food. Do not rub victims: instead, allow them to slowly warm themselves. This should suffice to treat the early stages of hypothermia. The early detection and treatment of mild hypothermia is the only way to prevent severe hypothermia, a critical condition.

Prickly Heat This itchy rash is caused by excessive perspiration trapped under the skin. It usually strikes people who have just arrived in a hot climate. Keeping cool, bathing often, drying the skin and using a mild talcum or prickly heat powder, or resorting to air-conditioning, may help.

Sunburn In the tropics, the desert or at high altitude you can get sunburnt surprisingly quickly, even through cloud. Use a sunscreen, a hat, and a barrier cream for your nose and lips. Calamine lotion or a commercial, after-sun preparation are good for mild sunburn. Protect your eyes with good-quality sunglasses, particularly if you will be near water, sand or snow.

Infectious Diseases

Bilharzia Also known as schistosomiasis, this disease is transmitted by minute worms. They infect certain varieties of freshwater snails found in rivers, streams, lakes and particularly behind dams. The worms multiply and are eventually discharged into the water. Risk areas in Kenya include Lake Victoria, the estuary area of the Tana River and around Kitui and Taveta.

The worm enters through the skin and attaches itself to your intestines or bladder. The first symptom may be a general feeling of being unwell, or a tingling and sometimes a light rash around the area where it entered. Weeks later a high fever may develop. Once the disease is established, abdominal pain and blood in the urine are other signs. The infection often causes no symptoms until the disease is well established (several months to years after exposure) and damage to internal organs irreversible.

Avoiding swimming or bathing in freshwater where bilharzia is present is the main method of preventing the disease. Even deep water can be infected. If you do get wet, dry off quickly and dry your clothes as well.

A blood test is the most reliable way to diagnose the disease, but the test will not show positive until a number of weeks after exposure.

Diarrhoea Simple things such as a change of water, food or climate can all cause a mild bout of diarrhoea, but a few rushed toilet trips with no other symptoms is not indicative of a major problem.

Dehydration is the main danger with any diarrhoea, particularly in children or the elderly as dehydration can occur quite quickly. Under all circumstances *fluid replacement* (at least equal to the volume being lost) is the most important thing to remember. Weak black tea with a little sugar, soda water, or soft drinks allowed to go flat and diluted 50% with clean water are all good. With severe diarrhoea, a rehydrating solution is preferable to replace minerals and salts lost.

Commercially available oral rehydration salts (ORS) are very useful; add them to boiled or bottled water. In an emergency you can make up a solution of six teaspoons of sugar and half a teaspoon of salt to a litre of boiled or bottled water. You need to drink at least the same volume of fluid that you are losing in bowel movements and vomiting. Urine is the best guide to the adequacy of replacement – if you have small amounts of concentrated urine, you need to drink more. Keep drinking small amounts often. Stick to a bland, fat-free diet as you recover.

Gut-paralysing drugs such as loperamide or diphenoxylate can be used to bring relief from the symptoms, although they do not actually cure the problem. Only use these drugs if you do not have access to toilets, eg, if you *must* travel. Note that these drugs are not recommended for children under 12 years.

In certain situations, antibiotics may be required: diarrhoea with blood or mucus (dysentery), any diarrhoea with fever, profuse watery diarrhoea, persistent diarrhoea not improving after 48 hours and severe diarrhoea. These suggest a more serious cause of diarrhoea, and in these situations gut-paralysing drugs should be avoided.

In these situations, a stool test may be necessary to diagnose what bug is causing your diarrhoea, so you should seek medical help urgently. Where this is not possible the recommended drugs for bacterial diarrhoea (the most likely cause of severe diarrhoea in travellers) are norfloxacin 400mg twice daily for three days or ciprofloxacin 500mg twice daily for five days. These are not recommended for children or pregnant women. The drug of choice for children would be co-trimoxazole with dosage dependent on weight. A five-day course is given. Ampicillin or amoxycillin may be given in pregnancy, but medical care is necessary.

Two other causes of persistent diarrhoea in travellers are giardiasis and amoebic dysentery.

Giardiasis is caused by a common parasite, *Giardia lamblia*. Symptoms include stomach cramps, nausea, a bloated stomach, watery, foul-smelling diarrhoea and frequent gas. Giardiasis can appear several weeks after you have been exposed to the parasite. The symptoms may disappear for a few days and then return; this can go on for several weeks.

Amoebic dysentery, caused by the proto-zoan *Entamoeba histolytica*, is characterised by a gradual onset of low-grade diarrhoea, often with blood and mucus. Cramping abdominal pain and vomiting are less likely than in other types of diarrhoea, and fever may not be present. It will persist until treated and can recur and cause other health problems.

You should seek medical advice if you think you have giardiasis or amoebic dysentery, but where this is not possible, the recommended drugs are either tinidazole or metronidazole. Treatment is a 2g single dose of tinidazole or 250mg of metronidazole three times daily for five to 10 days.

Fungal Infections These infections occur more commonly in hot weather and are usually found on the scalp, between the toes (athlete's foot) or fingers, in the groin and on the body (ringworm). You get ringworm (which is a fungal infection, not a worm) from infected animals or other people. Moisture encourages these infections.

To prevent fungal infections, wear loose, comfortable clothes, avoid artificial fibres, wash frequently and dry yourself carefully. If you do get an infection, wash the infected area at least daily with a disinfectant or medicated soap and water, and rinse and dry well. Apply an antifungal cream or powder such as tolnaftate. Try to expose the infected area to air or sunlight as much as possible and wash all towels and underwear in hot water, change them often and let them dry in the sun.

For women, fungal vaginal infections are characterised by a rash, itch and discharge and can be treated with a vinegar or lemon-juice douche, or with yoghurt. Nystatin, miconazole or clotrimazole pessaries or vaginal cream are the usual treatment.

Hepatitis A common disease worldwide, hepatitis is a general term for inflammation of the liver. There are several different viruses that cause hepatitis, and they differ in the way that they are transmitted. The symptoms are similar in all forms of the illness, and include fever, chills, headache, fatigue, feelings of weakness and aches and pains, followed by loss of appetite, nausea, vomiting, abdominal pain, dark urine, light-coloured faeces, jaundiced (yellow) skin and yellowing of the whites of the eyes.

People who have had hepatitis should avoid alcohol for some time after the illness, as the liver needs time to recover.

Hepatitis A is transmitted by contaminated food and drinking water. You should seek medical advice, but there is not much you can do apart from resting, drinking lots of fluids, eating lightly and avoiding fatty foods. **Hepatitis E** is transmitted in the same way as hepatitis A; it can be particularly serious in pregnant women.

There are almost 300 million chronic carriers of **hepatitis B** in the world. It is spread through contact with infected blood, blood products or body fluids, for example through sexual contact, unsterilised needles and blood transfusions, or contact with blood via small breaks in the skin. Other risk situations include having a shave, tattoo or body piercing with contaminated equipment. The symptoms of hepatitis B may be more severe than type A and the disease can lead to long-term problems such as chronic liver damage, liver cancer or a long-term carrier state. **Hepatitis C and D** are spread in the same way as hepatitis B and can also lead to long-term complications.

There are vaccines against hepatitis A and B, but there are currently no vaccines against the other types of hepatitis. Following the basic rules about food and water (hepatitis A and E) and avoiding risk situations (hepatitis B, C and D) are important preventative measures.

HIV & AIDS Infection with the human immunodeficiency virus (HIV) may lead to acquired immune deficiency syndrome (AIDS), which is a fatal disease. Any exposure to blood, blood products or body fluids may put the individual at risk. The disease is often transmitted through sexual contact or dirty needles – vaccinations, acupuncture, tattooing and body piercing can be potentially as dangerous as intravenous drug use. HIV/ AIDS can also be spread through infected blood transfusions; donors in Kenya are not consistently screened for HIV/AIDS.

It is impossible to detect the HIV-positive status of an otherwise healthy-looking person without a blood test. As with other sexually transmitted diseases, using a condom, although not 100% reliable, is effective in preventing infection. If you do need an injection, ask to see the syringe

AIDS in Kenya

Like most of its neighbours, Kenya is in the grip of a devastating AIDS epidemic. There are 2.5 million Kenyans with full-blown AIDS and nearly 700 people die every day from the disease. AIDS is predominately a hetrosexual disease in Kenya and now strikes all classes of people. At least 890,000 children have been orphaned and many others are infected while in the womb.

Teachers have been badly affected – at least 18 die daily – because they are predominantly in the 20 to 29 age group that's most affected by HIV/AIDS, and Kenya is facing an education crisis as a result, leaving even fewer people to spread the AIDS-awareness message. Around 85% of prostitutes are affected, and younger sex workers are doubly vulnerable, due to the widespread belief that AIDS can be avoided or cured by sleeping with younger partners.

Drug treatments that are available in the West to increase the lifespan of AIDS sufferers and reduce the risk of infection passing to the foetus in HIV-infected women remain well beyond the financial reach of most Kenyans, few of whom have access to even basic health care. The problem is unlikely to improve as long as Western drug companies refuse to allow developing countries to produce much cheaper generic versions of their products. Currently, the coast of treating a single AIDS victim for a year is US$34,000, while the annual wage of most people in Kenya is under US$500.

---

unwrapped in front of you, or take a needle and syringe pack with you.

Fear of getting HIV should never preclude treatment for serious medical conditions.

Intestinal Worms These parasites are most common in rural, tropical areas. The different worms have different ways of infecting people. Some may be ingested via food such as undercooked meat (eg, tapeworms) and some enter through your skin (eg, hookworms). Infestations may not show up for some time, and although they are generally not serious, if left untreated some can cause severe health problems later. Consider having a stool test when you return home to check for these and determine appropriate treatment.

Meningococcal Meningitis This serious disease can be fatal. There are recurring epidemics in sub-Saharan Africa. A fever, severe headache, sensitivity to light and neck stiffness, which prevents forward bending of the head, are the first symptoms. There may also be purple patches on the skin. Death can occur within a few hours, so urgent medical treatment is required.

Treatment consists of large doses of penicillin given intravenously, or injections of chloramphenicol.

Sexually Transmitted Diseases (STDs) HIV/AIDS and hepatitis B can be transmitted through sexual contact – see earlier entries in this section for more details. Other STDs include gonorrhoea, herpes and syphilis. Sores, blisters or rashes around the genitals and discharges or pain when urinating are common symptoms. In some STDs, such as wart virus or chlamydia, symptoms may be less marked or not observed at all, especially in women. Chlamydia infection can cause infertility in men and women before any symptoms have been noticed. Syphilis symptoms eventually disappear completely, but the disease continues and can cause severe problems in later years. While abstinence from sexual contact is the only 100% effective prevention, using condoms is also effective. The treatment of gonorrhoea and syphilis is with antibiotics. The different STDs each require specific antibiotics.

Typhoid This fever is a dangerous gut infection caused by contaminated water and food. Medical help must be sought.

In its early stages, sufferers may feel they have a bad cold or flu on the way, as early symptoms are a headache, body aches and a fever that rises a little each day until it is around 40°C (104°F) or more. The pulse is often slow relative to the degree of fever present – unlike a normal fever where the pulse increases. There may also be vomiting, abdominal pain, diarrhoea or constipation.

In the second week, the high fever and slow pulse continue and a few pink spots may appear on the body; trembling, delirium, weakness, weight loss and dehydration may occur. Complications such as pneumonia, perforated bowel or meningitis may occur.

Insect-Borne Diseases

Filariasis, leishmaniasis, sleeping sickness, typhus and yellow fever are all insect-borne diseases, but they do not pose a great risk to travellers. For more information on them, see Less Common Diseases later in this section.

Malaria This serious and potentially fatal disease is spread by mosquito bites. If you are travelling in endemic areas – which now includes most of Kenya – it is extremely important to avoid mosquito bites and to take tablets to prevent this disease. Although the risk is lower above 2600m, malaria is now a remote risk in Nairobi and elsewhere in the highlands. Symptoms range from fever, chills and sweating, headache, diarrhoea and abdominal pains to a vague feeling of ill-health. Seek medical help immediately if malaria is suspected. Without treatment malaria can rapidly become more serious and can be fatal.

If medical care is not available, malaria tablets can be used for treatment. You need to use a malaria tablet that is different from the one you were taking when you contracted malaria. The standard treatment dose of mefloquine is two 250mg tablets and a further two six hours later. For Fansidar, it's a single dose of three tablets. If you were previously taking mefloquine and cannot obtain Fansidar, then other alternatives are Malarone (atovaquone-proguanil; four tablets once daily for three days), halofantrine (three doses of two 250mg tablets every six hours) or quinine sulphate (600mg every six hours). There is a greater risk of side effects with these dosages than in normal use if used with mefloquine, so getting medical advice is preferable. Be aware also that halofantrine is no longer recommended by the WHO as emergency standby treatment, because of its side effects, and should only be used if no other drugs are available.

Travellers are advised to prevent mosquito bites at all times. The main messages are as follows:

- Wear light-coloured clothing.
- Wear long trousers and long-sleeved shirts.
- Use mosquito repellents that contain the compound DEET on exposed areas (prolonged overuse of DEET may be harmful, especially to children, but the use of repellant is considered preferable to being bitten by disease-transmitting mosquitoes).
- Avoid perfumes or aftershave.
- Use a mosquito net impregnated with mosquito repellent (permethrin) – it may be worth taking your own.
- Impregnating clothes with permethrin effectively deters mosquitoes and other insects.

Cuts, Bites & Stings

See Less Common Diseases for details of rabies, which is passed through animal bites.

Cuts & Scratches Wash well and treat any cut with an antiseptic such as povidone-iodine. Where possible avoid bandages and Band-Aids, which can keep wounds wet. Coral cuts are notoriously slow to heal and, if they are not adequately cleaned, small pieces of coral can become embedded in the wound.

Bedbugs & Lice Bedbugs live in various places, but particularly in dirty mattresses and bedding, evidenced by spots of blood on bedclothes or on the wall. Bedbugs leave itchy bites in neat rows. Calamine lotion or a sting-relief spray may help.

Lice cause itching and discomfort. They make themselves at home in your hair (head lice), your clothing (body lice) or in your pubic hair (crabs). You catch lice through direct contact with infected people or by sharing combs, clothing and the like. Powder or shampoo treatment will kill the lice, and infected clothing should then be washed in very hot, soapy water and left in the sun to dry.

Bites & Stings Bee and wasp stings are usually painful rather than dangerous. However, in people who are allergic to them, severe breathing difficulties may occur and require urgent medical care. Calamine lotion or a sting-relief spray will give relief, and ice packs will reduce the pain and swelling. There are some spiders with dangerous bites, but antivenins are usually available. Scorpion stings are notoriously painful and some Kenyan species are extremely venomous.

There are other fish and sea creatures that can sting or bite dangerously or which are dangerous to eat – seek local advice.

Jellyfish Avoid contact with these sea creatures, which have stinging tentacles – seek local advice on where they frequent. Stings from most jellyfish are simply rather painful. Dousing in vinegar will deactivate any stingers that have not 'fired'. Calamine lotion, antihistamines and analgesics may reduce the reaction and relieve the pain.

Leeches & Ticks Leeches may be present in damp rainforest conditions; they attach themselves to your skin to suck your blood. Trekkers often get them on their legs or in their boots. Applying salt or a lighted cigarette end will make them fall off. Do not pull them off, as the bite is then more likely to become infected. Clean and apply pressure if the point of attachment is bleeding. An insect repellent may keep them away.

You should always check all over your body if you have been walking through a potentially tick-infested area as ticks can cause skin infections and other more serious diseases. Kenya has huge populations of domestic and wild mammals, so ticks are a risk is any rural area. If a tick is found attached, press down around the tick's head with tweezers, grab the head and gently pull upwards. Avoid pulling the rear of the body as this may squeeze the tick's gut contents through the attached mouth parts into the skin, increasing the risk of infection and disease. Smearing chemicals on the tick will not make it let go and is not recommended.

Snakes Kenya has numerous venomous snakes, including one of the most deadly of all, the black mamba. To minimise your chances of being bitten always wear boots, socks and long trousers when walking through undergrowth where snakes may be present. Don't put your hands into holes and crevices, and be careful when collecting firewood.

Snake bites do not cause instantaneous death and antivenins are available in Kenya, but it can take a long time to reach medical care and air evacuation may be necessary. In the meantime, you should immediately wrap the bitten limb tightly, as you would for a sprained ankle, and then attach a splint to immobilise it. Keep the victim still and seek medical help, if possible with the dead snake for identification. Don't attempt to catch the snake if there is a possibility of being bitten again. Tourniquets and sucking out the poison are now comprehensively discredited.

Less Common Diseases
The following diseases pose a small risk to travellers, and so are only mentioned briefly. Seek medical advice if you think you may have any of these diseases.

Cholera This is the worst of the watery diarrhoeas and medical help should be sought. Outbreaks of cholera are generally widely reported, so you can avoid problem areas. *Fluid replacement is the most vital treatment* – the risk of dehydration is severe as you may lose up to 20L a day. If there is a delay in getting to hospital, then begin taking tetracycline. The adult dose is 250mg four times daily. It is not recommended for children under nine years nor for pregnant women. Tetracycline may help shorten the illness, but adequate fluids are required to save lives.

Filariasis This is a mosquito-transmitted parasitic infection found in the coastal zone. Possible symptoms include fever, pain and swelling of the lymph glands; inflammation of lymph drainage areas; swelling of a limb or the scrotum; skin rashes; and blindness. Treatment is available to eliminate the parasites from the body, but some of the damage already caused may not be reversible. Medical advice should be obtained promptly if the infection is suspected.

Leishmaniasis This is a group of parasitic diseases transmitted by sandflies, which are found throughout the Kenyan highlands. Cutaneous leishmaniasis affects the skin tissue causing ulceration and disfigurement, and visceral leishmaniasis affects the internal organs. Seek medical advice, as laboratory testing is required for diagnosis and correct treatment. Avoiding sandfly bites is the best precaution. Bites are usually painless, itchy and yet another reason to cover up and apply repellent.

Rabies This fatal viral infection is present in Kenya, and its incidence is rising in urban areas due to the presence of feral dogs. Many animals can be infected (such as dogs, cats, bats and monkeys) and it is their saliva that is infectious. Any bite, scratch or even lick from an animal should be cleaned immediately and thoroughly. Scrub with soap and running water, and then apply alcohol or iodine solution. Medical help should be sought promptly to receive a course of injections to prevent the onset of symptoms and death.

Sleeping Sickness Around Lake Victoria and along the Tanzanian and Ugandan borders, tsetse flies may carry trypanosomiasis, or sleeping sickness. The tsetse fly is about twice the size of a housefly and recognisable by the scissor-like way it folds its wings when at rest. Only a small proportion of tsetse flies carry the disease, but it is a serious disease, which can be fatal without treatment. No protection is available except avoiding the tsetse fly bites. The flies are attracted to large moving objects such as safari buses, to perfume and aftershave and to colours such as dark blue. Swelling at the site of the bite, five or more days later, is the first sign of infection; this is followed within two to three weeks by fever. There is an upsurge in tsetse fly numbers after the rains (July).

Tetanus This disease is caused by a germ that lives in soil and in the faeces of horses and other animals. It enters the body via breaks in the skin. The first symptom may be discomfort in swallowing, or stiffening of the jaw and neck; this is followed by painful convulsions of the jaw and whole body. The disease can be fatal. It can be prevented by vaccination.

Tuberculosis (TB) This is a bacterial infection usually transmitted from person to person by coughing, but which may be transmitted through consumption of unpasteurised milk. Milk that has been boiled is safe to drink, and the souring of milk to make yogurt or cheese also kills the bacilli. Travellers are usually not at great risk as close household contact with the infected person is usually required before the disease is passed on. If you are to be in a situation where you may be exposed to TB, you may need to have a TB test before you travel as this can help diagnose the disease later if you become ill.

Typhus This disease is spread by ticks, mites or lice. It begins with fever, chills, headache and muscle pains followed a few days later by a body rash. There is often a large painful sore at the site of the bite and nearby lymph nodes are swollen and painful. Typhus can be treated under medical supervision. Seek local advice on areas where ticks pose a danger and always check your skin carefully for ticks after walking in a danger area such as a tropical forest. An insect repellent can help, and walkers in tick-infested areas should consider having their boots and trousers impregnated with benzyl benzoate and dibutylphthalate.

Yellow Fever This viral disease is endemic in many African and South American countries and is transmitted by mosquitoes. The initial symptoms are fever, headache, abdominal pain and vomiting. Seek medical care urgently and drink lots of fluids.

SOCIAL GRACES
Dress
Despite their often exuberant and casual approach, Kenyans are generally quite conservative, and are particularly concerned with modesty in dress. T-shirts and shorts are almost unheard of and while foreign men may *just* be able to pull it off, you may feel like the only person at the wedding who came in casual dress! Shirts are an obsession for Kenyan men and almost everyone wears one, often with a sweater or blazer.

In the cities, women can also get away with shorts and T-shirts, but again it won't be greatly appreciated. On the Muslim-dominated coast, particularly in Lamu, women should wear tops that cover the shoulders and skirts or pants that reach at least to the knees. Many Kenyan Muslims are now adopting full *purdah*, which covers everything but the eyes, so attitudes to female modesty are only likely to become stronger.

When doing official business with civil servants and embassy staff, your position will be enhanced if you're smartly dressed and don't look like you've just spent five weeks in the back of a truck!

Photographing People
Kenya's wildly photogenic tribal people are generally less-than-wildly enthusiastic about being photographed, and with good reason. Most are simply sick of being photographed.

Some tribespeople in the north will get very upset if you photograph them at all, believing that photography in some way steals a part of their soul. If you snatch a shot you'll be in a lot of trouble. Always ask first and respect the people's wishes.

WOMEN TRAVELLERS

Within Kenyan society, women are poorly represented in positions of power, and the few high-profile women in politics run the same risks of violence as their male counterparts. However, in their day-to-day lives, Kenyans are generally respectful towards women, although white women in bars will attract a lot of interest from would-be suitors. Most are just having a go and will give up if you tell them you aren't interested. The only place you are likely to have problems is at the beach resorts on the coast. Here women may even be approached by male prostitutes. It's always best to cover your legs and shoulders when away from the beach so as not to offend local sensibilities.

With the upsurge in crime in Nairobi and along the coast, women should avoid walking around at night. The ugly fact is that men are likely to be just robbed, while rape is a real risk for women. Lone night walks along the beach or through quiet city streets are a recipe for disaster, and criminals usually work in gangs, so take a cab, even if you're in a group.

Regrettably, black women in the company of white men are assumed to be prostitutes, and can face all kinds of discrimination from hotels and security guards. They may also be approached by Kenyan hustlers who believe that they will be willing to help them rip off the white 'customer' they're with. They can avoid the worst of this by taking taxis between hotels and restaurants etc.

GAY & LESBIAN TRAVELLERS

There is a widespread perception across Africa that homosexuality is an un-African phenomenon, introduced to the continent by European colonials. It goes on covertly of course, particularly on the coast, but under Kenyan law, homosexuality is punishable by up to 14 years in prison. According to the UN, sex between gay men accounts for only 5% to 10% of HIV/AIDS cases in Kenya. Despite the best efforts of international aid organisations, condoms are still as unpopular with Kenya's gay community as they are in the wider community.

Although there are probably more gays and lesbians in Nairobi, the coast is more tolerant of gay relationships, at least privately. There's even a Swahili word for gay; *msenge*. Lamu has long been considered a paradise getaway for gay couples, but it's no longer as tolerant as it once was. In 1999, a couple were taken into protective custody in Lamu to shield them from an angry mob of locals who were opposed to their plans for a gay wedding.

The closest Kenya has to a 'scene' is the very unofficial gay night at Gypsy bar in Westlands in Nairobi on Tuesday. The website **W** www.purpleroofs.com/africa/kenyata .html lists a number of gay or gay-friendly tour companies in Kenya and around the world who may be able to help you plan your trip. For luxury, all-inclusive packages, the travel agents **Atlantis Events** (**W** *www.atlan tisevents.com/*) and **David Tours** (**W** *www .davidtours.com/kenya*) can arrange anything from balloon safaris to luxurious coastal hideaways, all with a gay focus.

DISABLED TRAVELLERS

Travelling in Kenya is not easy for disabled travellers, but it's not impossible. Very few tourist facilities are geared up for disabled people, and those that are, are restricted to the expensive hotels and lodges. However, if you're polite you're likely to get assistance from people wherever you need it.

In Nairobi, only the ex-London taxi cabs are spacious enough to accommodate a wheelchair, but many safari companies have experience taking disabled people out on safari. The travel agent, **Travel Scene Services** (**☎** *02-215404, fax 225156;* **e** *travelscene@ insightkenya.com*) has lots of experience with disabled travellers.

Many of the hotels owned by **Lonrho Hotels** (*Nairobi* **☎** *02-216940, fax 216796;* **W** *www.lonrhohotels.com*) can make provisions for disabled people – Mount Kenya Safari Club has it's own wheelchair for guests' use. In Amboseli National Park, the **Ol Tukai Lodge** (*in Nairobi* **☎** *02-540780, fax 540821*) has two disabled-friendly cottages.

For further information about disabled travel contact the following.

Access-Able Travel Source (**☎** 303-232 2979, fax 239 8486; **e** access-able@home.com; **W** www.access-able.com) PO Box 1796, Wheatridge Co, USA

Holiday Care Service (**☎** 01293-774535, fax 771500, minicom 776943; **W** www.ukstroke .com/holidaycare) 2nd floor, Imperial Bldgs, Victoria Rd, Horley, Surrey, UK, RH6 7PZ

In Kenya, the **Association for the Physically Disabled of Kenya** (☎ 02-224443, fax 219541; e apdk@iconnect.co.ke; APDK House, Lagos Rd, Nairobi; PO Box 46747) may also be able to help disabled visitors.

SENIOR TRAVELLERS

Although there are no tour companies set up specifically for senior travellers, the more-expensive tours cater well to seniors' requests and requirements. Before you book, ask the operator what they can do to help make your trip possible and comfortable. The luxury-tour and safari business is well used to older travellers, and wildlife drives and other safari activities are great for older people. One company that has a good reputation for catering to seniors is **Eastern & Southern Safaris** (☎ 02-242829, fax 253894; e info@essafari.co.ke; 4th floor, Twiga Towers, Moi Ave, Nairobi).

You may be able to find other senior-friendly companies on the website of **Wired Seniors** (w wiredseniors.com), which has travel-links from around the world.

TRAVEL WITH CHILDREN

Many parents regard Africa as just too dangerous for travel with children, but it is possible, and even easy, if you're prepared to spend a little more and take the luxury-safari and lodge route or spend most of your time on the coast. Most hotels will not charge for children under two years of age. Those aged between two and 12 years, who share their parents' room, are usually charged at 50% of the adult rate. You'll also get a cotbed thrown in for this price. Budget hotels are probably best avoided for reasons of hygiene.

When on safari, hotels and lodges with a pool will keep your kids amused between wildlife drives. Be warned that some exclusive lodges, including Treetops, the Ark and the Shimba Rainforest Lodge, impose an age limit for children; typically they must be aged at least eight to qualify. If camping, be alert for potential hazards such as mosquitoes, dangerous wildlife and campfires. It's particularly important to consider the risks posed to children by tropical diseases – talk to your doctor to get the best advice. Mosquito repellents with high levels of DEET may be unsuitable for young children.

Street food is also likely to be risky, as is unwashed fruit. Letting your children run around bare foot is usually fine on the beach (beware of sea urchins!), but may be risky in the bush because of thorns, bees, scorpions and snakes. Hookworm and bilharzia are also risks.

Travelling between towns in Kenya is not always easy with children. Car sickness is one problem, and young children tend to be seen as wriggling luggage, so you'll often have them on your lap. Seatbelts are rare in taxis and accidents are common but a child seat brought from home that clips onto seatbelts is a good idea if you're hiring a car or going on safari. The journey to and from the coast by train is highly enjoyable for people of all ages.

Canned baby foods, powdered milk, disposable nappies and the like are available in most large supermarkets, but are expensive. Bring as much as possible from home, together with child-friendly insect repellent (this can't be bought in Kenya).

In Nairobi, the Langata Giraffe Centre, David Sheldrick Wildlife Trust, National Museum and its snake park and aquarium, Nairobi National Park and the Railway Museum are all good for children. Bomas of Kenya has a good children's playground.

For further invaluable advice see Lonely Planet's *Travel with Children* by Cathy Lanigan.

DANGERS & ANNOYANCES
Crime

It is a sad fact that crime is rife in Kenya. It ranges from petty snatch theft and mugging to violent armed robbery, carjacking and even white-collar crime and corruption. The wealthy are content to surround themselves with more and more armed guards and razor-wire and little is done to address the causes of the problem. As a visitor, you needn't feel paranoid, but you should always keep your wits about you, particularly at night.

Perhaps the best advice for when you're walking around cities and towns is not to carry anything valuable with you – that includes jewellery, watches, cameras, bumbags, day-packs and money. Most hotels provide a safe or secure place for valuables, although you should be cautious of the security at some budget places. Cheap digital watches and plastic sunglasses can be brought in Kenya for under KSh100 and you won't miss them if they get taken.

A pair of lionesses stalking their prey

Visitors to Chyulu Hills National Park observing the wildlife

Hunting Thomson's gazelles

A clutch of ostrich eggs on the plains

Grevy's zebra

Wildlife-viewing tower, Samburu National Reserve

While pick-pocketing and bag-snatching are the most common crimes, armed muggings do occur in Nairobi and on the coast (see the relevant chapters for more details). However, they usually occur at night or in remote areas, so always take taxis after dark or along lonely dirt roads. Conversely, snatch-and-run crimes happen more in crowds. If you suddenly feel there are too many people around you, or think you are being followed, dive straight into a shop and ask for help.

A moneybelt is still a sensible place to keep cash and other valuables, but if you get mugged, it'll be the first thing they ask for. More ingenious tricks include tucking money etc. into a length of elasticised bandage on your arm or leg, or creating a hidden pocket inside your trousers. If you don't actually need your credit card, travellers cheques or cash with you, they'll almost always be safer locked away in your hotel safe.

Luggage is an obvious signal to criminals that you've just arrived. When arriving anywhere by bus, it's sensible to take a 'ship-to-shore' approach, getting a taxi directly from the bus station to your hotel. You'll have plenty of time to explore once you've safely stowed your belongings. Also, don't read this guidebook or look at maps on the street – it attracts unwanted attention.

In the event of a crime, you should report it to the police, but this can be a real procedure. You'll need to get a police report if you intend to make an insurance claim. In the event of a snatch theft, think twice before yelling 'Thief!'. It's not unknown for people to administer summary justice on the spot, with sometimes-fatal results for the criminal.

In August 1998 the US Embassy in Nairobi was bombed (see the boxed text 'Embassy Bombings' in the Nairobi chapter). As the country was returning to normality, the car bombing of the Paradise Hotel, north of Mombasa, occurred in November 2002 (see the boxed text 'Suicide Attack in Kenya' in the Facts about Kenya chapter). It is likely that these were isolated incidents and that Western travellers to Kenya can expect to have a trouble-free time in the country.

Although crime is a fact of life in Kenya, it needn't spoil your trip. Above all, don't make the mistake of distrusting every Kenyan just because of a few bad apples.

Confidence Tricks

In Nairobi and on the coast you'll almost certainly come across people who play on the emotions and gullibility of foreigners. People with tales about being 'refugees' can sound very convincing, but they all end up asking for money. If you do give any, expect to be 'arrested' by 'plain-clothes police', complete with 'police' ID cards, who then extract a 'fine' on the basis that 'it's illegal to give money to refugees'. This is probably the most common scam in Nairobi and it's probably best to ignore all such requests for money.

Be sceptical of anyone who claims to recognise you in the street – it's unlikely that any ordinary person is going to be *this* excited by seeing you twice. On the coast, anyone who makes a big show of inviting you into the hospitality of their home probably has ulterior motives. The usual trick is to bestow some kind of gift upon the delighted traveller, who is then emotionally blackmailed into reciprocating to the order of several hundred shillings.

The 'university scam' is another old faithful. A well-dressed young guy will usually start up a conversation and soon discover, by some fantastic coincidence, that you happen to be from the same place he's going to university next year! Sooner or later there'll either be a request for money or they'll ask to see your credit card to know 'what kind they might need'. The result will be either emotional blackmail or daylight robbery. Don't fall for it.

In Nakuru, a trick that's been popular for years involves tourists with cars. Locals

---

Street Kids

Nairobi has huge problems with street children, many of whom are AIDS orphans, who trail foreigners around asking for food or change. It's up to you whether you give, but if you do, the word will go around and you won't get a moment's peace. It's also debatable how much your donations will help as the older boys operate like a mini-mafia, extorting money from the younger kids.

If you want to help out, money might be better donated to the charity **Homeless Children International – Kenya** (☎ 02-573013; W www.homelesskids.org/kenya), which works to improve conditions for these children.

splash oil on your wheels, then tell you the wheel bearings, differential or something else has failed, and direct you to a nearby garage where their friends will 'fix' the problem – for a substantial fee. Don't trust people who gesticulate wildly to you as you are driving along, indicating your front wheels are wobbling. Chances are, if you stop you'll be relieved of your valuables.

Banditry

Wars in Somalia, Sudan and Ethiopia have all had their effect on the stability and safety of northern and northeastern Kenya. AK-47s have been flowing into the country for many years and the papers are filled with stories of hold-ups, shoot-outs, cattle-rustling and general lawlessness. Bandits and poachers infiltrating from Somalia have made the northeast of the country particularly dangerous and with the American 'War on Terror' shutting down the funding for many warring factions within Somalia, these problems are only going to get worse. In the north, the problem is armed tribal wars and cattle rustling across the Sudanese border. There are Kenyan bandits too, of course, but cross-border problems seem to account for most of the trouble in the north of the country.

Despite all the headlines, tourists are rarely targeted, as much of the violence and robbery takes place far from the main tourist routes. However, you should check the situation locally before taking the bus from Malindi to Lamu or between Garsen and Garissa or Thika.

The area along the Ethiopian and Sudanese borders is also very risky, with vehicles travelling in convoys with armed guards to/from Moyale.

LEGAL MATTERS

All drugs, except *miraa* (a leafy shoot with amphetamine-like effects) are illegal in Kenya. Marijuana (or *bhang*) is widely available, but highly illegal and possession carries a penalty of up to 10 years. Dealers are common on the beaches north and south of Mombasa and frequently set up travellers for sting operations for real or phoney cops to extort money.

African prisons are unbelievably harsh places; don't take the risk. Note that *miraa* is illegal in Tanzania.

BUSINESS HOURS

Government offices are open Monday to Friday from 8am or 8.30am to 1pm, and 2pm to 5pm. Some businesses also open on Saturday morning from 8.30am to 12.30pm.

Banking hours are Monday to Friday from 9am to 3pm. Banks are also open on the first and last Saturday of the month from 9am to 11am. In tourist resorts such as Malindi and Diani Beach, Nairobi and Mombasa there are branches of Barclays Bank that open Monday to Saturday until 4.30pm or 5pm. Forex bureaus are typically open 9am to 5pm Monday to Friday and 9am to noon on Saturday. Barclays Bank at Nairobi's Jomo Kenyatta International Airport is open 24 hours and is the only bank open on Sunday.

PUBLIC HOLIDAYS & SPECIAL EVENTS

Kenya's many tribal groups have their own local festivals, but they're private affairs and you'll stand little chance of getting to see them. Animal sacrifices and ritual circumcision are common events so this may not be a bad thing!

Muslim festivals, especially Ramadan, are significant events along the coast. The Maulid Festival at Lamu celebrates the birth of the Prophet Mohammed with several community events. This will be celebrated on 14 May 2003, 2 May 2004, and 21 April 2005. Many places to eat in the coastal region close until after sundown during the Muslim fasting month of Ramadan. This will run from 27 October 2003, 15 October 2004 and 5 October 2005. Mombasa holds a carnival in November with music and dance.

Public Holidays

1 January	New Year's Day
March/April	Good Friday & Easter Monday
1 May	Labour Day
1 June	Madaraka Day
10 October	Moi Day
20 October	Kenyatta Day
12 December	Independence Day
25 December	Christmas Day
26 December	Boxing Day

ACTIVITIES
Diving & Snorkelling

There is a string of marine national parks spread out along the coast between Shimoni and Malindi (see The Coast chapter for further details), with plenty of opportunities for snorkelling and scuba diving. However, snorkellers are discouraged from wearing flippers (fins) due to damage to the coral. The better marine parks are further from Mombasa at Wasini Island, to the south of Mombasa, and at Malindi and Watamu, north of Mombasa.

There are distinct seasons for diving in Kenya. October to March is the best time, but during June, July and August it's often impossible to dive due to poor visibility caused by silt flowing from some of the rivers on the coast. In 1997, there was a huge coral die-off as part of the warming of the ocean attributable to El Nino and global warming. However, the coral is slowly recovering and there are thousands of colourful fish species and even marine mammals.

If you aren't certified to dive, almost every hotel and resort on the coast can arrange an open-water diving course. By international standards, they aren't cheap – a five-day PADI certification course will cost US$350 to US$450. Trips for certified divers with two dives go for around US$90. The cheapest way to dive is on dhow tours to Wasini, where you only pay US$50 for two dives, although you have to pay for the tour as well.

Nairobi Sailing and Sub Aqua Club (☎ 501250; Nairobi Dam, Langata Rd) offers British Sub Aqua Club diver training and runs diving trips to the coast between September and April.

If you're going to scuba dive on the coast, note that the only decompression chamber in the region is in Mombasa and is run by the Kenyan navy.

Windsurfing & Sailing
Most resort hotels south and north of Mombasa have sailboards for hire, and conditions are ideal – offshore reefs protect the waters, and winds are usually reasonably strong and constant. Rates for hiring sailboards vary from KSh400 to KSh700 per hour; instruction is also available. The sheltered channel between Lamu and Manda Islands is one of the best places to windsurf on the coast.

Kilifi, Mtwapa and Mombasa all have sailing clubs, and smaller freshwater clubs can also be found at Lake Naivasha and Lake Victoria, which both have excellent windsurfing and sailing. If you're experienced, you may pick up some crewing at the various yacht clubs, although you'll need to become a temporary member. While it isn't hands on, a traditional dhow trip out of Lamu is an unforgettable experience.

Trekking
Mt Kenya is the obvious trekking choice, but other promising and relatively unexplored territory includes Mt Elgon on the Ugandan border, the Cherangani Hills and Kerio Valley east of Kitale, the Matthews Range and Ndoto Mountains north of Isiolo, the Loroghi Hills north of Maralal, the Mau Forest near Nakuru and even the Ngong Hills close to Nairobi.

For more trekking information refer to the relevant chapters in this book, get hold of a copy of Lonely Planet's *Trekking in East Africa*, or contact the **Mountain Club of Kenya** (MCK; ☎ 02-501747; W www.mck.or.ke) at Wilson Airport (see Things to See & Do in the Nairobi chapter). Its website has good advice on Mt Kenya as well as on technical climbing and trekking throughout Kenya. Also, **Kilimanjaro Adventure Travel** (W www.kilimanjaro.com) has information on mountaineering, trekking and adventure travel in Tanzania and Kenya.

Gliding & Flying
The **Gliding Club of Kenya** (☎ 0171-55261, fax 55040; e gliding@africaonline.co.ke; W www.kenyatravel.de) has its headquarters in Mweiga near Nyeri in the Aberdares – see Nyeri in The Central Highlands chapter for more information.

Flying lessons are easily arranged in Nairobi and are much cheaper than in Europe, the USA and Australasia. Contact the **Aero Club of East Africa** (☎ 02-608990) and **Ninety-Nines Flying Club** (☎ 02-500277), both at Wilson Airport.

Ballooning
Balloon trips in the wildlife parks are an absolutely superb way of seeing the savanna plains and, of course, the animals. The experience of floating silently above the plains with a 360° view of everything beneath you, is incomparable – it's definitely worth saving for.

The flights typically set off at dawn and go for about 1½ hours after which they put down and you tuck into a champagne breakfast. After that, you'll be taken on a wildlife drive in a support vehicle and returned to your lodge. Flights are currently available in the Masai Mara for around US$380. Check out the following two companies.

Adventures Aloft (☎ 02-221439) Eagle House, Kimathi St, Nairobi. This company operates out of Mara Fig Tree Lodge and you can book in Nairobi, at the Fig Tree Lodge or any other lodge in the Masai Mara.

Balloon Safaris Ltd (☎ 02-605003; W www.balloonsafaris.com) Wilson Airport, Nairobi. This company operates out of Keekorok Lodge so you can book through Block Hotels in Nairobi (☎ 02-540780, fax 544948) or at Keekorok Lodge or any other lodge in the Masai Mara. The flights depart from Keekorok Lodge.

Fishing

The **Kenya Fisheries Department** (02-742320; Museum Hill Rd, opposite National Museums of Kenya) operates a number of fishing camps in various parts of the country, but they're difficult to reach without your own vehicle and directions from the Fisheries Department, from whom you'll also need to get a fishing licence.

The deep-sea fishing on the coast is some of the best in the world and various private companies and resorts in Shimoni, Diani Beach, Mtwapa, Watamu and Malindi can arrange fishing trips. Boats cost from US$250 to US$500 and can usually fit four or five anglers. You'll pay the same price if it's just you in the boat. The season runs from August to April.

For freshwater fishing, there are huge Nile perch as big as a person in lakes Victoria and Turkana, and some of the trout fishing around the Aberdares and Mt Kenya is quite exceptional. See the Safaris chapter for more details of fishing safaris in Kenya.

Fishing licences for Mt Kenya, Mt Elgon and the Aberdare National Parks can be obtained from the respective park gates at a cost of KSh200 per day. In addition to this fee, park visitors are required to pay the daily park entry fee and Kenya Wildlife Service (KWS) guide fee at KSh500 per day.

White-Water Rafting

The Athi/Galana River has substantial rapids, chutes and waterfalls and there are also possibilities on the Tana River and Ewaso Ngiro River near Isiolo. The most exciting times for a white-water rafting trip are from late October to mid-January and from early April to late July when water levels are highest.

The people to talk to are **Savage Wilderness Safaris** (☎/fax 02-521590; e whitewater@alphanet.co.ke.org; W www.whitewaterkenya.com; Sarit Centre, Westlands, PO Box 1000, Nairobi), run by charismatic Mark Savage. Depending on water levels, rafting trips of up to 450km and of three weeks duration can be arranged, although most trips last one to four days and cover up to 80km.

One of the most popular short trips (US$95 per person, one day) is on the Tana River, northeast of Nairobi, which covers grade two to five rapids. Overnight trips with more time spent on the river cost US$140. Also possible are three-day adventures on the Athi River, southeast of Nairobi (US$380 per person plus US$95 per extra day) and the Ewaso Ngiro River, northwest of Isiolo (US$450 per person with additional days at US$105).

The above prices include transport from Nairobi, tented accommodation, good quality food, soft drinks and beer. You are also provided with all necessary rafting equipment including life jackets and helmets. At least four people are required for the Tana trips and at least six for the other rivers.

Cycling

An increasingly large number of companies are offering cycling and mountain-biking trips in Kenya.

Popular locations include the edge of the Masai Mara, Hell's Gate National Park, the Central Highlands and the Kerio Valley. Companies include **Sana Highlands Trekking Expeditions** (☎ 02-227820, fax 218336; W www.sanatrekkingkenya.com) and **Bike Treks** (☎ 02-446371, fax 442439; e biktreks@form-net.com; W www.angelfire.com/sk/biketreks).

Many local companies and places to stay can arrange bicycle hire all over the country, allowing you to cycle through places such as Arabuko Sokoke Forest Reserve and Hell's Gate National Park. Hire is usually between KSh300 and KSh500 per day. See Bicycle in the Getting Around chapter for more information on cycling in Kenya. For details of companies offering cycling safaris, see the Safaris chapter.

COURSES
Language
If you intend to spend considerable time in Kenya, learning Swahili is an excellent idea. Taking a language course (or any course) also entitles you to a 'Pupils' Pass', an immigration permit allowing continuous stays of up to 12 months. You may have to battle with bureaucracy and the process may take months, but it can be worth it. The best language school is run by the Anglican Church of Kenya (ACK).

The fee for a Pupil's Pass varies. A charge will be levied by your school for sorting out the paperwork so expect to pay around KSh2500 for a one-year pass. A deposit of KSh5000 or a letter of guarantee by an approved body registered in Kenya (your language school) is required along with two photographs and a copy of your passport (if applying from overseas). Check out the following language schools.

ACK Language & Orientation School (☎ 02-721893, fax 714750) Bishops Rd, Upper Hill (PO Box 47429), Nairobi. Full-time courses (US$450) last 14 weeks and take up five hours a day. More flexible is private tuition, which costs US$4 per hour. Study materials will cost around US$40.

Language Center Ltd (☎ 02-569531/2, fax 569533) Ndemi Close off Ngong Rd (PO Box 40661), Nairobi. This is a good cheaper option; classes cost KSh250 per hour in a group or KSh450 for one-on-one tuition, and you can study two, three or seven days a week.

Trans Africa Language Services (☎ 02-561160, fax 566231) Joseph Kang'ethe Rd off Ngong Rd (PO Box 72061), Nairobi. This company offers a full-time, four-week course (four hours per day, five days per week), but staff seem to be unmotivated and teaching materials are limited.

Codelink Training Services (☎ 02-252092, fax 211701) 2nd floor, Gilfillan House, Kenyatta Ave (PO Box 60713), Nairobi. Codelink offers flexible courses costing around KSh250 per hour.

WORK
It's difficult, although by no means impossible, for foreigners to find jobs. The most likely areas in which employment might be found are in the safari business, teaching, advertising and journalism. Except for teaching, it's unlikely you'll see jobs advertised, and the only way you'll find out about them is to spend a lot of time with resident expats. However, as in most countries, the rule is that if an African can be found to do the job, there's no need to hire a foreigner.

The most fruitful area in which to look for work, assuming that you have the relevant skills, is the 'disaster industry'. Nairobi is awash with UN and other aid agencies servicing the famines in Somalia and southern Sudan and the refugee camps along the Kenyan border with those countries. But keep in mind that the work is tough, often dangerous and the pay low.

Work permits and resident visas are not easy to arrange. A prospective employer may be able to arrange them relatively painlessly but, usually, you will find yourself spending a lot of money and time in Nairobi at the **immigration office** (☎ 02-332110; ground floor, Nyayo House, cnr Kenyatta Ave & Uhuru Hwy).

Voluntary Conservation & Development Work
Taita Discovery Centre (in Nairobi ☎ 02-331191, fax 330698; W www.savannahcamps .com) is an offshoot of Savannah Camps & Lodges. This purpose-built conservation research centre covers 68,000 hectares of the Taita and Rukinga ranches near Tsavo West National Park and forms a vital migration corridor for elephants and other animals between Tsavo and the foothills of Mt Kilimanjaro.

Courses on a huge range of conservation topics are run here along with hands-on projects in conservation and the local community. However, doing good work doesn't come cheap. The cost is US$177 per week for a minimum of four weeks, and you'll have to make your own arrangements for getting to the sanctuary, or take a package from Nairobi or Mombasa that includes flying doctor membership (US$120 return).

Another good organisation is **Kenya Youth Voluntary Development Projects** (☎ 02-225379, fax 225379; e kvdakenya@yahoo .com; 4th floor, Gilfillan House, Kenyatta Ave, PO Box 48902, Nairobi). A variety of three- to four-week projects are possible, including road building, health education and clinic construction. There's a US$200 registration fee and camping accommodation is provided.

Inter-Community Development Involvement (ICODEI; ☎ 0337-30017, fax 30680; W www.volunteerkenya.org; Reverend Reuben

Lubanga, PO Box 459, Bungoma), run in conjunction with the University of Indiana in the USA, offers a number of longer community projects focusing on health issues such as AIDS awareness, agriculture and conservation. The cost is US$1300 for the first month and US$120 per extra week. This includes a three-day Masai Mara safari.

The Wakuluzu Trust, at Colobus Cottage in Diani Beach, and the Elsamere Conservation Centre, on Lake Naivasha, also take paying volunteers (see The Coast and The Rift Valley chapters for further information).

A number of foreign organisations can also assist with volunteer work. The **Voluntary Service Overseas** (☎ 020-8780 2266, fax 8780 1326; **e** enquiry@vso.org.uk; **w** www.vso.org .uk; 317 Putney Bridge Rd, London SW15 2PN) can provide placements for professionals. Also check out **Volunteer Work Information Service** (**w** www.workingabroad.com), **Global Volunteers** (**w** www.globalvolunteers.org) and **Coordinating Committee for International Voluntary Service** (**w** www.unesco.org/ccivs).

ACCOMMODATION

Kenya has a good range of accommodation options from the very basic, KSh150 a night cubicle hotels with hardboard partitions between the rooms, to luxury tented camps with every amenity, hidden away in the national parks, which can run to US$500 a night! However, there are also camp sites, budget tented camps, simple bandas (often wooden huts) and cottages inside most of the parks.

During the low season many companies offer excellent deals on accommodation on the coast and in the main wildlife parks, often tying in airlines to create packages aimed at the local and expat market. The website of **Let's Go Travel** (**w** www.letsgosa fari.com) displays almost all the major hotels in Kenya, giving prices and descriptions.

Although most mid-range and top-end places quote prices in US dollars, payment can be in local currency. Note that most places have separate rates for residents, and these are often much less than the nonresident rates. Rates quoted in this book are nonresident rates unless stated otherwise.

Camping

There are many opportunities for camping in Kenya and it is worth considering bringing a tent, although gear can also be hired in Nairobi and around Mt Kenya. There are camp sites in just about every national park or reserve, though these are usually very basic. There'll be a toilet block with a couple of pit toilets, and usually a water tap, but very little else. Private sites are few and far between but they do offer more facilities. Often it's possible to camp in the grounds of a hotel in rural towns and Nairobi has some good private camp sites. Camping in the bush is possible but security would be a major concern; don't even think about it on the coast.

Bandas

These are basic huts and cottages, usually with some kind of kitchen and bathroom, that offer excellent value for budget travellers. There are KWS bandas at Shimba Hills, Tsavo West, Meru, Mt Elgon and near the marine reserves at Malindi and Shimoni. Some are wooden huts, some are thatched stone huts and some are small brick bungalows with solar-powered lights, and facilities range from basic dorms and squat toilets to kitchens and hot water provided by wood-burning stoves. The cost varies from US$10 to US$20 per person. **Let's Go Travel** (☎ 02-340331; **e** info@letsgosafari.com; **w** www .letsgosafari.com) in Nairobi is the agent for an increasing number of bandas. You'll need to bring all your food, bedding and firewood.

Hostels

The only youth hostel affiliated with Hostelling International (HI) is in Nairobi. It has good facilities and is a pleasant place to stay, but there are plenty of other cheaper choices, which are just as good. Other places that call themselves 'youth hostels' are not members of HI and standards are variable.

Hotels & Guesthouses

Real bottom-end hotels (often known as 'board and lodgings' to distinguish them from '*hotels*', which are often only restaurants) are widely used as brothels and tend to be very rundown. Security at these places is virtually nonexistent; the better ones are set around courtyards and are clean if not exactly comfortable. Expect singles/doubles to cost around KSh150/250.

Things usually improve dramatically if you have a dollar or two more to spend. For around KSh300/600, you will usually get a clean room with bathroom (soap and towel supplied). These places often have a cheap restaurant and a lively (ie, noisy) bar and offer a degree of security.

Better all round are the mid-range hotels, which go from KSh600 to KSh1000 for a single. You can expect all the basic comforts and sometimes even touches of luxury such as towels, soap, toilet paper, clean sheets, a table and chair, and often a telephone and room service. Bear in mind, though, that 'a self contained room' in Kenya only means you get your own bathroom.

At the top end of the market, you can pay anything from US$30 to US$500 per person, and you'll usually get air-conditioning, cable TV, phones, reliable hot showers and, as often as not, a swimming pool and at least one bar and restaurant. The more expensive places tend to be wonderful, although sometimes there doesn't seem all *that* much difference between a US$200 a night room and a US$30 a night room! Most of the big international chain hotels are represented here and there are a few splendid old colonial places with tons of atmosphere.

If you intend to stay in any of the top-end hotels, it's important to know that the price depends on the season. The high season generally runs from 16 December to 31 March and from 1 July to 31 August. The shoulder season is from 1 September to 15 December and the low season from 1 April to 30 June. Prices go up higher still over the Christmas and New Year periods.

Safari Lodges

Hidden away inside or on the edges of national parks are some fantastic safari lodges. These are usually visited as part of organised safaris and you'll pay much more if you just turn up and ask for a room. Some of the older places are trading heavily on their more glorious past, but the best places feature five-star rooms and soaring *makuti*-roofed bars and restaurants overlooking waterholes full of wildlife. Staying in at least one good safari lodge is recommended, if only to see how the other half live! Rooms range from US$120 to US$500 in the high season, but tend to come down a lot in the low season.

Tented Camps

As well as lodges, many camps contain some wonderful luxury tented camps. These places tend to occupy wonderfully remote settings, usually by rivers or other natural beauty spots, and feature large comfortable safari tents with beds and furniture and bathrooms (usually with hot running water!). There are a few moderately priced options in Tsavo East National Park but most of the camps are very exclusive and the tents are pretty much five-star hotel rooms under canvas. Rates range from US$30 a night all the way up to US$600 or higher and many guests fly in on charter planes.

Beach Resorts

Much of the coast, from Diani Beach to Malindi, is taken up by huge luxury beach resorts. Most offer a fairly similar experience, with swimming pools, watersports, bars, restaurants, mobs of souvenir vendors on the beach and 'tribal' dance shows in the evening. They aren't all bad, though, and a handful of them have been very sensitively designed. Quality seems to improve the further you get from Mombasa. Nightly rates vary from US$40 per person at the small family resorts to US$500 at top-end places.

African Safari Club

Although it's package tourism at it's most developed, the **African Safari Club** *(UK* ☎ *020-8466 0014, fax 8466 0020;* e *info@ africansafariclub.com;* w *www.africansafari club.com)* has some splendid properties on the coast and in several of the national parks. The company even has it's own airline ferrying in guests from Europe. There are African Safari Club resorts at Watamu, Kilifi, Shanzu Beach and Kikambala on the coast and in Tsavo East and Masai Mara. Rates are typical for upmarket resorts, but are included as part of holiday packages.

FOOD
Local Food

Although there is some more interesting Kenyan food, most of what travellers encounter are tough meat stews and curries with a filler such as rice, potatoes or other stodgy starches (see Main Dishes for a full description of these). They'll fill you up but it's really just survival food for the locals offering maximum filling-up potential at minimum cost. Vegetarians will really struggle as meat features in almost every dish.

The most basic local eateries are usually known as *hotels* or *hotelis* and often only

Kenya's National Dish

Vegetarians beware – *Nyama choma* or barbecued meat is Kenya's unofficial national dish and it's a red-blooded, hands-on affair. Most places have their own butchery on site, and *nyama choma* is usually purchased by weight, often as a single hunk of meat. Half a kilogram is usually enough for one person (taking into account bone and grizzle), and it'll be brought out to you chopped into small bite-sized bits with vegetable mash and greens. Goat is the most common meat, but you'll see chicken, beef and even antelope and zebra in some of the upmarket places.

Don't expect *nyama choma* to melt in the mouth, though. It's often tough as old boots and you'll need a good half hour at the end of the meal to work over your gums with a toothpick. Copious quantities of Tusker beer tend to help it go down. That said, there's at least one restaurant – the Carnivore in Nairobi – that has elevated *nyama choma* into a gourmet experience. It's regarded as one of the 50 best restaurants in the world, so they must be doing something right!

open during the daytime. You may find yourself having dinner at 5pm if you rely on these places. However, if you have the resources, even in smaller towns it's usually possible to find a restaurant that offers more variety at a higher price. Often these places are connected with the mid-range and top-end hotels and are usually open in the evening.

Apart from the ubiquitous *nyama choma*, (barbecued meat; see the boxed text 'Kenya's National Dish'), the most distinctive African food is found on the coast. Swahili dishes reflect the history of contact with the Arabs and other Indian Ocean traders – coconut and spices are used heavily – and the results can often be excellent, although the Indian food available on the coast is often better still. Most restaurants serve curries and Indian-inspired dishes such as masala chips (ie, with a curry sauce) as well as Kenyan dishes.

Sambusas, deep-fried pastry triangles stuffed with spiced mincemeat, are obvious descendants of the Indian samosa. The best *sambusas* are crisp and spicy but more often you'll get limp greasy pastry with a bland mince filling, like an English Cornish pasty. Another simple snack you'll see everywhere is the *mandazi*, a semi-sweet, flat doughnut that makes up the backbone of an African breakfast. They're eaten on their own or used to soak up sauces, but they're best in the morning when they're freshly made – they turn stale and hard as the day goes on.

Something you don't come across very often, but which makes an excellent snack meal, is *mkate mayai* (literally 'bread eggs'), a wheat dough pancake, filled with minced meat and egg and fried on a hotplate. Other street snacks include roasted corn cobs (cost-

ing just a few shillings), and deep-fried yams, eaten hot with a squeeze of lemon juice and a sprinkling of chilli powder.

Strictly for the brave is *mursik*, made from milk fermented with grass ash and cow's urine in smoked gourds. Although it tastes and smells revolting, it contains compounds that reduce cholesterol, enabling the Maasai to live quite healthily on red meat, milk and blood. You may be able to sample it at villages in the Mara.

Main Dishes Most dishes are based around stewed meat, accompanied by starch of some sort. Perhaps some potato or other vegetables thrown into the mix, but the meat is often as tough as leather. Beef, goat and mutton are most common.

Starch comes in five major forms: potatoes, rice, chapati, *matoke* and *ugali*. The Kenyan chapati is an obvious Indian influence, *matoke* is mashed plantains (green bananas), while *ugali* is maize meal cooked into a thick porridge until it sets hard, then is served up in flat slabs. It's incredibly stodgy, almost totally devoid of any flavour and tends to sit on the stomach like a royal corgi, but most Kenyans swear by it. It's filling, but you'll rarely find yourself saying 'you know what, I really fancy some *ugali*...'.

Another noteworthy staple, especially in the Central Highlands, is *irio* (*kienyji* in Swahili), a Kikuyu dish made from mashed greens, potatoes and boiled corn or beans. Also common is *mukimo* a kind of hash made from sweet potatoes, corn, beans and plantains. Vegetarians can find *githeri*, a mix of beans and corn, and cooked red kidney beans in most local eateries.

Western dishes such as roast chicken and steak are staples in more upmarket restaurants found in the bigger towns. It's perfectly good food, but it can get a little boring after a while.

Menus, where they exist in the cheaper places, are usually just a chalked list on a board on the wall. In better restaurants, they are usually written just in English. See the Language chapter at the back of this book for a list of the main words you are likely to come across when trying to decipher Swahili menus or buy food in the market.

Fruit
Because of the country's varied climate, there's often an excellent array of fruits to be found. Depending on the place and the season, you can buy mangoes, papaya, pineapple, passion fruit, guavas, oranges, watermelon, custard apples, bananas (of many varieties), tree tomatoes and also coconuts. Prices are cheap and the quality is very high.

Fast Food
The eating of fast food has taken off in a big way and virtually every town has a place serving greasy but cheap chips, burgers, sausages, pizzas and fried chicken. Lashings of tomato ketchup and chilli sauce are used to help the stodge go down. A number of South African fast-food chains have taken hold in Nairobi. Branches of Steers, Nandos, Chicken Inn and Creamy Inn are springing up all over the place.

Vegetarian
Vegetarians are really only catered for in Indian restaurants across the country, some of which are exclusively vegetarian, or at the more-expensive restaurants that serve international cuisine in Nairobi. Away from the two main cities there are virtually no vegetarian dishes to accompany the starch. Beans will figure prominently in any vegetarian's culinary encounters in Kenya! Buying fresh fruit and vegetables in the market can help relieve the tedium of ordering around the meat on restaurant menus.

Self-Catering
Preparing your own food is a viable option if you are in a place that supplies a kitchen or if you're camping and carrying cooking gear. Every town has a market, and there's usually an excellent range of fresh produce. Western-style supermarkets are found in major towns.

DRINKS
Nonalcoholic Drinks
Tea & Coffee Despite the fact that Kenya grows some excellent tea and coffee, getting a decent cup of either can be difficult, as the best stuff is exported.

Tea *(chai)* is the national obsession and is drunk in large quantities, but it bears little resemblance to what you might be used to. As in India the tea, milk and masses of sugar are boiled together and stewed for ages and the result is milky and horrendously sweet. It's often better when spiced as *chai masala*. For tea without milk ask for *chai kavu*.

As for coffee, the stuff you get served is often sweet and milky and made with a bare minimum of instant coffee. In Nairobi, there are a handful of coffee houses serving very good Kenyan coffee, and you can usually get a good filter coffee at any of the big hotels. With all the Italian tourists who visit the coast, you can now get a decent cappuccino pretty much anywhere between Diani Beach and Lamu.

Soft Drinks All the old favourites are here, including Coke, Sprite and Fanta, but they go under the generic term of soda and are available everywhere. As with beer, prices vary depending on where you buy it. In most places you pay around KSh20 per bottle but in the more exclusive places you can pay up to KSh100. Stoney's ginger ale (known just as Stoney's) is hugely popular, as is Vimto, a fizzy fruity concoction that has a taste that grows on you.

Juice With all the fresh fruit on offer in Kenya, fruit juices are a national obsession and the best on offer are breathtakingly good. All rely on modern blenders, however, so there's no point asking for a fruit juice during a power cut. Prices range from KSh30 to KSh150. Although you can get juices made from almost any fruit, the nation's favourite is passion fruit. It is known locally simply as passion, although it seems a little odd asking a waiter or waitress whether they have passion and how much it costs!

Pineapple, orange and mango also feature on most menus. If you're worried about hygiene, the bottled juices produced by the Picana company are also very good.

Alcohol

Beer Kenya has a thriving local brewing industry and formidable quantities of beer are consumed. However, you'll usually be given a choice of 'warm' or 'cold' beer. 'Why warm?' you might ask as your face wrinkles in horror! Most Kenyans appear to prefer it that way.

The local beers are Tusker, White Cap and Pilsner (all manufactured by Kenya Breweries) and they're sold in 500ml bottles. Tusker comes in three varieties, Tusker Export, Tusker Malt Lager and just plain Tusker, which are all basically the same product with different labels (although locals swear they can tell the difference). Guinness is also available but tastes and looks nothing like the genuine Irish article. Castle (a South African beer) is made under licence in Kenya by, you've guessed it, Kenya Breweries.

Other local bottled drinks include Hardy's cider, Redd's (a sort of apple alcopop) and Kingfisher (another fruity concoction that's available in several awful flavours).

Beers are cheapest when bought from a supermarket, where a 500ml bottle will cost you around KSh45. If bought from a normal bar, you are looking at KSh80. Bought at a bar in a five-star hotel, though, beer can cost up to KSh200.

Wine Kenya has a fledgling wine industry and the Lake Naivasha Colombard wines are said to be quite good. This is something that cannot be said about the most commonly encountered Kenyan wine – papaya wine. Quite how anyone came up with the idea of trying to reproduce a drink made from grapes using papaya instead is a mystery, but the result tastes foul and even smells unbearable.

On the other hand, you can get cheap imported South African, European and even Australian wine by the glass for around KSh150 in Nairobi restaurants. In the big supermarket chains such as Nakumatt and Uchumi, you can pay anything from between KSh500 and KSh1500 for a bottle of South African wine.

Lethal Brew

Kenya has a long tradition of producing its own bootleg liquor, but you should steer well clear of *chang'a*. In November 2000, a batch of the brew laced with methanol killed more than 130 people and hospitalised 500 others. The drink, Sorghum Baridi, from Central Province, contains so much methyl alcohol that the bottles are actually cold to the touch! Perhaps the most dangerous *chang'a* comes from Kisii, and is fermented with marijuana twigs, cactus mash, battery alkaline and formalin. Needless to say these brews can have lethal effects on your health, including permanent blindness, mental illness and even death.

Local Brews Although it is strictly illegal for the public to brew or distil liquor, this still goes on. *Pombe* is the local beer, usually a fermented brew made with bananas or millet and sugar. It shouldn't do you any harm. The same cannot be said for the distilled drinks known locally as *chang'a*, which are laced with genuine poisons. See the boxed text 'Lethal Brew' for more on *chang'a*.

ENTERTAINMENT
Bars

Almost equal to the Kenyan love of dancing is the Kenyan love of beer – they consume massive amounts of the stuff, and there are bars everywhere. These range from flash five-star places where waiters wear bow ties, to local *dukas* where the beer is warm, the floor earthen and the noise-level high. Dancing is spontaneous and can break out at any time. Note that some bars in tourist areas or transport hubs are full of prostitutes and the endless offers of company can be quite demoralising.

Discos

Kenyans love to party and you'll always find a disco in the main towns. Nairobi has half a dozen, and they are great places to spend an evening. They work on a familiar system of cheap entry for ladies, and are often pick-up joints of the highest order. Prostitution, alas, is rife. The extravagant discos on the coast also offer huge floor shows, usually Las Vegas–style song-and-dance extravaganzas.

Live Music

The *Daily Nation* on Saturday has a listing of who's playing where across the country. It will give you an idea of the popular venues – concerts of note are advertised well in advance. Posters are also a source of information, although you can't beat word of mouth.

The really big gigs are often sponsored by tobacco or drinks companies and take place in the Carnivore restaurant or at the racecourse in Nairobi. They are quite an experience.

See Music in the Facts about Kenya chapter for details on Kenya's contemporary performers.

Cinemas

There are cinemas in Nairobi, Mombasa and other major towns. The movies vary from Indian Bollywood hits to trashy Hollywood ultra-violence. Although occasional Hollywood blockbusters are shown in Nairobi and Mombasa, it's Indian movies that everyone wants to see! The price is a bargain; usually around KSh200.

Small video theatres are common and popular throughout Kenya. Cheap enough for just about anyone (KSh15), they play a heady mix of Hong Kong martial-art movies as well as Hollywood violence or soft-porn straight-to-video flicks. Film quality (of the reel and the aesthetics) varies. Some places even show European soccer matches via satellite, or on video.

Dance, Theatre & Performance

There are a number of contemporary dance troupes and theatre groups in Kenya, although the majority of performances take place in Nairobi. The Phoenix and Miujiza Players, Mbalamwezi Theatre Group, plus the La Campagnie Gaara and Bakututu dance groups, and Sigana Troupe, are all names to look out for. Other than in purpose-built theatres, plays and performances are often held in the various foreign cultural centres in Nairobi, Mombasa and Kisumu.

For more details on the Kenyan scene contact the **Mzizi Arts Centre** (☎ 785086; *5th floor, Buru Buru centre, Mumias South Rd*) and check in Saturday's *Daily Nation* to see what's on across the country (see also Entertainment in the Nairobi chapter and Arts in the Facts about Kenya chapter).

Safari Rally

Known originally as the Coronation Rally (in honour of Queen Elizabeth II), the first event was held in 1953, when 56 local European drivers took off for a 5000km tour of East Africa with just a couple of spare tyres in the boot. Until 1972, all the winners were Kenyan, but highly sponsored international race teams now dominate the rally and the locals rarely get a look in. Perhaps the most famous Kenyan driver ever was Joginder Singh, known across the nation as the 'Flying Sikh', who won three times. The last Kenyan to win the race was Ian Duncan in 1994. Although the rally is now backed up by helicopters and support vehicles, the roads here still eat rally cars for breakfast. Only 14 of the 48 cars in the 2002 rally finished, little changed from the figures for the first rally back in 1956. It's an unique experience and everyone, from city slickers to Maasai shepherds, stops what they're doing to watch the cars speed by.

SPECTATOR SPORTS

Soccer is a big deal in Kenya. People are nuts about it, and the big teams draw big crowds. Harambee Stars, AFC Leopards and Mathare United are among the best teams in the Kenyan Premiership. The grounds and pitches are not on a par with those in Europe, but the action is fast, furious and passionate – passion that at times spills out on the terraces. Tickets to a game cost between KSh300 and KSh600 and it's quite an experience. Check out the *Daily Nation* for fixtures.

Kenyan long-distance runners are among the best in the world, although much of their competitive running takes place outside the country. Even trials and national events in Kenya sometimes fail to attract these stars, despite these events being flagged in the press well in advance. **Moi Stadium** (*Thika Rd*), outside Nairobi, is a popular venue for events.

The East African Safari Rally hits Kenya in March, usually over the Easter weekend. If you're here, the spectacle is worth seeking out. Times and routes are published in the *Daily Nation* or you can contact the **Automobile Association of Kenya** (☎ 02-720383; *Hurlingham shopping centre*) in Nairobi.

SHOPPING

Kenya is an excellent place for souvenirs, although much of the cheap stuff is mass-produced for the tourist trade. Look carefully at what's available before parting with your money. It is illegal to export some wildlife products (see Customs earlier in this chapter).

Nairobi and Mombasa are the main souvenir centres, but many of the items come from other regions, so it's often possible to pick them up where they are made. It's certainly possible to buy something that will look good in your living room without spending a fortune, but, these days, something of genuine quality and artistry is going to cost real money. This particularly applies to *makonde* carvings, jewellery and paintings. In some cases, you can be talking about thousands of US dollars.

Local people are sometimes willing to swap their handicrafts for Western clothing (especially T-shirts), shoes and the like, but it's important to remember Kenyans need your money more than an old T-shirt – paying a fair price can make a real difference to the lives of villagers whose only income comes from selling goods to tourists. Keep this in mind when arguing over a few cents.

Posting things of small value home is usually straightforward and secure (see Post & Communications earlier in this chapter). There are dozens of souvenir shops at the airport, but prices there are extremely high.

Baskets

Kiondos (sisal baskets) are an extremely popular Kenyan souvenir. They come in a variety of sizes, colours and configurations with many different straps and clasps. Expect to pay around US$2 for a basic basket, and up to US$10 for a large one with leather trim. Some of the finer baskets have baobab bark woven into them and this bumps up the price considerably. Reed baskets, widely used as shopping bags, cost less than KSh50.

Fabrics & Batik

Kangas and *kikois* are the local sarongs and serve many purposes. *Kangas* are colourful prints on thin cotton that are sold in pairs, one to wrap around your waist and one to carry a baby on your back. Each bears a Swahili proverb. Biashara St in Mombasa is the *kanga* centre in Kenya, and you'll pay upwards of US$3 for a pair, depending on quality. *Kikois* are made with a thicker, striped cotton and are simpler and more colourful. They are originally from Lamu and this is still the best place to buy them.

Batik cloth is another good buy and there's a tremendous range, but the better prints are not cheap and the tradition was imported from elsewhere. You can expect to pay US$4 upwards for batiks on cotton, and thousands of shillings for batiks on silk.

Woodcarvings

These are easily the most popular Kenyan souvenir, and a painted wooden giraffe is an instant marker of a trip to East Africa. Much of the stuff on offer is of dubious taste, but there is some very fine work available. The most famous woodcarvings here are the *makonde*–style effigies (which are made by the Akamba people from around the Tanzanian border), which are traditionally carved from ebony, a very black, heavy wood. They often feature wildlife, towers of thin figures and slender Maasai figurines. However, be aware that ebony is a threatened wood (see the boxed text 'Good Wood' earlier in this chapter).

If possible, buy from one of the many nonprofit handicraft cooperatives around the country rather than souvenir shops; these people need all the help they can get. Heavy bargaining is necessary if you buy from market stalls or tourist shops. You can pay anything from KSh200 up to hundreds of US dollars for a large and intricate piece.

Soapstone

Easily carved soapstone is used to make popular chess sets, ashtrays and abstract organic-looking sculptures. Kisumu on Lake Victoria is the best place to buy, although soapstone souvenirs are sold and produced across the country, most notably in Kisii. The only problem is that soapstone is quite fragile and heavy to carry round.

Jewellery

Most jewellery on sale in Kenya is of tribal origin, although very little is the genuine article. The colourful Maasai beaded jewellery is the most striking and the most popular, and is very distinctive. Necklaces, bangles and wristlets are widely available and beadwork is used on all sorts of knick-knacks, from hair-slides to wallets. Prices are high, but there's lots of work involved in making them. None of the 'elephant hair' bracelets sold by hawkers in Nairobi are the real thing – most are simply reed grass covered in boot polish.

Tribal Souvenirs
Traditional tribal objects are very popular. Spears are particularly sought after and come apart into several sections, making them easy to transport. Like the painted leather shields, most are mass-produced for the tourist market. Turkana wrist knives and Maasai knives forged from car shock absorbers are also high kudos souvenirs.

Decorated Maasai calabashes, traditionally used to store *mursik* (see Food earlier), are eye-catching but tend to pong a bit. All sorts of masks are available, although few are used in rituals today. The three-legged African stool is another very popular souvenir, and *shukas* (Maasai blankets) and shoes made from old car tyres are cheap, unusual souvenirs.

Getting There & Away

Unless you are travelling overland from Southern Africa or Egypt, flying is the most convenient – and just about the only – way to get to Kenya. Nairobi is a major African hub and flights between Kenya and the rest of Africa are easy to come by and relatively cheap. It's important to note that the pricing and availability of flights are highly seasonal. Conveniently for Europeans, the cheapest fares usually coincide with the European summer holidays – from June to September. It's often possible to pick up an economy return ticket from London for about UK£400. However, during December and January, prices soar and availability plummets.

It's also worth checking out cheap charter flights to Mombasa from Europe, although these will probably be part of a package deal to a hotel resort on the coast. Prices are often absurdly cheap and there's no obligation to stay at the resort you're booked into. Many African (and other) airlines have gone bust in the aftermath of 11 September 2001, so the be aware that information in this chapter is particularly vulnerable to change.

A few adventurous and resourceful souls with their own vehicles still travel overland to Kenya from Europe, but most routes pass through either several war zones and should only be considered after some serious planning and preparation. See Land later in this chapter for more details.

AIR
Airports
Most international flights to and from Nairobi are handled by Jomo Kenyatta International Airport, 15km southeast of the city. By African standards it's a pretty well-organised place, with two international terminals, a smaller domestic terminal and an incredible number of shops selling expensive souvenirs. You can walk easily between the terminals. If you're flying out of here, note that loose or 'insecure' (fragile) items have to be wrapped up in plastic film (which costs KSh250 to KSh400).

Some flights between Nairobi and Kilimanjaro International Airport or Mwanza in Tanzania, as well as many domestic flights, use Wilson Airport, which is about 6km south of the city centre on Langata Rd.

Warning
The information in this chapter is particularly vulnerable to change: Prices for international travel are volatile, routes are introduced and cancelled, schedules change, special deals come and go, and rules and visa requirements are amended. Airlines and governments seem to take a perverse pleasure in making price structures and regulations as complicated as possible. You should check directly with the airline or a travel agent to make sure you understand how a fare (and ticket you may buy) works. In addition, the travel industry is highly competitive and there are many lurks and perks. The upshot of this is that you should get opinions, quotes and advice from as many airlines and travel agents as possible before you part with your hard-earned cash. The details given in this chapter should be regarded as pointers and are not a substitute for your own careful, up-to-date research.

The other arrival point in the country is Moi International Airport in Mombasa, 9km west of the centre, but this is mainly used by charter airlines.

Tickets
There is no advantage in buying a one-way ticket to Nairobi and then buying another one-way ticket back home from there. You'll end up paying more than the cost of a return ticket in the first place. You may also run foul of immigration on arrival in Kenya without an onward ticket and be forced to buy one on the spot – an expensive exercise.

Second-hand tickets are now impossible to use. Quite simply, if your boarding card and passport don't match, you're stuffed. Also note that you can't get a standby flight to Kenya unless you're an airline employee.

The airport departure tax for international flights is usually included in the cost of your plane ticket.

Airlines Kenya Airways is the main international and domestic airline servicing the country, but British Airways' subsidiary Regional Air is servicing an increasing number of international routes. See Getting There &

Away in the Nairobi chapter for contact details of airlines serving Kenya.

USA All flights from the USA to Nairobi go via Europe. Through tickets are easy to get from travel agents, but it's often cheaper to buy a discounted ticket to London, Amsterdam or Brussels, and then connect to Kenya from there; see UK and Continental Europe later for more details. However, North West Airlines is affiliated with KLM and Kenya Airways and offers speedy connections through London or Amsterdam.

San Francisco is the discount air-ticket capital of America, although ticket consolidators can also be found in Los Angeles, New York and other big cities. The *New York Times*, the *Los Angeles Times*, the *Chicago Tribune* and the *San Francisco Examiner* all produce weekly travel sections in which you will find a number of ads fro travel agencies.

With its recent buyout of Council Travel, **STA Travel** (☎ 800 777 0112; W *www.sta travel.com*) is now the biggest discount travel agent in the US. There are offices in Boston, Chicago, Miami, New York, Philadelphia, San Francisco and other major cities. Call or visit its website for office locations.

Return tickets to Nairobi from New York can cost as little as US$1300 in the low season; from Los Angeles, a return ticket costs about US$1500.

Canada The fares offered by Canadian discount air-ticket sellers (consolidators) tend to be about 10% higher than those sold in the USA. The *Globe & Mail*, the *Toronto Star*, the *Montreal Gazette* and the *Vancouver Sun* are good places to look for cheap fares.

Travel CUTS (☎ 800 667 2887; W *www .travelcuts.com*) is Canada's national student travel agency and has offices in all major cities. **STA Travel** has branches in Toronto and Vancouver – contact its head office (☎ 1-888 427 5639, fax 416-925 6300; W *www.sta travel.ca; 200 Bloor St West, Toronto, M5S1T8*) for more information.

Air France, KLM and British Airways offer flights from Toronto to Nairobi for US$1900 to US$2500. As with flights from the USA, it may be cheaper to fly to Europe first, and pick up a cheap onward ticket.

UK Airline ticket discounters are known as bucket shops in the UK. Despite the some-

what disreputable name, there is nothing under-the-counter about them. Discount air travel is big business in London.

One of the best bucket shops in the capital is **Flightbookers** (☎ 020-7757 2000; W *www .ebookers.com; 177-178 Tottenham Court Rd, London W1P 9LF*). This company offers consistently cheap fares and has an excellent online booking system, which allows you to book seats from various countries in Europe, including the UK, Ireland, France, Germany, Holland and Spain. Flightbookers has a bureau de change and travel vaccination clinic at its London office. Another recommended bucket shop is **Trailfinders** (☎ 020-7938 3939; W *www.trailfinders.com; 194 Kensington High St, London W8 7RG*), which can also fix you up with immunisations, insurance and visas. There are loads of others – look in the travel sections of the weekend broadsheets, such as the *Independent* and the *Sunday Times* or the entertainment magazine *Time Out*.

For students or travellers aged under 26, the best youth and student travel agency around the UK is **STA Travel** (☎ 020-7361 6161; W *www.statravel.co.uk; 86 Old Brompton Rd, London SW7 3LQ*), which has 50 branches in the UK. The other big international student player, **USIT Campus** went under in 2002.

The average price of an airline ticket from London to Nairobi is around UK£500 return. Airline competition is fierce and cheap deals are often offered by the likes of Swiss Airlines and Kenya Airways (often as low as UK£300 return). It can also sometimes be cheaper to pick up a discount flight to Brussels with Easyjet or one of the other budget airlines and then connect through to Nairobi with SN Brussels Airlines, which consistently undercuts the bigger European carriers (see Continental Europe following).

Around-the-world (RTW) ticket is another option if you have the time, but the most common African stop is Johannesburg – any ticket that includes Nairobi is usually much more expensive (between UK£1100 and UK£1400). It may be cheaper to buy an RTW ticket via Johannesburg and then buying a ticket on to Nairobi from there.

Charter flights can work out as a cheaper alternative to scheduled flights and the package may also include accommodation, which you aren't obliged to stay in if you want to travel around the country. **Somak**

(☎ 020-8903 8526; ⓔ flights@somak.co.uk; ⓦ www.somak.co.uk) is probably your best bet for good deals.

Continental Europe Currently, the cheapest way to get to Kenya from Europe is with the newly resurrected SN Brussels Airlines (formerly Sabena) via Entebbe or Kigali. Fares from Brussels are often hundreds of euros cheaper than from other European cities (around €450), so it may be worth picking up a cheap connection to Brussels with one of the budget airlines and then connecting to Africa from there. In Belgium, **Acotra Student Travel Agency** (☎ 02-512 86 07; Rue de la Madeline, Brussels) and **WATS Reizen** (☎ 03-226 16 26; de Keyserlei 44, Antwerp) are both well-known agencies.

Kenya Airways' link with KLM means that you can also fly from regional airports across Europe, via Amsterdam, to Nairobi. In the Netherlands, **NBBS Reizen** (in Amsterdam ☎ 020-624 09 89; Rokin 66) is the official student travel agency. There are several other agencies around the city – **Malibu Travel** (☎ 020-626 32 30; Prinsengracht 230) can be recommended. From Amsterdam, as from most European cities, return fares range from €560 to €800, depending on the season.

STA Travel, the international student and young person's travel giant, has branches in many European nations, including Austria (ⓦ www.oekista.at), Denmark (ⓦ www.sta travel.dk), Finland (ⓦ www.statravel.fi), Germany (ⓦ www.statravel.de), Norway (ⓦ www.statravel.no) and Sweden (ⓦ www .statravel.se).

There are also many STA-affiliated travel agencies across Europe. Visit ⓦ www.sta travelgroup.com/thmenu.htm to find an STA partner close to you. Useful STA-affiliated companies include: **Voyages Wasteels** (in France ☎ 01 43 25 12 52, fax 01 43 25 46 25; 11 Rue Dupuytren, 756006 Paris); **Viagi Wasteels** (☎ 06-445 6679, fax 445 6685; Via Milazzo 8/C, 00185 Rome); and **Robissa Travel Bureau** (☎ 01-321 1188, fax 321 1194; 43 Voulis St, GR-105 57, Athens).

France has a network of student travel agencies that can supply discount tickets to travellers of all ages. **OTU Voyages** (☎ 0825 004 027, fax 01 46 33 19 98; ⓦ www.otu.fr; central office 39 Ave Georges Bernanos (5e) Paris) has 28 branch offices around the country. **Acceuil des Jeunes en France** (☎ 01 42

77 87 80, fax 01 42 77 70 48; 119 Rue Saint Martin (4e) Paris) is another popular discount travel agency in France. One cheap option is **Nouvelles Frontières** (☎ 08 03 33 33 33; ⓦ www.nouvelles-frontieres.com; 5 Ave de l'Opéra (1er) Paris), which often offers cheap tickets to Mombasa with its own charter airline, Corsair.

Because of the Swiss Airlines connection, Switzerland is also a good place to buy discount air tickets to Nairobi. **SSR Voyages** (☎ 01-297 11 11; ⓦ www.ssr.ch; Leonhardstrasse 10, Zurich) specialises in student, youth and budget fares. There are branches in most major cities.

Australia & New Zealand Getting to Kenya from Australia or New Zealand is harder than you might expect as none of the trans-Asian airlines fly to Nairobi (and that includes Qantas and Air New Zealand). The most direct route from Australia to Kenya is via Mauritius with Air Mauritius, but the cheapest tickets are usually via the Persian Gulf with Gulf Airlines or Emirates or with South African Airways (SAA) via Johannesburg. Return fares typically cost A$2250 to A$2600 from Sydney or Melbourne and around A$2300 from Perth.

Two well-known agents for cheap fares in Australia are **STA Travel** (☎ 1300 733 035; ⓦ www.statravel.com.au; main office 260 Hoddle St, Abbotsford, Vic 3067) and **Flight Centre** (Australia-wide ☎ 133 133; ⓦ www .flightcentre.com.au; central office 82 Elizabeth St, Sydney, NSW 2000). Both have offices throughout Australia and at university campuses – call or visit their websites for details. Cheap air fares are also advertised in the travel sections of weekend newspapers, such as the *Age* in Melbourne and the *Sydney Morning Herald*.

A RTW ticket or an Australia/New Zealand to Europe round-trip ticket, with stopovers in Asia and Africa, is something else to think about. Having Nairobi added to such a ticket bumps up the price a little and you may have to go through several travel agents before you find someone who can put a good deal together.

In New Zealand, the *New Zealand Herald* has a good travel section with plenty of advertised fares. **Flight Centre** (☎ 09-309 6171, countrywide 0800 233 544; ⓦ www.flightcentre.co.nz; National Bank Towers, 205-225

Queen St, Auckland) has many branches throughout the country. **STA Travel** (☎ 09-309 9723; **W** www.statravel.co.nz; Level 8, 229 Queen St, Auckland) has offices in Auckland as well as in Hamilton, Palmerston North, Newmarket, Wellington, Dunedin and Christchurch. The fare from Auckland to Nairobi with Emirates or SAA is around NZ$2740 to NZ$2950.

Indian Subcontinent There are plenty of flights between East Africa and Mumbai (Bombay), due to the large Indian population in East Africa. Although most of India's discount travel agents are in Delhi, there are also some reliable agents in Mumbai. In Mumbai, try **STIC Travels** (☎ 022-218 1431; 6 Maker Arcade, Cuffe Parade) or **Transway International** (☎ 022-262 6066; 2nd floor, Pantaky House, 8 Maruti Cross Lane, Fort). **STA** has an office in New Delhi (☎ 011-336 7860; **e** fareinfo@isicweb.net; Room 2, Hotel Janpath, Janpath).

Typical fares from Mumbai to Nairobi are about US$320/370 one way/return. **Kenya Airways** (in Nairobi ☎ 02-3207 4100) and **Air India** (in Nairobi ☎ 313300) offer flights.

Middle East For the Middle East, **Kenya Airways** (in Nairobi ☎ 02-3207 4100) and **Egypt Airways** (in Nairobi ☎ 02-226821) serve Cairo several times a week (US$440, return fares only). From Mombasa, **Oman Air** (☎ 011-224400; Moi Ave, Mombasa) has twice-weekly flights to Dubai and Muscat. Emirates and Gulf Airlines both have numerous flights from Nairobi to destinations throughout the Middle East.

The Horn of Africa & Sudan There are regular direct flights between Nairobi and Addis Ababa with both **Ethiopian Airlines** (in Nairobi ☎ 02-330837) and **Kenya Airways** (in Nairobi ☎ 02-3207 4100). A return fare on Ethiopian Airways is about US$355.

Several airlines serve Sudan, Eritrea and Djibouti, where your security can't always be guaranteed, and even war-torn Somalia. Kenya Airways and **Regional Air** (in Nairobi ☎ 02-311584) fly between Khartoum and Nairobi several times a week; one-way/return flights cost US$270/380. Some flights continue on to Djibouti (US$640 return) and Asmara in Eritrea (US$690 return). The regional carriers **African Express**

Airways (in Mombasa ☎ 011-433851) and **Da'allo Airlines** (in Nairobi ☎ 02-317318) have flights between Nairobi and Djibouti (US$320 return).

Tanzania & Uganda With the demise of Air Uganda, **Kenya Airways** (in Nairobi ☎ 02-3207 4100) is now the principal carrier flying between Nairobi and Entebbe (34km south of Kampala). There are three or four flights daily and the one-way/return fare is US$200/350. If the new Ugandan airline AfricaOne gets off the ground, there should be more choice on this route.

If you're heading to Tanzania, Kenya Airways and **Air Tanzania** (in Nairobi ☎ 02-336224) offer cheap daily flights between Dar es Salaam and Nairobi (US$230/430 one way/return). The cheapest way to get to the island of Zanzibar is with **Air Kenya** (☎ 02-501601; **e** resvns@airkenya.com), based at Nairobi's Wilson Airport. There are flights daily except Wednesday from Nairobi (US$180/250) and four flights a week from Mombasa (US$100/200). Air Kenya frequently offers fantastic promo fares of US$100 return.

Another way to save money is to pick up a cheap, advance-purchase ticket from Nairobi to Mombasa with Flamingo Airlines (see the Getting Around chapter for further information) and then connect to Zanzibar from there. Kenya Airways also has daily flights to Zanzibar from Jomo Kenyatta International Airport.

Several airlines fly daily from Nairobi to Kilimanjaro International Airport near Moshi, including Air Kenya, Ethiopian Airlines and **Precision Air** (☎ 02-822111 ext 5169; Jomo Kenyatta International Airport). The one-way/return fare is US$135/270. Precision Air also has flights to Mwanza on Lake Victoria on Monday, Wednesday and Friday (US$200).

Indian Ocean Islands There are several flights weekly between Nairobi and the magical islands of Madagascar, Mauritius, the Seychelles and the Comores. Flights to/from Madagascar are about US$480 return with **Air Madagascar** (in Nairobi ☎ 02-225286); cheaper deals crop up from time to time. A return ticket to Mauritius from Nairobi is roughly US$500 with **Air Mauritius** (in Nairobi ☎ 02-229166) or **British**

Airways *(in Nairobi ☎ 02-244430)*. Kenya Airways and British Airways both serve the Seychelles for US$350 to US$550 return. For Moroni in the Comores, **African Express Airways** *(in Mombasa ☎ 011-433851)* has flights on Saturday only (US$220/320 one way/return).

South Africa The only direct flights between Kenya and South Africa go to/from Johannesburg. Kenya Airways and **SAA** *(in Nairobi ☎ 02-227486)* both have daily flights for around US$380/620 one way/return.

In Johannesburg, the **South African Student's Travel Services** *(☎ 011-716 3045)* has an office at the University of the Witwatersrand. **STA Travel** *(☎ 011-447 5551)* has an office in Johannesburg on Tyrwhitt Ave in Rosebank.

Flight Centres has a partner office in Cape Town *(☎ 021-556 8490, fax 556 8492; e wacpt@iafrica.com; 15a Mansell Ave, Killarney Gardens, PO Box 50425, Cape Town)*.

Other Parts of Africa Nairobi is a major African hub and there are good connections to Malawi, Zambia and Zimbabwe. As an indication of prices, one-way/return flights to Lusaka in Zambia cost US$250/350 with Kenya Airways or Regional Air; flights to Harare in Zimbabwe cost US$270/400 with Kenya Airways or Air Zimbabwe; while flights to Blantyre or Lilongwe in Malawi cost US$300/455 with Kenya Airways or Air Malawi. **Worldwide Adventure Travel** *(☎ 04-728092, fax 704794; e wathre@ comone.co.zw; Travel Centre, 5th floor, 93 Jason Moyo Ave, PO Box 7071, Harare)* is the sister organisation of Flight Centres in Nairobi, and has years of experience in the budget travel business.

From Nairobi there are also flights to Burundi, Cameroon, Côte d'Ivoire, Congo (Zaïre) and Ghana with Kenya Airways and other carriers.

Travellers with Specific Needs

If you have special needs of any sort, you should let the airline know as soon as possible so it can make arrangements accordingly. You should give the airline a reminder when you reconfirm your booking and again as you check in at the airport. See Disabled Travellers in the Facts for the Visitor chapter for more general information.

LAND
Border Crossings

The main border crossings into Kenya are at Namanga, Taveta and Lunga Lunga (for Tanzania), Busia and Malaba (for Uganda) and at Moyale (for Ethiopia). All are open 24 hours. Visas are typically available on arrival for most nationalities, but you should contact your nearest Kenyan diplomatic office to get the most-up-to-date information. Moneychangers are always present and visa fees can be paid in local currency or US dollars. You should carry several passport photos with you for immigration forms. Note that a single-entry Kenyan visa will also allow you to visit Uganda and Tanzania. The land borders with Sudan and Somalia are closed indefinitely.

From Europe

There were once several breathtaking overland routes to Kenya via North or West Africa, but most of these are now totally out of bounds due to the ongoing unrest in Algeria, Somalia, southern Sudan, Eritrea and Congo (Zaïre) – the list goes on. Most overland tour companies coming from North or West Africa now fly their clients to Kenya after travelling most of the way by truck. To try and make the same journey using public transport or hitching would be an endeavour fraught with peril.

The most realistic route to take for travellers with their own vehicle cuts through Tunisia, Libya, Egypt, Sudan and Ethiopia. At the time of writing, it was much easier for those on motorbikes.

Starting in Genoa (Italy), catch the ferry to Tunisia and then head east through Libya to Egypt. Be aware that you'll need to have a Libyan visa before you set off. Cut down to Lake Nassar and then cross to Wadi Halfa in Sudan. Motorbikers can take the ferry, but 4WD owners have to negotiate with the owners of a motor-powered pontoon that can transport 16 vehicles across the lake for a total of US$2000. Once in northern Sudan, pass through Khartoum and cross into Ethiopia at Metema (see Ethiopia later for more details).

If you're planning to ship your vehicle to Kenya, be aware that port charges in Kenya are very high. For example, a Land Rover shipped from the Middle East to Mombasa is likely to cost US$1000 just to get off the ship and out of the port. This is almost as much as the cost of the shipping. Putting a vehicle into the Mombasa port costs about US$600 on top of this. There are numerous shipping agents in Nairobi and Mombasa willing to arrange everything for you, but check all the costs in advance.

Tanzania

There are several land borders between Kenya and Tanzania, most of which can be reached by public transport. The exception is the crossing from the Serengeti to Masai Mara, which can only be undertaken with your own vehicle. The border at Oloitokitok near Mt Kilimanjaro is closed to tourists, although you may be able to temporarily cross on a tour from the Kibo Slopes lodge in Oloitokitok (see Oloitokitok in the Southern Kenya chapter for more information). Train services between the two countries have been suspended.

Mombasa to Tanga/Dar es Salaam Numerous buses run along the coast road from Mombasa to Tanga and Dar es Salaam, crossing the border at Lunga Lunga/Horohoro. Most people travel on through buses from Mombasa, but its easy enough to do the journey in stages by local bus or matatu.

In Mombasa, buses to Dar es Salaam leave from Jomo Kenyatta Ave, near the junction with Mwembe Tayari Rd. **Interstate 2000** (☎ 011-490776) has an office opposite the Kobil petrol station on Jomo Kenyatta Ave and offers daily buses to Tanga (KSh400) and Dar es Salaam (KSh800). Buses leave Mombasa at 7am and 6pm, returning from Dar es Salaam at the same times. **As-Salaam**, by the Total petrol station on Jomo Kenyatta Ave, has buses at 8.30am and 6pm (KSh400/1000 to Tanga/Dar es Salaam). Several small companies have desks on the roadside near the Interstate 2000 office and offer buses and matatus to Tanga for KSh400 – most services leave between 9am and noon. **Al Yumeiny** is a reliable company.

In Dar es Salaam, buses leave from the Mnazi Mmoja bus stand on Bibi Titi Mohamed Rd, near Uhuru and Lindi Sts, along the southeast side of Mnazi Mmoja Park.

If you want to do the journey in stages, there are frequent matatus to Lunga Lunga from the Mombasa ferry jetty at Likoni. A matatu can then take you the 6.5km between the two border posts. On the Tanzanian side, there are regular matatus from Horohoro to Tanga (see Lunga Lunga in The Coast chapter for more details).

Mombasa to Arusha/Moshi A number of rickety local buses leave Mombasa every evening, bound for Moshi and Arusha in Tanzania. There are occasional morning services, but most buses leave around 7pm from Mombasa or Arusha. Fares are around KSh500 to Moshi (six hours) and KSh800 to Arusha (7½ hours). In Mombasa, buses leave from in front of the Mwembe Tayari Health Centre on Jomo Kenyatta Ave.

Buses cross the border at Taveta, which can also be reached by train or matatu from Voi (see Taveta in the Nairobi to the Coast chapter for more details).

Nairobi to Arusha/Moshi You have a choice of ordinary buses or much more comfortable minibus shuttle services between Nairobi and Arusha. Each takes about four hours and neither requires a change of service at the border at Namanga. Riverside Shuttle and Davanu Shuttle both offer convenient services from central Nairobi.

Riverside Shuttle (☎ 02-229618; 3rd floor, Pan-African Insurance Bldg, Kenyatta Ave, Nairobi) has minibuses from Nairobi to Arusha at 8am and 2pm daily from in front of its office by the Standard Chartered Bank (US$25). From Arusha to Nairobi, buses leave at 8am and 2pm from Riverside's **office** (☎ 057-2639) next to the Chinese restaurant on Sokoine Rd. The 8am service from Nairobi continues to Moshi (US$30), returning at 11.30am from Moshi. If you bargain hard you may be able to pay the resident rate of KSh1000/1500 (TSh10,000/15,000).

Davanu Shuttle (☎ 02-316929, 4th floor, Windsor House, University Way, Nairobi) also has daily minibuses between Nairobi and Arusha at 8am and 2pm (US$30). Again, the 8am bus continues to Moshi (US$35). In Nairobi, buses leave from outside the New Stanley Hotel on Kimathi St, also picking up at Windsor House on University Way and the Norfolk Hotel on Harry Thuku Rd. In Arusha, the Davanu **office** (☎ 057-8142) is at the Adventure Centre on Goliondoi Rd.

The big advantage of both these services is being able to board the bus in the comparative sanity of downtown Nairobi. There are often touts at Jomo Kenyatta International Airport in Nairobi advertising a direct shuttle bus service from the airport to Arusha for about $30, but they just bring you into Nairobi where you join one of the regular shuttles.

Full-sized buses are much cheaper, but most leave from the hectic River Rd area in Nairobi; thefts are common there so watch your baggage. **Akamba** (☎ 02-340430; Lagos Rd) has a 7am bus for KSh750 (TSh7500). Buses from Nairobi to Dar es Salaam (see Nairobi to Dar es Salaam following) also travel via Arusha. Small local buses leave from in front of the Goldline office on Accra Rd between 7am and 8am daily, charging KSh700 to Arusha, KSh1000 to Moshi.

It's also easy, though less convenient, to do this journey in stages, since the Kenyan and Tanzanian border posts are next to each other at Namanga. There are several nice places to stay in Namanga if you want to break the journey (see Namanga in the Southern Kenya chapter).

Nairobi to Dar es Salaam Several companies have buses from Nairobi to Dar es Salaam. Taqwa buses (KSh1400, 12 hours) leave at 8pm daily from near the Falcon office on Accra Rd in Nairobi. **Scandinavia Express** (☎ 02-247131; River Rd) offers luxury buses from its River Rd office at 6.30am (KSh2800), while **Akamba** (☎ 02-340430; Lagos Rd) has a 7am bus for KSh1500.

Serengeti to Masai Mara Theoretically it's possible to cross between Serengeti National Park and Masai Mara National Reserve with your own vehicle, but you'll need all the appropriate vehicle documentation (including insurance and entry permit).

Nairobi/Kisumu to Mwanza The road is sealed all the way from Kisumu to just short of Mwanza in Tanzania offering a convenient route to the Tanzanian shore of Lake Victoria. From Nairobi, probably the most comfortable way to go is with **Scandinavia Express** (☎ 02-247131; River Rd), which has a daily bus to Mwanza at 9pm (KSh1200, 12 hours). **Akamba** (☎ 02-340430; Lagos Rd) also has a bus at 9pm (KSh900).

From Kisumu a bus leaves for the Tanzanian border at Isebania/Sirari at 8.30am Sunday to Friday (KSh400). Buses going to Mwanza (KSh500, four hours) leave frequently from Kisii. Matatus head to Mwanza from the Tanzanian side of the border.

Uganda

The main border post for overland travellers is Malaba, with Busia being an alternative if you are travelling via Kisumu. Numerous bus companies run between Nairobi and Kampala, or you can do the journey in stages via Malaba or Busia.

Nairobi to Kampala Various companies cover the Nairobi to Kampala route. From Nairobi, and at the top end of the market, **Scandinavia Express** (☎ 02-247131; River Rd) has a luxury bus at 8pm (KSh1700), while **Akamba** (☎ 02-340430; Lagos Rd) has two daily buses; an ordinary bus at 9pm (KSh990) and a 'Royal Executive' bus with movies and a drinks service that departs at 7am (KSh1900). All buses take about 10 to 12 hours and prices include a meal at the halfway point. In Kampala, Akamba's office (☎ 250412) is on Dewinton St. Akamba also has a service to Mbale in Uganda at 9pm (KSh800, 10 hours).

From Accra Rd in Nairobi, **Falcon** (☎ 02-229692) has a daily bus to Kampala at 8pm (KSh800), while Taqwa has a bus at 7pm (KSh1000). Further north on Accra Rd, **Gateway Bus Services** (☎ 02-318256) has buses to Kampala via either Busia or Malaba at 8pm (KSh800).

If you want to do the journey in stages, Akamba has morning and evening buses from Nairobi to Malaba (KSh550, six hours) and a daily direct bus from here to Kampala at noon (Royal service KSh1100, six hours). There are also regular matatus to Malaba (KSh650) from Cross Rd.

The Ugandan and Kenyan border posts at Malaba are about 1km apart, so you can walk or take a *poda-poda* (bicycle taxi). Once you get across the border, there are frequent matatus until the late afternoon to Kampala (USh 6000, three hours), Jinja (USh 5000, two hours) and Tororo (USh 2500, less than one hour). If you're travelling in the opposite direction and don't want to travel overnight, you could spend the night in Bungoma (45 minutes east of Malaba).

Buses and matatus also run from Nairobi or Kisumu to Busia, from where there are regular connections to Kampala and Jinja.

Ethiopia

With the ongoing problems in southern Sudan, and Somalia, Ethiopia offers the only viable overland route north from Kenya. The security situation around the main entry point at Moyale remains fluid, and, although the border is usually open, security problems have forced its closure several times. Cattle and goat rustling is rife in the area, triggering frequent cross-border tribal wars, so check the security situation carefully before attempting this crossing.

As it is, all vehicles travelling between Marsabit or Isiolo and Moyale must travel in convoy with armed guards. Convoys leave around the break of dawn, but if you miss the main convoy, it's possible to arrange a private armed escort for around US$30. If you don't have your own transport, lifts can be arranged with the trucks in the main convoy from Isiolo for around KSh1000 (or KSh500 from Marsabit).

On the Ethiopian side, a bus leaves Moyale for Addis Ababa at around 6am, so you'll need to stay overnight as the border is only open from 6am to 6pm.

After clearing Kenyan immigration and customs you will arrive at the Ethiopian customs post where officials will ask how much money (cash and travellers cheques) you have. This will be entered into your passport alongside your visa stamp. After customs, there's a 2km walk into town where you have to go to immigration for an entry stamp. It's a good idea to find a hotel before you go through the immigration formalities so that you don't have to carry all your gear.

Be aware that a yellow fever vaccination is required to cross either border at Moyale. Unless you fancy being vaccinated at the border, get your jabs in advance and remember to keep the yellow fever certificate with your passport. A cholera vaccination may also be required. If you plan to continue north from Ethiopia through Sudan, you'll have to go to Addis Ababa to get your Sudanese visa.

For those coming to Kenya with their own vehicle, there are two choices after passing through Addis Ababa. You can travel south to Moyale, or take the more demanding route southwest to the Omo River and onto the northeastern tip of Lake Turkana at Fort Banya (just a point on the map). There is no border post at Fort Banya, so you must already possess a Kenyan visa and get it stamped in Nairobi – immigration officials are quite used to this, although not having an Ethiopian exit stamp is a problem if you want to re-enter Ethiopia. This route is risky and fuel stops are few and far between.

Somalia & Sudan

There's no way you can get overland from Kenya to war-ravaged Somalia at present (unless you're part of a refugee aid convoy) as the Kenyan government has closed the border to try and stop the flow of poachers, bandits and weapons into Kenya.

Kenya has recently staged a series of meetings aimed at ending the civil war between the Islamic government of Sudan and the Christian and animist tribes in the south of the country. If these talks go anywhere, the Kenya–Sudan border may reopen, although currently it's only possible to travel between the two countries via Metema on the Ethiopian border (see Ethiopia earlier for more details the route into Ethiopia).

SEA & LAKE

At the time of writing there were no ferries operating on Lake Victoria, although there's been talk for years of services restarting.

Tanzania

It's theoretically possible to travel by dhow between Mombasa and the Tanzanian islands of Pemba and Zanzibar, but first of all you'll have to find a captain who's making the journey and then you'll have to bargain hard to pay a reasonable amount for the trip. Perhaps the best place to ask about sailings is at Shimoni, south of Mombasa. There is a tiny immigration post here, but there's no guarantee they'll stamp your passport so you might have to go back to Mombasa for an exit stamp.

The ferry, MS *Sepideh*, operated by **Zanzibar Sea Ferries Ltd** (*in Zanzibar ☎ 054-33725; in Dar es Salaam ☎ 051-38025; in Pemba ☎ 054-56210; in Mombasa ☎ 011-311486*) was intended to provide a sea ferry between Mombasa, Tanga, Pemba, Zanzibar and Dar es Salaam, but it no longer includes Mombasa on its route. More luxurious cruise liners still ply the route, but they are unlikely to pick up short-haul passengers.

Dhows do sail between small Kenyan and Tanzanian ports along Lake Victoria, but many are involved in smuggling (fruit mostly!) and are best avoided.

ORGANISED TOURS

It's possible to get to Kenya as part of an overland truck tour originating in Europe or other parts of Africa (many also start in Nairobi bound for other places in Africa). See the Safaris chapter for details of safaris that are specific to Kenya.

Most companies are based in the UK or South Africa, but Flight Centres is a good local operator with offices in Nairobi, Harare and Cape Town. Trips can last from just a few weeks to epic grand tours, which last up to 13 weeks – details can be found on the websites of the following companies.

Acacia Expeditions (☎ 020-7706 4700, fax 8706 4686; e acacia@afrika.demon.co.uk; w www.acacia-africa.com) 23a Craven Terrace, London W2 3QH

African Routes (☎ 031-569 3911, fax 569 3908; w www.africanroutes.co.za) PO Box 1835, Durban, South Africa

Dragoman (☎ 01728-861133, fax 861127; e info@dragoman.co.uk; w www.dragoman.co.uk) 99 Camp Green, Kenton Rd, Debenham, Suffolk IP14 6LA

Explore Worldwide (☎ 01252-760000, fax 760001; w www.exploreworldwide.com) 1 Fredrick St, Aldershot, Hampshire, GU11 1LQ

Flight Centres (☎ 02-210024, fax 332407; e fcswwat@form-net.com) Lakhamshi House, 2nd floor, Biashara St, Nairobi; (☎ 021-556 8490, fax 556 8492; e wacpt@iafrica.com) 15a Mansell Ave, Killarney Gardens (PO Box 50425), Cape Town; (☎ 04-728092, fax 704794; e wathre@comone.co.zw) Travel Centre, 5th floor, 93 Jason Moyo Ave, (PO Box 7071), Harare

Gametrackers Ltd (☎ 02-338927, fax 330903; w www.gametrackers.com) Nginyo Towers, 5th floor, cnr Koinange & Moktar Daddah Sts (PO Box 62042), Nairobi

Guerba Expeditions (☎ 01373-858956, fax 858351; e info@guerba.co.uk; w www.guerba.co.uk) Wessex House, 40 Station Rd, Westbury, Wiltshire BA13 3JN; (☎ 02-352430; e guerba@africaonline.co.ke) Guerba (Kenya) Ltd (PO Box 43935), Nairobi

Getting Around

Kenya is an easy place to get around thanks to an extensive internal air network, bus routes and the few working rail lines that remain from the East African Railway. For short hops and some longer trips, matatus (usually gaudily decorated Nissan minibuses) and shared taxis (known locally as Peugeots), supplement the bus services. The cheapest way to travel is by bus, followed by matatu, Peugeot and private taxis. Travelling by train is comparatively expensive if you go 1st or 2nd class (which is recommended) but is more comfortable and safer.

AIR
Domestic Air Services

With the creation of Kenya Airways' budget airline, Flamingo, there are now three main domestic carriers offering scheduled flights within Kenya. With all these airlines book well in advance (essential during the tourist high season). You should also remember to reconfirm return flights at least 48 hours before departure, especially those that connect with an international flight. Otherwise, you may find your seat has been reallocated.

Kenya Airways Most of Kenya Airways' domestic routes have been taken over by Flamingo Airlines. The national carrier *(head office ☎ 02-229291; Barclays Plaza, Loita St, Nairobi)*, currently only has flights from Nairobi to Mombasa, with six or seven daily departures in each direction. Full-fare tickets cost KSh6250/12,500 one way/return, but rates drop to KSh4000/8000 if you buy a ticket 14 days in advance, and to KSh3450/6900 if you buy 21 days in advance.

Flamingo Airlines Kenya Airways' subsidiary, Flamingo Airlines *(☎ 02-3207 4340;* W *www.flamingoairlines.com; lower ground floor, Barclays Plaza, Loita St, Nairobi)* has at least three daily flights between Nairobi and Kisumu (KSh4100 one way, one hour), and also one or two flights a day to Malindi (KSh4100, 1¼ hours).

There are daily flights to Lamu (KSh7700, 1¼ hours), Eldoret (KSh4100, one hour), and Lokichoggio (US$180, two hours; flights leave from Wilson Airport). Tickets can be booked online on the Flamingo website.

There's a discount of around 20% if you book more than seven days in advance, or 50% if you book more than 30 days in advance.

Regional Air (British Airways) British Airways' subsidiary, **Regional Air** *(in Nairobi* ☎ *02-311623;* W *www.regionalair.net; mezzanine floor, Grand Regency Hotel, Loita St; in Mombasa* ☎ *011-229777; TSS Towers, Nkrumah Rd)* has three daily flights between Nairobi and Mombasa on weekdays, two flights on Saturday and one flight on Sunday (KSh4000/8000 one way/return, one hour).

Air Kenya The excellent small carrier **Air Kenya** *(in Nairobi* ☎ *02-501601;* e *resvns@ airkenya.com;* W *www.airkenya.com)* operates out of Nairobi's Wilson Airport and has numerous daily flights to tourist destinations across Kenya using both large and small turboprop aircraft.

There are two or three daily flights between Nairobi and Mombasa (US$70, 1¼ hours), and daily services from Nairobi to Amboseli (US$88, 45 minutes), Kiwayu Island (US$156, 1¾ hrs), Lamu (US$135, 1¼ hours), Lewa Downs (US$120, one hour), Masai Mara (US$107, 45 mins), Malindi (US$70, 1¼ hours), Nanyuki (US$63, or US$84 in the reverse direction, 45 minutes), Samburu (US$100 to US$120, one hour) and Ukunda (US$70, two hours).

From Mombasa, there are daily connections to Malindi (US$25, 30 minutes), Lamu (US$98, 1¼ hours) and Kiwayu (US$150, 1½ hours).

Other Private Airlines Chartering a small plane saves you time and is the only realistic way to get to some parts of Kenya, but it's an expensive business. It may be worth considering if you can get a group together. For a three-day trip to Sibiloi National Park on the west of Lake Turkana from Nairobi you can expect to pay around US$350 to US$400 each if five people are sharing.

There are dozens of charter companies operating out of Nairobi's Wilson Airport – **Excel Aviation** *(☎ 02-601764, fax 501751)*, **Z-Boskovic Air Charters** *(☎ 02-501210, fax 505964)* and **Blue Bird Aviation** *(☎ 02-602338, fax 602337)* can be recommended.

Ask around at the **Aero Club** (☎ 02-608990), at Wilson Airport, to see if any pilots are prepared to offer a cheap charter.

Several small, charter-type airlines run occasional scheduled flights from Nairobi, Malindi, Lamu and Mombasa – see Getting There & Away under those towns for details.

Domestic Departure Tax

There is a KSh100 departure tax on all domestic flights. Unless you charter a plane this will be included with your ticket price.

BUS

Kenya has an extensive network of long- and short-haul bus routes, operated by a variety of private and state-owned companies that offer varying levels of comfort, convenience and roadworthiness. Buses are considerably cheaper than taking the train or flying and services are frequent, fast and often quite comfortable. However, many travellers are put off taking buses altogether by the diabolical state of Kenyan roads.

In general, if you travel during daylight hours, buses are a fairly safe way to get around and you'll certainly be safer in a bus than in a matatu. The best buses are saved for long-haul and international routes and offer DVD movies, drinks, toilets and reclining, airline-style seats. There's usually a significant price-hike for these so-called 'executive' services, though.

Most bus companies have a ticket agent at important stops along the way where you can book a seat. Don't sit at the back (you'll be thrown around like a rag doll on Kenyan roads), or right at the front (you'll be able to see the oncoming traffic, which is usually a terrifying experience).

The government bus line, **Kenya Bus Services** (KBS; ☎ 02-229605), runs the local buses in Nairobi and also offers long-haul services to most major towns around the country. Its buses tend to be slower than those of the private companies, but are probably safer for this reason.

Of the private companies, **Akamba Bus Service** (☎ 02-340430) has the most comprehensive network, and has a good, but not perfect, safety record. Other big players are Coastline Safaris, Mombasa Raha (Mombasa Liners), Interstate 2000, Scandinavia Express, Falcon, Busstar, Busscar and Eldoret Express. Many bus drivers operate on

a mixture of adrenaline, *miraa* (a leafy shoot with amphetamine-like effects) and blind faith, so be ready for a white-knuckle ride.

There are a few security considerations to think about when taking a bus in Kenya. Some routes, most notably the roads from Malindi to Lamu, Garsen to Thika and Isiolo to Marsabit are prone to attacks by *shiftas* (bandits) and vehicles have to travel either in convoys or with armed escorts – always check things out locally before you travel. Another possible risk is drugged food and drink – if you want to reach your destination with all your belongings, politely refuse any offers of drinks or snacks from strangers.

In the area north of Maralal and Marsabit, your only means of transport will be to get a ride in a truck. You will need to pay for this.

MATATU

Most locals chose to travel via the unique transport phenomenon that is the matatu (the name comes from 'three', because when matatus first started running it cost three coins to travel). These can be anything from dilapidated Peugeot 504 pick-ups with a cab on the back, to shiny, brightly painted 20-seat minibuses complete with mega-decibel stereos. The most common vehicles are white Nissan minibuses (many local people prefer the name 'Nissans' to matatus), which are designed to take 18 passengers, but often carry many, many more.

Many are daubed with colourful graffiti reflecting what's currently hip in Kenya, and most seem to be driven by madmen who seem to have no concept of personal danger. To be fair, vehicle owners put a lot of pressure on the crews to maximise profits, but drivers are notorious for blind overtaking, and the majority of car crashes in Kenya involve at least one matatu. Many drivers also chew *miraa* leaves to stay awake beyond what is a reasonable or safe time.

Under no circumstances should you sit in the 'death seat' next to the matatu driver. Most matatu crashes are head-on collisions. Play it safe and sit in the middle seats away from the window. Of course, many travellers use matatus and, in some cases, there is no alternative, but if there is a bus, train or plane, take that in preference.

You can always find a matatu going to the next town or further afield, so long as it's not too late in the day. Simply ask around among the drivers at the park. Matatus leave when full and the fares are fixed. It's unlikely you will be charged more money than other passengers.

PEUGEOTS (SHARED TAXIS)

Shared Peugeot taxis are a good alternative to matatus. Although you're still likely to be whisked along at breakneck speed, at least it will be in a vehicle that has a sporting chance of stopping quickly if the need arises. The vehicles are usually Peugeot 505 station wagons (hence the local name) that take seven to nine passengers and leave when full.

They take less time to reach their destinations than the matatus as they go from point to point without stopping, and are more expensive. Many companies have offices around the Accra, Cross and River Rds area in Nairobi, and serve destinations mostly in the north and west of the country.

TRAIN

The Uganda Railway was once the main artery of trade in East Africa, but these days the network has dwindled to a just a handful of routes. In recent years the trains to Kisumu, Eldoret, Malaba, Uganda and Tanzania have all been suspended. However, the night train between Nairobi and Mombasa is still one of the great rail journeys in Africa. Passengers in 1st and 2nd class are treated to the full colonial experience, including a silver-service dinner in the dining car, served up by waiters in starched white uniforms.

The journey takes around 13 hours, leaving Nairobi at 7pm weekdays and arriving in Mombasa somewhere between 8.30am and 11am the next morning. Although it's slower than the bus, the train is much more comfortable than flying or taking the bus or matatu, and you can also get a cold beer delivered at any time during the journey. The dining car is a great place to meet other travellers and hook up for safaris or travel along the coast. And, despite the railway's accident record, the train is still much safer than going along the Nairobi–Mombasa highway.

Classes

There are three classes on the Nairobi to Mombasa line, but only 1st and 2nd class can be recommended. Third class is seats only and security can be a real problem.

Tickets in 1st and 2nd classes include meals (dinner and breakfast) and bedding. Note that passengers are divided up by gender.

First class consists of two-berth compartments with a washbasin, wardrobe, drinking water and a drinks service. Second class consists of plainer, four-berth compartments with a washbasin and drinking water. No compartment can be locked from the outside, so remember not to leave any valuables lying around when you leave. You might want to padlock your rucksack to something during dinner and breakfast. Always lock your compartment from the inside before you go to sleep.

Meals are served in an old-fashioned dining car, and typically consist of stews, curries or roast chicken served with rice and vegetables. There's always a vegetarian option. Tea and coffee is included; sodas (soft drinks), bottled water and alcoholic drinks are not, so ask the price before accepting that KSh1500 bottle of wine! Cold beer is available at all times in the dining car and can be delivered to your compartment.

The only downside to the train is the price of tickets. Nonresidents pay a hefty KSh3000/2100 for 1st/2nd class. Children from three to 11 years pay KSh1830/1380.

Reservations

You must book in advance for both 1st and 2nd class – two to three days is usually sufficient – otherwise you'll probably find there are no berths available. Visa credit cards are accepted for railway bookings. If you book by phone, you'll need to arrive early to pay for your ticket and make sure you're actually on the passenger list. Compartment and berth numbers are posted up about 30 minutes prior to departure.

Booking offices are in Nairobi (☎ 02-221211 ext 2700/2) and Mombasa (☎ 011-312231).

Voi-Taveta Service

The only other passenger service operating is the twice-weekly train between Voi and Taveta on the Tanzanian border (see Voi in the Southern Kenya chapter for details).

CAR & 4WD

Many travellers bring their own vehicles into Kenya as part of overland trips and, expense not withstanding, it's a great way to see the country at your own pace. Otherwise, there are numerous hire-care companies who can rent you anything from a small hatchback to Toyota Land Cruiser 4WDs, although hire rates are some of the highest in the world.

Private Vehicles

If you bring your own vehicle to Kenya you should be given a free three-month permit at the border on entry, so long as you have a valid *carnet* for it. If you don't have a *carnet* you should be able to get a free one-week permit at the border, which can be extended. Get in touch with the **Automobile Association of Kenya** *(☎ 02-723195)*, in the Hurlingham shopping centre in Nairobi, to check the latest requirements. Foreign-registered vehicles with a seating capacity of more than six people are not allowed into Kenyan national parks and reserves. Jeeps should be fine, but VW Kombis and other camper vans may have problems.

Road Rules

You'll need your wits about you if you're going to tackle driving in Kenya. Driving practices here are some of the worst in the world and all are carried out at breakneck speed. Indicators, lights, horns and hand signals can mean anything from 'I'm about to do something incredibly dangerous' to 'Hello *mzungu* (white person)!' and should never be taken at face value. Kenyans also habitually drive on the opposite side of the road when there's a break in the traffic – flashing your lights at the vehicle hurtling towards you should be enough to persuade the driver to get back into their own lane. Never drive at night unless you absolutely have to as few cars have adequate headlights and the roads are full of pedestrians and cyclists. Drunk driving is also very common.

Due to the volatile security situation, there are certain routes where you must obtain police permission before setting out. Obtaining permission is usually just a formality, but vehicles are required to travel with armed guards and, usually, in convoy. The main stretches where this applies are: between Isiolo and Marsabit (and on to Moyale); the dirt track from Amboseli National Park to Tsavo West National Park; between Malindi and Lamu; and the Garsen–Garissa–Thika road.

Road Distances (km)

	Busia	Embu	Isiolo	Kakamega	Kericho	Kisumu	Kitale	Lodwar	Malindi	Meru	Mombasa	Nairobi	Nakuru	Namanga	Nanyuki	Nyeri	Voi
Busia	---																
Embu	610	---															
Isiolo	569	184	---														
Kakamega	95	525	481	---													
Kericho	218	395	351	130	---												
Kisumu	138	475	431	50	80	---											
Kitale	154	511	467	109	230	158	---										
Lodwar	440	691	735	395	522	443	285	---									
Malindi	1087	657	877	999	869	949	985	1141	---								
Meru	565	154	56	477	347	427	463	729	864	---							
Mombasa	969	618	759	881	751	831	867	1120	118	746	---						
Nairobi	482	131	272	394	264	368	380	599	605	259	521	---					
Nakuru	325	288	244	237	107	211	223	442	762	240	644	157	---				
Namanga	661	314	524	596	469	548	563	779	430	468	409	180	337	---			
Nanyuki	487	131	84	399	269	349	385	651	795	78	677	190	175	380	---		
Nyeri	508	88	140	420	290	370	406	601	752	136	634	150	151	330	58	---	
Voi	811	460	601	723	593	673	709	960	281	588	160	329	486	249	519	476	---

Road Hazards

As well as other vehicles, there are a number of other hazards to watch out for on Kenyan roads. Most roads are severely eroded at the edges, reducing the carriageway to a single lane, which is usually occupied by whichever vehicle is bigger in any given situation. There are *some* good roads in Kenya, but those in the north and east of the country are particularly poor. The main Mombasa–Nairobi–Malaba road (A104) is badly worn due to the constant flow of traffic.

Roads in national parks are all *murram* (dirt) and have been eroded into bone-shaking corrugations through overuse by safari vehicles. Keep your speed down and be careful when driving after rain. Although some dirt roads can be negotiated in a 2WD vehicle you'll be much safer in a 4WD. Always carry drinking water, emergency food and, if possible, spare fuel.

On all roads, be very careful of pedestrians and cyclists – you don't want to contribute any more to the death toll on Kenya's roads. Animals are another major hazard in rural areas, be it monkeys, herds of goats and cattle or lone chickens with a death wish.

Parking

In small towns and villages, parking is usually free but there's a pay-parking system in Nairobi, Mombasa and other main towns. Attendants issue one-day parking permits for KSh50 to KSh70, which are valid anywhere in town. If you don't get a permit, you're liable to be wheel-clamped and getting your vehicle back will cost you at least KSh2000. It's worth staying in a hotel with secure parking if you can afford it.

Fuel Costs

At the time of research, in Nairobi, regular petrol was KSh50 per litre, super KSh55 and diesel was KSh44. Rates creep steadily up the further you get from the capital.

Rental

Hiring a vehicle to tour Kenya (or at least the national parks) is an expensive way of seeing the country, but it does give you freedom of movement and is sometimes the only way of getting to the more remote parts of the country.

However, unless you're sharing with several people, it's likely to cost more than you'd pay for an organised camping safari with all meals.

Unless you're just planning on travelling on the main routes between towns, you'll need a 4WD vehicle. None of the car-hire companies will let you drive 2WD vehicles on dirt roads, including those in the national parks, and if you ignore this proscription and have an accident you will be personally liable for any damage to the vehicle.

Costs Starting rates for rental almost always sound very reasonable, but once you factor in mileage and the various types of insurance you'll be lucky to pay less than KSh6000 per day for a saloon car or KSh7000 per day for a small 4WD. As elsewhere in the world, rates come down rapidly if you take the car for more than a few days.

Vehicles are usually rented with either an allowance of 100km to 200km per day (in which case you'll pay an extra fee for every kilometre you go over), or with unlimited kilometres, which is often the best way to go. Rates are usually quoted without insurance and you'll be given the option of paying an extra KSh1200 per day for insurance against collision damage and KSh800 a day for insurance against theft. It would be financial suicide to hire a car in Kenya without both kinds of insurance. Otherwise, you'll be responsible for the full value of the vehicle if it's stolen or damaged.

Even if you have collision and theft insurance, you'll still be liable for an excess of KSh2000 to KSh150,000 (depending on the company). Always check this before signing. You can usually reduce the excess to zero by paying another KSh700 per day for an Excess Waiver. Note that tyres, damaged windscreens and loss of the tool kit are always the hirer's responsibility, though.

As a final sting in the tail, you'll be charged 16% value added tax (VAT) on top of the total cost of hiring the vehicle. Any repairs that you end up paying for will also have VAT on top. And a final warning – always return the vehicle with a full tank of petrol. If you don't, the company will charge you twice the going rate to fill the tank.

Deposits There's a wide variation in the deposit required on hired vehicles. It can be as much as the total hire charges (base rate and kilometre) plus whatever the excess is on the collision damage waiver. You can cover this with either cash, signed travellers cheques (returnable) or – credit card.

One-Way Rates If you want to hire a vehicle in one place and drop it off in another there will be additional charges. These vary depending on the vehicle, the company and the pick-up and drop-off locations. In most cases, count on paying KSh10,000 between Nairobi and Mombasa and about KSh5000 between Mombasa and Malindi.

Drivers' Licences An international driver's licence or your own national driving licence is a standard requirement. Some companies stipulate a minimum age of 23 years but, with others, it is 25. Some companies prefer a licence with no endorsements or criminal convictions, and most require you to have been driving for at least two years. You will also need acceptable ID such as a passport.

Maintenance It's *generally* true to say the more you pay for a vehicle, the better condition it will be in. The larger companies are usually in a better financial position to keep their fleet in good order. Whoever you hire from, be sure to check the brakes, the tyres (including the spare), the windscreen wipers and the lights before you set off.

The other factor is what the company will do for you (if anything) if you have a serious breakdown. The major rental companies *may* deliver a replacement vehicle and make arrangements for recovery of the other vehicle at their expense, but with most companies you'll have to get the vehicle fixed and back on the road, and then try and claim a refund.

Driving to Tanzania & Uganda Only the larger (and more expensive) companies cater for this and there are large additional charges. Expect to pay around US$150 for sorting out all the documentation, insurance, permits etc with Budget, Hertz or Avis.

Rental Agencies At the top end of the market are some international companies. All have airport and town offices in Nairobi and Mombasa. Of these, Budget/Payless is probably the best value. Note that the excess after collision and theft insurance is around KSh40,000 – it's well worth paying for the Excess Waiver (see Costs earlier).

Avis (☎ 02-311331, 220465) College House, University Way, Nairobi; (☎ 02-822186) Jomo Kenyatta International Airport, Nairobi; (☎ 011-223048) Southern House, Moi Ave, Mombasa; (☎ 011-424021) Moi International Airport, Mombasa

Budget/Payless Rent-a-Car (☎ 02-223581, fax 223584; e carrental@budget-kenya.com) Hilton Hotel, Mama Ngina St, Nairobi; (☎ 02-822370) Jomo Kenyatta International Airport, Nairobi; (☎ 011-221281, fax 221282) Sarova House, Moi Ave, Mombasa; (☎ 011-434021/3) Moi International Airport, Mombasa

Hertz (☎ 02-248777, fax 217533; e info@hertz .utc.co.ke) Cnr Muindi Mbingu & Kaunda Sts, Nairobi; (☎ 02-822339) Jomo Kenyatta International Airport, Nairobi; (☎ 011-316333) UTC Bldg, Moi Ave, Mombasa; (☎ 011-433211) Moi International Airport, Mombasa; (☎ 0123-20040) Harambee Rd, Malindi

Cheaper but reliable companies with well-maintained vehicles include:

Avenue Car Hire (☎ 02-33216, fax 216923; e info@avenuecarhire.com; w www.avenue carhire.com) Avenue Service Station, Kenyatta Ave, Nairobi

Central Rent-a-Car (☎ 02-222888, fax 339666; e cars@carhirekenya.com; w www.car hirekenya.com) ground floor, Sixeighty Hotel, Muindi Mbingu St, Nairobi

Glory Car Hire (☎ 02-225024, fax 331533) Diamond Bldg, Tubman Rd, Nairobi; (☎ 011-313561, fax 221196) Moi Ave, Mombasa

Habib's Cars Ltd (☎ 02-220463, fax 220985; e habibtours@attmail.com) Agip House, Haile Selassie Ave, Nairobi

Central Rent-a-Car is certainly the best in this category, with a well-maintained fleet of fairly new vehicles and a good back-up service. Its excess liability is also the lowest (KSh2000). Apart from Central, all of these companies have steep excesses. Glory levies a staggering KSh150,000 excess – enough to bankrupt even the most well-heeled traveller!

MOTORCYCLE

A few expats have off-road (trail) motorcycles, but they aren't seen as a serious means of transport, which is a blessing considering the lethal nature of the roads.

On the coast, it is possible to hire off-road motorcycles, mopeds (light motorcycles) and quads (called trucks) at Diani Beach and Bamburi Beach, although most people just use them to zip up and down the beach road. **Fredlink Co Ltd** (☎ 2468; e fredlink@swift mombasa.com; Diani Plaza, Diani Beach) rents out 350cc trail bikes and Yamaha scooters, and also arranges motorcycle safaris. See the Safaris and The Coast chapters for further information.

BICYCLE

Kenya has seen a huge influx of cheap imported Chinese bicycles. Loads of Kenyans get around by bicycle. If you intend to cycle in Kenya – and plenty of hardy cyclists tour the country every year – do as the locals do and get off the road whenever you hear a car coming. No matter how experienced you are, it would be suicidal to attempt the road from Nairobi to Mombasa on a bicycle.

Cycling is easier in rural areas, and you'll usually receive a warm welcome in any villages you pass through. Many local people operate *poda-podas* (short-haul bicycle taxis), so repair shops are becoming increasingly common along the roadside. Be wary of cycling on dirt roads as punctures from thorn trees are a major problem.

The hills of Kenya are not particularly steep but can be long and hard. You can expect to cover around 80km per day in the hills of the western highlands, somewhat more where the country is flatter.

It's possible to hire mountain bikes in an increasing number of places, and several tour operators now offer biking safaris (see Activities in the Facts for the Visitor chapter for details). Hell's Gate National Park near Naivasha is particularly popular for mountain biking.

For a good introduction to cycling in Kenya, read Dervla Murphy's book *The Ukimi Road*, which covers her trip from Kenya to Zimbabwe in 1992 – it's a little dated, but the road conditions she describes are very much the same!

HITCHING

Hitchhiking is never entirely safe in any country in the world, and we don't recommend it. Travellers who decide to hitch should understand that they are taking a small but potentially serious risk. People who do choose to hitch will be safer if they travel in pairs and let someone know where they are planning to go. Also, beware of drunken drivers.

Although it's risky, many locals have no choice but to hitch, so people will know what you're doing if you stick your thumb out on the roadside. However, most Kenyan drivers will expect a contribution towards petrol, so make it clear from the outset if you are expecting a free ride.

Foreign drivers will be approached all the time by Kenyan hitchers, and giving a lift to a jeep full of Maasai is certainly a memorable cultural experience. If you're hoping to hitch into the national parks, you'll have to rely on coming across tourists who don't mind taking a stranger along on their safari; your best chance is to try at the main gates to the parks. But you'll very likely need patience.

BOAT
Lake Victoria

There has been speculation for years that ferry transport will start again on Lake Victoria, but for now, the only boats operating are 10m-long motorised canoes going to Mfangano, Rusinga and Takawiri islands from Mbita Point, near Homa Bay. There is no reliable boat transport connecting Kisumu, Kendu Bay and Homa Bay.

Dhow

Sailing on a traditional Swahili dhow along the East African coast is one of Kenya's most memorable experiences.

Dhows are commonly used to get between the islands in the Lamu archipelago and the mangrove islands south of Mombasa (see The Coast chapter for more details) but, for the most part, these operate more like dhow safaris than as public transport.

Although some trips are luxurious, the trips out of Lamu are more basic. When night comes you simply bed down wherever there is space. Seafood is freshly caught and cooked on board on charcoal burners, or else barbecued on the beach on the surrounding islands.

Most of the smaller boats rely on the wind to get around so it's quite common to end up becalmed until the wind picks up again. Some boats, however, have been fitted with outboard motors so that progress can be made even when there's no wind.

The larger dhows are all motorised and some of them don't even have sails.

Safaris

PLANNING A SAFARI

The chances are that as soon as you arrive in Kenya, you'll be looking to join a safari (and even if you aren't, touts from the safari companies will certainly come looking for you!) It's possible to arrange everything for yourself if you hire a vehicle, but there are lots of things you need to sort out (see Do-It-Yourself Safaris later in this chapter) and it's easier and cheaper to go with an organised group. There are an incredible number of companies out there offering an incredible variety of itineraries so it's a good idea to shop around and find a company that best fits your requirements. Depending on your tastes, you can travel by minibus, 4WD, truck, camel, cycle, airplane or even on foot in some places. More than a few travellers book the first safari that fits their budget and end up feeling that they should have chosen something else; a bit of legwork visiting the various companies may save you a lot of time trying to get a refund if the safari isn't what you thought you had booked.

Choosing a Safari

There are essentially two broad types of organised safaris – those where you camp and those where you stay in lodges or luxury tented camps at night. Some budget companies also have their own lodges on the outskirts of parks, which tend to be cheaper, although you'll often lose quite a bit of time shuttling between the lodge and the parks.

Whatever type of accommodation you choose, safaris typically start and end in either Nairobi or Mombasa, although there are a handful of exceptions to this. Most companies use either large Toyota Land Cruiser jeeps or Nissan Urvans (effectively matatus), which have hatches in the roof for wildlife viewing, often with some kind of shade over the top. This safe vantage point from which to take photos is something you'll miss out on if you hire your own car. Some of the bigger companies also use open-sided trucks (see Truck Safaris later), which achieve the same effect. A few companies offer you the opportunity to take walking or cycling safaris (see later in this chapter for details).

As well as transfers to and from Nairobi or Mombasa and also between the parks, safari

companies offer two wildlife drives per day. Each drive typically lasts two to 2½ hours and the best (in terms of sighting animals) are those that start at 6.30am or 4pm, when animals are at their most active. Bear in mind that if you arrange a half-day visit to any park as part of your safari, the chances are you won't be visiting at prime viewing time.

For more information about camping or lodge and tented camp safaris, including some companies that offer these safaris, see those entries later in this chapter.

Which Parks? Once you've decided on the type of accommodation and where you want to leave from you'll need to pick your parks.

Some travellers choose to maximise their chance of seeing the 'Big Five' (elephant, rhino, leopard, lion and buffalo) by visiting one of the more open but crowded parks such as Amboseli or Masai Mara, and often end up with a lot of 'lions-in-front-of-a-jeep' type photos. Others prefer to view wildlife in the less disturbed wilderness of the African bush. While they see less wildlife at many of the other parks due to denser vegetation, nothing can beat the sensation of having a pool of basking hippos all to yourself.

People who are interested in more specific pursuits such as bird-watching, fishing or tribal culture will find that some parks (and companies) are better suited to their needs than others (see Specific-Interest Safaris later in this chapter).

We've tried to give an impression of what you can expect to find at the various parks (see National Parks & Reserves in the Facts for the Visitor chapter and individual park entries), but the wildlife is mobile and does not always want to be seen, so there's no guarantee you'll see every species described in the wildlife books.

You should also give some thought to how far the various parks are away from each other, as it's quite easy to spend half your safari driving between the parks if you're not careful. This is a frequent complaint on shorter safaris or a safari that includes half-day excursions. If time is a factor (and/or cost) pick parks that are close together, Amboseli and Tsavo West, for example, or both Tsavo East and Tsavo West.

Itineraries Whether you take a camping or lodge safari, there's a plethora of options ranging from two to 15 days and, in some cases, up to six weeks, visiting parks in neighbouring countries as well. If possible, it's best to go on a safari for at least five days (preferably longer); otherwise a good deal of your time will be taken up driving to and from the national parks and Nairobi. Much more than 10 days and the endless bumpy roads and tracks may start to wear you down. You'll also see a great deal more on a longer safari and have a much better chance of catching sight of all the major animals. In addition, you may also get a chance to spend some time with local tribespeople on a longer safari. The short trips also make stops in tribal villages, but these are normally just

a quick souvenir and photo opportunity, and can be a bit demoralising.

A three-day safari from Nairobi typically takes you either to Amboseli or Masai Mara. A four-day safari might take you to Amboseli and Tsavo, or to Amboseli and Masai Mara or to Samburu and Buffalo Springs, but you'd be pushing it to get to three parks in four days. A five-day safari could take you to Amboseli and Tsavo, or to Masai Mara and Lake Nakuru, whereas a six-day safari may include lakes Nakuru, Bogoria and Baringo plus Masai Mara, or alternatively Lake Nakuru, Masai Mara and Amboseli. On a seven-day safari, you could expect to visit at least two of the Rift Valley lakes plus Masai Mara and Amboseli, whereas on an 11-day safari you could take in either two or more of the Rift Valley lakes plus Masai Mara, Amboseli and Tsavo, or Samburu and Buffalo Springs, Meru, Lake Nakuru and Masai Mara. Only a few companies build Meru into their regular itineraries, though.

In the high season, many companies have daily or every second day departures to the most popular national parks – Amboseli, Masai Mara and Tsavo – since there's high demand. To the less frequented parks such as Samburu and Buffalo Springs, Shaba and Meru, they generally leave only once or twice per week. In addition, most companies will leave for any of the most popular national parks at any time so long as you have a minimum number of people wanting to go – usually four. Due to the slump in tourism, some companies will *only* leave if they have the minimum number of clients, especially in the low season. If you are on your own, you may have to hang around for a while to be bundled together with a larger group.

It obviously makes a lot of sense to either book ahead or get a group together yourself rather than just turn up and expect to leave the next morning. Advance booking is a good idea for the Lake Turkana safaris (see later in this chapter) since they're heavily subscribed in the high season. It's also essential for any of the more exotic options described under Other Safaris later in this chapter.

Other Issues As a general rule, on all safaris, you'll be left to your own devices between late morning and mid-afternoon (except for lunch), although if you're on a camping safari you may be taken to a lodge to relax over a cold beer or have a swim in the pool. You may also be taken to a lodge after the late-afternoon wildlife drive for the same thing before returning to camp for dinner. Either way, you've got lots of time to kill between wildlife drives so a good book to read will be a life-saver.

A bit of patience and the ability to go with the flow is the key to having a good time on safari. There is so much wildlife here that almost everyone finishes the day elated at having spotted some animal or other.

When to Go

Wildlife can be seen at all times of year, but the migration patterns of the big herbivores (which in turn attract the big predators) are likely to be a major factor in deciding when to go. From July to October, huge herds of wildebeests and zebras cross from the Serengeti in Tanzania to the Masai Mara, and Amboseli also sees huge herds at this time. This is probably prime viewing time as the land is parched, the vegetation has died back and the animals are obliged to come to drink at the ever-shrinking waterholes. However, most safari companies increase their rates at this time.

The long rains (from March to June) and short rains (from October to November) transform the national parks into a lush carpet of greenery. It's very scenic, but it does provide much more cover for the wildlife to hide behind and the rain can turn the tracks into impassable mush. Safaris may be impossible on the lowland parks during either rainy season.

Booking

Many travellers prefer to get all the planning done before they arrive in the country and book from abroad, either through travel agents or directly with companies. Many safari operators now take Internet bookings (see Digital Resources in the Facts for the Visitor chapter and individual company entries later in this chapter). However, if you do this, you may have to pay by credit-card over the Internet or on the telephone – not always a safe thing to do – and you have no assurance that you'll get what you've paid for until you arrive in Kenya.

There is less risk of being sold something different to what you expected if you visit the various companies in person and talk through the kind of package you're looking for. A good starting point is to visit one of the travel agents in Nairobi or Mombasa and get as many leaflets as you can get your hands on. You can then make an informed choice about which companies to visit. Bear in mind that once you enter a safari company office, the staff may be reluctant to let you walk out without a firm booking. This is more of a problem in the budget places, so be firm and say no if what they're offering isn't exactly what you're looking for. You can also book directly with the travel agents, although you'll usually pay a little more than if you negotiate directly with the companies.

A third way, and one which many people are railroaded into, is to accept the help of a safari tout. These people will approach you almost as soon as you step off the plane in Nairobi and try to get you signed up for a safari then and there. They're not all bad guys and the safari you end up with may be fine, but you'll pay a mark up to cover their commission, while the experience of being hemmed in on all sides by touts and agents trying to make a sale can be exasperating. At most of the budget companies, it's not even worth trying to enter the office without a tout as they wait by the door and escort every customer inside.

The service provided by even the best safari companies can vary, depending on the driver, the itinerary, the behaviour of the wildlife, acts of God such as flat tyres and breakdowns and, of course, the attitude of the passengers themselves. It's possible for a good company to provide a bad safari and bad companies to occasionally shine. It's also a volatile market and a company that has a good reputation one year can go to the dogs the next. We recommend some of the better companies later in this chapter, but this shouldn't take the place of hands-on research once you arrive in the country. It's worth getting in touch with the **Kenyan Association of Tour Operators** (KATO; ☎ 02-225570, fax 218402; W www.katokenya.org; PO Box 48461, Nairobi) before making a booking. They may not be the most powerful regulatory body in the world, but most reputable safari companies are members and going with a KATO member will give you *some* recourse to appeal in case of conflict.

(Continued on page 97)

WILDLIFE GUIDE

PRIMATES

Bushbabies Greater bushbaby *Otolemur crassicaudatus* (pictured); East African lesser bushbaby *Galago senegalensis*

Named for their plaintive wailing calls (the calls of lesser bushbabies are rarely noticed), bushbabies are nocturnal primates with small heads, large rounded ears, thick bushy tails and enormous eyes. Greater bushbabies are dark brown; tiny lesser bushbabies are light grey with yellow on their legs. Both species are often in family groups of up to six or seven, but they usually forage alone for sap, fruit, insects and, in the case of greater bushbabies, lizards, nestlings and eggs. Lesser bushbabies make spectacular treetop leaps.

Size: Greater bushbaby 80cm in length, including 45cm tail; weight up to 1.5kg. Lesser bushbaby 40cm in length; weight 150g to 200g. **Distribution:** Lightly wooded savanna to thickly forested areas; greater and lesser bushbabies occur mostly in southern and central Kenya. **Status:** Common but strictly nocturnal.

Vervet Monkey *Cercopithecus aethiops*

Conspicuous inhabitants of the woodland-savanna, vervet monkeys are easily recognised by their grizzled grey hair and black face fringed with white. The male has a distinctive bright-blue scrotum, an important signal of status in the troop. Troops may number up to 30. Vervet monekys have a sophisticated vocal repertoire, with, for example, different calls for different predators. They are diurnal and forage for fruits, seeds, leaves, flowers, invertebrates and the occasional lizard or nestling. They rapidly learn where easy pickings can be found around lodges and camp sites, but become pests when they are accustomed to being fed.

Size: Up to 130cm long, including 65cm tail; weight 3kg to 9kg; male larger than female. **Distribution:** All savanna and woodland habitats. **Status:** Very common and easy to see.

Blue (Samango) Monkey *Cercopithecus mitis*

Similar to vervet monkeys, but slightly larger and much darker, blue monkeys have a grey to black face, black shoulders, limbs and tail, and a reddish-brown or olive-brown back. They are more arboreal than vervet monkeys and generally prefer dense forest and woodland rather than savanna. They feed largely on fruit, bark, gum and leaves. Social groups may be as large as 30 but generally number between four and 12. The groups usually consist of related females and their young, and a single adult male. Their broad diet allows them to occupy relatively small home ranges.

Size: 140cm long, including 80cm tail; weight normally up to 15kg, but as much as 23kg; male larger than female. **Distribution:** Throughout most evergreen forests and forest patches. **Status:** Locally common; active by day; often difficult to see in foliage.

Eastern Black-and-White Colobus
Colobus guereza

This colobus is glossy black with a white face, bushy white tail, and a white fur 'cape'. Newborns are initially white, gaining their adult coat at around six months. The black-and-white colobus spends most of its time in the forest canopy, where it feeds mostly on leaves. Its low-energy diet means it is relatively inactive but it makes spectacular leaps when moving through the treetops. The ready availability of its food enables it to survive on quite small home ranges, usually maintained by troops of up to 12 animals, consisting of a dominant male, females and young.

ARIADNE VAN ZANDBERGEN

Size: 140cm long, including 80cm tail; weight 3.5kg to 10kg; male larger than female. **Distribution:** Forests in western Kenya; the similar Angolan black-and-white colobus *(C. angolensis)* can be found in southeast Kenya. **Status:** Locally common; active during the day but often difficult to see among foliage.

Baboon *Papio cynocephalus*

Baboons are unmistakable. The yellow baboon *(P. c. cyno-cephalus)* and the olive baboon (*P. c. anubis;* pictured) are named for their differing hair colour. Baboons live in troops of between eight and 200; contrary to popular belief there is no single dominant male. Social interactions are complex, with males accessing only certain females, males forming alliances to dominate other males, and males caring for un-related juveniles. Baboons forage in woodland-savanna for grasses, tubers, fruits, invertebrates and occasionally small vertebrates. Ever opportunistic, baboons often visit camp sites and may become (dangerous) pests.

JASON EDWARDS

Size: Shoulder height 75cm; length 160cm, including 70cm tail; weight up to 45kg; male larger than female, and twice as heavy. **Distribution:** The yellow baboon is common in central and eastern Kenya; the olive baboon is more common in western Kenya. **Status:** Abundant.

CARNIVORES

Pangolin *Manis temminckii*

Ground pangolins are covered with large rounded scales over the back and tail, and have a sparse covering of hair on the face and underbelly. They subsist entirely on ants and termites that they excavate from termite mounds, rotting wood and dung heaps. Pangolins (which are also known as scaly anteaters) walk on the outer edges of their paws with their claws pointed inwards, leaving a distinc-tive track.

ANDREW VAN SMEERDIJK

Size: Length 70cm to 100cm; weight 5kg to 15kg **Distribution:** Throughout Kenya, apart from the north-east, in many habitats except dense forest. **Status:** Relatively uncommon; nocturnal and difficult to see.

MITCH REARDON

Jackals Golden jackal *Canis aureus;* black-backed jackal *Canis mesomelas* (pictured); side-striped jackal *Canis adustus*

Golden jackals are often the most numerous carnivores in open savanna and are very active by day. Black-backed jackals have a mantle of silver-grey hair and black-tipped tails; they are the most common night scavengers. Side-striped jackals are the least common. They're grey with a light stripe along each side and a white-tipped tail. All have similar social and feeding behaviour. Pairs are long-lasting and defend small territories. Jackals scavenge from the kills of larger predators but are also efficient hunters.

Size: Shoulder height 38cm to 50cm; length 95cm to 120cm, including 25cm to 40cm tail (shortest in the golden jackal); weight up to 15kg. **Distribution:** Throughout Kenya, preferring open plains and woodlands; side-striped jackal most abundant in well-watered wooded areas. **Status:** Abundant in parks; and settled areas.

JASON EDWARDS

Bat-Eared Fox *Otocyon megalotis*

The huge ears of these little foxes detect the faint sounds of invertebrates below ground, before they unearth them in a burst of frantic digging. Bat-eared foxes eat mainly insects, especially termites, but also wild fruit and small vertebrates. They are monogamous and are often seen in groups comprising a mated pair and offspring. Natural enemies include large birds of prey, spotted hyenas, caracals and larger cats. They will bravely attempt to rescue a family member caught by a predator by using distraction techniques and harassment, which extends to nipping larger enemies on the ankles.

Size: Shoulder height 35cm; length 75cm to 90cm, including 30cm tail; weight 3kg to 5kg. **Distribution:** Throughout Kenya; absent from mountainous habitat and dense forest. **Status:** Common, especially in national parks; mainly nocturnal but often seen in the late afternoon and early morning.

MITCH REARDON

Wild Dog *Lycaon pictus*

Wild dogs' blotched black, yellow and white coat, and their large, round ears, are unmistakable. They live in packs of up to 40, though usually 12 to 20. Wild dogs are endurance hunters; the pack chases prey until exhaustion, then cooperates to pull it down. They are widely reviled for eating their prey alive, but this is probably as fast as 'cleaner' methods used by other carnivores. Mid-sized antelopes are their preferred prey, but wild dogs can take animals as large as buffaloes. They require enormous areas of habitat and they are among the most endangered carnivores in Africa.

Size: Shoulder height 65cm to 80cm; length 100cm to 150cm, including 35cm tail; weight 20kg to 35kg. **Distribution:** Much reduced, now restricted to the largest protected areas, including Tsavo National Park. **Status:** Highly threatened: numbers reduced by persecution, disease and habitat loss.

Cape Clawless Otter *Aonyx capensis*

Similar to European otters, but much larger, Cape clawless otters are a glossy chocolate brown with a white or cream-coloured lower face, throat and neck. Only the hind feet are webbed, and, unlike the front feet of most otters, the front feet of Cape clawless otters end in dexterous, humanlike fingers with rudimentary nails. Otters are very entertaining to watch, being active and vocal – their repertoire includes whistles, mews and chirps. They are active during early morning and evening, though they become nocturnal in areas where they are hunted by humans. Their main foods include fish, freshwater crabs and frogs.

ROGER DE LA HARPE/GALLO IMAGES

Size: Length 105cm to 160cm, including 50cm tail; weight up to 30kg. **Distribution:** Large freshwater bodies and along coastlines across Kenya. **Status:** Locally common; active both day and night but usually seen in the early morning and late afternoon.

Honey Badger (Ratel) *Mellivora capensis*

Pugnacious and astonishingly powerful for their size, honey badgers have a fascinating relationship with honey guide birds. Honeyguides lead them to bees' nests, which honey badgers rip open for honey, and in doing so provide honeyguides access to their favoured food – beeswax. Honey badgers are omnivorous, feeding on small animals, carrion, berries, roots, eggs, honey and social insects (ants, termites and bees) and their larvae. Their thick, loose skin is an excellent defence against predators, bee stings and snake bites. Honey badgers are best viewed in parks, where they sometimes scavenge from bins.

LORNA STANTON/GALLO IMAGES

Size: Shoulder height 30cm; length 95cm, including 20cm tail; weight up to 15kg. **Distribution:** Widespread in Kenya, apart from the northeast, in most habitat types. **Status:** Generally occurs in low densities, but populations are sustainable; apparently active by day in parks but nocturnal in areas of human habitation.

Genets Small-spotted genet *Genetta genetta;*
large-spotted genet *Genetta tigrina* (pictured)

Relatives of mongooses, genets resemble slender domestic cats, with foxlike faces. The two species can be differentiated by the tail tips – white in the small-spotted, black in the large-spotted. The former also has a crest along the spine, which it raises when threatened. All-black individuals of both species may occur, particularly in mountainous regions. Genets are solitary, sleeping by day in burrows, rock crevices or tree hollows. They hunt on land and in trees, feeding on rodents, birds, reptiles, eggs, insects and fruits. Genets deposit their droppings in latrines, usually in open sites.

DENNIS JONES

Size: Shoulder height 18cm; length 85cm to 110cm, including 45cm tail; weight up to 3kg. **Distribution:** Throughout Kenya. **Status:** Very common but strictly nocturnal; often the most common small carnivore seen at night.

MITCH REARDON

Mongooses

Many of the small animals that dash in front of cars in Africa are mongooses. A few species, such as the dwarf mongoose (*Helogale parvula*) and the banded mongoose (*Mungos mungo;* pictured) are intensely social, keeping contact with twittering calls while foraging. Others, such as the slender mongoose (*Galerella sanguinea*) – with a black-tipped tail that it holds aloft when running – and the white-tailed mongoose (*Ichneumia albicauda*), are usually solitary. Family groups are better at spotting danger and raising kittens. Collectively, they also intimidate much larger enemies. Invertebrates are their most important prey.

Size: Ranging from the dwarf mongoose at 40cm in length and up to 400g in weight, to the white-tailed mongoose at 120cm and up to 5.5kg. **Distribution:** Throughout Kenya. They prefer open to closed woodlands and wooded savanna. **Status:** Common; sociable species are diurnal, while solitary species are generally nocturnal.

LUKE HUNTER

Aardwolf *Proteles cristatus*

Smallest of the hyena family, aardwolves subsist almost entirely on harvester termites (which are generally ignored by other termite eaters because they are so noxious), licking more than 200,000 from the ground each night. Unlike other hyaenids, they don't form clans; instead, they forage alone and mates form only loose associations with each other. The male assists the female in raising the cubs, mostly by babysitting at the den while the mother forages. Aardwolves are persecuted in the mistaken belief that they kill stock, and may suffer huge population crashes following spraying for locusts (the spraying also kills termites).

Size: Shoulder height 40cm to 50cm; length 80cm to 100cm, including tail of up to 25cm; weight 8kg to 12kg. **Distribution:** Widespread in savanna and woodland habitats from the south of Kenya into the country's arid north. **Status:** Uncommon; nocturnal but occasionally seen at dawn and dusk.

MITCH REARDON

Spotted Hyena *Crocuta crocuta*

Widely reviled as scavengers, spotted hyenas are highly efficient predators with a fascinating social system. Females are larger than, and dominant to, males and have male physical characteristics, including an erectile clitoris that renders the sexes virtually indistinguishable. Clans, which can contain dozens of individuals, are led by females. Spotted hyenas are massively built and appear distinctly canine, but they are more closely related to cats than dogs. They can run at a speed of 60km/h and a pack can easily dispatch adult wildebeests and zebras. Their 'ooo-oop' call is one of the most distinctive East African night sounds.

Size: Shoulder height 85cm; length up to 180cm, including tail of up to 30cm; weight up to 80kg. **Distribution:** Throughout Kenya, increasingly restricted to conservation areas. **Status:** Common where there is suitable food and often the most common large predator in protected areas; mainly nocturnal but also seen during the day.

Serval *Felis serval*

The first impression one gains of servals – tall, slender, long-legged cats – is that they look like small cheetahs. The tawny to russet-yellow coat has large black spots, forming long bars and blotches on the neck and shoulders. All-black individuals occasionally occur. Other distinguishing features include large upright ears, a long neck and a relatively short tail. Servals are associated with vegetation near water and are most common in flood-plain savanna, wetlands and woodlands near streams. They are rodent specialists, feeding on mice, rats and springhares. Birds, small reptiles and occasionally the young of small antelopes are also taken.

DAVID WALL

Size: Shoulder height 60cm; length up to 130cm, including tail up to 30cm; weight up to 16kg. **Distribution:** Well-watered habitats throughout Kenya. **Status:** Relatively common but mainly nocturnal, sometimes seen in the early morning and late afternoon.

Caracal *Felis caracal*

Sometimes called African lynxes due to their long, tufted ears, caracals are robust, powerful cats that prey mostly on small antelopes, birds and rodents but also take prey much larger than themselves. Long back legs power prodigious leaps – they even take birds in flight. Caracals are largely solitary, and although male–female pairs may associate more than most other cats, females raise their one to three kittens alone. The sandy body colour is excellent camouflage, but the ears and face are strikingly patterned in black and white and are highly mobile and expressive – features used for visual signalling.

DAVID WALL

Size: Shoulder height 40cm to 50cm; length 95cm to 120cm, including tail up to 30cm; weight 7kg to 18kg; male slightly larger than female. **Distribution:** Throughout Kenya. **Status:** Fairly common but largely nocturnal and difficult to see.

Leopard *Panthera pardus*

Leopards are heard more often than seen; their rasping territorial call sounds very much like a saw cutting through wood. Supreme ambush hunters, leopards stalk close to their prey before attacking in an explosive rush. They eat everything from insects to zebras, but antelopes are their primary prey. Leopards are highly agile and climb well, spending more time in trees than other big cats – they hoist their kills into trees to avoid losing them to lions and hyenas. They are solitary animals, except when a male and female remain in close association for the female's week-long oestrus.

ROB DRUMMOND

Size: Shoulder height 50cm to 75cm; length 160cm to 210cm, including 70cm to 110cm tail; weight up to 90kg; male larger than female. **Distribution:** Widely spread throughout Kenya; of all the big cats, the most tolerant of human activity. **Status:** Common but, being mainly nocturnal, they are very difficult to see.

Lion *Panthera leo*

Lions spend the night hunting, patrolling territories (of 50 to 400 sq km) and playing. They live in prides of up to about 30, comprising four to 12 related females, which remain in the pride for life, and a coalition of unrelated males, which defend females from foreign males. Young males are ousted from the pride at the age of two or three, becoming nomadic until around five years old, when they are able to take over their own pride. Lions hunt – certainly as a group, perhaps cooperatively – virtually anything, but wildebeests, zebras and buffaloes are their main targets.

Size: Shoulder height 120cm; length 250cm to 300cm, including tail up to 100cm; weight up to 260kg (male), 180kg (female). **Distribution:** Largely confined to protected areas and present in all savanna and woodland parks in Kenya. **Status:** Common where they occur; mainly nocturnal but easy to see during the day.

Cheetah *Acinonyx jubatus*

The world's fastest land mammals, cheetahs can reach speeds of over 105km/h but become exhausted after a few hundred metres and therefore usually stalk prey to within 60m before unleashing their tremendous acceleration – three out of every four hunts fail. Cheetahs prey on antelopes weighing up to 60kg as well as hares and young wildebeests and zebras. Litters may be as large as nine, but in open savanna habitats most cubs are killed by other predators, particularly lions. Young cheetahs disperse from the mother when aged around 18 months. The males form coalitions; females remain solitary for life.

Size: Shoulder height 85cm; length up to 220cm, including tail up to 70cm; weight up to 65kg. **Distribution:** Largely restricted to protected areas or the regions surrounding them; shuns densely forested areas. **Status:** Uncommon, with individuals moving over large areas; frequently seen in national parks.

UNGULATES

African Elephant *Loxodonta africana*

Elephants usually live in groups of 10 to 20 females and young, congregating in larger herds at common water and food resources. Bulls live alone or in bachelor groups, joining herds when females are in season. A cow may mate with many bulls. Vocalisations include a deep rumble felt as a low vibration, and a high-pitched trumpeting given in threat or when frightened. Consuming 250kg of vegetation daily, elephants can decimate woodlands, but this may be part of the savanna's natural cycle. They live for up to 100 years.

Size: Shoulder height up to 4m (male), 3.5m (female); weight five to 6.5 tonnes (male), three to 3.5 tonnes (female). **Distribution:** Widely distributed in Kenya apart from the north. **Status:** Very common in most of the larger national parks.

Hyraxes Rock Hyrax *Procavia johnstoni* (pictured);
Yellow-Spotted Rock Hyrax *Heterohyrax brucei*

Hyraxes (or dassies) occur nearly everywhere there are
mountains or rocky outcrops. They are sociable, living in
colonies of up to 60. Despite resembling large guinea pigs,
hyraxes are actually related to elephants. Yellow-spotted
hyraxes are distinguished by the presence of a prominent
white spot above the eye. Hyraxes spend much of the day
basking on rocks or chasing other hyraxes. If accustomed to
humans they are often approachable, but will dash off if
alarmed, uttering shrill screams. Rocks streaked white by
hyraxes' urine are often an indicator of a colony's presence.

Size: Rock hyrax length up to 60cm; weight up to 5.5kg. Yellow-spotted length up to 50cm; weight up to
2.5kg. **Distribution:** Both species are very widely distributed throughout Kenya. **Status:** Common; regularly
inhabit areas around lodges, where they become tame.

Burchell's Zebra *Equus burchelli*

Thousands of Burchell's zebras (one of three zebra species
in Africa) join blue wildebeests on their famous mass migration. The zebras' sociality centres on harems of five to
six mares defended by a single stallion. Larger herds are
usually temporary aggregations of smaller groups. Stal-
lions may hold a harem for 15 years, but they often lose
single mares to younger males, which gradually build up
their own harems. When pursued by predators, zebras
close ranks as they run off, making it hard for any individual to be singled out for attack. And yes, it's true – a
zebra's stripes are as individual as a human's fingerprints.

Size: Shoulder height 1.4m to 1.6m; length 2.2m to 2.6m; weight up to 390kg; females are slightly smaller
than males. **Distribution:** Burchell's zebra in and around parks throughout Kenya; Grevy's zebra only in
northern Kenya. **Status:** Very common and easily seen.

Black (Hook-Lipped) Rhinoceros *Diceros bicornis*

Poaching for horns has made rhinoceroses Africa's most
endangered large mammal. In many countries rhinos have
been exterminated and the white rhino *(Ceratotherium
simum)* is now very rare in East Africa (it remains numerous in Southern Africa). The smaller of the two species,
black rhinos are more unpredictable and prone to charging
when alarmed or uncertain about a possible threat. They
use their pointed, prehensile upper lip to feed selectively on
branches and foliage. Black rhinos are solitary and aggressively territorial, usually only socialising during the mating
season; however, they may form temporary associations.

Size: Shoulder height 1.6m; length 3m to 4m; weight 800kg to 1400kg; front horn up to 130cm long.
Distribution: Restricted to relict populations in a few reserves; black best seen in Nairobi National Park; white
best seen in Lake Nakuru national Park. **Status:** Highly endangered in Kenya but seen in protected areas.

Warthog *Phacochoerus aethiopicus*

Warthogs grow two sets of tusks: their upper tusks grow as long as 60cm, their lower tusks are usually less than 15cm long. Females have a pair of distinctive facial warts under the eyes; males have a second set of warts further down the snout. Sociality varies, but groups usually consist of one to three sows and their young. Males form bachelor groups or are solitary, only associating with females during oestrus. Warthogs feed mainly on grass, but also on fruit and bark. In hard times, they grub for roots and bulbs. They den in abandoned burrows or excavate their own burrows.

Size: Shoulder height 70cm; weight up to more than 100kg, but averages 50kg to 60kg; male larger than female. **Distribution:** Throughout Kenya except in dense rainforest and mountains above 3000m. **Status:** Common, diurnal and easy to see.

Hippopotamus *Hippopotamus amphibius*

Hippos are found close to fresh water, spending most of the day submerged and emerging at night to graze on land. They can consume about 40kg of vegetation each evening. They live in large herds, tolerating close contact in the water but foraging alone when on land. Adult bulls aggressively defend territories against each other and most males bear the scars of conflicts (often a convenient method of sexing hippos). Cows with calves are aggressive towards other individuals. Hippos are extremely dangerous when on land and kill many people each year, usually when someone inadvertently blocks the animal's retreat to the water.

Size: Shoulder height 1.5m; weight 1000kg to 2000kg; male larger than female. **Distribution:** Usually found near large areas of fresh water throughout Kenya. **Status:** Common in major water courses and easy to see.

Giraffe *Giraffa camelopardalis*

There are several distinctly patterned subspecies of giraffe, including reticulated giraffes and Masai giraffes, which are more common. A giraffe's neck has seven cervical vertebrae – the same as all mammals. The 'horns' (knobs of skin-covered bone) of males have bald tips; females' are covered in hair. Giraffes form loose, ever-changing groups of up to 50; females are rarely seen alone, while males are more solitary. Browsers, giraffes exploit foliage out of reach of most herbivores – males usually feed from a higher level than females. Juveniles are prone to predation and lions even take adults; giraffes are most vulnerable when drinking.

Size: Height 3.5m to 4.5m (female), 4m to 5.5m (male); weight 700kg to 1000kg (female), 900kg to 1400kg (male). **Distribution:** Reticulated giraffe occurs in northern Kenya; Masai giraffe is widespread southwest of Nairobi extending into Tanzania; Rothschild's giraffe is restricted to western Kenya near Lake Baringo. **Status:** Relatively common and easy to see.

Bushbuck *Tragelaphus scriptus*

Shy and solitary animals, bushbucks inhabit thick bush close to permanent water, where they browse on leaves at night. Bushbucks are chestnut to dark brown in colour and have a variable number of white vertical stripes on the body between the neck and rump, as well as a number of white spots on the upper thigh and a white splash on the neck. Normally only males grow horns, which are straight with gentle spirals and average about 30cm in length. When startled, bushbucks bolt and crash loudly through the undergrowth. They can be quite aggressive and even dangerous when cornered.

Size: Height at shoulder 80cm; weight 45kg to 80kg; horns up to 55cm long; male larger than female. **Distribution:** Throughout the region, favouring denser habitats. **Status:** Common, but shy and difficult to see.

Kudus Greater kudu *Tragelaphus strepsiceros* (pictured); lesser kudu *Tragelaphus imberbis*

Greater kudus are Africa's second-tallest antelope; males carry massive spiralling horns (the largest of any antelope). They are light grey in colour, with six to 12 white stripes down the sides. Lesser kudus have 11 to 15 stripes; males are blue-grey and females are bright rust coloured. In both species, one to three females and their young form groups, and are joined by males during the breeding season. Kudus are browsers, finding their diet in woodland-savanna with fairly dense bush cover. Strong jumpers, they flee with frequent leaping, clearing obstacles more than 2m high.

Size: Greater kudu shoulder height 1.2m to 1.5m; weight 190kg to 320kg. Lesser kudu shoulder height 95cm to 110cm; weight 90kg to 110kg. Males larger than females. **Distribution:** Greater kudu can be found throughout Kenya, except in the driest areas; lesser kudu prefer the arid regions of northern Kenya. **Status:** Greater kudu scattered; lesser kudu common.

Eland *Taurotragus oryx*

Africa's largest antelope, elands are massive. The horns of both sexes average 65cm, spiralling at the base then sweeping straight back. The male has a distinctive hairy tuft on the head, and stouter horns. Herds consist of adults, adults and young, or sometimes just young – group membership and composition change often. The most common large groups consist of 10 to 60 females and young. Males are less gregarious, coming together more sporadically and in smaller numbers, but one or more often join female-and-young herds. Aggregations up to 1000 form where new grass is growing.

Size: Shoulder height 1.5m to 1.8m (male), 1.25m to 1.5m (female); weight 450kg to 950kg (male), 300kg to 500kg (female); horns up to 100cm long. **Distribution:** Patchy distribution in arid zones; best seen in Nairobi and Tsavo National Parks. **Status:** Low density but relatively common and easy to see.

African Buffalo *Syncerus caffer*

Both sexes of African buffaloes have distinctive curving horns that broaden at the base to meet over the forehead in a massive 'boss' – the female's are usually smaller. Local populations of buffaloes inhabit large home ranges and at times herds of thousands form, but the population's social organisation is fluid: groups of related females and their young coalesce and separate into larger or smaller herds; males associate with the females during breeding, and at other times they form male herds or are solitary. Although generally docile, buffaloes can be dangerous – especially lone bulls, and females protecting their young.

Size: Shoulder height 1.6m; weight 400kg to 900kg; horns up to 1.25m long; female somewhat smaller than male. **Distribution:** Widespread, but large populations only occur in parks. **Status:** Common and may be approachable where protected.

Common (Grey) Duiker *Sylvicapra grimmia*

One of the most common small antelopes, common duikers are usually solitary, but are sometimes seen in pairs. They are greyish light brown in colour, with a white belly and a dark-brown stripe down the face. Only males have horns, which are straight and pointed and rarely grow longer than 15cm. Duikers are predominantly browsers, often feeding on agricultural crops. This habit leads to them being persecuted outside conservation areas, although they are resilient to hunting. Common duikers are capable of going without water for long periods, but they will drink whenever water is available.

Size: Shoulder height 50cm; weight 10kg to 20kg; females slightly larger than males; horns up to 18cm. **Distribution:** Throughout Kenya. **Status:** Common; active day and night, but more nocturnal where disturbance is common.

Waterbuck *Kobus ellipsiprymnus*

Waterbucks have a shaggy, brown coat and white rump, face and throat markings; only males have horns. Females have overlapping ranges, coming and going to form loose associations of normally up to a dozen animals. Young, nonterritorial males behave similarly. Mature males hold territories, onto which females wander (nonterritorial males are also often allowed access). These essentially independent movements sometimes produce herds of 50 to 70. They always stays near water and are good swimmers, readily entering water to escape predators. Their oily hair has a strong, musky odour, potent enough for humans to smell.

Size: Shoulder height 1.3m; weight 200kg to 300kg (males), 150kg to 200kg (females); horns up to 100cm. **Distribution:** Wet areas throughout Kenya. **Status:** Common and easily seen.

Reedbucks Common reedbuck *Redunca arundinum;* Bohor reedbuck *Redunca redunca* (pictured); mountain reedbuck *Redunca fulvorufula*

Brown common reedbucks are found in woodland areas; yellowish bohor reedbucks are prevalent on floodplains; greyer mountain reedbucks inhabit grassy hill country. All have white underparts; males have forward-curving horns. Common reedbucks form pairs, though mates associate only loosely; female mountain reedbucks form small groups that range over the territories of several males. Bohor males have ranges that overlap those of females. Reedbucks whistle when advertising territories or when alarmed.

Size: Common reedbucks shoulder height 90cm; weight 70kg; horns up to 45cm. Bohor 30% smaller; mountain 30% smaller again. Males larger than females in common and bohor; sexes similar size in mountain. **Distribution:** Throughout Kenya wherever suitable well-watered grasslands occur. **Status:** Common.

Roan Antelope *Hippotragus equinus*

Roan antelopes are among Africa's rarest and largest antelopes. Their coats vary from reddish-fawn to dark reddish-brown, and have white underparts and a mane of stiff, black-tipped hairs. Their faces are black and white, their long, pointed ears tipped with a brown tassel. Both sexes have long backward-curving horns. They prefer sites with tall grasses, shade and water. Herds of normally less than 20 females and young range over the territories of several adult males; other males form bachelor groups. Female herds of up to 50 are common – herds are larger during the dry season when food and water are more localised.

Size: Shoulder height 1.4m; weight 200kg to 300kg; horns up to 100cm. Females smaller than males and have shorter horns. **Distribution:** Mostly at Ruma National Park near Lake Victoria. **Status:** Populations are declining and the species is threatened in Kenya; easily seen where present.

Sable Antelope *Hippotragus niger*

Widely considered the most magnificent of Africa's antelopes, sable antelopes are slightly smaller than roan antelopes, but are thicker set; and have longer horns, often reaching more than 100cm. Sables have a white belly and face markings; females are reddish brown, while mature males are a deep, glossy black. They favour habitat slightly more wooded than that of roan antelopes. Social organisation of the two species is also very similar, but sable female-and-young herds are slightly larger – usually 10 to 30, but up to 70 or so. Both species are fierce fighters, and are even known to kill attacking lions.

Size: Shoulder height 1.35m; weight 180kg to 270kg; horns up to 130cm long – the male's are longer and more curved than the females. **Distribution:** Mostly at Shimba Hills National Reserve. **Status:** Common and easily seen.

ANDREW VAN SMEERDIJK

Oryx *Oryx gazella*

Well adapted to aridity, oryxes can survive without drinking. To conserve water, they let their body temperature rise to levels that would kill most mammals. Oryxes are solid and powerful; both sexes carry long, straight horns. Principally grazers, they also browse on thorny shrubs. In areas with abundant water and food, populations are sometimes resident and adopt a social system like that of roan antelopes. More usually, nomadic herds number around a dozen, but can total up to 60. Herds normally contain males and females, but there are strict hierarchies within the sexes. Herds, especially if small, may also be single sex.

Size: Shoulder height 1.2m; weight 170kg to 210kg (males), 120kg to 190kg (females); horns up to 110cm. **Distribution:** Beisa oryx in northern Kenya; fringe-eared oryx in southern Kenya. **Status:** Relatively common and easy to see, but shy.

DENNIS JONES

Hartebeest *Alcelaphus buselaphus*

Hartebeests are red to tan in colour, medium-sized and easily recognised by their long, narrow face and short horns. In both sexes, the distinctively angular and heavily ridged horns form a heart shape, hence their name, which comes from Afrikaans. Hartebeests prefer grassy plains but are also found in sparsely forested savanna and hills. Dominant males defend territories, which herds of females and their young pass through; other males move in bachelor groups. Herds typically number up to about a dozen (male herds are generally smaller), but aggregations of hundreds and (in the past) thousands also occur.

Size: Shoulder height 1.2m; weight 130kg to 170kg (males), 115kg to 150kg (females); horns up to 85cm. **Distribution:** Wide ranging; Coke's hartebeest, also known as 'Kongoni', is common in Kenya; Jackson's hartebeest is confined to areas near Lake Victoria. **Status:** Common.

DENNIS JONES

Topi *Damaliscus lunatus*

Topis are reddish brown, with glossy violet patches on the legs and face. The horns, carried by both sexes, curve gently up, out and back. Their social system is highly variable. In grassy woodlands, males hold territories with harems of up to 10 females. On floodplains with dense populations, nomadic herds of thousands may form, males establishing temporary territories whenever the herd halts. Elsewhere, males gather on breeding-season display grounds; females visit these 'leks' to select their mates. Both sexes often stand on high vantage points (commonly termite mounds) to view their surroundings and as territorial advertisement.

Size: Shoulder height 1.2m; weight 110kg to 150kg (male), 75kg to 130kg (female); horns up to 45cm. **Distribution:** Widespread throughout medium-length grasslands, common in the Masai Mara National Reserve. **Status:** Common.

Blue Wildebeest *Connochaetes taurinus*

Blue wildebeests are gregarious, and in some areas form herds up to tens of thousands strong, often in association with zebras and other herbivores. Wildebeests are grazers, and move constantly in search of good pasture and water, preferring to drink daily – this gives rise to the famous mass migration in the Serengeti–Masai Mara ecosystem. Elsewhere, especially where food and water are more permanent, groups of up to 30 are more usual, with larger congregations being less frequent and more temporary. In both situations, males are territorial and attempt to herd groups of females into their territory.

DENNIS JONES

Size: Shoulder height 1.4m; weight 140kg to 230kg (females), 200kg to 300kg (males); horns up to 85cm; male larger than female. **Distribution:** Throughout parks in the south of Kenya. **Status:** Very common; 1.5 million occur in the Serengeti–Masai Mara ecosystem.

Klipspringer *Oreotragus oreotragus*

Small, sturdy antelopes, klipspringers are easily recognised by their tip-toe stance – their hooves are adapted for balance and grip on rocky surfaces, enabling them to bound up impossibly rough and steep rockfaces. Klipspringers normally inhabit rocky outcrops; they also sometimes venture into adjacent grasslands, but always retreat to the rocks when alarmed. Klipspringers form long-lasting pair bonds and the pair occupies a territory, nearly always remaining within a couple of metres of each other. When disturbed, the pair often gives a duet of trumpet-like alarm calls.

DAVID WALL

Size: Shoulder height 55cm; weight 9kg to 15kg; horns up to 15cm; female larger than male. **Distribution:** Rocky outcrops and mountainous areas throughout the region. **Status:** Common but wary; often seen standing on high vantage points.

Steenbok *Raphicerus campestris*

Steenboks are pretty and slender antelopes; their back and hindquarters range from light reddish-brown to dark brown with pale underparts markings. The nose bears a black, wedge-shaped stripe. Males have small, straight and widely separated horns. Although usually seen alone, it's likely that steenboks share a small territory with a mate, but only occasionally does the pair come together. Steenboks are active in the morning and afternoon and by night; they may become more nocturnal where frequently disturbed. If a predator approaches they lie flat with neck outstretched, zigzagging away only at the last moment.

DENNIS JONES

Size: Shoulder height 50cm; weight up to 16kg; horns up to 19cm; female a little larger than male. **Distribution:** Restricted to central and northern Kenya. **Status:** Relatively common, but easily overlooked.

WILDLIFE GUIDE

Kirk's Dik-Dik *Madoqua kirkii*

Dik-diks are identified by their miniature size, the pointed flexible snout and a tuft of hair on the forehead; only the males have horns. Dik-diks are monogamous and pairs are territorial. If one is seen, its mate is usually nearby, as well as that year's young. Territories are marked by up to a dozen large piles of dung placed around the boundary. Both members of the pair, and their young, use the dung piles, placing their deposits as part of an elaborate ceremony. Dik-diks feed by browsing on foliage and, being well adapted to their dry environments, don't drink.

Size: Shoulder height 35cm to 45cm; weight 4kg to 7kg; horns up to 12cm. **Distribution:** Throughout Kenya. **Status:** Common but wary and easy to miss; active day and night.

Impala *Aepyceros melampus*

Often dismissed by tourists because they are so abundant, impalas are unique antelopes with no close relatives. Males have long, lyre-shaped horns averaging 75cm in length. They are gregarious animals, forming resident herds of up to 100 or so. Males defend female herds during the oestrus, but outside the breeding season they congregate in bachelor groups. Impalas are known for their speed and ability to leap – they can spring as far as 10m in one bound, or 3m into the air. They are the common prey of lions, leopards, cheetahs, wild dogs and spotted hyenas.

Size: Shoulder height 85cm; weight 40kg to 80kg; horns up to 90cm; male larger than female. **Distribution:** Savanna regions from central Kenya extending south. **Status:** Very common and easy to see.

Gazelles Thomson's gazelle *Gazella thomsonii*
(pictured); Grant's gazelle *Gazella granti*

Among the most common medium-sized antelopes, gazelles are often the main prey of predators – so they are very fleet of foot and wary of attack. Thomson's gazelles are smaller and form large aggregations (often of many thousands) on the open plains. They often occur with impala-sized Grant's gazelles, which lack the distinctive black side stripe of the 'tommy'. The social structure is flexible; herds often consist of females and young, with males defending territories around the feeding grounds of females.

Size: Thomson's gazelle shoulder height 65cm; weight 15kg to 30kg; horns up to 45cm. Grant's gazelle shoulder height 85cm; weight 40kg to 80kg; horns to 80cm. Females of both smaller than males and have much smaller horns. **Distribution:** Thomson's and Grant's gazelle common in savanna and woodland. **Status:** Very common.

(Continued from page 96)

Accreditation by the **Kenya Professional Safari Guides Association** (☎ 02-609355, 609365) is also a good indicator of quality.

One thing to look out for whomever you book with is client swapping. Quite a few companies will shift clients on to other companies if they don't have enough people to justify running the trip themselves. This does ensure that trips actually depart on time and saves travellers days of waiting for a safari to fill up, but it does undermine consumer trust. Reputable companies will usually inform you before they transfer you to another company. In any case, it may not be the end of the world if you end up taking your safari with a different company to the one you booked with; just make sure the safari you booked and paid for is what you get.

The brochures for some safari companies may give the impression that they offer every conceivable safari under the sun, but in fact, many companies also advertise trips run by other companies. While it's not the most transparent way to do business, again, it needn't be the end of the world. A reliable company will normally choose reliable partners, and you're only really likely to come unstuck at the budget end of the market. Sadly, the only way some of the shoddier operators can get business is through touts, and these companies employ all sorts of tricks to cut costs, including not maintaining their vehicles, entering national parks through side entrances to avoid fees, and employing glorified matatu drivers with little knowledge of the wildlife as guides.

Be particularly careful of safari companies in Nairobi. Some of these guys don't actually run *any* of their own safaris, and are basically just travel agents. If you book with one of these operators and anything goes wrong, or the itinerary is changed without your agreement, you have very little comeback and it'll be virtually impossible to get a refund. Unfortunately, it's often hard to tell which are genuine safari companies and which are agents. One trick is to pick up half a dozen leaflets from various companies and compare the wording – you'll find that quite a few are identical! If you want to know who you're dealing with throughout, go with one on the more expensive agents and confirm exactly who will be operating which parts of the trip, particularly if you are detouring to Tanzania or Uganda.

We welcome all feedback on your safari experiences and will try to incorporate it into future editions of this book.

Costs

With all this competition, prices are remarkably standard across different companies, but the determining factors are always going to be the type of accommodation, the places you want to visit, the season you visit and the duration of the safari. In general, the longer you go for, the less you pay per day. Whichever type of safari you choose, be aware that you generally get what you pay for. A high degree of personal involvement in camp chores and a willingness to eschew creature comforts usually guarantees a lower price. If you want the opposite, it will cost you more.

There's a good argument for spending a bit more on your safari and using a reliable vehicle. Too many budget companies are notorious for breakdowns and we get a flood of letters every year from travellers who spent at least one day of their safari waiting for a tow truck or mechanic.

For camping safaris with no frills you are looking at an all-inclusive price of between US$65 and US$80 per day. The price includes transport, food (three meals per day), park entry and camping fees, tents and cooking equipment. Rates per day usually decrease if you go for more than three days or so, but if you want to go all out and take on a safari of 11 days or more, prices tend to increase as there's a lot more organisation involved. Putting up the tent is usually your responsibility – the guide will be far too busy preparing dinner to sort out all the camping arrangements. You'll usually be expected to share a tent even if you're travelling alone, although you can pay a single supplement of around 25% of the daily safari rate and have the tent to yourself. Sleeping-bag hire is typically US$10 on top of the safari price.

The prices for safaris that involve staying in lodges or tented camps are considerably higher. Here you're looking at a minimum of US$180 per person per night in the lodges and up to US$350 in the luxury tented camps (these prices will drop in the low season). These prices are based on the assumption that you will share accommodation, but if you want a room to yourself, there's usually a single-room supplement of around 25%, although it can be as high as 50%! Rates of all places to stay inside national parks are inflated due to the location so you may not get as much luxury as you might expect for US$200!

Remember that at the end of one of these safaris your driver/guide and the cook(s) will expect a reasonable tip. This is only fair since wages are low and they will have made a lot of effort to make your trip memorable. Remember that other travellers are going to follow you and the last thing anyone wants to find is a disgruntled driver/guide who couldn't care less whether you see wildlife or not. At the time of research, a good tip was around KSh150 per guide/cook per person per day – in other words, what you would spend on a couple of drinks.

Many safaris feature side trips to *manyattas* (tribal villages), which provide an opportunity for displaced villagers to make a bit of income from tourism, either posing for photographs or selling you souvenirs. Guides and drivers usually levy a fee of around US$10 per head for this, but often this money goes into the driver's pocket. If you visit a *manyatta*, insist that the driver gives the tribespeople their due!

What to Bring

Unless you are organising your own trip from scratch, any organised safari will provide camping gear or accommodation and all meals, plus drinking water and soft drinks. Beer is usually extra, so you may want to bring your own to keep down costs. Sleeping bags can usually be hired from your safari company or local outfitters. If you're planning to attempt the Mt Kenya trek it's probably worth bringing a decent three-season bag from home.

You'll need to bring enough clothing and footwear for hot days and cold nights, but the amount of baggage that you'll be allowed to bring is limited. Excess gear can usually be stored at the safari company's offices. Don't forget to bring a pocket-knife and a torch (flashlight) – the company will provide kerosene lanterns for the camp but it's unlikely they'll be left on all night.

'Luxury' items such as toilet paper and mosquito nets are generally not provided, so you'll need to bring your own. Mosquito nets

---

Minimal Impact Safaris

In their quest for the perfect photo opportunity, some safari drivers do crazy things. A healthy dose of common sense goes a long way, but too many drivers are under too much pressure to please their clients, with little regard for the effects on wildlife. In the interests of the animals, please observe the following:

- Never get out of your vehicle, except at designated points where this is permitted. The animals may look tame and harmless enough, but this is not a zoo – the animals are wild and you should treat them as such.
- Never get too close to the animals and back off if they are getting edgy or nervous. Stress can alter the animals' natural behaviour patterns and could make the difference between this year's lion cubs surviving or getting killed by other predators.
- Animals always have the right of way. Don't follow predators as they move off – you try stalking something when you've got half a dozen minibuses in tow!
- Keep to the tracks. One of the biggest dangers in the parks today is land degradation from too many vehicles crisscrossing the countryside. Amboseli and Masai Mara can both end up looking as though the East African Safari Rally has been run entirely within the park by the end of the season. The tyre tracks act as drainage channels for the rain and erode the soil, which affects the grasses that attract the herbivores, which attract the predators. Ask your driver to stick to the main trails.
- Don't light fires except at camp sites, and dispose of cigarettes carefully. An old film case is the best place for cigarette butts and they can then be disposed of outside the park.
- Don't litter the parks and camp sites. Unfortunately, the worst offenders are safari drivers and cooks who toss everything and anything out the window. It won't do any harm to point out to them the consequences of what they're doing, or clean it up yourself.

---

can often be hired and insect repellent, skin cream and mosquito coils are always a good idea. There are few shops in the bush, so sanitary towels, medicines and other important items should all be brought with you.

TYPES OF SAFARI
Camping Safaris

Camping safaris cater for budget travellers, the young (or young at heart) and those who are prepared to put up with a little discomfort to get the authentic bush experience. At the bottom of the price range, you'll have to forgo luxuries such as flush toilets, running water and iced drinks, and you'll have to chip in to help with chores such as putting up the tents and helping prepare dinner. Showers are provided at some but not all camp sites, although there's usually a tap where you can scrub down with cold water. The price of your safari will include three meals a day cooked by the camp cook(s), although food is of the 'plain-but-plenty' variety.

There are more comfortable camping options, where there are extra staff to do all the work, but they cost more. A number of companies have also set up permanent camp sites in the Masai Mara and Samburu National Reserves where you can just drop into bed at the end of a dusty day's drive. At the top end of this market are some very plush, luxury, camping safaris that utilise permanent camp sites with showers and tents fitted with mosquito nets, beds and sheets. These are described under Lodge & Tented Camp Safaris later in this chapter.

Whatever you pay, you'll end up hot, tired, and dusty at the end of the day, but you're guaranteed to sleep well, and few things can match the thrill of waking up in the middle of the African bush with nothing between you and the animals except a sheet of canvas and the dying embers of last night's fire. It's not at all unusual for elephants or hippos to trundle through the camp at night, or even the occasional lion, and, so far, no-one has been eaten or trampled on.

Another plus for these safaris is that you'll probably find yourself with travellers from the four corners of the earth.

Reliable companies at the time of writing include the following.

Best Camping Tours (☎ 02-229667, fax 217923; W www.kenyaweb.com/bestcampingtours) Norwich Union House (opposite Hilton Hotel), Mama Ngina St (PO Box 40223), Nairobi. This popular and reliable company offers budget camping safaris on all the main routes including Amboseli or Masai Mara (three to four days) and Amboseli and Tsavo West (four days). Longer seven- and eight-day safaris visit various combinations of Amboseli, Tsavo West, the Rift Valley lakes, Masai Mara, Mt Kenya, Samburu, and Lake Nakuru. It also runs trips into Tanzania. The average cost is around US$80 per day.

Bushbuck Adventures (☎ 02-532090, fax 521505; e bushbuck@arcc.or.ke; W www.kilimanjaro.com /safaris/bushbuck) Peponi Rd, Nairobi. Bushbuck is a small company specialising in personalised safaris. It has a private, semi-permanent camp in the northwest corner of the Masai Mara. As a result, it's relatively expensive, but some company profits are put into conservation projects. Prices range from US$150 per person per day for five people to US$340 for one person.

Flight Centres (☎ 02-210024, fax 332407; e fc swwat@form-net.com) Lakhamshi House, 2nd floor, Biashara St, Nairobi. This company acts as an informal broker for camping safaris in Kenya. It can shop around for you and is a good barometer of quality. It also runs a few of its own safaris (see Truck Safaris later in this chapter).

Gametrackers Ltd (☎ 02-338927, fax 330903; W www.gametrackers.com) Nginyo Towers, 5th floor, cnr Koinange & Moktar Daddah St (PO Box 62042), Nairobi. Also long established and usually reliable, this company offers a full range of camping and lodge safaris around Kenya, including the remote parks around Lake Turkana (as part of an eight- to 10-day circuit). There are also short excursions to Nairobi National Park, walking treks in Aberdare National Park, camel safaris (see Other Safaris later in this chapter), Mt Kenya treks and numerous long-haul trips to Tanzania, Uganda and further afield. For shorter safaris, rates are usually around US$65 per day, plus US$15 for sleeping bags. The longer trips depart on set dates, outlined on its website.

Kenia Tours and Safaris (☎ 02-223699, fax 217671; W www.keniatours.com) 4th Floor, Jubilee Insurance Bldg, Wabera St (PO Box 19730), Nairobi. Using minibuses and 4WD vehicles, Kenia offers basic camping, comfortable camping and lodge-based safaris to the major national parks, including the Aberdare National Park. It has a good reputation within the industry and can also offer tailor-made packages elsewhere in Kenya. Safaris typically last seven days and visit Masai Mara, Lake Nakuru and Amboseli, Samburu or the Rift Valley lakes. The cost is around US$65 to US$75 for basic camping, US$85 to US$95 for comfortable camping and US$125 to US$135 upwards in lodges. This company has been known to swap clients with Savuka.

Ketty Tours (☎ 011-315178, fax 311355; e ket ty@africaonline.co.ke) Diamond Trust House, Moi Ave (PO Box 82391), Mombasa. This company specialises in short tours of the coastal region (Wasini, Shimba Hills, Gede etc) and into Tsavo East or West. However, it also offers camping safaris to all the usual parks from two to 10 days. Prices typically start at US$100 per person per day for a camping safari and US$120 to US$150 for a luxury trip.

Planet Safari Adventure (☎ 02-229799, fax 211899; ⓦ www.planetkenyasafaris.com) Sona-lux House, 9th floor, Moi Ave (PO Box 79347), Nairobi. This popular company has pretty much cornered the budget market and receives equal amounts of praise and criticism from travellers. Its big advantage over other budget operations is the use of Land Cruiser 4WDs, although mini-buses are also used, but we've had quite a few reports of breakdowns. If you book with Planet you get a couple of nights dorm accommodation in rooms (with kitchen) adjacent to its office. All the major Kenyan parks are visited and camping safaris cost US$65 to US$70 per person per day while luxury, lodge-based safaris cost around US$160 per person per day. It can also organise trekking trips to Mt Kenya (US$65 per day) and camping safaris in Tanzania. Planet has a desk at Jomo Kenyatta International Airport, and untold numbers of touts downtown.

Primetime Safaris (☎ 02-215773, fax 217136; ⓔ primesaf@africaonline.co.ke) Contrust House, 9th floor, Moi Ave (PO Box 56591), Nairobi. An-other big budget player that's widely touted, Primetime offers similar trips to Planet for simi-lar rates. We've received several good and a few bad reports, so make sure you know exactly what you're getting. The standard five-day Masai Mara trip will cost around US$65 a day.

Safari Camp Services (☎ 02-228936, fax 212160; ⓔ safaricamp@kenyaweb.com; ⓦ www.safari campserv.com) Barclays Plaza, Loita St (PO Box 44801), Nairobi. This company was one of the first camping safari companies in Kenya and has been operating successfully for two decades. Run by the colourful Dick Hedges, it was re-sponsible for the legendary Turkana Bus (see Lake Turkana Safaris later in this chapter) and you'll hear nothing but praise for its operation. Shorter itineraries include the Wildlife Bus, which visits Samburu, Lake Nakuru and Masai Mara (US$645, seven days, two or three departures every month, on Saturday) and a four-day Masai Mara trip (US$375, several departures every month). Safari Camp Services also provides camel safaris (see Camel Safaris later in this chapter) and other tailor-made safari options.

Safari Seekers (☎ 02-226206, fax 334585; ⓦ sa fari-seekers.kenyaweb.com) Jubilee Insurance Exchange Bldg, 5th floor, Kaunda St (PO Box 9165), Nairobi; (☎ 011-220122, fax 228277) Ground Floor, Diamond Trust Arcade, Moi Ave (PO Box 88275), Mombasa. This company has been operating for some years and gets consis-tently good reports. It has its own permanent camp sites in Amboseli, Samburu and Masai Mara, and runs camping and lodge safaris both in Kenya (ex-Nairobi and Mombasa) and Tanza-nia (ex-Arusha) as well as mountain climbing on Mt Kenya (six days) and Kilimanjaro (seven days), plus trips into Uganda. All-inclusive camp-ing safaris cost US$80 to US$105 per person per day (plus US$10 per person per trip for sleeping bag hire). Departures are at least once a week, or any time with at least four people. Safari Seekers also offers air safaris to Amboseli and Masai Mara with accommodation at luxury lodges or tented camps from US$200 to US$225 a day.

Savuka Tours & Safaris (☎ 02-225108, fax 215256; 4th Floor, Pan-African Insurance Build-ing, Kenyatta Ave (PO Box 20433), Nairobi. This is a big budget operator but its touts are extremely persistent and mob travellers in downtown Nairobi. The rates are cheap, but its camp in the Masai Mara is 40 minutes from the nearest gate. On the other hand, we've had many positive reports from customers; make sure you know how much time you'll actually spend inside the parks. The usual Mara, Am-boseli, Lake Nakuru and Samburu itineraries are available and rates for camping safaris start at US$65 to US$70 per day.

Special Camping Safaris Ltd (☎/fax 02-350720; ⓔ scs@iconnect.co.ke; ⓦ www.camping-sa faris.com) Whistling Thorns, near Kiserian, Isinya/Kiserian Pipeline Rd (PO Box 51512), Nairobi. This small family-run company offers good trips to Masai Mara (US$495, four days), Masai Mara and the Rift Valley lakes (US$625, six days), and a Game Safari Special that takes in Masai Mara, lakes Naivasha, Nakuru, Bogo-ria, and Baringo, Maralal, Samburu and the Mt Kenya foothills (US$1050, 10 days). All these rates are based on four people.

Several readers have recommended **Saferide Safaris** (☎ 02-253129, fax 335561; ⓦ www .saferidesafaris.com; Avenue House, Kenyatta Ave, PO Box 57662, Nairobi) and **Eastern & Southern Safaris** (☎ 02-242828, fax 253894, ⓦ www.essafari.co.ke; Twiga House, 4th floor, Muranga'a Rd, PO Box 43332, Nairobi).

Lodge & Tented Camp Safaris

If you can't do without your luxuries, there is another whole side to the safari business, a world of luxurious lodges with swimming pools and bars overlooking secluded water-holes, and wonderfully remote tented camps that recreate the way wealthy hunters used to travel around Kenya a century ago. Some of the lodges are beautifully conceived and the locations are to die for, perched high above huge sweeps of savanna or waterholes teeming with African wildlife. Most are set deep within the national parks, so the safari drives offer maximum wildlife-viewing time. All have African-themed decor to put you in the mood. A lot of the environmental bad habits of the 1980s, leopard-baiting for example, are falling out of favour.

Most lodge guests are on package tours and prefer to view the wildlife from relative comfort, rather than getting up close and personal with the African bush. For our money, budget camping safaris and luxury tented safaris are the most atmospheric way to experience the national parks, but if you have the cash, it's worth staying at the occasional lodge to get a decent meal and shower.

In the lodges you can expect rooms with bathrooms or cottages with air-conditioning, international cuisine, a terrace bar beneath a huge *makuti* canopy with wonderful views, a swimming pool, wildlife videos and other entertainments and plenty of staff on hand to cater for all your requirements. Some of the lodges have accumulated quite a menagerie of semi-tame monkeys and other small mammals. The well-fed rock hyraxes at the Voi Safari Lodge in Tsavo East are so relaxed that you may have to shoo them out of your room. Almost all lodges have a waterhole, and some have a hidden viewing tunnel that leads right to the waterside. Some also put out salt to tempt animals to visit.

The luxury tented camps tend to offer semi-permanent tents with fitted bathrooms (hot showers come as standard), beds with mosquito nets, proper furniture, fans and gourmet meals, served al fresco in the bush. These places are even more luxurious than the lodges, and tend to be *very* expensive; many of the guests fly in on charter planes, which should give you some impression of the kind of budgets we're talking about.

Some of the companies listed for camping safaris also provide lodge-based safaris, but the following are big reliable operators who have been around for years. Most are members of KATO. In and around Mombasa, most bookings are done through hotels.

Abercrombie & Kent Ltd (☎ 02-334955, fax 215752; W www.abercrombiekent.com) 6th & 7th Floor, Bruce House, Standard St (PO Box 59749), Nairobi; (☎ 011-316549, fax 314734) Palli House, 3rd floor, Nyerere Ave (PO Box 90747), Mombasa

Big Five Tours & Safaris (☎ 02-228352, fax 337965; W www.bigfiveafrica.com) Phoenix House, Kenyatta Ave, (PO Box 10367) Nairobi; (☎ 011-311426, fax 311498) Ambalal House, Nkrumah Rd (PO Box 86922), Mombasa

Kuldip's Touring Company (☎ 011-223780, fax 313347; W www.kuldiptourskenya.com) Mji Mpya Rd, off Moi Ave (PO Box 82662), Mombasa

Pollman's Tours & Safaris (☎ 02-500386, fax 544639; W www.pollmans.com) Pollman's House, Mombasa Rd (PO Box 45895), Nairobi; (☎ 011-312565, fax 314502) Taveta Rd (PO Box 84198), Mombasa

Private Safaris (☎ 02-530601, fax 543438; W www.privatesafaris.co.ke) Twinstar Tower, Mombasa Rd (PO Box 45205), Nairobi; (☎ 011-316685, fax 315850) Safari House, Kaunda St (PO Box 85722), Mombasa

Somak Travel (☎ 02-535508/9, fax 535175; W www.somak-nairobi.com) Somak House, Mombasa Rd (PO Box 48495), Nairobi; (☎ 011-487349, fax 487353) Somak House, Nyerere Ave (PO Box 90738), Mombasa

Southern Cross Safaris (☎ 02-884712, fax 884723; W www.southerncrosssafaris.com) Symbion House, Karen Rd (PO Box 24584), Nairobi; (☎ 475074, fax 473533) The Kanstan Centre (near Nyali Bridge), Malindi Rd (PO Box 99456), Mombasa; (☎ 0123-30547, fax 30032) Malindi Complex, Lamu Rd, Malindi

United Touring Company (UTC; ☎ 02-331960, fax 331422; W www.unitedtouring.com) Fedha Towers, cnr Muindi Mbingu and Kaunda Sts (PO Box 42196), Nairobi; (☎ 011-316333, fax 314549) Moi Ave (PO Box 84782), Mombasa

Prices are similar across these companies. Abercrombie & Kent use Land Cruiser 4WDs, while the others tend to use minibuses. Most offer trips to the main national parks – including Masai Mara, Samburu, Nakuru and Tsavo East and West – and tend to focus on short trips of four to eight days. For a four-day Masai Mara safari you're looking at around US$600 per person in the low season and US$800 in the high season.

OTHER SAFARIS
Flying Safaris

These safaris essentially cater for the well-off who want to fly between remote airstrips in the various national parks and stay in luxury tented camps. If money is no object, you can get around by a mixture of charter and scheduled flights and stay in some of the finest camps in Kenya; arrangements can be made with any of the lodge and tented-camp safari operators. Flying safaris to Lake Turkana and Sibiloi National Park are common, and most safari companies will be able to sort out a country-wide itinerary. Safari Camp Services and Safari Seekers (see Camping Safaris earlier in this chapter) can both arrange reasonably priced flying safaris. Quite a few of the special-interest safari operators (see later in this chapter) use light aircraft to save time.

Truck Safaris

Overlanding is a common element of many people's travels through Africa. Although most are bound for elsewhere in Africa – Harare or Cape Town are particularly popular – a few Kenya-only trips are available in converted flat-bed trucks that can carry up to 24 passengers.

Below is a list of the most popular outfits with tours within Kenya. For information on companies that include Kenya as part of an overland trip, see Organised Tours in the Getting There & Away chapter.

Acacia Expeditions (☎ 020-7706 4700, fax 8706 4686; ⓔ acacia@afrika.demon.co.uk; ⓦ www .acacia-africa.com) 23a Craven Terrace, London W2 3QH. As well as overland trips, Acacia runs shorter trips within Kenya, including, a four-day Masai Mara package (US$625 plus a local payment of US$90), four- and six-day packages to Masai Mara and Lake Nakuru (US$635 plus US$170 and US$895 plus US$149, respectively), a five-day Mt Kenya trek (US$1165 plus US$40) and also an eight-day Kenya Wildlife Safari (US$1195 plus US$40).

Flight Centres (☎ 02-210024, fax 332407; ⓔ fc swwat@form-net.com) Lakhamshi House, 2nd floor, Biashara St, Nairobi. As well as international overland trips (see Organised Tours in the Getting There & Away chapter), this company has a four-day Masai Mara and Lake Naivasha trip for just US$155, plus a US$120 kitty.

Guerba Expeditions (☎ 01373-858956, fax 858351; ⓔ info@guerba.co.uk; ⓦ www.guerba .co.uk) Wessex House, 40 Station Rd, Westbury, Wiltshire BA13 3JN; (☎ 02-352430; ⓔ guerba@ africaonline.co.ke) Guerba (Kenya) Ltd (PO Box 43935), Nairobi. This excellent outfit has deep Kenyan roots. Truck safaris in clude an eight-day tour covering the Masai Mara and lakes Nakuru and Naivasha for UK£375 (plus UK£165 kitty) and a 16-day trip that goes to wildlife parks and the lakes for UK£1015 (not including kitty). Its Kenya Family Safari & Coast package (15 days; Masai Mara, lakes Nakuru and Naivasha, Amboseli) takes children over eight years old.

Lake Turkana Safaris

There can be few travellers who come to Kenya who do not relish the expedition through the semiarid wilds of Samburu National Reserve and up to the legendary Lake Turkana (Jade Sea). To get an idea of the country you will pass through, see the South of Turkana and East of Turkana sections in the Northern Kenya chapter.

These safaris all use open-sided 4WD trucks that take up to 18 people and two to three staff (cook, driver and courier). You will need to set aside a minimum of seven days to complete the journey. Routes vary depending how long you go for – some take in lakes Bogoria and Baringo and others include Samburu and Buffalo Springs National Reserves: some take in both of these options – but virtually all of them pass through the town of Maralal where you'll spend the night.

Bushbuck Adventures (☎ 02-532090, fax 521505; ⓔ bushbuck@arcc.or.ke; ⓦ www.kilimanjaro .com/safaris/bushbuck) Peponi Rd, Nairobi. This company offers 10-day Lake Turkana safaris on request. Itineraries are tailor-made and tend to keep away from the usual routes. Trips often include guided walks, allowing meetings with Rendille and Samburu tribespeople. The Ndoto Mountains, Matthews Range, Shaba National Reserve and Chalbi Desert can all be included.

Gametrackers (☎ 02-338927, fax 330903; ⓦ www.gametrackers.com) Nginyo Towers, cnr Koinange & Moktar Daddah St (PO Box 62042), Nairobi. Gametrackers offers a 10-day and eight-day option to Lake Turkana and is the only company to include Marsabit National Park. Its 10-day safari takes in Mt Kenya, Samburu National Reserve, Marsabit, Chalbi Desert, Lake Turkana, Maralal and Lake Baringo. It costs US$550 (plus a local payment of US$110 per person). The eight-day option visits Lake Baringo, Maralal, Lake Turkana and the Samburu National Reserve. It costs US$415 (plus a local payment of US$75 in Turkana). Both safaris use a powerboat for a short excursion on the lake and traditional Turkana huts make up Gametracker's camp beside the lake 10km south of Loyangalani. Gametrackers also offers a 10-day combined Lake Turkana and camel safari (see Camel Safaris later in this chapter).

Sana Highlands Trekking Expeditions (☎ 02-227820, fax 218336; ⓦ www.sanatrekking kenya.com) 4th Floor, Sonalux House, Moi Ave (PO Box 39439), Nairobi. This company offers an eight-day Turkana Bus trip to Lake Turkana, via Lake Baringo, Maralal and Samburu. The cost is around US$650 per person based on four people.

Safari Camp Services (☎ 02-28936, fax 212160; ⓔ safaricamp@form-net.com; ⓦ www.safari

campserv.com) Barclays Plaza (PO Box 44801), Nairobi. This group blazed the trail 20 years ago and has run more than 1000 safaris. There are two options: its Turkana Bus and the Vanishing Africa safari. The Turkana Bus is the economy option and takes in Maralal, Lake Turkana, Wamba and also Samburu National Reserve (US$555 per person, seven days, departs twice monthly in high season). This itinerary also forms part of the 14-day Camel Train that includes a camel trek in the Ndoto Mountains (see Camel Safaris later in this chapter). Vanishing Africa is more upmarket and visits Masai Mara, lakes Naivasha, Nakuru and Baringo, Maralal, South Horr, Lake Turkana and Samburu National Reserve over 14 days. Lodge accommodation is used wherever possible – private camp sites elsewhere. As a result, it's considerably more expensive at US$2650 and only departs on set dates – contact the company for more information.

Camel Safaris

This is a superb way of getting right off the beaten track and into areas where vehicle safaris don't or can't go. Most camel safaris go to the Samburu and Turkana tribal areas between Isiolo and Lake Turkana and you'll have a chance to experience nomadic life and mingle with tribal people. Wildlife is also plentiful, although it's the journey itself that is the main attraction.

You have the choice of riding the camels or walking alongside them and most tribes are led by experienced Samburu *moran* (warriors) and accompanied by English-speaking tribal guides who are well versed in bush lore, botany, ornithology and local customs. Most travelling is done as early as possible in the cool of the day and a camp site established around noon. Afternoons are time for relaxing, guided walks and showers before drinks and dinner around a camp fire.

All companies provide a full range of camping equipment (generally including two-person tents) and ablution facilities, but they vary in what they require you to bring. Some even provide alcoholic drinks, although normally you pay extra for this. The typical distance covered each day is 15km to 18km so you don't have to be super fit.

The following companies offer camel safaris of varying lengths:

Bobong Camp Site (☎ 0176-32718; e olmaisor@africaonline.co.ke) PO Box 5, Rumuruti or con-

tact Kembu Camp Site (see the Northern Kenya chapter for details). This remote camp site, 18km north of Rumuruti, offers some of the cheapest camel safaris in Kenya – KSh750 per day for basic hire of one camel and a handler, no other equipment included. You can create your own package with the owners and pretty much roam where you want to. Organised Turkana and Samburu cultural visits can be arranged for KSh5000.

Desert Rose Camels (w www.eco-resorts.com/desertrose.htm; book through the website or Safari Camp Services – see later). Safaris leave from the Desert Rose lodge in Baragoi (see the Northern Kenya chapter) for the Matthews Range, Ndoto Mountains and Mt Nyiru, between Wamba and South Horr. The exact route depends on the season and the number of days you have available. All trips use experienced Samburu camel handlers and guides. Desert Rose prefers a minimum of six days for a safari and the rates for this are around US$250 per person per day; less for large groups.

Safari Camp Services (☎ 02-228936, fax 212160; w www.safaricampserv.com) Barclays Plaza (PO Box 44801), Nairobi. Camel trekking is now possible as part of the Turkana Bus tour (see Lake Turkana Safaris earlier in this chapter). The Short Camel Train Walk (US$635) includes the first and last parts of the Turkana Bus tour with a four-day camel trek in and around Mt Nyiro in the middle. This trip lasts nine days and does not include Lake Turkana. The Full Camel Train Walk (US$1080) lasts 14 days and includes all the Turkana Bus tour sights with four days trekking beginning after Lake Turkana.

Yare Safaris Ltd (☎/fax 02-214099, 0368-2295; e travelkenya@iconnect.co.ke) 1st Floor, Union Towers, Mama Ngina St (PO Box 63006), Nairobi. Yare offers a seven-day safari to Maralal, where Yare have bandas and a camp site. The actual trek starts at Barsalinga on the Ewaso Ngiro River (which flows through Samburu and Buffalo Springs National Reserves). A support vehicle carries the luggage ahead of the camels to the next camp site. The cost is US$495 per person, which includes everything except a sleeping bag, items of a personal nature and alcoholic drinks. Short custom packages are also available.

Walking & Cycling Safaris

For the keen walker or cyclist and those who don't want to spend all their time in a safari minibus, there are a number of options. For information on treks in Mt Kenya National Park, see that section in the Central Highlands chapter.

Bike Treks (☎ 02-446371, fax 442439; e bik treks@form-net.com; w www.angelfire.com/sk/biketreks), Kabete Gardens, Westlands, Nairobi. This company offers walking and cycling as well as combined walking/cycling safaris. Its shortest safari is a three-day Masai Mara combined trip, and there are also six-day walking trips to the Loita Plains and Maasai land west and south of Narok, which includes a full-day wildlife viewing drive in the Masai Mara. For cyclists there's a six-day safari through the heart of Maasai land including a full-day wildlife drive in the Masai Mara. A minimum of three people guarantees departure on any of these safaris. Rates are about US$120 per person per day, including food, accommodation, bicycles and/or guides, but not sleeping-bag hire (around US$15 extra).

Bushbuck Adventures (☎ 02-532090, fax 521505; e bushbuck@arcc.or.ke; w www.kilimanjaro.com/safaris/bushbuck) Peponi Rd, Nairobi. As well as budget camping safaris Bushbuck offers customised safaris for individuals and groups that usually involve hiking. The most intensive itinerary is a 14-day trip to the Aberdares, Mt Kenya and Shabu National Reserve. Rates are around US$150 to US$170 per person per day.

Gametrackers (☎ 02-338927, fax 330903; w www.gametrackers.com) Nginyo Towers, cnr Koinange & Moktar Daddah St (PO Box 62042), Nairobi. This company offers a four-day walking safari into the Aberdare National Park. Departures are on demand with at least five people required. Expect to pay around US$350.

IntoAfrica (☎/fax 0114-255 5610; e enquiry@intoafrica.com; w www.intoafrica.co.uk) 59 Langdon St, Sheffield, UK, S11 8BH. This environmentally and culturally sensitive company places an emphasis on fair trade and offers a variety of routes up Mt Kenya as well as cultural treks with Maasai people in the Chyulu Hills and Tsavo West National Parks. Safaris usually work out to be around US$128 per person per day, based on a minimum of two. See Cultural Safaris later for more culturally focused safaris.

Sana Highlands Trekking Expeditions (☎ 02-227820, fax 218336; w www.sanatrekking kenya.com) 4th Floor, Sonalux House, Moi Ave (PO Box 39439), Nairobi. This company specialises in hiking safaris to Mt Kenya, Kilimanjaro and Aberdare National Park. There's also shorter trips to the Loita Hills southwest of Nairobi and cultural packages focusing on local tribes. Its nine-day package includes walks in the Cherengani Hills, Saiwa Swamp, Kakamega Forest and visits to the Rift Valley lakes and Masai Mara (US$630 per person, based on four people).

Sirikwa Safaris (☎ 0733-793524, or through Soy Trading ☎ 0325-20061) Kitale. This outfit is run by Jane & Julia Barnley from their farmhouse/guesthouse and camp site about 20km outside Kitale on the Lodwar road. They have considerable knowledge of routes and camp sites in the Cherangani Hills and can provide field guides (KSh400 per day), guided bird-watching walks (KSh1200 per day) and porters (KSh200 per day). They can also arrange trips to Kakamega Forest, Saiwa Swamp National Park, Mt Elgon, Kongelai Escarpment, Tata Falls, Turkwel Gorge and Cherangani Hills.

Ontdek Kenya (☎ 0171-30326; w www.ontdek kenya.com) PO Box 2352, Nyeri. This small operator has been recommended by several readers and offers walking trips around the Rift Valley lakes and Mt Kenya.

Special-Interest Safaris

Bird-Watching Most of the safari companies listed in this chapter offer some kind of bird-watching safaris, but quality varies. For the very best Kenya has to offer, contact **East African Ornithological Safaris** (EAOS; ☎ 02-331191, fax 330698; e eaos@africa online.co.ke; w www.savannahcamps.com/eaos/index.html; Fedha Towers, 11th floor, Standard St, Nairobi), who are part of the Savannah Camps & Lodges group. EOAS offers 13-day specialist bird-watching extravaganzas that take in Mt Kenya, the Rift Valley lakes, Kakamega Forest Reserve, the Masai Mara National Reserve and Lake Victoria.

Top-class lodges are used throughout this trip and the cost, based on two people sharing, works out at US$2880/3600 per person in the low/high season.

There are monthly departures throughout the year. This company was set up by one of the best ornithologists in Kenya.

Motorcycling A company that operates out of Diani Beach, **Fredlink Co Ltd** (☎ 0127-2468; e fredlink@swiftmombasa.com; w www.motorbike-safari.com; Diani Plaza), runs motorcycle safaris to the Taita Hills and the Kilimanjaro foothills, supported by a Land Rover. Large 350cc trail bikes are used and the six-day trips include a wildlife drive in Tsavo West National Park and two nights' lodge accommodation.

The cost is KSh57,800 per rider, and this includes meals, camping, guides, fuel and a support vehicle.

Fredlink also rents 350cc motorcycles or modern 50cc scooters for KSh2300/1300 per day and can arrange custom-guided motorcycle tours for around KSh7000 per day. Check its website for more information.

Fishing Kenya offers some wonderful fishing, but most trips are geared to wealthy visitors. Perhaps the grandest option is a flying trip to **Rutundu Log Cabins** *(book with Let's Go Travel ☎ 02-340331; W www.lets gosafari .com; singles/doubles self-catering US$413/825, full board US$484/968)* in Mt Kenya National Park. Both Lake Rutundu and Lake Alice, a two-hour drive to the south, are well stocked with rainbow trout, while the nearby Kazita Munyi River is stocked with brown trout. Rods, flies, boats and guides are all available.

The cabins are comfortable and well-equipped and return charter flights here from Nanyuki are around US$250.

East Africa Ornithological Safaris (see Bird-Watching earlier) also offer flying trips to Lake Rutundu, plus Lake Victoria (for Nile perch) and Malindi (for billfish and sharks). Trips last 11 days and cost a whopping US$6700 per person, based on two people sharing.

For shorter fishing excursions, **Lonrho Hotels Kenya** *(☎ 02-216940, fax 216796; W www.lonrhohotels.com)* offers popular half-day flying trips from the Mara Safari Club to Lake Victoria for Nile perch fishing (US$425 per person) and half-day river and lake fishing trips (for trout) from the Mount Kenya Safari Club (US$29 per person). Similar Lake Victoria trips can be booked through Let's Go Travel.

Cultural Safaris With ecofriendly lodges now springing up all over Kenya, local tribespeople are becoming increasingly involved with tourism, and there are a growing number of companies offering cultural safaris that allow you to interact with the tribes in a far more personal way than the rushed souvenir stops that the mainstream tours make at Maasai villages. The best of these options combine volunteer work with more conventional tour activities and provide accommodation in tents, ecolodges and village houses.

One good company to talk to is **Eco-Resorts** *(☎ 0122-32161; e melinda@eco-re sorts.com; W www.eco-resorts.com; PO Box 120, Watamu)*, which offers a variety of volunteer and cultural packages around Kenya.

Another good company to consider, **Into-Africa** *(☎/fax 0114-255 5610; e enquiry@in toafrica.com; W www.intoafrica.co.uk; 59 Langdon St, Sheffield, UK, S11 8BH)* runs seven- and 14-day 'fair-traded' trips providing insights into African life and directly supporting local communities. Its Wild Kenya and Kenya Insights safaris explore cultures *and* offer wildlife viewing. Accommodation is in hotels, bush camps and also permanent tented camps.

Trips leave on scheduled dates and cost around US$128 per person per day; if you have a group, you can pay more and begin the trip when you want.

Many of the Lake Turkana safaris covered earlier include the opportunity to trek to Rendille and Samburu villages and interact with the tribespeople.

DO-IT-YOURSELF SAFARIS

This is a viable proposition in Kenya if you have some camping equipment and can get a group together to share the costs of renting a vehicle (see Car & 4WD Rental in the Getting Around chapter).

Doing it yourself has several advantages over organised safaris. The main ones are flexibility and being able to choose your travelling companions. The disadvantage is the cost and the fact that whoever is driving is going to be too busy concentrating on the road to notice much of the wildlife. Vehicle breakdowns, security and a lack of local knowledge are also a big worry.

Maps are hard to find, particularly for remote areas, and if you do break down and don't have breakdown cover or have no way of contacting the car-hire company, you're well and truly on your own.

With an appropriate vehicle, all accommodation options are open to you, even out-of-the-way places, and camping and using bandas are two good ways to keep down your costs. **Let's Go Travel** *(☎ 02-340331; e info@letsgosafari.com; W www .letsgosafari.com)* is probably the best outfit to contact for this type of accommodation.

If you want to hire camping equipment (anything from a sleeping bag to a folding toilet seat, tent or mosquito net) the only place to go is **Atul's** *(☎ 02-225935; PO Box 43202, Biashara St, Nairobi)*. Identification, such as a passport, is required and advance booking is recommended and saves time. If you'd like an equipment list before going to Kenya, write ahead. Expect to pay KSh220 per day for a sleeping bag with liner, KSh450 for a two-person dome tent and KSh100 per day for gas stove (gas canisters are extra).

On most items there is a deposit of KSh2000 to KSh3000. For longer trips, it may work out cheaper to buy some things at the big Uchumi supermarkets in Nairobi, which sell cheap plastic plates, stoves, chairs etc.

As far as costs go, it's probably true to say that organising your own safari will cost at least as much, and usually more, than going on a cheap organised safari. It's not a good idea to go on a do-it-yourself safari as just one person; if you do have to change a tyre in lion country, you'll want someone to watch your back!

Nairobi

☎ 02 • pop 2.5 million

Nairobi is a completely modern creation and almost everything here has been built in the last 100 years. Until the 1890s, this was just an isolated swamp, but as the rails of the East Africa railway fell into place across the nation, a depot was established on the edge of a small stream known to the Maasai as *uaso nairobi* (cold water). Nairobi quickly developed into the administrative nerve-centre of the Uganda Railway. In 1901, the capital of the British Protectorate was moved here from Mombasa and the future of the city on the swamp was assured. Even when the first permanent buildings were constructed, Nairobi remained a real frontier town, with rhinos and lions freely roaming the streets and lines of iron-roofed bungalows stretching ignominiously across the plain.

Once the railway was up and running, wealth began to flow into the city. The colonial government built some grand hotels to accommodate the first tourists to Kenya – big game hunters, lured by the attraction of shooting the country's almost naively tame wildlife. There was even a special chair on the front of the train to enable visiting dignitaries to bag lions and elephants on the trip from Mombasa to the capital. Almost all of the colonial-era buildings, though, were replaced by bland modern office buildings during the burst of new construction that followed Uhuru (Independence) in 1963.

Today Nairobi is a busy city of 2.5 million, with large communities of expats, people from the Indian subcontinent and refugees from surrounding nations. It's the largest city between Cairo and Johannesburg and is set to grow bigger, particularly in Nairobi's notorious shantytowns. Kibera, just southwest of the centre, is the largest slum in Africa, home to one-third of the city's population. Poverty and crime here are endemic and even water is provided by illegal pipelines, controlled by local gangsters. The Moi government had a policy of 'relocation', which involved bulldozing the shanties and shifting the hapless occupants to camps further from the city, so it's no surprise that Nairobi has a terrible problem with street crime.

At the other end of the scale are the smart new skyscrapers of downtown and the outer

Highlights

- Stepping back into Kenya's ancient history at the National Museum of Kenya
- Bargaining for souvenirs and curios at the City Market, Westlands Triangle Curios Market and Nairobi's many craft emporiums
- Catching up on Western foods, fashions and films after long trips in the bush at Nairobi's air-con malls and shopping centres

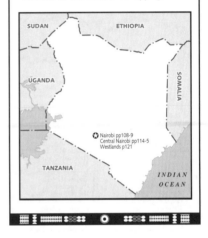

southern garden suburbs of Langata and Karen, which are home to well-heeled English expats and which even resemble English country villages. This area is described in the Nairobi's Southern Outskirts section of the Around Nairobi chapter.

In Nairobi you'll see huge contrasts, with the wealthiest citizens living in Western-style luxury just metres from unskilled workers who earn less than US$1 per day. It's a humbling experience and should give you food for thought about the vast economic divide between Africa and the West.

The central business district is clean, tidy and pleasant, but it doesn't have much atmosphere. More interesting is the busy River Rd area, just one block east of the centre, from where a huge bus and matatu (minibus) network fans out across the nation. The streets here are abuzz with energy, opportunism and aspiration, where office workers, shopkeepers, market traders and

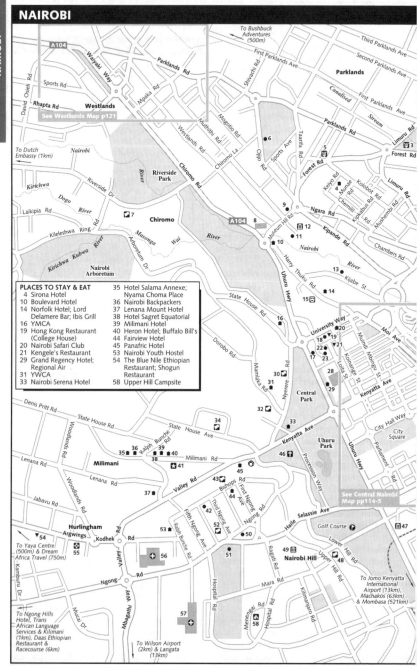

NAIROBI

See Westlands Map p121

See Central Nairobi Map pp114-5

PLACES TO STAY & EAT

4 Sirona Hotel
10 Boulevard Hotel
14 Norfolk Hotel; Lord Delamere Bar; Ibis Grill
16 YMCA
19 Hong Kong Restaurant (College House)
20 Nairobi Safari Club
21 Kengele's Restaurant
29 Grand Regency Hotel; Regional Air
31 YWCA
33 Nairobi Serena Hotel
35 Hotel Salama Annexe; Nyama Choma Place
36 Nairobi Backpackers
37 Lenana Mount Hotel
38 Hotel Sagret Equatorial
39 Milimani Hotel
40 Heron Hotel; Buffalo Bill's
44 Fairview Hotel
45 Panafric Hotel
53 Nairobi Youth Hostel
54 The Blue Nile Ethiopian Restaurant; Shogun Restaurant
58 Upper Hill Campsite

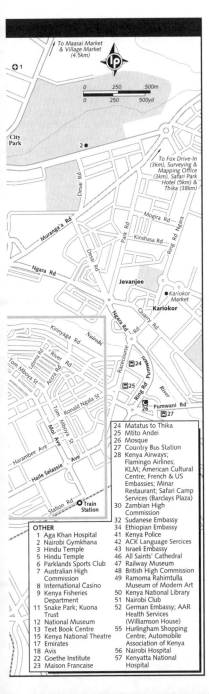

24 Matatus to Thika
25 Mtito Andei
26 Mosque
27 Country Bus Station
28 Kenya Airways;
   Flamingo Airlines;
   KLM; American Cultural
   Centre; French & US
   Embassies; Minar
   Restaurant; Safari Camp
   Services (Barclays Plaza)
30 Zambian High
   Commission
32 Sudanese Embassy
34 Ethiopian Embassy
41 Kenya Police
42 ACK Language Sercices
43 Israeli Embassy
46 All Saints' Cathedral
47 Railway Museum
48 British High Commission
49 Ramoma Rahimtulla
   Museum of Modern Art
50 Kenya National Library
51 Nairobi Club
52 German Embassy; AAR
   Health Services
   (Williamson House)
55 Hurlingham Shopping
   Centre; Automobile
   Association of Kenya
56 Nairobi Hospital
57 Kenyatta National
   Hospital

OTHER
1 Aga Khan Hospital
2 Nairobi Gymkhana
3 Hindu Temple
5 Hindu Temple
6 Parklands Sports Club
7 Australian High
   Commission
8 International Casino
9 Kenya Fisheries
   Department
11 Snake Park; Kuona
   Trust
12 National Museum
14 Text Book Centre
15 Kenya National Theatre
17 Emirates
18 Avis
22 Goethe Institute
23 Maison Francaise

students mingle with budget travellers, street children, vagrants, prostitutes and thieves. Throughout the city, a thin veneer of security is provided by *askaris*, security guards equipped with sticks, who are nonetheless expected to defend shops, households and vehicles against criminals, some of whom tote automatic weapons!

From a traveller's perspective, Nairobi is a place to get business done – be it changing money, arranging visas or organising camping safaris to Kenya's national parks – and to avail yourself of Western luxuries that may be hard to find elsewhere in the region. It's a cosmopolitan place, with cinemas showing Western blockbusters, air-con shopping malls and restaurants serving food from all over the globe. There are also some excellent nightspots where party people can catch up with the latest in Western and African music over an ice-cold Tusker beer. It's a great place to stay for a while and party hard, but stay too long and you'll spend a fortune.

Whatever you do here, you'll need to keep your wits about you. Nairobi is in the grip of a seemingly endless crime-wave, and heavy-handed policing and political disputes often result in violent demonstrations, particularly when the government embarks on one of its slum-clearing sprees. Religious violence is also on the increase. In 1998 the US embassy on Moi Ave was blown up by militants linked to Osama Bin Laden, killing more than 200 Kenyans (see the boxed text 'Embassy Bombings'). More recently, there have been riots between Muslim and Christian youths, linked to the demolition of hawker stalls adjacent to mosques. Another hassle you'll face is persistent touts who roam the streets flogging cheap safaris. Because of these problems, many expats stick to the suburbs, which have huge shopping centres and hundreds of restaurants, bars and shops.

ORIENTATION

The compact city centre is in the area bounded by Uhuru Hwy, Haile Selassie Ave, Tom Mboya St and University Way. Kenyatta Ave divides this area in two; most of the important offices and Nairobi's government offices lie to its south, while there are some top-end and mid-range hotels, the City Market and more offices to its north. The main budget travellers' accommodation is northeast of the centre, on the eastern side of Tom Mboya St. This area has a bad reputation for robbery, so be careful here. Cheap hotels and many matatu depots and bus company offices can be found around Latema, Accra and River Rds. The Country Bus Station, departure point for many destinations on Lake Victoria, is southeast of this area on Landhies Rd, while the train station is just south of the centre near the junction of Moi Ave and Haile Selassie Ave.

Various suburbs surround this area. Southwest of the centre, beyond Uhuru and Central parks, are Upper Hill, Milimani and Hurlingham, with the youth hostel, camp sites and more mid-range hotels. Further out are the expat enclaves of Langata and Karen, Wilson Airport and the main gate to Nairobi National Park. The country's main airport, Jomo Kenyatta International Airport, is southeast of the centre, south along Uhuru Hwy, which continues on to Mombasa. The residential areas to the east of the centre are home to huge refugee communities.

North of the centre are the University of Nairobi, the National Museum, still more top-end hotels, and the expat-dominated suburb of Westlands, home to large European and Indian communities. There are loads of places to eat here and Westlands is easily accessible by matatu from the city centre.

Maps

Of the many available maps of Nairobi – none of which are all that good – the best is probably the *City of Nairobi: Map & Guide* (produced by Survey of Kenya) in English, French and German with a red front cover. It covers the suburbs as well as having a detailed map of the central area, but it's now difficult to get. Also adequate, with hotels and places of interest marked, is the 1:125,000 *Nairobi Map & Guide* (KSh180) published by Tourist Maps.

Much better, though bulkier, is *Nairobi AtoZ* (Kenway Publications; KSh375), by RW Moss. Like the equivalents in other countries, the AtoZ covers the city in detail.

INFORMATION
Tourist Offices

Remarkably, there is no tourist office in Nairobi and you'll have to glean what you can from a handful of free booklets, which take a bit of effort to hunt down. *What's On?* is available from travel agents, airline offices

and some hotels; it has extensive listings. The similar monthly *Going Out* is available on Flamingo Airlines flights and in the Flamingo office in Barclays Plaza on Loita St. Some cinemas have copies of *Going Places* and *Having Fun*, which have similar listings.

The vast noticeboards at the Sarit Centre in Westlands and Yaya Centre in Hurlingham are good places to look for local information. All sorts of things are advertised here, including courses in foreign languages, cars and motorcycles for sale and houses for rent.

Money

At Jomo Kenyatta International Airport there is a branch of **Barclays Bank** *(open 24 hrs daily)*, with an ATM, as well as several Kenyan banks. Barclays has numerous branches (with ATMs) around town that are typically open from 9am to 3pm weekdays and 9am to 11am on the first and last Saturday of each month. Downtown branches with guarded ATMs include those on Mama Ngina St, Muindi Mbingu St and on the corner of Kenyatta and Moi Aves. There are also branches in the Sarit Centre and on Woodvale Grove in Westlands and the Yaya Centre in Hurlingham.

The other big bank here is **Standard Chartered Bank**, which opens the same hours as Barclays and has numerous downtown branches with ATMs; the most convenient is on Kenyatta Ave. For Western Union money transfers, the **Postbank** *(open 8.30am-4pm Mon-Fri & 8.30am-11am Sat)* is on Kenyatta Ave, near Wabera St.

Foreign-exchange bureaus offer slightly better rates for cash. There are dozens of options in the town centre, so it's worth strolling around to see who is currently offering the best deal. Most display the day's rates in the window, with euros, British pounds, US dollars, South African rand, Canadian and Australian dollars, and Ugandan and Tanzanian shillings widely accepted. Options include the following.

Capital Bureau de Change (☎ 251704) Jubilee Insurance Bldg, Wabera St
Crown Bureau de Change (☎ 250720) Mama Ngina St
Goldfield Forex (☎ 244554) Fedha Towers, Kaunda St
Greenland Forex (☎ 246644) Uganda House, Kenyatta Ave
Middletown Forex (☎ 212227) Standard St

If you're up in Westlands, **Travellers Forex Bureau** *(☎ 447204)* in the basement of the Mall shopping centre is a good choice.

American Express *(☎ 222906; Hilton Hotel; open 8.30am-4.30pm Mon-Fri)* buys and sells travellers cheques and looks after mail for clients (see Post & Communications in the Facts for the Visitor chapter).

Post & Communications

Post The vast **main post office** *(Kenyatta Ave; open 8am-6pm Mon-Fri, 9am-noon Sat)* is a well-organised air-con edifice close to Uhuru Park. There's a very basic poste restante service in the same office as the parcel desk, where you'll need to bring your parcels – unwrapped – so the contents can be examined (bring a roll of parcel wrapping paper and parcel tape so you can seal the package once it's been inspected – you can buy these at **Seal Honey**, nearby on Kenyatta Ave). Around the back of the main building is the **EMS** desk, where you can send packages by courier for much less than the rates charged by any of the private couriers.

If you just want stamps, there are **post offices** on Haile Selassie Ave, Moi Ave and Tom Mboya St and in the Sarit Centre and on Mpaka Rd in Westlands. All are open the same hours. The Moi Ave office is a good place to send parcels – packing boxes are available for KSh50 to KSh70.

Of the private couriers, **DHL** *(☎ 534988; International House, ground floor, Mama Ngina St)* is reliable; there's a handy branch in the Sarit Centre, Westlands.

Telephone & Fax Public phones are common in Nairobi but many just don't work. A quieter place to make calls is at **Telkom Kenya** upstairs at the main post office and open the same hours. There are dozens of pay phones here and you can buy phonecards. Many stands downtown sell Telkom Kenya phonecards and top-up cards for prepaid mobile phones (see Post & Communications in the Facts for the Visitor chapter).

Alternatively there are numerous private agencies in the centre of town offering international telephone services. Typical charges for calls or faxes are KSh150 to KSh200 per minute or page to almost anywhere in the world. Try **Danas Communication Centre** *(☎ 223655; 20th Century Cinema Bldg, 1st floor, Mama Ngina St)*. The cheapest option is the Internet-phone (that's calls made over the Internet) and fax service at **Lazards** *(Data Centre Bldg, 3rd floor, Kenyatta Ave; open 7am-10pm daily)*. International phone calls here cost as little as KSh20 per minute to the USA or Europe and international faxes start at KSh60 per page.

Email & Internet Access There are literally hundreds of Internet cafés in downtown Nairobi, most of them tucked away in anonymous office buildings in the town centre. Surfing prices vary from KSh1 to KSh3 per minute and the speed is usually pretty good.

A reliable Internet café is **Capital Realtime** *(☎ 219843; Lonhro House, Standard St; open 8.30am-7.30pm Mon-Fri & 10am-4pm Sat)* with dozens of terminals. Another good place is **Lazards** (see Telephone & Fax earlier), which has lots of terminals. There's an Internet café in the main post office.

The Vine, downstairs in the Mall in Westlands, charges KSh2 per minute, but there are more machines and faster connections at **Cyberking** *(☎ 440644; Madonna House, Westlands Rd)*, which charges KSh2 per minute and is open daily.

At the airport, you can access the Internet at **Bon Voyage** *(☎ 822700)* for KSh4 per minute.

Travel Agencies

One of the best agencies (if not the best) is **Flight Centres** *(☎ 210024, fax 332407; ⓔ fcswwat@arcc.or.ke; Lakhamshi House, 2nd floor, Biashara St)*. This company has been doing discounted air tickets for years and is totally switched on to the backpacker market. It also acts as a broker for camping safaris and runs overland trips across Africa.

Also highly recommended is **Let's Go Travel** *(☎ 340331, fax 336890; ⓔ info@lets gosafari.com; Caxton House, Standard St)*, near Koinange St. There are also branches in Westlands *(☎ 447151, fax 447270; ABC Place, Waiyaki Way)* and Karen shopping centre *(☎ 882505, fax 882171)*. This place is very good for flights, safaris and pretty much anything else you might need. It publishes an excellent price list of hotels, lodges, camps and bandas (huts) in Kenya (which is also on its website ⓦ www.lets gosafari.com), and acts as main booking agent for many off-the-beaten-track and unusual options.

Also very sharp is **Dream Travel Africa** (☎ 572139, fax 577489; e dreamtravel@form -net.com; Galana Rd), just off Argwings Kod-hek Rd. It has set up the ecofriendly Dream Camp in the Masai Mara.

A good upmarket operator with offices around Africa and the Indian Ocean Islands is **Bunson Travel** (☎ 221992, fax 214120; W www.bunson.co.ke; Pan-African Insurance Bldg, Standard St).

Visa Extensions
Visas can be renewed at the **immigration office** (☎ 222022; Nyayo House, cnr Kenyatta Ave & Uhuru Hwy; open 8.30am-12.30pm & 2pm-3.30pm Mon-Fri) – you'll need two passport photos and KSh2200 for a three-month extension and visas are issued the same day (see Visas in the Facts for the Visitor chapter for general information).

Bookshops
Text Book Centre (☎ 449680; Parklands Rd) on the ground floor of the Sarit Centre, West-lands must be one of the best bookshops in East Africa. The selection is enormous, including not only imported Western books and glossy coffee table tomes, but maps and titles by African writers. There is a sister shop on Kijabe St, north of the city centre, but it isn't as well stocked.

Other excellent bookshops include **Book-point** (☎ 211156; Moi Ave), **Book Villa** (☎ 223379; Standard St) and **Westland Sun-dries Bookshop** (☎ 212776; Kenyatta Ave), which has a branch in Westlands (☎ 446406; Ring Rd, Westlands). In the Yaya Centre in Hurlingham, **Bookstop** (☎ 714547) is very well-stocked with coffee table books, maps and new and second-hand novels.

For newspapers and magazines, there are dozens of street hawkers selling current editions of the daily papers and old editions of Western magazines.

Libraries
The main public library in Nairobi is the **Kenya National Library** (☎ 2725550; Ngong Rd; open 8am-6.30pm Mon-Thur, 8am-4pm Fri & 9am-5pm Sat), on the far side of Uhuru Park. There's a smaller collection at the **McMillan Memorial Library** (☎ 221844; Banda St; open 9am-6pm Mon-Fri, 9.30am-4pm Sat), a lovely colonial-era building near the main mosque.

Cultural Centres
All the foreign cultural organisations have libraries open to the public. There's no fee except at the American Cultural Center and the British Council, which you can join as a temporary member for around KSh250. Maison Francaise is particularly good at showcasing Kenyan and African performing arts. Its Le Jardin Cafe serves some of the best coffee in Nairobi. The addresses are:

American Cultural Center (☎ 240290) Barclays Plaza, 3rd floor, Loita St. Open 9am-4.30pm Mon, Tues & Thur, 9am-1pm Wed & 9am-4.15pm Fri
British Council (☎ 334855, e information@britishcouncil.or.ke) ICEA Bldg, 1st floor, Kenyatta Ave. Open 10am-6pm Tues-Fri & 10am-1pm Sat
Goethe Institute (☎ 224640, e bibl-Nairobi@goethe.or.ke) Maendeleo House, cnr Monrovia & Loita Sts. Open 10am-12.30pm Thur-Tues, 2pm-5pm Mon-Fri
Japan African Culture Interchange Institute (☎ 340230, fax 339081, e jinfocul@japan embassy.or.ke) ICEA Bldg, Kenyatta Ave. Open 8.30am-12.30pm & 1.30pm-5pm Mon-Fri
Maison Francaise (☎ 336663, fax 336253, e mfcultural@iconnect.co.ke, W ambafr .iconnect.co.ke, Maison Francaise Bldg, off Loita St. Open 8.30am-6.30pm Mon-Fri & 8.30am-5pm Sat
Nairobi Cultural Institute (☎ 569205) Ngong Rd. It holds lectures and other functions of local cultural interest.

Camping Equipment
If you want to hire camping equipment (any-thing from a sleeping bag to a folding toilet seat) the only place to go is **Atul's** (☎ 225935; Biashara St). The kit available is by no means mountaineering quality, but it will see you through a lightweight camping trip. Rates are not cheap and you'll have to leave a deposit.

Before paying to hire, have a scoot around the big **Uchumi** supermarkets in the Sarit Centre in Westlands and beside the train station. Other good camping suppliers include **Kenya Canvas Ltd** (☎ 333509; Muindi Mbingu St) and **X-treme Outdoors** (☎ 722224; Yaya Centre) in Hurlingham.

Photography
Shops selling and developing film are com-mon across Nairobi (see Photography & Video in the Facts for the Visitor chapter) and most can also do instant passport-size

Embassy Bombings

On a quiet morning in August 1998, the US embassy in Nairobi was torn apart by a massive explosion, which sent debris showering onto Haile Selassie Ave and ripped through office buildings, buses and private cars. Once the smoke had cleared, the full extent of the devastation became apparent; more than 4500 seriously injured and 224 dead, almost all of them Kenyan civilians.

The car-bombing, and the simultaneous bombing of the US embassy in Dar es Salaam, was quickly traced to Islamic militants opposed to America's presence in the Middle East, linked to a then little-known Saudi dissident called Osama Bin Laden. Four suspects from Tanzania, Jordan, Lebanon and Saudi Arabia were subsequently convicted in New York on murder and conspiracy charges.

However, many victims and relatives were angered by the lenient sentences given to the perpetrators, and the compensation awarded to victims of the September 11 attacks in the US have vastly outstripped the meagre payments made to victims of the Kenyan bombing. Another source of contention is the memorial gardens created on the site of the former embassy, which has a KSh20 entrance fee, putting it beyond the reach of many ordinary Kenyans.

With the compensation package set to run out in 2002, there is a growing sense of despair among victims and relatives that contributes to rising anti-American feeling. Many are angrily suggesting that the attacks of September 11 could have been avoided altogether if America had been willing to address threats of terrorism in Africa four years earlier.

---

photographs. Stocks of film are pretty poor outside Nairobi so stock up here before you go on safari. We can recommend **Elite Camera House** (☎ 224521; Kimathi St), near Oakwood Hotel, which offers reductions for bulk purchases. There are plenty more camera shops on Mama Ngina St.

For processing, the best options are **Fuji Colour Centre** (IPS Bldg, Standard St) and **Kodak Photo Xpress** (Fedha Towers, Standard St). Processing and printing costs KSh480 to KSh650 for a 36-exposure film, depending on the print size.

If you're interested in hiring an SLR camera and lenses, contact **Expo Camera Centre** (☎ 336921; e expophoto@africaonline.co.ke). There's a branch on Mpaka St in Westlands (☎ 441253).

Laundry

Laundries are few and far between in Nairobi. Most people rely on the laundry services offered by most hotels (although these are priced by the item and can work out pretty expensive). One of the few laundrettes in Nairobi is **Lavage Laundrette & Dry Cleaners** (☎ 227196; Mpaka Rd, Westlands), which will wash and dry your clothes for KSh110 per kilogram; drop your laundry off by 8am if you want it back the same day.

For dry cleaning, try **White Rose Drycleaners** (☎ 227724; Kenyatta Ave), across

the road from the main post office. There are numerous other branches across Nairobi.

Medical Services

There is a **doctor's surgery** (☎ 333977; Bruce House, 3rd floor, Standard St; open 8.30am-4.30pm Mon-Fri) that is used to travellers turning up convinced they have the ebola virus and the like. For a consultation and blood tests you'll pay around KSh1800. There's a **dentist** on the same floor.

KAM Pharmacy (☎ 251700; Executive Tower, IPS Bldg, Kimathi St) is a one-stop shop for medical treatment. There's a pharmacy on the ground floor, a doctor's surgery on the 1st floor and a laboratory on the 2nd. Consultations cost KSh1000.

Otherwise go to outpatients at either **Nairobi Hospital** (☎ 722160) off Valley Rd or the **Aga Khan Hospital** (☎ 740000; Third Parklands Ave). Avoid the Kenyatta National Hospital because, although it's free, stretched resources mean you may come out with something worse than what you went in with.

AAR Health Services (☎ 715319; Williamson House, Fourth Ngong Ave) is probably the best of a number of private ambulance and emergency air-evacuation companies (see Travel Insurance in the Facts for the Visitor chapter). It also runs a private clinic (☎ 446201) at the Sarit Centre in Westlands.

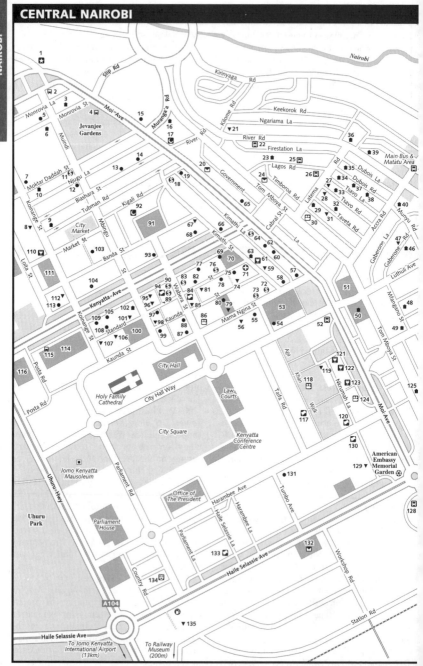

CENTRAL NAIROBI

CENTRAL NAIROBI

NAIROBI

```
0       125      250m
0       125      250yd
```

PLACES TO EAT
8 Alan Bobbe's Bistro
21 Supreme Restaurant; Mayur Restaurant
27 Prestige Palace
28 New Flora Restaurant; Friendship Corner
31 Taj
47 Malindi Dishes
56 Nairobi Java House
59 Burger Dome
67 The Smart Place
74 Tanager Chinese Restaurant
79 Pekeshe Coffee House; Expo Camera House; (Jubilee Insurance Exchange Building)
81 Pasara Cafe; Capital Realtime Internet; South African Embassy; South African Airways
85 Trattoria
95 Simmers
96 La Scala
98 Panda Chinese Restaurant; Goldfield Forex
101 Restaurant Akasaka
106 Dragon Pearl
107 Beneve Coffee House
112 Mandy's
119 Seasons Restaurant
129 Tamarind Restaurant
135 Nyama Choma Stands

OTHER
1 Police
2 Davanu Shuttle (Windsor House)
4 Bus Stop (for Westlands)
5 Kenya Bus Service Office
7 Gametrackers Ltd
11 Barclays Bank
12 Kenya Canvas Ltd
13 Atul's (Camping Gear)
14 Flight Centres
15 Eastern & Southern Safaris
17 Khoja Mosque
18 Standard Chartered Bank
19 Glory Car Hire
20 Post Office
22 Scandinavia Express
24 Post Office
25 Akamba Bus Office
26 Coastline Safaris
30 Odeon Cinema
41 Falcon; Interstate 2000 Offices
42 Narok Line & Molo Line Services
43 Crossland Services
44 Matatus to Naivasha & Namanga (Tanzania)
45 Buses to Kisii & Migori
51 National Archives
52 Metro Shuttle Bus Stand
54 Budget Car Hire
55 British Airways; DHL; Swiss, Italian, Spanish & Rwandan Embassies (International House)
57 Yare Safaris
58 Best Camping Safaris

PLACES TO STAY
3 Parkside Hotel
6 Comfort Inn
9 Embassy Hotel
10 Terminal Hotel; Dove Cage Restaurant; Down Town Hotel
16 Meridian Court Hotel
23 Marble Arch Hotel
29 Iqbal Hotel
32 Oriental Palace Hotel
33 Hotel Greton
34 Nyandarua Lodging
35 Safety Line Lodge
36 New Kenya Lodge
37 Hotel Africana
38 Wilton Gateway Hotel
39 Evamay Lodge
40 Sirikwa Hotel
46 Abbey Hotel
48 Orchid Hotel
49 Terrace Hotel
50 Ambassadeur Hotel; Hornbill Pub
53 Hilton Hotel; Jockey Pub; American Express; Kumbu Kumbu
63 Oakwood Hotel; Adventures Aloft; Elite Camera House
70 New Stanley Hotel, Thorn Tree Cafe
102 Sixeighty Hotel; Central Car Hire
125 Princess Hotel

60 Primetime Safaris
61 Taco
62 Planet Safari Adventures; Sana Highlands Trekking Expeditions
64 Barclays Bank
65 Bookpoint
66 Nakumatt Supermarket
68 Saferide Safaris
69 Westlands Sundries Bookshop
71 Doctor's Surgery; KAM Pharmacy
72 Crown Bureau de Change
73 Barclays Bank
75 Fuji Colour Centre; Book Villa
76 Middletown Forex
77 Riverside Shuttle; Savuka Tours & Safaris
78 Gallery Watatu
80 Safari Seekers
81 Bunson Travel
83 Standard Chartered Bank
84 Austrian Embassy
86 20th Century Cinema; Dancing Spoon; Danas Communication Centre
87 Kenia Tours & Safaris
88 Akamba Bus Office; Capital Bureau de Change
89 Greenland Forex
90 Postbank
91 McMillan Memorial Library
92 Jamaa Mosque
93 British Council; Japanese Embassy (ICEA Building)
94 Ugandan High Commission
97 Kodak Photo Express; UTC
99 Hertz
100 Bruce House; Doctors Surgery; Calypso; Ethiopian Airlines; Abercrombie & Kent
103 Pan-African Gallery
104 Codelink; Kenya Youth Voluntary Development Projects
105 Lazards
108 Let's Go Travel
109 Big Five Tours & Safaris; Seal Honey
110 New Florida
111 Air Tanzania
113 White Rose Drycleaners
114 Main Post Office; Telkom Kenya
115 Bus & Matatu Stop (for Hurlingham & Milimani)
116 Immigration (Nyayo House)
117 Tanzanian Embassy; Walkers
118 Nairobi Cinema
120 Congo (Zaïre) Embassy
121 Green Corner
122 Taco Bell
123 Florida 2000; Water Margin
124 Kenya Cinema Plaza; Zanze Bar
126 KBS Bus Station
127 Uchumi Supermarket
128 Matatus to Wilson Airport; Nairobi National Park; Langata & Karen
130 Indian High Commission; Air India
131 Treasury
132 Post Office
133 Canadian Embassy
134 Professional Centre

NAIROBI

Emergency

For the police or an ambulance, call ☎ 999 but don't rely on their prompt arrival. For less urgent police business call ☎ 240000. In a medical emergency call the **Aga Khan Hospital** (☎ 740000). It's reliable and has a 24-hour casualty section. The Amref flying-doctor service is on ☎ 501280 and AAR Health Services are on ☎ 717376.

NATIONAL MUSEUM

This museum (☎ 742131, fax 741424; W www .museums.or.ke; Museum Rd; adult/child KSh200/100; open 9.30am-6pm daily) off Museum Hill Rd is well worth an afternoon's look. Housed in a grand building set in leafy grounds, the museum has an interesting range of cultural and natural history exhibits. One of the major attractions is the Peoples of Kenya series of tribal portraits by Joy Adamson (of *Born Free* fame). They are a fantastic record and an amazing achievement. Upstairs are huge galleries of stuffed birds (at least 900 specimens) and animals, and good ethnographical displays on the various Kenyan tribal groups. Downstairs, there are re-creations of rock art from Tanzania, an exhibition of hominid fossils from Lake Turkana, and fossil, mineral and shell displays. There are temporary exhibits in the outlying gallery, covering topics such as Swahili and Indian subcontinent culture in Kenya. Local artists exhibit in the Gallery of Contemporary East African Art. Volunteer guides offer tours in English, German, Spanish and French; it's worth booking them in advance and there's no direct charge for their services, although a donation to the museum is appropriate.

In the grounds, there's a **snake park** (adult/child KSh200/100; open 9.30am-6pm daily) where you can see black mambas, some sad-looking crocodiles and giant *dudus* (creepy crawlies – see the boxed text 'Dudus' in The Coast chapter). Nearby is the **Kuona Trust**, a nonprofit art studio where Kenyan artists can gather and express themselves. You're welcome to wander around but ask before taking photos. The guided nature trail in the grounds isn't particularly exciting.

NATIONAL ARCHIVES

Opposite the Ambassadeur Hotel is the distinctive **National Archives** (☎ 749341; Moi Ave; open 8.30am-4.30pm Mon-Fri, 8.30am-1pm Sat). It's a grand building and the gallery inside features documents and an interesting collection of photographs and paintings of Mzee Kenyatta and former President Moi visiting different countries and shaking hands with dignitaries. There are also displays of handicrafts.

RAILWAY MUSEUM

Reached by a long lane beside the train station or a short cut across the vacant land next to the Shell petrol station on Haile Selassie Ave is this interesting little **museum** (Station Rd; adult/student/child KSh200/100/20; open 8.15am-4.45pm daily). The main collection is housed in an old railway building, and consists of relics from the East African Railway. There are train and ship models, photographs, tableware and oddities from the history of the railway, which include the Engine Seat that allowed visiting dignitaries such as Theodore Roosevelt to shoot wildlife from the front of the train.

Nairobbery

Nairobi, or 'Nairobbery' as it is often referred to by residents, is now regarded as the most dangerous city in Africa, beating Johannesburg two years running for all acts of crime. There are robberies, muggings and car-jackings every day in the city, and a recent survey revealed that 37% of Nairobi residents had been mugged in the past year!

However, the majority of these crimes happen in the suburbs or shantytowns. The area bound by Kenyatta Ave, Moi Ave, Haile Selassie Ave and Uhuru Hwy is comparatively safe, if you follow a few simple precautions as suggested in Dangers & Annoyances in the Facts for the Visitor chapter.

Danger zones include the area around Latema and River Rds – unfortunately, where many bus depots and budget hotels are located – and Uhuru Park, which divides the Milimani Rd area from downtown.

During the day, you should just about be alright if you don't show any obvious signs of wealth, but at night mugging is a risk anywhere. Take a taxi, even if you're only going a few blocks. This will also keep you safe from the attentions of Nairobi's prostitutes, who flood into downtown after dark.

In the grounds are dozens of fading locos in various states of disrepair, dating from the steam days to Independence (which puts the newer trains on a par with those still being used on the Nairobi to Mombasa line). You can walk around the carriages at your leisure. At the back of the compound is the steam train used in the movie *Out of Africa*. It's a fascinating introduction to this important piece of colonial history.

PARLIAMENT HOUSE

If you fancy a look at how democracy works in Kenya, it's possible to obtain a permit for a seat in the public gallery at **parliament house** *(☎ 221291; Parliament Rd)*. If parliament is out of session, you can tour the buildings by arrangement with the sergeant-at-arms.

MZIZI ARTS CENTRE

This arts centre *(☎ 785086; Buru Buru centre, 5th Floor, Mumias South Rd)* is a good place to view contemporary Kenyan art, craft, dance, literature and performance art. 'Cultural Personality Evenings' (when Kenyan cultural stars give lectures) and sigana performances are held here (see Entertainment in the Facts for the Visitor chapter for more information on the performing arts).

ART GALLERIES

There are few public art galleries in Nairobi, but several shops here sell work by local artists and welcome browsers. At the National Museum, the **Gallery of Contemporary East African Art** is worth a look. In Upper Hill, **Ramoma Rahimtulla Museum of Modern Art** *(☎ 729181; Rahimtulla Tower, Upper Hill Rd)*, is a small gallery that promotes and sells work by Kenyan artists. Of the private galleries, the longest established is **Gallery Watatu** *(☎ 228737; Lonrho House, Standard St)* and it has regular exhibitions and a permanent display.

Work by many contemporary Kenyan and African artists are often displayed in the foreign cultural centres and in various museums.

KENYATTA CONFERENCE CENTRE

It's well worth visiting this grand architectural statement of Kenyan independence on the City Square. The building is looking a little worn these days, but the **viewing platform** *(adult/child KSh200/100)* on the roof offers wonderful views over Nairobi. You can really appreciate how small Nairobi is from up here, and on clear days, you can see aircraft coming in to land over the Nairobi National Park. You're allowed to take photographs from the viewing level but not elsewhere in the building. Access is sometimes restricted when there's a conference in progress.

CLUBS & SOCIETIES

There are lots of specialist clubs and societies in Nairobi and many of them welcome visitors.

East African Wildlife Society (☎ 574145) Riara Rd, Kilimani, PO Box 20110. This society is at the forefront of conservation efforts in East Africa and publishes an interesting bimonthly magazine, *Swara*. Annual membership costs KSh3000, which includes subscription to *Swara* (US$65 if you want the magazine sent by airmail rather than surface mail).

Friends of Nairobi National Park (Fonnap; ☎ 500622, fax 505866) Kenya Wildlife Service (KWS) Headquarters, Langata Rd, PO Box 42076. The society aims to protect the migration routes between the Masai Mara and the national park. Annual membership is US$30 and there are meetings on the first Sunday of every month at the main gate of Nairobi National Park, usually with a guest speaker.

Mountain Club of Kenya (MCK; ☎ 501747, W www.mck.or.ke) Wilson Airport; PO Box 45741. The club meets at 8pm every Tuesday at the clubhouse at Wilson Airport. Members organise frequent climbing and trekking weekends around the country and have a huge pool of technical knowledge about climbing in Kenya.

East Africa Natural History Society (aka Nature Kenya; ☎ 3749957, W www.naturekenya.org) National Museum of Kenya, off Museum Hill Rd, PO Box 44486. Members meet outside Nairobi Museum at 8.45am every Wednesday for enjoyable half-day bird-watching outings close to town. Annual membership is KSh500.

Sports

The following private clubs offer facilities for tennis, squash and cricket and some also cater for football and hockey. All are out in the 'burbs and tend to be rather snooty. Membership fees of up to KSh800 per day apply.

Impala Club (☎ 565684) Ngong Rd
Nairobi Club (☎ 725726) Ngong Rd
Nairobi Gymkhana (☎ 741310) Cnr Rwathia & Forest Rds
Parklands Sports Club (☎ 745164) Ojijo Rd

NAIROBI

SWIMMING POOLS

Most international tourist hotels have swimming pools that can be used by nonguests for a daily fee of between KSh200 and KSh500. Hotels with heated pools near the city centre include **Norfolk Hotel** (☎ 250900; Harry Thuku Rd), **Nairobi Safari Club** (☎ 251333; University Way), **Grand Regency Hotel** (☎ 211199; Loita St) and **Milimani Hotel** (☎ 2722358; Milimani Rd, Milimani).

ORGANISED TOURS

There's not much to see in downtown Nairobi, but most of the travel agents and safari operators in Nairobi (see the Safaris chapter for details of tour operators) can take you on a tour of the National and Railway Museums, parliament and the market for around US$35. Also popular are trips to suburban attractions, such as Nairobi National Park (US$55), the Bomas of Kenya (US$40) or the Karen Blixen Museum and Langata Giraffe Sanctuary (US$45) – see the Around Nairobi chapter for more on these attractions. The Safari chapter also details longer tours/safaris operating out of Nairobi.

For an introduction to the world of *jua kali* – Kenya's open-air manufacturing industry – **People to People Tourism** (☎ 781531, fax 330170; ⓦ www.peopletopeopletourism .com) combines tours of the usual tourist sights with visits to *jua kali* workshops producing crafts and other goods.

PLACES TO STAY – BUDGET
Camping

Highly recommended is **Upper Hill Campsite** (☎ 720290; campsite@alphanet.co.ke; Menengai Rd, Upper Hill; camping per person KSh250, dorm beds KSh250-300, singles/ doubles KSh600/800), off Hospital Rd near the Indonesian embassy. It offers camping and rooms in a pleasant and secure compound and there's a great little restaurant and bar. There is always an interesting group of backpackers and overlanders in residence. Facilities include hot showers, a fireplace with comfortable chairs, and a collection of books and games. There's an area where you can carry out vehicle maintenance and the owners can help you find a mechanic. The city is a 15-minute walk away or you can take bus or matatu No 18 from Kenyatta Ave to the Kenyatta National Hospital, which is just around the corner.

Another fine option is the camping ground of Nairobi Park Services, located just west of Nairobi National Park. See Nairobi National Park in the Around Nairobi chapter for details.

Youth Hostels & Backpackers

Between Valley and Ngong Rds, **Nairobi Youth Hostel** (☎ 2723012; Ralph Bunche Rd, Upper Hill; beds in 16-bed dorm KSh400, in 3- or 4-bed room KSh450, in twins KSh500, 3-person self-catering flats KSh1500) is well looked-after and is a good place to meet other travellers. The dorms and rooms are spotlessly clean and open all day, and the showers are always wonderfully hot. The flats have a small kitchen and sleep three but are often booked up. A year's membership to Hostelling International (HI) costs KSh400, or you can pay a KSh100 surcharge per day. The friendly wardens will lock up gear safely for a small charge and there's a restaurant, TV room and safari desk. The notice board here is also worth a look for travel partners, things to sell etc. Any matatu or bus going down either Valley or Ngong Rds will drop you off at Ralph Bunche Rd. Many people have been robbed returning to the youth hostel by foot after dark; always take a matatu or taxi during this time.

YMCA (☎ 2724116; ⓔ ymca@iconnect .co.ke; State House Rd; self-contained singles/ doubles KSh940/1480; singles/doubles with shared bathroom KSh690/1180) is an OK place with secure parking and a range of passable rooms. Rates include the daily membership fee.

YWCA (☎ 724699; ⓔ ywca@iconnect.co .ke; Mamlaka Rd; rooms with bathroom KSh650-1200), off Nyerere Rd, is a poorer choice. The grounds are a mess and the rooms are overpriced. There are usually rooms for women available, but most of the men's rooms are booked out long-term by students. There's a big, popular cafeteria, though.

Nairobi Backpackers (☎ 724827; ⓔ nbo backpackers@yahoo.com; Milimani Rd, Milimani; dorm beds KSh500, singles/twins KSh1000/1200), near Hotel Salama Annexe, is a comfortable house with clean airy rooms, but slightly high rates. It's set in a secure garden and rooms are spotless. Rates include breakfast.

Hotels – City Centre

There are numerous budget hotels in Nairobi between Tom Mboya St and River Rd. The area is a bit rough, so you'll have to be careful with your belongings when you walk around, and always take taxis at night. Security problems aside, these places are handy for the buses and close to the centre, but all suffer from water shortages and there's often only water for a couple of hours a day.

New Kenya Lodge (☎ 222202, fax 603560; River Rd; dorm beds KSh250, singles with shared bathroom KSh300, singles/doubles with bathroom KSh500/600) at the Latema Rd intersection is a bit of a legend among budget travellers and is still cheap, although it's past its best. Accommodation is basic but clean and there's supposedly hot water in the evenings. There's a good notice board here and the lodge also runs its own safaris, although we've had bad reports. If it's full, they can put you up in the **New Kenya Lodge Annexe** around the corner on Duruma Rd.

Iqbal Hotel (☎ 220914; Latema Rd; dorm beds KSh280, singles/doubles/triples KSh400/600/960) has been popular for years and its probably the best of the cheapies. The rooms are basic but passable and the shared bathrooms are clean. There's supposedly hot water in the morning but you have to be up early. Baggage is safe and there's a storeroom where you can leave excess gear for KSh40 per day. It's very secure and the askari (security guard) can arrange taxis at reasonable prices.

Two other places on Dubois Rd, just off Latema Rd, are **Nyandarua Lodging** and the plainer **Safety Line Lodge** (☎ 221578). At around KSh250/300 for singles/doubles, they are much cheaper than the Iqbal, but the single rooms are just glorified closets.

Most of the other rock-bottom hotels in this area are brothels or somewhere for drunks with a few shillings left to sleep off their hangovers, and can't be recommended.

Princess Hotel (☎ 214640; Tom Mboya St; singles KSh500-650, doubles KSh800) has OK rooms despite the dingy foyer, and the staff are friendly. Rooms are bright and come with bathroom, and the cost includes a good breakfast. The hotel has its own bar and restaurant with good food.

Terrace Hotel (☎ 221636; Ronald Ngala St; singles/doubles/triples KSh450/700/1200) has worn but spacious and clean rooms with bathroom and hot water. There's a butchery, bar and restaurant where you can get stews and nyama choma (barbecued meat) for under KSh100.

Hotel Africana (☎ 220654, fax 331886; Dubois Rd; singles/doubles/triples KSh450/600/900) has clean bright rooms and is quite well looked after. For some reason, only the 2nd floor gets hot water in the mornings, so the rooms on the 1st and 3rd floors are cheaper! The Coffee House restaurant here specialises in Indian vegetarian food.

Orchid Hotel (formerly Dolat Hotel; ☎ 228 663; Mfangano St; singles/doubles/triple with bathroom KSh610/735/1200) is one of the best places in the budget category. Rooms are large and bright and have reliable hot water and quite a few travellers stay here. The staff are friendly and it's good value for money.

Sirikwa Hotel (☎ 226687; cnr Munyu & Accra Rds; singles/doubles/triples KSh600/800/1250) is also a good place, although perhaps overpriced. Rooms are clean and have hot water, a bathroom and a phone. Security is good and there's a TV room. Breakfast is available for KSh100 per person.

Wilton Gateway Hotel (☎ 341664, fax 341627; Dubois Rd; singles/doubles with bathroom KSh600/800) is a decent hotel used by Kenyan salesmen, with a bar and restaurant and comfortable rooms.

PLACES TO STAY – MID-RANGE
City Centre – East of Moi Ave

Opposite Malindi Dishes, **Abbey Hotel** (☎ 243256, fax 247729; Gaberone Rd; singles/doubles with bathroom KSh950/1350) is a good central choice. Rooms are spacious and light and there's hot water on demand (although with a slightly scary-looking heater plugged into the shower head). It has a nice atmosphere despite being in the thick of the action. There's a butchery, bar and restaurant where you can get cheap Kenyan food, including nyama choma. The rates include breakfast.

Evamay Lodge (☎ 212784, fax 212605; cnr River & Duruma Rds; singles/doubles/triples with bathroom KSh700/1000/1300) is not bad value and prices include breakfast. The hot water is reliable here.

Hotel Greton (☎ 242893/4, fax 242892; Tsavo Rd; singles/doubles/triples KSh950/1200/1700) is a quiet and friendly place between Latema and Accra Rds. The rooms are old but comfortable and have hot showers. Rates include breakfast.

Ambassadeur Hotel (☎ 335803, fax 336 860; Tom Mboya St; singles/doubles/triples US$39/50/69), right opposite the National Archives, is a vast hotel that's become a local institution. Rooms have TV, phones and a bathtub; they are chintzy but comfortable.

North of Latema Rd are several mid-range hotels in this downmarket part of town. Some are overpriced, but the following two places are good value.

Marble Arch Hotel (☎ 245656, fax 245724; e marblearchhotel@swiftkenya.com; Lagos Rd; singles/doubles/triples KSh3600/5400/6600, suite KSh9750) is a very popular conference hotel with good facilities, including a vast restaurant, a bar and a coffee shop. It's got a lively atmosphere, but can get a bit frantic when the Mombasa Baptist Church, Nairobi Association of Small Businesses and Bible Truth Society are all in town! Rooms have wall-to-wall carpets, TV, phone and a real bathtub. Room rates include breakfast.

Meridian Court Hotel (☎ 333916, fax 333658; Muranga'a Rd; e meridian@arcc .or.ke; singles/doubles/triples KSh3200/3900/4200) is fantastic value for money. The vast suite-like rooms have a fridge, phone, a lounge with a TV and a tub with 24-hour hot water. Rooms are spotless and there's a sports bar with pool tables and a Chinese restaurant.

City Centre – West of Moi Ave

Terminal Hotel (☎ 228817, fax 220075; Moktar Daddah St; singles/doubles/triples with bathroom KSh1000/1300/1600) is easily the best option in this price range. Staff are friendly and helpful and the rooms are clean, spacious and well-appointed. Soap, towels and toilet paper are provided and there's hot water around the clock. Security is excellent, rooms are fairly quiet and there's a notice board downstairs. The Dove Cage restaurant next door (see Places to Eat) is a popular meeting place for travellers and overland groups. Children with adults are charged KSh50 per day. You can store excess baggage here for KSh30 per article per day.

Down Town Hotel (☎ 310485, fax 310435; Moktar Daddah St; singles/doubles KSh1000/1200), nearby, has a few more frills, but isn't quite as welcoming. It's still a good choice though, and the rooms have mosquito nets and bathrooms with reliable hot water.

Embassy Hotel (☎ 224087, fax 224534; Tubman Rd; singles/doubles/triples KSh1000/1500/1600) is a somewhat older place opposite the city market. All rooms have bathroom, hot water, soap, towels and toilet paper. The hotel has its own bar and restaurant where you can get meals and breakfast.

Parkside Hotel (☎ 214154, fax 334681; Monrovia St; singles/doubles/triples KSh1500/2100/2800) is opposite Jevanjee Gardens and is another good choice. Staff are very friendly and the hotel has a restaurant. All rooms have bathrooms with hot showers and it's very popular with volunteer workers. Breakfast is included (although bed only costs KSh200 less per person).

Comfort Inn (☎ 316666, fax 317610; cnr Muindi Mbingu & Monrovia Sts; singles/doubles/triples/quads US$25/40/50/60) is an extremely comfortable new hotel that is already gaining a reputation with travellers and volunteer workers. There's a bar, restaurant and coffee shop (serving great breakfasts – see Places to Eat) and rooms are nicely furnished, with bathroom and phone. Rates include breakfast.

Oakwood Hotel (☎ 220592, fax 332170; Kimathi St; singles/doubles/triples US$50/66/70) in the heart of town, opposite the New Stanley Hotel, is a fine choice. It's a little expensive, but the panelled-wood interior is attractive and the location is excellent. All the rooms have bathroom, TV and phone, and breakfast is included. The same owners run the Fig Tree Lodge in the Masai Mara.

Sixeighty Hotel (☎ 332680, fax 332908; Muindi Mbingu St; doubles from KSh2400) is a comfortable, modern hotel in the thick of things.

Milimani & Hurlingham

Most of the mid-range hotels in this area are along Milimani, Ralph Bunche and Bishops Rds. Many are popular with travellers as well as UN staff and other nongovernmental organisations.

Heron Hotel (☎ 720740, fax 721698; e herco@iconnect.co.ke; Milimani Rd; singles/doubles KSh750/890, 1-bedroom single/double apartment KSh1750/2400, 2-bedroom apartment KSh3800) is perched behind the infamous Buffalo Bill's. The facilities here are very good, but with the red-light antics going on out front, the atmosphere is a little seedy. Also, there have been reports of thefts from rooms here. If you feel like taking the risk, all rooms have bathrooms with hot water and there's a swimming pool and sauna.

Milimani Hotel (☎ 2722358, fax 2724685; Milimani Rd; singles/doubles KSh3500/5000), next door, is a decent business-class hotel tucked in among apartment buildings. It's popular with expats and facilities include a swimming pool (nonguests KSh150), bar, beer garden, restaurant and guarded parking. Rates include breakfast. The service is very good. Meals in the restaurant cost KSh450 for a buffet lunch and KSh600 for dinner.

Hotel Sagret Equatorial (☎ 2720933; Milimani Rd; singles/doubles with bathroom KSh1925/2750), near Ralph Bunche Rd, is a big pastel-coloured Art Deco hotel. It's quite atmospheric but expensive for what you get. Rates include breakfast. The hotel has its own bar and restaurant (very popular for nyama choma) and there's guarded parking.

Hotel Salama Annexe (☎ 2729272; Milimani Rd; singles/doubles KSh1200/1500, camping per person KSh150-200), where Milimani Rd turns into a dirt road, is a quieter place with a nyama choma restaurant. It's rather old-looking but there's secure

parking and it's possible to camp here. Room rates include breakfast.

Lenana Mount Hotel (☎ 717044, fax 719394; e lenanamounthotel@iconnect.co .ke; singles/doubles KSh2900/4000), not far away on Ralph Bunche Rd, is great value for money. Tidy and spacious rooms have phone and satellite TV, and there's secure parking and a pool.

Fairview Hotel (☎ 2711321, fax 2721320; e reserv@fairviewkenya.com; Bishops Rd; singles/doubles from KSh4900/6900, family room per double KSh7400, plus KSh1800 per child under 12) is one of the best places in this price range. Behind Panafric Hotel and surrounded by pleasant gardens, it caters mainly for businesspeople and families, but makes a good first port of call when arriving in the country. There are a number of different classes of room all with bathroom, satellite TV and phones. All prices include breakfast, with the lunch/dinner buffet costing KSh900/1000. There's a good pool, too.

Parklands & Westlands

Sirona Hotel (☎/fax 742730; Kolobot Rd, Parklands; singles/doubles US$30/40), on the

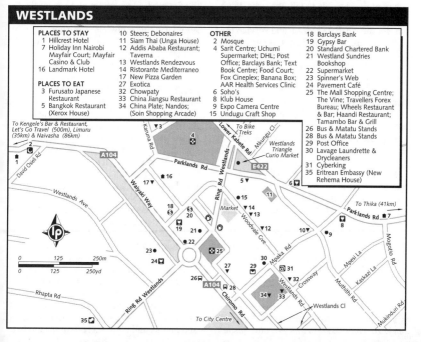

fringes of this residential area north of the National Museum, is a popular choice. Safari companies sometimes use this hotel to accommodate their clients. It's a pleasant and peaceful hotel, with a large open-plan restaurant and bar area with a pool table and a relaxing beer garden, although it's a little tired-looking. Safe parking is available.

Considering the number of restaurants and shopping centres in Westlands, it's surprising how little accommodation there is here. **Hillcrest Hotel** (☎ 448046, fax 444208; *Waiyaki Way, Westlands; singles/doubles with bathroom KSh1400/1800*) is the only mid-range choice. It's set in a grounds just back from Waiyaki Way. Rooms are clean and well maintained and the general atmosphere is pleasant and relaxed. There's a restaurant and safe parking.

PLACES TO STAY – TOP-END

In a city the size of Nairobi there are naturally many top-of-the-range hotels, but you don't always get the same standard of luxury that you get from similar hotels in other countries. You may get a better deal if you book through a travel agent. In the low season, you *may* be able to talk the rates down. All the following rates include breakfast, but *not* the steep 28% VAT and service tax.

Several exclusive little hotels can also be found in the wealthy southern outer suburbs of Langata and Karen. For details, see the Around Nairobi chapter.

City Centre

Most of Nairobi's best hotels are clustered around the town centre.

New Stanley Hotel (☎ 228830, fax 229388; *e gm@thestanley.sarova.com; cnr Kimathi St & Kenyatta Ave; singles/doubles US$195/210*) is as central as you can get. There's been a Stanley Hotel in Nairobi since 1902, but the current site has only been in use since 1912 and the latest version of the Stanley is quite a modern construction. It still has a certain colonial charm though, and there's a popular restaurant, coffee shop and bar. Rooms are decked out in mock-Victorian style and have air-con, cable TV and phone. Facilities include a rooftop swimming pool, two restaurants, a pub and a ballroom.

The **Hilton Hotel** (☎ 250000, fax 250099; *e rm_nairobi@hilton.com; Mama Ngina St; singles/doubles US$170/210, executive singles/ doubles with complimentary bar US$230/ 265*), with its distinctive towers on the corner of Moi Ave, has all the usual Hilton facilities including a rooftop swimming pool, restaurant and well-appointed rooms.

Grand Regency Hotel (☎ 211199, fax 217120; *e gregency@africaonline.co.ke; between Loita St & Uhuru Hwy; singles/doubles from US$200/240*) is a well-located upmarket place. For these rates you get comfortable rooms, a pool, restaurant and bar.

Nairobi Safari Club (☎ 251333, fax 224625; *e info@nairobisafariclub.com; University Way; suites singles/doubles from US$180/220*), in Lilian Towers, is a vast and very exclusive luxury hotel. All the rooms here are suites and the price includes taxes and temporary membership to the club, which qualifies you for almost nothing. The pool is free but you'll have to pay KSh800 per day to use the gym and health centre.

Nairobi Serena Hotel (☎ 313800, fax 725184; *e nairobi@serena.co.ke; singles/ doubles US$275/325, suites US$400-700*), on the edge of Central Park between Kenyatta Ave and Nyerere Rd, is a recent creation and imaginatively designed. It's owned by the Serena Lodges group and has all the facilities you'd expect from a five-star hotel. Avoid walking anywhere from here at night. Meals cost US$14 (breakfast), US$20 (lunch) and US$22 (dinner) plus taxes.

Norfolk Hotel (☎ 250900, fax 336742; *Harry Thuku Rd; singles/doubles in main block US$250/290, suites US$320-500*), just outside the city centre, is Nairobi's oldest hotel. Built in 1904, it was *the* place to stay during colonial days. It's still extremely popular among those with a taste for nostalgia and money to spend. The old-world charm has been retained despite the fact that facilities have been brought up to modern international standards. Breakfast is US$17 and lunch and dinner are US$22. The stylish Ibis Grill Restaurant is one of the best in Kenya, and the Lord Delamere terrace bar and restaurant is a great place for a drink and snack.

Boulevard Hotel (☎ 227567, fax 334071; *e hotel@hotelboulevardkenya.com; Harry Thuku Rd; singles/doubles/triples KSh5140/ 6680/7980*), near the junction of Uhuru Hwy and Museum Hill Rd, is a little further from the centre. Set in a large garden, the hotel offers rooms with bathroom, balcony and phone, and there's a restaurant and beer garden. Matatus used to lose control on Chiromo Rd and plunge into the swimming pool here quite regularly, but there's now a heavy-duty fence to protect bathers.

Milimani
Panafric Hotel (☎ 720822, fax 726356; e gm@ panafric.sarova.co.ke; Kenyatta Ave; singles/ doubles/triples US$82/107/119), part of the Sarova Hotels chain, is across Uhuru Park from the downtown area. It's a large, multi-storey and modern hotel with all the facilities you'd expect. The service is good here.

Westlands
Landmark Hotel (☎ 448713/7, fax 446159; e landmark@africaonline.co.ke; singles/doubles US$122/150), which belongs to the Block Hotels chain, is off Waiyaki Way. It's a well-run hotel and it's better value than the places in the city centre. There's a pool and several restaurants, and guests are offered a free shuttle bus between the hotel and downtown.

Holiday Inn Nairobi Mayfair Court (☎ 3740920, fax 3748823; e ekatam@africa online.co.ke; Parklands Rd; singles/doubles US$110/125) is tucked between the suburbs of Westlands and Parklands. It is a large, colonial-style hotel situated in beautifully maintained grounds. There are two swimming pools, restaurants, a health club and boutiques, while the Mayfair Casino & Club is just next door.

Thika Road
Safari Park Hotel (☎ 802493, fax 802477; e sales@safaripark.co.ke; Thika Rd; singles/ doubles US$190/210, double suites US$250-1000) is a few kilometres out of the centre. Set on a 25-hectare site, this swish hotel features soaring makuti (palm leaf) roofs, lots of woodwork, a huge landscaped pool and lush gardens. It's a fine place to retreat from the city and facilities are top class. There is a free shuttle bus into town for guests.

PLACES TO EAT
Lunch is the main meal of the day for many Kenyans and this is what the cheaper restaurants cater for. Nairobi is well stocked with places to eat. You can get a good Kenyan meal for under KSh100 in a coffee shop or workers canteen, while a meal at a European, Chinese or Indian restaurant will usually cost at least KSh500.

If you want a full meal in the evening it generally involves eating from a mid-range (or better) restaurant, or from a barbecue at a bar. Many restaurants transform into bars in the evening, so you'll often find that you're the only person eating.

Many restaurants downtown don't open for dinner, though, so you may have to head to the suburbs, which offer dozens of choices of cuisine from all over the world. The main eating centre is the suburb of Westlands, about 2km northwest of the downtown area. There are also some good choices in Hurlingham.

Most of the more expensive restaurants are licensed and offer beer, wine and spirits but the major exceptions are the Indian vegetarian restaurants that usually offer only fruit juices and tea or coffee. All of the posher places accept credit cards and most add 17% VAT to the bill.

There are few places to stay with facilities for self-caterers, but you can buy ingredients for snack lunches etc from the many supermarkets downtown and in the suburbs. The massive **Uchumi supermarket** chain has megastores in the Sarit Centre in Westlands, and next to the train station on Haile Selassie Ave, plus dozens of small supermarkets dotted around town. **Nakumatt** is Uchumi's main rival, and has a convenient branch on Kenyatta Ave.

Breakfast
Many of the Kenyan and Swahili restaurants covered later in this section serve very cheap, traditional African breakfasts of mandazi (fried sweet Kenyan bread) and tea or coffee for under KSh30. Eggs cooked various ways and Indian breakfast foods such as samosas (stuffed meat parcels) and idli (South Indian rice dumplings) with curry sauce are also widely available.

Nairobi Java House (☎ 313564; Mama Ngina St; fresh coffee KSh50; open 7am-8.30pm Mon-Sat) serves some of the best coffee in Kenya, and also has plenty of cakes and other sweet treats. It's nicely laid out and very popular so you may have to share a table.

Pekeshe Coffee House (Mama Ngina St), across the road, is similar, but not quite so plush.

Dove Cage Restaurant (Moktar Daddah St) offers good-value set breakfasts from KSh70.

Comfort Inn (see Places to Stay) in Koinange St is another great place for breakfast and it's also open on Sunday. Set breakfasts with fruit, fresh juices, fried bacon, sausage and eggs, toast and jam, and tea or coffee cost KSh300. It's open from 8am.

For a breakfast splurge, try the buffets at the major hotels, which offer the works – fruit juices, yogurt, cereals, porridge, eggs, bacon, beans, sausages, toast, fruits, cakes – you name it. Among the top-end hotels the best-value buffet is at the **Thorn Tree Cafe** in the New Stanley Hotel (all-day fried breakfast KSh420, continental buffet breakfast KSh650, full English buffet breakfast KSh1000). If you'd like to breakfast in colonial nostalgia then the **Norfolk Hotel** would have to be the choice – if you don't mind shelling out KSh1350.

Fast Food

Traditionally Nairobi's office workers have relied on budget canteens and coffee shops for cheap meals, but this is rapidly changing with the arrival of various South African and European fast-food chains. **Nandos** (Portuguese peri-peri chicken), **Steers** (hamburgers), **Chicken Inn** (fried chicken), **Creamy Inn** (milkshakes), **Pizza Inn** and **Debonairs** (pizza) have all arrived in Nairobi, and all have branches downtown.

Wimpy, an English fast-food chain that now serves Kenyan food, has branches on Kenyatta Ave. These places have the usual range of snacks and meals (burgers, sausages, eggs, fish, chicken, milk shakes etc) costing up to KSh250. They're open from 8am to 8pm Monday to Saturday.

Burger Dome (Mutual Bldg, Kimathi St; mains from KSh150) is a very popular local burger place with good cheap meals. **Walkers** (Reinsurance Plaza, Aga Khan Walk; fast food from KSh130) is similar.

That English staple, fish and chips, has caught on in a big way in Nairobi and it appears on the menu at most cheap places. Also hugely popular are Kenya's favourite sausages, **Farmer's Choice**, and Kenya's favourite chicken, **Kenchic**. These two companies supply most of the budget restaurants in Nairobi and you'll see their logo in restaurant windows all over town. Kenchic, the state chicken enterprise, even has its own franchises, with dozens of chickens slowly roasting in the windows.

In Westlands, the **Sarit Centre** (Parklands Rd) has a huge food court on the 2nd floor with a variety of small restaurants and fast-food places, including Indian, Chinese, Italian and African food. There's also a Wimpy and Southern Fried Chicken. You can get a meals here for KSh200 to KSh400. There's a similar food court at the **Yaya Centre** in Hurlingham – the best-value choice is the **Coffee Cream** coffee shop, which serves lunches of a different cuisine daily for around KSh250 to KSh350.

Restaurants

Kenyan & Swahili There are cheap eateries frequented by city workers concentrated around City Hall and in the streets around River and Latema Rds. These places serve local dishes such as stew and curry and you can get a whole meal for less than KSh100. Most work like school canteens; you just queue up with a tray and select your food from heated trays at the front of the restaurant.

Lunch and dinner usually consist of stew or curry and rice or *ugali* (corn starch), with assorted fried greens on the side. More interesting side dishes include *matoke* (mashed plantains and maize) or *maharagwe* (kidney beans). Other local favourites are fried chicken and fish in batter, grilled tilapia (a type of fish) and steaks, with or without pepper sauce. All these come with chips, which are also served as a stand-alone meal covered in masala (curry) sauce.

Malindi Dishes (Gaberone Rd; meals KSh70-170; open 8am-8.45pm daily) is a great little Swahili canteen. As the name suggests, this place serves great food from the coast, including *pulao* (curried rice), biryanis and coconut fish, with side dishes such as *ugali*, naan (Indian bread) and rice. You'll get a grand feed here, but it's a Muslim place, so it's closed for prayer at lunch time on Friday.

Prestige Palace (Tsavo Rd; meals KSh100-140) is a popular local canteen in the River Rd area serving curry and naan, fish and chips, grilled tilapia and other familiar dishes, plus very cheap snacks such as masala chips (just KSh55).

The Smart Place (Banda St; meals KSh120-220; open 8am-8pm Mon-Sat) is a highly recommended Muslim restaurant. The food is excellent and cheap and it's justifiably popular with worshippers at the nearby Jamaa mosque. Service is fast and the fried tilapia and Swahili stews and curries are excellent. All come with *ugali* or rice and greens.

Dove Cage Restaurant (☎ 242194; Moktar Daddah St; mains from KSh150), next to Terminal Hotel in central Nairobi, is an excellent little place if you're staying in the Koinange St area. Western and Kenyan meals are cheap and the service is fast and friendly. Breakfasts here are good value.

Mandy's (Koinange St; mains KSh180-240), is another good place for lunch, with staples such as steak, burgers, curries and stews. It's very popular so you'll probably have to share a table.

Beneve Coffee House (cnr Standard & Koinange Sts; meals under KSh200) has a tasty selection of self-service food ranging from stews to curries, fish and chips, samosa, pasties and a host of other choices. It's good value, but closed on weekends.

Calypso (Bruce House, Standard St; meals KSh150-250) is a basement canteen serving good African and Western canteen meals. It's open all day during the week, but only at lunch time on Saturday.

Pasara Cafe (☎ 338247; Lonrho Bldg, Standard St; lunches KSh170-275) is a stylish, modern café on the ground floor of the blueglass Lonrho Building. It attracts loads of businesspeople on working lunches and it's a great place for a breakfast. As well as canteen meals, there are sandwiches, baguettes and fresh salads. The staff are friendly and if you come here often they'll make you feel like a local.

Simmers (☎ 217959; cnr Kenyatta Ave & Muindi Mbingu St; mains under KSh160) is a huge, partly open-air restaurant and bar that serves cheap African lunches during the day. Fish stew with *ugali* and greens will set you back KSh220. In the evenings it transforms into a lively bar with live bands (see Entertainment).

The **Dancing Spoon Cafe & Wine Bar** (☎ 227581; 20th Century Cinema Bldg, 1st floor, Mama Ngina St; dishes KSh200-300) is next to the 20th Century Cinema. The Western and Kenyan food here is well above average and it's a great place for a steak and beer before you take in a movie.

Seasons Restaurant (Nairobi Cinema, Uchumi House, off Aga Khan Walk; mains KSh150-270) serves the same purpose as the Dancing Spoon and has a large cheap menu of Kenyan and Western favourites. There's

also a bar and beer garden that's popular with locals.

Wheels Restaurant (☎ 445899; Waiyaki Way, Westlands; mains KSh150-300) is a Kenyan restaurant and bar with a huge rooftop terrace above the Mall shopping centre. By nightfall, it's more of a drinking than eating place.

Nyama Choma Kenyans tend to give short shrift to vegetarianism – *nyama choma* (barbecued meat; see the boxed text 'Kenya's National Dish' in the Facts for the Visitor chapter) is the national dish and there are some amazing restaurants in Nairobi where you can really do this in style. Should the fancy take you, you can sample ostrich, zebra, hartebeest, eland, gazelle and even crocodile (like a sweet chicken). The meat is generally fabulous and is served as rare or as well-done as you like it. However, these places categorically do not cater to vegetarians.

The two most famous *nyama choma* restaurants are the Carnivore in Langata and The Horseman in Karen. For details, see Places to Eat under Nairobi's Southern Outskirts in the Around Nairobi chapter.

Nyama Choma Place (Milimani Rd; meals KSh400-600 plus drinks), at Sagret Hotel (see Places to Stay), is highly rated by Kenyans. There's a butchery here where you select your meat and then it's tossed on the barbie – any day of the week you'll see clouds of delicious-smelling smoke rising from the restaurant. It's best to come in a group as meat is sold in the form of whole goat legs or complete racks of ribs. Chips or *ugali* are available with the roast.

A definite step down the scale, but worth it for the atmosphere, are the **nyama choma stalls** near the Railway Museum, behind the Shell petrol station on Haile Selassie Ave. This is a very popular place among the city's office workers and, although foreigners are a rare sight, you'll be warmly welcomed. Here you can eat good *nyama choma* for around KSh150 and sample many other Kenyan dishes such as *matoke*.

Ethiopian Some distance from the centre is **Daas Ethiopian Restaurant** (☎ 712106; Lenana Rd; meals including drinks KSh400-500), which is in an old house, off Ngong Rd (signposted) about halfway between Kenyatta

NAIROBI

Hospital roundabout and Dagoretti Corner. The decor includes many Ethiopian artefacts and there's often live music in the evening. Meals based around excellent *injera* (unleavened bread) are eaten with the fingers.

Blue Nile Ethiopian Restaurant (☎ 723471; *Argwings Kodhek Rd; mains KSh300-500)* in Hurlingham is also good and has live bands on Friday, Saturday and Sunday.

Addis Ababa Restaurant (☎ 447321; *Woodvale Grove, Westlands; mains KSh400-500)* is easily missed as it's tucked away up some stairs, but serves good Ethiopian food and often has live music. It's closed Sunday lunchtime.

Indian Westlands is the centre of Nairobi's Indian population, but there are a few budget options downtown as well.

Taj (*Taveta Rd; mains KSh80-100)*, around the corner from Iqbal Hotel, is a very cheap and cheerful Indian canteen. Food is basic but very cheap.

Supreme Restaurant (☎ 331586; *River Rd; thali meals KSh170-250)*, near the gyratory at the junction with Tom Mboya St, offers excellent Indian (Punjabi) vegetarian thalis, consisting of various curries, rice, dhal (lentil soup), *bhajia* (vegetables fried in lentil flour) and chapatis. It also has superb fruit juices. Upstairs is **Mayur Restaurant** (*buffet lunch/dinner KSh280/300)*, which has a good reputation for Indian vegetarian food.

New Flora Restaurant (*Tsavo Rd; mains KSh100-200; open 10.30am-8.30pm)* is a good-value canteen place serving kebabs, chicken tikka, biryanis (rice with a curry topping), and curries.

Minar Restaurant (☎ 444656; *Loita St; buffet lunch KSh520, mains KSh280-800; open noon-3pm & 6.30pm-10pm daily)* used to have several branches in the city centre, but now there's just one, in the basement courtyard at the Barclays Plaza Building. It specialises in *mughlai* dishes and offers good all-you-can-eat buffet lunches and plenty of vegetarian dishes.

Haandi (☎ 448294/5; *Mall shopping centre, 1st floor, Ring Rd, Westlands; mains KSh600-935; open noon-2.30pm & 7pm-11pm daily)* is widely regarded as the best Indian restaurant in Kenya. There are an incredible 101 items on the menu, including wonderful *mughlai* meat dishes and loads of vegetarian curries.

Chowpaty (☎ 748884; *Shimmers Plaza, Westlands Rd; mains KSh200-350)* is a great Indian vegetarian restaurant. The menu reads a bit like a manifesto for vegetarianism, but the food is excellent and includes lots of South Indian dishes such as *dhosa* (lentil pancakes stuffed with vegetable curry).

Exotica (☎ 448887; *off Chiromo Rd; mains KSh180-300; open 7am-late daily)* is a fast-food type place that's always full of Indian expats. There are stuffed chapatis, curries and Western dishes such as chicken wings and burgers (non-beef).

Chinese Nairobi has plenty of Chinese restaurants but they aren't a cheap option. Almost all offer 'large' portions (good for two) and 'small' portions (enough for one). Food is generally excellent, but all these places add 17% VAT to the bill, so the prices soon mount up.

Hong Kong Restaurant (☎ 228612; *College House, Koinange St; small dishes from KSh260, large dishes from KSh340)* is a bright red Chinese restaurant with good food. It's the cheapest Chinese option in town and is accordingly popular.

Dragon Pearl (☎ 338863; *Bruce House, Standard St; mains KSh430-700; open 11am-3pm & 6pm-10.30pm)* is decked out with Chinese furniture and offers huge portions. Even the 'small' portions here are massive.

Tanager Chinese Restaurant (☎ 221615; *Rehema House, Kaunda St; mains KSh280-330; open 11am-11pm daily)* is a cheap and simple Chinese place right in the city centre.

Panda Chinese Restaurant (☎ 213018; *Fedha Towers, cnr Kaunda & Muindi Mbingu Sts; mains KSh380-1500; weekday business lunches KSh520)* is a newly opened and very classy Chinese restaurant. The staff bend over backwards to serve and the Chinese food is the best we found in Nairobi.

Water Margin Chinese Restaurant (☎ 0733 588347; *Commerce House, Moi Ave; mains KSh300-550; open 11am-2.30pm & 6pm-6am daily)*, attached to the Florida 2000 nightclub, has decent food and is open all night for hungry revellers.

Up in Westlands are several more Chinese restaurants worth seeking out.

China Jiangsu Restaurant (☎ 444748; *Westlands Rd; mains KSh200-500; open 11am-2.30pm & 6pm-10pm daily)* is a stylish rooftop restaurant above the Soin shopping centre. Prices are very reasonable considering the classy surroundings. Meals come in small or large portions.

China Plate (☎ 445661; Soin Arcade, Mpaka Rd; meat mains KSh580, vegetarian mains KSh390) is more of a fast-food place, but it's got a nice open-air terrace and food is still good. It's popular with locals and there are some OK vegetarian choices.

Japanese There are a few fine eateries catering to Nairobi's Japanese community.

Restaurant Akasaka (☎ 220299; Standard St; mains KSh380-500), opposite Bruce House, is a wonderful Japanese restaurant. It's always a little quiet, but this fits the stylish Japanese decor and the food is very authentic. There's even a *tatami* room (reserve in advance) where you can eat at traditional low tables. Akasaka offers the full range of Japanese cuisine including *udon* noodles, sushi sets, tempura, teriyaki and sukiyaki as well as great miso soup. Good-value set lunches are available for around KSh400.

Shogun (☎ 716080; Roughton Court Plaza, Argwings Kodhek Rd; meals around KSh700; open 12.30pm-2pm Tues-Fri & 6pm-10.45pm Tues-Sun), in Hurlingham, has a very nice atmosphere and fine authentic Japanese food.

Furusato Japanese Restaurant (☎ 442508; Karuna Rd, Westlands; set meals KSh700-1400), behind the Sarit Centre, is a very stylish place with grand set Japanese meals including sushi, *teppanyaki* and tempura. The sushi and sashimi here are delicious. Reservations are recommended.

Thai Westlands has two good Thai options, both open for lunch and dinner daily.

Bangkok Restaurant (☎ 3751311; Parklands Rd; mains KSh300-500), in Rank Xerox House, has been in business for a number of years and has a good reputation for authentic Thai food.

Siam Thai (☎ 751727; Unga House, Muthithi Rd; mains KSh230-600) also has a very good reputation. Unga House can be reached from either Woodvale Grove or Muthithi Rd. This attractive restaurant has an extensive menu.

International There are some good but expensive restaurants serving cuisine from around the world – mostly grills, steaks and Western dishes such as pasta.

Thorn Tree Cafe (cnr Kimathi St & Kenyatta Ave; mains KSh300-500), once a legendary meeting place with a message board for travellers and a vast thorn tree in the courtyard, has suffered from a rather sterile renovation. The old tree was cut down some years back but the replacement is getting to a fair size, and the noticeboard is still there. While the set breakfasts are a recommended splurge (see Breakfast earlier), lunch and dinner are good but expensive.

Kengele's Bar & Restaurant (☎ 344335; Koinange St; mains KSh390-600; Mon-Fri lunch buffet KSh490; open 9.30am-10.30pm) is a popular but expensive bar-cum-restaurant with good but expensive food. There are burgers, grills, Mexican, African, Western and Asian options and the open-air balcony is a nice place to dine. There's a second branch in ABC Place in Westlands (☎ 447944).

Tamambo Bar & Grill (☎ 448064; Mall shopping centre, Waiyaki Way, Westlands; mains KSh480-1500) is a very stylish restaurant and cocktail bar. It's decked out with native artefacts and serves upmarket seafood and grilled meat dishes.

Ibis Grill (☎ 250900; mains KSh1300-3300) at the Norfolk Hotel is a world-class restaurant that specialises in *nouvelle cuisine*, blending African and international styles. If flambéd impala grabs your fancy, bring the credit card – few mains are under KSh1500!

Alan Bobbe's Bistro (☎ 226027; Cianda House, Koinange St; mains KSh950-1200), a posh French place set back from Koinange St, is arguably one of the best restaurants in Kenya. The French food here is truly excellent – including such treats as trout with almonds and calamari Provencale – but it's not cheap. Reservations and smart attire are recommended. Look out for the 'French poodle' sign on Koinange St.

Italian With Kenya's huge Italian expat population, it's not surprising that there are some good Italian choices here.

Trattoria (☎ 340855; cnr Wabera & Kaunda Sts; mains KSh400-500; open 7.30am-midnight daily) is a very popular downtown restaurant offering excellent pizzas, pasta and gelati. The atmosphere and food are excellent and it's packed every night.

La Scala (☎ 332130; Phoenix House Arcade, Standard St; open 7am-10pm Mon-Fri, 7am-8.30pm Sat & Sun) is a pleasant low-key place that caters mainly to Kenyans. It's friendly and relaxed and you can get fresh salads as well as pasta and pizzas. It's popular with dating couples and the food is modestly priced.

There are also three choices in Westlands.

Taverna (☎ 445234; Woodvale Grove; mains KSh550-1300) is quite sophisticated, with lots of pasta choices and good seafood.

Ristorante Mediterraneo (☎ 447494; Woodvale Grove; mains from KSh380), almost next door, is another posh Italian option, and has a nice Mediterranean atmosphere.

New Pizza Garden (Waiyaki Way; pizzas & grills KSh360-650), part of Landmark Hotel (see Places to Stay), has excellent pizzas and a nice garden setting. There's often live music on Sunday afternoon. The pizza garden is just over the road from the hotel.

Seafood Nairobi's best seafood restaurant is **Tamarind** (☎ 338959; Nkrumah Lane; mains about KSh800-1800; open 2.30pm-4.30pm & 8.30pm-midnight daily) in the National Bank Building, between Harambee Ave and City Hall Way. It serves splendid seafood cooked in all manner of exotic styles – from European and Asian to coastal Swahili – and the stylish dining room is decked out in sumptuous Arabic-Moorish style. Smart dress is expected and you'll need to budget at least KSh1500 for the full works, more if you want wine and crab, prawns or lobster.

ENTERTAINMENT

For information on all entertainment in Nairobi and for big music venues in the rest of the country, get hold of the *Saturday Nation*, which lists everything from cinema releases to live music venues. There will also be plenty of suggestions on the website Ⓦ www.goingoutguide.com, run by the magazine *Going Out*.

Bars

Many of Nairobi's bars are restaurants during the day and bars at night. Most have TVs showing CNN or KTV and many have dance floors where the locals get up and dance at the drop of a hat. Foreign women will probably draw attention at these bars, but it's likely to be more genteel at the classier places downtown.

Thorn Tree Cafe (cnr Kenyatta Ave & Kimathi St), in New Stanley Hotel, is a little soulless, but it's a calm place for a beer and

is very popular with Westerners. There are often live bands here and you can always watch CNN if the music fails to excite.

Zanze Bar (☎ 222532; Moi Ave), on the top floor of Kenya Cinema Plaza, is a lively and friendly bar with pool tables, a dance floor, cheap beer and snack food. During the week things are fairly quiet, but from Friday to Sunday it rocks until the early hours. It's much more relaxed than nearby Florida 2000.

Pasara Cafe (Lonrho House, Standard St) becomes a classy bar in the evenings and pulls in a high-flying crowd of city workers. It's open till late from Monday to Friday.

There are number of cheap but very rough-and-ready bars on Latema Rd. These places aren't recommended for female travellers, and even male drinkers should be a little careful. One option is **Friendship Corner**. There are some safer and friendlier watering holes around Tom Mboya St and Moi Ave.

Green Corner (☎ 335243; Nkrumah Rd) is a very popular after-work bar and restaurant with DJs or live bands most nights of the week. It's upstairs in Tumaini House, opposite Nairobi Cinema.

Taco Bell (Moi Ave), around the corner, is also very popular with Kenyan city workers. It's on the 1st floor and has DJs from Thursday to Sunday. We suspect that the Taco Bell Corporation of the USA doesn't know they've borrowed the name. **Taco** (Kimathi St) is almost identical.

Hornbill Pub (Tom Mboya St), at the Ambassadeur Hotel, is a dark but friendly bar in the thick of things, with cold Tusker and sizzling *nyama choma*.

Buffalo Bill's (Milimani Rd, Milimani), in front of Heron Hotel, is a Nairobi institution, although not a very wholesome one. This long-running bar and restaurant is the centre of Nairobi's prostitution scene, and while it's considered upmarket compared with some pick-up joints, it's still deeply seedy. Aside from the lonely expat males and hard-selling bar girls, plenty of travellers drop in for the Wild West atmosphere. It's certainly an experience...

A less seedy option is the nearby bar at the **Nyama Choma Place** (Milimani Rd), in Hotel Salama Annexe. It's a friendly place and gets very lively most evenings.

Those looking for more genteel surroundings in which to sip their beer could try the **Ngong Hills Hotel** (Ngong Rd) or the

Children at Sunday School, Nairobi

Jamaa Mosque, Nairobi

Mask in craft shop, Nairobi

APPRECIATE   WILDLIFE

Street scene with a message; Koinage St, Nairobi

Waiting for a phone, Nairobi

Nation House, Nairobi

Three-wheeled transport on the streets of Nairobi

Lord Delamere bar at the **Norfolk Hotel**. Beers are around KSh180 and there's a minimum charge for nonguests.

Jockey Pub (*Hilton Hotel, Mama Ngina St*) is a cosy English-style pub, but nonguests have to spend a minimum of KSh2000! There's a free yard of ale if can drink it in under three minutes without stopping – the current record is a staggering 22 seconds.

Some of the most popular bars among foreigners and expats are in Westlands.

A good fun local drinking hole is **Wheels Restaurant & Bar** (*Mall shopping centre, Waiyaki Way*). It pulls in a lively crowd and there's a rooftop drinking terrace.

Gipsy Bar (*☎ 440836; Woodvale Grove*), opposite Barclays Bank, is still one of the most popular bars in Westlands, pulling in a mixed crowd of Kenyans, expats and prostitutes. Snacks are available and there's decent Western and African music. Tuesday is an informal gay night, although it's very low-key.

Soho's (*☎ 3745710; Parklands Rd*) is lively and popular, and pulls in a smart Kenyan and expat crowd. As well as beers, there's a good selection of wines and cocktails.

Klub House (*☎ 749870; Parklands Rd*), further west past the Holiday Inn, has more pool tables than anyone else and is a good place to party until late. Music is latino, Caribbean and African.

Discos

There's a good selection of discos in the centre of Nairobi and there are no dress codes, although there's an unspoken assumption that males will do as the locals do and at least wear a shirt and long trousers. Beer in all these places is reasonably priced at about KSh100 but other drinks, especially imported ones, are more expensive. Snacks and meals are available at all of them.

The most popular discos in the centre of town are **Florida 2000** (*☎ 229036; Moi Ave*) near City Hall Way and **New Florida** (*☎ 215014; cnr Koinange & Banda Sts*), known locally as the 'Mad House', which is housed in the bizarre spacecraft-like building above the Kobil petrol station on Koinange St. Entry is usually free before 9pm; thereafter it's KSh150 for men and KSh75 for women. Both places close at 6am and are steamy, frantic places, filled with drinkers, dancers and prostitutes. It's mayhem, but it can be good fun if you're in the right mood.

Close to the roundabout at the bottom of Museum Hill is a complex containing the boisterous **Mamba International Nightclub** (*☎ 743807*), the **Toona Bar & Restaurant** (*☎ 3742600*) and the **International Casino** (*☎ 742600*). It's a loud, showy nightspot and is favoured by wealthy young Indians, which means it's not quite as full-on as the Floridas.

Simba Saloon (*☎ 501706; admission KSh200*), next door to the Carnivore in Langata, is a huge, partly open-air bar and disco that pulls in a huge crowd on Wednesday, Friday and Saturday. There are video screens, a huge dance floor, several bars, a bonfire in the garden and unashamedly Western music. It's packed with wealthy Kenyans, expat teenagers, travellers and workers with non-governmental organisations and it's easily the best night out in town. The return cab fare from downtown with waiting is KSh1200.

Pavement Café (*☎ 4441711; Waiyaki Way, Westlands*) is another throbbing nightspot that rages till late. Wednesday, Friday and Saturday are disco nights, Thursday is salsa night and there are also Sunday jazz sessions.

Live Music

Citi Cabanas (*☎ 820992; Airport North Rd*), on the road to Mombasa before the turn-off to the airport, is a good venue. The clientele are mainly middle-class Kenyans looking to let their hair down. A variety of bands play out there.

Simmers (*cnr Kenyatta Ave & Muindi Mbingu St*) has a great atmosphere and is highly recommended for a beer in the evening. This open-air bar has live African bands every evening – everything from Kenyan a cappella music to Congolese *lingala* – and the dance floor is always buzzing. There are prostitutes here but they'll only bother you if you show an interest.

Green Corner (see Bars earlier) has live bands on Thursday and Sunday. Bands are normally Kenyan or Congolese. The **Toona Tree Bar** at the International Casino on Museum Hill has live bands on Friday and also Saturday.

Cinemas

Nairobi is a good place to take in a few films at a price substantially lower than what you'd pay back home. The upmarket cinemas show a mix of Western blockbusters and even more popular Indian blockbusters. The latter are often subtitled so you can understand what's happening in between the big song-and-dance numbers. Tickets range from KSh150 to KSh240.

Kenya Cinema Plaza (☎ 227822; Moi Ave), **20th Century** (☎ 210606; Mama Ngina St) and **Nairobi Cinema** (☎ 338058; Uchumi House, Aga Khan Walk) are comfortable modern cinemas in the centre with two screens apiece.

Fox Cineplex (☎ 227959; Sarit Centre, Westlands) is a good modern cinema on the 2nd floor of the Sarit Centre, but seats here are a whopping KSh300.

There are also several very cheap local cinemas that show a mix of Indian, South African and Western films, but the films are often scratched. Centrally located cinemas include the **Odeon** on Latema Rd and the **Cameo** on Kenyatta Ave.

If you have a car, there are a couple of drive-in cinemas in the 'burbs, both with cafés and bars. The best is the **Belle-Vue** (☎ 505779; Mombasa Rd), or there's the **Fox Drive-In** (☎ 802293; Thika Rd).

Theatre
Phoenix Players puts on regular performances at the **Professional Centre** (☎ 225506; Parliament Rd). Many of the plays are by foreign playwrights, but a good proportion are by Kenyans. Tickets cost KSh650.

Kenya National Theatre (☎ 225174; Harry Thuku Rd), opposite Norfolk Hotel, is the major theatre venue in Nairobi. As well as contemporary and classic plays, there are special events such as beauty pageants, which are less high-brow but still culturally interesting. Ticket prices start at KSh100.

For African theatre, the foreign cultural centres (see Cultural Centres earlier in this chapter) are often the places to head for. Also, check the *Daily Nation* to see what's on.

SHOPPING
Nairobi is a good place to pick up souvenirs but prices are typically higher than elsewhere in the country. The centre of the Nairobi's souvenir trade used to be the Blue Market on Tubman Rd but the compound was destroyed by rioting youths during a dispute over a new parking area for the Jamaa Mosque. The souvenir business has shifted to the **City Market** (Muindi Mbingu St), which has dozens of stalls selling wood

carvings, drums, spears, shields, soapstone, Maasai jewellery and clothing. It's a hectic place and you'll have to bargain hard (and we *mean* hard), but there's plenty of good stuff on offer. Near the Sarit Centre in Westlands, **Triangle Curios Market** (Parklands Rd), is cheaper and there are lots of genuine tribal objects such as Turkana wrist knives and wooden headrests. The **Kariokor Market** (Racecourse Rd), northeast of the city centre, is another cheap option.

Every Friday, there's a popular **Maasai Market** held at the Village Market, an upmarket shopping complex far out in the 'burbs on Limuru Rd. Souvenirs on offer include beaded jewellery, gourds, baskets and other Maasai crafts, but you'll have to bargain hard. The market is open from early morning to late afternoon. You can get here by matatu No 106 from near the train station.

There are loads of souvenir shops downtown, and in the area northwest of Kenyatta Ave, but prices tend to be a bit high. Most places sell exactly the same stuff, but there are a few speciality shops with better-than-average crafts. Other options include the following places.

Spinners Web (☎ 440882; Viking House, set back from Waiyaki Way, Westlands) works with workshops and self-help groups around the country. It's a bit like a handicrafts version of Ikea, with goods displayed the way they might look in Western living rooms, but there's some good stuff on offer, including carpets, wall hangings, ceramics, wooden bowls, baskets and clothing.

For upmarket souvenirs from around Africa, there are a number of pricey emporiums with wonderful pieces from Kenya, Mali, Ethiopia and other countries. **Kumbu Kumbu** (☎ 222074; Hilton Arcade) and **Pan-African Gallery** (Market Lane) are good choices in town. The latter company also supplies the souvenir shops at the National Museum, Karen Blixen Museum and many of the big hotels.

Utamaduni (☎ 890464; Bogani East Rd, Langata), in the southern 'burbs is a charitable organisation that sells African crafts. See the Around Nairobi chapter for more details.

Another good charitable venture is the **Undugu Craft Shop** (☎ 443525; Woodvale Grove) in Westlands. This nonprofit organisation supports community projects in Nairobi and has very good-quality crafts. In the Sarit

Centre in Westlands, **Banana Box** (☎ 581267) works in conjunction with community projects and refugee groups and offers modern uses for traditional objects.

If you want fine Kenyan art, a good place to check out what's happening is **Gallery Watatu** (☎ 228737; Standard St) on the 1st floor of Lonhro House. There's a permanent display here and many of the items are for sale, but be prepared to part with at least KSh20,000 for something small and KSh100,000 for one of the wonderful animal paintings by Elijah Ooko. It is also worth checking out the **Gallery of East African Contemporary Art** at the National Museum, the **Ramoma Rahimtulla Museum of Modern Art** in Upper Hill and the **Mzizi Arts Centre** (Buru Buru centre, 5th floor, Mumias South Rd). See earlier in this chapter for more details on these last two.

GETTING THERE & AWAY
Air
International airlines with offices in Nairobi include:

Air France (☎ 822202) Jomo Kenyatta International Airport
Air India (☎ 313300) Jeevan Bharati House, 1st floor, Harambee Ave
Air Madagascar (☎ 225286) Hilton Hotel, 1st floor, City Hall Way
Air Malawi (☎ 240965) International House, mezzanine floor, Mama Ngina St
Air Mauritius (☎ 229166) International House, mezzanine floor, Mama Ngina St
Air Tanzania (☎ 336224) Chester House, Koinange St
Air Zimbabwe (☎ 339522) Sasini House, Loita St
British Airways (☎ 244430) International House, 11th floor, Mama Ngina St
Da'allo Airlines (☎ 317318) City House, 5th floor, Wabera St
Egypt Air (☎ 226821) Hilton Arcade, off City Hall Way
Emirates (☎ 211187) VPT Tower, 20th floor, Uhuru Hwy
Ethiopian Airlines (☎ 330837) Bruce House, Muindi Mbingu St
Gulf Airlines (☎ 241123) International House, ground floor, Mama Ngina St
Kenya Airways (☎ 3207 4100) Barclays Plaza, ground floor, Loita St
KLM-Royal Dutch Airlines (☎ 3207 4100) Barclays Plaza, ground floor, Loita St
South African Airways (SAA; ☎ 227486) Lonrho House, 2nd floor, Standard St
Swiss (☎ 250288) Ambank House, University Way

As well as the national carrier, Kenya Airways, several other airlines have domestic flights within Kenya. Domestic airline offices include:

Air Kenya (☎ 501601, 501421, 605745) Wilson Airport, Langata Rd
Flamingo Airlines (☎ 3207 4340) Barclays Plaza, lower ground floor, Loita St
Regional Air (☎ 311584, 311623) Grand Regency Hotel, Loita St

Domestic services out of Jomo Kenyatta International Airport are offered by Kenya Airways and its subsidiary, **Flamingo Airlines**. Kenya Airways has six or seven daily flights to Mombasa, while Flamingo operates to Eldoret, Kisumu, Lamu, Malindi and Lokichoggio. Fares come down rapidly if you can book more than a week in advance (if not possible, it's best to book through a travel agent).

Three other carriers serve Mombasa. British Airways' subsidiary, **Regional Air** has three daily flights on weekdays, two flights on Saturday and one flight on Sunday. **Air Kenya**, based at Wilson Airport, has daily flights to Mombasa, Malindi, Lamu, Nanyuki and Ukunda (near Diani Beach) as well as many national parks and some international destinations in Tanzania. **African Express Airways** (☎ 824333) flies from Jomo Kenyatta International Airport to Mombasa on Saturday only.

Fares given below are one way (return fares are double):

destination	fare	frequency
Amboseli	US$88	once daily
Eldoret	KSh4100	once daily
Lamu	from KSh7700	twice daily
Lewa Downs	US$120	once daily
Kisumu	KSh4100	three daily
Kiwayu	US$156	once daily
Lokichoggio	US$180	once daily
Malindi	from KSh4100	three daily
Masai Mara	US$107	twice daily
Mombasa	from KSh4000	at least nine daily
Nanyuki	US$63	once daily
Samburu	US$100	twice daily
Ukunda	US$70	once Tues-Fri & Sun

The check-in time for all domestic flights is 30 minutes before departure and the baggage allowance is often only 15kg as there isn't much space on the smaller turboprop aircraft. All flights are nonsmoking. Make sure you reconfirm flights with airlines 48 hours before departure or you could lose your seat.

Bus

In Nairobi, most long-distance bus company offices are in the River Rd area, clustered around Accra Rd and the surrounding streets. Numerous companies do the run to Mombasa, including Akamba, Busscar, Busstar, Coastline Safaris, Mash Express and Mombasa Raha/Mombasa Liners. Most services leave in the early morning or late in the evening and the trip takes eight to 10 hours with a meal break on the way. Buses leave from outside each company's office and fares range from KSh400 to KSh700. **Coastline** (☎ 217592; Accra Rd) buses are the most comfortable and expensive.

Akamba (☎ 340430; Lagos Rd) is the biggest private bus company in the country and has an extensive network. It's not the cheapest, but is probably the safest and most reliable company. It has buses to Eldoret, Isiolo, Homa Bay, Kakamega, Kisii, Kisumu, Kitale, Malaba, Mombasa, Nanyuki, Naivasha, Kampala (Uganda) and Dar es Salaam (Tanzania). Buses leave from Lagos Rd and there's also a booking office on Wabera St (☎ 215449), near City Hall.

The government-owned **Kenya Bus Service** (KBS; ☎ 229605) is another large and reliable operator that is cheaper than Akamba, but the buses are much slower. Its main depot is east of the centre on Uyoma St, but there's a downtown booking office (☎ 246093) on the corner of Muindi Mbingu and Monrovia Sts. There are loads of buses to Kisumu and Kakamega and less frequent services to Busia, Eldoret, Homa Bay, Kitale and Malaba.

The Country Bus Station on Landhies Rd is a hectic, disorganised place with buses running to Busia, Eldoret, Kakamega, Kisumu, Machakos, Nyeri, Nakuru, Nanyuki, Malaba and Meru. All buses have their destinations displayed in the window. Eldoret Express is the biggest operator here and has plenty of buses to Kisumu and the Ugandan border while Busscar has very frequent buses to Machakos. See the Getting Around and Getting There & Away chapters for more details on other bus companies operating out of Nairobi. Typical fares include the following.

destination	fare (Ksh)	duration (hrs)
Arusha (Tanzania)	750-800	4
Dar es Salaam (Tanzania)	1400-1500	12
Eldoret	350-500	3
Embu	220	1½
Homa Bay	420	6
Kakamega	400-500	5
Kampala (Uganda)	800-900	10-12
Kisii	350	4
Kisumu	400	4
Kitale	400	5
Machakos	70	1
Malindi	500	8
Mombasa	450-550	7
Meru	250	3
Mwanza (Tanzania)	1200	12
Nyeri	150	1½
Naivasha	130	1
Nanyuki	200	2
Nakuru	180	2

Shuttle Minibus

Shuttle minibuses run from Nairobi to Kampala (Uganda), and to Arusha and Moshi in Tanzania (see the Getting There & Away chapter for details).

Matatu

Most matatus leave from Latema, Accra, River and Cross Rds and fares are similar to the buses. The biggest operator here is **Crossland Services** (☎ 245377; Cross Rd) which serves Busia (KSh600, six hours), Eldoret (KSh350, three hours), Kericho (KSh340, three hours), Kisii (KSh400, four hours), Kisumu (KSh450, four hours), Kitale (KSh450, five hours), Naivasha (KSh130, one hour), Nakuru (KSh180, two hours) and Nanyuki (KSh250, two hours). On the same road are **Molo Line Services** (☎ 336363) with matatus to Eldoret, Naivasha, Nakuru and Kisumu, and **Narok Line** (☎ 212437), which serves Kisii and Narok (KSh200, two hours).

Other companies are located on the surrounding streets. Head to Accra Rd for matatus to Chogoria (KSh250, 2½ hours), Embu (KSh160, 1½ hours), Meru (KSh250 to KSh300, three hours) and Nanyuki (KSh250, 2½ hours). Matatus leave from Latema Rd for Nyahururu (KSh250, two hours) and Nyeri (KSh170, two hours). There are loads of matatus to Naivasha

(KSh110) and the Tanzanian border at Namanga (KSh200, two hours) from the corner of Ronald Ngala St and River Rd. For Thika (KSh50, 40 minutes) go to the Total petrol station on Racecourse Rd.

Peugeots (Shared Taxis)
Like matatus, most of the companies offering Peugeot shared taxis have their offices around the Accra, River and Cross Rds area. One reliable company is **Crossland Services** (☎ 245377; Cross Rd), which has cars to Eldoret, Kericho, Kitale and Nakuru. Other companies serve Isiolo, Kisumu, Meru and Malaba. Fares are about 20% higher than doing the same journeys by matatu. Most services depart in the morning.

Train
Nairobi train station has a **booking office** (☎ 221211 ext 27002; open 9am-noon & 2pm-6.30pm daily). The evening train to Mombasa is the only service currently running from Nairobi (see the Getting Around chapter). Trains in either direction leave at 7pm daily, but you'll need to arrive early as seats are only assigned at the last minute. The trains reach their destinations between 9am and 11am the following morning and meals and bedding are included. Fares are KSh3000/2100 in 1st/2nd class, both of which are quite comfortable. The train is a good place to meet up with other travellers heading to the coast. It's advisable to book a few days in advance.

Nairobi train station also has a left-luggage office; it's always open when trains arrive (around 9am) and depart (around 7pm), but is erratically staffed at other times. The service costs KSh80 per item per day.

GETTING AROUND
To/From Jomo Kenyatta International Airport
The international airport (☎ 822111) is 15km out of town off the road to Mombasa. There's now a dedicated (small blue) airport bus run by Metro Shuttle (part of Kenya Bus Service), which can drop you off at hotels in the city centre. Going the other way, the main departure point is across from the Hilton Hotel on City Hall Way. The journey takes about 40 minutes and costs US$5 per person. Buses run every half-hour from 8am to 8.30pm daily. Buses stop at all the air terminals.

A cheaper way to get into town is city bus No 34 but a lot of travellers get ripped off on this bus or when they step off the bus in the centre. Never take your hand off your valuables and have small change handy for the fare. If you don't mind taking the risk, the buses run from 5.45am to 9.30pm weekdays, 6.20am to 9.30pm on Saturday and 7.15am to 9.30pm on Sunday. The last few evening services may not run. Heading to the airport, bus 34 runs west along Kenyatta Ave.

A much safer option is to take a taxi, which will usually costs about KSh1000 in either direction. If you book at one of the 'information' desks at the airport, you'll still end up in a public taxi, but it isn't any more expensive. If you arrive at night, a taxi is pretty much your only option.

To/From Wilson Airport
To get to Wilson Airport (☎ 501941) for light-aircraft services to Mombasa, Malindi, Lamu etc or for charter flights, the cheapest option is to take bus or matatu No 15, 31, 34, 125 or 126 from Moi Ave. The fare is KSh20. A taxi from the centre of town will cost you KSh600 to KSh800 depending on the driver. In the other direction, you'll have to fight the driver down from KSh1000. The entrance to the airport is easy to miss; it's just before the large BP petrol station.

Bus
The ordinary city buses are run by **Kenya Bus Service** (KBS; ☎ 229707) but hopefully you won't need to use them much. Forget about them if you have a backpack – you'll never get on, and even if you do, you'll never get off! Most buses pass through downtown, but the main KBS terminus is on Uyoma St, east of the centre.

Useful buses include No 46 from Kenyatta Ave for the Yaya Centre in Hurlingham (KSh10) and No 23 from Moi Ave at Jevanjee Gardens for Westlands (KSh10). There are buses services to Westlands and the Yaya Centre about every 20 minutes from 6am to 8pm Monday to Saturday.

There's also a useful Metro Shuttle bus service to Ngong Rd and Karen, passing the Karen Blixen Museum. Buses run from 6am to 7.30pm Monday to Saturday, and 7am to 6.30pm Sunday. They leave from in front of the Hilton. All these services cost KSh20 to KSh40, depending on where you get off.

Matatu

If you don't mind taking your life in your hands, there are frequent matatus that follow the same routes as buses, with the same route numbers. For Westlands, you can pick up No 23 on Moi Ave or Latema Rd. No 46 to the Yaya Centre stops in front of the main post office and Nos 125 and 126 to Langata leave from in front of the train station. As usual, you should keep an eye on your valuables on all matatus.

Car

See Car & 4WD in the Getting Around chapter for comprehensive information on car hire, road rules and conditions. If you do hire a car, beware of wheel-clampers. Parking in the centre is by permit (KSh70 per day), available from the parking attendants who roam the streets in bright yellow or red jackets. If you park overnight in the street in front of your hotel, the guard will often keep an eye on your vehicle for a small consideration.

Taxi

Other than the fleet of old London cabs, Nairobi taxis rate as some of the least roadworthy motor vehicles in the world. You'll be lucky to get seat belts or working brakes, and shattered windscreens and asthmatic engines are par for the course. Because people are compelled to use them due to Nairobi's endemic street crime, taxis are overpriced, but you've little choice, particularly at night. Taxis don't cruise for passengers, but you can find them parked on every other street corner in the city centre. At night they're outside restaurants, bars and nightclubs.

Fares around town are pretty standard. Any journey within the downtown area costs KSh200, from downtown to Milimani Rd costs KSh300, and for longer journeys such as Westlands or the Yaya Centre, fares range from KSh400 to KSh500. From the city centre to the Carnivore restaurant is KSh700 one way, or KSh1200 for a return trip with waiting.

Around Nairobi

There are a number of interesting attractions, most within an hour's drive or matatu (minibus) ride from Nairobi, which are easily reachable on day trips. If you don't have time for a long safari, Nairobi National Park starts right on the edge of town. Further afield are the lush areas around Karen, the Ngong Hills and mysterious Lake Magadi, one of Kenya's many soda lakes. Southeast of Nairobi on the road to Mombasa, is Machakos, the former capital of the British East Africa Protectorate. Northeast of the capital are the towns of Kiambu and Thika, while Limuru – with it's tea plantations and nearby views into the Rift Valley – is a short distance northwest, on the road to Naivasha and the Rift Valley.

Apart from these excursions, it's also possible to take a long day trip to either Mt Longenot, Mt Suswa, Lake Naivasha or Hell's Gate National Park (see the Rift Valley chapter), or Ol Donyo Sabuk (see the Central Highlands chapter).

Nairobi's Southern Outskirts

Though it's a part of ever-sprawling Nairobi, this well-to-do area has a different feel to the rest of the city. In places it is almost European and there are some interesting things to do in this area, as well as some excellent dining and accommodation options.

BOMAS OF KENYA

The Bomas of Kenya (☎ 02-891801; Langata Rd; nonresident adult/child KSh600/300, resident KSh100/25; performances 2.30pm Mon-Fri, 3.30pm Sat & Sun) is a cultural centre at Langata, near the main gate to Nairobi National Park. The talented dance team here perform traditional dances and songs taken from the country's 16 ethnic groups and it's quite a spectacle, although it is very touristy. If you bring a video camera there's an extra KSh500 charge.

Bus or matatu No 125 or 126 from the train station on Haile Selassie Ave will get you there in about half an hour. Get off at Magadi Rd, from where it's about a 1km

Highlights

- Getting up close and personal with the giraffes at Langata Giraffe Centre
- Spotting lions and rhinos at Nairobi National Park, just a few kilometres from central Nairobi
- Visiting tea plantations, caves and expat getaways at Limuru and Kiambu and in the Ngong Hills
- Visiting the Carnivore for a *nyama choma* (barbecued meat) feast and dancing till dawn at the Simba Saloon, next door, Nairobi's leading nightspot
- Taking in the views from the roads around Limuru as you descend into the Rift Valley

National Parks & Reserves: Nairobi National Park

Around Nairobi p136
🔾 Nairobi NP p137
Machakos p142
Thika p144
Langata & Karen p139

walk; it's clearly signposted on the right-hand side of the road.

NAIROBI NATIONAL PARK

This somewhat underrated park *(nonresident adult/child US$23/10, residents KSh500/200, vehicle KSh200; smartcard required)* is the most accessible of all Kenya's wildlife parks, being only a few kilometres from the city centre. It's possible to visit as part of a tour or even by public transport as the park runs its own wildlife bus (Sunday only).

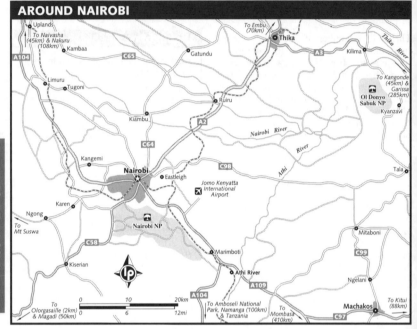

AROUND NAIROBI

AROUND NAIROBI

The park has been around since 1946 and wildlife here is plentiful despite the backdrop of looming skyscrapers and the roar of jets coming into land at Jomo Kenyatta International Airport. You stand a good chance of seeing gazelles, warthogs, zebras, giraffes, ostriches, buffaloes, lions, cheetahs and leopards. The landscape is mixture of savanna and swampland and is home to the highest concentration of black rhinos in the world (over 50). By the main gate is the site where former President Moi famously burned ten tons of ivory in 1989 in protest at the international trade in ivory.

The wetland areas are home to more than 550 recorded species of bird – more than in the whole of the UK! – attracting many bird-watchers.

Nairobi National Park is not fenced and wildlife is still able (for the time being) to migrate along a narrow wildlife corridor to the Rift Valley. The concentrations of wildlife are higher in the dry season as animals migrate into the park where water is almost always available. Keeping the migration pathway open is one of the principal aims of the Friends of Nairobi National Park campaign (see Things to See & Do in the Nairobi chapter).

The headquarters of the **Kenya Wildlife Service** *(KWS; ☎ 02-602345, fax 505866; ⓔ kws@kws.org)* is at the park entrance. There's an office right by the gate that sells and recharges smartcards, plus a small education centre. Nearby is the **Nairobi Safari Walk** *(nonresident adult/child US$8/5, residents KSh500/100; open 8.30am-5.30pm)* a sort of zoo-meets-nature boardwalk with lots of birds and other wildlife. The nearby **Animal Orphanage** charges the same rates, but it's basically a rather poor zoo and not a patch on the David Sheldrick Wildlife Trust (see following).

Nairobi Park Services has a fine camp ground on the edge of the national park (see Places to Stay, later). **Ranger's Restaurant**, by the main gate, is a plush overpriced place used by tour groups, and nothing on the menu is under KSh800.

Getting There & Away
The cheapest way to see the park is with the 'Park Shuttle,' a big KWS bus that leaves the main gate at 3pm Sunday for a 2½-hour

NAIROBI NATIONAL PARK

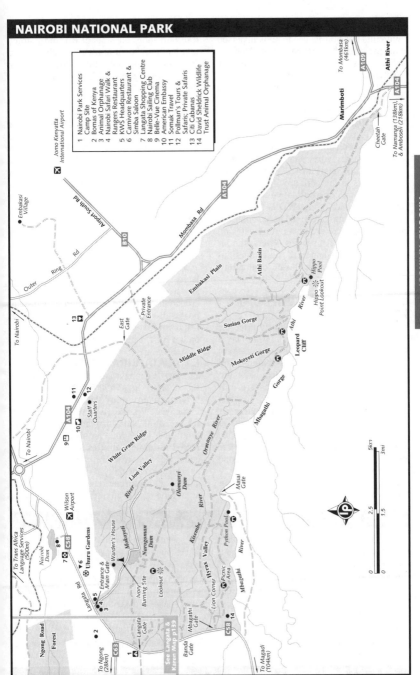

1 Nairobi Park Services
  Camp Site
2 Bomas of Kenya
3 Animal Orphanage
4 Nairobi Safari Walk &
  Rangers Restaurant
5 KWS Headquarters
6 Carnivore Restaurant &
  Simba Saloon
7 Langata Shopping Centre
8 Nairobi Sailing Club
9 Belle-Vue Cinema
10 American Embassy
11 Somak Travel
12 Pollman's Tours &
  Safaris; Private Safaris
13 Citi Cabanas
14 David Sheldrick Wildlife
  Trust Animal Orphanage

See Langata &
Karen Map p139

AROUND NAIROBI

tour of the park. The cost is US$20/5 per adult/child and you'll need to book in person at the main gate by 2.30pm. Matatu Nos 125 and 126 pass the park entrance (45 minutes).

Alternatively, most safari companies (see the Safari chapter and Organised Tours in the Nairobi chapter) offer tours of the park. Half-day packages usually depart twice a day at 9.30am and 2pm and cost US$55 to US$75. These companies also offer combined trips with the Bomas of Kenya and lunch at the Carnivore restaurant (see Places to Eat & Drink, later) for US$75 to US$130.

The roads in the park are OK for 2WDs but hire companies won't let you drive their cars on dirt roads, so a 4WD is the way to go. The main entrance to the park is on Langata Rd, but there are also public gates on Magadi Rd. The Athi River Gate at the far end of the park is handy if you're continuing on to Mombasa, Amboseli or the Tanzanian border.

DAVID SHELDRICK WILDLIFE TRUST

The trust was established shortly after the death of David Sheldrick in 1977. David and his wife Daphne pioneered techniques of raising orphaned black rhinos and elephants and reintroducing them back into the wild. Rhinos and elephants are still reared on site and can be viewed between 11am and noon daily. There's no charge for visiting, but a donation of around KSh300 per person would be appropriate. There's a **gift shop and information centre** (☎ 02-891996, fax 890053) and usually someone around to answer questions.

From outside Development House on Moi Ave take bus or matatu No 125 or 126 and ask to be dropped off at the KWS central workshop, on Magadi Rd (the journey takes about 50 minutes). It's about 1km from the workshop gate to the Sheldrick centre; it's signposted but KWS staff can give directions.

UTAMADUNI

A charitable organisation set in a large colonial house near the Langata Giraffe Sanctuary, Utamaduni (☎ 890464; Bogani East Rd, Langata) has excellent crafts from around Africa. Every room has a theme. A portion of all proceeds goes to the Kenya Wildlife Foundation.

BUTTERFLY AFRICA

This **butterfly sanctuary** (☎ 884972; Dagoretti Rd; W www.african-butterfly.org; open 9am-4.30pm daily; nonresident adult/child KSh400/200, residents KSh200/100) is housed in a large greenhouse full of tropical plants. There are loads of exotic butterflies fluttering around the place and some interesting display boards. It's out past the Karen roundabout on Dagoretti Rd; you can get here from Moi Ave on the No 111 bus or matatu.

LANGATA GIRAFFE CENTRE

The giraffe centre (☎ 02-891658; off Koitobos Rd; adult/child KSh500/250; open 10am-5.30pm daily), run by the African Fund for Endangered Wildlife (AFEW), is about 18km from central Nairobi, reached by Langata South Rd. Here you can observe and hand feed Rothschild's giraffes from a raised circular wooden structure, which is quite an experience, especially for children. There's a display of information about giraffes, and across the road is an interesting self-guided

Ngong Races

Three Sundays a month, hundreds of Nairobi residents flee the noise and bustle of the city for the much more genteel surroundings of the Ngong Hills Racecourse, on Ngong Rd just east of Karen. The races are quite a spectacle, if only for the contrast between the well-heeled race-goers in the members enclosure and the cheering hopefuls in the public stands. In the past, races had to be cancelled because of rogue rhinos on the track, but things are much more orderly these days. The races are all rumoured to be rigged, of course, but that doesn't diminish the enthusiasm of the punters. Entry is KSh250 and you can bet as little as KSh20, so everyone should be able to afford a flutter. There are three races every month – call the **Jockey Club** (☎ 02-566108) for race dates. You can get here on bus or matatu No 24 from Haile Selassie Ave in the city, but keep an eye on your winnings on the bus home!

forest walk. Booklets are available from the ticket office.

To get here from central Nairobi, take matatu No 24 to the Hardy Estate shopping centre in Langata and walk from there, or take matatu No 126 to Magadi Rd and walk through from Mukoma St.

KAREN BLIXEN MUSEUM

This **museum** (☎ 882779; Karen Rd; open 9.30am-6pm daily; nonresident adult/child KSh200/100, resident KSh50/20) is the farmhouse where Karen Blixen, author of *Out of Africa*, lived between 1914 and 1931. She left after a series of personal tragedies, but the lovely colonial house has been preserved as a museum. It was presented to the Kenyan government at Independence by the Danish government along with the adjacent agricultural college. It's set in lovely gardens and is quite an interesting place to wander around. The museum is about 2km from Langata Rd.

Just down the road is **Karen Blixen Coffee Garden**, a smart upmarket restaurant and a very popular pub. Also here are **Karen Blixen Cottages**. For more details see Places to Stay and Places to Eat & Drink, respectively, later.

The easiest way to get here is via the Karen Metro Shuttle Bus from opposite Hilton Hotel on City Hall Way. A taxi will cost about KSh900 one way. You can also come on an organised tour.

NGONG HILLS

The green and fertile Ngong Hills were where many white settlers set up farms in the early colonial days. It's still something of a white enclave, and here and there in the hills are perfect reproductions of English farmhouses with country gardens full of flowering trees – only the acacias remind you that you aren't in the Home Counties of England.

The hills provide some excellent walking, but robbery is a risk so it makes sense to go on an organised tour or pick up an escort from Ngong police station or the KWS office in Ngong. Close to the summit of the range, Point Lamwia, is the grave of Denys George Finch-Hatton, the famous playboy and lover of Karen Blixen. A large obelisk east of the summit on the lower ridges marks his grave. The stone is inscribed with Coleridge's *The Rime of the Ancient Mariner*,

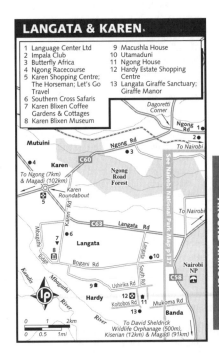

LANGATA & KAREN

1 Language Center Ltd
2 Impala Club
3 Butterfly Africa
4 Ngong Racecourse
5 Karen Shopping Centre; The Horseman; Let's Go Travel
6 Southern Cross Safaris
7 Karen Blixen Coffee Gardens & Cottages
8 Karen Blixen Museum
9 Macushla House
10 Utamaduni
11 Ngong House
12 Hardy Estate Shopping Centre
13 Langata Giraffe Sanctuary; Giraffe Manor

one of Finch-Hatton's favourite poems. The hills still contain plenty of wildlife (antelopes and buffaloes are common) and there are legends about a lion and lioness standing guard at Finch-Hatton's graveside.

In the foothills of the Ngong Hills is **Whistling Thorns**, which is an excellent place to stay in the area. See Places to Stay, later.

PLACES TO STAY
Karen & Langata

Nairobi Park Services (☎/fax 890325; e nps@swiftkenya.com; Magadi Rd; camping per person US$3, dorm beds US$6, doubles/triples US$15/18) is set in a quiet residential area on the edge of Nairobi National Park, about 1km from the junction with Langata Rd. Established by two former overland drivers, it's set in a garden with a great wood-finished bar and restaurant with satellite TV, cold beers and cheap meals. There are vehicle work bays (mechanics and tools can be arranged) so it's a good pit stop for overland trucks and those with their own vehicle. Security is tight and parking costs US$2 per vehicle per night. To get here from the centre,

Karen Blixen

The suburb of Karen takes its name from Karen Blixen, aka Isak Dinesen, a Danish coffee planter and lady aristocrat, who went on to become one of Africa's most famous writers. Although she lived a life of genteel luxury on the edge of the Ngong Hills, her personal life was full of heartbreak. After her first marriage broke down, she began a secret affair with the British playboy Denys Finch-Hatton, who was killed in a plane crash during one of his frequent flying visits to Tsavo National Park.

Blixen subsequently returned to Denmark where she began her famous memoir *Out of Africa*. The book is probably one of the definitive tales of European endeavour in Africa, but Blixen was passed over for the 1954 Nobel Prize for Literature in favour of Ernest Hemingway. She died from malnutrition at her family estate in Denmark in 1962.

Her house in Karen was donated to Kenya at Independence by the Danish government and has now been turned into a museum. *Out of Africa* was subsequently made into a movie starring Meryl Streep, Robert Redford and one of the retired locos from the Nairobi Railway museum!

take a No 125 or 126 bus or matatu from near the train station on Haile Selassie Ave; the entrance is opposite the Langata Gate to the national park.

Several exclusive little hotels can be found in these wealthy suburbs.

Macushla House (☎ 891987, fax 891971; Nguruwe Rd, Langata; singles/doubles US$95/170) is a beautiful place, more like a private house, catering for just 10 guests. Located west of the Langata Giraffe Centre, it has a swimming pool, beautiful gardens, an excellent restaurant and the rates, which include breakfast, are really very reasonable all things considered.

Ngong House (☎/fax 891856, fax 890674; e ngonghouse@form-net.com; Ndovo Rd off Langata Rd South; singles/doubles full board US$435/580), also a short walk from the giraffe centre, is an altogether different sort of hotel. The four luxurious tree-houses are set on 4m-high stilts, with fine views out across the Ngong Hills. Rates include transfers and all meals and drinks, and a number of free

small excursions are provided. It's a magical place, but you pay for it.

Giraffe Manor (☎ 891078; e giraffem@kenyaweb.com; w www.giraffemanor.com; singles/doubles full board US$350/540) was built in 1932 in the style of a typical English country manor. The elegant house is situated on 56 hectares, much of which is given over to the giraffe centre next door on Mukoma Rd. The food is excellent (you dine as the personal guests of the owners) and you may have a Rothschild's giraffe peering through your bedroom window first thing in the morning.

Karen Blixen Cottages (☎ 882130, fax 882508, 336 Karen Rd; per person US$170), near the Karen Blixen museum, is a lovely cottage complex set in a pretty garden. Rates include breakfast.

Contact the **Langata Link** (☎ 891314; e the_link@swiftkenya.com) for more information about hotels and restaurants in Langata and Karen.

Ngong Hills

One excellent place to stay in the Maasai land foothills of the Ngong Hills is **Whistling Thorns** (☎/fax 02-350720; e scs@iconnect.co.ke; Isinya/Kiserian Pipeline Rd, near Kiserian, PO Box 51512; camp sites KSh250, with tent KSh450, cottage doubles with bathroom per person KSh2500-3500). There's a swimming pool, pool table and restaurant. There are also horses for riding at KSh1200 per hour and numerous walking trails in the area. Cottage rates include breakfast.

To get here, take bus or matatu No 111 or 126 from Moi Ave to Kiserian and change at the Total petrol station to a Isinya/Kajiado matatu. Ask to be dropped at Whistling Thorns, which is 200m from the roadside. Count on a two-hour trip from door to door from central Nairobi.

PLACES TO EAT & DRINK

Karen Blixen Coffee Garden (☎ 02-882138; pizzas KSh300-500, mains KSh500-860), just down the road from the Karen Blixen Museum, is a smart, upmarket restaurant set in a veritable English country garden. The food is excellent and there's a friendly and very popular pub here that attracts a good mixed crowd in the evenings.

Carnivore (☎ 02-501709; just off Langata Rd, near Wilson Airport; set barbecue meals

KSh1250), sets the standard in *nyama choma* (barbecued meat). The staff here put on an incredible show and Carnivore was recently voted one of the 50 best restaurants in the world! At the entrance is a huge barbecue pit laden with skewers of beef, pork, lamb, chicken and farmed game meats such as zebra, hartebeest, ostriche and crocodile. On every table there's a wooden carousel of salads and sauces topped by a flag and, as long as the flag is flying, waiters will keep bringing the meat, which is carved right at the table. Assuming you have any space left, dessert and coffee are also included in the set price.

At lunchtime, it's possible to get to the Carnivore by matatu No 126 from the centre – the turn-off is signposted just past Wilson Airport, from where it's a 1km walk. At night, you're best off hiring a cab for the return trip. The driver will wait for you outside and the fare will be about KSh1200.

The very popular **Simba Saloon** disco and bar is next door. It's huge and gets the crowds on Wednesday, Friday and Saturday nights (see Entertainment in the Nairobi chapter for more details).

The Horseman (☎ 02-884560; Karen shopping centre, Langata Rd; game meats KSh680-1000, other mains KSh300-500; open 10am-11pm daily) is a similar meat-eaters' paradise to the Carnivore. Housed in a perfect re-creation of an English pub are three restaurants, two open-air and one indoors, set in a leafy compound straight out of rural Surrey, England. One of the restaurants specialises in game meat, one serves pizzas and the other place offers Chinese, Indian and Kenyan food. It's highly rated by locals and the cosy bar is open till late.

South of Nairobi

LAKE MAGADI

The most southerly of the Rift Valley lakes in Kenya, Lake Magadi is rarely visited by tourists because of its remoteness, although it actually makes an easy day trip from Nairobi if you have your own vehicle or hire a taxi for the day. The most mineral-rich of the soda lakes, it is almost entirely covered by a thick encrustation of soda that supports many flamingos and other water birds and gives the landscape a weird lunar appearance, somewhere between Ice Station Zebra and Mission to Mars!

A causeway leads across the most visually dramatic part of this strange landscape to a viewpoint on the western shore. It's worth a drive if you have a 4WD, or otherwise you can head to the hot springs further south. The springs aren't particularly dramatic, but you can take a dip in the deeper pools, and there are large numbers of fish there that have adapted to survive in the hot water. You may run into local tribespeople, particularly Maasai, who will offer to show you the way and 'demonstrate' everything for you.

The thick soda crust is formed when the mineral-rich water, pumped up from hot springs deep underground, evaporates rapidly in the 38°C temperature to leave a mineral layer. A soda-extraction factory 'harvests' this layer and extracts sodium chloride (common salt) and sodium carbonate (soda), which are then put straight onto trains to Mombasa.

The town of Magadi is purely a company town for factory staff and their families; it was originally built by the multinational ICI and is now run by the unimaginatively named Magadi Soda Co. Facilities in town are limited, but you will find a couple of small bars, restaurants and shops, as well as a large swimming pool, which appears to be a bit of a social centre (a sign says 'Residents Only', but the staff appear to be flexible about this).

Some years ago, Magadi was the site of a major rescue operation when drought threatened hundreds of thousands of young flamingos that had soda encrustations on their feathers.

Olorgasailie Prehistoric Site

Located 40km north of Magadi, a number of important archaeological finds were made at this site by Louis and Mary Leakey in the 1940s, including hand axes and stone tools thought to have been made by *Homo erectus* about half a million years ago. Fossils have also been discovered and some have been left in place, protected from the elements by shade roofs (sadly the famous 'elephant butchery' site is not one of these). A guided tour (KSh200) is available and there are numerous notice boards and displays.

Places to Stay

Magadi is best visited from Nairobi or the Ngong Hills; **Whistling Thorns** (see Places to Stay under Nairobi's Southern Outskirts, earlier in this chapter) at Kiserian is conveniently placed. A new ecolodge has opened near Magadi itself, but it's about 50km past the lake, so unless you're very keen or very fussy you're probably better off camping. There's no shortage of space – ask at the roadblock for the best spot.

At Olorgasailie there is a useful **camp site** (*camping KSh200, single/double bandas KSh500/800*), which is not a bad place to stay for the night. You'll need to bring your own food, bedding and drinking water, though. It can get pretty windy out here, but you'll certainly feel like you're out in the bush and it's likely you'll have the place to yourself.

Getting There & Away

The C58 road from Nairobi is in good condition, although there is very little traffic on it after Kiserian. Akamba no longer run bus services here and there seems to be only one matatu a day to Nairobi (KSh200), leaving in the morning and returning to Magadi in the evening.

MACHAKOS
☎ 0145

A decade or so before Nairobi was even established, Machakos was the site chosen by the Imperial British East Africa company as an upcountry trading post, principally because of the reputation of the Akamba people as middlemen between the Swahili of the coast and the Maasai and Kikuyu inland. The cooperation of these two warlike tribes was essential for anyone who wished to reach the shores of Lake Victoria and, when diplomacy didn't work, the British resorted to railroading – literally – building a railway right through the middle of the Maasai and Kikuyu territory. Topography meant that the railway passed west of Machakos, so the provincial headquarters shifted to Nairobi in 1901.

The centre of the former Akamba territory (see the special section 'Tribes of Kenya' for more details) Machakos is still a busy place, although these days it's African rather than expat in nature. Being at a lower altitude than Nairobi, it avoids the cloud that hangs over the capital and it's hemmed in by attractive hills and valleys. There are no attractions as such, but the nice unhur-

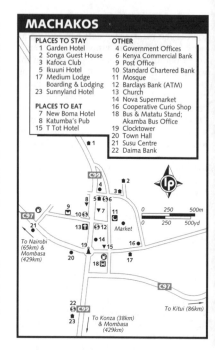

MACHAKOS

PLACES TO STAY
1 Garden Hotel
2 Songa Guest House
3 Kafoca Club
5 Ikuuni Hotel
17 Medium Lodge
     Boarding & Lodging
23 Sunnyland Hotel

PLACES TO EAT
7 New Boma Hotel
8 Katumba's Pub
15 T Tot Hotel

OTHER
4 Government Offices
6 Kenya Commercial Bank
9 Post Office
10 Standard Chartered Bank
11 Mosque
12 Barclays Bank (ATM)
13 Church
14 Nova Supermarket
16 Cooperative Curio Shop
18 Bus & Matatu Stand;
     Akamba Bus Office
19 Clocktower
20 Town Hall
21 Susu Centre
22 Daima Bank

ried pace of life and African atmosphere make it a good place to come and unwind after the urban insanity of Nairobi.

The best walking options are south of the centre, with numerous trails leading up to farms in the surrounding hills. Apparently, there's a magnetic hill a few kilometres from town that has its own laws of gravity, but you'll need local help to find the spot and we can't vouch for what you'll find when you get there!

Information

There are Barclays and Standard Chartered Banks with ATMs on the main road through town. There's an **Internet café** that charges KSh2.50 per minute in the Susu Centre, opposite the Total garage on the main road to the Nairobi–Mombasa highway. A handy place to buy crafts is the **Cooperative Curio Shop**, which employs local artisans.

Places to Stay

Songa Guest House (*doubles with bathroom KSh250*), beside a maize field just north of the market, is friendly and it's one of the cheapest places to stay.

Medium Lodge Boarding & Lodging *(doubles downstairs KSh150, upstairs KSh180)*, close to the market, is very basic but it's also friendly and cheap. The downstairs rooms get some noise from the disco in the basement at weekends.

Ikuuni Hotel *(☎ 21166; singles with shared bathroom KSh600, doubles with bathroom 1000)* is a better bet, the staff are friendly and its tidy rooms circle a courtyard. Sheets are washed and ironed(!) daily and there's a bar and restaurant.

Kafoca Club *(☎ 21933; singles/doubles with shared bathroom KSh300/400, singles with bathroom KSh1000)* is not far from Ikuuni Hotel. It's a little faded, but everything is clean, and the staff are friendly. There's a very popular bar, beer garden and restaurant and guarded parking.

Sunnyland Hotel *(☎ 20402; singles/doubles KSh450/700)* is one of the best places to stay. It is out along the road to Kitui next to Daima Bank. All rooms have new beds and linen and bathrooms with hot water; they're good value.

Garden Hotel *(☎ 20037, fax 21515; standard singles/doubles with bathroom KSh1830/ 3290, suite singles/doubles KSh3740/4860)*, past the government offices in the north of Machakos, is the best hotel in town. It is a huge and busy conference hotel with its own restaurant, bar and beer garden and a range of rooms at different prices. Rates include breakfast. Camping may be possible in the grounds.

Places to Eat

There are few restaurants other than those at the hotels. Quite a few hotels on the road next to the open-air market and around the bus/matatu stand do standard African fare.

T Tot Hotel *(snacks & meals KSh20-80)*, right in the centre of town, is hard to beat. It's clean, well organised, has an incredible number of waiters and the samosas, stews and side dishes are top class.

Katumba's Pub features an upstairs bar and restaurant with a veranda overlooking the street. There's also a pool table. **New Boma Hotel**, across the road, is similar.

Sunnyland Hotel has a good restaurant serving stews, curries and fried chicken, while **Garden Hotel** is a good place for a splurge. The buffet lunch or dinner here costs KSh475; breakfast is KSh300.

Getting There & Away

The Machakos bus station is behind the Mobil petrol station. The best way to get here is to a take a matatu from the country bus station on Landhies Rd in Nairobi (KSh70, one hour). There are also very frequent Busscar buses for KSh60 to KSh70.

There's an Akamba office at the bus station and it's possible to book transport to destinations throughout Kenya, mostly travelling via Nairobi. There's a direct service to Mombasa at 10am and 8.30pm (KSh450, six hours).

North of Nairobi

KIAMBU

The main reason to come to Kiambu, 15km northeast of Nairobi, is to visit **Paradise Lost** *(☎ 315273; e paradiselostcaves@yahoo.com; Kiambu Rd; admission US$10; camping KSh400, tents can be provided)*, an attractive picnic spot around 20km from Nairobi. Here are some 2.5-million-year-old caves set in 52 acres of forest and there's a waterfall and scenic dam where you can go fishing or swim (the owners insist there are no crocodiles!). Free boats are provided and horse and camel rides are also possible. You can get here by matatu No 100 from Racecourse Rd in Nairobi.

THIKA

☎ 0151

Thika is not much more than a busy little agricultural service town, and there aren't many of those famous flame trees to be seen. But if you feel the need to get out of Nairobi quickly (and who doesn't?) it's just 41km down the road. However, you may feel that any town that has to put up signs prohibiting people from dropping cremated ashes in the river should be avoided!

The town's only 'attractions' as such are the **Chania Falls** and **Thika Falls**, about 1km north of the centre of town on the edge of the busy Nairobi–Nyeri road. They're more popular with school trips than tourist buses, but are pleasant enough. The large **market** on the eastern edge of town is also worth a look, particularly for patterned sarongs and *shukas* (Maasai blankets), which are much cheaper here than in Nairobi.

Not far from Thika is one of Kenya's smaller national parks, **Ol Donyo Sabuk**,

AROUND NAIROBI

THIKA

PLACES TO STAY	4 Medical Centre
5 New Fulilia Hotel	6 Sagret Hotel (closed)
20 December Hotel	7 Local Matatus
	8 Mambu & Net Stop Cybercafes
PLACES TO EAT	11 Mathai Supermarket
9 Generations Cafe	12 Long-distance Matatus
10 Prismos Hotel	13 Thika Arcade
14 Macvast Executive	15 Matatus to Nairobi
Restaurant Two	16 Clock Tower
	17 Standard Chartered Bank
OTHER	18 Post Office
1 Hindu Temple	19 Kenya Commercial Bank
2 Jain Temple	21 Kenya Commercial Bank
3 Sikh Temple	22 Barclays Bank (ATM)

which can be reached by public transport from here (see the Central Highlands chapter for more details).

Places to Stay & Eat

If you decide to stay, there's a reasonable choice of accommodation, although the budget end of the scale gets pretty shabby and the cheapest places tend to be seedy late-night drinking establishments.

New Fulilia Hotel (☎ 31286; Uhuru St; singles KSh300), not to be confused with the scuzzy New Fulilia 1987 on Kame Nkrumah, is not as good as it used to be but is probably still the best of the cheapies, with a lively bar/restaurant.

Vybestar Thika Inn (☎ 22357; Kenyatta Hwy; singles/doubles KSh500/800), behind

the Caltex petrol station just outside town, is relatively new but has already gained a reputation as 'Thika's Carnivore,' with people coming all the way from Nairobi for *nyama choma* and a lively disco. Fortunately the rooms are set slightly away from the bar area, with phones, mosquito nets, steamy showers and nice linen. They're probably the best value in town.

December Hotel (☎ 22140; Commercial St; singles/doubles KSh600/1000), near the post office, is more of a mid-range place, with attached bar, restaurant and coffee bar. It's a touch overpriced but the rooms are large and clean and some have phones and balconies. The **Chania Tourist Lodge**, west of town, is similar but even more expensive.

Blue Post Hotel (☎ 22241; e bluepost@ wananchi.com; singles/doubles KSh1300/ 1600), close to the busy highway near the Chania River, is a surprisingly tourist-class place. The setting is lovely and the rooms with balconies overlooking the falls are excellent, but the other wings are pretty disappointing. The hotel has a rather average restaurant (lunch/dinner KSh550), a bar and the Cascades disco.

For a good meal in a regular restaurant try the amazingly named **Macvast Executive Restaurant Two** (Commercial St), **Prismos Hotel** (Kane Nkrumah St) or **Generations Cafe**. Thika also has some of the cheapest Tusker in Kenya, from KSh55 a bottle.

Getting There & Away

Matatus leave from a number of places around Thika. The main matatu stand, used chiefly by local matatus, is near Sagret Hotel; most long-distance matatus leave from around Workshop Rd and Commercial St. Destinations include Nairobi (KSh50, 40 minutes), Embu (KSh120, one hour), Nakuru (KSh180, two hours), Naivasha (KSh150, 1½ hours) and Nyeri (KSh150, 1½ hours). The road east to the coast isn't particularly secure. Matatus east towards Ol Donyo Sabuk (KSh50, 45 minutes) should be fine, but the bus route to Mombasa may be risky.

In Nairobi, matatus for Thika leave from the Total service station on Racecourse Rd.

LIMURU

About 30km northwest of Nairobi, Limuru possibly has even more of a European feel than the Ngong Hills, except here there are vast coffee and tea plantations blanketing the rolling hills, cut by swathes of conifer and eucalypt forest. The village itself is unremarkable, but there are some interesting detours in the surrounding hills.

On the road from Rwaka to Limuru via Banana Hill, is **Kentmere Club** (☎ 0154-50625, fax 50588; Tigoni), a perfect English farmhouse, hidden away in the Kenyan countryside. It's officially a private club, but you can become a day member for KSh60 and there's a very good restaurant and peaceful guesthouse, with rooms for KSh2503/3707/4961 for singles/doubles/triples. Gourmet three-course meals cost KSh1200.

Visits to a nearby tea estate are organised by **Mitchell's Kiambethu Tea Farm** (☎ 73084) at Tigoni. Trips start at 11am daily and finish at 2.30pm. The cost is KSh1200/600 per adult/child including food, but you must book in advance. You can also get here on a tour from Nairobi – try **Let's Go Travel** (☎ 02-340331, fax 336890; e info@letsgosafari .com). To get to Tigoni, take a No 106 matatu

to Banana Hill, and change to a No 116 matatu there. The No 116 passes the Tea Farm and the Kentmere Club.

The best places to see the escarpments of the Rift Valley are the roads that descend into the valley just past Limuru. The views are stunning; if you're on the new road, which runs direct to Naivasha, Mt Longonot is directly in front, while the plains of the Maasai sweep away to the south towards the Masai Mara National Reserve.

The old road, northwest of Limuru, was originally built by Italian POWs in WWII (there's a memorial chapel halfway down) and goes past the turn-offs for Mt Longonot, the Masai Mara and Hell's Gate. It's now been resurfaced and is in better condition than the 'new' road!

A number of viewpoints are signposted along these roads and are generally the safest places to stop. Predictably, there are souvenir stalls at all these places, selling Maasai blankets, sheepskin hats and other trinkets; there are few bargains to be found because of the number of tourists passing through.

AROUND NAIROBI

Southern Kenya

The region between Nairobi and Mombasa is home to some impressive national parks and nature reserves, most importantly Tsavo National Park, Kenya's largest, and Amboseli. Also here are some interesting community-run nature projects and the African towns of Voi, Wundanyi and Taveta, which are worth a detour on your way to the coast or Tanzania. This interesting region also includes the traditional homeland of the Akamba people – known to them as Ukambani – and the eastern extremity of the Maasai territory.

The towns here are easily accessible by public transport. However, for the national parks you're probably best off taking an organised safari from Nairobi. If you really must visit the parks independently, it may be possible to arrange transport to one of the budget tented camps in Tsavo East from Voi, or there's a remote chance of hitching a lift with a private safari party at the main gates to Tsavo East and Tsavo West. Wildlife drives and guided walks can be arranged at many of the lodges and camps and local safaris can also be arranged through Kibo Slopes Cottages near Oloitokitok.

AMBOSELI NATIONAL PARK

Amboseli *(nonresident adult/child per day US$30/10, resident KSh500/200, camping US$10/2; vehicle per day KSh200, smartcard required)* is the second most popular park in Kenya after the Masai Mara, mainly because of the spectacular backdrop of Africa's highest peak, Mt Kilimanjaro, which broods over the southern boundary of the park.

At 392 sq km, Amboseli is a small park and it lacks the profusion of animal species found in the Masai Mara, but the landscape provides limited cover for wildlife, so you have a good chance of seeing some of the larger predators. The vegetation here used to be much denser, but rising salinisation, damage by elephants and irresponsible behaviour by safari vehicles has caused terrible erosion. Amboseli can turn into a real dustbowl in the dry season.

Buffaloes, lions, gazelles, cheetahs, wildebeests, hyenas, jackals, warthogs, zebras, Masai giraffes and baboons are all present, but the last few black rhinos were moved to Tsavo West in 1995 after a sustained period

Highlights

- Watching an elephant herd at dawn at the foot of Mt Kilimanjaro in Amboseli National Park

- Visiting one of the community and privately run wildlife sanctuaries between Amboseli and Tsavo National Parks and taking a bush walk with a Maasai guide

- Taking in the incredible landscapes at Tsavo West National Park, including the epic Shetani Lava Flow and the hippo pools at Mzima Springs

- Appreciating the vast open spaces and rhinos and elephants covered in red dust at Tsavo East National Park

of poaching. In the permanent swamps of Enkongo Narok and Olokenya, large elephant herds can be seen grazing with Mt Kilimanjaro in the background – it's probably the definitive Kenyan wildlife shot and almost every visitor ends up with an 'elephants in front of Mt Kilimanjaro' photo in their album.

Erosion and grass die-off is having a dramatic effect at Amboseli and it's only a matter of time before the lack of food makes the animals move on. It's important for vehicles to stick to the defined tracks to avoid making things any worse. Hopefully others will follow suit and the grasslands that drew all these animals here in the first place can be preserved.

Places to Stay & Eat

The **camp site** is just inside the southern boundary of the park, with toilets, an unreliable water supply (bring your own) and a bar selling warm beer and sodas (soft drinks). It's fenced off from the wildlife so you can walk around safely at night. *Don't* keep food in your tent, though, as baboons often visit during the day looking for an easy feed. A buffet lunch at any of the big lodges will cost US$16 to US$20.

The two lodges in the centre of the park have grand views of Mt Kilimanjaro.

Amboseli Lodge *(in Nairobi ☎ 02-227136, fax 219982; full board per person US$40 in low*

season, singles/doubles full board US$117/ 180 in high season) consists of a number of comfortable cottages dotted around an expansive lawn and garden with sweeping views. There's a swimming pool and quite a few tour groups drop in for lunch (US$16).

Ol Tukai Lodge *(in Nairobi ☎ 02-540780, fax 540821; singles/doubles US$120/180 in low season, US$130/200 in high season)* belongs to the Block Hotels group. It's a splendid place, with soaring *makuti* roofs and tranquil shaded gardens. The split-level bar has wonderful views and the overall atmosphere is of peace and luxury. There's a pool here and two of the attractive wooden cottages have wheelchair access.

Amboseli Serena Lodge *(in Nairobi ☎ 02-2710511, fax 2718100; ⓔ mktg@serena.co.ke;*

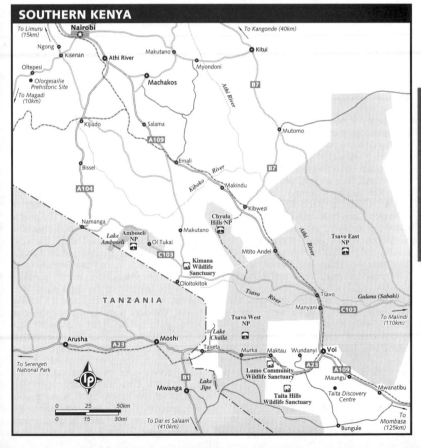

SOUTHERN KENYA

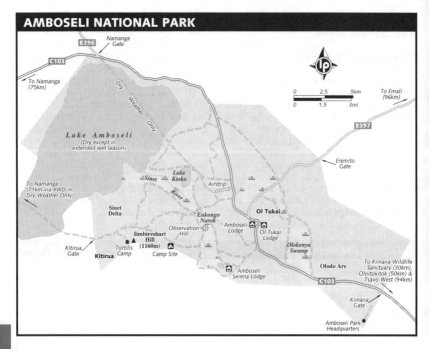

AMBOSELI NATIONAL PARK

full board per person in low season US$75, singles/doubles with full board US$205/250 in high season) is a posh Serena hotel near the southern perimeter of the park. The adobe-style cottages make a change from the usual *makuti*, and there's a pool and pleasant gardens. The nearby Enkongo Narok swamp ensures constant bird and animal activity.

Tortilis Camp (in Nairobi ☎ 02-604053, fax 604050; ⓔ safaris@chelipeacock.coke; singles/doubles with full board US$212/424 in low season, US$310/520 in high season), further west, near the public camp site, is a wonderfully conceived place with a perfect Mt Kilimanjaro vista. The shady lounge and dining areas are elevated to exploit the views, while the permanent tents nestle among a stand of *Acacia tortilis* trees. It's very ecofriendly – food is cooked without using firewood and solar power heats the water. The lodge also grows its own organic vegetables in a huge vegetable garden. Nature walks with trained Maasai guides can be arranged.

Getting There & Away

Air Air Kenya has daily flights between Wilson Airport in Nairobi and Amboseli. These depart from Nairobi at 7.30am and take about an hour (US$88 one way). The return flight leaves Amboseli at 8.30am. You'll need to arrange with one of the lodges or a safari company for a vehicle to meet you at the airstrip.

Car & 4WD The usual approach to Amboseli is via Namanga, 165km south of Nairobi on the Tanzanian border. The road is sealed and in surprisingly good condition from Nairobi to Namanga, but the 75km dirt road to the Namanga Gate can be fiercely corrugated (allow around four hours to reach Amboseli from Nairobi). In the dry season, it is also possible to enter through Kitirua Gate, but this is a bumpy old road and it's hard to follow. The track branches right off the main Namanga to Amboseli road after about 15km.

Some people also enter from the east via the Amboseli–Tsavo West road, although this track is in a terrible state and shouldn't even be considered in a conventional vehicle. During the 1990s, there were some bandit attacks in this area, so vehicles have to travel in convoys accompanied by armed guards, which leave the Kimana Gate of Amboseli at around 7am, 9am and 2pm.

Book in advance at either the Amboseli Serena or Ol Tukai lodges. Allow 2½ hours to cover the 94km from Amboseli to the Chyulu Gate of Tsavo West.

Although some roads in Amboseli are probably manageable in a 2WD, no self-respecting car-hire company will let you bring one in. A 4WD is the way to go. Petrol is available at the Amboseli Serena Lodge.

AROUND AMBOSELI

There are several private sanctuaries and numerous luxury tented camps hidden away in the bush between Amboseli and Tsavo West National Parks, offering plentiful wildlife, fine views of Mt Kilimanjaro and a level of peace and quiet that is sadly missing from some parts of Amboseli.

The only access to this area is the poorly maintained dirt track leading west from Emali (on the Nairobi–Mombasa highway) to Oloitokitok on the Tanzanian border, or the even more diabolical road between Amboseli and Tsavo West.

Namanga, on the opposite side of the park, is the main border crossing into Tanzania and has a few good places to stay.

Bissel

On your way from Nairobi to Namanga, it's worth stopping in the little community of Bissel, a vibrant Maasai township with a busy market where you can buy all sorts of Maasai goods. You'll be a bit of a novelty, but people are very friendly.

Namanga
☎ 0303

A large township has grown up around the Tanzanian border at Namanga and it's a good place to break the journey from Nairobi to Arusha or Amboseli. The border crossing is open 24 hours and the two border posts are almost next to each other, so you can walk across. There are numerous moneychangers on the Kenyan side of the border (however, don't believe anyone who says you can't take Kenyan shillings into Tanzania or vice versa!).

Numerous Maasai women come here to sell bead jewellery and other Maasai crafts. There's some great stuff on offer, but you'll have to bargain fiercely. There are some nice places to stay and overland groups pass through quite regularly, so there's a decent

chance of finding a lift into Amboseli or across the border.

Namanga Safari Lodge (☎ 32216; camping KSh150, doubles KSh500) has cheap and cheerful accommodation in a garden full of stucco animals. It also serves cheap meals.

Namanga River Hotel (☎ 32059; singles/doubles KSh1480/2770, camping per person KSh300) is a posher affair with nice cottages, a good restaurant and bar, plus a shady camping area set among acacia trees. It's often booked out by overland groups. Meals cost around KSh500.

Getting There and Away   The large Kobil petrol station marks the turn-off to Amboseli and is a good place to ask around for lifts. Fill your tank here if you're driving into Amboseli.

Buses from Nairobi to Arusha pass through daily (KSh250, two hours). There's an Akamba bus office at the Kobil petrol station, where you can book onto the morning service to Arusha. Several other companies also cover this route. Matatus also run here from the petrol station at the junction of River Rd and Ronald Ngala St in Nairobi (KSh200). Peugeots (shared taxis) on this route charge KSh300.

On the Tanzanian side of the border, there are matatus and Peugeots to Arusha (KSh200 to KSh250, 1½ hours). For more details on getting to/from Tanzania see the Getting There & Away chapter.

Kimana Wildlife Sanctuary

About 30km east of Amboseli, close to the road that connects Amboseli to Tsavo West, is this 40-hectare **wildlife sanctuary** (admission per person US$10, vehicle KSh100). It's owned and run by local Maasai and wildlife is probably just as plentiful here as in Amboseli. The sanctuary was set up with the help of Usaid and the KWS in 1996 and is doing quite well, particularly now that the African Safari Club have built a lodge and tented camp here. The dirt road going west from Emali (on the Nairobi–Mombasa highway) to Oloitokitok passes the entrance to the reserve, but you'll need a vehicle to enter the sanctuary itself.

There's officially no need to join the Tsavo convoy if you're coming from Amboseli, but the area south of Kimana has a reputation for banditry.

Places to Stay There are three guarded camp sites *(camping KSh150)* within the sanctuary.

Close to Kimana village on the edge of the sanctuary, **Kimana Zebra Lodge** and **Kimana Twiga Luxury Camp** are run by the private African Safari Club (see African Safari Club under Accommodation in the Facts for the Visitor chapter).

Numerous luxury camps are dotted in the bush just off the road between Kimana and Tsavo West.

Nyati Safari Camp *(☎ 0122-32506; ⓦ www .nyaticamp.com; singles/doubles in low season US$85/150, in high season US$100/180)* is a very stylish Italian-run operation with just 10 tents aligned to face Mt Kilimanjaro. It's 16km outside Tsavo West.

Campi ya Kanzi *(Nairobi ☎ 02-605349, fax 605391; ⓦ www.campiyakanzi.com; singles/ doubles from US$480/740)* is a luxury tented camp on a 400-sq-km Maasai-run conservation project. It's centred on a nostalgically decorated stone cottage and offers extremely comfortable tents with fine views.

Oloitokitok

At the end of the road from Emali is this dusty little border post. Non-Kenyans aren't allowed to cross into Tanzania here, though, except as part of a tour with **Kibo Slope Safaris** *(☎ 0302-22091, fax 22427; doubles in low season KSh1600, singles/doubles in high season US$30/60)*, which also operates a lodge close to Oloitokitok. Rates include breakfast and meals are available.

It's possible to get here by matatu from Emali (KSh300), but it's a bumpy, dusty ride.

MAKINDU

This dusty junction town, 45km northwest of Mtito Andei is worth a visit for the **Makindu Handicraft Cooperative Society**, a community project that employs 120 displaced Akamba people who produce excellent woodcarvings from renewable woods (see the boxed text 'Good Wood' in the Facts for the Visitor chapter). The Sikh and Muslim faiths are vying for the attention of the townspeople here with two huge hospitals and religious centres. The Sikh *gurdwara* (pilgrim's hostel) welcomes visitors and you can stay here overnight for a small fee.

The best place to stay around here is **Hunter's Lodge** *(☎ 0302-22469; singles/doubles*

KSh1520/2530)* a few kilometres down the road towards Nairobi. It's a relaxed hotel with comfortable rooms that look over a pond and there are massive marabou storks in the acacia trees. The restaurant serves big buffet meals for KSh725.

CHYULU HILLS NATIONAL PARK

Northwest of Tsavo West National Park are the dramatic **Chyulu Hills** *(adult/child US$15/ 5)*, a collection of ancient volcanic cinder cones. The hills were gazetted as a national park in 1983 and have splendid views of Mt Kilimanjaro and populations of elands, giraffes, zebras and wildebeests, plus a small number of elephants, lions and buffaloes.

Within the Chyulu Hills is the longest **lava tube** in the world – Leviathan – formed by hot lava flowing beneath a cooled crust, but you'll need full caving equipment to explore it. Caving and trekking trips in the hills may be possible with **Savage Wilderness Safaris Ltd** *(in Nairobi ☎/fax 02-521590; ⓔ white water@alphanet.co.ke.org; ⓦ www.whitewater kenya.com; Sarit Centre, Westlands, PO Box 1000, Nairobi)*.

Although there's loads to see, the park lacks even basic infrastructure. Memories of the forced evictions of squatters by KWS guards in the 1980s are still fresh in the minds of local people and it's only in the last year, with heavy investment from the charity Care for the Wild International, that any serious attempt has been made to open up the park. The **park headquarters** *(☎ 0302-22483; PO Box 458, Kibwezi)* are being developed close to Kibwezi on the Nairobi–Mombasa highway and a **public camp site** is being built nearby at Kiboko further northwest on the main highway.

For the time being, the best access is on the west side of the park, from the track between Amboseli and Tsavo West. The track into the hills from the park headquarters on the east side of the park is extremely hard going. Be careful when driving through Kibwezi – baboons have taken to harassing passing cars and buses for food.

At the time of research, the closest place to stay to the park was the excellent **Ol Donyo Wuas** *(in Nairobi ☎ 02-882521, fax 882728; ⓔ bonham.luke@swiftkenya.com; full board per person US$395, single supplement US$100)*, an innovative ecolodge that recycles water and uses solar power. The cottages here are built from local materials and US$20 per guest per day is donated to fund local community projects, including conservation, water projects and health services. Rates include wildlife drives, horse riding and the Big Five can all be seen in the surrounding wildlife sanctuary.

Another option is **Nyati Safari Camp** (see Kimana Wildlife Sanctuary earlier in this chapter).

Getting There & Away

Until the road from Kibwezi is brought up to standard, your best bet to get here is the 4WD track that branches off the Amboseli–Tsavo West road about 10km west of Chyulu Gate. Ol Donyo Wuas can be reached via this track, although most guests fly in on air charters from Nairobi.

The park headquarters is signposted just outside Kibwezi, about 41km northwest of Mtito Andei on the main Nairobi–Mombasa highway.

SHETANI LAVA FLOW & CAVES

About 4km west of the Chyulu Gate of Tsavo West National Park on the road to Amboseli are the spectacular **Shetani lava flows**. This vast expanse of folded black lava spreads for 50 sq km across the savanna at the foot of the Chyulu Hills. The last major eruption here is believed to have taken place around 200 years ago, but there are still few plants among the cinders. It's possible to follow the lava flows back from the Amboseli–Tsavo West road to the ruined cinder cone of Shetani (from the Swahili for 'devil') at the foot of the Chyulu Hills. The views are spectacular, but be wary of wildlife in this area.

Nearby are the **Shetani Caves**, which are also a result of volcanic activity. You'll need a torch (flashlight) if you want to explore the caves, but be watchful for wildlife and watch your footing on the razor-sharp rocks.

TSAVO NATIONAL PARK

At nearly 22,000 sq km, Tsavo is the largest national park in Kenya and for administrative purposes, it has been split into Tsavo West National Park (9000 sq km) and Tsavo East National Park (11,747 sq km), which are divided by the Nairobi–Mombasa highway (A109). Both parks feature some excellent scenery but the undergrowth is considerably higher than in Amboseli or Masai Mara, so

it takes a little more effort to spot the wildlife, particularly the big predators. The compensation for this is that the landscapes are some of the most dramatic in Kenya and the parks see comparatively few visitors, compared to the hordes who descend on Amboseli and the Masai Mara.

The northern half of Tsavo West is the most developed, with a number of excellent lodges and several places you can get out of your jeep or minibus and walk, including the Mzima Springs (with plenty of hippos) and the Chaimu Crater. The landscape here is made of volcanic hills and sweeping expanses of savanna. The southern part of the park, on the far side of the dirt road between Voi and Taveta on the Tanzanian border, is rarely visited.

Tsavo East is more remote, but there are a number of lodges, and, refreshingly, a number of independent budget tented camps, where you can stay for as little as US$30. Most of the action here is concentrated along the Galana River; the north part of the park is bandit country and isn't really secure. The landscape here is drier, with rolling plains hugging the edge of the Yatta Escarpment, a vast prehistoric lava flow.

During the dry season, the landscape in both parks is dusty and parched, but it erupts into colour at the end of the wet season, although, of course, there's more greenery to hide the wildlife at this time.

Both parks were once the lands of the Orma, Watta, Maasai and Kamba people, but all the villagers were displaced when the park was gazetted. Some of these people have now established community wildlife sanctuaries on the outskirts of the park (see later in this section). Tsavo had terrible problems with poachers during the 1980s, when the elephant population dropped from 45,000 to just 5000 and rhinos were almost wiped out entirely. Populations are slowly recovering and there are now about 8000 elephants in the two parks, but less than 100 rhinos, down from about 9000 in 1969. The last few years have seen a worrying upsurge in poaching.

Information

Entry is US$27/10 per adult/child per day, vehicles cost KSh200 and camping is US$10 per adult. However, the two parks are administered separately so you have to pay separate entrance fees for each. Both use the smartcard system – you'll need enough credit for your vehicle, entry fee and any camping charges for as long as you're staying. Smartcards can be bought and recharged at the Voi Gate to Tsavo East.

There's a small **visitor centre** *(admission free; open 8am-5pm)* near the Mtito Andei Gate to Tsavo West, with interesting displays on conservation issues and some of the animals and birds in the park.

All track junctions in Tsavo East and Tsavo West have numbered and signposted cairns, which in theory makes navigation fairly simple. In practice, the signposts are often missing and the numbering system is confusing so you'll need a map. Survey of Kenya publishes a *Tsavo East National Park* map (KSh500), and a newer *Tsavo West National Park* map (KSh700). Both are available from the visitor centre at Tsavo West. Tourist Maps' *Tsavo National Parks* (KSh250) covers both parks.

Fuel is available at Kilaguni Serena and Ngulia Safari lodges in Tsavo West, and at Voi Safari Lodge in Tsavo East.

Tsavo West National Park

This fine national park covers a huge variety of landscapes, from swamps and natural springs to rocky peaks, extinct volcanic cones and rolling plains. It's easily the more beautiful of the two parks, but wildlife can be hard to spot because of the dense scrub. Birds are very common and there are large populations of elephants, zebras, hippos and leopards. Lions are out there, but they tend to stay hidden.

The focus is **Mzima Springs**, which produces an incredible 93 million gallons of fresh water a day. The springs are the source of the bulk of Mombasa's fresh water and you can walk down to a large pool that is a favourite haunt of hippos and crocodiles. There's an underwater viewing chamber, which unfortunately just gives a view of thousands of primeval-looking fish. Be a little careful here – both hippos and crocs are not to be trifled with.

Chaimu Crater, just southeast of Kilaguni Serena Lodge and the **Roaring Rocks** viewpoint nearby, can be climbed in about 15 minutes. The views from either spot are stunning, with falcons, eagles and buzzards whirling over the plains. While there is little danger walking these trails, be aware

that the wildlife is still out there so keep your eyes open.

Another attraction is the **Ngulia Rhino Sanctuary**, at the base of Ngulia Hills, part of the Rhino Ark programme. It's close to Ngulia Safari Lodge, but a long drive from anywhere else. The 70-sq-km area is surrounded by a metre-high electric fence and provides a measure of security for the park's last 49 black rhinos. There are driving tracks and waterholes within the enclosed area and there's a good chance of seeing one of these elusive creatures. Large numbers of elephants, buffaloes and other species have also moved into the enclosure.

Some of the more unusual species to look out for in the park include the naked mole rat, which can sometimes be seen kicking sand from its burrows, and the enigmatically named white-bellied go-away bird, which is often seen perched in dead trees. Red-beaked hornbills and bateleur eagles are also common. Look out for dung beetles rolling huge balls of elephant dung along the tracks.

It's possible to go **rock-climbing** at Tembo Peak and the Ngulia Hills but you'll need to arrange this with the **park warden** *(☎ 0302-22483; PO Box 71, Mtito Andei)*. This area is also fantastic for birdlife and there's a very reliable hippo pool on the Mukui River, near the Ngulia Safari Lodge.

Lake Jipe, (pronounced *ji-pay*) at the southwest end of the park, is reached by a desperately dusty track from near Taveta. The lodge here has closed down, but there's a basic camp site and bandas where you can hire boats to take you hippo and crocodile spotting on the lake (US$5). Huge herds of elephants come to the lake to drink and large flocks of migratory birds stop here from February to May.

Places to Stay – Budget & Mid-Range

Tsavo West has several basic camp sites with good bathroom and shower blocks. Currently, the **public camp sites** *(camping per person US$8)* are at Komboyo, near the Mtito Andei Gate, and at Chyulu, just outside the Chyulu Gate. There are also a number of **special camp sites**; their locations change from time to time so check with the warden (☎ 03202-22483). Write to: Assistant Director, Tsavo West National Park, PO Box 71, Mtito Andei.

TSAVO EAST & WEST NATIONAL PARKS

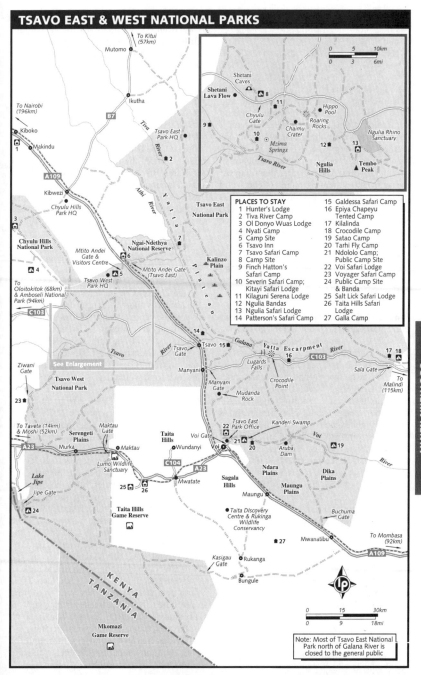

To Kitui
(57km)

Mutomo

Ikutha

To Nairobi
(196km)

Kiboko

Makindu

B7

Tiva River

Tsavo East
Park HQ

2

Shetani
Caves

Shetani
Lava Flow

8

11

Chyulu
Gate

Chaimu
Crater

Roaring
Rocks

Hippo
Pool

Ngulia Rhino
Sanctuary

9

10

Mzima
Springs

Tsavo River

12

13

Ngulia
Hills

Tembo
Peak

A109

Kibwezi

Chyulu Hills
Park HQ

3

Chyulu Hills
National Park

4

Athi River

Yatta

Tsavo East
National Park

Ngai-Ndethya
National Reserve

6

Mtito Andei
Gate &
Visitors Centre

Mtito Andei Gate
(Tsavo East)

Tsavo West
Park HQ

5

To
Oloitokitok (68km) &
Amboseli National
Park (94km)

C103

7

Kalinzo
Plain

Plateau

PLACES TO STAY
1 Hunter's Lodge
2 Tiva River Camp
3 Ol Donyo Wuas Lodge
4 Nyati Camp
5 Camp Site
6 Tsavo Inn
7 Tsavo Safari Camp
8 Camp Site
9 Finch Hatton's
   Safari Camp
10 Severin Safari Camp;
   Kitayi Safari Lodge
11 Kilaguni Serena Lodge
12 Ngulia Bandas
13 Ngulia Safari Lodge
14 Patterson's Safari Camp
15 Galdessa Safari Camp
16 Epiya Chapeyu
   Tented Camp
17 Kilalinda
18 Crocodile Camp
19 Satao Camp
20 Tarhi Fly Camp
21 Ndololo Camp;
   Public Camp Site
22 Voi Safari Lodge
23 Voyager Safari Camp
24 Public Camp Site
   & Banda
25 Salt Lick Safari Lodge
26 Taita Hills Safari
   Lodge
27 Galla Camp

Ziwani
Gate

Tsavo West
National Park

23

To Taveta (14km)
& Moshi (52km)

A23

Murka

Serengeti
Plains

Maktau
Gate

Maktau

Lumo Wildlife
Sanctuary

Taita
Hills

Wundanyi

C104

Mwatate

25 **26**

Taita Hills
Game Reserve

Lake
Jipe

Jipe Gate

24

14

Tsavo
Gate

Tsavo **15**

Galana

Yatta Escarpment

River

17 18

16

C103

Sala Gate

To
Malindi
(115km)

Manyani

Lugards
Falls

Crocodile
Point

Manyani
Gate

Mudanda
Rock

Tsavo East
Park Office

22

21

20

Kanderi Swamp

Aruba
Dam

Vol

19

River

Voi Gate

Voi

Ndara
Plains

Dika
Plains

Sagala
Hills

Maungu

Maungu
Plains

Taita Discovery
Centre & Rukinga
Wildlife
Conservancy

Buchuma
Gate

27

Mwanatibu

To Mombasa
(92km)

A109

Kasigau
Gate

Rukanga

Bungule

KENYA

TANZANIA

Mkomazi
Game Reserve

See Enlargement

Tsavo

River

Tsavo
Gate

0   5   10km
0   3   6mi

0   15   30km
0   9   18mi

Note: Most of Tsavo East National
Park north of Galana River is
closed to the general public

LP

Down on Lake Jipe are some simple **bandas** *(KSh1000)* and a **camp site** *(camping per person KSh150).*

Ngulia Bandas *(book through Let's Go Travel ☎ 02-340331, fax 214713;* e *info@lets gosafari.com; 3-person bandas KSh3000),* on the edge of Ngulia Hills, offers accommodation in cheap bandas with a bathroom and kitchen. Bedding, towels, mosquito nets and kerosene lanterns are provided, but you'll need to bring everything else with you, including drinking water. Eating at nearby lodges is usually only an option at lunchtime.

Outside Mtito Andei Gate in the village of the same name, there are plenty of cheap and basic **board and lodgings** but most serve as brothels for long-haul truck drivers. The Shell, Total, Caltex petrol stations have **roadhouses** serving cheap meals and drinks.

Tsavo Inn *(☎/fax 0147-30092; singles/ doubles KSh3600/4500)* is outside the park, opposite the Mtito Andei Gate. It's pleasant but overpriced and there's no particular reason to stay here.

Places to Stay – Top End At Kitani, **Severin Safari Camp** *(in Mombasa ☎ 011-485001, fax 48521;* e *severin@severin-sea-lodge.com; singles/doubles US$80/160 in low season, US$156/240 in high season)* is a brand new and very attractive complex of tents under thatched canopies. Tents have bathroom, mosquito nets and nice furnishings. The **Kitani Safari Lodge**, about 2km further on, is owned by the same company. After renovations are complete, it should offer similar standards but in self-catering bandas.

Ngulia Safari Lodge *(☎ 0147-30000, fax 30006;* e *ngulialodge@kenya-safri.co.ke; singles/doubles with full board US$100/160 in low season, US$150/200 in high season)* is a curiously unattractive building in a spectacular location. The surrounding Ngulia Hills attract loads of birds and the lodge puts out bait for leopards, which guarantees you a sighting, although not a place in animal welfare heaven! There are views over a water hole on one side and the Ngulia Rhino Sanctuary on the other.

Kilaguni Serena Lodge *(☎ 0302-22471/5, fax 22470; rooms per person US$60 in low season, US$185/250 in high season; double suites US$450)* is now owned by the Serena Group and it's an attractive place, with a splendid bar and restaurant overlooking a busy waterhole – the vista stretches all the way from Mt Kilimanjaro to the Chyulu Hills. Guided walks in the nearby Seven Sisters Hills are possible and the suites here are truly luxurious.

Finch Hatton's Safari Camp *(aka Kambi ya Simba; in Nairobi ☎ 02-310355/6, fax 217778;* e *finchhattons@iconnect.co.ke; singles/ doubles full board US$210/285 in low season, US$260/370 in high season)* is a very upmarket tented camp with bone china and gold shower taps. The lodge is named after Denys Finch-Hatton, the playboy hunter and lover of Karen Blixen, who died at Tsavo. It's situated among springs and hippo pools in the west of the park. In keeping with the colonial mood, guests are requested to dress for dinner. The camp has it's own airstrip (flights from Nairobi cost US$300).

Voyager Safari Camp *(in Nairobi ☎ 02-446651, fax 446533;* e *info@heritagehotels .co.ke; singles/doubles full-board US$111/150 in low season, US$185/250 in high season)* is by the Zimani Gate at the southwest end of the park. It's another luxury tented place and as well as wildlife walks, you can visit WWII battlefields and Grogan's Castle, a fortress-like hilltop residence built in the 19th century by Ewart Grogan, who became famous for walking from Cape Town to Cairo to prove his love for a woman!

Getting There & Away The main access to Tsavo West is through the Mtito Andei Gate on the Mombasa–Nairobi highway in the north of the park, where you'll find the park headquarters and visitor centre. The main track cuts straight across to Kilaguni Serena Lodge and Chyulu Gate. Security is a problem here, so vehicles for Amboseli travel in armed convoys, leaving the Kilaguni Serena Lodge at 8am and 10am.

Another 48km southeast along the main road is the Tsavo Gate. It is handy for the Ngulia hills lodges and the rhino sanctuary. Few people use the Maktau Gate on the Voi–Taveta road in the south of the park.

Even assuming you had your own 2WD (hire companies would never let you bring one of theirs here), the tracks here are only really suitable for 4WDs. The roads in the south of the park are particularly challenging.

If you want to try and hitch through the park, you may stand a remote chance from near the main gate in Mtito Andei.

Tsavo East National Park

The landscape in Tsavo East is flatter and drier, despite the fact that one of Kenya's largest rivers flows through the middle of the park. The main track through the park follows the Galana River from the Voi Gate to the Sala Gate. The park headquarters, where you can charge and buy smartcards, is at Voi Gate.

Much of the wildlife spotting is concentrated on the Galana River, which has plentiful crocs and hippos. There are several places along the river where you can, with caution, get out of your vehicle. Most scenic are **Lugards Falls**, a wonderful landscape of water-sculpted channels, and **Crocodile Point**, where you may see hippos and crocs. There are usually armed guards around, but you shouldn't get too close to the water. Kudus, waterbucks and dik diks are common along the river banks. Also of interest is the **Mudanda Rock**, towering over a natural dam near the Manyani Gate, which attracts elephants in the dry season.

The bush is thinner than in Tsavo West, so wildlife is easier to spot, although it's not as plentiful. The rolling hills in the south of the park are home to large herds of elephants, usually covered in red dust. The action is concentrated around the waterhole at Voi Safari Lodge, and the **Kanderi Swamp**, which is home to a profusion of wildlife and the public camp site. You can expect elephants to stroll through the camp site in the evenings. Further into the park, 30km east of Voi gate, is the **Aruba Dam** built across the Voi River, which also sees loads of wildlife. A lodge has been under construction here for some time.

The area north of the Galana River is dominated by the Yatta Escarpment, a vast prehistoric lava flow, but unfortunately much of this area is off limits due to the ongoing campaign against poachers. During the 1980s, the rhino population here was decimated and there are worrying signs that poaching is on the increase. Four rhinos and ten elephants were killed here by Somali poachers in 2001, the first such killings in years. Some observers suggest the increase in poaching is due to America's war on terror, which has closed down the sources of the funding for many warlord factions in Somalia.

Until their partial translocation to Tsavo East, the sole surviving population of hirola antelope was found near the Kenya–Somali border in the south Tana River and

Man-eaters of Tsavo

The maneless lions of Tsavo National Park have a reputation as the fiercest predators in Africa. During the construction of the Uganda railway in the 19th century, just two of these lions ate their way through an incredible 140 Indian workers in the course of a single year! The surviving workers soon decided that the lions had to be ghosts or devils, due to their uncanny ability to slip into the fiercely guarded camps, remove sleeping victims from their tents and vanish with the bodies into the night without a sound.

A series of ever more ingenious traps was devised by the chief engineer, Colonel JH Patterson, but each time, the lions evaded them, striking unerringly at weak points in the camp defences. In one trap, three goats were tied to a 110kg metal rail, but one of the lions dragged the entire trap into the bush while Patterson blasted his gun impotently into the darkness. Patterson was finally able to bag the first lion by hiding on a flimsy wooden scaffold baited with the corpse of a donkey that the lions had killed the previous night. The second man-eater was dispatched a short time later from a tree where the lion had chased a gang of Indian workers the night before, although it took six bullets to bring the massive beast down.

The dead lions were eventually sold to the Chicago Field Museum, where they can still be seen today. Recent research has shown that the lions had badly damaged teeth, which may have driven them to abandon their normal prey and become man-eaters. Patterson wrote a best-selling book about the experience, The Man-Eaters of Tsavo, which was later filmed as The Ghosts and the Darkness, with the addition of an American sidekick to sell the story to Hollywood audiences. Although there's been nothing to compare to this since, at least six local people were attacked by lions at Tsavo from 1995 to 2000, so be a little cautious when walking at Chaimu Crater, Mzima Springs or Lugards Falls!

Garissa districts. Intense poaching (for meat) and habitat destruction have reduced their numbers from an estimated 14,000 in 1976 to a pitiful 450 today, 97 of them being in Tsavo East. There are also around 48 black rhinos, moved here from Nairobi National Park, although how long they last in this hard-to-police sanctuary remains to be seen.

Places to Stay – Budget There's a single camping area with basic toilets at **Ndololo** *(camping per person US$8)*, near Kanderi Swamp. Elephants wander through here all the time. You can always pop in for a beer or a meal at Ndololo Camp if you book in advance. There are also a few **special camp sites**, which move from year to year – inquire with the KWS at Tsavo in advance.

Ndololo Camp *(☎ 0147-30050, fax 30285; e info@tsavoparkhotel.com; singles/doubles/ triples in safari tents with full board US$40/ 60/80)*, nearby, is a great-value tented camp run by the owners of Tsavo Park Hotel in Voi. The 15 comfortable tents have beds, mosquito nets, and a canvas toilet and shower cubicle. The buffet lunch costs KSh750. The camp offers nature walks.

Tarhi Fly Camp *(in Mombasa ☎/fax 011-487378; e kedev@africaonline.co.ke; safari tents with bathroom per person US$35 plus $12 camping fee)* is another reasonably priced tented camp. It's right on the edge of the Voi River about 14km east of Voi Gate and it's a lovely peaceful spot. Rates include meals and wildlife walks with a Maasai guide.

If you want cheap accommodation but don't want to camp, you can stay in Voi (see later in this chapter).

Places to Stay – Top End Just 4km from Voi Gate, **Voi Safari Lodge** *(☎ 0147-30019, fax 30080; e voilodge@kenya-safari.co.ke; singles/doubles with full board in low season US$100/160, in high season US$150/200)* is a cracking lodge owned by Kenya Safari Lodges and Hotels. It's perched on the edge of an escarpment overlooking an incredible sweep of savanna, with a natural waterhole that attracts elephants, buffaloes and the occasional predator. Rather chubby rock hyraxes sun themselves on every ledge. Facilities include a pool and several restaurants and bars.

Satao Camp *(book through Southern Cross Safaris in Mombasa ☎ 011-475074, fax 471257; e sales@southerncrosssafaris.com; singles/ doubles US$120/170)* on the Voi River is a popular upmarket tented camp. It's nicely laid out and you can take guided bush walks (US$30) and hire jeeps for wildlife drives (US$100 per day).

Let's Go Travel *(☎ 02-340331, fax 214713; e info@letsgosafari.com)*, in Nairobi, handles bookings for the next three tented camps.

Epiya Chapeyu Tented Camp *(singles/ doubles US$70/140)* is another tented camp in a lovely palm-shaded glade by the Galana River. Wildlife walks and drives are available. It's closed April to July.

Patterson's Safari Camp *(singles/doubles from US$85/120)*, further west, is another tented camp with the usual self-contained safari tents. It's a relaxed place, only 9km from Tsavo Gate, and it sits on the spot where Patterson finally hunted down the man-eaters of Tsavo.

Tsavo Safari Camp, beside the Athi River in the northern part of the park, close to Mtito Andei Gate, used to be one of the nicest places to stay, but with the demise of the Kilimanjaro Safari Club, its future is uncertain.

Galdessa Safari Camp *(in Nairobi ☎ 02-574689, fax 564945; e mellifera@swiftkenya .com; w www.galdessa.com; singles/doubles US$336/512)* on the Galana River, 15km west of Lugards Falls, is very close to the rhino sanctuary and is heavily involved in rhino conservation. It's very ecofriendly but frighteningly expensive. It's closed in May.

Tiva River Camp *(book through Rove Africa Safaris ☎ 02-512862, fax 512493; e safaris@ roveafrica.com; singles/doubles US$450/690)* is an exclusive, mobile tented camp on the banks of the Tiva River in the north of the park. It's known for it's guided bush walks. The camp is closed June to October.

Just outside the Sala Gate are several private camps. The private African Safari Club (see Accommodation in the Facts for the Visitor chapter) owns the tented **Crocodile Camp**, close to the gate.

Kilalinda *(in Nairobi ☎ 02-605349, fax 605391; w www.privatewilderness.com/ kilalinda_int.htm; singles/doubles from US$480/ 740)* is a very fine ecolodge that was built without felling any trees. Guests pay a US$20 conservation fee that goes into local community projects and maintaining the surrounding wildlife reserve.

Getting There & Away Most tourist safaris enter Tsavo East via the Sala Gate, where a good dirt road runs east for 110km to Malindi (see Organised Tours under Malindi in The Coast chapter for details). If you're coming from Nairobi, the Voi Gate (just behind the village of same name) and the Manyani Gate (on the Nairobi–Mombasa highway) are just as accessible.

AROUND TSAVO
There are some interesting detours along the road between Voi and Taveta, which cuts though the southern part of Tsavo West. There are a number of private and community-owned nature reserves in the bush on the edge of Tsavo West.

Wundanyi
The provincial capital, Wundanyi, is an interesting little place set high up in the Taita Hills. It's a nice place to retreat if the heat of Tsavo gets too much and numerous trails crisscross the cultivated terraced slopes around town leading to dramatic gorges, waterfalls, cliffs and jagged outcrops. It's easy to find someone to act as a guide, but stout walking boots and a head for heights are essential. Needless to say, the views are spectacular.

Other attractions in the hills include the butterflies of **Ngangao Forest** (a 6km matatu ride northwest to Werugha), the huge granite **Wesu Rock** that overlooks Wundanyi and the **Cave of Skulls** where the Taita people once put the skulls of their ancestors. The original African violets were discovered here and the UNDP/GEP East Africa Cross Border Biodiversity Project office has more information about local fauna and flora.

The town market – hidden away behind the buildings on the hilltop – sells very cheap *loofas* (sponges made from the insides of a kind of squash).

Places to Stay & Eat The best option in town is **Wundanyi Lodge** (☎ 0148-2029; singles/doubles KSh200/250). It's a simple, friendly courtyard place around the back of the Centre Shop at the top of the hill. Rooms are clean and tidy.

Hotel Hills View (☎ 0148-2417; doubles KSh200), about 500m outside town opposite Wesu Rock, has a good cheap bar and restaurant but rooms are only average.

The best place to eat in town is the **Tsavo Hill Cafe**, just down from the matatu station. It's a popular place, open all hours and steak and chips costs KSh100.

A favourite local drinking hole is **Taita Paradise**, a cosy little bar on several levels, tucked away behind Wundanyi Lodge.

Getting There & Away From Voi, on the Nairobi–Mombasa highway, there are frequent matatu services to Wundanyi (KSh90). Leave Wundanyi by around 8.30am if you want to connect with the morning buses to Nairobi out of Voi. There are also direct matatus between Wundanyi and the Kobil petrol station at the junction of Jomo Kenyatta Ave and Mwembe Tayari Rd in Mombasa (KSh260).

Taita Hills
South of the dirt road from Voi to Taveta, are the Taita Hills, a fertile area of verdant hills and scrub forest, a far cry from the semiarid landscape of Tsavo. Within the hills is the private **Taita Hills Game Reserve** (admission US$23), covering an area of 100 sq km. The landscape is dramatic and all the plains wildlife is here in abundance. If you stay at one of the lodges here, you can take a nocturnal wildlife drive.

The two lodges at Taita Hills are owned by the Hilton Hotel chain, but only the **Salt Lick Safari Lodge** (☎ 0147-30243, fax 30007; singles/doubles/triples US$285/325/380) is normally used. It's a weird complex of mushroom-like houses on stilts surrounding a waterhole, but the facilities are luxurious. The bougainvillea-covered **Taita Hills Safari Lodge** is only used if the Salt Lick Safari Lodge is full. Children under five are not admitted.

Lumo Community Wildlife Sanctuary
This innovative new reserve of 657 sq km was formed from three community-owned ranches in 1996. It's partly funded by the EU and involves local people at every stage of the project, from the park rangers to senior management. Birdlife is plentiful and all the 'Big Five' are here, as well as several war

relics from WWI. The park is set to open in late 2003 and the entry fee is likely to be US$10 to US$15. There are also plans for a tented camp and camp site. For more information, call the **sanctuary offices** (☎ 0147-2234) in the village of Maktau, near Maktau Gate. The sanctuary lies on the Voi–Taveta road so you can get here by public bus, matatu and the Voi–Taveta train even stops near the entrance. The rangers may be able to arrange a wildlife drive or guide for a fee.

Taveta

This dusty little town sits on the Tanzanian border on the way to Moshi and Arusha. There's a busy market here on Wednesday and Saturday, when people trek into town from remote villages on both sides of the border selling everything from bananas and baskets to mobile-phone chargers.

There's a branch of Kenya Commercial Bank with a bureau de change and a Kobil petrol station. The border is open 24 hours but the border posts are 4km apart so you'll have to take a *poda-poda* (bicycle taxi) for KSh30. On market days, trucks provide the same service for KSh20. From Holili on the Tanzanian side, there are matatus to Moshi (TSh500), where you can change on to Arusha (TSh1000).

There are a handful of places to stay here if you want to stop and explore the surrounding countryside.

Challa Hotel (☎ 0149-2212; singles/doubles KSh500/1000) is the largest building in town. It's behind the market and the friendly staff can arrange tours to Lake Challa and further afield. Rooms have mosquito nets and bathroom and there's a restaurant and bar.

There are also several cheap **board and lodging** places on the same road, charging KSh100 to KSh200.

Getting There & Away Numerous matatus head to Voi throughout the day (KSh200, two hours), or there are buses to Nairobi via Voi every evening at 10pm (KSh400, eight hours). From Tuesday to Friday there are also morning buses to Mombasa (KSh300, three hours).

On Wednesday and Saturday, a tiny train leaves Voi at 5am, returning from Taveta at 2pm (2nd/3rd class KSh205/100, five hours). It's tortuously slow, but skirts the national park, Lumo Wildlife Sanctuary and Taita

Hills Game Reserve, so you've a good chance of seeing wildlife.

Lake Challa

This deep and spooky crater lake is about 10km north of Taveta. There are grand views across the plains from the crater rim, near the defunct Lake Challa Safari Lodge, with the mysterious lake shimmering hundreds of metres below. The Lake gained notoriety in early 2002 when a gap-year student was killed by crocodiles here. You can walk around the crater rim and down to the water but be very careful near the water's edge, and under no circumstances consider swimming.

The road to Challa turns off the Voi–Taveta road on the outskirts of Taveta, by the second police post. On Taveta market days (Wednesday and Saturday), there are local buses to Challa village (KSh50), which pass the turn-off to the crater rim.

Rukinga Wildlife Conservancy

This private reserve southeast of Voi covers 68,000 hectares of ranch land between Tsavo East and Tsavo West. **Savannah Camps & Lodges** (in Nairobi ☎ 02-331191, fax 330698; ⓦ www.savannahcamps.com) holds an exclusive tourism concession in the area, which is rich in wildlife. The Taita Discovery Centre inside the sanctuary runs environmental education and bush adventure courses for a minimum of four weeks (see Courses in the Facts for the Visitor chapter).

Accommodation is provided by the **Galla Camp** (book through Savannah Camps & Lodges ☎ 02-331191; singles/doubles US$194/252), a luxury tented camp within the sanctuary. It is very well run and there are loads of conservation type activities you can get involved with.

VOI
☎ 0147

Voi is a busy junction town at the intersection of the Nairobi–Mombasa highway and the road to Moshi in Tanzania via Taveta. The Voi Gate to Tsavo East National Park is just east of the town, and Voi has plenty of cheap places to stay, which is great for travellers who can't afford the safari lodges inside the park. There's a lively market and a general air of affluence and activity, and there are some nice walks in the surrounding hills.

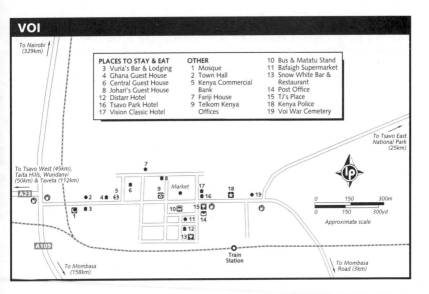

VOI

To Nairobi
(329km)

PLACES TO STAY & EAT	OTHER	10 Bus & Matatu Stand
3 Vuria's Bar & Lodging	1 Mosque	11 Bafaigh Supermarket
4 Ghana Guest House	2 Town Hall	13 Snow White Bar &
6 Central Guest House	5 Kenya Commercial	Restaurant
8 Johari's Guest House	Bank	14 Post Office
12 Distarr Hotel	7 Fariji House	15 TJ's Place
16 Tsavo Park Hotel	9 Telkom Kenya	18 Kenya Police
17 Vision Classic Hotel	Offices	19 Voi War Cemetery

To Tsavo East
National Park
(25km)

To Tsavo West (45km),
Taita Hills, Wundanyi
(50km) & Taveta (112km)

Market

0   150   300m
0   150   300yd
Approximate scale

To Mombasa
(158km)

Train
Station

To Mombasa
Road (3km)

There is a bureau de change at the Kenya Commercial Bank (but no ATM), on the main road through town. If you need print and slide film for a trip into Tsavo, go to the Bafaigh supermarket (just behind the bus station). There are plenty of phones at the Telkom Kenya office on the main road. Behind the Telkom office is Fariji House, with a **doctor's surgery** (☎ 30139), Internet café and bookshop.

Places to Stay & Eat

For ultra-cheap lodging-type rooms, try **Central Guest House** near the Kenya Commercial Bank or **Vuria's Bar & Lodging** on the main road. Rooms cost around KSh150/200 at both. On the edge of Tsavo East near the Voi Gate are a handful of mediocre lodges, but they're demoralising places to stay.

Vision Classic Hotel (☎ 0722-660113; singles/doubles KSh300/500), next door to Tsavo Park Hotel, is an OK-value place offering clean rooms with bathroom.

Johari's Guest House (☎ 30493; singles/doubles KSh200/300) is a cheap courtyard place one block north of the main road through Voi. It's spotlessly clean, which is appropriate as it's also a drycleaners.

Distarr Hotel (☎/fax 30277; singles/doubles with bathroom KSh400/500), the large white building downhill from the bus station, is probably the best-value place in town. It's a

spotlessly clean Muslim-run place and there's a very good cheap restaurant downstairs serving stews and *ugali*, curries and steak and chips (KSh90 to KSh200), plus good juices.

Ghana Guest House (☎ 30291; singles/doubles with bathroom KSh450/550) is a large yellow building back towards the Nairobi–Mombasa highway, with clean and quiet rooms.

Tsavo Park Hotel (☎ 30050, fax 30285; ✉ info@tsavoparkhotel.com; singles/doubles KSh1200/1800) in the centre of town is a good place to go if you want a hot shower and satellite TV. It's clean and well-run and the rooms aren't bad value, although not all have TVs. Rates include breakfast, and there's a good-value restaurant (buffet lunch KSh300). The same people run the Ndololo Camp in Tsavo East, and transfers into the park can be arranged.

Most of the guesthouses have reasonable (cheap) restaurants and there are a number of food *dukas* and cafés around the bus and matatu stand. Probably your best options are the **Tsavo Park Hotel** and **Distarr**.

For a lively night out, **Snow White Bar & Restaurant** and **TJ's Place**, which is near the market, are popular bars with pool tables. As Voi is a transport hub, there's a low-key prostitution scene servicing the truck drivers, which can be a hassle in some bars.

SOUTHERN KENYA

Getting There & Away

There are plenty of buses and matatus to Mombasa (KSh200, three hours), and buses to Nairobi (KSh400 to KSh700, five to six hours) pass through town at around 10.30am and midnight. Busstar, Busscar, Mombasa Raha and Akamba all have offices at the bus station. There are daily matatus to Wundanyi (KSh90, one hour) and Taveta on the Tanzanian border (KSh200, two hours).

The **train station** *(☎ 30100)* is south of the town cemetery at the east end of Voi.

From Monday to Friday, there are trains to Mombasa (1st/2nd class KSh1410/1130) at around 4am and Nairobi (1st/2nd class 2100/1475) at around 11pm.

At the time of writing, there was also a train to Taveta at 5am on Wednesday and Saturday (2nd/3rd class KSh205/100, five hours), returning the same day at 2pm. The train also stops at Maktau, near the Lumo Community Wildlife Sanctuary.

See the Getting There & Away chapter for information about travel to Tanzania.

Dancers performing, near Nairobi

The wonderous but rarely visited Lake Magadi

Marabou storks along the road to Lake Magadi

Dry grassland and flamingos, Amboseli NP

Maasai herding cattle at sunset, southern Kenya

An outrageous ostrich, Chyulu Hills National Park

Safari camp site, Tsavo West National Park

Rhino conservation education for children

The Coast

This cannot be less than natural beauty, the endless sand, the reefs, the lot, are completely unmatched in the world.

Ernest Hemingway

The coast of Kenya is one of the nation's premier attractions, with a chain of splendid beaches stretching most of the way from Tanzania to the Somali border. Offshore are extensive coral reefs, with excellent diving and snorkelling, while dotted along the coast are traditional Swahili villages and the ruins of Arab-Muslim city states. It's a wonderful area, and after a hot and dusty safari, almost everyone heads for the coast to unwind.

Mombasa is the main city on the coast and has been, at various times, a Swahili city-state, the capital of Portuguese East Africa, an Omani provincial capital and the railhead for the British East Africa railway. After the cool highlands, Mombasa's steamy tropical climate takes some getting used to, but the city is the major hub for transport north and south along the coast and the old part of the city is well worth exploring.

North and south of Mombasa are some of the finest beaches in Africa. A staggering number of beach hotels and resorts are crammed into this small stretch of coast. The big developments are at Diani Beach, Bamburi, Shanzu, Watamu and Malindi, but there are also some wonderfully peaceful getaways tucked away between the megaresorts, most notably at Tiwi Beach, just south of Mombasa.

During the 1970s and '80s, Kenya was promoted heavily as a 'sea and sand' destination and there was a not-entirely unfair perception that the sole purpose of the Kenya Tourist Board was to prop up the personal fortunes of hoteliers on the coast.

These days, publicity and investment is distributed a bit more fairly, and nature reserves such as the Arabuko Sokoke Forest Reserve (excellent for birdlife), and the Shimba Hills National Reserve and Mwaluganje Elephant Sanctuary (which are both prime locations to spot elephants) have received much needed cash injections.

Offshore are the coral reefs of the Mombasa, Malindi, Watamu, Diani-Chale and

Highlights

- Hiking through Arabuko Sokoke Forest on the trail of rare birds and the golden-rumped elephant shrew
- Reliving the Swahili past at the magnificent ruined city of Gede
- Walking back through the centuries in the narrow alleyways of Lamu town
- Drifting along on a dhow cruise through the Lamu archipelago and swimming under the stars off Kiwayu Island
- Enjoying sandy beaches and seafood banquets in the ancient town of Malindi
- Snorkelling with the myriad fishes and colourful coral at the Kisite-Mpunguti and Watamu Marine National Parks
- Tracking elephants and the rare sable antelope at Shimba Hills National Reserve and Mwaluganje Elephant Sanctuary

Major National Parks & Reserves

Shimba Hills National Reserve, Mwaluganje Elephant Sanctuary, Arabuko Sokoke Forest Reserve, Tana River Primate National Reserve, Malindi Marine National Park, Watamu Marine National Park, Kisite-Mpunguti Marine National Park

Kisite-Mpunguti Marine Parks, which provide some excellent diving and snorkelling. Big-game fishing is also very popular along the coast, although this sits a little uneasily

161

THE COAST

To Garissa (75km)

To Garissa (75km)

SOMALIA

Arawale NR

Hola

Ijara

Dodori River

Boni NR

Tana River Primate NR

Duldul River

Bodhei

Dodori NR

Kiunga Marine NR

Bargoni

Kiwayu Island

B8

Hindi

Paté
Paté Island

Kiwayu Island

Tana

Garsen

Witu C112

Manda Island

Lamu
Lamu Island

Lamu Archipelago

River

Kipini

B8

Ungwana Bay

Gandi

Marafa Depression

INDIAN

Tsavo East NP

Galana

Marafa

River

Gongoni

OCEAN

To Manyani (75km)

C103

Mambrui

Sala Gate

River

Malindi

Malindi Marine NP

Arabuko Sokoke Forest Reserve

Gede

Gede Ruins

Malindi Marine Reserve

Rare

Watamu

Watamu Marine NP

River

Bamba

Watamu-Malindi Marine NR (Coral Gardens)

Buchuma Gate

Mnarani

Kilifi

Takaungu

To Voi (61km) & Nairobi (395km)

A109

Kaloleni

B8

Vipingo

Kikambala Beach

Mwaluganje Elephant Sanctuary

Mariakani

Mtwapa

Jumba la Mtwana

Baobab Adventure

MOMBASA

Kinango

Kwale

Shelly Beach

Mombasa Marine Park

Ramisi

C106

Tiwi

Tiwi Beach

Shimba Hills NR

Ukunda

Diani Beach

Mwabungu

River

Gazi Beach

Msambweni

Chale Island

Lunga Lunga

A14

Bodo

Ramisi

Funzi Island

Horohoro

Shimoni

Vanga

Wasini Island

TANZANIA

Kisite-Mpunguti Marine NP

To Tanga (50km)

0   25   50km
0   15   30mi

with the marine environmental protection message the government is trying to put across.

These days, there is also a growing interest in Swahili culture and history, although the slave trade is still something of a taboo subject. Archaeologists have unearthed a number of ancient Swahili ruins, most notably at Gede and Kilifi, and these are well worth exploring. For a taste of living Swahili culture, you can't beat a trip to the gorgeous island of Lamu, up by the Somali border. It's possible to take dhow trips to even more remote Swahili islands from Lamu, and many mangrove islands south of Mombasa can also be visited by dhow.

If you're planning to visit in the low season, it's well worth contacting one of the big travel agents to see if any cheap flight-and-accommodation packages are available. There's no obligation to spend your whole trip in the hotel, and the combined cost of accommodation and the flight will often be less than the cost of a scheduled airline ticket to Nairobi.

History

Little is known about the pre-Arabic cultures along the coast as the tribes who lived here were decimated by the slave trade and absorbed into the later Swahili culture. One belief that still persists among the Mijikenda (the nine coastal tribes) is the importance of sacred forests, known as *kayas*. There are strict rules about who can enter these places of power, and sacrifices and ritual burials were often conducted in the forests in the past. Few *kayas* remain, but the incredible biodiversity of the coastal woodland at Diani Beach, Tiwi Beach and other places is partly a result of centuries of conservation by the Mijikenda.

The first overseas visitors were Shirazi Arabs from Persia, who were lured here in the 6th century by rumours of a bottomless supply of ivory. At first, the traders lived a peripatetic existence, sailing south along the coast during the northeast monsoon, and returning home to Arabia under the southwest monsoon, but trading communities were soon established on easily defensible islands such as Lamu, Manda, Pemba and Zanzibar. A healthy trade grew up exporting ivory, tortoiseshell, gold and animal skins to Asia and the Middle East.

By the 9th century, a series of fully fledged city-states, known collectively as 'Zinj el Barr' (from the Arabic term for black Africans) were spread out along the coast and the first African slaves began to appear in Arabia. For the next nine hundred years, between two and twenty thousand slaves were removed from their tribes annually from East Africa and shipped to households and plantations in other parts of East Africa or Iraq and Oman.

In the process, there was considerable intermarriage between Arabs and Africans, giving rise to the Swahili culture, which still dominates the coast. Powerful dynasties were established at Kilwa (in present-day Tanzania), Malindi, Paté (in the Lamu archipelago) and Mombasa, where the Mazrui clan became one of the most powerful families in East Africa.

The first Arab domination of the coast ended in the early 16th century, when the Portuguese embarked on a campaign to end the Arab trade monopoly in the Indian Ocean. Dom Francisco de Almeida set sail for Mombasa in 1505 with a huge armada of 23 men-of-war and captured the city in just 1½ days. In the process, Mombasa was completely levelled. So much loot was gathered that a substantial amount of it had to be left behind when the fleet sailed for India, for fear of overloading the ships.

Mombasa was soon rebuilt and saw a few decades of calm before the Portuguese once again sailed over the horizon in 1528. This time it was Nuña da Cunha who captured the city, first by diplomacy (offering to act as an ally to Mombasa in its disputes with Malindi, Pemba and Zanzibar) and then by force. As soon as the winds were right, he burned the city to the ground and sailed on to Goa.

Trade was the primary concern of the Portuguese and they didn't exercise direct control over the administration of the coastal cities. However, absurd tributes were demanded from the locals for the privilege of being vassals to the Portuguese crown. Perhaps, unsurprisingly, the Swahilis did not take kindly to becoming slaves themselves and rebellions were very common throughout the 16th and 17th centuries.

The Portuguese made a bid for permanency in 1593 with the construction of Fort Jesus on Mombasa island, but it quickly became a symbolic target for rebel leaders and

The Slave Trade

Although the Arab-Swahili island states along the East African coast have a reputation as spice islands, the history of the region is inextricably linked to the slave trade. Between the 7th and 19th centuries, Arab and Swahili traders removed somewhere in the region of four million slaves from East Africa to households and plantations across the Arab-controlled world.

At first, slaves were often obtained through trade with war-like tribes in the interior, but as the industry developed, vast slave caravans set off into the African interior, bringing back tons of plundered ivory and tens of thousands of men, women and children. Of these, fewer than one in five survived the forced march from the plains to the coast, either dying of disease or being executed for showing signs of weakness along the way.

Although some slaves married their owners and gained freedom – one of the most notorious Swahili slave traders, Tippu Tip, was himself the grandson of a freed slave – the experience of most slaves was much harsher. Thousands of African boys were surgically transformed into eunuchs to provide servants for Arabic households and an estimated 2.5 million young African women were sold as concubines for harems.

After the East African slave trade was finally brought to a close in the 1870s under pressure from Britain, the Swahili communities along the coast went into steady decline, although illicit trading continued right up until the 1960s, when slavery was finally outlawed in Oman. These days, this painful chapter of African history is little discussed by Kenyans, who prefer to look forward as a unified Christian, tribal and Muslim nation.

was besieged countless times. During the 17th and 18th centuries, Mombasa changed hands dozens of times before the Portuguese finally gave up their claim to the coast in 1729.

Behind the scenes, the Swahilis were also fighting for their lives against aggressive African tribes, including the Galla people from Somalia and the fearsome cannibalistic Zimba from Malawi. The demise of the Swahili city-states along the coast is now widely attributed to these warlike tribal groups.

It has become fashionable to portray the Portuguese as the villains of the piece, but the sultans of Oman, who defeated the Portuguese and occupied Fort Jesus after an incredible 33-month siege in 1698, were no more popular with the locals. Despite their shared faith, the Swahilis staged countless rebellions against the Omani rulers, even passing Mombasa into British hands from 1824–26 to keep it from the sultans of Oman.

Things only really quietened down after sultan Seyyid Said of Oman moved his capital from Muscat to Zanzibar in 1832.

Seyyid Said established huge clove plantations along the coast, creating a massive upsurge in the demand for slaves. The slave caravans of the 19th century had a devastating effect on the East African population. European explorers such as Livingstone reported massacres and human rights abuses, which galvanised the British public to put a stop to slavery once and for all.

Through a mixture of political savvy and implied force, the British government was eventually able to pressure Seyyid Said's son, Barghash, to ban slavery, marking the beginning of the end for Arab rule on the coast. The Zanzibar slave market closed forever in 1873.

Britain may have had ulterior motives, of course. As part of the treaty, the British East Africa Company took over administration of the interior of the country. However, a 16km-wide coastal strip was recognised as the territory of the sultan and was leased by the British from him in 1887, first for a 50-year period and then permanently.

Mombasa was subsequently to become the most important city in British East Africa as the railhead for the Uganda railway. In 1920, Kenya became a fully fledged British colony with its capital in Nairobi, and Mombasa was made capital of the separate British Coast Protectorate of East Africa.

Upon Kenyan independence in 1963, the last Sultan of Zanzibar gifted the protectorate to the new Kenyan government.

Mombasa

☎ 011 • pop 653,000

Mombasa is the largest city on the Kenyan coast and also the largest coastal port in East Africa. The population is overwhelmingly African, many of whom are Swahilis, but there are a remarkable range of races and cultures here, from Africans to British expats, Omanis, Indians and Chinese. Indians are the largest minority, descendants of Hindu and Muslim labourers and engineers brought here by the British to build the East African Railway, and the population as a whole is predominantly Muslim.

The city sprawls across a low-lying island at the mouth of a broad inlet, which provides a fantastic natural anchorage for ships. Traders have been coming here since at least the 12th century and goods from Kenya, Uganda, Rwanda, Burundi and eastern Congo (Zaïre) all pass through here on their way overseas.

Tourism is also a big industry in Mombasa, although most visitors stay in the beach resorts north and south of the city.

Mombasa is a fairly typical modern African town, but the pace of life is far more relaxed than in Nairobi and the climate is tropical after the coolness of the highlands. The most interesting part of Mombasa is the characterful Old Town, with its narrow, winding alleyways and historic Swahili houses. In the middle of the Old Town are the remains of Fort Jesus, which played a pivotal role in the various power struggles over the dominion of East Africa.

The island is linked to the mainland by a causeway (which carries the road and rail links to Nairobi), a bridge (connecting the island to the north coast) and a vehicle ferry (which serves the south coast). In recent years, Mombasa has spread onto the mainland both north and south of the island.

Orientation

The main thoroughfare in Mombasa is Digo Rd and its southern extension Nyerere Ave, which run north-south through the city. The ferry to Likoni and the south coast leaves from the southern end of Nyerere Ave, near the Nakumatt superstore.

Running west from the junction between Nyerere Ave and Digo Rd is Moi Ave, where you'll find the tourist office and the famous sculpted 'tusks', a metal archway over the road in the shape of a pair of elephant tusks. Heading east from the same junction, Nkrumah Rd provides the easiest access to the Old Town and Fort Jesus.

North of the centre, Digo Rd becomes Abdel Nasser Rd, where you'll find many of the bus stands for Nairobi and destinations north along the coast. There's another big group of bus offices west of here at the intersection of Jomo Kenyatta Ave and Mwembe Tayari Rd. The train station is at the intersection of Mwembe Tayari and Haile Selassie Rds.

Maps Choices are limited but your best option is the 1:10,000 *Streets of Mombasa Island* map produced by Coast Map Services (KSh230). It was updated in 2000 and shows many of the city's hotels, banks, restaurants and other useful places.

Information

Tourist Offices The Mombasa & Coast Tourist Office (☎ 225428; e mcta@ikenya .com; Moi Ave; open 8am-noon & 2pm-4.30pm Mon-Fri, 8am-noon Sat) is just past the famous tusks. It has a limited stock of leaflets but staff are helpful and can help arrange accommodation, safaris etc.

Money There are several branches of **Barclays Bank** in town – the most useful is on Nkrumah Rd (open 9am-3pm Mon-Fri, 9am-11am Sat). **Standard Chartered Bank** has its main branch (with an ATM) at Treasury Square on Nkrumah Rd (open the same hours). The **Postbank** (Meru Rd) is the local agent for Western Union money transfers.

There are also a number of foreign-exchange bureaus including **Pwani Forex Bureau** (☎ 221727; Digo Rd), opposite the main market, and the **Fort Jesus Forex Bureau** (☎ 316717; Ndia Kuu Rd), in front of the fort entrance. They're both open Monday to Friday from 8.30am to 5pm and 8.30am to 1pm on Saturday. American Express is represented by **Express Kenya** (☎ 312461; PO Box 90631, Nkrumah Rd) – mail can be held here for card-holders.

Outside these hours you can change money at major hotels, although rates are usually poor. The exchange rates are generally slightly lower than in Nairobi, especially for travellers cheques.

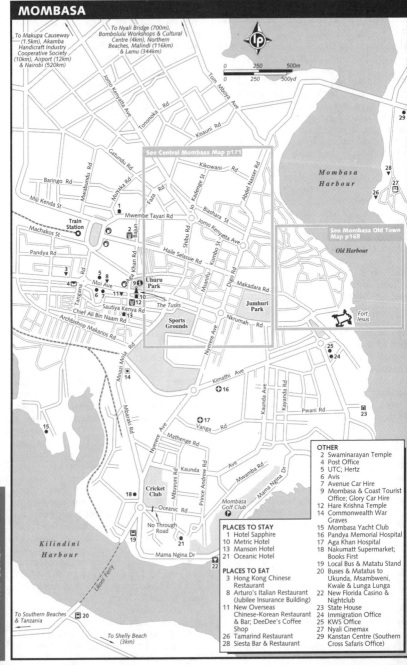

MOMBASA

To Makupa Causeway
(1.5km), Akamba
Handicraft Industry
Cooperative Society
(10km), Airport (12km)
& Nairobi (520km)

To Nyali Bridge (700m),
Bombolulu Workshops & Cultural
Centre (4km), Northern
Beaches, Malindi (116km)
& Lamu (344km)

Mombasa
Harbour

See Central Mombasa Map p171

See Mombasa Old Town
Map p168

Old Harbour

Mombasa
Harbour

Train
Station

Uhuru
Park

The Tusks

Sports
Grounds

Jumhuri
Park

Fort
Jesus

Kilindini
Harbour

Cricket
Club

Mombasa
Golf Club

No Through
Road

To Southern Beaches
& Tanzania

To Shelly Beach
(3km)

PLACES TO STAY
1 Hotel Sapphire
10 Metric Hotel
13 Manson Hotel
21 Oceanic Hotel

PLACES TO EAT
3 Hong Kong Chinese
Restaurant
8 Arturo's Italian Restaurant
(Jubilee Insurance Building)
11 New Overseas
Chinese-Korean Restaurant
& Bar; DeeDee's Coffee
Shop
26 Tamarind Restaurant
28 Siesta Bar & Restaurant

OTHER
2 Swaminarayan Temple
4 Post Office
5 UTC; Hertz
6 Avis
7 Avenue Car Hire
9 Mombasa & Coast Tourist
Office; Glory Car Hire
12 Hare Krishna Temple
14 Commonwealth War
Graves
15 Mombasa Yacht Club
16 Pandya Memorial Hospital
17 Aga Khan Hospital
18 Nakumatt Supermarket;
Books First
19 Local Bus & Matatu Stand
20 Buses & Matatus to
Ukunda, Msambweni,
Kwale & Lunga Lunga
22 New Florida Casino &
Nightclub
23 State House
24 Immigration Office
25 KWS Office
27 Nyali Cinemax
29 Kanstan Centre (Southern
Cross Safaris Office)

THE COAST

Post & Communications The main post office *(Digo Rd; open 8am-6pm Mon-Fri, 9am-noon Sat)* is right in the city centre. There are numerous cardphones dotted around town – the **Telkom Kenya** offices on Nkrumah Rd and Moi Ave have the most reliable phones. For cheaper long-distance calls, head to **Global Post Services** *(☎ 315370, fax 316695; Maungano Rd; open 7.30am-11pm)*; international calls to most destinations cost around KSh100 per minute. The owner, Rashmi, is a source of useful tourist information and a capable 'fixer' who can deal with just about any problem.

The best place to access Hotmail, Yahoo etc is the air-con Internet café in the **Blue Room Restaurant** *(Haile Selassie Rd; open 9am-9.30pm daily)* where access costs; KSh2 per minute. There are dozens of terminals and the connection is reliable. Other good Internet places include **Mombasa Coffee House** and **Uunet Online Cafe**, both on Moi Ave, which charge KSh1 per minute.

Government Offices Visas can be extended at the **immigration office** *(☎ 311745; Mama Ngina Dr)* in the Uhuru ni Kari building, just behind Treasury Square.

You'll find the **Kenya Wildlife Service** *(KWS; ☎ 312744/5; Mama Ngina Dr; open 6am-6pm daily)* at Nguua Court, just in front of the Uhuru ni Kari building. You can buy and charge national-park smartcards here.

Bookshops Far and away the best bookshop in Mombasa is **Books First** *(☎ 313482; Nyerere Ave)* in the Nakumatt supermarket, close to the Likoni ferry. It's incredibly well stocked, with everything from novels to maps and coffee-table books on Africa.

The **Bahati Book Centre** *(☎ 223598; Moi Ave)* is the only downtown bookshop with a decent stock of books and maps. Maps are also available at **City Bookshop** *(☎ 313149; Nkrumah Rd)*, next to the Kenya Cinema.

Libraries The **Mombasa Area Library** *(☎ 226380; Msanifu Kombo Rd; open 9.30am-6pm Mon-Thur, 9.30am-4pm Fri, 8am-5pm Sat)* has a fairly extensive English-language section.

Left Luggage The left-luggage service at the train station costs KSh80 per item per day. The office always opens when the trains arrive or depart, but staffing is only intermittent at other times.

Photography Despite Mombasa being a major tourist centre, slide film and fast print film (above ASA 100) can be hard to find – bring supplies from Nairobi. **Photocine** *(Moi Ave)* usually has slide film in stock.

Medical Services The best hospitals in Mombasa are the **Aga Khan Hospital** *(☎ 227710/13; Vanga Rd)* and the **Pandya Memorial Hospital** *(☎ 314140/1; Dedan Kimathi Ave)*. You must pay for all services and medication upfront, so have travel insurance handy.

Emergency In an emergency, contact the **police hotline** on ☎ 222121 or ☎ 999. **AAR Health Services** is on ☎ 312405 (24 hours).

Dangers & Annoyances Mombasa is safer than it has been in years, although you should still take taxis rather than walking around alone at night. You need to be more careful on the beaches north and south of town (see the South of Mombasa and North of Mombasa sections later in this chapter). The Likoni ferry is another bag-snatching hotspot.

A new development is the upsurge in anti-Western sentiment among some Kenyan Muslims. Demonstrations against Israel and America are becoming increasingly common in Mombasa; visitors should keep a low profile during any escalation of violence in the Middle East.

Malaria is another risk on the coast so remember to take your antimalaria drugs (see Health in the Facts for the Visitor chapter for more information).

Fort Jesus

Mombasa's biggest tourist attraction dominates the harbour entrance at the end of Nkrumah St. It's still an imposing edifice, despite being partially ruined. The fort was built by the Portuguese in 1593 to enforce their rule over the coastal Swahilis, but they rarely managed to hold onto it for long. It changed hands at least nine times in bloody sieges between 1631 and 1875, before finally passing into the hands of the British.

An Italian architect, Joao Batista Cairato, who had done a lot of work for the Portuguese in Goa, designed the fort. There are

THE COAST

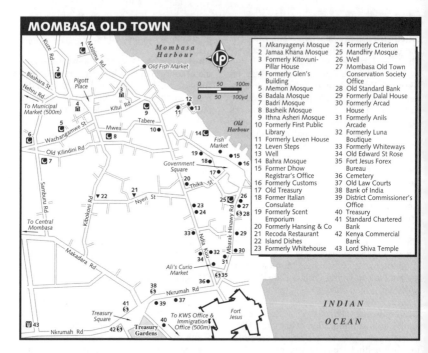

MOMBASA OLD TOWN

1 Mkanyagenyi Mosque
2 Jamaa Khana Mosque
3 Formerly Kitovuni-
   Pillar House
4 Formerly Glen's
   Building
5 Memon Mosque
6 Badala Mosque
7 Badri Mosque
8 Basheik Mosque
9 Ithna Asheri Mosque
10 Formerly First Public
   Library
11 Formerly Leven House
12 Leven Steps
13 Well
14 Bahra Mosque
15 Former Dhow
   Registrar's Office
16 Formerly Customs
17 Old Treasury
18 Former Italian
   Consulate
19 Formerly Scent
   Emporium
20 Formerly Hansing & Co
21 Recoda Restaurant
22 Island Dishes
23 Formerly Whitehouse
24 Formerly Criterion
25 Mandhry Mosque
26 Well
27 Mombasa Old Town
   Conservation Society
   Office
28 Old Standard Bank
29 Formerly Dalal House
30 Formerly Arcad
   House
31 Formerly Anils
   Arcade
32 Formerly Luna
   Boutique
33 Formerly Whiteways
34 Old Edward St Rose
35 Fort Jesus Forex
   Bureau
36 Cemetery
37 Old Law Courts
38 Bank of India
39 District Commissioner's
   Office
40 Treasury
41 Standard Chartered
   Bank
42 Kenya Commercial
   Bank
43 Lord Shiva Temple

some ingenious elements in its design, including the angular configuration of the west walls, which make it impossible to attack one wall without being a sitting duck for soldiers on the opposite battlements.

These days the fort houses a **museum** *(nonresident adult/child under 12 KSh200/ 100; open 8.30am-6pm daily)* built over the former barracks for the garrison. The exhibits are mostly ceramics, reflecting the variety of cultures that traded along the coast, but include other interesting odds and ends donated from private collections or dug up from sites along the coast. Also displayed are finds from the Portuguese frigate *Santo António de Tanná*, which sank off the fort during the siege in 1698, and a few anthropological displays about the coastal tribes, including an interesting display on *kaya* forests.

Exploring the battlements and ruined buildings within the compound is just as interesting. The **Omani house** in the San Felipe bastion in the northwestern corner of the fort, was built in the late 18th century and houses a small exhibition of Omani jewellery. Nearby is a ruined church and a huge well and cistern. The **eastern wall** of the fort

includes an Omani audience hall (now covered by a 2nd storey, but still complete with official inscriptions – and unofficial graffiti) and the **Passage of the Arches** (a passage cut through the coral giving access to the sea).

Most of the coach tours arrive here late in the morning, so if you come early, you may have the place to yourself. Many official and unofficial guides will offer their services. Many people prefer to buy the official *Fort Jesus* guide booklet (KSh60) from the ticket desk and go it alone. Guide booklets for the Old Town are also available here.

The Old Town

While Mombasa's Old Town doesn't quite have the medieval charm of Lamu or Zanzibar, it's still an interesting area to wander around. The houses here are characteristic of coastal East African architecture, with ornately carved doors and window frames and fretwork balconies, designed to protect the modesty of the female inhabitants. Sadly, many of these were destroyed in the days when Mbarak Hinawy Rd was the main access to the port. There is now a preservation order on the remaining doors and balconies, so further losses should hopefully be prevented. The **Mombasa Old Town Conservation Society** (☎ *312246, fax 226302; Mbarak Hinawy Rd)* is encouraging the renovation of many dilapidated buildings in the Old Town.

Apart from Ndia Kuu Rd, where the well-preserved Swahili houses have all been turned into souvenir shops, there is little evidence from the outside of what these buildings were once used for. To flesh out the history of old Mombasa, it's worth picking up a copy of the booklet *The Old Town Mombasa: A Historical Guide* (KSh100) from the tourist office or Fort Jesus. This excellent guide features a good map and a building-by-building account of interesting structures in the Old Town, including the **Leven Steps** near the waterfront, site of the former British colonial administration, where there's an ancient well.

Early morning or late afternoon is the best time to walk around as there's more activity, although most houses are residential these days and the streets are always rather quiet. The winding alleyways linking the Old Town to Digo Rd are livelier, with market traders selling everything from *kangas* and mobile-phone accessories to baobab seeds and fried taro roots. **Biashara St** is the main market street for clothes, while **Neru Rd**, behind the municipal market, has wall-to-wall tailors' shops.

Religious Buildings
Mombasa has some interesting mosques, but non-Muslims are usually not permitted to enter. You can look from the outside, though, and it's worth seeking out the 16th-century **Mandhry Mosque**, opposite the conservation office in the Old Town and the similar **Basheikh Mosque** nearby. The colourful modern **Memon Mosque**, just off Samburu Rd, is also interesting.

You'll get a warm reception at the Hindu **Lord Shiva Temple** on Mwinyi Ab Rd, which has an interesting sculpture garden, and the **Swaminarayan Temple** on Haile Selassie Rd, which has some wonderfully ornate painted doors and vivid paintings from Hindu mythology. Shoes should be removed before entering.

Old Law Courts
The old law courts on Nkrumah Rd have been converted into an informal **museum** *(open 8am-6pm daily; admission free)* with displays of Kenyan crafts and votive objects from various tribal groups.

Sailing
If you can sail, it may be worth joining **Mombasa Yacht Club** (☎ *223580)*. Temporary membership costs KSh100/500 per day/week. Wednesday is club night (where qualified sailors may be able to talk you into some crewing) and there are usually races on Sunday. Those hoping to hitch a lift on a passing yacht will have a better (though remote) chance at Moorings restaurant in Mtwapa or the Kilifi Boatyard.

Golf
Also out of town is **Mombasa Golf Club** (☎ *222620; Mama Ngina Dr)*, perched on the southeastern edge of the island. Day membership is KSh1500, clubs cost KSh700 per day and caddies cost KSh100 per nine holes.

Organised Tours
A number of tour companies have branches in Mombasa (see the Safaris chapter for more details) and offer tours of the Old Town and Fort Jesus (US$50 per person) plus safaris to Shimba Hills National Reserve and Tsavo East and Tsavo West National Parks. Most safaris are expensive lodge-based operations, but there are a few camping safaris to Tsavo East and Tsavo West National Parks.

Numerous activities are possible both north and south of Mombasa and many operators can pick you up from hotels in town. See the North of Mombasa and South of Mombasa sections later for more details.

Harbour Cruises Luxury dhow cruises around the harbour are very popular in Mombasa, and not-withstanding the price, they are an excellent way to see the harbour, Old Town and Fort Jesus and get a slap-up meal at the end of it.

Topping the billing is Tamarind Dhow, run by the posh **Tamarind Restaurant** (☎ *471948;* @ *info@tamarinddhow.com)* in Nyali. The cruise embarks from the jetty below the Tamarind Restaurant, and includes a harbour tour and a fantastic meal. The lunch cruises leave at noon and cost US$32/16 per adult/child. Longer and more splendid evening cruises leave at 6pm and

Dhows

Arabic dhows have been sailing along the coast of East Africa for centuries, and numerous dhow ferries still operate between the mangrove islands that line the Kenyan coast. These ancient vessels are distinguished by their triangular sails (lateens), although today, many rely on a mixture of sail and motor power to get around. Dhows range considerably in size, from huge ocean-going *jahazi*, with broad hulls designed to withstand constant bumping along rocky shores and coral reefs, to small *kijahazi*, used as ferries and fishing boats up and down the coast. Kenyan *jahazi* have a perpendicular bow while Zanzibar dhows have sloping bows, but you're only likely to see these larger boats on dhow tours around Mombasa. *Kijahazi* are much more common and are widely used around the Lamu archipelago. There are excellent models of the various types of the dhow in the Lamu Museum.

cost US$70/35. There is a choice of seafood, steak or vegetarian dishes. Prices include a complimentary cocktail and transport to and from your hotel.

The other big operator is **Jahazi Marine** (☎ 472213, 487366; ℮ jahazi@africaonline .co.ke), which offers evening dhow cruises on Monday and Wednesday to Saturday. The cruise includes a meal in Fort Jesus, which looks spectacular at night when it's lit up by spotlights.

You can also head on to the Bora Bora International Nightclub in Bamburi. The full deal, including transfers to and from your hotel, costs US$70.

Special Events

Mombasa holds a lively **carnival** every November with street parades, floats and lots of music.

Places to Stay

There are plenty of budget choices in Mombasa, as well as some excellent mid-range hotels, but there are few top-end options. Many people choose to skip Mombasa and head straight for the beaches to the north and south (see the South of Mombasa and North of Mombasa sections later).

Places to Stay – Budget

Most of the cheap choices are close to the bus stations on Abdel Nasser Rd and Jomo Kenyatta Ave.

New People's Hotel (*Abdel Nasser Rd; singles/doubles with shared bathroom KSh200/ 320, with bathroom KSh300/400*) is very convenient for buses to Lamu and Malindi. It's a bit of a dosshouse and gets loads of noise from traffic and the Noor Mosque next door, but you can't argue with the prices. There's a good, cheap restaurant downstairs (see Places to Eat).

The Muslim-owned **Ramadhan Guest House** (☎ 229965; *Abdel Nasser Rd; 2-bed rooms & shared bathroom KSh400*) is further up the road, near the Mombasa Raha (Mombasa Liners) office. Rooms are airy and bright, with fans and nets.

Tana Guest House (☎ 490550; *cnr Mwembe Tayari & Gatundu Rds; singles/ doubles/triples KSh300/400/600*), on the other side of town, is a simple but friendly place close to the Jomo Kenyatta Ave bus stations, and rooms are clean and tidy.

Coast Pride Hotel (☎ 494152; *Mwembe Tayari Rd; doubles with fan & bathroom KSh500*), nearby, is another friendly choice with a simple restaurant.

Beracha Guest House (☎ 224106; *Haile Selassie Rd; singles/doubles with shared bathroom KSh350/450, with bathroom KSh500/ 600*) is right in the thick of things, opposite the Shell petrol station on Haile Selassie Rd. It's good value for money and staff are friendly, but rooms are variable. Breakfast is included and there's a cheap restaurant.

Metric Hotel (☎ 222155; *Moi Ave; doubles/ twins with shared bathroom KSh400/500, VIP doubles with bathroom KSh600*) is tucked away in a close off Moi Ave near the tusks. It mainly caters to Kenyans, and, although small, the rooms are clean with fans and nets.

Evening Guest House (☎ 221380; *Mnazi Moja Rd; singles with shared bathroom KSh400, doubles with bathroom KSh600*) is good value and clean but it's slightly seedy (condoms are available at reception!). The simple rooms have nets and fans and the hotel has its own bar and restaurant.

Glory Hotel Annex (☎ 220419; *Sautiya Kenya Rd; singles/doubles without bathroom KSh400/700, singles/doubles with bathroom KSh600/900*) is hidden in a small close just off Sautiya Kenya Rd. Rooms are acceptable

CENTRAL MOMBASA

PLACES TO STAY
1 Tana Guest House;
   Coast Pride Hotel
12 New People's Hotel
21 Excellent Hotel
22 Royal Court Hotel;
   Tawa Terrace
24 Glory Bed & Breakfast
30 Beracha Guest House
34 Hotel Hermes
42 Glory Guest House
50 Glory Hotel Annexe
51 Evening Guest House
56 Hotel Splendid
71 New Palm Tree Hotel

PLACES TO EAT
19 Fayaz Baker &
   Confectioners
20 Roasters Choice
23 New Chetna Restaurant
26 Aridi 4 Restaurant
27 Blue Room Restaurant;
   Internet Café

32 Baron Restaurant & Pub
38 Splendid View Restaurant
40 Shehnai Restaurant
41 Pistacchio Café
43 Mombasa Coffee House
47 Wimpy; Salt 'n' Sweet
48 Le Bistro; Rozina House
   Restaurant & Café
55 Anglo Swiss Bakery
59 Mombasa Meeting Point
60 Fontanella Steakhouse &
   Beer Garden

OTHER
2 Automobile Association of
   Kenya; Akamba Office
3 Mombasa Raha (Mombasa
   Liners) Office
4 Mash Express Office
5 Coastline Safaris Office
6 Matatus to Voi & Wundanyi;
   Kobil Petrol Station
7 Buses to Dar es Salaam &
   Tanga

8 Buses to Arusha & Moshi
   (Mwembe Tayari Health
   Centre)
9 KBS Bus Station
10 Noor Mosque
11 Buses & Matatus to Malindi
13 Interstate 2000 Office
14 Falcon & Busscar Offices
15 Busstar Office
16 TSS Express Office
17 Pwani Forex Bureau
18 Barclays Bank (ATM)
25 Mombasa Area Library
28 Mombasa Tailoring Mart
29 Khonzi Mosque
31 City Grocers
33 Main Post Office
35 Sheikh Jundoni Mosque
36 Voda Taxis
37 Global Post Services
39 Unik Car Hire & Safaris
44 Sky Bar & Restaurant
45 Postbank
46 Budget Car Hire

49 Bahati Book Centre
52 Casablanca Restaurant &
   Club
53 Uunet Online Cafe
54 Ketty Tours; Safari Seekers
57 Photocine
58 Telkom Kenya
61 Royal Casino; Salambo Club
62 Postbank
63 Regional Air; Air Kenya
64 Ambalal House; Kenatco
   Taxis; Big Five Tours &
   Safaris
65 Kenya Airways; Flamingo
   Airlines
66 Toyz Disco
67 Express Kenya (American
   Express)
68 Afro Bar
69 Kenya Cinema; City
   Bookshop
70 Barclays Bank (ATM)
72 Telkom Kenya
73 Holy Ghost Cathedral

To Makupa Causeway (3km),
Akamba Handicraft Industry
Cooperative Society (11km),
Airport (25km) &
Nairobi (521km)

To Mobasa Raha
(Mombasa Liners) &
Tawakal Offices (100m),
Ramadhan Guest House
(300m), Northern Beaches,
Malindi (118km) &
Lamu (345km)

To Train
Station (400m)

Mwembe Tayari Rd

Jomo Kenyatta Ave

Joe Kadenge St

Abdel Nasser Rd

Bungoma Rd

Biashara St

Shibu Rd

Jomo Kenyatta Ave

Nehru Rd
To Old Town

Main
Market

Hospital St

Kombo St

Konzi St

Turkana St

Langoni Rd

Old Kilindini Rd
To Old Town

To Train
Station
(400m)

Haile Selassie Rd

Maungano Rd

Msanifu Rd

Taita St

Digo Rd

Makadara Rd

Uhuru
Gardens

To Mombasa & Coast
Tourist Office (100m)

Meru Rd

Gusii St

Meru Rd

Mui Ave

Jumhuri
Park

Sautiya Kenya Rd

Nyerere Ave

Mikindani St

To Fort
Jesus (600m)

Mnazi Moja Rd

Sports
Grounds

Nirji Mpye Rd

To Nakumatt
Supermarket (1km)
& Likoni Ferry (1.5km)

Nkrumah Rd

THE COAST

and have a fan and a washbasin, but the atmosphere isn't particularly friendly. The Glory chain has several other guesthouses dotted around town and a car-hire company.

Places to Stay – Mid-Range

Excellent Hotel *(☎ 227683, 311744; Haile Selassie Rd; B&B singles/doubles with bathroom KSh800/1000)* is very good value. It's popular with travellers. There's a restaurant and rooftop bar where live bands sometimes play (closed on Sunday).

Glory Bed & Breakfast *(☎ 220265; Haile Selassie Rd; singles with/without bathroom KSh700/500, doubles 1000/800, triples 1400/1200)* is across the road and rooms are adequate, if a little cramped. As with the other Glory hotels, security has been a problem here in the past, although there haven't been any reports recently. Rooms have fans but no nets and the rates include breakfast.

Hotel Splendid *(☎ 221694, fax 312769; Msanifu Kombo St; singles KSh700-900, doubles KSh1100-1800)* has a nice atmosphere and tries hard to live up to its name. The more expensive rooms have TVs, minibars and balconies. Rates include breakfast, and there's a popular moderately priced rooftop restaurant that catches sea breezes.

Hotel Hermes *(☎ 313599; Msanifu Kombo St; singles/doubles with bathroom & air-con KSh700/1000)*, near the Sheikh Jundoni Mosque, is well maintained and the rooms are huge, but it cops a bit of noise from the mosque and the matatus on Msanifu Kombo St. Rates include breakfast.

Glory Guest House *(☎ 223239; Shibu Rd; singles/doubles with shared bathroom KSh600/1000, with bathroom & fan KSh800/1200, VIP singles/doubles with air-con & fridge KSh1000/1500, triples with/without bathroom KSh1900/1600)* is a bit of a walk from the centre, but rooms are well-maintained and breakfast is included. Security has been a problem in the past at all the Glory accommodation in Mombasa and at this one in particular.

New Palm Tree Hotel *(☎ 315272, fax 222669; Nkrumah Rd; singles/doubles KSh944/1416)* is a fine, colonial-era hotel with a wonderful sense of fading grandeur. It's a great place to stay and the rooms are all upstairs, set around a spacious open courtyard furnished with tables and chairs. Downstairs is a good, reasonably priced restaurant and a friendly bar. Rooms are comfortable, spotlessly clean and have fans and bathrooms, and the prices include breakfast. There's secure parking behind the hotel.

Places to Stay – Top End

At all the following places breakfast is included in the price.

Manson Hotel *(☎ 222419, fax 222420; Kisumu Rd; singles/doubles with bathroom KSh1350/1650, singles/doubles/triples with bathroom & air-con KSh1650/2000/2600)* is hidden away in a quiet residential neighbourhood and is well looked after. Security is tight, and its facilities include a restaurant, TV and pool room.

Hotel Sapphire *(☎ 491657; fax 495280; Mwembe Tayari Rd; singles/doubles/triples KSh1900/2700/3600)* is close to the train station and facilities here are good, although the architects made a few curious decisions when they designed this place. All rooms have a bathroom, air-con and satellite TV. There's also a swimming pool (sometimes empty) and two restaurants, the Sapphire (Chinese) and Mehfil (Indian).

Royal Court Hotel *(☎ 223379, fax 312398; e royalcourt@swiftmombasa; Haile Selassie Rd; singles/doubles KSh2650/3450)* towards the train station is the best place in this price range. It's a stylish business hotel and the rooms are nicely decorated and have air-con and satellite TV. There are great views (and excellent food) at the Tawa Terrace restaurant on the roof (see Places To Eat).

Oceanic Hotel *(☎ 223496, fax 229022; singles/doubles KSh1500/1800)* was once a luxurious place to stay, but it's looking pretty old these days. However, the facilities are still good – including several restaurants and a pool – and most rooms have cracking sea views. You can walk here from the Likoni ferry, but you'll have to go around the long way via Kaunda Ave if you're coming by car.

Places to Eat

Snacks & Fast Food There are dozens of inexpensive local cafés and restaurants serving stews, curries, fish and chips, fried chicken and snacks such as samosas, *bhajai* (vegetables fried in a lentil batter) and *kachori* (spiced potato in batter).

Fayaz Baker & Confectioners *(Jomo Kenyatta Ave)* bakes up excellent cakes and muffins – great for a breakfast on the run.

Anglo-Swiss Bakery *(Meru Rd)* is another good place for cakes.

Roasters Choice *(☎ 230117; Msanifu Kombo St; mains from KSh150)* has a slightly dingy interior, but it's popular with locals and serves good, cheap food.

Blue Room Restaurant *(☎ 224021; Haile Selassie Rd; snacks KSh20-50, full meals KSh150-300; open 9am-9.30pm daily)* is hugely popular for its canteen meals – anything from cakes to curries, steaks and pizzas. It looks like a school canteen and operates in the same way but food is good and there's no waiting. There's also a good Net café and a highly recommended ice-cream parlour here.

Aridi 4 Restaurant *(Turkana St; mains KSh90-250; open 7am-8.30pm daily)* is a friendly and good-value local place with superb juices and the usual array of grills, burgers and fried chicken.

DeeDee's Coffee Shop *(☎ 220336; Moi Ave; set lunches KSh130-200)* is a colourfully decorated place with murals and a mock-up of a dhow in the dining room. Snacks and coffee are available all day and there are good-value set lunches.

Mombasa Coffee House *(Moi Ave; open daily)* is a good place for fresh coffee and snacks, with some fast Internet-connected computers.

Rozina Cafe *(☎ 311107; Moi Ave)* is part of the much posher Rozina House Restaurant (see Restaurants). There's a good selection of snack meals and it's cheap as chips. Nearby **Salt 'n' Sweet** and **Wimpy** are similar.

New People's Hotel *(Abdel Nasser Rd; meals KSh90-180)* is a huge café next to the Noor Mosque. It's very popular with worshippers, and so tends to have an almost exclusively male clientele. The biryanis (rice with curried meat) are good value.

Restaurants There's a great selection of restaurants in Mombasa.

Swahili Lots of small restaurants on the edge of the Old Town serve great Swahili cuisine.

Recoda Restaurant *(☎ 312969; Nyeri St; mains & kebabs around KSh160)* is very popular with locals. It's only open in the evening, but tables are set up along the street and you can sample excellent Swahili dishes such as beans in coconut, grilled fish, meat, superb chapatis and salad under a tropical sky. This is a Muslim restaurant so

there are no alcoholic drinks and it's closed all day until after sunset during Ramadan.

Island Dishes *(cnr Nyeri St & Kibokoni Rd; mains KSh50-120)* is just around the corner and is run by two Omani brothers. The food is excellent and comes in huge portions. Dishes vary from day to day; lamb biryani, coconut fish and curries normally feature.

Indian Since many of the restaurants in Mombasa are Indian-owned you can find excellent curries and lunchtime thalis (set meals, consisting of several dishes served on a single plate).

New Chetna Restaurant *(☎ 224477, Haile Selassie Rd; vegetarian mains from KSh200-280)* is a very popular South Indian vegetarian restaurant. The food here includes *masala dosa* (curried vegetables inside a lentil flour pancake) and *idli* (rice dumpling) and the KSh200 thali (set meal) is great value. For desert, there's a shop at the front selling Indian sweets.

Splendid View Restaurant *(☎ 487270; Maungano Rd; tandoori dishes KSh150-350; open 11.30am-2pm & 5.30pm-10.30pm Mon-Sat, 4.30pm-11.30pm Sun)* is opposite the Splendid Hotel (hence the name). The tandoori chicken and shish kebabs are possibly the best on the coast, served with piping hot naan bread. Most locals come for takeaway meals, but you can eat in and there are fruit juices and lassi (yogurt drinks) to wash down your meal.

Shehnai Restaurant *(☎ 312492; Maungano St; veggie mains from KSh290, meat dishes from KSh370; open noon-2pm & 7pm-10pm Tues-Sun)*, in the centre of town just off Haile Selassie Rd, specialises in *mughlai* cuisine and has a huge menu. It's very popular with well-heeled Indian families and the food is authentic and very good.

Chinese There are a number of good Chinese restaurants in Mombasa, although most also double as bars, so you may be the only person eating.

Mombasa Meeting Point *(☎ 315098; Nyerere Ave; mains with rice or noodles KSh400-600)* has incredibly chintzy decor but serves great Korean and Chinese food. You can't miss this place – look for the party lights in the windows.

New Overseas Chinese-Korean Restaurant & Bar *(☎ 230729; Moi Ave; mains KSh220-*

480) has the longest name in Mombasa and spangley decor similar to the Meeting Place. There are loads of seafood choices – a Chinese or Korean feast will set you back about KSh800.

Hong Kong Chinese Restaurant *(☎ 485422; Moi Ave; mains KSh230-490)*, further past Tangana Rd, is also recommended. It's open for lunch and dinner daily and most dishes come in either small (good for one) or large (good for two) portions.

International Very popular with locals is **Baron Restaurant & Pub** *(☎ 314971; Digo Rd; mains KSh150-450)*, which has a good range of grills, curries and *nyama choma* (barbecued meat). The upstairs balcony is a fine place for a beer.

Pistacchio Café *(☎ 221989; Meru Rd; buffet lunch KSh395; open 9am-10pm Mon-Sat)* is Swiss run with excellent ice cream and popular lunchtime buffets – usually a mixture of Indian and Western dishes. À-la-carte dishes such as spaghetti are also served.

Fontanella Steakhouse & Beer Garden *(☎ 223756; City House, Moi Ave; mains KSh150-200)* is a popular open-air place in an atrium off Moi Ave, with good Western-inspired food. Steaks are KSh200 and *nyama choma* costs around KSh100 per 250g.

Le Bistro *(☎ 229470; Moi Ave; starters KSh100, mains KSh225-300; lunch buffet KSh250; open 10am-11pm daily)* is a great place for dinner, with a friendly cocktail bar and fantastic European-influenced food. The salads and pizzas are highly recommended. There's a great-value, lunchtime buffet from Monday to Saturday. The restaurant is close to the tusks statue by the tourist office – look out for the Maasai doorman.

Rozina House Restaurant *(☎ 311107, Moi Ave; mains from KSh650)* is next door and serves expensive seafood dishes. The food is good, but the atmosphere would be better if there wasn't so much hard-sell at the door. Cheaper meals are available at the café.

Tawa Terrace *(☎ 223379; Haile Selassie Rd; fish & chips KSh300, lobster KSh1100)*, on the roof at the Royal Court Hotel, has grand views and recommended food.

Arturo's Italian Restaurant *(☎ 226940; Moi Ave; pasta, risotto & secondi platti KSh400-700; open lunch & dinner Mon-Sat)*, in the Jubilee Insurance building, is a great little Italian restaurant with authentic food.

Tamarind Restaurant *(☎ 471747; Silos Rd, Nyali; seafood mains KSh780-1900)* is certainly up there with the very best restaurants in Kenya. It's housed in a grandly conceived, Moorish building on the shore facing Mombasa island and there's a waterside terrace festooned with bougainvillea. Prices reflect the calibre of the place – lobster flambéed in cognac and simmered in white wine is KSh275 per 100g – and it's well worth the splurge. A taxi between town and the Tamarind costs KSh500.

Siesta Bar & Restaurant *(☎ 474896; Nyali Rd, Nyali; mains KSh390-580; open from 5pm daily)* is an atmospheric open-air Mexican restaurant, set in a fine garden overlooking the water. It's great for a sunset beer and the Mexican food is highly recommended.

Self Catering If you are putting your own food together, or want to stock up with goodies to take down the coast, **City Grocers** *(Haile Selassie Rd)* is well stocked, although the **Nakumatt supermarket** *(Nyerere Ave)*, close to the Likoni ferry, has a far better selection. Fruit and vegetables are available in the **main market** on Digo Rd or from old-fashioned **fruit carts** on Biashara St and Haile Selassie Rd. Other vendors around Biashara St and Samburu Rd sell *haluwa* (an Omani dessert, similar to nutty Turkish delight), fried taro roots, sweet baobab seeds and sugared doughnuts.

Entertainment

Bars & Discos There are plenty of good drinking holes in Mombasa and many restaurants cater primarily to drinkers in the evening.

Afro Bar *(Nkrumah Rd)* is a popular after-work drinking hole and you can get snacks such as *nyama choma* with your beer.

Casablanca Restaurant & Club *(Mnazi Moja Rd)* is a loud bar that pulls in a lot of Westerners, but also a lot of prostitutes. Still, the music is good, there's a nightly disco and the beers are wonderfully cold.

Sky Bar & Restaurant *(☎ 315165; Moi Ave)*, not far from the tusks statue, is a pretty seedy drinking hole with plastic chairs and lots of prostitutes. Most travellers only come here to play on the pool tables.

Toyz Disco *(☎ 313931; Baluchi St; entry KSh50-100)* is a loud and lively Kenyan nightspot just off Nkrumah Rd. A rather ominous sign outside announces that drugs, nudity, fighting and weapons are banned, but it's perfectly friendly inside. Entry is free for women before 10pm. Expect plenty of gangsta rap and jangly Congolese music.

Royal Casino *(cnr Moi Ave & Digo Rd)* has a number of pool tables and a bar as well as the slots and gaming tables. On Wednesday you can see some of the only stand-up comedy in Kenya.

Salambo Club *(☎ 220180; Moi Ave)*, next door, is a popular hang-out for Kenyans, with loud Lingala music and cold beers.

The most lively nightclub and disco is **New Florida Casino & Nightclub** *(☎ 316810; Mama Ngina Dr; entry men/women KSh150/70)*. Built right on the seashore and enclosing its own swimming pool, it's owned by the same people who run the Florida clubs in Nairobi and offers much the same atmosphere and clientele. The extravagant Las Vegas–style floorshows are quite an experience. Friday, Saturday and Sunday are the big party nights.

For live music try **Hotel Splendid** or **Excellent Hotel**, which sometimes have live bands playing on the roof terrace. Keep an eye out for the posters on Nkrumah Rd advertising reggae concerts and other events.

Cinemas Mombasa has a couple of cinemas.

Kenya Cinema *(☎ 312355; Nkrumah Ave; admission KSh120-150)* is an appealing old movie house, which screens regular Hindi movies (often with English subtitles) and occasional Western blockbusters.

Nyali Cinemax *(☎ 470000; Nyali Centre, Nyali Rd, Nyali; admission KSh300)* is a plush, new cinema close to Tamarind Restaurant.

Shopping
Moi Ave has loads of souvenir shops, but prices are high and every shop seems to stock exactly the same stuff. Almost every building on Ndia Kuu Rd in the Old Town is now a souvenir emporium.

For better crafts visit **Bombolulu Workshops & Cultural Centre** *(☎ 471704; w www.apdkbombolulu.com; tours per nonresident adult/child KSh320/150; open 8am-6pm Mon-Sat)*. This nonprofit organisation produces crafts of a very high standard and gives vocational training to hundreds of physically disabled people. You can visit the showroom to buy jewellery, clothes, carvings and other crafts and tour the workshops and mock-ups of traditional homesteads in the grounds, where various cultural activities take place. The turn-off for the centre is on the left about 3km north of Nyali bridge. It's easy to get here by a Bombolulu matatu (KSh20) from Msanifu Kombo St.

Akamba Handicraft Industry Cooperative Society *(☎ 432241; Airport Rd; open 8am-5pm Mon-Fri, 8am-noon Sun)* employs an incredible 10,000 people from the local area. It's also a nonprofit organisation and produces very fine animal woodcarving. Kwa Hola/Magongo matatus run right past the gates (pick them up from the Kobil petrol station on Jomo Kenyatta Ave). Many coach tours from Mombasa also stop here.

Biashara St, west of the Digo Rd intersection, is the centre for *kikoi*, brightly coloured woven sarongs for men, and *kangas*, printed wraps worn by women. *Kangas* come as a pair – one for the top half of the body and one for the bottom – and are marked with Swahili proverbs. You may need to bargain, but what you get is generally what you pay for; bank on about KSh300 for a pair of *kangas* or a *kikoi*.

Mombasa has an incredible number of skilled tailors and you can have a safari suit or shirt custom-made in a day or two for an incredible price. **Mombasa Tailoring Mart** *(☎ 226859; Digo Rd)* is recommended; tailored African-style shirts cost from KSh1250 and full safari suits start at KSh2750. There are numerous other choices on Nehru Rd, behind the Municipal Market.

There are stalls selling sisal baskets and spices in and around the Municipal Market, but you'll rarely pay fair prices as touts loiter around the market and 'accompany' tourists to the stalls for a commission.

Getting There & Away
Air Every couple of hours during the day, **Kenya Airways** *(☎ 221251, fax 313815; TSS Towers, Nkrumah Rd; ☎ 443400; Moi International Airport)* flies between Nairobi and Mombasa (KSh6250 one way, one hour). It's much cheaper if you book more than 14 days in advance. Remember to reconfirm your return seat a day or so before travelling.

British Airways' subsidiary, **Regional Air** *(☎ 229777; TSS Towers, Nkrumah Rd)* has three daily flights between Nairobi and Mombasa Monday to Friday, two flights on

Saturday and one flight on Sunday (KSh4000 one way).

Air Kenya *(☎ 229777; TSS Towers, Nkrumah Rd; ☎ 433982 Moi International Airport)* has two or three daily flights between Wilson Airport in Nairobi and Mombasa (US$70, 1¼ hours). There are daily flights to Lamu (US$98, 1¼ hours) via Malindi (US$25, 30 minutes). Air Kenya also has three weekly flights to Zanzibar.

African Express Airways *(☎ 433851)* flies from Mombasa to Nairobi (KSh4300) at 5pm on Saturday only.

Oman Air *(☎ 224400; Moi Ave)* has twice-weekly flights to Dubai and Muscat.

Bus & Matatu Most bus offices are either on Jomo Kenyatta Ave or Abdel Nasser Rd. Services to Malindi and Lamu leave from Abdel Nasser Rd, while buses to Tanzania leave from the junction of Jomo Kenyatta Ave and Mwembe Tayari Rd. Kenya Bus Service (KBS) has suspended all its services in and around Mombasa for the foreseeable future.

For buses and matatus to the beaches south of Mombasa you first need to get off the island via the Likoni ferry (see Boat under Getting Around following). Frequent matatus run from Nyerere Ave to the ferry.

Nairobi There are dozens of daily departures in either direction (mostly in the early morning and late evening). Companies include:

Akamba (☎ 490269) Jomo Kenyatta Ave
Busscar (☎ 222854) Abdel Nasser Rd
Busstar (Nairobi ☎ 02-219525) Abdel Nasser Rd
Coastline Safaris (☎ 312083) Mwembe Tayari St
Falcon (Nairobi ☎ 02-229662) Abdel Nasser Rd
Mash Express (☎ 432723) Jomo Kenyatta Ave
Mombasa Raha (Mombasa Liners; ☎ 225716) Abdel Nasser Rd; Jomo Kenyatta Ave

The trip to Nairobi takes anywhere from eight to 10 hours and includes a meal break about halfway – fares vary from KSh400 to KSh700. **Coastline** is the most expensive but its buses are very comfortable. The noon and 10.30pm **Mombasa Raha** (Mombasa Liners) buses are deluxe services with DVD movies (KSh550). Most companies have at least four departures daily, with the exception of **Akamba**, which just has a morning and evening service.

All buses travel via Voi (KSh300), which is also served by frequent matatus from the Kobil petrol station on Jomo Kenyatta Ave (KSh200). Several companies have buses across the country to towns near Lake Victoria, but all go via Nairobi.

Heading North There are numerous daily matatus and small lorry-buses to Malindi, leaving from in front of the Noor Mosque on Abdel Nasser Rd. Buses take up to 2½ hours (KSh100), matatus about two hours (KSh120).

Tawakal, Interstate 2000, Mombasa Raha (Mombasa Liners) and **TSS Express** have buses to Lamu at around 7am (be at the office 30 minutes early) from their offices on Abdel Nasser Rd. Buses take around seven hours to reach the Lamu ferry at Mokoke (KSh400).

Heading South Regular buses and matatus leave from the Likoni ferry terminal and travel along the southern coast. See individual entries in the South of Mombasa section for details.

For Tanga and Dar es Salaam in Tanzania, **Interstate 2000, As-Salaam, Al Yumeiny** and other companies have daily departures at around 7am and 6pm from their offices on Jomo Kenyatta Ave, near the junction with Mwembe Tayari Rd.

Dubious-looking local buses heading to Moshi and Arusha leave from in front of the Mwembe Tayari Health Centre in the morning or evening. See the Getting There & Away chapter for more details.

Train The popular overnight train to/from Nairobi is a great place to meet other travellers and hook up for safaris or travel on the coast. Trains leave at 7pm in either direction, arriving the next day somewhere between 8.30am and 11am. The fares are KSh3000/2100 in 1st/2nd class and include dinner, breakfast and bedding – reserve as far in advance as possible. The **booking office** *(☎ 312231)*, at the station in Mombasa, is open from 8am to 7pm daily.

Boat In theory it's possible to get a ride on a dhow to Pemba, Zanzibar or Dar es Salaam in Tanzania, but it's generally more trouble than it's worth. You might have a better chance down the coast at Shimoni. There were no ferry services at the time of writing, but there's always a chance that services between Mombasa and Tanzania may start up again. See Sea & Lake in the Getting There & Away chapter.

Getting Around

To/From the Airport There is currently no public transport to/from the airport, so you're best off taking a taxi – the official fare to central Mombasa is KSh610. Coming from town, the usual fare is KSh700, but you'll have to bargain down hard from KSh1000.

If you don't have much luggage, you can take a Kwa Hola/Magongo matatu from the Kobil petrol station on Jomo Kenyatta Ave to just beyond the Akamba Handicrafts Cooperative on Airport Rd for KSh20 and walk the last few kilometres.

Matatu Matatus charge KSh10 to KSh20 for short hops. For the Likoni ferry and Nakumatt supermarket, matatus run south along Nyerere Ave (the main post office on Digo Rd is a good place to board). For Bombolulu and Bamburi, matatus run along Msanifu Kombo St.

Car & Motorcycle The **Automobile Association of Kenya** (AA; ☎ 492431; Jomo Kenyatta Ave) is between the Total petrol station and KBC bank.

There's not much to choose between the hire-car companies in town apart from the possible insurance excesses (see Car Rental in the Getting Around chapter). Rates are the same as in Nairobi – about KSh7000 per day for a small jeep and KSh6000 per day for a saloon car. None of these companies will let you take a 2WD car into Shimba Hills National Reserve or the Mwaluganje Elephant Sanctuary. Companies which have offices in Mombasa include the following.

Avenue Motors (☎ 225126) Moi Ave
Avis (☎ 223048) Southern House, Moi Ave (☎ 424021) Moi International Airport
Budget (☎ 221281, fax 221282) Sarova House, Moi Ave (☎ 434021-3) Moi International Airport
Glory (☎ 313561, fax 221196) Moi Ave
Hertz (☎ 316333) UTC Building, Moi Ave (☎ 433211) Moi International Airport
Unik Car Hire & Safaris (☎ 314864) Fatemi Bldg, Maungano Rd

Be aware of Glory's high insurance excess (KSh150,000).

Taxi Mombasa taxis are as expensive and run down as those in Nairobi, only harder to find. A good place to start looking is in front of the Express Travel office on Nkrumah Rd. Assume it'll cost KSh200 to KSh300 from the train station to the city centre. Two reliable companies are **Kenatco** (☎ 227503; Ambalal House, Nkrumah Rd) and **Voda Taxis** (☎ 222788; Maungano Rd).

Boat The Likoni ferry connects Mombasa Island with the southern mainland and runs at frequent intervals during the night and day. There's a crossing every 20 minutes on average between 5am and 12.30am, less frequently outside these times. It's free to pedestrians and KSh40 for a car. To get to the ferry from the centre of town, take a Likoni matatu from outside the main post office on Digo Rd (KSh10).

South of Mombasa

The main attraction south of Mombasa is the string of gorgeous beaches stretching most of the way to the Tanzanian border. However, the immaculate white sand can vanish under mounds of seaweed between March and December. Attempts at removing the troublesome weed have met with mixed results as the weed beds play an important role in protecting the sand. Some resorts have been left sitting high and dry as the sand has been eroded from the beaches.

Offshore are the Diani-Chale and Kisite-Mpunguti Marine National Parks, which protect some impressive coral reefs. Scuba diving, snorkelling and glass-bottomed boat trips are all popular activities. The reef protects the beaches from sharks, so there is no danger to swimmers at the beach resorts along the coast.

Diani Beach is where you'll find most of the big resorts and hotels, but the beach is better and more tranquil at low-key Tiwi Beach, just to the north, which has several budget places to stay. Dhow trips to the mangrove islands of Funzi and Wasini near the Tanzanian border offer a chance to experience what the coast was like before the big hotels arrived.

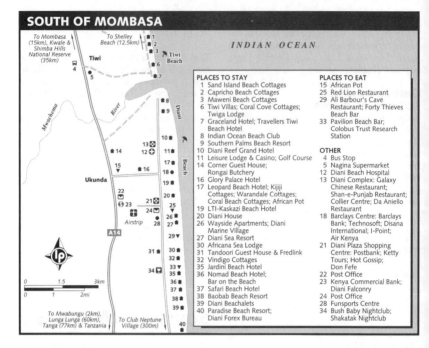

SOUTH OF MOMBASA

To Mombasa (15km), Kwale & Shimba Hills National Reserve (35km)

To Shelley Beach (12.5km)

Tiwi

Tiwi Beach

INDIAN OCEAN

Mwachema River

Diani Beach

Ukunda

Airstrip

A14

0   1.5   3km
0   1   2mi

To Mwabungu (2km), Lunga Lunga (60km), Tanga (77km) & Tanzania

To Club Neptune Village (300m)

PLACES TO STAY
1   Sand Island Beach Cottages
2   Capricho Beach Cottages
3   Maweni Beach Cottages
6   Tiwi Villas; Coral Cove Cottages; Twiga Lodge
7   Graceland Hotel; Travellers Tiwi Beach Hotel
8   Indian Ocean Beach Club
9   Southern Palms Beach Resort
10 Diani Reef Grand Hotel
11 Leisure Lodge & Casino; Golf Course
14 Corner Guest House; Rongai Butchery
16 Glory Palace Hotel
17 Leopard Beach Hotel; Kijiji Cottages; Warandale Cottages; Coral Beach Cottages; African Pot
19 LTI-Kaskazi Beach Hotel
20 Diani House
26 Wayside Apartments; Diani Marine Village
27 Diani Sea Resort
30 Africana Sea Lodge
31 Tandoori Guest House & Fredlink
32 Vindigo Cottages
35 Jardini Beach Hotel
36 Nomad Beach Hotel; Bar on the Beach
37 Safari Beach Hotel
38 Baobab Beach Resort
39 Diani Beachalets
40 Paradise Beach Resort; Diani Forex Bureau

PLACES TO EAT
15 African Pot
25 Red Lion Restaurant
29 Ali Barbour's Cave Restaurant; Forty Thieves Beach Bar
33 Pavilion Beach Bar; Colobus Trust Research Station

OTHER
4   Bus Stop
5   Nagina Supermarket
12 Diani Beach Hospital
13 Diani Complex: Galaxy Chinese Restaurant; Shan-e-Punjab Restaurant; Collier Centre; Da Aniello Restaurant
18 Barclays Centre: Barclays Bank; Technosoft; Disana International; I-Point; Air Kenya
21 Diani Plaza Shopping Centre: Postbank; Ketty Tours; Hot Gossip; Don Fefe
22 Post Office
23 Kenya Commercial Bank; Diani Falconry
24 Post Office
28 Funsports Centre
34 Bush Baby Nightclub; Shakatak Nightclub

SHELLY BEACH

Right across the water from Mombasa island, Shelly Beach isn't a bad place to swim if you just want a day trip from Mombasa. There are a few faded hotels and the beach is passable, although there's lots of seaweed. The turn-off to Shelly Bay is just south of the Likoni ferry jetty, immediately after the bus stand. Matatus hang around at the junction offering transfers to the beach (KSh30).

TIWI BEACH
☎ 0127

This wonderfully undeveloped beach is reached by two dirt roads that wind their way through the coastal scrub about 20km south of Likoni. It's a world away from the beach resorts and bustle of Diani Beach and most of the places to stay are cottages set in quiet gardens that run right down to the sand. There are a handful of low-key restaurants and bars here if you don't feel up to catering for yourself.

Tiwi is a tranquil spot but it's still very popular with those in the know, so you should book well ahead if you intend to visit during the high season (Easter, August

to early September and Christmas and New Year). Beach boys are fairly prevalent at the southern end of Tiwi, but are almost unheard of on the private beaches at the northern end of the strip.

Places to Stay & Eat

The places to stay here are divided into two groups, linked by a bumpy track just inland from the beach. The first group of three is reached by a *murram* (dirt) track that turns off the main road about 18km south of Mombasa.

Sand Island Beach Cottages (*☎/fax 51233;* e *sandisland@africaonline.co.ke; 2-person cottages KSh2100, 3-6 person cottages from KSh2700)* has a number of lovely colonial-style cottages with excellent kitchens, set in a tidy garden. Nearby Sand Island is a lovely place to relax and catch some sun. Rates increase by 20% in the high season, and linen, mosquito nets and fans are all provided. There's an in-house cook who can prepare meals for you, and fresh fruit is available from the orchard.

Capricho Beach Cottages (*☎/fax 51231;* e *capricho@tiwibeach.com; 2-person cottages*

THE COAST

Safety on the Coast

Security from crime along the coast has improved in recent years, but you still need to be careful around the popular resorts. Muggings are still a risk on the minor roads that run between the main Mombasa to Tanzania road and the various beach resorts along the coast. Take a taxi or matatu, particularly at night.

All the resorts and cottages on the coast employ *askaris* (guards) to keep out undesirables, but once you're on the beach, it's easy to become a target for 'snatch and run' crimes. Leave watches, wallets, jewellery and other items of value in your room.

Beach boys – young Kenyan men who walk up and down the beaches selling everything from woodcarvings to marijuana and sexual favours – are a feature of life at the big resorts and their dogged persistence can wear you down. A polite refusal should be enough to persuade them to take whatever it is they're offering elsewhere.

KSh1900, 4-person cottages KSh2400-2800, 6-person cottages KSh3100) is peaceful and well set-up for families, although there are lots of hidden costs. The self-catering cottages are set in a pleasant garden. There's a KSh200 charge per person to use the swimming pool and a KSh70 charge per person for linen and mosquito nets. Cooks/cleaners can also be hired for KSh250 per day. Prices rise by 20% in high season.

Maweni Beach Cottages (☎ 51008; fax 51225; e julianestephan@kenyasouthcoast .com; 1-bedroom cottage KSh1360, 2-bedroom cottages KSh2540-2820, 3-bedroom cottage KSh3170) consists of attractive *makuti*-roofed cottages overlooking a peaceful cove.

Facilities are good and the owners are friendly and helpful. All the cottages have kitchens.

The other group of places is about 2km further south near the village of Tiwi. A clearly signposted dirt road leads from the highway to Graceland Hotel and Travellers Tiwi Beach Hotel at the southern end of the group. Just before the Graceland, a track branches north to Twiga Lodge, Coral Cove Cottages and Tiwi Villas.

Travellers Tiwi Beach Hotel (☎ 51202, fax 51207; e travhtls@africaonline.co.ke; singles/ doubles half-board US$68/90 in low season, US$90/121 in high season) is just north of Diani on the northern bank of the Mwachema River. Accommodation is in huge *makuti*-roofed barns, which house package tourists by the hundreds.

There are excursion packages to the Travellers Mwaluganje Elephant Camp available for US$78 for a day trip and US$158 overnight (see Mwaluganje Elephant Sanctuary later in this chapter).

Graceland Hotel (Tiwi Sea Castles; ☎/fax 51048, e gracelandhotel@myrealbox.com; singles/doubles KSh1980/2640, 1-bedroom cottages KSh6600-7920, 2-bedroom cottages KSh10,560) is a lovely informal resort with a peaceful, relaxed atmosphere, a pool and a good restaurant and bar. Accommodation is in well-maintained rooms with bathroom, mosquito nets and fans, or in cottages that sleep two to four people.

Twiga Lodge (☎ 51267, 51097; camping per person KSh150, singles/doubles KSh600/1200, cottages KSh1200) has long been *the* place to stay at Tiwi and it's probably the best place on the south coast to meet other travellers. The beachfront camping ground is popular with overland tour groups and almost everyone ends up in the restaurant and bar in the evenings (meals cost KSh200 to KSh300). Some of the rooms and cottages are a little old, but a new accommodation block is being constructed on the beach. There was a problem with theft here a few years back, but things seem to be OK these days. You should still be careful, though, not to leave valuables lying around.

Coral Cove Cottages (☎ 51295, fax 51062; e coralcove@tiwibeach.com; small 2-person cottage KSh800-1800, 2-person beach cottage KSh3200, 4-person cottage KSh2500-4500) is a fantastically friendly place, with tame monkeys, cats, dogs, geese and ducks and a wide variety of comfy, nicely decorated cottages. The larger cottages have kitchens and cooks/cleaners can be hired for KSh350 per day. It's a fine place to stay and the owners go out of their way to help their guests.

Tiwi Villas (☎ 51265; ☎ 0722-724153; doubles KSh1000-1800, 4-person cottages KSh1500-2500) sits on a small coral cliff above the beach. It's a peaceful place and the *makuti*-roofed cottages are good value for money. Cottages have nets and fans but have no cooking facilities.

If you stay at Coral Cove or Tiwi Villas, you can always get a meal or beer at Twiga Lodge next door.

Self-caterers can pick up supplies from the **Nagina supermarket** and the fruit and vegetable **duka** (small shop) near the turn-off to Travellers Tiwi Beach Hotel. Also, men on bicycles carrying fruit, vegetables and fresh fish tour the cottage complexes during the day.

Getting There & Away
Buses and matatus from Likoni to Ukunda can drop you at the start of either road down to Tiwi (KSh30) – keep an eye out for the signs to Capricho Beach Cottages or Travellers Tiwi Beach Hotel. This second road is much easier to find.

Although it's only 3.5km to the beach, both access roads are notorious for muggings so wait for a lift from one of the many cars that pass this way or catch one of the ancient waiting taxis (KSh300). Heading back to the highway, any of the places to stay can call ahead for a cab.

DIANI BEACH
☎ 0127
Diani Beach is where the overwhelming majority of beach tourists from Europe end up, and it's one continuous strip of souvenir stalls, beach houses and all-inclusive luxury resorts. If that's your cup of tea, Diani is unlikely to disappoint, but if it's peace and tranquillity you're after, you may be better off heading to one of the smaller resorts elsewhere on the coast.

Although the beach is wonderfully white and the resorts are very grand, the strip is looking a little drab in places. Diani is still recovering from the downturn in tourism following the infamous 'ethnic cleansing' of Likoni and Ukunda before the 1997 elections, and several hotels, restaurants and shopping centres here have folded due to lack of business.

Most visitors are on all-inclusive package tours from Europe, which has sadly killed off trade for many of the independent restaurant and bars at Diani. There are also a handful of budget options.

As at Tiwi Beach, make advance bookings for any of the cheaper places at Diani during the high season. If you intend to stay for some time and are part of a big group, scan

---

Diani Shipwreck

As well as diving the reefs of Diani Beach, divers can now visit Kenya's first purposely sunk shipwreck, the MFV *Alpha Funguo*. This 15m tuna fishing boat was scuttled off the edge of the reef in February 2002 and is already accumulating some impressive marine growth. Among other fish seen here are graceful lionfish and a giant 2m-long grouper. The wreck lies in 28m of water and all the scuba companies at Diani Beach offer trips for around US$90 with two dives.

---

the ads beside the road and in the shopping centres to secure a cheap private lease at one of the beach houses along the strip. Good package deals to the coast, either from within Kenya or from Europe, are often available at travel agencies.

Orientation
The town of **Ukunda**, which is on the main Mombasa–Tanzania road is the turn-off point for Diani Beach and has a post office, a bank, several shops and a number of basic lodging houses and restaurants. From there, a tarmac road runs about 2.5km to a T-junction with the beach road, where you'll find everything Diani has to offer.

Information
Tourist Offices You can get tourist information from the private **i-Point** (☎ 2234; e *diani@technosoftkenya.com; Barclays Centre; open 8.30am-6pm Mon-Fri, 9am-4pm Sat*), including the *Diani Beach Tourist-Guide* (KSh50), which lists most places to stay, eat and shop.

Money Located in the Barclays Centre, almost opposite the Ukunda Rd junction, **Barclays Bank** has an ATM, and there's a bureau de change at the **Kenya Commercial Bank** back on the highway in Ukunda. Both banks open 9am to 3pm Monday to Friday and 9am to 11am Saturday.

You can change travellers cheques and cash at **Diani Forex Bureau** (☎ 3595; open *9am-4pm Mon-Fri, 9am-noon Sat*) at the southern end of the beach. For Western Union money transfers, visit the **Postbank** in the Diani Plaza Shopping Centre.

Post & Communications The Diani **post office** *(open 8am-12.30pm & 2pm-5pm Mon-Fri, 9am-noon Sat)* is housed in a hut by the turn-off to the Ukunda airstrip. There's also a **post office** in Ukunda near the Kenya Commercial Bank.

For email and Internet access try **Technosoft** *(☎ 3386)* and **Disana International** *(☎ 2080)* in the Barclays Centre; both charge KSh5 per minute for surfing. Disana also has reasonable international telephone and fax rates. Further south, **Hot Gossip** *(☎ 3101; Legend Pavilion; Internet access KSh10 per minute; open 9am-7pm Mon-Sat)* has fast connections and also offers international phone and fax services.

Medical & Emergency Services Open 24 hours, **Diani Beach Hospital** *(☎ 2435)* is about 1km north of the Ukunda Rd junction. There are several doctor's surgeries in Diani – try **Dr Vargazee** *(☎ 2588)* in the Diani Sea Resort arcade.

Diani **police** can be contacted on ☎ 2229.

Dangers & Annoyances Crime is an occasional problem at Diani. See the boxed text 'Safety on the Coast' earlier is this chapter for more information.

Things to See & Do

There are a handful of attractions in the area, although most are normally visited on organised tours (see Organised Tours later).

One local option is the **Diani Falconry** *(☎ 0722-884238; Ukunda; adult/child KSh300/150; open 8am-6pm daily)*, behind the Kenya Commercial Bank on the main highway.

If you want water sports, approach one of the big hotels – the Safari Beach Hotel, Jardini Beach Hotel and Africana Sea Lodge are probably the most approachable. Two-person **sailboats** (toppers; plastic hulled sailboats that you sit on, rather than in) can be hired for KSh600 per hour or KSh2000 per day from the **Forty Thieves Beach Bar** *(☎ 2033)* in the central area of Diani Beach.

All the big resorts have **diving schools** and charge standard rates – PADI open-water courses cost US$480 and reef trips with two dives cost US$90. The Diani Marine Village dive resort (see Places to Stay) is the best place to approach if you aren't staying at a big hotel. Most dive sites here are under 29m and there's even a purposely sunk shipwreck (see the boxed text 'Diani Shipwreck').

There's a **golf course** at the Leisure Lodge & Casino on the northern section of the beach. It's open to nonguests for US$30 per day, and caddies and clubs can be hired for around US$20 for 18 holes.

Camel rides are available along the beach for around KSh500 per hour (negotiable).

Organised Tours

Several companies offer **dhow trips** further down the coast to either Funzi or Wasini Islands (see Funzi Island and Wasini Island

---

Colobus Climbing Frames

Once common all along the coast, the Angolan black and white colobus *(Colobus angolensis palliatus)* is now restricted to a few isolated pockets of forest south of Mombasa. Easily identifiable by the distinctive white tufts of hair on their cheeks and shoulders, colobus monkeys have no thumbs and take their name from the Greek word *kolobos* meaning 'maimed'.

The **Colobus Trust** *(☎ 0147-3519, fax 3223;* e *wakuluzu@colobustrust.org)* was established in Diani Beach in 1997 after a survey revealed that almost a fifth of the remaining 200 monkeys had been killed in the preceding four months. The main culprits were big hotels, which were destroying the monkey's habitat, and tour buses and trucks, which killed huge numbers of monkeys on the roads. Colobus eat the leaves of certain coastal trees and are particularly vulnerable to habitat destruction.

Funded by international volunteers, the Colobus Trust has set up 23 rope ladders between the trees on either side of the Diani Beach Rd, allowing the monkeys to safely cross from one side to the other. It seems to be working, as there are now believed to be nearly 400 colobus.

Guided walks leave from the research station near the Africana Sea Lodge at 10am and 2pm daily to see the colobus in their natural habitat. Tours are free but a donation of around KSh300 per person is appropriate. The trust also runs wildlife education and awareness for local people and staff of big hotels.

THE COAST

later in this chapter). Day safaris to Shimba Hills National Reserve or Mwaluganje Elephant Sanctuary typically cost around US$100 including lunch and park entry fees; **Ketty Tours** (☎ 3582; Diani Plaza shopping centre) is a reliable operator. Cheaper trips may be available with smaller safari companies at Diani. See the boxed text 'Colobus Climbing Frames' for details on guided forest walks.

Places to Stay – Budget
There are few budget choices here, and none fulfil the vision of a tropical beach holiday. Beach access can be a problem as few of the big hotels will let nonguests walk through their compounds – your best bet is the path beside the defunct Tradewinds Hotel.

In Ukunda, **Corner Guest House** (doubles KSh400) is the best of a number of basic lodging places near the Diani junction; rooms are simple but clean with fans and nets.

Halfway down the road to Diani from Ukunda, **Glory Palace Hotel** (☎ 3392; singles/ doubles with fan KSh800/1200, singles/ doubles with air-con KSh1000/1500) has clean but rather spartan rooms. There is a restaurant and a decent-sized swimming pool.

Tandoori Guest House (☎ 2106; doubles with bathroom KSh600) is the only budget choice along the beach strip. It's south of the Ukunda junction in the Diani Plaza shopping centre and offers large plain rooms with fans, nets and bathrooms, above a restaurant.

Places to Stay – Mid-Range
The following places are all on the beach road. Unless otherwise indicated, all are self-catering and kitchen facilities are provided.

North of Ukunda Junction Just north of the turn-off for Ukunda, **Coral Beach Cottages** (☎ 2206, fax 3428; 2-bedroom cottages KSh3000, seafront 2-bedroom cottages KSh3500, 3-bedroom cottage KSh4500) has large, well-appointed cottages set in a neat garden. The atmosphere is pleasant and relaxed. The excellent African Pot restaurant is right at the entrance gate.

Mixed together in the forest just north of the Word of Life religious centre are **Warandale Cottages** (☎/fax 2187; 1-/2-/3-bedroom cottages from KSh1850/2350/4750) and **Kijiji Cottages** (☎ 2186; 2-/3-bedroom cottages KSh3500/4500). The characterful cottages

are set along winding paths and there are two reception offices at the entrance to the complex. The architecture is unique and facilities are excellent. There is a swimming pool and a secluded beach that's often cut off from the beach boys by the tide. Rates almost double in high season.

Southern Palms Beach Resort (☎ 3721, fax 3381; e saleem@africaonline.co.ke; singles/ doubles half board KSh2500/3500 in low season, KSh3500/5000 in high season) is a gigantic, mass-market hotel consisting of tall accommodation blocks with makuti roofs. Everywhere you look there are bars and swimming pools. It's lively enough, if you like that sort of thing, but the ever-present askaris (guards) are a bit oppressive.

South of Ukunda Junction South of the junction, options include the following.

Vindigo Cottages (☎ 2192; 2-/3-/4-person cottages KSh1500/3000/2500) is a slightly ramshackle complex of cottages but rates are reasonable. There are no fans but cottages catch the sea breeze and all have nets. A few larger cottages are also available.

Wayside Apartments (☎ 3119; 1-bedroom apartments KSh2700, 2-bedroom apartments KSh4000, 3-bedroom apartments KSh6700) is a neat and well-run complex of modern apartments opposite the derelict Tradewinds Hotel. There's a good communal pool and bar but no sea view. Prices rise during high season.

Diani Marine Village (☎ 2367, fax 3452; e dimarine@africaonline.co.ke; B&B per person US$35) is primarily a dive resort, but the rooms are very attractive, with fans, nets, stone floors and four-poster beds. Lunch and dinner is available.

Nomad Beach Hotel (☎ 2155, fax 2391; e nomad@swiftmombasa.com; bandas/cottages US$30/45 in low season, US$80/90 in high season), a relaxed place, is made up of simple, comfortable cottages and bandas on the edge of the beach. The attractive grounds are shaded by palms, and there's a nice informal atmosphere. The bar on the beach is a local favourite and nonguests are welcome.

Safari Beach Hotel (☎ 2726, fax 2357; singles/doubles KSh2650/3700 in low season, KSh3880/4900 in high season), is part of the Alliance group. Accommodation is in two-storey, thatched, round buildings, and the general decor is quite tasteful. It's a good place for people with kids and there's lots of activities on offer.

Diani Beachlets (☎ 2180; twin bandas with shared kitchen & bathroom KSh450, maisonettes with bathroom KSh1167-1350, beachside 2-/3-bedroom cottages KSh2065/2646) at the southern end of the beach is a little old but it's probably the best bet for backpackers. The bandas and maisonettes sleep two people and the seafront cottages sleep four to six people. Rates drop by 30% in the low season.

Paradise Beach Resort (☎ 3595, fax 3404; cottages KSh3500/7000 in low season, KSh3500/7000 in high season) is behind Diani Beachlets. Although the grounds are a little plain, it's right by the beach and the Indian owners are friendly and helpful. Cottages are spacious, with three bedrooms, kitchen and a dining/lounge area.

Places to Stay – Top End

There are at least 13 flashy resort complexes and hotels spread out north and south along the beach strip, as well as a few that didn't survive the downturn in tourism. The hotels and resorts here cater mostly to package tourists from Europe and offer restaurants, bars, discos, pools, water sports and 'animations' – song and dance extravaganzas loosely based on African dances. Most hotels have desks for tours and activities in the area (see Things to See & Do earlier). The prices listed include breakfast.

North of Ukunda Junction Perched on some small cliffs above the ocean is **Leopard Beach Hotel** (☎ 2721, fax 3424; e leopard@iconnect.co.ke; singles/doubles US$45/90 in low season, US$100/140 in high season). The recent refurbishment has paid off and the compound of low *makuti*-thatched buildings, divided by ponds and pools, is very attractive. Posher suites are available.

Leisure Lodge & Casino (☎ 2620, fax 2046; e leisure@africaonline.co.ke; rooms full board US$55 in low season, US$90 in high season) has good sports facilities, including an 18-hole golf course across the road (see Things to See & Do earlier), but the buildings are rather drab.

Diani Reef Grand Hotel (☎ 2723, fax 2196; e dianireef@kenyaweb.com; singles/doubles half board US$115/170 in low season, US$170/240 in high season) is one of the few Diani hotels with access for disabled people. The buildings are bland but the gardens are full of palms and bougainvilleas and there are loads of restaurants and bars. Guests are greeted with a fresh coconut to drink when they arrive.

Indian Ocean Beach Club (☎ 3730, fax 3557; e iobc@africaonline.co.ke; singles/doubles half board US$134/167 in low season, US$210/263 in high season) is a tasteful, low-key hotel in the Moorish style on the edge of the Mwachema River. It's one of the more sensitively designed places, with some nice Swahili touches and a degree of style sadly lacking elsewhere.

Diani House (☎ 3487, fax 2412; e aceltd@africaonline.co.ke; per person half/full board US$185/215) is a beautiful, colonial-style house facing the ocean, set in a gorgeous garden. The same people own the Mukurumuji Tented Camp up in the Shimba Hills (an overnight excursion there is possible for US$115).

South of Ukunda Junction Right by the junction, just south of the Barclays Centre, is **LTI–Kaskazi Beach Hotel** (☎ 3725, fax 2233; e kaskazi@africaonline.co.ke; singles/doubles US$65/100 in low season, US$170/220 in high season). The architecture is Arab influenced and rooms have some nice touches. There are restaurants, pool and bars descending to the ocean. High-season rates are a little high for what you get.

Diani Sea Resort (☎ 3081/3, fax 3439; e dianisea@africaonline.co.ke; singles/doubles US$43/62 in low season, US$92/132 in high season) is an attractive, red-tiled place tucked away behind a shopping arcade. There are nice, stepped gardens and the atmosphere is peaceful and unhurried. Facilities include tennis courts, a good pool and a dive centre.

Africana Sea Lodge (☎ 2060/9, fax 3439; singles/doubles KSh3750/6090) and **Jardini Beach Hotel** (☎ 2622, fax 2269; singles/doubles KSh4000/6800) are both owned by the Alliance Hotels group. Africana Sea Lodge is the better of the two with accommodation in pleasant one-storey *makuti* huts and excellent water-sports facilities, including a dive school. High-season rates are 30% higher.

Baobab Beach Resort (☎ 2623, fax 2032; singles/doubles all-inclusive US$47/93 in low season, US$117/215 in high season) is tucked away in densely forested grounds. The forest is teeming with monkeys and the facilities are very good, although the buildings could have been more sensitively designed.

Club Neptune Village *(☎ 3620, fax 3019;* e *neptune@africaonline.co.ke; singles/doubles KSh4400/6400)* is right at the end of Diani Beach Rd. Rooms are in two-storey *makuti*-thatched cottages and there are several large pools, restaurants and bars down by the beach. Rates increase by KSh750 in high season.

Places to Eat

African Pot *(☎ 3564; mains from KSh285; side dishes KSh40-90)* is just before the entrance to Coral Beach Cottages. It serves extremely fine Swahili and Kenyan food. As well as *nyama choma*, there are Indian-inspired coastal dishes such as chicken *palak* and *matoke* (cooked green bananas). There's a sister restaurant in Ukunda, right by the junction to Diani.

Ali Barbour's Cave Restaurant *(☎ 2033; fish dishes from KSh850, other mains from KSh700; open from 7pm daily)* is a very sophisticated seafood restaurant built into a coral cave near the Diani Sea Lodge and open to the stars. Food is excellent – lobster served however you like it costs KSh1850. It's quite an experience, but you should take a taxi to/from the door as people have been mugged walking down the track to the restaurant.

Forty Thieves Beach Bar *(☎ 2033; grills & burgers KSh280-400)* is owned by the same people as Ali Barbour's and is probably the most popular budget eating and drinking place at Diani. There are comfortable recliners under a *makuti* canopy right by the sand and burgers, steaks and fish and chips feature prominently on the menu. You can hire boats here and the evening discos pull in a lively crowd (see Entertainment).

Pavilion Beach Bar *(dishes around KSh390)* is in front of the defunct Two Fishes Hotel and has a familiar menu of grills and burgers. It has live bands on Sunday afternoons. It's best approached from the beach.

Shan-e-Punjab *(☎ 2116; Diani Complex; mains KSh300-500)* is a very popular Indian restaurant opposite the Diani Reef Grand Hotel. A wide range of curries are on offer, including some vegetarian options. The same owners run the supermarket in the Diani Complex.

Galaxy Chinese Restaurant *(☎ 2529; Diani Complex; mains KSh370-670)*, next door, specialises in Chinese food. This restaurant also has a branch in Bamburi Beach.

Da Aniello Restaurant *(Collier Centre; pasta & pizzas KSh350-550; closed Wed)* is a new Italian place with a traditional pizza oven. There's an al-fresco dining area and food is very good.

Red Lion Restaurant *(☎ 3497; mains KSh380-550; closed Mon)* is a peaceful and friendly Italian restaurant, with decent pasta and other Italian favourites. It's open for lunch and dinner.

There are several other restaurants spread out along the strip that now only open for breakfast and lunch, but may soon not open at all. Apart from the above, many of the beach hotels offer weekend buffet lunches and dinners that are open to nonguests. The Sunday buffet lunch (KSh500) at the **Nomad Beach Hotel** is probably the best deal.

Don Fefe *(Legend Pavilion)* serves incredible gelati (Italian ice cream) – the passion fruit gelati is so good (KSh50 per scoop).

For self-caterers, there are **supermarkets** in most of the shopping centres at Diani, or simple **dukas** in Ukunda. **Rongai Butchery**, in Ukunda, is highly recommended for *nyama choma* and fresh meat for beach barbecues.

Entertainment

There are a few good nightspots outside the main hotels.

Forty Thieves Beach Bar (see Places to Eat earlier) is easily the best bar in Diani and there are theme nights every night of the week. Wednesday, Friday and Saturday are disco nights, Tuesday and Thursday are movie nights, and there are live bands on Sunday afternoons. It's open until the last guest leaves.

Bar on the Beach, on the beach at Nomad Beach Hotel (see Places to Stay earlier), is a local favourite and another good choice for party-people. Nonguests are welcome. There are cold beers and dancing.

Opposite the closed-down Two Fishes Hotel are **Bush Baby Nightclub** *(☎ 3111)* and **Shakatak Nightclub** *(☎ 3124)*. Both are pick-up joints of the highest order, but they're quite good fun if you don't mind the seedy atmosphere.

In Ukunda are several African bars where you can find local music and (unfortunately) lots of prostitutes. **Hollywood Restaurant** is better than most and sometimes shows movies in the evening.

Getting There & Around

Air There are flights Sunday, Monday and Wednesday to Friday (US$70 one way) between Nairobi's Wilson Airport and the Ukunda airstrip with **Air Kenya** (☎ 3153; Barclays Centre).

Bus & Matatu Diani is the most accessible beach if you're using public transport. Numerous matatus run south from the Likoni ferry directly to Ukunda (KSh50, 30 minutes) or further south to Msambweni and Lunga Lunga. From the Diani junction in Ukunda, matatus run down to the beach all day for KSh20, heading north first along the strip and then south.

Car & Motorcycle Cars can be hired from **Lexus/Leisure Car Hire** (☎ 3374; Diani Sea Resort arcade) and **Glory Car Hire** (☎ 3076; Diani Beach shopping centre), near the Ukunda junction. Glory has a shockingly high insurance excess. See Car & 4WD in the Getting Around chapter for general information on car hire.

Fun Sports Centre (☎ 0733-760637), opposite the Red Lion Restaurant, rents out quads (beach 'trucks') for KSh1000 per hour or KSh8000 per day. A valid passport, drivers licence and a KSh2000 deposit are required.

Motorcycles can be hired from **Fredlink Co** (☎ 2468; e fredlink@swiftmombasa.com; Diani Plaza) near Tandoori Guest House. With the first 100km included, 350cc trail bikes cost KSh2300 per day and Yamaha scooters cost KSh1300 (unlimited kilometres costs KSh3300/2300 for bikes/scooters). A full motorcycle licence, passport and credit card or cash deposit are required. This company also runs motorcycle safaris (see Special-Interest Safaris in the Safaris chapter for more details).

SHIMBA HILLS NATIONAL RESERVE

This 320-sq-km reserve (adult/child US$23/10; open 6am-6pm daily) lies directly inland from Diani Beach and covers a wonderful landscape of steep-sided valleys, rolling hills and lush pockets of tropical rainforest.

It's a popular detour from Diani and the Shimba Hills are home to numerous elephants, a healthy population of leopards and a vast abundance of birdlife. You may also spot the reserve's most famous resident – the rare sable antelope. This tall, regal antelope has a striking black-and-white coat and long, curved horns and is now protected after the sable population plummeted to less than 120 animals in the 1970s.

Most people enter the park through the main gate, about 5km beyond Kwale, but you can also enter via Shimba Gate, about 1km further on, or the Kidongo Gate at the southern end of the park (turn off the coast highway at Mwabungu, about 7km south of Ukunda). Numerous 4WD tracks connect the various observation points in the reserve; Marere Dam and the forest of Mwele Mdogo Hill are recommended for birdlife.

Highly recommended guided forest walks are run by the **Kenya Wildlife Service** (KWS; ☎ 0127-4159; PO Box 30, Kwale) from the Sheldrick Falls ranger post at the southern end of the park down to scenic Sheldrick Falls on the Machenmwana River. There's a peaceful swimming hole at the base of the falls and a snack picnic is included in the price (KSh500 per person). Walks leave the ranger post at 11am Thursday to Tuesday and last around two hours. It may be possible to walk elsewhere in the park with a ranger escort – call for more information.

Places to Stay

The **public camp site** (camping per adult US$10) and excellent round **bandas** (per person US$20) are superbly located on the edge of an escarpment close to the main gate, with stunning views down to Diani Beach. Monkeys sit in the trees around the camp, and very tame zebras occasionally warm themselves by your campfire. It's also possible to camp at **Hunter's Camp** close to Sheldrick Falls.

Shimba Rainforest Lodge (☎ 0127-4077, Nairobi ☎ 02-535412, fax 02-545954; singles/doubles full board US$114/143 in low season, US$238/297 in high season), owned by Block Hotels, is a good Treetops-style affair with a walkway through the rainforest and a viewing platform and bar. Children under seven years are not admitted. The waterhole here attracts quite a lot of wildlife, including leopards.

THE COAST

Mukurumuji Tented Camp *(☎/fax 0127-2412; e aceltd@africaonline.co.ke; per person full board US$94)* is set on a forested hill perched above the Mukurumuji River on the southern boundary of the park. Guests can take advantage of walking trips along the river and over to Sheldrick Falls. Transfers from Diani cost US$10 each way or you can take an excursion package from Diani House at Diani Beach, including transfers from the south coast, a trip to Shimba Hills or Mwaluganje Elephant Sanctuary and all meals for US$196 per person.

There are a few options found in Kwale itself. **Golden Guest House** *(singles/doubles KSh350/500)* is close to the turn-off to Mwaluganje Elephant Sanctuary on the edge of the village and has pleasant rooms with nets and bathroom around a courtyard garden. It's signposted from the road.

Getting There & Away

You'll need a 4WD to enter the Shimba Hills, but hitching may be possible at the main gate. From Likoni, small lorry-buses (No 34) to Kwale and Tiribe pass the main gate (KSh40). Most visitors come on overnight safari packages, but the Mukurumuji Tented Camp can organise transfers from Diani if you're staying there.

MWALUGANJE ELEPHANT SANCTUARY

This sanctuary *(☎ 0127-4121; e mes@swift mombasa.com; adult/child US$15/2; vehicles KSh150-200; open 6am-6pm)* is a good example of community-based conservation and most local people are shareholders in the project. It was opened in October 1995 to create a corridor along an ancient elephant migration route between the Shimba Hills National Reserve and the Mwaluganje Forest Reserve and comprises 2400 hectares of rugged, beautiful country along the valley of the Cha Shimba River.

More than 150 elephants live in the sanctuary and you're likely to see a large variety of other fauna and flora including rare cycad forest (this primitive palm-like plant species is over 300 million years old). There's a good information centre close to the main gate and a second ticket office on the outskirts of Kwale.

Travellers Mwaluganje Elephant Camp *(in Mombasa ☎ 011-485121/6, fax 485678;*

Mwaluganje ☎ 0127-51202/5, fax 51207; e travhtls@swiftmombasa.com; overnight singles/doubles accommodation package with transfers & wildlife drives US$228/356) is a rather fine place to stay. There's a waterhole and accommodation is in permanent tents. Most come here on overnight packages, which include transfers from the south coast and wildlife drives. Cheaper packages are available if you're already a guest at the Travellers Tiwi Beach Hotel in Tiwi Beach (see Tiwi Beach earlier in this chapter).

Close to the waterhole is a **camp site** *(camping per person KSh100)* surrounded by an electric fence.

The main entrance to the sanctuary is about 13km northeast of Shimba Hills National Reserve on the road to Kinango. A shorter route runs from Kwale to the Golini Gate passing the Mwaluganje ticket office. It's only 5km but the track is 4WD only.

BETWEEN DIANI BEACH & FUNZI ISLAND

There are several worthwhile detours between Diani and Funzi Island.

About 20km south of Ukunda, at the tip of a mangrove peninsula, is gorgeous **Chale Island**, a tropical getaway with a fine beach and supposedly therapeutic mud. Most visitors come here on health retreats at the upmarket resort of **Chale Paradise Island** *(☎ 0127-3235, fax 3319; office opposite LTI Kaskazi Hotel, Diani Beach; singles/doubles including meals & transfers US$150/200)*. Having beauty treatments using Chale's famous 'Fangomud' cost US$58 per day, including massage and a vitamin cocktail.

A few kilometres further south, down another dirt track branching off the main road, is Gazi Beach, where you'll find **Seahorse Dhow** *(☎ 0127-2423, fax 2421; office in Collier Centre, Diani Beach)*. This company offers dhow trips to a nearby island, including a seafood lunch, snorkelling and a guided walk (US$60 from Gazi, US$65 with transfers from south coast hotels). There are also powerboat trips to Kisite-Mpunguti Marine National Park (see later in this chapter) with lunch and snorkelling for US$65 (US$75 from south coast hotels).

FUNZI ISLAND

Funzi is a small mangrove island about 35km south of Diani. As with other islands along the coast, dhow tours to the village at the southern tip of Funzi are becoming increasingly popular, and crocodiles and dolphins can be spotted in the inlets.

While luxury trips are available, this is one of the easiest places to sort out your own boat trip. In the mainland village of **Bodo**, west of Funzi, boatmen offer dolphin-spotting trips in the bay for around KSh700 per person with lunch, and crocodile-spotting expeditions up the Ramisi River for around KSh1200. Trips include a visit to Funzi village and a barbecue seafood lunch. Tsumo Juma and Fuka Hassan are two reliable boatmen.

A **restaurant** and **lodge** has been set up on the island – camping is around KSh300, bandas cost KSh1500 and the money goes to local community projects. Bring supplies with you, including drinking water.

Funzi Sea Adventures (☎ 0127-2044, fax 2346; ☒ funzicamp@africaonline.co.ke; office in Diani Villas, Diani Beach) runs more luxurious dhow trips to Funzi Island and up the Ramisi River. Trips cost US$55 including food, drink and transfers. Children are half-price. Staying overnight at their island camp cost US$140/70 per adult/child. It's stunning and much quieter than Wasini Island.

The easiest way to get onto the island is from Bodo. Take a matatu from Ukunda, northwest of Diani, heading south to Lunga Lunga. Get off at the Bodo turn-off. The village is another 2.5km along a dirt track – you can take a *poda-poda*. Try to arrive before 9am if you're planning a boat trip.

SHIMONI & WASINI ISLAND
☎ 0127

The village of Shimoni sits at the tip of a small peninsula, about 76km south of Likoni and close to the Tanzanian border. Dhow trips to nearby Wasini Island and the coral reefs of Kisite-Mpunguti Marine National Park have become a big industry here, and every morning a convoy of coaches arrives carrying tourists from the resorts at Diani Beach. The trips are well run, but you can easily organise your own trip directly with the boatmen.

Although tourism has definitely arrived in Shimoni, it's still a peaceful spot, particularly once the day-trippers have gone home. There are some interesting ruins and colonial graves in the village and villagers have opened up the old **slave caves** (adult/child KSh100/25; open 8.30am-10.30am & 1.30pm-6pm daily) as a tourist attraction, bringing in some much-needed income. There's no clear evidence that slavers actually used the caves, but it's an atmospheric place and it's interesting to hear about this little-discussed part of East African history.

Even though lots of people visit Wasini Island, it is still a delight. There are no roads or running water and the only electricity comes from generators.

There are several interesting things to see, including ancient **Swahili ruins** and the **'coral gardens'**, a bizarre landscape of exposed coral reefs that you can walk around (except at certain times of year when the sea floods it). Most people come here on organised dhow trips from Diani (see Organised Tours later).

Kisite-Mpunguti Marine National Park

Just off the south coast of Wasini Island, this marine reserve (adult/child US$8/5) is one of the best in Kenya. The park covers 28 sq km of pristine coral reefs and offers excellent diving and snorkelling. You have a reasonable chance of seeing dolphins in the Shimoni Channel and humpback whales are sometimes spotted between August and October.

There are various organised trips to the marine park (see Organised Tours later) but these tend to be expat ventures and don't contribute a great deal to the local community. It's easy to organise your own boat trip with a local captain – the going rate is KSh7000 per dhow, which covers up to 20 passengers and includes lunch and a walk in the coral gardens on Wasini Island. Masks and snorkels can be hired for KSh100 (fins are discouraged as they may damage the reef).

A good place to start looking for a boatman is the office of **KWS** (☎ 52027; open 6am-6pm daily), about 200m south of the main pier, where you'll also have to come to pay the entry fee to the reserve. The best time to dive and snorkel is between October and March.

Avoid June, July and August because of rough seas, silt and poor visibility. The marine life in the park may suffer if the planned port at Shimoni is ever completed (see the boxed text 'Mining, Multinationals and Marine Life').

Mining, Multinationals and Marine Life

Despite protests from environmental organisations, including the Kenya Wildlife Service (KWS), the Kenyan government has issued a licence to the Canadian mining giant Tiomin Resources Inc to develop Shimoni as a commercial port for the export of titanium dioxide ore. Environmentalists fear the project will lead to a huge increase in silt flowing into the ocean, choking the marine life of the Kisite-Mpunguti Marine National Park. Increased shipping in the channel is also likely to have a profound effect on resident dolphins and other marine mammals. Local people and international conservation organisations have set up the Coast Mining Rights Forum which is campaigning against the project. See the website of **Mining Watch Canada** (W *www.miningwatch.ca)* for more about the anti-Tiomin campaign.

Snorkelling & Diving

Masks and snorkels are for rent on the beach for KSh100. You'll need a boat to get out to the reef. Most trips to the park provide their own snorkelling gear. Certified divers can take dives with many of the tour companies (see Organised Tours following) or more expensively at Shimoni Reef Lodge or Pemba Channel Fishing Club (see Places to Stay & Eat). Dive courses and longer dive safaris are also possible in the Pemba Channel.

Deep-Sea Fishing

The Pemba Channel is famous for deep-sea fishing. The Pemba Channel Fishing Club (see Places to Stay & Eat) holds around 70% of the country's marlin fishing records. Boats cost from US$450 for nine hours (valid for up to four fishermen). This company promotes tag and release, which we strongly encourage (see the boxed text 'Tag & Release' later in this chapter).

Organised Tours

Various companies offer organised dhow tours out of Shimoni. Children pay half the adult price. Transfer to/from hotels on the south coast is usually available for an extra $20 per person.

The Friends of Kenyan Dolphins have set up the **Dolphin Dhow** (*☎/fax 2094;* e *dolphin@dolphindhow.com;* W *www.dolphindhow.com; office* ☎ *2144; Barclays Centre, Diani Beach),* a dolphin-spotting and snorkelling trip around Wasini Island. The dhow leaves from Shimoni jetty at 8.45am daily and costs US$75. The price includes snorkelling equipment, drinks, a Swahili seafood lunch and the marine park fees.

Wasini Island Restaurant & Kisite Dhow Tours (*☎ 2331, fax 3154;* e *kisite@africaon line.co.ke; office* ☎ *3055; Jardini Beach Hotel, Diani Beach)* runs popular snorkelling trips to the marine park including a nature walk on Wasini and a very good seafood lunch at the Wasini Island Restaurant. Trips leave at around 9am and cost US$60 from Shimoni jetty. Certified divers can take two scuba dives for an extra US$50. There are also wildlife-spotting safaris in the mangroves of Funzi Bay, including lunch at secluded Mwazaro Beach (US$70).

Pilli-Pipa (*☎/fax 2401; office* ☎ *3559, Collier Centre, Diani Beach)* is another expat-owned company offering full-day dhow trips to the marine park, this time with lunch at the Pilli-Pipa restaurant on Wasini Island. Again, trips leave at around 9am. The price is US$80, including lunch, snorkelling and alcoholic and soft drinks. If you come on a dhow trip, you can also avail yourself of some of the cheapest scuba diving on the Kenyan coast – certified divers pay US$25/40 for one/two dives.

Places to Stay & Eat

Camp Eden (*KWS* ☎ *52027; camping US$2, bandas per person US$10),* behind KWS headquarters, offers accommodation with 'birdsong and insect noise' in the tropical forest south of the main jetty. The airy bandas are well maintained and have mosquito nets. There's a camp site, a covered cooking area, pit toilets and showers. Bring supplies from Mombasa or Ukunda.

Shimoni Reef Lodge (*in Mombasa* ☎ *011-471771, fax 473969; B&B/half board/full board per person KSh2000/2800/3700 in low season, KSh2200/3200/4000 in high season)* is a pleasant resort-type place on a bluff that overlooks the Shimoni Channel. The Arabic-style cottages are open-plan and surround a pool, and there's a restaurant overlooking the ocean, but it can seem a little lonely here if there are no other guests.

Pemba Channel Fishing Club *(in Mombasa ☎ 011-313749, fax 316875; PO Box 86952, Mombasa; per person full board US$120 in low season, US$150 in high season)* is better still, with elegant colonial-style cottages around a swimming pool. Deep-sea fishing is possible (see earlier) and the quite Hemingway-esque restaurant and bar is excellent; nonguests are welcome but the cooks need prior warning.

Across the channel on Wasini Island, the only accommodation is at **Mpunguti Lodge** *(☎ 52288 at the local call box near the lodge; camping KSh300, doubles per person full board KSh1400)* in Wasini village, run by Masood Adullah. The pleasant rooms have mosquito nets, but water for showers has to be provided by the bucket. There's a pleasant camping area and a kitchen for guests. Bring supplies and alcoholic drinks from the mainland.

Smugglers Den Bar & Restaurant, close to the KWS compound in Shimoni, is a simple bar serving beers, *nyama choma* and snack food.

Getting There & Around

There are matatus every hour or so between Likoni and Shimoni (KSh100) until about 6pm. It's best to be at Likoni by 6.30am if you want to get to Shimoni in time to catch one of the dhow sailings.

The price of getting across the channel to Wasini Island depends to a degree on who you meet on arrival, how many are in your group and how affluent you look. The price per person is usually about KSh300 each way and boats leave when they have five passengers.

There are occasional dhows between Shimoni and Pemba in Tanzania, but you'll first have to use all your powers of persuasion to get the captain to take you on as a passenger and then bargain hard to get a reasonable price. Ask at the customs office in Shimoni to see if there are any sailings. There is a small immigration office at Shimoni, but you may have to get your exit stamp back in Mombasa if it's closed.

LUNGA LUNGA

There isn't much at Lunga Lunga apart from the Tanzanian border crossing, which is open 24 hours. It's 6.5km from the Kenyan border post to the Tanzanian border post at Horohoro – matatus run between the two border posts throughout the day (KSh20). From Horohoro, there are numerous matatus to Tanga (TSh200). Frequent matatus run to Lunga Lunga from Likoni, but most people take through buses from Mombasa to Tanga or Dar es Salaam.

North of Mombasa

Like the south coast, the coastline north of Mombasa has been extensively developed, although this trails off once you get north of Shanzu Beach. It's mostly set up for European package tourists on all-inclusive holidays, but there are some decent choices for independent travellers.

The northern beaches are also dogged by seaweed at certain times of year, but are usually clear between December and April. At other times, the sand can vanish under piles of black seaweed. The expensive resort hotels employ people to burn or bury the troublesome weed on the beach.

If you're on a budget, the chances are you'll be staying away from the beach, as the big hotels have grabbed most of the sand. The big hotels here are predictably luxurious but most of them are so self-contained that many of the guests don't see anything of Africa except Mombasa airport, the inside of minibuses, the hotel and Kenyan waiters.

Going north from Mombasa, the beaches are Nyali, Bamburi, Shanzu, Kikambala and Vipingo.

NYALI BEACH
☎ 011

Effectively a suburb of Mombasa, this is the first beach as you head north and take Nyali Rd. Nyali is a shopping hub for nearby Bamburi Beach. The Planet shopping centre has a branch of the excellent **Books First** bookshop chain, with fast connections at the Internet-café for KSh3 per minute.

Also in Nyali is the very posh **Nyali Golf Club** *(☎ 471589; day rates weekdays/weekends KSh2400/2600; open 8am-6pm daily)* set in ornamental gardens on Links Rd. Club hire is KSh1000.

The various hotels are clearly signposted from the various roundabouts on Links Rd.

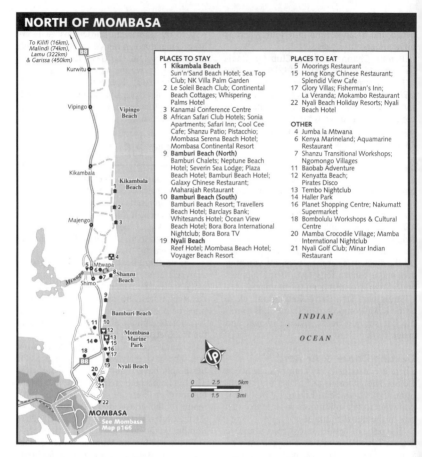

NORTH OF MOMBASA

To Kilifi (16km),
Malindi (74km),
Lamu (322km)
& Garissa (450km)

Kurwitu

Vipingo

Vipingo
Beach

Kikambala

Kikambala
Beach

Majengo

Mtwapa

Shimo

Shanzu
Beach

Bamburi Beach

Mombasa
Marine
Park

Nyali Beach

MOMBASA

See Mombasa
Map p166

INDIAN

OCEAN

0   2.5   5km
0   1.5   3mi

PLACES TO STAY
1 **Kikambala Beach**
   Sun'n'Sand Beach Hotel; Sea Top
   Club; NK Villa Palm Garden
2 Le Soleil Beach Club; Continental
   Beach Cottages; Whispering
   Palms Hotel
3 Kanamai Conference Centre
8 African Safari Club Hotels; Sonia
   Apartments; Safari Inn; Cool Cee
   Cafe; Shanzu Patio; Pistacchio;
   Mombasa Serena Beach Hotel;
   Mombasa Continental Resort
9 **Bamburi Beach (North)**
   Bamburi Chalets; Neptune Beach
   Hotel; Severin Sea Lodge; Plaza
   Beach Hotel; Bamburi Beach Hotel;
   Galaxy Chinese Restaurant;
   Maharajah Restaurant
10 **Bamburi Beach (South)**
   Bamburi Beach Resort; Travellers
   Beach Hotel; Barclays Bank;
   Whitesands Hotel; Ocean View
   Beach Hotel; Bora Bora International
   Nightclub; Bora Bora TV
19 **Nyali Beach**
   Reef Hotel; Mombasa Beach Hotel;
   Voyager Beach Resort

PLACES TO EAT
5 Moorings Restaurant
15 Hong Kong Chinese Restaurant;
   Splendid View Cafe
17 Glory Villas; Fisherman's Inn;
   La Veranda; Mokambo Restaurant
22 Nyali Beach Holiday Resorts; Nyali
   Beach Hotel

OTHER
4 Jumba la Mtwana
6 Kenya Marineland; Aquamarine
   Restaurant
7 Shanzu Transitional Workshops;
   Ngomongo Villages
11 Baobab Adventure
12 Kenyatta Beach;
   Pirates Disco
13 Tembo Nightclub
14 Haller Park
16 Planet Shopping Centre; Nakumatt
   Supermarket
18 Bombolulu Workshops & Cultural
   Centre
20 Mamba Crocodile Village; Mamba
   International Nightclub
21 Nyali Golf Club; Minar Indian
   Restaurant

Mamba Crocodile Village

This place (☎ 472803; ℮ mamba@africaon
line.co.ke; nonresident adult/child KSh450/
250; open 8am-6pm) is a bizarre combination of crocodile farm, animal park, sports
bar and also a nightclub (see Entertainment
later).

The crocodile village located opposite
Nyali Golf Club on Links Rd. While it's interesting to see the crocodiles in various
stages of their development, the knowledge
of their impending reincarnation as belts and
handbags dampens the thrill somewhat.
There's a croc feeding show at 5pm.

Also here is a botanical garden, aquarium
and snake park, which you have to pay for
separately (KSh150/70 for a nonresident
adult/child).

Places to Stay

There are several upmarket choices, but
only one budget option.

Glory Villas (☎ 474758; Mwea Tabere St; 4-
person cottages KSh3000, singles/doubles
KSh800/1500) is a complex of odd conical
towers with makuti roofs behind the Planet
shopping centre. It's not exactly cheap and
Nyali Beach is a 15-minute walk away, but
there's a pool and restaurant.

Fisherman's Inn (☎/fax 471278; Mwamba
Dr; singles/doubles KSh1800/2200, self-
catering apartments KSh4500) is reached via
a turn-off just before the Planet shopping
centre. It's very friendly and intimate with
a lovely Moorish foyer and well-appointed
rooms. The apartments can sleep up to five
and there's a swimming pool and restaurant.

THE COAST

Walk through the Reef Hotel to get to the beach.

Nyali Beach Holiday Resorts (☎ 472325, fax 472402; Beach Rd; singles/doubles KSh2200/3800 in low season, KSh3000/5500 in high season) is a low-key place popular with Kenyan families. It's less luxurious than the other resorts around here, but you still get a pool, restaurant and bar and the rates are very reasonable.

Nyali Beach Hotel (in Nairobi ☎ 02-535412; fax 545954; Beach Rd; singles/doubles half board US$118/147, deluxe rooms US$120/160) is the first big hotel north of Mombasa. This place is a classy and very expensive Block Group hotel on a good beach and facilities are excellent; add 30% to 40% in the high season.

Voyager Beach Resort (in Nairobi ☎ 02-446651; fax 446600; e reservations@voyagerresorts.co.ke; Barracks Rd; singles/doubles US$157/212 in low season, US$196/265 in high season) is a rather striking, nautically themed place perched on the rocks at the end of Nyali Beach. The facilities are good and there are several pools, restaurants and bars.

Mombasa Beach Hotel (☎ 471861, fax 472970; e mombasabeachhotel@kenya-safari.co.ke; per person half board US$50 in low season, US$65 in high season) is the first place on the beach proper. It's a rather institutional complex of 1970s blocks and shows its age.

Reef Hotel (☎ 471771, fax 474194; singles/doubles US$40/50 in low season, US$70/85 in high season) is slightly faded, but still attracts plenty of Kenyans as well as foreign tourists. The beach is good and there are the usual pools, restaurants etc.

Places to Eat

La Veranda (☎ 485482; Mwea Tabere St; pizzas & pasta KSh350-600) is a reliable Italian restaurant with a big pizza oven, al-fresco veranda dining and reasonable prices. It's behind the Planet shopping centre.

Mokambo Restaurant (☎ 0733-795173, Mwamba Dr; mains KSh400-580), next to Fisherman's Inn, is a very stylish place run by a friendly Italian family. Food is great and it's open daily.

Minar Indian Restaurant (☎ 471220; Links Rd; mains KSh280-800) is inside the posh Nyali Golf Club so you can play a round before dinner. As with other branches of the Minar chain, the food is very good.

The Planet shopping centre has a big **Nakumatt supermarket**, which should be able to provide anything self-caterers need.

Entertainment

The main nightspot in Nyali is the totally over-the-top **Mamba International Nightclub** (☎ 475180; Mamba Crocodile Village; admission KSh150; open nightly). It's one of the most popular nightspots close to Mombasa – it's a wonder the poor crocs get any sleep!

Getting There & Away

From Mombasa, Nyali Beach is reached via Nyali Rd, which branches off the main road north just after Nyali Bridge. There are regular matatus to/from Mombasa.

BAMBURI BEACH
☎ 011

The next beach heading north is Bamburi, which has huge hotels, boisterous nightclubs and some good restaurants. Offshore is the **Mombasa Marine Park**, which has impressive marine life, although it cops some pollution from the industries in the area. On land, Bamburi is dominated by the Bamburi Cement Company. The beach hotels begin just north of the junction between Links Rd and the main highway north from Mombasa.

There's a branch of **Barclays Bank** (open 9am-3pm Mon-Fri 9am-11am Sat) next to Whitesands Hotel.

The most popular public beach is **Kenyatta Beach**, beside the infamous Pirates Disco. Loads of Kenyans come here and you can hire tyre inner tubes to splash around with (KSh50 per hour). Glass-bottomed boats to the marine park cost around KSh1000 per boat (not including park fees).

Baobab Adventure

The cement workings at the Bamburi Cement Company (☎ 485901; w www.kenyabeach.com/baobabfarm/) used to be an eyesore until the creation of this ingenious complex of nature trails and wildlife sanctuaries. The main attraction is **Haller Park** (nonresident adult/child KSh450/225; open 8am-5pm daily), which includes a wildlife sanctuary, crocodile farm, fish farm, reptile park and drive-through giraffe compound. Giraffes are fed at 11am and 3pm; hippos at 4pm.

Also here are the **Bamburi Forest Trails** (nonresident adult/child KSh200/100; open

THE COAST

6.30am-5.30pm daily), a network of walking and cycling trails through reforested cement workings, with a butterfly pavilion displaying many coastal species. To the north of the main cement plant is **Nguuni Wildlife Sanctuary**, where herds of ostrich, eland and oryx are farmed. Tours must be booked.

The various parts of the Baobab Adventure are well-signposted from the highway north from Mombasa and have well-marked bus stops.

Places to Stay – Mid-Range

There are no budget choices here but there are some good mid-range places if you're travelling in a group.

Ocean View Beach Hotel (☎ 485953, fax 485953; singles/doubles/triples KSh2100/ 3500/4200) is a pleasant low-key place that has a go at providing all the facilities of the big hotels. It's popular with both Kenyans and foreign tourists.

Bamburi Beach Resort (☎ 485632, fax 315419; doubles KSh2500, 2-bedroom apartments KSh4000, 3-bedroom apartments KSh5000) is just beyond Travellers Beach Hotel. It's a tidy little apartment complex with direct access to the beach. Apartments have an outdoor kitchen and air-con. There's a nice pool and beachfront bar. Rates double at Easter and Christmas.

Bamburi Chalets (☎ 485706; 2-bedroom cottages KSh2500-3000) is right at the northern end of Bamburi Beach. The gardens are a bit overgrown but the cottages are attractive and open-plan. All have kitchens and there's a pleasant pool.

Places to Stay – Top End

Whitesands Hotel (☎ 485926, 485652; e whitesands@whitesands.sarova.co.ke; singles/doubles half board US$60/120 in low season, US$130/160 in high season) is possibly the best resort hotel on this section of coast, with good service, thoughtful design and high standards. There are lovely meandering pools and water-sports facilities and it fronts directly onto the sand.

Travellers Beach Hotel (☎ 485121, fax 485674; e travhtls@africaonline.co.ke; singles/doubles half board US$65/85 in low season, US$85/114 in high season) is a modern, quite stylish place fronted by a huge triangular makuti building. All rooms face the sea and facilities are good.

Bamburi Beach Hotel (☎ 485611, fax 485900; saleem@africaonline.co.ke; singles/ doubles KSh3400/4500 in low season; KSh4500/6000 in high season) is a big resort towards the north end of the strip. The decor is a bit of a free-for-all but facilities are OK.

Plaza Beach Hotel (☎ 485321, fax 485325) is an attractively nostalgic beach hotel nearby. It was under renovation at the time of writing but should be open by the time you read this.

Severin Sea Lodge (☎ 4855001, fax 485212; e severin@severin-sea-lodge.com; singles/doubles half board US$37/74 in low season, US$129/156 in high season) has accommodation in appealing cottages running down to the beach and there are some nice bars and restaurants, including a funky restaurant in a converted dhow.

Neptune Beach Hotel (☎ 485701/3; e neptune@africaonline.co.ke; singles/doubles with breakfast KSh2900/4600, full board KSh3300/5400) is a huge pink block that mainly caters to European package tourists. The building sticks out like a sore thumb, but facilities are okay.

Places to Eat

There are several small restaurant chains with branches in Bamburi.

Splendid View Cafe (☎ 487270) serves Indian mughlai cuisine, plus a handful of Western dishes that appeal to package tourists. There are good special deals for around KSh250, plus Sunday seafood barbecues for KSh450. It's right at the start of the strip.

The **Hong Kong Chinese Restaurant** (☎ 485422) next door serves good Chinese food.

Maharajah Restaurant (☎ 485895; veggie mains from KSh320, meat dishes from KSh500; open dinner Wed-Mon, lunch Sat & Sun) is a stylish Indian restaurant at the entrance to the Indiana Beach Hotel with good veggie and nonveggie food.

Galaxy Chinese Restaurant (☎ 485611; Bamburi Beach Hotel; mains KSh370-670) is a good Chinese restaurant. There's another branch in Diani Beach.

Entertainment

Bamburi is known for its infamous nightclubs, which pull in a slightly wild crowd of locals, tourists, prostitutes and hustlers.

Lamu woman at her doorway

Elephants, Shimba Hills National Reserve

The *mirhab* at the Great Mosque, Gede ruins

Snorkelling with interested observers, Malindi Marine National Park

Peaceful beach, Watamu

Coral archway in Fort Jesus, Mombasa

View along Harambee Ave, Lamu

Traditional dhow, north coast beach

Old laneway, Lamu

Coast Phone Numbers

In recent years, the telephone network on the coast has descended into anarchy. Many places north of Mombasa are now entirely reliant on prepaid mobile phones. Until the phone network is upgraded and restored, there's a chance that phone numbers between Nyali and Malindi may be out of order.

Pirates (☎ 486020; Kenyatta Beach; admission KSh200) is a huge complex of water slides and bars and it rocks on until late nightly.

Bora Bora International Night Club (☎ 486421; admission men/women KSh170/100; open from 9pm, closed Tues) is known for its over-the-top cabaret shows.

Tembo Nightclub (☎ 485078, men/women KSh150/80; open until 5am Sun-Thur, to 6am Fri & Sat) is another loud and very popular nightspot beside the highway in Bamburi. There are several bars.

Getting There & Around
Buses and matatus to Malindi or Mtwapa stop at Bamburi (KSh40). For the Baobab Adventure, there are bus stops in front of both the Haller Park and the main Bamburi Cement Company gate.

You can hire quads (beach 'trucks') at **Bora Bora ATV** (☎ 485026), in front of the Bora Bora International Club; rates are KSh800 per hour or KSh5000 per day.

SHANZU BEACH
☎ 011

This busy beach resort is dominated by the private African Safari Club, which operates no less than a chain of six luxury hotels on the beach.

The beach is lovely, but away from the all-inclusive places, Shanzu has a seedy side, with several 'short stay' hotels and bars catering to European sex tourists.

There are loads of souvenir stalls and the **Shanzu Transitional Workshop** run by the Girl Guides Association, provides training for handicapped women; attractive clothes and other items are made using traditional Swahili fabrics.

Nearby is **Ngomongo Villages** (☎ 486254; W www.ngomongo.com; adult/child KSh500/250; open 9am-5pm daily), a curious enterprise that attempts to give visitors a glimpse of all of Kenya's tribal groups in one place. Although it's touristy stuff, the tours are good fun and you can try your hand at various tribal activities, such as Maasai dancing, archery and pounding maize.

Places to Stay & Eat
The upmarket **Coral Beach**, **Shanzu Beach**, **Palm Beach**, **Paradise Beach**, **Dolphin** and **Flamingo Beach** hotels are owned by the African Safari Club, (see African Safari Club under Accommodation in the Facts for the Visitor chapter).

Safari Inn (☎ 485094; singles/doubles KSh500/800) and also **Sonia Apartments** (☎ 485196; doubles KSh1000) are two budget places in the Shanzu shopping arcade, but both are seedy pick-up joints for prostitutes, and staff may be a bit surprised if you ask for a room for the whole night!

Mombasa Continental Resort (☎ 485811, fax 485437; e msaconti@africaonline.co.ke) is an another big upmarket hotel. It's currently being renovated, but there can be no guarantee it will reopen.

Mombasa Serena Beach Hotel (☎ 485721, fax 485453; e mombasa@serena.co.ke; singles/doubles half board US$90/180 in low season, US$190/250 in high season, garden room supplement US$25 in low season) has a wonderfully executed Moorish theme with lots of sculpted plaster.

It seems very intimate despite its size. Although it's expensive, it's well appointed and the beach is wonderful.

Most visitors to Shanzu eat at their hotels, but there are several restaurants in the Shanzu shopping centre offering almost identical menus of pizzas and other European favourites for between KSh350 and KSh500. **Pistacchio** and **Shanzu Patio** are the most appealing.

For cheap local food, **Cool Cee Cafe**, beside the curio market, serves good stews, matoke etc for under KSh150.

Getting There and Away
Matatus plying the route between Mombasa and Malindi or Mtwapa pass the turn off to Shanzu (KSh40). There are direct matatus between Mtwapa and the beachfront at Shanzu (KSh20), so it may be worth coming here first.

THE COAST

MTWAPA
☎ 011

This small fishing village has a handful of upmarket places to eat with fine views of Mtwapa creek.

Most travellers come here for the gourmet meals and dhow tours offered by **Kenya Marineland** *(☎ 485248; e kml@africaonline.co.ke)*, towards the mouth of Mtwapa Creek. These trips include a visit to the Marineland aquarium, morning and afternoon cruises along the coast with various entertainments and lunch at the waterside **Aquamarine** restaurant. It's not a bad trip and the food at the restaurant is excellent – the price is US$70/35 per adult/child including food and transfers to/from hotels on the north and south coast.

Moorings Restaurant *(☎ 485260; mains KSh380-500)* is a popular expat hang-out on a floating pontoon on the north shore of Mtwapa Creek. Once you get past the culture shock of stepping back in time into the British Empire, it's a fine place for a beer and serves great seafood.

There's a small chance of finding crewing work or a lift along the coast here. Waterskiing can be arranged and small motorboats can be hired for KSh2000 per hour. The turn-off is just after the Mtwapa bridge – follow the signs down to the water's edge.

Several companies based in Mtwapa offer deep-sea fishing for marlin and other large billfish. Try **Hallmark Charters** *(☎ 485680)* or **Howard Lawrence-Brown** *(☎ 486394)*. As always, we recommend that fish are tagged and released (see the boxed text 'Tag & Release' later in this chapter).

Jumba la Mtwana

This national monument *(nonresident adult/child KSh200/100)* is just north of Mtwapa Creek. The ruins are from a 15th-century Swahili slaving settlement, and some interesting structures remain, of which the **Mosque by the Sea** stands out. There are three other mosques on the site and evidence of extensive sanitation facilities in all the main buildings. A handy small guidebook may be available from the ticket office for KSh20.

The nearby beach is delightful. The site is a 3km walk down a dirt track, signposted from the highway about 1km north of Mtwapa bridge.

Getting There & Away
The road through Mtwapa is in a terrible state and all traffic slows to a crawl to avoid the potholes. There are very regular matatus to Mombasa (KSh30) and Malindi (KSh70).

KIKAMBALA & VIPINGO
☎ 0125

These two remote beaches are reached by long winding dirt roads and both have a peaceful, unspoilt atmosphere. The coast at Vipingo is particularly beautiful and the reef comes right up to the beach. The peaceful nature of this area was, temporarily, literally blown apart when the Paradise Hotel in Kikambala was the target of a car bomb attack in November 2002 (see the boxed text 'Suicide Attack in Kenya' in the Facts about Kenya chapter).

Places to Stay & Eat
Kanamai Conference Centre *(☎ 32046; Kikambala Beach; camping per person KSh120, dorm beds KSh400, singles/doubles KSh1200/1400, 1-/2-/3-bedroom cottages KSh1650/2150/2450)* is a Christian conference centre and has a tranquil, laid-back atmosphere. Alcohol is prohibited, but there's a cafeteria serving breakfast (KSh200), lunch (KSh300) and dinner (KSh350). All the rooms and cottages are simple but comfortable and have bathrooms. It's reached via a 3km dirt track, signposted from the main road just before Kikambala township.

Whispering Palms Hotel *(☎ 32004/6, fax 32029; e whispers@africaonline.co.ke; singles/doubles half board KSh2100/3600 in low season, KSh2900/5200 in high season)* is a fading 1960s holiday resort set in palm gardens a few kilometres up the beach from Kanamai. It's a little forlorn, but the rooms aren't bad for the money and the beach here is wonderfully wild and untamed. Follow the track past Le Soleil Beach Club (signposted from the highway).

Continental Beach Cottages *(☎ 32190; 2-person/4-person cottages KSh1500/3250, per person half/full board KSh1150/1450)*, next door, is a quiet little place with a beach bar and a nice pool.

The cottages are neat and well looked after with kitchens and air-con and the gardens face onto a quiet stretch of beach. Grills and other meals cost around KSh250 in the restaurant.

Le Soleil Beach Club (☎ 32604, fax 32164; e lesoleil@africaonline.co.ke; singles/doubles/ triples US$45/60/85 in low season, US$85/ 115/140 in high season) is a big beach resort with modernist white blocks and the usual array of pools, bars and restaurants.

Sun 'n' Sand Beach Hotel (☎ 32621, fax 32133; e admin@sunnsand.co.ke; singles/ doubles all-inclusive US$80/120 in low season, US$90/140 in high season) deserves its reputation as the best hotel for kids along the north coast, and there are loads of pools to splash about in. It's a popular place, but it's intelligently laid out so it doesn't feel crowded. Accommodation is in large well-cared for *makuti*-roofed blocks. Children are charged 50% of the adult rate. The turn-off is well signposted from the highway.

On the road down to the Sun 'n' Sand are **Sea Top Club** (☎ 0733-549849; doubles KSh500) and **NK Villa Palm Garden** (☎ 0733-813208; doubles KSh800). Both have restaurants and tidy rooms with bathrooms. NK Villa also has a pool.

Getting There and Away

It is possible to come here by public transport (Mombasa–Malindi matatus and buses pass along the highway) but all of the places to stay are a long way from the highway and walking isn't recommended on the smaller tracks. Probably the best option is to get off at the clearly marked turn-off to Sea 'n' Sand and pick up a taxi in front of the resort.

If you have your own transport, Kanamai is reached by a signposted track near Majengo. Le Soleil, Whispering Palms and Continental Beach Cottages are reached via another turn-off 3km further north. Sea 'n' Sand, Sea Top Club and NK Villa Palm Garden are reached by a third road signposted about 1km further along the highway.

KILIFI

☎ 0125

Like Mtwapa to its south, Kilifi is a scenic river estuary that has become something of an expat hideaway. Many white Kenyans have yachts moored in the creek and there are numerous beach houses belonging to artists, writers and adventurers from around the globe.

The main reason for most to come here is to stay at one of the pleasant beach resorts at the mouth of the creek or to visit the in-

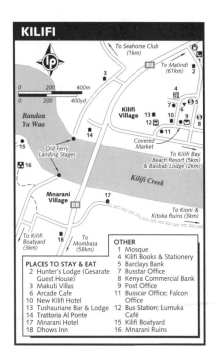

KILIFI

0   200   400m
0   200   400yd

To Seahorse Club (1km)
B8 To Malindi (61km)

Bandan Ya Waa

Kilifi Village 13 12

Old Ferry Landing Stages

Covered Market

To Kilifi Bay Beach Resort (5km) & Baobab Lodge (2km)

Kilifi Creek

Mnarani Village B8

To Kioni & Kitoka Ruins (3km)

To Kilifi Boatyard (3km)   18   To Mombasa (58km)

PLACES TO STAY & EAT
2 Hunter's Lodge (Gesarate Guest House)
3 Makuti Villas
6 Arcade Cafe
10 New Kilifi Hotel
13 Tushauriane Bar & Lodge
14 Trattoria Al Ponte
17 Mnarani Hotel
18 Dhows Inn

OTHER
1 Mosque
4 Kilifi Books & Stationery
5 Barclays Bank
7 Busstar Office
8 Kenya Commercial Bank
9 Post Office
11 Busscar Office; Falcon Office
12 Bus Station; Lumuka Café
15 Kilifi Boatyard
16 Mnarani Ruins

teresting ruins of Mnarani, high on a bluff on the north bank of the creek.

Information

Kilifi consists of the small village of Mnarani (or Manarani) on the southern bank of the creek and Kilifi village on the northern bank, where you'll find the post office, bus station, markets and the budget hotels. Also here are **Barclays Bank** (open 9am-3pm Mon-Fri, 9am-11am Sat), with an ATM, and the **Kenya Commercial Bank**, with a bureau de change, open the same hours. For email, go to **Kilifi Books & Stationery** (☎ 25408), near the Busstar office, where Internet access costs KSh5 per minute.

Kilifi Creek is a popular anchorage spot for yachties sailing along the coast, and if you're looking for a ride you *may* find something at the **Kilifi Boatyard** (☎ 25067), south of Kilifi town.

Mnarani

The ruins (nonresident adult/child KSh100/ 50; open 7am-6pm) are high on a bluff just above the old ferry landing stage on the southern bank of Kilifi Creek surrounded by

THE COAST

huge baobabs. Only partly excavated, the site was occupied from the end of the 14th century to around the first half of the 17th century, when it was abandoned following sieges by Galla tribespeople from Somalia and the failure of the water supply.

The best preserved ruin is the **Great Mosque** with its finely carved inscription around the *mihrab* (the niche in a mosque showing the direction of Mecca). Also here are a group of **carved tombs** (including a restored pillar tomb), a small mosque dating from the 16th century and parts of the town wall and a gate.

Tucked away in the woods are all manner of other ruins, including a small mosque and dozens of unexcavated ruins, and a huge baobab tree, rumoured to be the largest on the coast. There's a human-made hole in the side of the tree where local people leave offerings. The path up to the ruins (about 300m long) is clearly signposted off the tarmac road behind Mnarani village.

Mnarani was associated with the smaller settlements of **Kioni**, past Mnarani Club, and **Kitoka**, about 3km southeast of Mnarani Club on the northern bank of Takaungu Creek. All these settlements were ruled over by Mombasa and are now ruined. If you want to visit, it's best to find a guide to show you the way.

Kilifi Creek

The **beach** on either side of the creek is very pleasant and doesn't suffer the same seaweed problems as the beaches further south, but most of the frontage is private property. Hotels and local fishermen can arrange **sailing trips** around the creek for about KSh500.

Places to Stay – Budget & Mid-Range

Most cheap option are near the bus station, but most are pretty seedy cubicle-type dosshouses.

Tushauriane Bar & Lodge (☎ 22521; singles/doubles KSh150/300) is a bright yellow building behind the bus station. The simple rooms here just contain a bed and mosquito net, but are clean and cheap.

Hunter's Lodge (Gesarate Guest House; singles/doubles KSh120/240) is a small but clean courtyard place near the mosque and petrol station north of the centre.

Dhows Inn (☎ 22028; singles/doubles with breakfast KSh550/800) is on the main road

south of Kilifi Creek, opposite the entrance to the Mnarani Club. It's a small but well-maintained roadhouse with a number of decent doubles with bathrooms set around a garden. It's within easy walking distance of the Mnarani ruins, and there's a popular bar and restaurant. If you come by bus from Mombasa, get dropped outside the door to avoid a long walk.

Trattoria Al Ponte (☎ 22141, ☎ 0733-846495; doubles per person KSh600) overlooks the creek immediately north of the bridge. It's primarily a restaurant and bar but there are nice rooms at the back. When we visited, this place was being renovated, so call ahead to make sure rooms are still available.

Makuti Villas (☎ 22415; doubles or twins KSh1000) is great value. The very stylish stone-floored rooms are housed in *makuti* huts and have nets and fans. There's a bar and restaurant where you can get meals for around KSh200.

Places to Stay – Top End

Kilifi Bay Beach Resort (☎ 22264, fax 22258; e madahold@kenyaweb.com; singles/doubles US$72/104 in low season, US$110/185 in high season) is about 5km north of Kilifi on the coast road. It's a pleasant, small resort with a nice beach but prices are high for what you get. Its partner hotel, **Baobab Lodge** (☎ 22570, fax 22264), 3km back towards Kilifi, is barely hanging on these days – call ahead to see if it's still open.

Mnarani Club (in Mombasa ☎ 011-22318, fax 22200; singles/doubles full board US$125/205 in low season, US$170/300 in high season), on the southern side of Kilifi Creek, is a very stylish resort complex with a great *trompe l'oeil* pool which seems to blend into the ocean. There's a beach and loads of water sports are possible. The hotel has a no-children policy.

Seahorse Club, about 1.5km down a dirt road on the northern side of the creek, is a particularly good hotel in the African Safari Club group (see African Safari Club under Accommodation in the Facts for the Visitor chapter). The accommodation is in lovely cottages on either side of a long lily pond.

Places to Eat

New Kilifi Hotel (mains KSh80-120), towards the post office, is a very popular local canteen with good biryanis (rice and curried meat), plus the usual stew and *ugali* (maize meal) options. **Lumuka Cafe** at the bus station is similar.

Arcade Cafe *(mains KSh130-450; open 7am-7.30pm Mon-Sat)*, in the Kilifi shopping arcade, is spic and span. Samosas, steaks and stews are its mainstays.

Dhows Inn *(mains KSh150-300)*, on the southern side of the creek, has a limited menu of meat and seafood dishes but the food is usually good.

Kilifi Boatyard *(☎ 25067; seafood mains KSh350)* has a very nice, sand-floored café serving excellent seafood and cold beers to expat boating types. It's a long walk from town down a dirt road that branches off the highway opposite the Kilifi Plantation, just south of Kilifi. A taxi from Kilifi will cost KSh600 return.

If it's up and running, **Trattoria Al Ponte** *(mains KSh400)* serves good Italian fare and has a pleasant terrace restaurant that looks over the creek.

Getting There & Away
All the buses and matatus travelling between Mombasa and Malindi stop at Kilifi; the fare from Kilifi to either destination is KSh50. **Falcon**, **Busstar** and **Busscar** all have offices here for their Nairobi–Malindi route; buses to Mombasa and on to Nairobi leave at around 7.45am (KSh450).

WATAMU
☎ 0122
About 24km south of Malindi, Watamu is another popular beach resort with good sand beaches and plenty of resorts. Offshore is the southern part of Malindi Marine Reserve, and the unspoilt forests of Arabuko Sokoke Forest Reserve and the Swahili ruins of Gede are both a short distance away.

The coast at Watamu is broken up into three separate coves divided by eroded rocky headlands and there are a number of similar islands just offshore. Each of the bays becomes a broad white strand at low tide, and many people walk across to nearby islands to sunbathe and swim. Like the southern resorts, Watamu is inundated with seaweed at certain times of year, but the sand is usually clear between December and April.

Although Watamu is primarily a tourist resort, Swahili fishers still moor their

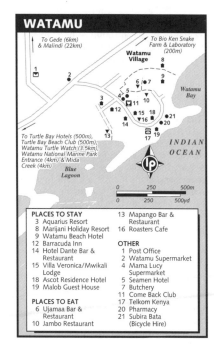

WATAMU

To Gede (6km) & Malindi (22km)
To Bio Ken Snake Farm & Laboratory (200m)
Watamu Village
Watamu Bay
INDIAN OCEAN
To Turtle Bay Hotels (500m), Turtle Bay Beach Club (500m); Watamu Turtle Watch (3.5km), Watamu National Marine Park Entrance (4km) & Mida Creek (4km)
Blue Lagoon

| 0 | 250 | 500m |
| 0 | 250 | 500yd |

PLACES TO STAY
3 Aquarius Resort
8 Marijani Holiday Resort
9 Watamu Beach Hotel
12 Barracuda Inn
14 Hotel Dante Bar & Restaurant
15 Villa Veronica/Mwikali Lodge
18 Ascot Residence Hotel
19 Malob Guest House

PLACES TO EAT
6 Ujamaa Bar & Restaurant
10 Jambo Restaurant

13 Mapango Bar & Restaurant
16 Roasters Cafe

OTHER
1 Post Office
2 Watamu Supermarket
4 Mama Lucy Supermarket
5 Seamen Hotel
7 Butchery
11 Come Back Club
17 Telkom Kenya
20 Pharmacy
21 Subira Bata (Bicycle Hire)

dhows just metres from the sunbathing tourists and a village of mud-walled houses sits immediately behind the resorts. Most accommodation is set up for package tourists, but a handful of places cater to more modest budgets.

Orientation
Most resorts are south of Watamu, on the road that runs down to KWS headquarters, but the Watamu Beach Hotel and the cheap guesthouses are reached by the U-shaped road which leads down to the old village. The village itself is something of a maze; the main track from the Watamu Beach Hotel through to the Mama Lucy supermarket is easy to follow. The access road to the northernmost beach branches off this track by the Seamen Hotel.

Information
There is no information office, but a website (W www.watamu.org) has information about things to do in the area. There's a post office near the junction of the coast road and the road to Gede and numerous cardphones in front of the Telkom office in the

centre of the village. Internet access is available at the **Watamu Supermarket** on the coast road for KSh15 per minute.

There are now no banks in Watamu, so your only options are the bureaus de change at the big hotels. If you need to use an ATM, your nearest choices are Kilifi and Malindi.

Bio Ken Snake Farm & Laboratory

This excellent snake farm (☎ 32303; adult/child under 12 KSh500/free; open 10am-noon & 2pm-5pm daily) is by far the best of the snake parks along the coast. It's run by James Ashe, a former curator from the National Museums of Kenya, and the farm is a non-profit organisation, providing free antivenin wherever it is needed in Kenya.

Ashe is also an expert on Kenyan reptiles and *dudus* (literally, creepy crawlies – see the boxed text 'Dudus' later). The centre is just north of Watamu village on the main beach road.

Watamu Marine National Park

The southern part of Malindi Marine Reserve, this marine park (adult/child US$8/5) includes some magnificent coral reefs and abundant fish-life. It lies around 2km offshore from Watamu. To get to the park, you'll need to hire a glass-bottom boat, which is easy enough at the **KWS** (☎ 32393; Plot 19, Watamu), at the end of the coast road, where you pay the park fees. For marine park trips, boat operators typically charge KSh800 per person or KSh4000 per boat, excluding park fees.

All the big hotels offer snorkelling trips to nonguests for around KSh800. The best are the 'snorkel safaris' run by zoologist

Richard Bennett at the **Turtle Bay Beach Club** (☎ 32003; adult/child KSh1380/690).

Mida Creek

The extensive mangrove forests around Mida Creek, just south of Watamu, support a huge number of bird species including the spectacular malachite kingfisher, yellow-billed stork and African fish eagle. It's a paradise for bird-watchers and there is some good snorkelling and scuba diving at the mouth of the creek (see following).

The head of the creek, the best area for viewing waterbirds, is reached by a dirt road opposite the main entrance to the Arabuko Sokoke Forest Reserve. The guides who work out of Arabuko Sokoke Forest Reserve run guided walks in the mangroves for KSh600 to KSh800 per day (see Arabuko Sokoke Forest Reserve later).

Many people also visit on boat tours (arranged through the hotels in Watamu), which visit a boardwalk and picnic ground on Sudi Island. At **Turtle Bay Beach Club** (☎ 32003) the tours cost KSh2000 per person.

Diving

With the marine park just offshore, diving is understandably popular. **Turtle Bay Aqua Ventures** (☎ 32008, fax 32266; e aquav@ africaonline.co.ke), at Ocean Sports Hotel, offers guided dives in the marine park for US$25 and an open-water PADI dive course for US$390. The best time to dive and snorkel is between October and March. Avoid June to August because of rough seas and poor visibility. Also popular are dive trips to the **Tewa Caves** at the mouth of Mida Creek, where a group of giant rock cod loiter menacingly at the bottom.

Tag & Release

While the idea of wrestling a huge marlin on the open sea has a powerful allure, catches of billfish in the Indian Ocean are getting smaller all the time. The biggest threat to big game fish is relentless overfishing by commercial tuna companies, who routinely hook other pelagic fish as so-called 'by-catch'. Pollution and falling stocks of prey species are also having a serious effect on game fish stocks. Some species are believed to have declined by as much as 80% since the 1970s and sharks are seen as particularly vulnerable.

You can do your bit to help sustain shark and billfish populations by tagging your catch and releasing it back into the ocean. Most deep-sea fishing companies provide anglers with a souvenir photo and official recognition of their catch, and then release the fish to fight another day, carrying tags which will allow scientists to discover more about these little-studied, but magnificent predators.

Turtles

Several species of marine turtle lay their eggs on the beaches around Watamu and **Watamu Turtle Watch** (☎ 32118; e aquav@africaon line.co.ke; Plot 18, Watamu) has set up a series of initiatives with local people to protect these threatened animals. Female turtles lay their eggs here between January and April. Contact the centre if you're interested in seeing this incredible natural spectacle.

Deep-Sea Fishing

If you want to ape the fish-wrestling antics of Ernest Hemingway, deep-sea fishing is possible at Ocean Sports Hotel and Hemingway's for around US$630 per boat (up to four anglers). People are more environmentally aware now than in Hemingway's day – tag and release is the way to go (see the boxed text 'Tag & Release').

Places to Stay – Budget & Mid-Range

There are several budget options in Watamu, although none of these are super-cheap – expect to pay at least KSh500 for a room.

Hotel Dante Bar & Restaurant (☎ 32243; doubles with bathroom KSh600) is a fading lodge with a frequently empty restaurant and large doubles with fans and nets. Rooms are OK, though the grounds look a little forlorn.

Villa Veronica/Mwikali Lodge (☎ 32083; doubles with bathroom KSh700), across the road, is the best value of the regular lodges. It's friendly, secure and family run. The spacious doubles are clean with fans, nets and fridges; rates include breakfast. Some rooms get noise from the nearby Come Back Club.

Malob Guest House (☎ 32260; doubles with bathroom KSh600), opposite Ascot Residence, is another good choice. Rooms with fans and nets are clean and well looked after, and are set around a peaceful courtyard.

Marijani Holiday Resort (☎/fax 32448; e marijani@swiftmalindi.com; singles/doubles with bathroom KSh1000/1400) is probably the best place to stay in the village. This discreet guesthouse offers spotless, stone-floored rooms in a large coral house close to the northernmost cove. To get here, take the road beside the Mama Lucy supermarket and turn left opposite Seamen Hotel in the middle of the village.

Ascot Residence Hotel (☎ 32326; e giulia@ swiftmalindi.com; singles/doubles KSh1500/ 2500, 2-/4-person apartments KSh3000/ 6000) is a very comfortable complex of tidy rooms and apartments set in a garden in the centre of Watamu village. Security is good and there's a pool and a fine pizza restaurant (see Places to Eat).

Places to Stay – Top End

Top-end hotels take up much of the beach frontage along the three coves.

There are two choices in the middle cove, right in front of Watamu village.

Aquarius Resort (☎ 0365-503387, fax 503393; e info@aquariuswatamu.com; per person half/full board KSh3000/3500) is a brand new place set back from the water, but with its own beachside restaurant and pool. The *makuti*-roofed buildings are set in a lovely garden and there are peaceful communal balconies overlooking the pool.

The **Barracuda Inn** (☎ 32509, fax 32296; e barracudaminn@swiftmalindi.com; singles/ doubles US$44/66 in low season, US$90/130 in high season), across from Aquarius, appeals to a younger Italian crowd. Rooms have balconies angled to catch the sea breeze and there's direct beach access.

Watamu Beach Hotel is a posh African Safari Club hotel that takes up most of the peninsula at the northeast end of Watamu (see African Safari Club under Accommodation in the Facts for the Visitor chapter).

Turtle Bay sports four big resorts. The closest to Watamu village is **Blue Bay Village** (☎ 32626, fax 32422; e bluebay@africaon line.co.ke; singles/doubles full board US$105/ 160, superior rooms from US$115/180), another Italian-dominated resort. It's quite thoughtfully laid out, with attractive villas set in an open-plan garden. There's a bar, restaurant and pool.

Ocean Sports Hotel (☎ 32008, fax 32266; e oceansps@africaonline.co.ke; singles/ doubles US$87/118 in low season, US$91/140 in high season, child under 12 low/high season US$22/27) is a small, informal, family-run resort with a deep-sea fishing slant. It's modest, but very relaxed and the clientele mainly consists of British expats.

Hemingway's Hotel (☎ 32624, fax 32256; e hemingways@swiftmalindi.com; singles/ doubles US$90/129 in low season, US$25/ 362 in high season), next door, has a strong deep-sea fishing theme and it's well cared for, but it's a little pricey. Loads of activities are possible and prices include free transport to and from Malindi airport (by prior arrangement) and snorkelling trips in the marine park, excluding national park fees.

Turtle Bay Beach Club (☎ 32003, fax 32268; e general.manager@turtlebay.co.ke; rooms per person US$48-72 in low season, US$63-95 in high season), at the far end of the cove, is a plush resort that mainly caters to Europeans on all-inclusive tours. There are various classes of rooms here and facilities are excellent. There are loads of excursions on offer, many of which are open to non-guests (call ahead).

Places to Eat
For local cuisine, there are several very cheap options tucked away in the lanes of Watamu village. Good choices include **Ujamaa Kwitu Bar & Restaurant** and **Jambo Restaurant**. Swahili dishes such as coconut fish and beef stews typically cost less than KSh150 and beer is available (not always cold).

Roasters Cafe (mains KSh130-200; open 24 hrs) is a hugely popular option with travellers, with grilled or stewed meat, fish and chicken served with side orders such as *ugali* or mashed potatoes.

Ascot Residence Hotel (dishes KSh400-800) has a very fine Italian restaurant, specialising in pizzas. There's a friendly central dining room and romantic tables for couples set in curtained gazebos in the garden.

Mapango Bar & Restaurant (☎ 32609; meals KSh400-750) is part of Aquarius Resort and diners can use its splendid pool. The menu consists mainly of European favourites such as pasta, steak and grilled swordfish. The restaurant is next to the ocean along the public access to the central cove at Watamu.

For a splurge, try the Sunday lunch buffets at the **Ocean Sports Hotel** or **Hemingway's Hotel** – the going rate is around KSh950 and half price for children.

The **Mama Lucy supermarket,** on the way out of Watamu, is handy for self-caterers and there's a good *halal* **butchery** near the village mosque.

Getting There & Away & Around
There are matatus between Malindi and Watamu throughout the day (KSh45, 30 minutes), from the old market in Malindi.

All matatus pass the turn-off to the Gede ruins (KSh25). For Mombasa, the easiest option is to take a matatu to the highway and flag down a bus or matatu from there.

Taxis loiter around outside Watamu Beach Hotel, charging KSh800 for a return trip to Gede and KSh1500 to Malindi.

Bicycles can be hired for KSh60 per hour or KSh300/400 per half/full day from **Subira Bata** shoe shop, opposite Ascot Residence Hotel.

ARABUKO SOKOKE FOREST RESERVE
Close to the marine park at Watamu, Arabuko Sokoke Forest Reserve (adult/child US$10/5) is the largest remaining tract of indigenous coastal forest remaining in East Africa. Gazetted in 2002 as an International Heritage Site, it's administered jointly by the Forestry Department and KWS, and contains an unusually high concentration of rare species, especially birds (240 species) and butterflies (260 species). A good deal of work has gone into involving the local community in the protection of the forest.

The most high-profile birds are: Clarke's weaver, found nowhere else in the world; the beautiful miniature Sokoke scops owl, only 15cm tall; the east coast akalat; the Sokoke pipit, the Amani sunbird; and the spotted ground thrush. The reserve's signature animal is the charming golden-rumped elephant-shrew – amazingly, it's related to the full-sized elephant. You may even see its much larger cousin trundling around the forest.

There's a good visitor centre at **Gede Forest Station** (☎ 0122-32420; open 8am-4pm daily) with displays on the various species here. The shop sells the excellent KWS/Forestry Department guide *Arabuko Sokoke Forest & Mida Creek* (KSh300) and Tansy Bliss's *Arabuko-Sokoke Forest – A Visitor's Guide* (KSh120). The noticeboard in the centre shows the site of recent wildlife sightings.

From the visitor centre, a series of nature trails and running tracks cut through the forest. There are more bird trails at **Whistling Duck Pools**, reached via the Mida Creek entrance to the reserve, and at **Kararacha Pools** and **Spinetail Way**, 16km further south. Near Kararacha is the **Singwaya Cultural Centre** where traditional dances can be arranged.

Trained bird and wildlife **guides** (☎ 0733-421194) can be hired for KSh400 for four hours, KSh600 for a full day and KSh400 for a highly recommended night walk (leav-

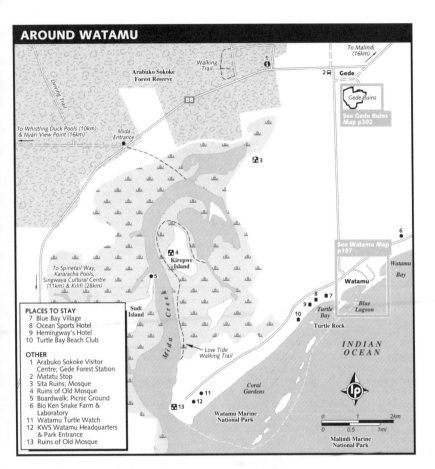

AROUND WATAMU

To Malindi
(16km)

Walking
Trail

Arabuko Sokoke
Forest Reserve

1

2 Gede

Gede Ruins

See Gede Ruins
Map p202

To Whistling Duck Pools (10km)
& Nyari View Point (16km)

Mida
Entrance

3

6

See Watamu Map
p197

Kirepwe
Island

4

Watamu
Bay

To Spinetail Way,
Kararacha Pools,
Singwaya Cultural Centre
(11km) & Kilifi (28km)

5

Watamu

8 7

9

Blue
Lagoon

10

Turtle
Bay

Turtle Rock

Sudi
Island

INDIAN
OCEAN

Low Tide
Walking Trail

PLACES TO STAY
7 Blue Bay Village
8 Ocean Sports Hotel
9 Hemingway's Hotel
10 Turtle Bay Beach Club

OTHER
1 Arabuko Sokoke Visitor
   Centre; Gede Forest Station
2 Matatu Stop
3 Sita Ruins; Mosque
4 Ruins of Old Mosque
5 Boardwalk; Picnic Ground
6 Bio Ken Snake Farm &
   Laboratory
11 Watamu Turtle Watch
12 KWS Watamu Headquarters
   & Park Entrance
13 Ruins of Old Mosque

Coral
Gardens

11

12

13

Watamu Marine
National Park

0   1   2km
0   0.5   1mi

Malindi Marine
National Park

ing the visitors centre at 6pm). They're very knowledgeable about the forest, and also offer walks in Mida Creek on the opposite side of the highway.

There are basic **camp sites** *(per person KSh200)* close to the visitor centre and further south near Spinetail Way. With permission, camping is also allowed deeper within the forest.

The forest is just off the main Malindi–Mombasa road. The main gate to the forest and visitor centre is about 1.5km west of the turn-off to Gede and Watamu, while the Mida entrance is about 3km further south. All buses and matatus between Mombasa and Malindi can drop you at either entrance. From Watamu, matatus to Malindi can drop you at the main junction.

GEDE RUINS

Some 4km from Watamu, just off the main Malindi–Mombasa road, are the famous Gede ruins *(adult/child KSh200/100; open 7am-6pm daily)*, one of the principal historical monuments on the coast. Hidden away in the forest is a vast complex of houses, palaces and mosques, made all the more mysterious by the fact that there are no records of Gede's existence in any historical texts.

Gede (or Gedi) was established and actively trading by at least the 13th century. Excavations have uncovered Ming Chinese porcelain and glass and glazed earthenware from Persia, indicating not only trade links, but a taste for luxury among Gede's Swahili elite. Within the compound are ruins of ornate tombs and mosques and the regal ruins

THE COAST

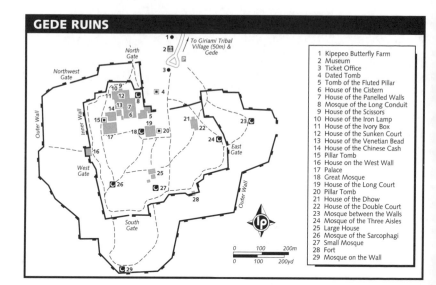

GEDE RUINS

To Giriami Tribal Village (50m) & Gede

North Gate

Northwest Gate

Outer Wall

Inner Wall

West Gate

South Gate

East Gate

Outer Wall

1 Kipepeo Butterfly Farm
2 Museum
3 Ticket Office
4 Dated Tomb
5 Tomb of the Fluted Pillar
6 House of the Cistern
7 House of the Panelled Walls
8 Mosque of the Long Conduit
9 House of the Scissors
10 House of the Iron Lamp
11 House of the Ivory Box
12 House of the Sunken Court
13 House of the Venetian Bead
14 House of the Chinese Cash
15 Pillar Tomb
16 House on the West Wall
17 Palace
18 Great Mosque
19 House of the Long Court
20 Pillar Tomb
21 House of the Dhow
22 House of the Double Court
23 Mosque between the Walls
24 Mosque of the Three Aisles
25 Large House
26 Mosque of the Sarcophagi
27 Small Mosque
28 Fort
29 Mosque on the Wall

0   100   200m
0   100   200yd

of a Swahili palace, further evidence of Gede's prosperity.

The city was inexplicably abandoned in the 17th or 18th century. The current wisdom is that a series of events weakened the city-state, including guerrilla attacks by the Galla tribe from Somalia and the cannibalistic Zimba people from near Malawi, and the removal of the sheikh of Malindi by the Portuguese in 1593. Then again, the reason could simply be that Gede ran out of water – at some stage the water table here dropped rapidly and some wells were deepened during the 17th century, yet none of the wells at Gede today have sweet water.

Whatever the reason for Gede's abandonment, the forest took over and the site was lost to the world until the 1920s. Since then, there have been extensive excavations, revealing the remains of substantial Swahili houses and complex sanitation facilities, including toilets and cisterns for ritual washing. The toilets are particularly impressive, consisting of paired cubicles containing a squat toilet and a stand for a washbasin. All the buildings here were constructed of coral rag, coral lime and earth and some have pictures incised into the plaster finish of their walls.

Two walls surround the site, the inner one of which was possibly built to enclose a smaller area after the city was temporarily

abandoned in the 15th to 16th centuries. Most of the interesting excavated buildings are concentrated in a dense cluster near the entrance gate, but there are dozens of other ruins scattered through the forest.

The ruins are very atmospheric and you'll often have the site to yourself if you visit early in the morning. Be a little careful as you walk around, because there are dozens of deep wells here.

Outside the site, by the car park, there's a small **museum** with displays of Arab jewellery and items found on the site, although the best stuff was taken to the Fort Jesus museum in Mombasa.

Gedi – Historical Monument (KSh30), a guidebook to the ruins with a map and descriptions of many buildings, should be available at the gate for KSh30.

The Tombs

On your right as you enter the compound is the **Dated Tomb**, so-called because of the inscription on the wall, featuring the Muslim date corresponding to 1399. This tomb has provided a reference point for dating other buildings within the complex. Next to it, inside the wall, is the **Tomb of the Fluted Pillar**, which is characteristic of such pillar designs found along the East African coast. The tomb is largely intact and was once decorated with ceramic dishes and coral bosses.

THE COAST

Great Mosque
The Great Mosque originally dates from the mid-15th century but was rebuilt a century later, possibly after damage sustained at the time of Gede's first abandonment. The mosque is of typical East African design with a *mihrab* or echo-chamber facing Mecca. You can see where porcelain bowls were once mounted in the walls flanking the *mihrab*. On the edge of the mosque is a ritual washing area, served by a conduit from a nearby well.

Palace
Behind the mosque are the ruins of an extensive palace (spread out over one-tenth of a hectare) thought to belong to the former ruler of Gede. This regal structure is entered through a complete arched doorway and many interesting features have been preserved, including a safe-room with no doors or windows, used to store valuables (the only entry would have been a small hatch high up in the wall).

Beside the palace is an annexe, built later than the main structure, consisting of four apartments with private courtyards.

Some of the walls contain square niches used for oil lamps and there is a well-preserved Swahili toilet. The palace also has a particularly fine pillar tomb.

One of the most interesting things found within the ruins was an earthenware jar containing a *fingo* or charm, thought to attract *djinns* (guardian spirits) who would drive trespassers insane.

The Houses
Most houses at Gede follow a traditional Swahili pattern, with a reception court at the front and separate living quarters for the master of the house and his wives. Around 14 have been excavated, most in a compact group beside the Great Mosque and the palace. They're named after particular features of their design or after objects found in them by archaeologists. The **House of the Cistern** and the **House of the Dhow**, outside the main complex, are particularly interesting, with ancient illustrations incised into their plaster walls.

Other Attractions
Numerous paths run through the woods from the main complex. The most interesting structures are southeast of the Great Mosque, including the **House of the Double Court** and the nearby **Mosque of the Three Aisles**, which has the largest well at Gede. There are numerous other structures on the forest.

Right by the main complex is the decorated north gate, where you'll find the **Giriama tribal village**, where the package tourists are entertained with 'traditional' Giriama dances. It's *very* contrived and the dancing girls' costumes look like a cross between a Hawaiian skirt and a tennis outfit.

Getting There & Away
The ruins lie just off the main highway near the village of Gede, on the access road to Watamu. The easiest way to get here is to take a Watamu-bound matatu and follow the well-signposted dirt road from Gede village – it's a 15-minute walk.

It's also possible to get a taxi to take you on a round trip from Malindi for about KSh800 with an hour or more to look around the site. This could be worthwhile if your time is limited.

KIPEPEO BUTTERFLY FARM
Right by the entrance to the Gede complex is this butterfly farm (☎ 32380; ⓔ kipepeo@ africaonline.co.ke; *nonresident adult/child KSh100/50; open 10am-5pm daily*), named for the Swahili word for butterfly. It was set up by a zoologist from the University of Nairobi. Locals are paid to collect live pupae from the Arabuko Sokoke Forest Reserve, which are hatched into butterflies and sold to foreign collectors and live exhibits in the UK and USA. The money is then ploughed back into conservation of the forests.

MALINDI & AROUND
☎ 0123
Malindi is effectively two towns in one, a historic Swahili township with a pedigree going back to the 12th century, and a modern holiday centre, with dozens of luxury resorts, bars, casinos and tourist shopping malls. From a tourist perspective, Malindi is all about beaches, and their brilliant white sand. Offshore are the coral reefs of the Malindi Marine Park, one of Kenya's best marine parks, with plenty of opportunities for snorkelling and diving.

The Swahili city-state of Malindi had its heyday in the 14th century, when it often

THE COAST

Dudus

Because of its lush climate, Kenya has some huge tropical bugs, known as *dudus* in Swahili. The locals have a fairly short temper with the insect world – all over the country, you'll see huge signs for a pesticide spray that 'kills all *dudus* dead!' – but these are fascinating creatures.

Arachnophobes should watch out for the plum-sized golden orb spider, with its famously strong web, and the delightfully named Mombasa golden starburst baboon spider, regarded as a 'small tarantula' since it only reaches 12cm in diameter! There are also several large species of scorpions, which are often seen after rain.

Perhaps Kenya's most notorious *dudu* is the safari ant. These huge red ants sweep across the countryside in huge columns consuming everything that lies in their path. Locally they're often known as 'army' or 'crazy' ants for their brutal search-and-destroy tactics. Tribespeople use the pincers of safari ants as improvised stitches for wounds.

An altogether friendlier species is the giant millipede, which can often be seen trundling through the forest on hundreds of pairs of tiny legs. Although these insect behemoths can reach 20cm in length, they only eat decaying wood and will roll themselves up into a defensive coil if approached.

rivalled Mombasa and Paté for control of this part of the East African coast. It was an important trading post and even the Chinese junks of Cheng Ho visited here in the 15th century. Malindi was also one of the few places on the coast to offer a friendly welcome to the early Portuguese mariners.

Malindi experienced a phenomenal tourist boom in the 1980s and the old town is surrounded by dozens of resorts, strung out along the beaches to the north and south. Many businesses suffered during the recent tourism downturn, but the place has received a huge cash injection from Italian tour operators. If you tire of pizzas and sun-loungers, the old part of town has a refreshingly African atmosphere.

Malindi is best visited in the high season, from August to January. At other times hotels are half empty and the bars and restaurants can feel lonely. Also, between March and June, brown silt flows out of the Galana River at the northern end of the bay, drastically reducing visibility in the marine park.

Orientation

The centre of Malindi is the area around the old market on Market Rd, is quite small, but the accommodation, restaurants and tourist malls are spread out north and south along the coast. Vasco da Gama and Mama Ngina Rds provide access to most of the resorts south of town, while the KWS headquarters is further south on Tourist Rd. The big shopping arcades and restaurant complexes are north of the centre on the road to Lamu; along its

length, the road changes its name from Uhura St to Harambee Rd and then to Lamu Rd.

The *Malindi Explorers' Map* (KSh250) is available from the supermarkets on Lamu and Harambee Rds.

Information

Tourist Offices At Malindi's tourist office (☎ 70747; 1st floor, Malindi Complex, Lamu Rd; open 8am-12.30pm & 2pm-4.30pm Mon-Fri) the staff are friendly but don't have much information. There are rumours that the office will move to the newly restored House of the Columns on the seafront.

Visa Extensions There's an **immigration office** (☎ 30876, Vasco da Gama Rd) next to the Jumaa Mosque and pillar tombs on the waterfront, but staff often refer travellers seeking visa extensions to Mombasa.

Money There is a branch of **Barclays Bank** (Harambee Rd; open 9am-4.30pm Mon-Fri, 9am-11am Sat) with an ATM. The nearby **Standard Chartered Bank** (Uhura St) also has an ATM and the **Kenya Commercial Bank** (Harambee Rd) has a bureau de change; both open similar hours to Barclays. Rates may be slightly better at the **Dollar Forex Bureau** (Harambee Rd). For Western Union money transfers, the **Postbank** is in the Malindi Complex on Lamu Rd.

Post & Communications The **post office** (Kenyatta Rd; open 9am-5pm Mon-Fri, 9am-noon Sat) can handle international parcels.

MALINDI

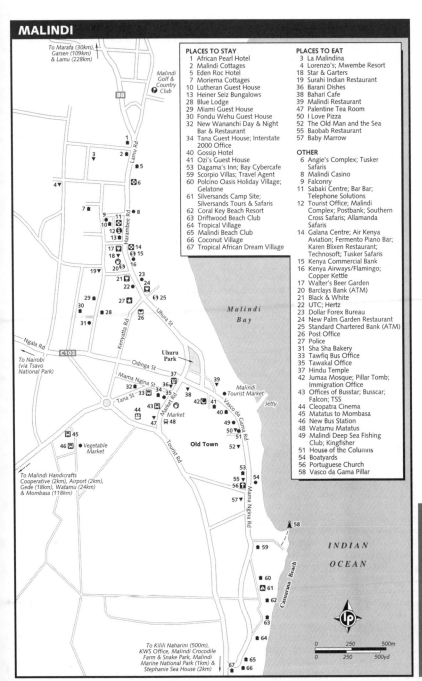

To Marafa (30km),
Garsen (109km)
& Lamu (228km)

Malindi
Golf &
Country
Club

Lamu Rd

Harambee Rd

Kenyatta Rd

Ngala Rd

To Nairobi
(via Tsavo
National Park)

Uhuru St

Uhuru Park

Odinga St

Mama Ngina St

Tana St

Market Rd

Market

Tourist Rd

Old Town

Vasco da Gama Rd

Mama Ngina Rd

Malindi Tourist Market

Jetty

To Malindi Handicrafts
Cooperative (2km), Airport (2km),
Gede (18km), Watamu (24km)
& Mombasa (118km)

Vegetable
Market

To Kilili Naharini (500m),
KWS Office, Malindi Crocodile
Farm & Snake Park, Malindi
Marine National Park (1km) &
Stephanie Sea House (2km)

*Malindi
Bay*

INDIAN

OCEAN

Casuarina Beach

0   250   500m
0   250   500yd

PLACES TO STAY
1 African Pearl Hotel
2 Malindi Cottages
5 Eden Roc Hotel
7 Moriema Cottages
10 Lutheran Guest House
13 Heiner Seiz Bungalows
28 Blue Lodge
29 Miami Guest House
30 Fondu Wehu Guest House
32 New Wananchi Day & Night
Bar & Restaurant
34 Tana Guest House; Interstate
2000 Office
40 Gossip Hotel
41 Ozi's Guest House
53 Dagama's Inn; Bay Cybercafe
59 Scorpio Villas; Travel Agent
60 Polcino Oasis Holiday Village;
Gelatone
61 Silversands Camp Site;
Silversands Tours & Safaris
62 Coral Key Beach Resort
63 Driftwood Beach Club
64 Tropical Village
65 Malindi Beach Club
66 Coconut Village
67 Tropical African Dream Village

PLACES TO EAT
3 La Malindina
4 Lorenzo's; Mwembe Resort
18 Star & Garters
19 Surahi Indian Restaurant
36 Barani Dishes
38 Bahari Cafe
39 Malindi Restaurant
47 Palentine Tea Room
50 I Love Pizza
52 The Old Man and the Sea
55 Baobab Restaurant
57 Baby Marrow

OTHER
6 Angie's Complex; Tusker
Safaris
8 Malindi Casino
9 Falconry
11 Sabaki Centre; Bar Bar;
Telephone Solutions
12 Tourist Office; Malindi
Complex; Postbank; Southern
Cross Safaris; Allamanda
Safaris
14 Galana Centre; Air Kenya
Aviation; Fermento Piano Bar;
Karen Blixen Restaurant;
Technosoft; Tusker Safaris
15 Kenya Commercial Bank
16 Kenya Airways/Flamingo;
Copper Kettle
17 Walter's Beer Garden
20 Barclays Bank (ATM)
21 Black & White
22 UTC; Hertz
23 Dollar Forex Bureau
24 New Palm Garden Restaurant
25 Standard Chartered Bank (ATM)
26 Post Office
27 Police
31 Sha Sha Bakery
33 Tawfiq Bus Office
35 Tawakal Office
37 Hindu Temple
42 Jumaa Mosque; Pillar Tomb;
Immigration Office
43 Offices of Busstar; Busscar;
Falcon; TSS
44 Cleopatra Cinema
45 Matatus to Mombasa
46 New Bus Station
48 Watamu Matatus
49 Malindi Deep Sea Fishing
Club; Kingfisher
51 House of the Columns
54 Boatyards
56 Portuguese Church
58 Vasco da Gama Pillar

THE COAST

There are several very good Internet cafés. **Technosoft** (☎ 31101; Galana Centre, Lamu Rd) is fast and reliable and charges KSh3 per minute. **Telephone Solutions** (☎ 30782; Sabaki Centre, Lamu Rd) has fast Internet access for KSh2 per minute. It also offers cheap international calls. A convenient choice if you're staying south of town is **Bay Cyber-cafe** (Vasco da Gama Rd), near Dagama's Inn, which charges KSh2 per minute.

Travel Agencies The most reliable travel agent in town is **Scorpio Villas** (☎ 31390, fax 21250; Mama Ngina Rd; @ scorpio@swiftma lindi.com), at the hotel of the same name.

Dangers & Annoyances Don't walk back to your hotel along the beach at night. In past years many people have been mugged, although there haven't been any incidents lately. The long dark walk from the restaurant strip at the north end of town to the resorts south of the centre should also be avoided at night – take a taxi.

Beach boys are the usual pain in the neck and as well as offers of sex and souvenirs, drugs are widely offered. This is often part of a sting in which phoney 'policemen' appear, confiscate the drugs and extract a large 'fine'. Drugs *are* illegal here, and being ripped-off is nothing compared to what will happen if you are arrested by a bona fide cop – either way, it isn't worth the risk.

Historic Buildings

The most famous monument, although it isn't particularly impressive, is the **Vasco da Gama Pillar** erected by the Portuguese explorer as a navigational aid in 1498. The coral pillar is topped by a cross made of Lisbon stone, which almost certainly dates from da Gama's time, and stands on the rocks at the northern end of Casuarina Beach, from where there are good views along the coast. To get here, follow the signs from the alley beside Scorpio Villas (see Places to Stay later).

Dating from the same time is the so-called **Portuguese church** (admission KSh200) that Vasco da Gama is reputed to have erected and where two of his crew are claimed to be buried. This may not be the case, but St Francis Xavier certainly visited on his way to India. The rest of the compound is taken up by the graves of Catholic missionaries. The

site is run by the National Museums of Kenya authority and donations are requested.

Opposite the boat jetty on the seafront is the town's principal mosque and the remains of the ancient **Jumaa Mosque and palace**. Within the compound is a large pillar tomb, but non-Muslims are not allowed to enter.

Most of the old part of Malindi is now made up of concrete houses, but there are a few traditional Swahili houses, including the newly restored **House of the Columns** (Vasco da Gama Rd) – the proposed site of a new museum and tourist office – and the **Hindu Temple** (Market Rd).

Malindi Marine National Park

Immediately offshore from Malindi and extending south as far as Watamu, this extensive marine park (nonresident adult/child US$8/5; open 7am-7pm daily) covers 213 sq km and protects some impressive coral reefs, although the piles of seashells on sale in Malindi may make you wonder just how much that protection is worth.

Despite the damage to the reef from shell collectors, careless snorkellers and hotel owners looking for decorative touches for their resorts, there is still some amazing marine life here, and there's always a chance you may see megafauna such as whale sharks and mako sharks. Note that underwater visibility is severely reduced by silt from the Galana River between March and June.

Most people visit on a snorkelling or glass-bottomed boat trip, which can be arranged at the **KWS office** (☎ 20845/31554; @ malindimnp@kws.org) on the coast road south of town. Boats only go out at low tide, so it's a good idea to call the KWS in advance to check the tide times. The going rate is around KSh3000 (per boat) for a two-hour trip, and masks and snorkels are provided. Alternatively, you can take a tour with any of the tour agencies in town.

The use of fins (flippers) is discouraged as there has been lots of damage here by inexperienced snorkellers. Walking atop the reef at low tide is another popular activity, which is doing irreparable damage and should be avoided.

The KWS compound sits on a lovely stretch of beach and there's a KWS camp site and bandas (see Places to Stay). You can also charge national park smartcards here for trips to Tsavo East and Tsavo West.

Malindi Crocodile Farm & Snake Park

This commercial crocodile farm *(☎ 20121; nonresident adult/child US$5/2; open 9am-5.30pm daily)* is just off the main road leading to the marine park, and obligingly, the crocs engage in a feeding frenzy at 4pm every Wednesday and Friday. Kids are more likely than adults to enjoy the spectacle without making the link between the smiling reptiles in the pens and the belts and wallets on sale in the foyer...

Falconry

The falconry *(adult/child KSh300/150; open 9am-5.30pm daily)*, near the town centre, has a number of caged birds of prey, as well as a huge tortoise roaming around. The displays are quite dramatic, but it's not the most prepossessing place.

Things to See & Do

With the marine park just offshore, **scuba diving** is a popular activity, although the visibility is greatly reduced by silt between March and June. All the big hotels have diving schools; the most approachable is **Scuba Diving Malindi** *(☎ 20155; Driftwood Beach Club)*. Single dives cost US$40 plus the park entry fee, while a PADI open-water diver course will cost US$350.

As you might expect with all the Hemingway allusions, **deep-sea fishing** is popular. **Kingfisher** *(☎ 21168; Vasco da Gama Rd)*, below the Malindi Deep Sea Fishing Club, is one of the best places on the coast to find a cheap private deep-sea fishing charter. It has a large fleet of boats and charges US$350 for a 'short day' of around six hours (up to four anglers). Tag and release is recommended (see the boxed text 'Tag & Release').

Malindi Golf & Country Club *(☎ 31402)*, a couple of kilometres north of town, is open to all comers on payment of a KSh100 daily membership fee. A round of golf here is KSh1200, club hire is KSh200 and caddies cost KSh100 for nine holes.

Organised Tours

Numerous safari companies operate from Malindi to Tsavo East National Park, entering the park via the Sala Gate. The going rate for a day trip to Tsavo East is US$120 per person. Reliable companies include the following.

Southern Cross Safaris (☎ 30547, fax 30032; e sxsmld@swiftmalindi)
Tusker Safaris (☎ 30525, fax 30868; e tuskeraf@ swiftmalindi.com) Angie's Complex, Lamu Rd
UTC (☎ 20040, fax 30443) Harambee Rd

These companies also offer trips to the Malindi Marine National Park (US$20) and Mida Creek (US$25). A cheaper choice is **Silversands Tours & Safaris** *(☎ 30014; Vasco da Gama Rd)*, next to the Silversands Camp Site.

Places to Stay – Budget

There is a camp site and bandas at the **KWS compound** *(☎ 20845/31554; Casuarina Beach; camping per person US$2, bandas per person KSh600)*. Water and bedding are provided and there's a kitchen you can use for KSh300. Mountain bikes can be hired for KSh200 per day.

Silversands Camp Site *(☎ 20412; camping per adult/child KSh150/75, 2-person banda with shared bathroom KSh460, bandas with bathroom KSh590)* is about 2km south of town along the coast road, just before the Driftwood Beach Hotel. It's very popular with travellers and there are good facilities but limited shade. The simple tented bandas face a lovely stretch of beach. Bicycles can be rented for KSh200 per day or KSh30 by the hour.

Tana Guest House *(☎ 20116; singles/ doubles with shared bathroom KSh300/400, singles/doubles with bathroom KSh500/600)* is the best cheap place in the old town, with large bright rooms with fan and mosquito nets set in a haven-like garden.

New Wananchi Day & Night Bar & Restaurant *(☎ 20584; Tana St; singles/doubles KSh200/250)* is a huge bar complex painted with Tusker beer adverts, with rooms upstairs. It's a real dosshouse, but it is cheap.

Most travellers prefer to stay in one of the hotels closer to the beach.

Ozi's Guest House *(☎ 20218; Vasco da Gama Rd; singles/doubles/triples KSh500/ 1000/1500)*, on the alley beside the Jamaa Masjid, is probably the best in this area. This friendly place is kept spotlessly clean, and the rooms all have bathrooms, fans and nets. Rates include breakfast.

Gossip Hotel *(☎ 20307; Vasco da Gama Rd; singles/doubles with bathroom KSh700/ 1200)* is a friendly, well-kept place, though it's heavily overpriced – try and negotiate a lower rate. Rates include breakfast. It's next to Metro Hotel, which seems to largely be a brothel.

Dagama's Inn *(☎ 31942; singles/doubles KSh500/600, with breakfast KSh600/800)* is a modern block with a *makuti* roof and slightly old-looking rooms. Quite a few travellers stay here and there's a decent restaurant downstairs. All rooms have nets, but only one has a fan.

There are several budget choices tucked away on the dusty streets behind Lamu and Nagala Rds.

Fondo Wehu Guest House *(☎ 30017; singles/doubles KSh450/1000)* is a good-value and friendly local guesthouse with a rooftop terrace. However, it's very hard to find. From Lamu Rd, turn off near Barclays Bank, then turn left at Suhari Restaurant – the guesthouse is down the alley next to the Sha Sha Bakery on the left-hand side. You'll probably have to ask directions.

Blue Lodge *(☎ 30246; singles/doubles with bathroom KSh350/400)*, opposite the turn-off to Fondo Wehu, is cheaper but much plainer. Rooms are spacious and have nets but no fans. There are good views from the top balcony.

Miami Guest House *(☎ 31029; singles with shared bathroom KSh500, doubles with bathroom KSh700)* is down the road towards Surahi Restaurant. There's an obvious sign, but its set back a bit from the road.

Lutheran Guest House *(☎ 21098; doubles/ triples/quads with shared bathroom KSh800/ 1200/1500, doubles with bathroom KSh1000, 2-bedroom cottages KSh1500)*, tucked away in the network of unsealed roads behind Lamu Rd, is a friendly little religious centre. Rooms and cottages have fans and nets and are set in a quiet garden. The rates include breakfast but alcohol is prohibited.

Places to Stay – Mid-Range

There are few places in this price range and tariffs vary according to the season.

Polcino Oasis Holiday Village *(☎/fax 31995; e oasis@africaonline.co.ke; 1-/2-bedroom apartments KSh1500/2500 in low season, KSh2000/3500 in high season)* is a vast *makuti*-roofed apartment block surrounding a truly vast pool. The shopping arcade has a pizzeria and a good ice-cream parlour.

Heiner Seiz Bungalows *(☎ 20978; Lamu Rd; singles/doubles KSh1500/1800; triples with kitchen KSh2000-2500)*, next to the Malindi Complex, is an attractive group of white cottages surrounding a pool. The cottages are divided into large and well-kept rooms with air-con and fridges. The triples are basically whole cottages with kitchens.

Malindi Cottages *(☎/fax 21071; Lamu Rd; 2-bedroom cottages KSh2000-2500)*, opposite Eden Roc Hotel, is looking pretty old and seedy, and the murky pool doesn't exactly inspire confidence.

Moriema Cottages *(☎ 31326; singles/ doubles KSh1000/2000).* tucked away in a quaint garden behind the Sabaki shopping centre is great value. Accommodation is in one-bedroom cottages with good kitchens. Rates include breakfast.

African Pearl Hotel *(☎ 31612; e african pearl@swiftmalindi.com; doubles with fan/air-con KSh1400/1800)* is an old-style hotel set in a very pleasant garden at the northern end of Malindi. Rooms are bright and airy and there's a pool and a decent restaurant and bar. It's very popular with nongovernmental organisation workers and expats.

Places to Stay – Top End

Melinda's top-range hotels are strung out along the beachfront both north and south of the town centre. All have swimming pools, restaurants and bars and most have water sports facilities and discos. The hotels south of town open right onto a wonderful stretch of beach, but those north of the centre are separated from the beach by a wide swathe of sand dunes. Unless otherwise stated, the following rates include breakfast.

Eden Roc Hotel *(☎ 20480, fax 21225; e edenroc@africaonline.co.ke; singles/doubles with fan KSh1960/3255, singles/doubles with air-con KSh2395/3595, single/double suites KSh3175/4230)* is the best choice north of town at this price range. It's one of the older resorts, and the beach is a long walk from the rooms, but it has a nice atmosphere.

South of town, the top-end hotels stretch all the way down to Casuarina Beach and the Malindi Marine Park.

Scorpio Villas *(☎ 20194, fax 21250; e scor pio@swiftmalindi.com; rooms per person B&B/full board US$25/40 in low season US$38/53 in high season)* is popular with older travellers. Villas are set in dense, well-tended tropical gardens and there are three pools, a restaurant and a good travel agent.

Lovely Silversands Beach is just 50m from the gate.

Coral Key Beach Resort *(☎ 30717, fax 30715; e coralkey@africaonline.co.ke; singles/doubles US$45/90 in low season, US$90/120 in high season)* is a massive mass-tourism place catering almost exclusively to young Italian couples. It's very lively, with activities such as water-volleyball and a climbing wall, and there are *loads* of pools.

Driftwood Beach Club *(☎ 20155, fax 30712; e driftwood@swiftmalindi.com; singles/doubles/triples KSh3800/5400/6750, 4-person cottages KSh7350, children 5-11 years in all rooms KSh750)* is further down the beach beyond Silversands Camp Site. It's a pleasant, low-key hotel used more by individual travellers than package groups. There are also posh luxury cottages. The restaurant, bar and other facilities are all open to nonguests for a temporary membership fee of KSh200/700 per day/week.

Tropical African Dream Village *(☎ 31673, fax 31872; e tropical@swiftmalindi.com; singles/doubles/triples US$63/88/119 in low season, US$90/126/157 in high season)* consists of three resorts around the intersection of Mama Ngina and Tourist Rds. The Tropical African Dream Village section on Tourist Rd is a rather grand complex of *makuti*-roofed plantation-style houses with a soaring *makuti*-roofed bar and restaurant. Around the corner, the Malindi Beach Club section has a glorious Swahili doorway and accommodation in cosy Moorish cottages, while the Coconut Village is a more predictable collection of *makuti*-roofed villas.

Kilili Baharini Resort *(☎ 20169, fax 20634; e kilili-resort@africaonline.co.ke; doubles from US$114 in low season; from US$218 in high season)* is a splendid Italian resort, with flamboyant decor and Swahili beds with mosquito nets set all over the complex so you can read and catch the sea breeze. It fronts directly onto the sand, and the light, spacious rooms are clustered in small groups around attractive pools.

Stephanie Sea House *(☎ 20720, fax 20613; e stephanie@swiftmalindi.com; singles/doubles/triples US$38/66/85 in low season, US$48/74/98 in high season)* is quite a long way south, just beyond the marine park headquarters. Predictably, it's Italian owned, and as long as you don't mind being an outsider to this set, it's a great place to stay.

Rooms have Swahili furniture and there's a good beachfront restaurant.

Places to Eat

In recent years, Malindi has been swamped by Italian cuisine and while it's often good, the endless pizza and pasta get pretty tiring.

Self-caterers should head to the **supermarkets** at the Sabaki Centre and in the arcade beside Barclays Bank.

African For those on a budget (or just bored of pizza), there are some good Swahili places in the old part of town, close to the old market. Many of these places close during the month of Ramadan.

Barani Dishes *(Market Rd; mains KSh40-100; open 6.30am-10pm daily)*, opposite Tana Hotel, is an incredibly popular local place serving *mishkaki* (beef kebabs), fish curries, soups, chicken and chips, and *mandazi* (fried African bread) for mopping up sauces.

Palentine Tea Room *(Market Rd; Swahili meals KSh80-100)*, is a recommended Muslim canteen opposite the old market, serving stews and curries and soups.

Bahari Cafe *(Vasco da Gama Rd; meals KSh70-220)*, close to the souvenir shops on Uhuru Park, is a bright little fast-food café serving biryanis.

Malindi Restaurant *(Vasco da Gama Rd; mains KSh70-220)*, across the road, is a popular open-air restaurant under a *makuti*-roof. Burgers, chicken and chips and other standard meals are cheap and it's an agreeable place for an evening beer.

Star & Garters *(☎ 31336; Lamu Rd; grills & other mains KSh190-250)* is a large *makuti*-roofed restaurant-come-bar with pool tables, cable TV, beers and quite reasonable food.

There are a few cheap options on Vasco da Gama Rd. **Baobab Restaurant** *(Vasco da Gama Rd; mains KSh250-600)*, on the seafront near the boatyards, is reasonably popular and offers reasonable Western and African food and beers. The seafood is a little expensive.

Western/Italian A popular hang-out for the deep-sea fishing crowd is **Malindi Sea Fishing Club** *(☎ 30550; Vasco da Gama Rd; mains KSh250-380; open until 8pm daily)*. The walls feature some huge stuffed sharks and billfish in dramatic poses. The seafood is excellent, but you have to pay a KSh100 temporary membership fee.

I Love Pizza (☎ 20672; Vasco da Gama Rd; pizzas KSh300-500, secondi platti from KSh600) is a very popular Italian restaurant on the seafront. It attracts a slightly snooty crowd, but the pizzas are excellent. It's open for lunch and dinner daily.

The Old Man and the Sea (☎ 20879; Vasco da Gama Rd; mains KSh350-600) is tucked away on the seafront in an old Moorish house, and serves incredibly good food in huge portions for very reasonable prices. The grilled kingfish is excellent. It's great for a romantic dinner and you can get decent wine by the glass for KSh110. VAT is added to the bill.

Baby Marrow (☎ 0733-542584; mains KSh400-1150; open for lunch & dinner) is a very stylish, partly open-air place with lots of seafood served in interesting sauces.

Polcino Oasis Holiday Village (mains KSh200-400) is a convenient option if you're staying at the Silversands camp site. There are good pizzas and pastas, plus wines and cold beer. Next door is the **Gelatone** ice-cream parlour, offering Malindi's best gelati (KSh50 a scoop).

In the north of town, along Lamu and Harambee Rds, are several options that cater to both package and independent travellers.

Copper Kettle (☎ 30786; mains KSh330-380) is an excellent Indian restaurant and coffee house with cheap Western meals and recommended *mughlai* cuisine. It's popular with travellers at lunch and dinnertime.

Bar Bar (Sabaki Centre; Lamu Rd; mains KSh250-400) is a perennially popular courtyard bar, restaurant and ice-cream parlour. The pizzas, pasta and the other Western favourites aren't bad, and there's nonstop Italian cable TV in the background. For a snack lunch, the panini and foccacia are recommended.

Karen Blixen Restaurant (☎ 0733-801215; Galana Centre; mains up to KSh350) is a new Italian terrace restaurant serving gnocchi, pasta and foccacias. It's also good for a morning cappuccino.

In the network of streets behind Lamu Rd are two very upmarket Italian restaurants, **La Malindina** (☎ 31440) and **Lorenzo's** (☎ 31758). Both are only open in the evening and serve set meals for around KSh2000. To get here, turn off Lamu Rd opposite the Regent Casino. Lorenzo's is straight ahead, near the private Mwembe Resort, while La Malindina is on a side road that branches off near the cemetery.

Entertainment

Bars Many tourist bars on Harambee and Lamu Rds are just glorified pick-up joints for prostitutes. Perhaps the most wholesome are **Star & Garters** (Lamu Rd) and **Black & White** (Harambee Rd), which are both open 24-hours and have regular live bands. **Walter's Beer Garden** (Harambee Rd) and **New Palm Garden Restaurant** (Harambee Rd) are much more seedy affairs.

Bar Bar (Sabaki Centre) is a popular place for a chilled-out beer in the evening and there's and a pool table.

Fermento Piano Bar (☎ 31780; Galana Centre, Lamu Rd) is a ritzy, air-con cocktail bar with posh drinks, such as strawberry margueritas, and a dance floor. It's young, trendy and Italian so wear your showiest outfit.

Malindi Sea Fishing Club (Vasco da Gama Rd) is a great place to sit with an icy Tusker looking out over the Indian Ocean, but it closes at 8pm. The friendly clientele are mainly British and white Kenyan. You'll need to pay the daily membership fee (KSh100).

Cinemas The small **Cleopatra Cinema** (Tourist Rd; seats KSh20) screens Indian blockbusters in the evenings and English premiership soccer in the afternoons.

Casinos With its ostentatious beach resorts and gourmet restaurants, it shouldn't be any surprise that casinos are big business in Malindi. **Malindi Casino** (☎ 30878; Lamu Rd) is by far the grandest. It's housed in a lovely, colonial-style building and the slot machines are open from 9am to 5am, while card tables open at noon. Admission is free (shoes are required) and the drinks and snacks are reasonably priced.

Shopping

The Malindi **curios market,** on the seafront near the Jumaa Mosque, has at least 30 stalls selling almost identical touristy souvenirs – you know what to expect. Prices and quality aren't bad, though you'll have to bargain hard. There are also numerous shops along Uhura St near the old town, with higher prices but usually more interesting items on offer. Avoid the shell vendors around Uhuru

Park – the shells on sale here are mostly plundered from the national park.

Another good place to buy handicrafts is at the **Malindi Handicrafts Cooperative** (☎ 30248), a community project on the outskirts of Malindi. It employs numerous local artisans, and the woodcarvings are of a high quality. To get there, turn-off the main road to Mombasa near the BP petrol station; the centre is 2km along a dirt road, opposite the community clinic.

Getting There & Away
Air A number of companies fly from Malindi to Lamu and Nairobi. For Nairobi, **Air Kenya** (☎ 30808; e resvns@airkenya.com; Galana Centre, Lamu Rd) has daily afternoon flights in each direction (US$70 one way, 1¼ hours). **Flamingo Airlines** (☎ 20237; Lamu Rd) flies the same route at least once a day (KSh4100 one way).

Air Kenya flies to Lamu (US$98 one-way, 35 minutes) every morning, returning in the afternoon. **Kas Kasi Aviation** (book through Allamanda Safaris ☎ 30526; e bryanp@swift malindi.com; Malindi Complex) offers flights between Malindi and Lamu on Wednesday and Sunday (US$60 one way). Flights leave Malindi at 7.30am and 4.30pm, returning from Lamu at 8.25am and 5.25pm.

Bus & Matatu The new bus station on the road towards Mombasa is only currently used by **Mombasa Raha** (Mombasa Liners), which has numerous daily buses to Mombasa (KSh100) and by small buses and matatus to Mombasa (KSh100).

For Nairobi, companies such as **Busstar**, **Busscar** and **Falcon** have offices opposite the old market in the centre of Malindi. There are daily departures at 7am and 7pm to Nairobi (KSh500, 10 hours).

Matatus to Watamu (KSh40) leave from the old market in town.

For Lamu, buses must travel in convoy with armed guards due to attacks by bandits and tribal wars in the area around Garsen and the Tana River. There haven't been any incidents lately, but the security situation could deteriorate at any time, so inquire locally about the current status of this road before travelling. Security aside, it's a slow, bumpy and uncomfortable journey, so fly if you can.

If you want to travel by bus, the journey takes at least eight hours between Malindi

and the ferry jetty at Mokowe, where boats meet the buses for the transfer to Lamu town; the fare is KSh300 to KSh400. Mombasa Raha (Mombasa Liners) and **TSS** have buses at 8.30am daily; **Interstate 2000** has a bus at 8am daily; and **Tawakal** has buses every other day at 7.30am. The ferry to Lamu from the mainland costs KSh40 and takes about 20 minutes.

Getting Around
You can rent bicycles from the **Silversands Camp Site**, the **KWS** and most of the bigger hotels for KSh200 to KSh500 per day. This is probably the best way to get around town unless you prefer to walk. Cycling at night is not permitted by the police.

Taxis are mainly concentrated along the road to Lamu between the post office and the Sabaki shopping centre, or in front of any of the big hotels south of town (the best place to start is in front of Coral Key Beach Resort). From the southern resorts, it costs KSh200 to Malindi town, KSh300 to the restaurant strip on Lamu Rd and KSh500 to the airport.

MARAFA DEPRESSION
This beautiful geological anomaly, also called **Hell's Kitchen**, Devil's Kitchen or Nyari (the Place Broken by Itself), lies about 30km directly northeast of Malindi near Marafa. Over the millennia wind and rain have eroded a ridge of sandstone into an amazing set of gorges. Most people visit on organised tours or by taxi (either way expect to pay about KSh3000).

Alternatively, there are one or two morning matatus from the new bus station in Malindi to Marafa village, from where it's a 30-minute walk to Hell's Kitchen. Guides are available in the village, but you may have to spend the night in one of the basic **lodges**, as all matatus travel in the morning.

TANA RIVER PRIMATE NATIONAL RESERVE
From Garsen, a nondescript town (with very basic hotels) on the road to Lamu, a rough road leads inland to hot and humid Garissa and on to Thika. About 40km north of Garsen on this road is the Tana River Primate National Reserve, established in 1976 to protect the remaining populations of the endangered crested mangabey and Tana River

Tana River Protests

The Tana River Primate Reserve has been earmarked for development into a national park, backed by the World Bank and IMF, but the plans would require thousands of local tribespeople to be relocated from their ancestral lands. There have been extensive protests against the plan by local people, who are already suffering from the ongoing tribal war between the Orma and Pokomo people over land rights in the area, which has killed hundreds in recent years.

Things came to a head in February 2001, when 300 naked women from surrounding villages stormed the research centre and attacked the scientists, a traditional gesture designed to shame enemies. Faced by such protests, the World Bank has suspended its funding and the KWS has put the plans on indefinite hold.

red colobus. Funded by the World Bank, the **Muchelelo Research Camp** was set up here in 1992 to study these rare primates, but plans to create a full-blown national park have faced considerable opposition from locals (see the boxed text 'Tana River Protests'). Entry to the park is free.

All roads into the area are prone to attacks by bandits and cannot currently be considered safe for travel, but should the security situation improve, visits to the reserve may be possible. Contact the **KWS** (☎ 02-602345) in Nairobi to find out the latest situation.

Lamu

☎ 0121

For most travellers, this ancient Swahili island state is the highlight of the coast. During the 1970s, Lamu picked up a reputation as the Kathmandu of Africa – a place of fantasy and other-worldliness, plucked straight from the pages of the Arabian Nights. It drew seekers of the miraculous, globetrotters and hippies who wanted to escape the trappings of Western society and get back to basics in a society that had somehow escaped the depredations of the 20th century. Less esoterically, they also found a ready supply of marijuana, which, for some, is still part of Lamu's appeal.

Although the culture, way of life and architecture of Lamu is very much intact, the first signs of change are becoming apparent in this deeply traditional society. Many wealthy Europeans – including the Prince of Hanover – have bought up property on the island, building flamboyant holiday houses on the beaches south of town. In response to this intrusion of Western influence, many locals are retreating into stricter forms of Islam, reducing the tolerant and relaxed atmosphere of the island.

The population is almost entirely Muslim and men still wear the full-length white robes known as *khanzus* and *kofia* caps, traditionally embroidered by women to pass the time while their husbands were away from the house. Older women dress in Swahili *kangas*, but simplified versions of the black wraparound *bui-bui*, common in many Arabic cultures, are the standard attire for younger women. Full *purdah*, which covers everything but the eyes, is becoming increasingly common.

Between the various islands of the archipelago, or along the coast, the main form of transport is the traditional dhow, and dhow trips to outlying islands are one of the must-do activities of any visit to Lamu. One of the most incredible spectacles on the coast is the century-old Maulid Festival, when the dances and celebrations still take place with complete disregard for camera-toting tourists.

Access to Lamu is by diesel-powered launch from the mainland or from the dirt airstrip on Manda Island. There is only one motor-powered vehicle on the island and most people use donkeys to carry things around. You'll often see locals tottering down the streets sitting side-saddle on one of these miniature beasts of burden.

History

Arab settlers established a busy trading post here at the start of the 16th century, exporting ivory, mangrove poles, tortoiseshell and thousands of African slaves, who were whisked away by dhow to Iraq, Oman and the burgeoning Arabic colonies elsewhere on the East African coast.

Initially, Lamu was a minor player in the East African power game, dominated by the nearby sultanate of Paté, but it rose to prominence in the 19th century, after defeating the forces of Paté in a battle at Shela

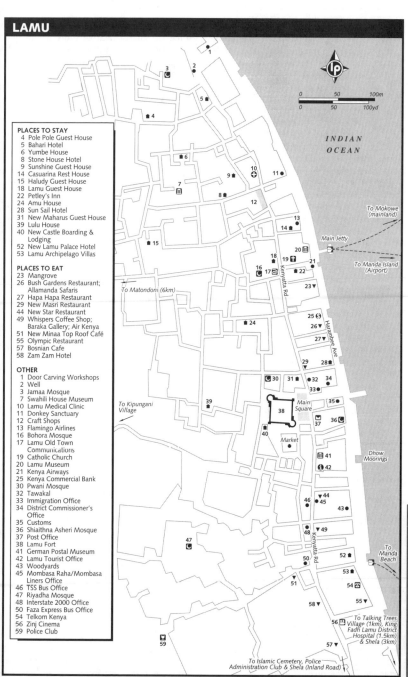

LAMU

INDIAN
OCEAN

To Mokowe
(mainland)

Main Jetty

To Manda Island
(Airport)

To Matondoni (6km)

To Kipungani
Village

Main
Square

Market

Dhow
Moorings

PLACES TO STAY
4 Pole Pole Guest House
5 Bahari Hotel
6 Yumbe House
8 Stone House Hotel
9 Sunshine Guest House
14 Casuarina Rest House
15 Haludy Guest House
18 Lamu Guest House
22 Petley's Inn
24 Amu House
28 Sun Sail Hotel
31 New Maharus Guest House
39 Lulu House
40 New Castle Boarding &
   Lodging
52 New Lamu Palace Hotel
53 Lamu Archipelago Villas

PLACES TO EAT
23 Mangrove
26 Bush Gardens Restaurant;
   Allamanda Safaris
27 Hapa Hapa Restaurant
29 New Masri Restaurant
44 New Star Restaurant
49 Whispers Coffee Shop;
   Baraka Gallery; Air Kenya
51 New Minaa Top Roof Café
55 Olympic Restaurant
57 Bosnian Cafe
58 Zam Zam Hotel

OTHER
1 Door Carving Workshops
2 Well
3 Jamaa Mosque
7 Swahili House Museum
10 Lamu Medical Clinic
11 Donkey Sanctuary
12 Craft Shops
13 Flamingo Airlines
16 Bohora Mosque
17 Lamu Old Town
   Communications
19 Catholic Church
20 Lamu Museum
21 Kenya Airways
25 Kenya Commercial Bank
30 Pwani Mosque
32 Tawakal
33 Immigration Office
34 District Commissioner's
   Office
35 Customs
36 Shiaithna Asheri Mosque
37 Post Office
38 Lamu Fort
41 German Postal Museum
42 Lamu Tourist Office
43 Woodyards
45 Mombasa Raha/Mombasa
   Liners Office
46 TSS Bus Office
47 Riyadha Mosque
48 Interstate 2000 Office
50 Faza Express Bus Office
54 Telkom Kenya
56 Zinj Cinema
59 Police Club

To Manda
Beach

To Talking Trees
Village (1km), King
Fadh Lamu District
Hospital (1.5km)
& Shela (3km)

To Islamic Cemetery, Police
Administration Club & Shela (Inland Road)

THE COAST

beach. At this time the twin cash-cows of ivory and slavery made Lamu a splendidly wealthy place, and most of the fine Swahili houses that survive today in Lamu were built during this period.

It all came to an end in 1873 when the British forced Sultan Barghash of Zanzibar to close down the slave markets. With the abolition of slavery, the economy of the island went into rapid decline. The city-state was incorporated into the British Protectorate from 1890, and became part of Kenya with independence in 1963.

Until it was rediscovered by travellers in the 1970s, Lamu existed in a state of humble obscurity, escaping the runaway development that happened elsewhere on the coast. Today, only Zanzibar can offer such a feast of Swahili culture and uncorrupted traditional architecture. In 2001 Lamu was added to Unesco's list of World Heritage Sites.

Orientation

Although there are several restaurants and places to stay along the waterfront, most of the guesthouses are tucked away in the confusing maze of alleys behind. Lamu's main thoroughfare is Kenyatta Rd, a long winding alley known popularly as 'Main St', which runs from the northern end of town past the fort and then south to the Muslim cemetery and the inland track to Shela.

The delightful village of Shela is home to Lamu's only resort and its finest beach, as well as several guesthouses in grand Swahili houses. Gorgeous Shela Beach continues for 12km along the Indian Ocean side of the island. Manda Beach lies just across the fast-moving Lamu channel from Shela.

Maps If you're going to stay long here the leaflet-map *Lamu: Map & Guide to the Archipelago, the Island & the Town* is worth buying (KSh300), assuming there are any in stock.

Information

Tourist Offices The tourist information office (☎ 33449; ℮ touristinformation@swift lamu.com; open 8am-9pm Mon-Sat & 8am-2pm Sun), just up from the waterfront near New Star Restaurant, is a commercial enterprise but it also provides fairly unbiased tourist information. Dhow tours can be arranged for reasonable prices.

Visa Extensions There's an **immigration office** (☎ 33032) near the fort where you should be able to get visa extensions, although travellers are sometimes referred to Mombasa.

Money The only bank on Lamu is **Kenya Commercial Bank** (open 9am-3pm Mon-Fri, 9am-11am Sat) on the waterfront. Unfortunately, it will only take Visa for cash advances. Beware of large commissions on cards and travellers cheques.

Post & Communications There are numerous cardphones outside the post office, but they're temperamental. Surprisingly, you can now send email from Lamu at reasonable prices: **Lamu Old Town Communications** (☎ 33411; Kenyatta Rd; open 9am-9pm) is close to the centre and charges KSh2 per minute. Connections aren't always reliable so keep your messages short. You can also make international calls and send faxes from here.

Bookshops Pretty much your only option these days is the bookshop at the **Lamu Museum**, specialising in Lamu and Swahili culture. *Lamu: A Study of the Swahili Town* is an authoritative book on the area.

Medical Services Built with Saudi Arabian money on the seafront towards Shela, the **King Fadh Lamu District Hospital** (☎ 33012) is one of the most modern and well-equipped hospitals on the coast. In the centre, the **Lamu Medical Clinic** (Kenyatta Rd, open 8am-9pm daily) is reliable.

Dangers & Annoyances Lamu has long been popular for its relaxed and tolerant atmosphere, but there are signs that this is changing.

In 1999 a gay couple who planned a wedding here was attacked by an angry mob and had to be evacuated under police custody. Whatever your sexuality, it's best to keep public displays of affection to a minimum and respect local attitudes to modesty.

Beach boys are also a growing problem in Lamu. Most loiter around the waterfront restaurants offering dhow trips, marijuana and other 'services'. Single women and even groups of female travellers are likely to have company wherever they go. There's not a lot you can do except politely turn down whatever it is they're offering...

Town Buildings

Lamu dates back to at least the late 14th century when the Pwani Mosque was built, but most buildings date from the 18th century. Traditional Swahili homes were build along rigid social lines, with separate quarters for men and women and audience halls that allowed men to receive guests without infringing on the privacy of their womenfolk.

Most buildings are constructed out of local materials, with cut coral-rag blocks for the walls, wooden floors supported by mangrove poles and intricately carved shutters for windows. Lavish decorations were created using carved plaster, and carpenters were employed to produce ornately carved window and door frames as a sign of the financial status of the owners.

Traditionally, Lamu houses had flat roofs that created a private world where women were free to talk and socialise – but many have recently been replaced by shady makuti-covered terraces. Although there have been concerns about the increasing use of imported materials, conservation efforts have largely paid off and the remaining carved doors and painted wooden beams are probably safe from plunder.

In recent years, there has been a real revival in woodcarving and you can see carved lintels and doors being made in workshops all over Lamu.

There are too many Swahili houses to recommend any particular examples here – chances are you'll be staying in a traditional Swahili home with all the above features. The grandest frontages are probably those on the waterfront, which feature some truly spectacular carved doors. There are also some ornate lintels featuring quotes from the Quran along Kenyatta Rd and in Shela.

The numerous mosques in Lamu give few outward signs of their purpose (few have minarets) and can be hard to distinguish from domestic buildings. The most appealing are the **Shiaithna-Asheri Mosque,** on the seafront, with its stucco minarets, and also the pillar-style **Mnarani Mosque** in Shela, behind Peponi Hotel.

Important religious ceremonies are concentrated around the Saudi-funded **Riyadha Mosque** at the back of Lamu.

Museums

All the museums and Lamu Fort are open from 8am to 6pm daily. Admission to each is KSh200/100 for a nonresident adult/child.

Lamu Museum Housed in a very grand Swahili warehouse on the waterfront near Petley's Inn, the Lamu Museum is an excellent introduction to the culture and history of Lamu Island. It's one of the most interesting small museums in Kenya, with displays on Swahili culture (including a reconstructed traditional Swahili house), the Maulid Festival, Lamu's nautical history and the tribes who used to occupy this part of the coast in pre-Muslim days, including the Boni, who were legendary elephant-hunters. The nautical section is particularly interesting, with models of the various types of dhow, including the sinister-looking slave dhows.

Pride of the collection are the remarkable and ornate *siwa* (ceremonial horns) of Lamu and Paté. Lamu's *siwa* is made of engraved brass but it pales beside the glorious ivory *siwa* of Paté, carved from a single massive elephant tusk. Both date from the 17th century. Swahili relics from Takwa and other sites in the archipelago are displayed the gallery downstairs.

Swahili House Museum If the Lamu Museum stokes your interest in Swahili culture then visit this beautifully restored traditional house tucked away off to the side of Yumbe House hotel. Inside you'll find a recreation of a working Swahili home, with cookware, beds and other furniture. The attendant will give you a whistle-stop but informative tour including some fascinating descriptions of the regimented lives of Swahilis in the 18th and 19th century.

Among other unusual details is the ceremonial death bed, where deceased family members lay in state before burial, and the echo chamber, designed so women could receive visitors, when their menfolk were away, without being seen. The museum is well signposted from Kenyatta Rd.

Lamu Fort The atmospheric Lamu Fort sits at the end of the parade of government buildings leading up from the main jetty. The building of this massive structure was begun by the Sultan of Paté in 1810 and completed in 1823. From 1910 right up to 1984 it was

THE COAST

used as a prison, but it has recently undergone a complete restoration and now houses an impressive and colourful illustrated walk-through display of the local environment and natural history (good fun for kids). The island's library is also housed here.

German Postal Museum In the late 1800s, the Germans regarded Lamu as an ideal base from where they could successfully and safely exploit the interior, before the British decided to nip the German expansion into Tanganyika in the bud. The German East Africa Company set up a post office near where the tourist office now stands and the old building is now a museum exhibiting photographs and memorabilia of that period.

Donkey Sanctuary

A man without a donkey, is a donkey.
                    Swahili proverb

Donkeys are still the main form of transport on Lamu, and their sanctuary *(admission free; open 9am-1pm Mon-Fri)* was established by the International Donkey Protection Trust of Sidmouth, Devon in the UK, to improve the health of Lamu's hard-working beasts of burden. The project provides free veterinary services to donkey-owners and tends to injured, sick or worn-out donkeys. To promote animal welfare, there's an annual donkey competition in March or April, with prizes for the best-cared-for donkey.

Beaches

There's no beach on the Lamu town waterfront, which is muddy and could use a major cleanup. For the full, white-sand experience you need to go to **Shela Beach**, a 40-minute walk or 10-minute trip by dhow from Lamu. This spectacular dune-backed beach runs for 12km around the headland, so you're guaranteed a private stretch of sand. At the start of the beach is an absurdly ostentatious mock-fort built by an Italian entrepreneur who had lots of money but dubious taste.

There's no surf at Shela village because it's still in the channel between Lamu and Manda Islands, which makes it good for windsurfing (equipment can be hired at Peponi and Talking Trees Village). For traditional surfing, there are real breakers at the mouth of the

channel, although this is also the realm of some substantial sharks.

Across the channel is smaller **Manda Beach**, which also has fine sand and is home to the Manda Beach Club where you can get a chilly Tusker or something fancy with a little umbrella in it. There are boats from New Lamu Palace Hotel to Manda at 10.30am, 1.30pm and 5.30pm (KSh600 return), or you can hire a boat from in front of Peponi Hotel for KSh300, or KSh600 if you want to be dropped off and picked up later.

Both beaches are good places to beachcomb for shells.

Villages

Shela This ancient Swahili village sits at the start of glorious Shela Beach. In many ways it seems even more medieval than Lamu, with few signs of modernity along its meandering alleyways. But the pleasing tidiness of Shela is mostly due to its large and affluent expat population – when Shela was established in the 17th century, it would have been far messier!

Shela's first residents were migrants from the abandoned settlement Takwa on Manda Island. The local people speak a distinct dialect of Swahili and you can see strong evidence of Omani ancestry in many people's faces. Although it's something of a European enclave, it's still an atmospheric place to wander around and the mood is as languorous and laid-back as it's always been.

To get to Shela, you can take a motorised dhow from the small jetty in Lamu for KSh100 per person (or KSh250 to KSh300 for a solo ride). Alternatively, you can walk it in about 40 minutes. The easiest way is to follow the harbour-front road and then follow the shoreline, though this may be partly flooded at high tide. When the tide is in, you can either wade through the sunken bits, or cut across to the inland path. If you want to follow the inland path all the way, it starts near the Islamic cemetery in Lamu.

Matondoni You'll see many dhows anchored along the waterfront at Lamu and at Shela in the harbour at the southern end of town, but if you want to see them being built or repaired the best place is at the village of Matondoni in the northwest of the island.

To get there you have a choice of walking (about two hours), hiring a donkey

(KSh400) or hiring a dhow (KSh2000 per boat, good for up to five people). Dhow captains often provide lunch.

Walking there is a little more problematic. First you have to find the track at the back of town, then head for the football pitch and follow the telephone wires that go to Matondoni. Ask directions from local people until you're sure you're on the right track.

Set off early if you are walking. There's a small café in Matondoni village, but no guesthouses. An impromptu group of travellers generally collects later in the afternoon so you can all share a dhow ride back to Lamu.

Kipungani At the southwest tip of Lamu Island is this small village where local people make straw mats, baskets, hats and *kifumbu*, used to squeeze milk from mashed coconut. It's a friendly place, and tea and snacks can be arranged, plus there's a beautiful empty beach nearby. It's a long, hot walk and the path is very hard to find. A better option is to visit on a dhow tour for about KSh5000 per boat (good for around five people). Prices include lunch.

Dhow Trips

Taking a dhow trip is almost obligatory and drifting through the mangroves is a wonderful way to experience the islands. You'll be approached by would-be captains almost as soon as you arrive but it's worth shopping around to find a captain you like and a price you're happy with. Prices vary depending on where you want to go and how long you go for; you can normally rely on around KSh400 to KSh500 per person, based on a group of four or five people. More than five isn't recommended as the boats aren't very big.

Most trips meander around the channel between Lamu and Manda Island, and the price includes fishing and snorkelling, although both can be disappointing as the fish tend to hide amongst the coral during the day. Longer trips head for Manda Toto Island, which has better snorkelling.

Lunch is usually served up on a beach on Manda Island and typically consists of a barbecue of anything you've caught, or simply barbecued bait! The better captains bring emergency fish with them just in case they aren't biting. Make sure you take a hat and some sunblock as there is rarely any shade on the dhows.

Dhow Eyes

Dependent on the wind and tides to carry them around, early Swahili traders lived in constant fear of colliding with coral reefs and sand banks. To minimise the chances of this happening, dhows were equipped with a pair of *ito*, wooden 'eyes', to allow the boat to see obstacles below the water and protect it from spells cast by enemies using the 'evil eye'. The tradition persists to this day on the East African coast, although the eyes are now symbolic, featuring emblems such as the star and crescent and the red flag of Zanzibar. Carpenters in Lamu do a lively business in ornamental *ito*, which make great souvenirs – certainly more interesting than the usual wooden giraffes and souvenir shields!

For something a bit more flashy, **Peponi Hotel,** at Shela, offers full-moon dhow cruises for KSh4500 (minimum eight people) including drinks, wine and a lobster dinner.

Multi-day trips head out to Paté or the still more remote island of Kiwayu (see Islands Around Lamu later).

Water Sports

Peponi Hotel at Shela has a water-sports centre. It runs water-skiing (KSh8000 per hour), windsurfing (KSh650 to KSh800 depending on your skill level), snorkelling (KSh200 per day for equipment) and scuba diving for certified divers between December and March (US$50 for a single dive or US$90 for two dives, at two sites including lunch).

Cheaper windsurfing gear is available at **Talking Trees Village**, on the waterfront between Lamu and Shela, for KSh400 per hour.

Special Events

The **Maulid Festival** celebrates the birth of the Prophet Mohammed. Its date shifts according to the Muslim calendar and it will fall on 14 May 2003, 2 May 2004, and 21 April 2005. The festival has been celebrated on the island for over 100 years and much singing, dancing and general jollity takes place around this time. Among the interesting traditional dances are the *goma* or cane-fighting dance – like a more aggressive form of Morris dancing – and the quivering-sword dance, where sword-wielding dancers set up a chorus of vibrating steel.

Organised events include swimming galas, poetry reading, donkey races for young boys and dhow races for all the dhow captains. Most of the celebrations are centred around the Riyadha Mosque, although there are loud celebrations at all of Lamu's mosques.

Other interesting celebrations include the **Cultural Festival** in the last week of August, with traditional dancing, displays of traditional crafts such as *kofia* embroidery and dhow races. The **Donkey Awards** in March/April are an unusual spectacle (see Donkey Sanctuary earlier).

Places to Stay – Budget

Lamu has been catering for budget travellers for several decades and still has loads of inexpensive guesthouses. Prices are remarkably consistent because of the competition for clientele, although you obviously get what you pay for. Rates go up by up to 50% from August to September and around Christmas and New Year.

At other times, there's plenty of scope for negotiation, particularly if you plan to stay for more than just a day or two. Touts will try and accompany you from the jetty and if you arrive with one of these hangers-on in tow, you'll pay more for your rooms.

If you plan on staying in Lamu for a while it's worth making inquiries about renting a house, so long as there's a group of you to share the cost.

The price per person will usually be similar to staying at a lodge, but you'll have the advantage of a place to yourself and the luxury of a kitchen. Houses are available in both Lamu and Shela – you'll need to ask around and see what is available (restaurants are usually a good place to start).

Lamu Town On the seafront near the main jetty, **Casuarina Rest House** (☎ 33123; *singles/doubles/triples with shared bathroom KSh300/500/700, singles/doubles with bathroom KSh400/800*) offers large, airy rooms with good views. It's a friendly place, there's a nice terrace and the rooms have fans and mosquito nets. Unfortunately, it's often full.

Lamu Guest House (☎ 33338; *singles/doubles with bathroom KSh500/700*), near the Lamu Museum on the waterfront, is very

good value, clean and tidy. The owner is very friendly and the rooms on the top floor catch the sea breeze.

New Castle Boarding & Lodging (*singles/doubles with shared bathroom KSh250/350*) is just behind the fort. It's a no-frills place, although rooms have nets and fans, and privacy can be a problem as the walls between the rooms don't reach the roof.

New Maharus Guest House (☎ 33001; *singles/doubles/triples KSh300/400/700*) is close to the main square. There's nothing 'new' about the place and only the doubles and triples have bathrooms.

Pole Pole Guest House (☎ 33344; *doubles KSh400-750*) is north of the centre of town and back from the waterfront. One of the tallest buildings in Lamu, it has bright doubles that have bathroom, fans and nets. There's a spacious, *makuti*-roofed area on top of the hotel with great views over the town. It's a good place to stay, but it relies heavily on touts so you may initially be quoted twice the above rates.

Haludy Guest House (*doubles from KSh500*) is a long way from the waterfront and is looking a little worn these days. However, there's a fridge and kitchen for self-caterers and the communal lounges are lovely.

Sunshine Guesthouse (*doubles/triples KSh400/600*), around the corner from Stone House Hotel, is a bit old-looking but it is cheap and there's a kitchen with a fridge for guests. Rooms have fans and bathrooms and there's a roof terrace. Entry is via the steps up over the alleyway.

Shela The only budget option near the beach is **Talking Trees Village** (aka *Dodo Village*; ☎ 3500, fax 33449; *camping per person KSh150-300; singles/doubles KSh1100/2100*) on the Shela–Lamu track. The beachfront lounge is a good place to hang out, but the camping area (50m back from the beach) has no shade.

Places to Stay – Mid-Range

Lamu Town North of the main jetty is **Bahari Hotel** (☎ 33172; *singles/doubles KSh600/1200*). It's fairly new with a pleasant rooftop area, but the rooms are variable. All rooms have bathroom, fans and mosquito nets. Prices include breakfast and are usually negotiable.

Stone House Hotel (☎ 33544, fax 33149; e kisiwani@swiftkenya.com; singles/doubles/triples KSh1950/2600/3800) is a wonderful old Swahili place with Escher-like stairways and a fine leafy courtyard. The hotel has its own superb rooftop restaurant (no alcoholic drinks) with excellent views over the town and waterfront. Add around 30% for half board and if it's the high season add another 10%. Rooms can be booked with Kisiwani Ltd (☎/fax 02-226384) in Nairobi.

Lulu House (☎ 33539; singles/doubles KSh500/800), another good hotel-style guesthouse, is hidden away in the maze of streets behind the fort. There's a nice garden courtyard and rooms are large and bright with fans and nets. As usual, there's a pleasant rooftop lounge area.

Yumbe House (☎/fax 33101; singles/doubles/triples KSh1100/2100/2900 in low season, KSh1290/2700/3860 in high season), close to the Swahili House Museum, is a tall Swahili house set around a leafy courtyard and with an airy rooftop terrace. The pleasant rooms have bathrooms (towels, soap and toilet paper provided), fridges, fans and nets and are spotlessly clean. If it's full, staff can refer you to its sister hotel **Yumbe Villas** a few blocks away.

Sun Sail Hotel (☎ 33269, fax 32077; downstairs singles KSh800, upstairs singles/doubles KSh1000/1500), right on the waterfront, has great views from some upstairs rooms, but the downstairs rooms are cramped. Still, it's clean and quiet and all rooms have fans, nets and bathroom. A large restaurant has been under construction here for years – perhaps it'll be open when you arrive.

Lamu Archipelago Villas (☎ 33247, fax 33368; singles/doubles KSh700/1500) is clean and modern but slightly soulless. The rooms have bathroom and fans, and rates include breakfast. It's right on the waterfront.

Amu House (☎/fax 33420; singles/doubles KSh1700/2300) is a beautifully restored, 16th-century house decorated with plaster carvings and furnished with local antiques. All rooms have a bathroom, fan, antique beds and nets and some have verandas. There's a restaurant, and rates include breakfast and transfers to and from Manda airport.

Shela Many houses are owned by expats (especially Italians) who have poured vast amounts of money into them but only live here for part of the year. At other times they can often be rented out so ask around in the restaurants in Shela. There are also a number of good, reasonably priced guesthouses in Shela.

Bahari Guest House & Restaurant (☎ 32046, fax 33029; doubles KSh2000-3000 in low season, KSh3000-5000 in high season) is on the shorefront between Peponi Hotel and Kijani House. Rooms open onto a wide balcony above the bay and have sea views, nets, fans and Swahili furniture. Rates include breakfast and you can often bargain down – aim for around KSh500 per person. It's highly recommended and the restaurant downstairs is good value.

Shella Pwani Guest House (☎ 33540; doubles KSh2000 in low season, KSh2500 in high season) is behind the shop selling kikois (sarongs), immediately behind Peponi Hotel. It's a lovely Swahili house with carved plasterwork and some rooms have fine sea views. There are fans and nets in all rooms.

White House Guest House, Shella Royal House and **Shella Rest House** (☎ 33091, fax 33542; e shella@africaonline.co.ke) are three lovely Swahili houses owned by a friendly family. Rates vary according to the season and include breakfast and staff, who can cook for you if required. All the houses have kitchens for guests. The White House is simplest, with large, bright rooms for KSh1000 to KSh4000; it's just behind the Pwani Guest House. Shella Royal Guest House is behind Kijani House, and it's grander with balcony dining areas on every floor; doubles vary from KSh1000 to KSh5000. Shella Rest House, near the Island Hotel, is the best of the three, with panoramic views from the rooftop terrace and rooms arranged in two-bedroom apartments, each with their own kitchen and bathroom. The apartments sleep four and cost KSh1500 to KSh5000.

Places to Stay – Top End

Lamu Town Right on the harbour next to the Lamu Museum is **Petley's Inn** (☎ 33107, fax 33378; singles/doubles with breakfast US$70/90, half board US$85/120), the top hotel in Lamu town. Originally set up in the late 19th century by Percy Petley – a somewhat eccentric English colonist who retired to Lamu – it has loads of traditional touches, and modern facilities, such as a rooftop bar and a swimming pool, have been subtly blended in. It's a fine place, although rates are steep considering what else you can get in Lamu. The rooftop bar is a great place for a beer, and set meals at the restaurant cost US$12 to US$15. Rates include transfers to and from Manda Island airstrip.

New Lamu Palace Hotel is owned by the same people who own Petley's Inn. It's not as sensitively designed, but rooms are smart and comfortable and there's a good restaurant and a bar serving alcohol. The problem is that you can rent a whole Swahili house for these prices! Rates and contact details are the same as for Petley's Inn.

Shela At the far end of Shela is **Peponi Hotel** (☎ 33421/3, fax 33029; e peponi@ users.africaonline.co.ke; standard singles/ doubles with breakfast US$155/195, superior singles/doubles with breakfast US$185/255), the top hotel on the island. It blends neatly into the surrounding Swahili buildings and offers a number of whitewashed cottages with their own verandas facing the channel between Lamu and Manda Islands. The stylish rooms are bright and airy and decked out with Swahili furniture. For full board add about 30%. The hotel has a very good watersports centre and there are a number of activities and equipment available both to guests and nonguests (see Water Sports earlier), plus a bar and upmarket restaurant. The hotel is closed during May and June.

Kijani House (☎ 33235/7, fax 33374; e ki jani@africaonline.co.ke; singles/doubles from US$120/180, full board from US$140/220) is on the waterfront in the middle of Shela village and is set in splendid gardens. Rooms are beautifully appointed, with fine Swahili furniture, and there are two swimming pools. Like Peponi, all manner of activities and trips can be arranged, and rates include boat transfers to and from Manda Island airstrip. The hotel is also closed in May and June. We have heard reports that Kenyans aren't all that welcome here.

Island Hotel (☎ 33290, fax 33568; e kisi wani@swiftkenya.com; singles/doubles/triples with breakfast US$51/72/98, with full board US$73/115/163), in the centre of Shela, is a superb Lamu-style house with a romantic rooftop restaurant (see Places to Eat). It's only five minutes' walk from the waterfront along the alley beside Kijani House, but you'll probably have to ask for directions.

The room rates include boat transfers to and from Manda Island airstrip. The hotel can also be booked through Kisiwani Ltd (☎/fax 02-446384) in Nairobi.

Kisiwani Ltd also rents out whole houses in Shela from US$170 to US$280 per day. Cooks and cleaners are provided and the houses sleep six to 10 people. **Mnarani House** is behind the Mnarani Mosque, while **Mtakuja House** and **Jasmine House** are behind Kijani House. You should book these houses well in advance.

Kipungani At the southwest end of Lamu Island is Kipungani where there's another top-end hotel called **Kipungani Explorer** (book through Heritage Hotels ☎ 02-4446651, 4446600; e info@heritagehotels.co.ke; singles/doubles US$296/400; closed Apr-June). It's very luxurious.

Places to Eat
Lamu It's important to know that all of the cheap places to eat and many of the more expensive restaurants are closed all day until after sunset during the month of Ramadan. If your hotel doesn't provide breakfast and lunch, you'll have to head to Whispers Coffeeshop, Petley's Inn, Lamu Palace Hotel or Peponi Hotel.

New Star Restaurant (mains KSh150-200) is one of the cheaper places to eat in Lamu. It mainly serves fast food such as fish and chips or stew and rice, but you can also get a few luxuries such as grilled lobster for just KSh450.

New Minaa Top Roof Café (meals under KSh100; open 6.30am-midnight), on the road up towards the Riyadha Mosque, is a bright, clean, rooftop café that serves Swahili favourites such as beef kebabs, maharagwe (beans in coconut milk), chicken tikka and samaki (fried fish). It's cheap and popular with both locals and travellers.

Other eateries well worth checking out are **Zam Zam Hotel**, **Bosnian Cafe** and **New Masri**, along the main street. Simple Swahili meals cost under KSh100 at all three places.

For consistently good food at reasonable prices there are a number of very popular makuti-roofed restaurants along the seafront. The menus at these places are almost identical, with fish, seafood, steaks and curries and all do magnificent juices and shakes served in British-style pint pots (KSh50 to KSh60).

These restaurants make a big song and dance about their lobster dinners, but these are generally small lobsters grilled and splashed with Swahili sauce. The huge mud crabs – known locally as 'monster crabs' – are better value.

Bush Gardens Restaurant *(mains KSh100-650)* has been popular for years and is where many people end up in the evening. There's no beer, but most people make do with *bao* (a traditional African board game) games to pass the time. The seafood is better than at most places in Lamu – the grilled Swahili-style barracuda costs KSh250, while the inevitable lobster cooked in coconut sauce is KSh650 – and the juices are recommended.

Hapa Hapa Restaurant *(mains KSh150-750)*, nearby, is another very popular choice with travellers, serving similar fare. The juices are very good and food is above average. It's also a good place for breakfast – traveller staples such as banana pancakes cost KSh60 to KSh100.

Mangrove *(mains KSh250-380)*, facing the main jetty, is decorated with nautical trinkets and it's very popular at lunchtime. The lobster costs KSh600. It's handy for a juice while you wait for a boat or to find your feet when you first arrive.

Olympic Restaurant *(mains KSh250-600)* is further south near the waterfront woodyards and serves the usual favourites. The owners are very friendly and for our money, this place does the best pineapple juice in Lamu.

Many travellers come across a man known as **Ali Hippy** who offers meals at his house. The meal usually includes lobster, crab, fish, coconut rice and vegetable stew and the whole family entertains you while you eat. Some people come away quite satisfied, but it's somewhat contrived and it's not unusual for the whole evening to be cancelled with no explanations. Expect to pay around KSh500.

Whispers Coffeeshop *(mains KSh240-450; open 9am-9pm)*, in the same building as the posh Baraka Gallery on the main street, is a great place for an upmarket meal, freshly baked cake or a real cappuccino. There's a lovely palm-shaded courtyard and simple meals such as pasta, fish and chips and pizza are available at lunch and dinner, even during Ramadan.

Petley's Inn and **New Lamu Palace Hotel** *(snacks KSh300-550, mains KSh650-1200)*

have gourmet restaurants serving a broader range of food than most restaurants on the island. Predictably, the menu focuses on upmarket seafood dishes, although you can get lobster for half these prices elsewhere on the waterfront. The big advantage here is that you can have a beer with your meal. Both restaurants are open during Ramadan and nonguests are welcome. There are also cheaper dishes such as burgers and spaghetti as well as the posh main courses.

Stone House Hotel *(meals KSh250-500; open noon-2pm & 7pm-9pm daily)* has a fine rooftop restaurant that catches the breeze. The wonderful panorama of the town and seafront is matched by the quality of the food. There are usually several choices for lunch or dinner and menus often feature crab and grilled barracuda. Only soft drinks are available.

Self-caterers should head to the main **market** next to the fort. The fruit and vegetables are cheap and fresh, and there's a slightly gory section where you can get meat and fish.

Shela There are several reasonably priced options in Shela, as well as a few good choices for a splurge.

Hidden away in the alleys behind the shorefront mosque is the tiny blue **Rangaleni Café**, which does the usual stew and *ugali* for around KSh60.

Stop Over Restaurant *(mains KSh150-500)*, on the beach at the northern end of Shela, is a good choice for breakfast, with a wide range of pancakes (KSh150 to KSh200) and omelettes (KSh150). Seafood and other main meals are cheap and well-prepared.

Bahari Guest House & Restaurant *(mains KSh250-500)*, on the foreshore between Kijani House and Peponi Hotel, is a nice terrace restaurant overlooking the water with a large menu. Lobster and chips here is just KSh500!

Barracuda Restaurant *(mains KSh350-500, lobster KSh800)*, at the Island Hotel, is ideal for a romantic night out. It's another rooftop place, looking out over the old village, and the seafood is excellent. Nonguests are welcome and prices are reasonable.

Barbecue Grill *(meals KSh500-1500)*, at Peponi Hotel, is a good place for a splurge, although it's not quite as grand as the prices suggest. The mainstay is seafood and the huge mudcrabs (KSh800) served here are recommended.

Shela's answer to Ali Hippy is **Ali Samosa** (☎ 32236; set dinners KSh1000), a former samosa-seller whose family has done rather well out of the tourist boom. The extremely good Swahili meals are served in a rooftop dining room in a house near the Shela Primary School. Ali can often be found at Peponi Hotel, or you can ask at the Shella Rest House, Shella Royal House and White House, which are run by Ali's brother.

Entertainment

Bars As a Muslim town, Lamu caters very poorly for drinkers. The three posh hotels – **Petley's Inn, New Lamu Palace Hotel** and **Peponi Hotel** – all have nice bars where you can sink a cold beer in stylish surroundings. In Lamu, Petley's has the edge as its terrace bar catches the breeze. Beers cost a steep KSh120.

Over at Shela beach, Peponi's bar resembles an English pub, and the terrace overlooking the water is a splendid place to watch the sunset, but the prices – KSh140 for a Tusker – may bring tears to the eyes.

During the day, the driftwood **Manda Beach Club** (Manda Island) is another great place for a beer or tropical cocktail. It's open all day and there are boat transfers from New Lamu Palace Hotel at 10.30am, 1.30pm and 5.30pm (KSh600). The last trip back leaves at 6pm.

Police Club, just south of the Riyadha mosque, is part of the Police Lines complex and serves warm beer.

Civil Servants' Club (admission KSh100), along the waterfront towards Shela village, is another place where you can get a drink.

There used to be a disco at Manda Beach, but it was closed down after protests by sleep-deprived locals. Today, the only option is the informal disco at the **Police Administration Club** (admission KSh50; open Fri & Sat night), south of town near the Muslim cemetery. There are cheap warm beers (KSh80) and a good-natured local crowd.

Cinema Lamu has two cinemas, both of them screening Bollywood blockbusters and English premiership soccer. Easiest to find is the **Zinj Cinema** on the main street at the southern end of town. Tickets cost a very reasonable KSh20.

Shopping

Along the seafront and in the suburbs surrounding Lamu town, you can see craftsmen carving traditional Lamu doors, furniture and window frames. Many now do a healthy sideline in picture frames, *bao* games, Quran stands, and traditional 'eyes' from Swahili dhows (see the boxed text 'Dhow Eyes' earlier), all of which make great souvenirs. For upmarket souvenirs from all over Africa, **Baraka Gallery,** on the main street, has a fine selection but stratospheric prices.

Getting There & Away

Air Three companies operate flights to/from Lamu. **Air Kenya** (☎ 33445; @ resvns@air kenya.com), at Baraka House, next to Whispers Cafe, offers daily afternoon flights between Lamu and Nairobi's Wilson Airport (US$135, 1¼ hours). There are also daily flights to Malindi (US$98, 35 minutes) and Kiwayu Island (US$65, 15 minutes).

Flamingo Airlines (☎ 33155) has an office on the seafront, near the Lamu Museum. There are daily afternoon flights between Lamu and the domestic terminal at Nairobi's Jomo Kenyatta International Airport for KSh7700. Fares come down dramatically if you can book more than a week in advance. Remember to reconfirm your flights at least a day before.

A much smaller operator is **Kas Kasi Aviation** (book through Allamanda Safaris ☎ 33285), next to Bush Gardens Restaurant on the waterfront. There are flights to Malindi on Wednesday and Sunday (US$60 one way), leaving at 8.25am and 5.25pm.

The airport at Lamu is on Manda Island and the ferry across the channel to Lamu costs KSh100. You will be met by 'guides' at the airport who will offer to carry your bags to the hotel of your choice for a small consideration (about KSh200). Many double as touts for places to stay in Lamu, so be cautious about accepting the first price you are quoted when you get to your hotel.

Bus Four bus companies operate between Mombasa, Malindi and Lamu: **Mombasa Raha** (Mombasa Liners), **TSS, Interstate 2000** and **Tawakal.**

There are booking offices for all these companies on the main street. The going rate to Malindi or Mombasa is KSh400 and all buses leave in a convoy at 7am (you'll need to be at the jetty at 6.30am for the boat to the mainland). It takes seven hours from Lamu to Malindi, and about 10 hours to Mombasa. Book early as demand is heavy.

Be aware of the dangers of *shiftas* (bandits) if you travel by bus between Lamu and Malindi (see Getting There & Away under Malindi earlier).

Getting Around

There are ferries (KSh40) between Lamu and the bus station on the mainland (near Mokowe). Boats leave when the buses arrive at Mokowe; in the reverse direction, they leave at around 6.30am to meet the departing buses. Ferries between the airstrip on Manda Island and Lamu cost KSh100 and leave about half an hour before the flights leave. Expect to pay KSh200 for a custom trip if you miss either of these boats.

Between Lamu village and Shela there are plenty of motorised dhows in either direction throughout the day until around sunset; these cost about KSh100 per person and leave when full. Alternatively, you can hire a whole boat for KSh250 to KSh300, or KSh400 after dark.

There are also regular ferries between Lamu and Paté Island (see Islands Around Lamu following).

Islands Around Lamu

The Islands of Manda, Paté and Kiwayu are even less developed than Lamu. The Swahili settlements of Takwa, Paté, Faza and Siyu (on Paté Island) date back to the 7th and 8th centuries and were once the major power-centres in the Lamu archipelago. In pre-Arab times, the islands were home to Bajun tribespeople, but that culture vanished almost entirely with the ascendancy of Arabic ideas.

Although affluent, the city-states existed in an almost perpetual state of war, fighting first against each other, then the Portuguese, then the Omani Arabs and finally the British, who were struggling to close down the slave trade. Swahili ruins can be found in numerous places on Paté and Manda Islands, most importantly at Takwa, which rivals Gede as one of the best-preserved sites on the coast.

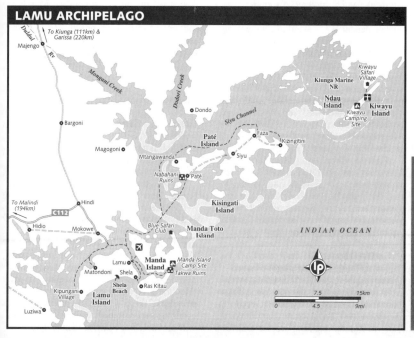

LAMU ARCHIPELAGO

Aside from ruins and traditional villages, there are wonderful beaches and some stunning coral reefs. Kiwayu, in the far north of the group, is part of the Kiunga Marine Reserve, and there are also fine reefs off tiny Manda Toto Island, west of Manda Island.

A popular activity while you're in Lamu is to take a dhow to one or more of these islands. You need a small group (six to eight people) to share costs, but you can easily put a group together by asking around the restaurants and budget hotels. There's a lot of competition and you'll be asked constantly by beach boys if you want to go on a trip, although these guys take a commission for bringing you to meet a particular boat captain.

The trips are usually great fun, but you should check out both the dhow and the crew before committing yourself. Make sure you know exactly how much you'll be paying and what that will include, to avoid misunderstandings and overcharging. Don't hand over any money until the day of departure except, perhaps, a small advance (say KSh500 per person) for food. On long trips, it's probably best to organise your own beer, soft drinks and bottled water supplies.

Dhows without an outboard motor are entirely dependent on wind to get them anywhere, although poling – or even pushing – the boat is fairly common along narrow creeks and channels. It's common to get becalmed or stuck on sand banks, so you'll just have to patient and wait until the wind picks up or the tide rises to move on. As the captain will certainly tell you, it's in God's hands. With this in mind, it's probably unwise to go on a long trip if you have a flight or other appointment to meet.

Likewise, dhows are dependent on the tides. You can't sail up creeks if the tide is out and there's not enough water to float the boat. This will be the main factor determining departure and return times (see the boxed text 'Dhows' earlier in this chapter for more information about this craft).

MANDA ISLAND

This is the easiest island to get to since it's just across the channel from Lamu. Almost everyone takes a half-day trip to the Takwa ruins at the head of the creek that almost bisects the island. The average cost of taking a dhow to Manda Island is around KSh1500

shared by however many people you can put together. Sometimes (but not always) this includes a barbecued fresh fish lunch, so settle this issue before you leave. You can also get there by motor launch, which isn't as romantic but will give you a little more time at the site before the tide gets too low for boats to negotiate the creek.

The extensive **Takwa ruins** (*adult/child KSh200/100*) are the remains of an old Swahili city that flourished between the 15th and 17th centuries. At its peak, there were at least 2500 people here, but the town was inexplicably abandoned in the 17th century and the people moved to Shela. The site is maintained by the National Museums of Kenya and the ruins include the remains of about 100 limestone and coral houses, all aligned towards Mecca.

The largest structure here is the **Jamaa mosque** (*Jamaa* means 'Friday'), which is well preserved and includes an unusual pillar atop the *mihrab*. Also here is a tomb dating from 1683 (1094 by the Islamic calendar). The settlement is surrounded by the remains of a wall and huge baobab trees dot the site.

Just off the northeast coast of Manda is **Manda Toto Island**, which offers some of the best snorkelling possibilities in the archipelago. The only way to get here is by dhow and you need a full day to get there and back from Lamu. Boat owners typically charge around KSh700 per person if there's a group of four or more, and masks and snorkels are provided.

Places to Stay

The only place to stay is the **camp site** adjacent to Takwa, but few people stay because facilities are minimal. Contact the Lamu Museum for bookings and information.

On the other side of the island is the **Blue Safari Club** (*in Nairobi ☎ 02-890184, fax 890096; ✉ info@bluesafariclub.com*), which is a US$500-a-night hideaway.

Getting There & Away

The trip across to Manda from Lamu takes about 1½ hours and can only be done at high tide because the inlet is too shallow at low tide. You may well have to wade up the final stretch, so wear shorts. Since you have to catch the outgoing tide, your time at the site will probably not be more than an hour.

Agama acquires mango peel, the Rift Valley

Njemps fisherman, Lake Baringo

White rhino strolls along a shore lined by flamingos, Lake Nakuru National Park

Hot springs, Lake Bogoria

Giant cactus tree, near Lake Naivasha

Waterfall, near Chogoria

Baobab Tree, Meru National Park, Central Highlands

Trekking in the higher reaches, Mt Kenya

View to the north from Point Lenana, Mt Kenya

Coffee plant

It's possible to walk to the Takwa ruins from the airstrip but it's around 3km and the path isn't clear. A boat transfer to the airport jetty costs KSh200.

Both Peponi Hotel and Kijani House in Shela offer tours to Takwa for around KSh1200 per person.

PATÉ ISLAND

There are a number of historical sites on Paté Island including Paté town, Siyu, Mtangawanda and Faza. All are still inhabited – mainly by fishers and mangrove-pole cutters – but very little effort has been put into preserving or clearing the remains of these once-powerful, Swahili city-states. The only foreigners who come to this island are those on dhow trips and the occasional archaeologist, so you can expect to be a novelty and treated with friendly curiosity, especially by the local children. Mosquitoes are a real pest and you're going to need insect repellent. Mosquito coils are for sale in the island's shops.

Accommodation and food on the island are easy to arrange with local families or there's the simple **Twaha Guest House** *(doubles KSh400)* in Paté village, plus one or two simple **restaurants** offering basic meals and tea. Paté village resembles a down-at-heel Lamu, but the **Nabahani ruins**, just outside town, are interesting, though they've never been seriously excavated or cleared.

Getting There & Away

A motor launch usually leaves Lamu Saturday to Thursday for Mtangawanda (about two hours), from where it's about an hour's walk to Paté town along a narrow footpath through thick bush and across tidal flats.

Boats continue around to Faza (about another two hours), also stopping at the mouth of the channel to Siyu, where small boats transfer passengers to shore. From Lamu the fare is KSh50 to Mtangawanda; boats leave from the jetty in front of the fort and times depend on the tides. If you're returning from Paté, ask locally to make sure the boat will be calling at Mtangawanda on the return trip from Faza to Lamu. If not, you may have to wait an extra day.

Siyu

Founded in the 15th century, Siyu was famous as a centre of Islamic scholarship and crafts. In its heyday (between the 17th and 19th centuries) it boasted some 30,000 inhabitants and was the largest settlement on the island. However, today less than 4000 people live here and there are few signs of its former cultural and religious influence.

The village is dominated by the ruins of a **huge fort**, which sits dramatically on the waterfront. Despite this grand structure, Siyu's demise came in 1847 when it was occupied by the Sultan of Zanzibar's troops. The fort has been well restored and there are some interesting Swahili relics inside.

The modern village displays little of Siyu's former glory and consists of simple mud-walled and *makuti*-roofed houses.

Getting There & Away The boat from Mtangawanda to Faza stops at the mouth of the mangrove-lined channel leading up to Siyu, where small canoes transfer passengers to the village. From Lamu the fare is KSh80. This service isn't always available, so you may have to walk from Paté or Faza.

From Paté it's about 8km to Siyu along a dirt track through the bush. The first part is tricky since there are turn-offs that are easy to miss so it's a good idea to take a guide with you as far as the tidal inlet (the boat captain can help to arrange this). From here on it's easy as the path bears left and then continues straight through to Siyu.

Faza

The biggest settlement on Paté Island, Faza is home to the district headquarters. The town has a chequered history, being almost totally destroyed by Paté in the 13th century and then again in the 16th century by the Portuguese in 1586. It was subsequently re-established and switched its allegiances to the Portuguese during their attempts to subdue Paté in the 17th century. With the demise of slavery, Faza faded away, but it's new status as an administrative centre is breathing some life back into the place.

The modern town is quite extensive and includes a post office, telephone exchange, the district headquarters, a simple restaurant, general stores and two guesthouses. The only historical relic is the ruined **Kunjanja Mosque** on the creek next to the district headquarters. Among the rubble is a beautifully carved *mihrab* and some fine Arabic inscriptions. Outside town is the tomb of **Amir Hamad**, commander of the Sultan of Zanzibar's forces, who was killed here in 1844 while campaigning against Siyu and Paté.

Places to Stay & Eat The two guesthouses – **Lamu House** and **Shela House** – are essentially family residences, but they can provide meals and a bedroom if you need somewhere to stay. The price is negotiable (expect to pay around KSh200 per person) and the families are very friendly.

The simple restaurant offers bean stews, tea and *mandazi* for just a couple of dozen shillings and is a popular meeting place for the men of the town.

Getting There & Away The inlet leading up to Faza from the main channel is deep enough at high tide to allow the passage of dhows and motor launches (although at low tide you'll have to walk in over the mud and sandbanks from the main channel).

The same motor launch that calls at Mtangawanda and Siyu finishes its journey at Faza, charging KSh150 from Lamu (Saturday to Thursday, four hours). Boats usually leave in the morning in either direction, but the exact ferry times depend on the tides so you should ask around the day before you leave.

Getting to Siyu from Faza involves a two-hour walk through *shambas* (small farms) and thick bush along an earth track. The path is confusing so it may be best to come with a guide from Faza – volunteers are sure to approach you.

KIWAYU ISLAND

At the far northeast of the Lamu archipelago, Kiwayu Island is part of the Kiunga Marine National Reserve.

It acquired a reputation some years ago as an exclusive hideaway for rock stars and other glitterati, but these types hang around at the luxury resort at the far end of the island and it's unlikely you'll be rubbing shoulders with them.

The main reason for coming here is to explore the coral reefs off the eastern side of the island, rated as some of the best along the Kenyan coast. For our money, the reefs at Watamu and Manda Toto Island are better, but the dhow trip here is still highly recommended.

The village on the western side of the island where the dhows drop anchor is quite small but it does have a general store with a few basics.

Places to Stay & Eat

Unless you can stretch to US$500 per night, the only place to stay is the **Kiwayu Camping Site** *(camping per person KSh150, bandas from KSh600)* run by a man named Qasim. The bandas are a bit run down but clean sheets, pillows and mattresses are provided as well as a kerosene lantern. There are basic toilet and saltwater shower facilities, and a covered dining and cooking area for campers and banda dwellers.

If money is no object, you could do worse than stay at the exclusive **Kiwayu Safari Village** *(☎ 02-604053, fax 604050; e safaris@chelipeacock.co.ke; doubles US$318-550)*; it's a splendid getaway, although you pay a premium for the privacy and isolation.

Getting There & Away

The most interesting way to get to Kiwayu is by dhow. The island usually forms part of a three- or five-day dhow trip from Lamu, usually with stops along the way. If there's sufficient wind, the return trip to Kiwayu from Lamu takes three days and two nights. Bank on around KSh1000 per person, based on a group of five or more.

High fliers tend to arrive by air. **Air Kenya** flies from Manda airstrip to Kiwayu (US$65 one way, 15 minutes, daily). These flights from Manda are usually add-ons to flights that originate from Mombasa or Nairobi.

THE COAST

The Rift Valley

What is known as the Rift Valley in Kenya is part of the Afro-Arabian rift system that stretches 6000km from the Dead Sea in the Middle East to Mozambique in southern Africa, passing through the Red Sea then Ethiopia, Kenya, Tanzania and Malawi. A western branch forms a string of lakes in the centre of the continent, including Albert and Edward on the Uganda–Congo (Zaïre) border, Kivu on the Congo (Zaïre)–Rwanda border, and Tanganyika on the Tanzania–Congo (Zaïre) border, which joins the main system at the northern tip of Lake Malawi.

In Kenya, the Rift Valley can be traced through Lake Turkana, the Cherangani Hills and lakes Baringo, Bogoria, Nakuru, El-menteita, Naivasha and Magadi. Together these areas make up some of Kenya's most interesting places to visit, from semidesert in the north to the lush hills in the west and the vast Maasai plains in the south before extending into Tanzania. Following this trail, you'll find a range of scenery and a profusion of birdlife and mammals that you're unlikely to come across anywhere else in the world. This chapter covers the Rift Valley attractions between Nairobi and Lake Baringo; lakes Magadi and Turkana are covered in the Around Nairobi and Northern Kenya chapters, respectively.

The central lakes and volcanoes covered in this chapter are the most accessible points of the Rift Valley system in Kenya and attract a huge number of tourists each year. The lakes are a naturalist's dream and a visit to at least one is a must; the dramatic volcanic landscapes around them provide the perfect backdrop for a classic African safari. This is an area not to be missed.

Soda Lakes

Because the shoulders of the Rift slope directly away from the valley, the drainage system in the valley is generally poor. In Kenya this has resulted in the formation of shallow lakes along the valley floor, some of which have no outlet. Owing to high evaporation the waters have become extremely concentrated, and the high alkalinity from the area's volcanic deposits provides the perfect environment for microscopic blue-green algae, which is food for tiny crustaceans and

Highlights

- Climbing the extinct volcanoes of Mt Longonot and Mt Suswa for incredible views from the crater rim
- Cycling or walking through the rugged landscapes of Hell's Gate National Park
- Discovering the prehistoric heritage of the region around Nakuru
- Comparing flamingos at the great soda lakes of Nakuru and Bogoria
- Snapping fish eagles in action at Lake Baringo

National Parks & Reserves: Hell's Gate National Park, Longonot National Park, Lake Nakuru National Park, Lake Bogoria National Reserve

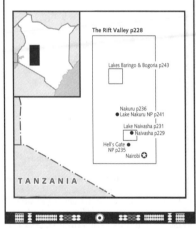

insect larvae. These in turn are eaten by certain species of soda-resistant fish.

The water of these soda lakes in Kenya (Bogoria, Nakuru, Elmenteita and Magadi) may feel strangely soapy to the touch and often doesn't smell too pleasant. However, the abundant algae, insect larvae, crustaceans and fish make these lakes a paradise for many species of water bird, which flock here in their millions.

Foremost among the birds is the deep-pink-coloured lesser flamingo that feeds on the blue-green algae. Also numerous are various species of duck, pelican, cormorant

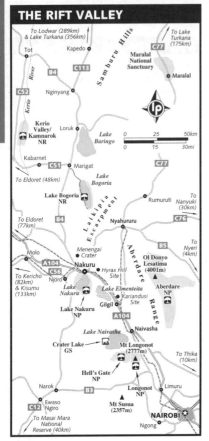

THE RIFT VALLEY

semi-active volcanoes; according to local legend, Mt Longonot erupted as recently as 1860! This continuing activity supports a considerable number of hot springs, as well as providing ideal conditions for geothermal power plants, which are becoming increasingly important for Kenya's energy supply.

Viewpoints

The stunning views of the escarpments of the Rift Valley can be seen from the roads that descend into the valley from just past Limuru. A number of viewpoints signposted along these roads are generally the safest places to stop. See Limuru in the Around Nairobi chapter for more details.

Getting There & Around

It's possible to take public transport to all of the Rift Valley lakes (and lakes Elmenteita, Baringo and to a lesser extent Bogoria can be explored on foot), but you'll need a vehicle to get inside Lake Nakuru National Park. If you want to explore the whole of the Kenyan Rift Valley lakes area it's a good idea to either join a tour group or get a group together and hire a vehicle.

LONGONOT NATIONAL PARK

For a different perspective on the Rift Valley, climbing to the rim of Mt Longonot (2777m), protected as a **national park** *(adult/child US$15/5)* 57km northwest of Nairobi, is hard to beat and offers some excellent views. The mountain is a fairly young, dormant volcano that retains the typical shape of these mountains, although it's far from a perfect cone.

Security has apparently improved in the park with increasing visitor numbers, but it is still worth taking a ranger with you, at least as far as the crater rim. The scramble up to the rim takes about 45 minutes from the parking area, and a further 2½ to three hours is needed to do a full circuit. If you're feeling game, there's a track leading down inside the crater to the bottom, although again it's worth getting a ranger to escort you.

The nearest roofed accommodation to the park is **Longonot Ranch** *(book through Safaris Unlimited ☎ 02-891168;* @ *safunlim@africa online.co.ke; singles/doubles full board US$250/ 350)*, a lovely old-style farmhouse reached from Moi South Lake Rd at Lake Naivasha. You can **camp** at the ranger station at the foot of the mountain; otherwise Naivasha is

and stork. The highest concentrations of these birds are found where food is most abundant, and this varies from year to year and lake to lake. Lake Nakuru, for instance, is currently looking very healthy but it sometimes almost dries up, forcing the birds to migrate to other soda lakes in the area.

Volcanoes

The other major feature of the Rift Valley here is its string of volcanic peaks and craters. Their eruptions not only provided the fertile soils that make this area such good agricultural land, but also formed the dramatic and varied landscape, which must rate among the most spectacular sectors of the entire Rift.

While most are now extinct, the valley still contains no fewer than thirty active or perhaps the best bet for cheap hotels. If you are on a day trip, you can leave your gear at the park office or the police station.

Getting There & Away

If you don't have your own transport it's easiest to take a matatu from Nairobi or Naivasha and get out at the Longonot National Park turn-off, just past the railway crossing. From there it is a 7km walk to the trailhead. Cars can be left safely at the parking area here.

MT SUSWA

Much less frequented than Longonot but arguably a far more interesting climb, this unique double-cratered volcano is well worth the effort it takes to get there. The steep outer crater protects a second inner crater, the rim of which peaks at 2357m and just begs to be trekked. There is also a network of apparently unexplored caves on the east side of the mountain.

To get here, turn left off the B3 Nairobi-Narok road and literally just head for the hill. The land here is owned by the local Maasai, who will show you the way around and usually allow you to camp (all for a fee, of course, of up to KSh300 per person). You'll need a 4WD to tackle the outer crater, although it's easy going after that.

NAIVASHA
☎ 0311

Sitting on the main road from Nairobi to Nakuru, Naivasha is essentially a service centre for the surrounding agricultural district. It offers little of interest to the traveller, although many do pass through here on the way to or from Mt Longonot, Hell's Gate National Park or Nakuru.

If you're going directly from Nairobi to Nakuru, the main road bypasses the town entirely.

The main point of stopping here is to load up with supplies before heading down to Lake Naivasha itself, as there are very limited stocks in the *dukas* (small shops) along the lakeshore road. However, it can also make a handy base for exploring Longonot and Hell's Gate if you don't want to stay in the parks.

Everything in town is in easy walking distance, and there is a good range of facilities. The **Barclays Bank** and **Kenya Commercial Bank** on Moi Ave keep normal Kenyan

PLACES TO STAY
1 Wambuku Inn
2 Four Seasons Boarding & Lodging
3 Sam's Holiday Inn; Rugia Communications
6 Ken-Vash Hotel
11 Kafico Lodge; Dancing Spoons Hotel
16 La Belle Inn
19 Othaya Annexe Hotel
22 Naivasha Silver Hotel; Jolly Cafe

PLACES TO EAT
8 Walk In Cafe
15 Jim's Corner Dishes
24 Bright Moon Chinese Restaurant

OTHER
4 Bus & Matatu Stand
5 Post Office
7 Bars & Inn's Nightclub
9 Supermarket
10 PolyClinic Hospital
12 Hindu Temple
13 Kenya Commercial Bank
14 Barclays Bank (ATM)
17 Supermarket
18 Beatman Club Sweat
20 Nairobi Matatu Booking Office & Local Matatus
21 Wagi Bureau
23 Matatus to Kongoni (Moi South Lake Rd)

banking hours; Barclays has an ATM. **Wagi Bureau** (Kenyatta Ave), which charges KSh4 per minute, and **Rugia Communications** (Mbaria Kaniu Rd), which charges KSh5 per minute, offer Internet services.

Places to Stay – Budget & Mid-Range

Naivasha has a good selection of no-frills budget hotels. Mid-range accommodation is a bit pricier than average, but secure parking comes as standard and you seem to get more furniture for your money here.

Four Seasons Boarding & Lodging (Mbaria Kaniu Rd; singles/doubles KSh130/200) is the cheapest place in town, but you really get what you pay for. Just up the road, opposite the bus stand, **Sam's Holiday Inn** (☎ 20810;

singles/doubles with bathroom KSh250/400) is considerably nicer.

Most other cheap dives can be found along Kariuki Chotara Rd; **Othaya Annexe Hotel** (☎ 0733-762969; singles with bathroom KSh300) is one of the better options here. It's getting a bit shabby on the outside but the rooms (no doubles) are pretty clean. The hotel has a balcony bar, a butchery, a bakery and a café downstairs.

Kafico Lodge (☎ 21344; Biashara Rd; singles/doubles with bathroom KSh300/500) is a large but unspectacular place above the Dancing Spoons Hotel. Using the secure parking gets your car washed for free!

Naivasha Silver Hotel (☎ 20580; Kenyatta Ave; singles/doubles with bathroom KSh400/600) was being redecorated at the time of research and looks like holding its own as the best mid-range place in town. Rooms have mosquito nets, hot water and big new double beds; there's an upstairs bar and restaurant.

Wambuku Inn (☎ 30287; Moi Ave; singles/doubles KSh700/1200) is a fairly new place and a reasonable option at this price, although the beds are slightly narrow and you don't get toilet seats.

Places to Stay – Top End

La Belle Inn (☎ 21007; Moi Ave; singles/doubles KSh1500/1900) is a classic colonial-style place, providing a popular rendezvous for locals and a convenient meal stop for safari companies. Rooms are generally nice, but some are better than others and you might expect more facilities for the price. There's a guarded car park, a restaurant and several bars; major credit cards are accepted.

Ken-Vash Hotel (☎ 30049; off Moi Ave; singles/doubles KSh1200/1800) is a large tourist-class place with less character than La Belle but slightly better-equipped rooms and thick shag carpets. It's not always the friendliest of places, but probably deserves more custom than it currently seems to get.

Lakeside Tourist Lodge (☎ 20856; Moi Ave; singles/doubles KSh1600/2000) is the latest newcomer to this category, but is so smart and clean that it ends up being entirely characterless – even the balconies only have views of a truck park.

Places to Eat

There are plenty of butcheries and small, cheap eating places around Naivasha. **Danc-ing Spoons Hotel** (Biashara Rd), **Walk In Cafe** (Kariuki Chotara Rd), **Jim's Corner Dishes** (Station Lane) and the delightfully pink **Jolly Cafe** (Kenyatta Ave) all serve standard main dishes for under KSh200.

Almost all the hotels here have reasonable restaurants, but for cuisine worthy of the name your only real option is **La Belle Inn** (meals from KSh300); the outdoor terrace is a great place for a drink or a meal, despite the occasional clouds of dust from the road. If you fancy something a bit different, the **Bright Moon Chinese Restaurant** (Moi Ave) is the only place offering a change in cuisine for kilometres.

There's a cluster of cheap bars on Kariuki Chokota Rd, although you'd have to be pretty brave to venture into most of them! **Inn's Nightclub** and the pleasant-sounding **Beatman Club Sweat** provide the local disco action.

Getting There & Away

Bus & Matatu The main bus and matatu station is off Mbaria Kaniu Rd, close to the municipal market. There are frequent buses and matatus leaving for Nairobi (KSh100, one hour), Nakuru (KSh100, one hour), Nyahururu (KSh150, 1½ hours), Thika (KSh150, 1½ hours) and all points west. Note that some matatus to Nairobi and all of those heading to Kongoni via Fisherman's Camp (KSh60, 45 minutes) leave from the stands on Kenyatta Ave.

LAKE NAIVASHA
☎ 0311

The area around Naivasha was one of the first settled by *wazungu* (whites) and was a favourite haunt of the decadent Happy Valley set in the 1930s. Along with Karen, near Nairobi, it's now probably the largest remaining settler and expat community in Kenya, and can have a distinctly resort-like feel to it in the high season, when it essentially becomes the Kenyan St Tropez!

The lake's level has risen and fallen over the years, as half-submerged fencing posts indicate. Early in the 1890s it dried up almost completely, but over the next 20 years it rose a phenomenal 15m and inundated a far larger area than it presently occupies. Recurring droughts in recent years have also affected the lake. It currently covers about 170 sq km and is home to an incredible variety of bird species, including the African fish eagle, which has experienced problems because of pollution.

Naivasha is a freshwater lake and its ecology is quite different from that of the Rift Valley's predominantly soda lakes. Since the lake water can be used for irrigation purposes, the surrounding countryside is a major production area for flowers, fresh fruit and vegetables, as well as beef cattle for domestic consumption and export. There's even a vineyard on the eastern shore. The flower market has become a major industry in the Naivasha area, as all the shade houses indicate. Flowers picked here in the early morning can be at flower auctions in the Netherlands the same day and sell for little more than half the price of those grown in Europe.

However, the success of such businesses is leading to the death of the very source of their creation. The ecology of the lake has been interfered with on a number of occasions, notably with the introduction of fish for sports fishing, commercial fish such as Nile perch, crayfish, the South American coypu (an aquatic rodent that initially escaped from a fur farm) and various aquatic plants, including the dreaded water hyacinth. The biggest threat has been from pesticide and fertiliser use in the area, which has made the level of pollutants in the lake dangerously high and seriously affected the fish eagles' breeding cycle.

For these reasons Naivasha has been a focus of conservation efforts in Kenya, and in 1995 the Lake Naivasha Riparian Association was formed to try and redress the balance by educating the estimated 300,000 people dependent on the lake about the environmental issues involved. As so much of the land is privately owned, the Elsamere Conservation Centre and other organisations are also trying to establish a code of conduct among the local growers that will maintain the biodiversity of the lake. The results are promising, but so far improvement has been slow, and further drops in the water level are predicted for the next 15 to 20 years.

Things to See & Do
On the western side of Lake Naivasha, north of the village of Kongoni, is **Crater Lake Game Sanctuary** *(admission KSh100)*, a small

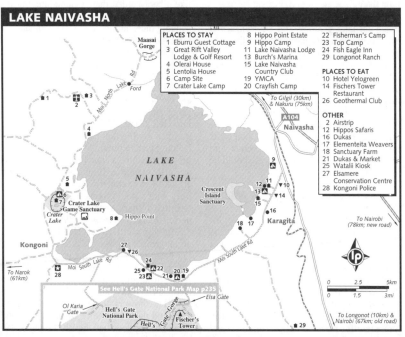

LAKE NAIVASHA

PLACES TO STAY	8 Hippo Point Estate	22 Fisherman's Camp
1 Eburru Guest Cottage	9 Hippo Camp	23 Top Camp
3 Great Rift Valley	11 Lake Naivasha Lodge	24 Fish Eagle Inn
Lodge & Golf Resort	13 Burch's Marina	29 Longonot Ranch
4 Olerai House	15 Lake Naivasha	
5 Lentolia House	Country Club	PLACES TO EAT
6 Camp Site	19 YMCA	10 Hotel Yelogreen
7 Crater Lake Camp	20 Crayfish Camp	14 Fischers Tower Restaurant
		26 Geothermal Club

OTHER
2 Airstrip
12 Hippos Safaris
16 Dukas
17 Elementeita Weavers
18 Sanctuary Farm
21 Dukas & Market
25 Watalii Kiosk
27 Elsamere Conservation Centre
28 Kongoni Police

Maasai Gorge

Moi North Lake Rd
Ford

To Gilgil (30km) & Nakuru (75km)

A104

Naivasha

LAKE NAIVASHA

Crater Lake Game Sanctuary

Crater Lake

Hippo Point

Crescent Island Sanctuary

Karagita

To Nairobi (78km; new road)

Kongoni

Moi South Lake Rd

To Narok (61km)

Moi South Lake Rd

See Hell's Gate National Park Map p235

Ol Karia Gate

Hell's Gate National Park

Elsa Gate

Hell's Gate Gorge

Fischer's Tower

To Longonot (10km) & Nairobi (67km; old road)

0   2.5   5km
0   1.5   3mi

park set around a beautiful volcanic crater. An excellent nature trail leads through the lush vegetation around the crater (a two-hour walk) and there is plenty of wildlife to see – over 150 species of bird have been spotted in this small area. There is a luxury lodge with a pleasant bar and restaurant by the crater lake itself and there's a camp site in the reserve (see Places to Stay following).

On the eastern side of the lake is **Crescent Island** (adult/child US$10/6), primarily a bird sanctuary you can visit by boat or car.

Just south of the lake is Hell's Gate National Park (see later in this chapter).

Elsamere Conservation Centre

A couple of kilometres past Fisherman's Camp on Moi South Lake Rd you'll find **Elsamere Conservation Centre** (☎ 21055, fax 21074; e elsa@africaonline.co.ke; admission KSh400; open 3pm-6pm daily), the former home of the late Joy Adamson of Born Free fame. She bought the house in 1967 with the view that she and her husband, George, might retire there. Adamson did much of her writing from Elsamere right up until her murder in 1980, although George never spent much time there.

The site is now a conservation centre focused on lake ecology and environmental awareness programs and is open to the public. The entrance fee includes afternoon tea on the lawn (with a chance to see the eastern black-and-white colobus monkeys), a visit to the memorial room and a showing of The Joy Adamson Story.

The only way to visit outside these hours is to sleep here (see Places to Stay following) or to book in for a meal – lunch costs KSh650/800 at weekdays/weekends and dinner is KSh1000. All bookings should be made in advance.

Places to Stay – Budget & Mid Range

Lake Naivasha is a very popular stopover for campers and overland companies, and the good range of budget accommodation reflects this.

Fisherman's Camp (☎ 30088; camping per person KSh200, dorm beds KSh300, bandas per person KSh800) on the southern shore of the lake is a perennial favourite and is usually busy, especially at weekends. You can hire a tent for KSh200 per person; there are

also some bandas with cooking facilities and two dorms. Nonguests pay a KSh100 entry fee, and meals cost around KSh250. You can also rent boats and bicycles here (see Getting Around later).

It's a huge, pleasant site but notoriously noisy, although there's usually enough room to get away from the worst of it. The bar and restaurant stay open until late, and it's worth camping well away from overland trucks – the sign saying 'no loud music allowed' is clearly some kind of joke! The hippos that once wandered around the camp site at night are now restricted to certain sections of grass by an electric fence, but there's still a real chance of seeing one of these great beasts grazing at night.

Top Camp (☎ 30276; camping KSh250, bandas KSh1000/1800), perched up the hill on the other side of the road, is run by the same company but is much smaller and quieter. The two- and four-bed bandas are unfancy but reasonable, and the views are superb.

Crayfish Camp (☎ 20239; e craycamp@ africaonline.co.ke; camping per person KSh150, doubles KSh2500, bandas per person KSh500), following Fisherman's lead, can seem more like a beer garden than a camp site, but it's not a bad option. The pricey new rooms are suitably nice, and the more basic bandas are OK; there's a restaurant and two bars, tent and bedding hire, pool tables, and kitchen facilities. Internet access is also available.

YMCA (☎ 0733-989493; camping per person KSh150, dorm beds KSh150-250, bandas per person KSh300-350) has a reasonable camp site, conveniently situated for walks into Hell's Gate. There are two dorms and a number of Spartan bandas; firewood and bedding can be provided for a small charge, or you can hire a tent for KSh200. Meals are also available (lunch KSh150, dinner KSh200). It's popular with Kenyans and gets busy with school groups during holidays.

Burch's Marina (☎ 21010; camping per person KSh200, rondavels KSh600, cottages KSh1500), about 1km past Hotel Yelogreen, is an idiosyncratic place ideal for those fleeing the noise of Fisherman's Camp and its ilk. There's a store selling basic provisions and a range of accommodation options here: the camp site is pleasant and well-shaded, with a well, hot showers and a communal cooking area, and there's a choice of basic twin-bed rondavels or four-bed family cottages (no bedding supplied). It can get pretty busy here, especially on Tuesdays and at weekends, so advance booking is mandatory.

Hippo Camp (*☎ 20639; camping US$5, single/double tents KSh600/800*), run by KWS, is a reasonable site with some slightly shabby permanent tents. The pricing policy seems a bit erratic and you may have to pay to get down to the lake from here.

Crater Lake Game Sanctuary (*☎ 20613; camping per person KSh150*) has a well-equipped camp site with running water (hot showers on request), a barbecue, eating area and decent toilets. Campers can use Crater Lake Camp's restaurant and bar (see Places to Stay – Top End), but if you want meals you should book in advance.

Fish Eagle Inn (*☎ 21158; e fish@africaon line.co.ke; camping per person KSh200, dorm beds KSh400, singles/doubles KSh1800/3200*), next to Fisherman's Camp, has some top-end facilities (sauna, pool, satellite TV etc), but the prices for even the smallest rooms would make Treetops blush. If you can afford to spring for them, the Jumbo House rooms are the only ones vaguely worth the money; you can take a dorm bed or camp for a rather more modest fee.

If you have your own transport, there are a couple of low-key self-catering places in the Green Park Development, near the airstrip. **Eburru Guest Cottage** (*book through Let's Go Travel ☎ 02-340331; e info@letsgosafari.com; singles/doubles KSh800/1200*) is probably the best value: two small buildings close to the main house contain two twin rooms, a lounge and kitchen. As you would expect at 2133m, the views across the lake to the Aberdares are quite stunning and zebras, elands, dik diks and gazelles are all reasonably common.

Places to Stay – Top End

Lake Naivasha Lodge (*☎ 20611, in Nairobi ☎ 02-224998, fax 230962; camping US$8, singles/doubles half board US$75/100 in high season*) is a very pleasant place virtually next door to Lake Naivasha Country Club, with spacious cottage-style rooms; prices were expected to go up for 2003. The only drawback here is the lack of lake frontage.

Elsamere Conservation Centre (*☎ 21055; e elsa@africaonline.co.ke; singles/doubles full board US$85/140*) offers very pleasant accommodation (full board only) in a great setting, and the staff are all very friendly. The

centre occasionally runs escorted trips to Hell's Gate and Mt Longonot. There is no bar here, but guests can bring their own booze.

The cumbersomely named **Great Rift Valley Lodge & Golf Resort** (*☎ 50048, in Nairobi 02-74888; e info@heritage-east africa.com; singles/doubles full board US$133/180 in low season, US$222/300 in high season*) is a good, new place on the edge of the Green Park development. The views are fantastic and the accommodation 'towers' sensitively designed, with a very high standard of decor and facilities. Cottages set away from the main site can also be rented on a self-catering basis; a wide range of activities is on offer for all guests.

Lake Naivasha Country Club (*☎ 21004, Nairobi ☎ 02-540780, fax 21161; e block naivasha@africaonline.co.ke; singles/doubles half board US$111/132 in low season, US$144/174 in high season*), a Block Hotels property, has a beautiful, expansive garden with lake access, a kids' playground, a pool and all the other facilities you'd expect. Excursions, bicycles and boat trips can all be arranged here; there is a daily membership charge of KSh100 for nonguests.

Crater Lake Camp (*☎ 20613; singles/doubles full board US$200/300 in low season, US$260/390 in high season*) is a luxury tented camp set among the trees and vegetation on the lakeshore. The food is good, the service excellent and you can explore the whole of the sanctuary on foot (maps are provided). Bookings can also be made through Let's Go Travel. The **restaurant** (*lunch KSh750, dinner KSh850*) and bar down by the lake are open all day.

There are a number of expensive home-stays, lodges and private houses on Moi North Lake Rd, which can be fascinating places to stay if you have the money. The following two places can be booked through **Let's Go Travel** (*02-340331; e info@letsgo safari.com*) in Nairobi.

Lentolia House (*☎ 0733-722835; exclusive use KSh15,000*) is a huge Edwardian-style house with 48 hectares of land down by the lakeshore. It is currently let on a self-catering basis (catered options are being planned) and sleeps 14, making it quite cost-effective for large groups.

Olerai House (*singles/doubles all-inclusive US$375/670*) is further down the lake road. There are just five rooms in this beautiful place, all of which have an Italian and French flavour.

For the ultimate in exclusivity, however, the two houses on the **Hippo Point Estate** are absolutely the *dernier cri* – at US$1000 a double, they don't come much fancier than this!

Places to Eat

If you're not eating at the hotels or camp sites listed earlier, head to the **Geothermal Club** *(meals KSh100-200)*, just east of Elsamere. Set in a beautiful spot looking down over the lake about 45 minutes' walk from Fisherman's Camp, this relaxed place caters for employees of the KenGen thermal power plant but will happily serve visitors. Cold beer (KSh65) is always available and there's a pool (KSh100) and a jetty onto the lake.

Hotel Yelogreen and **Fischers Tower Restaurant** are half-decent options for cheap meals if you're on the eastern side of the lake.

Shopping

There are a number of craft *dukas* and galleries off Moi South Lake Rd. **Elmenteita Weavers** *(open 9am-5.30pm daily)* is the pick of the bunch and sells hand-woven rugs, carpets, *kangas* (printed cotton wraparounds), baskets and the like. Quality is high and prices reflect this, but it's worth a look to see the weavers working.

Getting There & Away

Frequent matatus (KSh60) run along Moi South Lake Rd between Naivasha town and Kongoni on the western side of the lake, passing the turn-offs to Hell's Gate National Park and Fisherman's Camp.

From Kongoni it's 5km to Crater Lake. Those walking from here are advised to ask for an escort to the sanctuary as there have been muggings in the past.

There is one daily matatu along Moi North Lake Rd, leaving from the Total petrol station in Naivasha around 3pm. Returning to town you'll need to be on the road by about 7am, otherwise it's a long dusty walk.

Getting Around

Most of the lodges and camp sites listed earlier hire motorboats for trips on the lake; prices start around KSh2000 per hour at Hip-

pos Camp on Moi South Lake Rd, going up to US$60 per hour at Lake Naivasha Lodge. Boats from Fisherman's Camp (KSh2400 per hour) or Elsamere Conservation Centre (KSh2500 per hour) are generally reliable. Rowing boats (KSh200 per hour) are also available from Fisherman's Camp.

For trips to Crescent Island it's much cheaper to hire a boat from Burch's Marina or Lake Naivasha Country Club (KSh800 per person), as they are closer to the island. Watch out for the hippos! Alternatively, you can get there by land: the owner of Sanctuary Farm allows vehicles to enter the farm and drive across the causeway for a small fee. The farm is also a good place for horse riding.

Mountain bikes can also be hired from most sites; Fisherman's Camp and Fish Eagle Inn both charge KSh500 per day. You can get cheaper rates at various little places signposted off Moi South Lake Rd, such as Watalii Kiosk, but check the contraptions carefully before paying!

HELL'S GATE NATIONAL PARK

This dusty but dramatic Rift Valley park *(adult/child or student US$15/5)* is one of only two lowland parks that you can walk or cycle through without a ranger or guide (the other is Saiwa Swamp National Park near Kitale). It's well worth considering ditching your vehicle at the gate, as the looming cliffs and the Hell's Gate gorge are spectacular and the best bits are often inaccessible by road.

The park is home to a wide variety of bird and animal life. Zebras, Thomson's gazelles and baboons are all common, and you may even encounter the occasional cheetah, leopard or ostrich. Special interest is taken in birds of prey here and efforts are being made by the Kenya Wildlife Service (KWS), supported by the Naivasha Riparian Association, to reintroduce the rare lammergeyer; three captive-bred birds were released into the wild in April 2001, but sadly one was killed by a local farmer within two months.

The usual access point to Hell's Gate is through the main **Elsa Gate** 2km from Moi South Lake Rd, where there's an **information centre**. From here the road takes you past **Fischer's Tower**, a 25m-high column of volcanic rock named after Gustav Fischer, a German explorer who reached the area in 1882. Commissioned by the Hamburg Geographical Society to find a route from

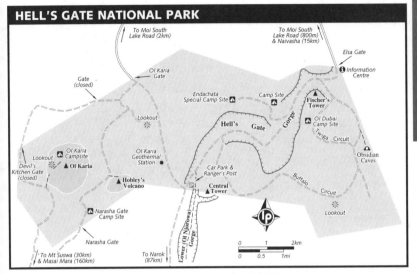

HELL'S GATE NATIONAL PARK

To Moi South Lake Road (2km)

To Moi South Lake Road (800m) & Naivasha (15km)

Elsa Gate

Information Centre

Ol Karia Gate

Gate (closed)

Endachata Special Camp Site

Camp Site

Fischer's Tower

Lookout

Hell's Gate

Gorge

Ol Dubai Camp Site

Twiga Circuit

Lookout

Ol Karia Campsite

Ol Karia

Ol Karia Geothermal Station

Obsidian Caves

Devil's Kitchen Gate (closed)

Hobley's Volcano

Car Park & Ranger's Post

Buffalo Circuit

Central Tower

Lookout

Narasha Gate Camp Site

Lower (Ol Njorowa) Gorge

Narasha Gate

To Mt Suswa (30km) & Masai Mara (160km)

To Narok (87km)

0   1   2km
0   0.5   1mi

Mombasa to Lake Victoria, Fischer was stopped here by territorial Maasai, who efficiently aborted his campaign by slaughtering almost his entire party.

The road continues through the steep-sided **gorge** (which together with the various towers in the park is very popular with climbers) and passes close to **Central Tower** (Embarta), a column of volcanic rock similar to Fischer's Tower but much larger. There is a picnic site and ranger's post close by, from where there is an excellent walk (in the dry season!) down into the **Lower (Ol Njorowa) Gorge**. The channels cut by the water are absolutely beautiful and the detour up the side gorge below Central Tower is equally rewarding. It's quite a steep descent and can be very slippery, but some steps have been cut into the rock and whole school parties manage it on a regular basis. You could easily spend a couple of hours wandering around this area.

The main road emerges at **Ol Karia Geothermal Station**, a power project utilising one of the hottest sources of natural steam in the world. The plumes of steam given off by the facility can be seen from many viewpoints in the park. It's also possible to have a look around part of the site; ask the guards at the gate nearby.

The round trip from the turn-off on Moi South Lake Rd to the shore of Lake Naivasha

via Elsa Gate and Ol Karia Gate is 22km; the distance between the two gates via Moi South Lake Rd is 9km. If you intend walking the whole way through the park, allow a full day, and take plenty of supplies. Drinking water is available only at the park's five camp sites. A good alternative is to hire a mountain bike from one of the camps beside the lake or ask around at Fisherman's Camp for a lift into the park.

If you want to explore further, the Buffalo Circuit takes you away from the usual tourist route and offers some fine views of the surrounding countryside, as well as passing some obsidian caves with fascinating formations. By turning west from Ol Karia Gate, you can also explore the volcanic landscape of the western side of the park; however, the two gates on the northwest corner of the park are locked, so there is no through route.

Camping (per person US$2) in the park is highly recommended. Ol Dubai and Naiburta camp sites are probably the best. See Lake Naivasha earlier in this chapter for details on other places to stay nearby and information on how to get to the park.

NAKURU
☎ 037

Nakuru is Kenya's fourth-largest town, situated in the centre of a rich farming area about halfway between Nairobi and Kisumu. It's a

THE RIFT VALLEY

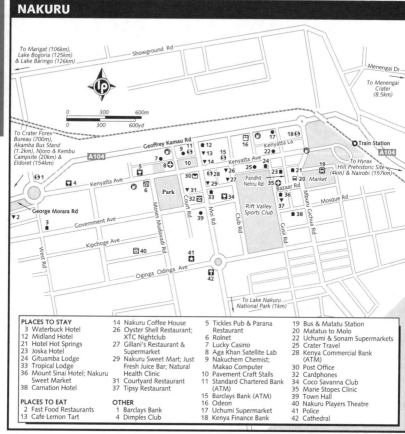

NAKURU

To Marigat (106km),
Lake Bogoria (125km)
& Lake Baringo (126km)

Showground Rd

Menengai Dr

To Menengai
Crater
(8.5km)

To Crater Forex
Bureau (700m),
Akamba Bus Stand
(1.2km), Njoro & Kembu
Campsite (20km) &
Eldoret (154km)

Geoffrey Kamau Rd

A104

Train Station

A104

To Hyrax
Hill Prehistoric Site
(4km) & Nairobi (157km)

Kenyatta Ave

Kenyatta La

Kenyatta Ave

Pandhit
Nehru Rd

Bazaar Rd

Market

Mburu Gichua Rd

Mosque Rd

George Morara Rd

Park

Court Rd

Moi Rd

Club Rd

Rift Valley
Sports Club

Gusii Rd

Government Ave

West Rd

Kipchoge Ave

Moses Mudavadi Rd

Oginga Odinga Ave

To Lake Nakuru
National Park (1km)

0   300   600m
0   300   600yd

PLACES TO STAY	14 Nakuru Coffee House	5 Tickles Pub & Parana	19 Bus & Matatu Station
3 Waterbuck Hotel	26 Oyster Shell Restaurant;	Restaurant	20 Matatus to Molo
12 Midland Hotel	XTC Nightclub	6 Rolnet	22 Uchumi & Sonam Supermarkets
21 Hotel Hot Springs	27 Gillani's Restaurant &	7 Lucky Casino	25 Crater Travel
23 Joska Hotel	Supermarket	8 Aga Khan Satellite Lab	28 Kenya Commercial Bank
24 Gituamba Lodge	29 Nakuru Sweet Mart; Just	9 Nakuchem Chemist;	(ATM)
33 Tropical Lodge	Fresh Juice Bar; Natural	Makao Computer	30 Post Office
36 Mount Sinai Hotel; Nakuru	Health Clinic	10 Pavement Craft Stalls	32 Cardphones
Sweet Market	31 Courtyard Restaurant	11 Standard Chartered Bank	35 Marie Stopes Clinic
38 Carnation Hotel	37 Tipsy Restaurant	(ATM)	39 Town Hall
		15 Barclays Bank (ATM)	40 Nakuru Players Theatre
PLACES TO EAT	OTHER	16 Odeon	41 Police
2 Fast Food Restaurants	1 Barclays Bank	17 Uchumi Supermarket	42 Cathedral
13 Cafe Lemon Tart	4 Dimples Club	18 Kenya Finance Bank	

pleasant, relatively modern town with a population of about 80,000 and all the usual
facilities. Most travellers spend only a short
time in the town itself, heading straight for
the big attraction of nearby Lake Nakuru
National Park; however, the town is generally relaxed enough to warrant a couple of
days' stay.

The volcanic Menengai Crater, a few kilometres from the centre, is also worth visiting,
and there are a couple of interesting prehistoric sites in the area (see Around Nakuru
later for more information).

Information

Changing money is no problem in Nakuru.
Crater Forex Bureau on George Morara Rd
is a short walk west of the town centre;

there are several banks with ATMs in town,
including a **Barclays Bank** on Kenyatta Ave.
Ask about the commission before changing
money here.

Internet services are available in various
places around town. **Makao Computer**,
above the Nakuchem chemist, is one of the
cheapest, with prices from KSh1 a minute.
Rolnet (Kenyatta Ave), which charges KSh3
per minute, is open on Sunday.

There are a number of travel agencies
here, most of which can arrange tours of
Lake Nakuru. **Crater Travel** (☎ 215019), off
Kenyatta Ave, is quite reputable.

The **Marie Stopes Clinic** and the **Aga
Khan Satellite Laboratory** offer a range of
health services, including blood tests for
malaria.

Places to Stay – Budget & Mid-Range

There is no camp site in Nakuru, but you can camp in Lake Nakuru National Park (see later in this chapter). Otherwise your best option is **Kembu Campsite** (☎ 61413; e ke mbu@net2000ke.com; camping per person KSh200, farmhouse per person KSh1500), an excellent farmyard site near Njoro, about 20km west of town. It's particularly popular with overlanders and has a large truck workshop on site; however, there is enough space for smaller parties not to be overwhelmed! A cottage (KSh900 per person) and tree house (KSh1200 per double) are also available, or you can take half board in the farmhouse itself.

Horse riding, mountain bike hire and various treks into the surrounding area can be arranged at Kembu. To get to the site, take a matatu heading to Molo (via Njoro; KSh80) and ask to be dropped at the sign, about 6km northeast of Njoro on the C56. It's also signposted from the A104.

The cheapest hotels in Nakuru can be found around Kenyatta Ave and Gusii Rd, near the bus and matatu stands and the main market. They're generally basic and can be noisy, but go for around KSh200.

Hotel Hot Springs (off Mburu Gichua Rd; singles/doubles with bathroom KSh250/500) is a bit dingy but not bad value for a single. The balcony restaurant is a great place to watch over the busy streetlife.

Gituamba Lodge (☎ 0722-235887; Gusii Rd; singles/doubles KSh260/340) is one of the better cheap options, with reasonably clean rooms and a few singles with bathroom (KSh310). Noise is still a problem – take a room on the top floor, away from the street and the very popular club/restaurant underneath.

Joska Hotel (☎ 212546; Pandhit Nehru Rd; singles with bathroom KSh300) is another good place. Rooms (no doubles) are not huge but are pretty well kept, and the street noise is not as bad as it could be in this area.

Tropical Lodge (☎ 42608; Moi Rd; singles/doubles KSh250/350) is far quieter, with large comfortable rooms, and isn't a bad choice if you don't mind minor privations such as small cockroaches and barely functional washbasins.

Mount Sinai Hotel (☎ 21779; Gusii Rd; singles/doubles with bathroom KSh350/500) is a big, clean place with plenty of rooms and sound security (iron bars all over!). The rooms are perhaps a bit pricey for what you get, but the views from the roof terrace are fantastic, and the ground floor restaurant is good value.

Carnation Hotel (☎ 43522; Mosque Rd; singles/doubles with bathroom KSh500/1000) is trying to lever itself into the mid-range category, with limited success. Prices include breakfast and security is good, but the rooms aren't really that much better than some of the cheaper options, and the shiny new brochure is misleading! Blackbird Tours is based here (see Getting There & Away under Lake Nakuru National Park).

Places to Stay – Top End

Most of the fancy lodges are in the national park, but Nakuru town also has a couple of upmarket options.

Midland Hotel (☎ 212125, fax 44517; Geoffrey Kamau Rd; singles/doubles KSh2300/3700) is the best place in this price range, with lots of wood panelling and wall-to-wall carpets. You get a choice of standard and superior rooms in two wings (doubles are generally nicer than singles), as well as three bars and two restaurants.

Waterbuck Hotel (☎ 215672; cnr Government Ave & West Rd; singles/doubles KSh1400/2400) is somewhat cheaper and has undergone recent renovations, including the addition of minibars, although the showers could still be nicer. Some rooms have small balconies. There is a fine courtyard restaurant and a pool bar, as well as guarded parking on site.

Places to Eat

There are several **fast-food places**, including a **Nandos**, on the way out of town past the A104 roundabout to the west.

Tipsy Restaurant (Gusii Rd; mains KSh90-130) is a favourite with local people, and offers reasonable value for Indian and Western-style food, although dishes can be a bit greasy. Next door, **Nakuru Sweet Mart** must be doing well, as it has opened a second outlet on Moi Rd; sweets, pastries and cakes are the staple produce, alongside Indian thali (plate meal) curries. The nearby **Cafe Lemon Tart** (Moi Rd; mains KSh100-200) is another bright and popular little place.

Gillani's Restaurant (*Club Rd; mains KSh120-220*) is a bit of an oddity, located inside the Gillani supermarket overlooking the aisles! However, there is a good choice of curries (including excellent chicken tikka) and other dishes, plus a TV and fish tanks for entertainment.

Going more upmarket, the **Courtyard Restaurant** (*off Court Rd; mains from KSh350*) is a smart joint with plenty of room and a varied menu, including an unusually good selection of vegetarian dishes. The open-air bars at the **Midland** and **Waterbuck** hotels (*meals around KSh400*) are also good places, specialising in barbecued chicken, and can get pretty crowded at lunch time.

For a more expensive treat, the **Oyster Shell Restaurant** (*Kenyatta Ave; mains KSh450-750*) is one of Nakuru's best eating houses, and is well worth the extra cash. The extensive menu includes western, Indian and even Indonesian dishes.

If you're just after a healthy drink, try the **Just Fresh Juice Bar** (*Moi Rd*), a funky little place run by two Australians; there's a Natural Health Clinic upstairs for the hippy hypochondriac in you. For a straightforward caffeine fix, **Nakuru Coffee House** (*Kenyatta Ave*) does the business and also sells excellent freshly roasted coffee.

There are plenty of **supermarkets** around for self-caterers.

Entertainment
Aside from the hotel bars, there are plenty of drinking establishments of various calibre in Nakuru. **Tickles Pub** (*Kenyatta Ave*), attached to the Parana Restaurant, is a relatively calm locals' place, while **Coco Savanna Club** (*Government Ave*) and **Dimples Club** (*Kenyatta Ave*) are more like 24-hour discos, with permanent pounding music, entry charges in the evenings and a clientele that includes pool sharks and some prostitutes.

The nearest you'll get to a proper nightclub here is **XTC**, above Oyster Shell Restaurant, which has decent equipment and a more varied music policy than other places, often hosting live bands. There is no cover charge and bar prices are dangerously close to the norm.

The **Odeon** (*Geoffrey Kamau Rd*) is a bit of a fleapit, but it's the only cinema in town; **Nakuru Players Theatre**, off Moses Mudavadi Rd, stages occasional Kenyan plays.

For those who like to be more pro-active with their cash, the **Lucky Casino** is just off Kenyatta Ave.

Getting There & Away
Bus & Matatu Buses, matatus and Peugeots (shared taxis) for destinations all over Kenya leave from the chaotic stands at the eastern edge of town, near the train station. There is also an Akamba depot in town for services to Nairobi and the west, but it's about 3km in the opposite direction, by the Agip petrol station on the A104 west of town.

There are regular matatu/Peugeot services to Naivasha (KSh100, 45 minutes), Nairobi (KSh150/300, 1½ hours), Nyahururu (KSh100, 45 minutes), Nyeri (KSh200, two hours), Eldoret (KSh200/250, two hours), Kitale (KSh200, two hours), Kisii (KSh200, four hours) and Kisumu (KSh250/300, 2½ hours).

Buses serve most of the same destinations at slightly cheaper rates, as well as going to Kampi ya Samaki (KSh200, two hours) for Lake Baringo.

Matatus to Molo leave from near the Total petrol station on Bazaar Rd.

AROUND NAKURU
Menengai Crater
Rising on the northern side of Nakuru, this 2490m-high extinct volcano provides stunning views over Lake Nakuru to the south and Lake Bogoria to the north, and makes for a great, if somewhat strenuous, couple of hours' walk.

The crater itself descends to 483m below the rim; a grim local legend has it that the little plumes of steam from the bottom are in fact the souls of defeated Maasai warriors, thrown into the crater after a territorial battle between factions, trying to make their way to heaven!

There are no matatus that go here; from Nakuru take a car or hire a taxi up Menengai Dr to the edge of the crater, about 8km out of town. If you do walk from Nakuru, be careful – there have been muggings on this route. There is a small group of *dukas* along the way where you can get basic meals, soft drinks and, of course, a Tusker or two for the road.

Hyrax Hill Prehistoric Site
This archaeological site (*open 9am-6pm daily; admission KSh200*) is 4km outside Nakuru;

local matatus to Naivasha/Nairobi will take you past the turn-off (about 1km from the site). A small visitor's leaflet is available from the site's museum.

Archaeological excavations were conducted here from 1937 until well into the 1980s, although the significance of the site was first mooted by Louis Leakey in 1926. Finds at the site indicate that three settlements were made here, the earliest possibly 3000 years ago, the most recent only 200 to 300 years ago.

From the museum at the northern end you can take a short stroll around the site, starting with the North-East Village where 13 enclosures, or pits, were excavated. Only Pit D, investigated in 1965, is still open. The North-East Village is believed to be about 400 years old; a great number of pottery fragments were found here, some of which have been pieced together into complete jars and are displayed in the museum.

From the village, the trail climbs to the scant remains of the stone-walled hill fort near the top of Hyrax Hill itself. You can continue up to the peak where there is a fine view of flamingo-lined Lake Nakuru.

On the other side of the hill, you come to the Iron Age settlement where the position of Hut B and Hut C is clearly visible. Just north of these huts, a series of burial pits containing 19 skeletons was found. The majority were male and lots of them had been decapitated, so a number of colourful explanations have been offered! Unfortunately, souvenir seekers have stolen the bones that were displayed here.

Virtually underneath these Iron Age burial pits, a Neolithic burial mound was discovered. A second Neolithic burial mound nearby has been fenced off as a display. Between the burial mound and the Nairobi road there are more Iron Age pits that were excavated in 1974.

The large collection of items found in these pits included a real puzzle – six Indian coins, one of them 500 years old, and two others dating from 1918 and 1919!

Finally, following the path back to the museum, there's a *bao* (a traditional African game that is played throughout East Africa) board carved in a large rock.

You are free to walk around the site yourself, but a guide is useful. You will be expected to give a small tip at the end.

Lake Elmenteita

Another of the major Rift Valley soda lakes, Elmenteita is not a national park – there are no entry fees and you can walk around the area, although there are few tracks and most of the land around the shoreline is privately owned.

Flamingo Camp (☎ 037-212382; camping per person KSh200, bandas KSh1500) is a good budget site right on the lakeshore. The site is secure (the guard dogs look like they bite!) with decent facilities, a restaurant and large semi-tented bandas; the design is apparently 'unmistakably English'!

Lake Elmenteita Lodge (☎ 0367-5040; singles/doubles US$100/180 in low season, US$180/230 in high season) is a beautiful colonial-style place set in lovely gardens, with excellent lake views and a full range of activities. Prices here seem to have shot up recently.

Delamere's Camp, one of the most exclusive lodges in Kenya, was closed for improvements at the time of writing but should reopen soon. Contact East African Ornithological Safaris (see Special-Interest Safaris in the Safari chapter) for further information.

There are frequent matatus along the A104 Naivasha–Nakuru road that will drop you at any of the signposted viewpoints on the escarpment above the lake, or at the turn-off for Flamingo Camp.

Kariandusi Prehistoric Site

The Kariandusi site (adult/child KSh200/100) is signposted off the main road from Naivasha to Nakuru, near Lake Elmenteita. It was at this site in the 1920s that the Leakeys discovered numerous obsidian and lava tools made by early humans between 1.4 million and 200,000 years ago. The excavations are there for you to see and the museum displays a brief history of early human life.

If you have a few minutes to spare and like caves, then continue 500m north to **African Diatomite Industries** (☎ 0367-5290) and have a look at its mining operation. Staff are happy to receive visitors and there is no charge. Diatomite is a white rock that has many plaster-like properties and numerous industrial applications. The mine itself looks like the set of a sci-fi movie: at the bottom of a deep pit you can take a guided walk around a network of circular tunnels, which were dug by hand into the brilliant white rock and are now home to thousands of bats.

LAKE NAKURU NATIONAL PARK

Created in 1961, this park *(adult/child US$30/10, vehicle KSh200)* covers 180 sq km and now rivals Amboseli as the second most visited park in Kenya after the Masai Mara. Like most of the other Rift Valley lakes, Lake Nakuru is a shallow soda lake. For a number of years the water level decreased steadily to the point where the lake was almost dry between the rains, forcing the huge flamingo population, once synonymous with the lake, to seek pinker pastures elsewhere, mainly on Lake Bogoria.

In recent years, pressures on the lake have increased. Pollution from Nakuru town, pesticide run-off from surrounding farms, and massive deforestation within the water catchment area have all caused concern. A long-running World Wildlife Fund (WWF, aka Worldwide Fund for Nature) project is making considerable progress in countering these problems, and the local afforestation programme celebrated the planting of its 10,001st indigenous tree seedling in May 2002. However, all visitors should still be aware of the delicate nature of the environment they are driving through.

On the positive side, the lake has been in recovery since the El Niño rains of 1997, and is currently around 3.5m deep, the deepest it has been for a decade. The flamingos are already starting to return in large numbers, but even without them Lake Nakuru has maintained a reputation as an ornithologists' paradise, with more than 400 bird species recorded here.

But there is much more to the park than just the lake. Areas of grassland, bush, euphorbia and acacia forests (look out for tree-climbing lions) and rocky cliffs support hundreds of species of bird and mammal. Warthogs are common all over the park, providing light relief from the 'serious' animals with their amusing gait and upright tails; right by the water you'll come across waterbucks and buffaloes, while Thomson's gazelles and reedbucks can be seen further into the bush and there's a good chance of seeing a leopard. Around the cliffs you may catch sight of hyraxes and birds of prey amid the countless baboons. A small herd of hippos generally frequents the northern shore of the lake.

The park is surrounded by a high electric fence, which keeps in a small number of black rhino and white rhino that were introduced from private ranches some years ago. The southern end of the lake is the best place to see white rhinos grazing close to the water's edge; the black rhinos, browsers by nature, are more difficult to spot.

Walking in the park is not permitted so you will either have to hitch a ride with other tourists (not easy), rent a vehicle or go on a tour (see Getting There & Away following). You can get out of your vehicle on the lakeshore and at certain viewpoints, but don't drive too close to the water's edge, as the mud is very soft! Take your cue from the tracks of other vehicles.

The main national park entrance is about 4km south of the centre of Nakuru. This is one of the parks for which you need one of the new smartcards; it's best to make sure you have this sorted beforehand, although there is an office by the main gate. An excellent map (KSh500) is available at the park gate and at KWS headquarters in Nairobi.

Places to Stay – Budget & Mid-Range

Backpackers' Camp Site *(camping per adult/child US$8/2)*, just inside the main park gate, is the main public camp site, with fresh water and long-drop toilets. You'll need to bring all your own food. Make sure tents are securely zipped up when you're away from them or the vervet monkeys and baboons will clean you out.

Makalia Public Camp Site is right at the far end of the park, by the (seasonal) Makalia Falls. Facilities here are not as good as at Backpackers' and it's harder to find, but the location is way nicer.

There are **special camp sites** dotted all over the park. They cost US$15 per person per day, plus the standard one-off KSh5000 set-up fee.

Wildlife Club of Kenya Youth Hostel *(☎ 037-850929; PO Box 33, Nakuru; camping per person KSh250, dorm beds KSh300)* is a nice, very friendly site with space for tents and small, clean dorms. The club also runs a self-catering **guesthouse** *(☎ 037-851559; beds per person KSh800)* nearby which is even better – facilities include hot showers and use

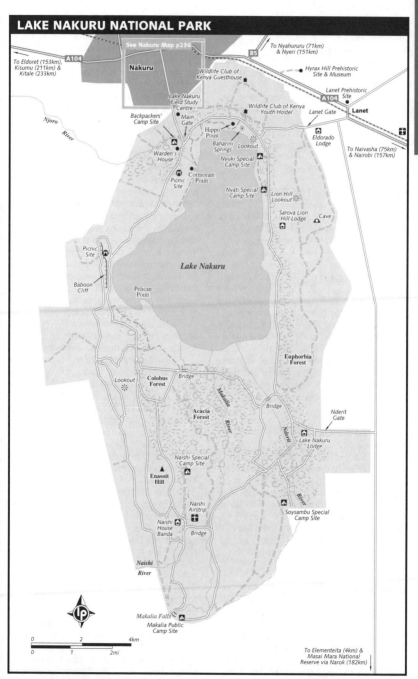

LAKE NAKURU NATIONAL PARK

See Nakuru Map p236

Nakuru

To Eldoret (153km), Kisumu (211km) & Kitale (233km)

A104

B5

To Nyahururu (71km) & Nyeri (151km)

Wildlife Club of Kenya Guesthouse

Hyrax Hill Prehistoric Site & Museum

Lanet Prehistoric Site

A104

Lanet Gate

Lanet

Njoro River

Lake Nakuru Field Study Centre

Backpackers' Camp Site

Main Gate

Hippo Point

Wildlife Club of Kenya Youth Hostel

Baharini Springs

Lookout

Eldorado Lodge

To Naivasha (75km) & Nairobi (157km)

Warden's House

Cormorant Point

Picnic Site

Nyuki Special Camp Site

Nyati Special Camp Site

Lion Hill Lookout

Sarova Lion Hill Lodge

Cave

Picnic Site

Lake Nakuru

Baboon Cliff

Pelican Point

Euphorbia Forest

Lookout

Colobus Forest

Bridge

Makalia River

Bridge

Nderit Gate

Acacia Forest

Nderit River

Lake Nakuru Lodge

Naishi Special Camp Site

Enasoit Hill

Naishi Airstrip

Naishi House Banda

Bridge

Soysambu Special Camp Site

Naishi River

Makalia Falls

Makalia Public Camp Site

0   2   4km
0   1   2mi

To Elementeita (4km) & Masai Mara National Reserve via Narok (182km) of kitchens with fridge, gas cooker and microwave! The caretaker may cook your food for you for a small fee.

Eldorado Lodge *(☎ 037-85491, fax 86493; camping per person KSh300, singles/doubles KSh1000/1500)* is actually outside the park, just past Lanet Gate, which may save you some park fees. It has a good-sized swimming pool, restaurant, bar and disco, and offers three-hour wildlife drives for KSh6500 per minibus. Rooms are expensive for what you get, but the lodge is very close to the park and you can also camp here.

Places to Stay – Top End

Sarova Lion Hill Lodge *(☎ 037-850235, Nairobi 02-713333; e reservations@sarova.co .ke; singles/doubles full board US$65/130 in low season, US$150/190 in high season, suites from US$385)* is the best lodge in the park, and possibly one of the best anywhere in Kenya. It has all the usual facilities, including a swimming pool, sauna and open-air bar/restaurant. The rooms are understated but nice, while the flashy suites are large and absolutely stunning. There is also a massive Presidential Suite with prices suitably beyond the reach of mere mortals!

Naishi House Banda *(US$200, with annexe US$250)*, at the southern end of the park, accommodates up to eight people in comfortable fully furnished rooms. Amenities here consist of decent showers and toilets plus kitchen, dining room and lounge.

Lake Nakuru Lodge *(☎ 037-850228, in Nairobi 02-212405, fax 230962; singles/ doubles full board US$150/180 in high season)*, 3km from the southern end of the lake, consists of a series of shingle-roofed octagonal cottages set in pleasant gardens, with trees planted by such luminaries as 'Bill's Band' and Miss Tourism Kenya. The usual facilities are available, along with activities such as horse riding (KSh850 per hour) and nature walks (KSh500). Low season discount is 40% off the normal rates.

Getting There & Away

If you don't have your own vehicle, the only way into the park from Nakuru is by taxi or on an organised tour, unless you're lucky enough to persuade a self-drive tourist to take you with them. A taxi costs around KSh1000 for three hours, although you'll have to bargain hard for this.

Alternatively, **Crater Travel** *(☎ 037-215019)* and **Blackbird Tours** *(☎ 037-40830)* in Nakuru can organise transport for you; a three-hour tour will cost around KSh4000 per vehicle, excluding park fees.

If you're driving, there's access from three points: the main gate, just outside Nakuru; Lanet, a few kilometres further along the Nairobi road; and Nderit Gate, near the southern end of the lake.

LAKE BOGORIA NATIONAL RESERVE

North of Nakuru off the excellent B4 highway, this reserve *(adult/child or student US$15/5, vehicle KSh200)* protects a shallow soda lake covering an area of 30 sq km with a maximum depth of 9m. It was listed as a Ramsar protected wetlands site in 2000. The journey here takes you through some dramatic changes of scenery, particularly around the equator, where the landscape turns dry and dusty, getting more forbidding the further north you go. As you approach Marigat the spectacular ridges and escarpments of the Tugen Hills come into view, and you will see an extraordinary number of huge termites' nests towering up from the reddish plains.

In recent years the lake achieved fame as 'the new home of the flamingo', with a migrant population of up to two million birds; this figure will decrease slightly now that Lake Nakuru is recovering from earlier droughts, but the spectacle is still quite something, and a visit can easily be combined with a trip to Lake Baringo.

The reserve is particularly well-run and some access on bicycle or foot is possible. There is plenty of wildlife in the park apart from the flamingos, including leopards, klipspringers, caracals and the rare greater kudu (it is one of the best places to see them in Kenya), but the modest **hot springs** and **geysers** are the other main attraction. The springs are hot enough to boil an egg, so don't get too close.

You can walk or cycle unaccompanied as far as the springs, but if you want to venture further into the park you'll need advance permission from the **warden** *(☎ 037-40746; PO Box 64, Marigat)*, and you may need to be accompanied by an armed ranger to keep you clear of the small buffalo population.

The eastern side of the lake is dominated by the sheer face of the Siracho Escarpment and the northwestern extremities of the Aberdares. To the south is a rather isolated wooded area popular with wildlife, especially greater kudu; the land to the west is hot and relatively barren.

In the past couple of years Bogoria has become more popular as a stop-off point for safari vehicles visiting Nakuru and Baringo, but few of these venture past the hot springs, and if you're walking you may well have the place to yourself.

For enthusiastic bird-watchers, **Kesubo Swamp**, just north of the park, is a haven for more than 200 species of bird, holding the Kenyan record for the largest number of species seen in one hour (96!). Ask at the warden's office for further details and to arrange a guide (around KSh250). There is also a **Tugen cultural village** about halfway down the road to the reserve, which is worth a visit to see what life would have been like for former President Moi's ancestors.

Places to Stay & Eat

There are three main camp sites at Bogoria: **Acacia** and **Fig Tree** at the southern end and the strangely named **VIPs** just outside Loboi Gate, all charging the usual US$8/2 for an adult/child.

Fig Tree Camp is probably the best of these, with a permanent freshwater stream shaded by huge fig trees; on the down side, baboons can be a nuisance, the long-drop toilets are pretty dodgy and the main road to the camp site is often flooded (there is another route but it's 4WD only).

Elsewhere the only available water is the totally unpalatable stuff from the lake, so bring your own supply for drinking.

Papyrus Inn *(☎ 037-43279; singles/doubles KSh500/700)*, just by Loboi Gate, has reasonable basic rooms with below-average shared facilities. It's very quiet most of the time, but there's a restaurant and bar and you may be able to hire a bicycle.

Lake Bogoria Hotel *(☎ 037-40748, in Nairobi 02-249055, fax 249066; singles/ doubles full board US$70/120)*, set in lovely grounds 2km before the same entry gate, is much more of a top-end option, with a choice of standard and VIP rooms. Tours of the lake can be organised for around KSh1000, and the restaurant is open to nonguests for lunch (US$15) and dinner (US$18).

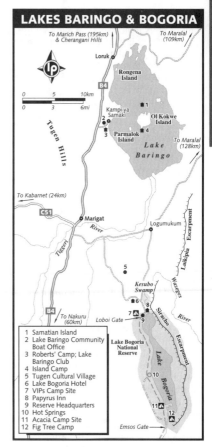

LAKES BARINGO & BOGORIA

1 Samatian Island
2 Lake Baringo Community Boat Office
3 Roberts' Camp; Lake Baringo Club
4 Island Camp
5 Tugen Cultural Village
6 Lake Bogoria Hotel
7 VIPs Camp Site
8 Papyrus Inn
9 Reserve Headquarters
10 Hot Springs
11 Acacia Camp Site
12 Fig Tree Camp

Some cheap accommodation is available in the nearby town of Marigat; try the **Marigat Inn** *(rooms from KSh250)*, about 1.5km north of town, or the more basic **Salama Lodge** *(rooms KSh250)*. The **Union Hotel** is OK for food. This area is also a good place to buy locally produced *asali* (honey), which is sold from countless roadside kiosks for around KSh150 for a vodka-bottle full.

Getting There & Away

There are two entrance gates to Lake Bogoria – Emsos in the south and Loboi in the north. The turn-off for Emsos is about 38km past Nakuru on the B4, but the route is poorly signposted and inaccessible without a serious 4WD.

Loboi Gate is a far more straightforward point of entry, reached by taking a turn-off shortly before Marigat. It's 20km from here to the actual gate along a good, sealed road that continues to the hot springs.

The nearest petrol is at the Esso petrol station on the main road at Marigat.

While getting to the park is easiest if you have your own vehicle, this is not essential: there are a couple of matatus from Marigat to Loboi at around 4.30pm, returning around 8am the following morning.

LAKE BARINGO
☎ 0328

The B4 continues up past Bogoria to **Kampi ya Samaki** *('registration fee' KSh200)* on the western shore of Lake Baringo, 15km north of Marigat. This small, quiet town used to be a fishing village, but droughts and over-fishing have virtually eradicated the indus-try, with the result that the local economy now depends almost entirely on tourism.

The lake, listed as Kenya's fourth Ramsar site in January 2002, is freshwater and has been plagued with problems over the past few years. Irrigation dams and droughts caused the water level to drop alarmingly, pushing the shoreline back several hundred metres; severe siltation due to soil erosion around the seasonal *luggas* (creeks) has meant the water is almost always muddy; and the lake has been overfished so badly that any tilapia caught these days are rarely more than 15cm long. The water level has risen again recently, but the situation is still very delicate, and with further droughts expected the ecosystem here remains at risk.

The lake, with its picturesque islands and encircling mountains, is still a spectacular sight nevertheless, and a popular place to visit. There's even an uninhabited 'Devil's Island' with a fearsome reputation among the normally prosaic locals, who won't go near the place at night, claiming you can see flames and hear screaming. So far no visitors have confirmed these sightings, but it sounds a bit more exciting than bird-watching!

Things to See & Do

Bird walks and boat rides are the most popu-lar activities around Lake Baringo, and the latter are touted as competitively as the Masai Mara is in Nairobi – there are boat of-fices all over town, and literally everyone

you talk to will claim to have access to a boat and be able to undercut anyone else's price. A speciality is a trip to see fish eagles feeding; the birds have learned to dive for fish at a whistle, making for great (if slightly contrived) photo opportunities.

The most reliable trips are probably the more expensive formal ones, which can be organised through either the Lake Baringo Community Boat Office (KSh2000 per boat per hour), Lake Baringo Club (KSh3000 per boat per hour or KSh800 per person per hour), Soi Safari Lodge (KSh3500 per boat, two hours) or Roberts' Camp (KSh2000 per boat per hour, up to seven people). Most of the trips offered by the smaller local hotels will actually be with Community boats.

Other activities can also be arranged from any of these places. Bird-watching tours to the dramatic cliffs close to the main road, where three quarters of Lake Baringo's 480 recorded bird species have been seen, are a popular sideline, and the rock is apparently suitable for technical climbing. Cultural tours to Pokot, Tugen and Njemps villages close to the lake are also common; the Njemps are local cousins of the Maasai and live on Ol Kokwe and Parmalok Islands and around the lakeshore, mainly practising pastoralism and fishing. You'll usually be allowed to walk

---

Baringo Wildlife

Crocodiles and hippos apart, Lake Baringo's main attraction is the birdlife and the lake is one of Kenya's bird-watching centres. Of the more than 1200 species of bird native to Kenya, more than 450 of them have been sighted here. People come from all over the world to try and catch a glimpse of something rare; Lake Baringo Club even has a resident or-nithologist who leads bird-watching walks and gives advice to guests. A few years ago she set a world record for the number of species seen in one 24-hour period – over 300!

There's a constant twittering, chirping and cooing of birds in the trees around the lake, in the rushes on the lake and on the steep face of the nearby escarpment. Even if you're not an avid 'twitcher', it's hard to resist setting off on a dawn bird walk, when you have a good chance of seeing hornbills or a magnificent eagle.

around freely and take photos, but in return you'll probably be hassled to buy handicrafts. There is a KSh500 charge for entering each village, on top of the price of your guide.

Lake Baringo Club (see Places to Stay) offers **bird walks** for KSh500 per person and **cultural visits** for KSh400 per person (less if you have your own transport), as well as **horse rides** for KSh1000 per hour and **camel rides** for KSh350 per half hour. Trips to Lake Bogoria cost KSh2500 per person (minimum two people), plus park fees. There's a slide show each evening featuring some of the more common birds sighted in the area.

Simose Internet, opposite the Club, can hook you up for a pretty extortionate KSh20 a minute.

Places to Stay – Budget & Mid-Range

Roberts' Camp (☎ 51403; PO Box 1051, Nakuru; camping per person KSh300, banda singles/doubles KSh500/1000, cottages KSh4000), next to Lake Baringo Club, is a very popular site right by the lake. Facilities include clean showers and toilets, plus the Thirsty Goat restaurant and bar (meals must be ordered in advance). As well as camping, there are three bandas and two excellent four-person cottages available, but you pay an extra KSh500 for bathroom and cooking facilities. Demand is heavy and it's best to book in advance through Mrs E Roberts.

Mzee Korby, the resident giant tortoise, is a pretty friendly beast, but campers need to exercise some common sense regarding the hippos, which may graze within just a metre of your tent at night. Ideally you should stay at least 20m away from them when you can, especially if they have young, and don't frighten them with headlights, torches (flashlights), loud noises or flash photography. No-one's been seriously hurt by a hippo in over 10 years here, but some readers have had decidedly close calls! Remember that they are wild animals and should be treated with respect.

There are a number of places to stay in Kampi ya Samaki, although none of them are great. **Lake View Lodge** (beds per person KSh100), overlooking the lake, is very cheap but very basic and a bit rundown. Bring your own padlock.

Lake Breeze Hotel (☎ 51464; camping per person KSh100, singles/doubles KSh300/500), just next door, is not a bad place in itself and the location is nice, but the staff can be a bit pushy.

Bahari Lodge (☎ 51408; singles/doubles KSh200/400) is popular with the drivers of safari vehicles, which is generally a good sign! The rooms are a little shabby but OK, and the restaurant and bar here are well-frequented in the evenings.

Harriers Lodge (☎ 514408; singles/doubles KSh200/400) may not be up to much in terms of facilities, but it's friendly, with cleanish rooms around a nice rear courtyard. You're likely to have the whole place to yourself.

Weavers Lodge (singles/doubles with bathroom KSh400/800) has cut its prices and is starting to win over some safari drivers from the Bahari. The rooms are a good size and come with fans, mosquito nets and comfortable beds; sadly toilet paper, soap and hot water are often lacking and the constant loud music from the bar can be a pain.

Places to Stay – Top End

Soi Safari Lodge (☎ 51242, in Nairobi 02-242725; e safaris-hotels@independent.co.ke; singles/doubles full board KSh3000/4500) is a brand new luxury hotel right on the lakeshore in Kampi ya Samaki. It's still pristine, but the rooms have a character of sorts, along with the usual mod cons and remote-controlled air con, and the staff try hard. There's a swimming pool, a large upstairs bar and a restaurant; the usual excursions are available.

Lake Baringo Club (☎ 51401, in Nairobi 02-540780; e blockbaringo@africaonline.co.ke; singles/doubles full board US$104/130 in low season, US$130/160 in high season), one of the Block Hotels chain, is a grand place next door to Roberts' Camp. The rooms are pleasant if uninspired, but the double beds are great! Facilities include swimming pool, games room, badminton court and library, and are open to nonguests for a fee (KSh150/200). It also offers excursions and other activities (see Things to See & Do earlier).

The following two places can be booked through **Let's Go Travel** (in Nairobi 02-340331; e info@letsgosafari.com). Full board for both includes return boat transfer, leaving from a jetty at the far northern end of Kampi ya Samaki. Guarded parking is available in town between the main street and the lakeshore.

Island Camp Baringo (☎ *singles/doubles full board US$200/275*), a luxury tented lodge on the extreme southern tip of Ol Kokwe Island, makes a perfect hideaway.

It's a beautifully conceived place with 23 double tents set among flowering trees, all looking out over the lake. Facilities include two bars, a swimming pool and water-sports equipment.

For a *truly* exclusive experience, though, **Samatian Island** (*per person full board US$379*) is the place to be. This tiny island, owned by the Roberts family, has just three chalets for rent, and the hefty price tag is worth it for the glorious isolation.

Places to Eat

Campers should bear in mind that, while some foodstuffs may be available at Roberts' Camp, fresh vegetables and fruit are generally in short supply and there's only a very limited stock available in Kampi ya Samaki. Bring much of what you need – Marigat usually has a good selection.

Those who want to splash out can eat at the restaurants at **Soi Safari Lodge** (*lunch/dinner KSh650/700*) or **Lake Baringo Club** (*lunch/dinner KSh870/990*). As you'd hope for this price, the food is mostly excellent, but drinks will bump up your bill quite a bit (KSh100/120 for a large Tusker).

In Kampi ya Samaki, cheap stodge is the order of the day; try the **Mombasa** and **Bethania** hotels or the **Zion Cafe** near the lake, but don't expect much choice – it helps if you like goat. **Lake Breeze Hotel** (*mains around KSh150*) has a slightly wider menu and can be a good place for a cold beer, but expect some unwanted attention. **Harriers Lodge** also picks up a small crowd in the evenings.

Getting There & Away

There are three buses per day between Kampi ya Samaki and Nakuru (KSh200, two hours), as well as infrequent matatus (KSh130) and Nissans (KSh150). From Kampi ya Samaki, much of the transport leaves early in the morning: the first bus departs around 6.30am. If you have difficulty finding direct transport to Nakuru, try heading to Marigat, where there are more frequent connections to Nakuru.

A gravel track connects Loruk at the top end of the lake with the Nyahururu to Maralal road. If you have your own transport it's a rough but bearable road; there's no public transport along it and hitching is extremely difficult. You can usually buy petrol at Lake Baringo Club; if you're heading northeast it's worth noting that after Marigat, there's no reliable supply until Maralal.

The Central Highlands

Densely populated and intensively cultivated, the Kenyan Central Highlands are very much the heartland of the country, not least because they are home to the politically favoured Kikuyu people (see the special section 'Tribes of Kenya'). The highlands form the eastern wall of the Rift Valley and consist of the Aberdares, which begin around Limuru and continue north up to Maralal, and the massif of Mt Kenya itself; within this area are the Aberdare and Mt Kenya National Parks, two of the region's major attractions. For ease of reference, the areas of the highlands that lie north of Rumuruti, Nanyuki and Meru are discussed in the Northern Kenya chapter.

The region is very fertile, well-watered and thickly forested in parts. The climate, likewise, is excellent for agriculture. Given these qualities, it's not surprising that the land was coveted by the white settlers who began arriving in ever-increasing numbers once the Mombasa–Uganda railway was completed. Here the settlers could grow anything year-round, particularly cash crops that were in demand in Europe. It's also not surprising that the Kikuyu eventually became so disenchanted with the loss of their best land that war erupted between the two groups in 1952, in the form of the Mau Mau rebellion (see History in the Facts about Kenya chapter). While not even the staunchest patriot could claim that the Mau Mau won, the uprising did force the British colonial authorities to reassess their position and ultimately to grant independence to the country.

White Kenyan farmers are still present in the area, but their holdings have been reduced and much of the land has been parcelled out among the Kikuyu. This subdivision, with its frequent encroachment on one of Kenya's few remaining large forested areas, has brought its own problems; water crises are frequent, soil erosion is a major threat and many plots are too small to support a family. Although there's still a great deal of forest remaining, demand for timber to be used as construction material and firewood (the most common form of fuel for cooking and heating) puts it at risk – a real danger given that much of Kenya is scrub and desert.

Highlights

- Reaching your peak in the heights of Mt Kenya
- Testing the waters at the dramatic Thomson's Falls
- Getting down and dusty in the backwoods of Meru National Park
- Soaring over the Aberdares with the Gliding Club of Kenya
- Ditching the hoi polloi for a top-end treat at Mt Kenya Safari Club
- Living like a Somali nomad at Nanyuki River Camel Camp

National Parks & Reserves:
Aberdare National Park, Mt Kenya National Park, Meru National Park, Mwea National Reserve, Ol Donyo Sabuk National Park

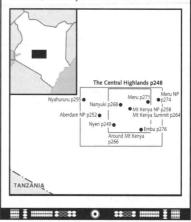

The Aberdares

The Aberdares stretch from South Kinangop, east of Naivasha, up as far as the Laikipia Escarpment northwest of Nyahururu. Known to the Kikuyu as Nyandarua (Drying Hide), the area was named after the president of the Royal Geographical Society by the explorer Joseph Thomson in 1884. The lower eastern slopes were long cultivated by the Kikuyu, while the higher regions, with peaks of up to

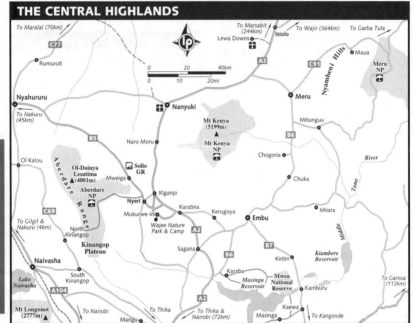

THE CENTRAL HIGHLANDS

cane, citrus fruits, bananas, tea, coffee and even that Australian import, macadamia nuts.

On a clear day (usually early morning), you can see Mt Kenya in all its snowcapped glory in the distance. Apart from this, however, it's hardly the most magnetic town in Kenya and few travellers stay more than a couple of nights.

4000m and covered in dense forests, bamboo thickets and mist-covered moors, were left to the leopards, buffaloes, lions and elephants.

The arrival of Europeans saw the establishment of coffee and tea plantations on the eastern side and wheat and pyrethrum (chrysanthemum) farms on the western slopes; unlike around Naivasha, most of this commercial land has now been returned to the Kikuyu.

NYERI & AROUND
☎ 0171

One of the largest towns in the Central Highlands, Nyeri is the administrative headquarters of Central Province and the usual gateway to Aberdare National Park. It's a lively place with a plethora of stores selling everything under the sun. It also has a good choice of hotels and restaurants.

In the early days of colonialism, Nyeri started life as a garrison town, but was quickly transformed into a trading and social centre for white cattle ranchers, coffee growers and wheat farmers. The area around the town is very green and is intensively cultivated for all manner of vegetables, sugar

Information

There are several places around the Ibis Hotel offering Internet services; **Dorpix Merchants**, which charges KSh3 to KSh5 per minute, is probably the best. Nyeri has three post offices, and there are plenty of cardphones. Both Barclays and Standard Chartered Banks have ATMs.

Things to See & Do

Lord Baden-Powell, founder of the international Scout Association movement, is buried in the cemetery behind St Peter's church. His former cottage (in the grounds of the Outspan Hotel) has been turned into a **museum** (admission KSh100).

Wildlife drives into Aberdare National Park can be organised through Aberdare

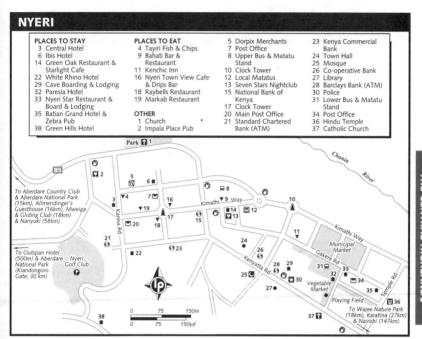

NYERI

PLACES TO STAY
3 Central Hotel
6 Ibis Hotel
14 Green Oak Restaurant & Starlight Cafe
22 White Rhino Hotel
29 Cave Boarding & Lodging
32 Paresia Hotel
33 Nyeri Star Restaurant & Board & Lodging
35 Batian Grand Hotel & Zebra Pub
38 Green Hills Hotel

PLACES TO EAT
4 Tayiri Fish & Chips
9 Bahati Bar & Restaurant
11 Kenchic Inn
16 Nyeri Town View Cafe & Drips Bar
18 Raybells Restaurant
19 Markab Restaurant

OTHER
1 Church
2 Impala Place Pub

5 Dorpix Merchants
7 Post Office
8 Upper Bus & Matatu Stand
10 Clock Tower
12 Local Matatus
13 Seven Stars Nightclub
15 National Bank of Kenya
17 Clock Tower
20 Main Post Office
21 Standard Chartered Bank (ATM)

23 Kenya Commercial Bank
24 Town Hall
25 Mosque
26 Co-operative Bank
27 Library
28 Barclays Bank (ATM)
30 Police
31 Lower Bus & Matatu Stand
34 Post Office
36 Hindu Temple
37 Catholic Church

Country Club, Outspan Hotel and also the Allmendinger's guesthouse. The Outspan charges KSh1500 per person, while the Aberdare Country Club charges US$169 per vehicle. See Places to Stay – Top-End for contact details.

A few kilometres north of Mweiga is **Solio Game Ranch** *(in Nairobi ☎ 02-240157, fax 240410)*, which has played a major part in preserving and breeding rhinos in Kenya. If you don't have your own vehicle, Aberdare Country Club organises tours for US$169 per vehicle plus KSh1600 per person.

The **Gliding Club of Kenya** *(☎ 55040; PO Box 926, Nyeri; ⓔ gliding@africaonline.co.ke)* has its headquarters at Mweiga, 18km north of Nyeri. If you fancy getting your head in the clouds, a 10-minute flight costs US$50. The managers, Peter and Petra Allmendinger, also run an excellent guesthouse (see Places to Stay – Top End).

Wajee Nature Park & Camp *(☎ 60359, in Nairobi ☎ 02-743615)* is a lovely little nature sanctuary and camp site (see Places to Stay, later) in the foothills of the Aberdare massif. The 10-hectare forest is criss-crossed with trails and is home to some rare forest birds;

a bird guide will cost about KSh300 per day, and you can borrow binoculars. Nature trails and traditional Kikuyu entertainment can also be arranged here.

The sanctuary is signposted from the main road 5km south of Nyeri and 2km north of Karatina. Coming from either direction you go to Mukurwe-ini (there are regular minibuses, known as matatus), then turn off the main road and head 3km south to Mihuti – the camp is another 1km south of the village.

Places to Stay – Budget & Mid-Range

Wajee Nature Park & Camp *(☎ 60359, Nairobi ☎ 02-743615; camping KSh300, bandas KSh1300, cottage KSh4200)* offers camping at a lovely nature sanctuary about 18km south of Nyeri. The camp site has good facilities, some three-person bandas (and a well-equipped cottage (maximum eight people). Meals are available (KSh300) or kitchen facilities with firewood and utensils can be provided for KSh500 per day.

There is plenty of cheap accommodation in Nyeri, but the real bottom-end places are

Behind the Beans

Kenya is a great place to buy coffee, and it's one thing you'll have no problem taking out of the country. However, next time you're sipping on a frappucino or demanding extra froth on your US$3 skinny latte, it's worth sparing a thought for Kenyan coffee farmers, who must number among the worst-exploited commodity producers in the world.

Coffee has become something of a *cause célèbre* recently with the September 2002 launch of Oxfam International's Make Trade Fair campaign, which highlights the huge gulf between farmers' earnings and the massive profits enjoyed by the multinational 'roasters' who package and distribute the product. According to the charity's report, coffee prices have slumped to a 30-year low, with farmers around the world receiving on average of around US$1 per kilogram; the international industry, however, is worth over US$2 billion annually, with consumer prices averaging US$15 per kilo. As the global market is hugely oversupplied, buyers can effectively force farmers to accept whatever price they offer.

Kenyan farmers have been hit particularly hard by the crisis, as most exporters buy through local co-operative societies and as little as US$0.10 from an average auction price of US$2.80 per kilo can reach the grower. For a country that exports up to 32,000 tons of coffee a year, this is obviously serious news.

While the Oxfam campaign has drawn worldwide attention to the problem, none of the big four roasters have yet pledged support, and it will be some time before such imbalances can be rectified.

perhaps best avoided. Acceptable options include the following.

Cave Boarding & Lodging (☎ 4223; off Kenyatta Rd; singles with bathroom KSh250) is slightly better than the name suggests, but there are definitely no frills here.

Paresia Hotel (☎ 2765; off Gakere Rd; singles/doubles with bathroom KSh300/500), a large modern tower block, is a touch shabby but has reasonable rooms with good security and some views over the town and the market.

Nyeri Star Restaurant & Board & Lodging (☎ 31083; Gakere Rd; singles/doubles with bathroom KSh300/500) is a bit brighter. You don't get much noise from the bus station outside, but the popular bar and restaurant inside can get quite lively.

Green Oak Restaurant (☎ 2726; off Kimathi Way; singles/doubles with bathroom KSh300/450) has some decent rooms at the back.

Ibis Hotel (☎ 4858; singles/doubles with bathroom KSh400/650), part of a small local chain, is good value, although not as well-equipped as its sister hotel in Nanyuki. There is a newly renovated covered courtyard, a bar and a restaurant downstairs.

Central Hotel (☎ 0722-667437; Kanisa Rd; singles/doubles with bathroom KSh450/550, suites KSh650) seems to have had a dramatic price crash, making it quite a bargain. It's a modern place with a good restaurant, a noisy bar and guarded parking.

White Rhino Hotel (☎ 30934; Kenyatta Rd; singles/doubles KSh500/1000) is appallingly maintained – only the bar has kept any of its colonial charm, probably because it's the only part that still sees regular crowds! The rooms are big but depressing and overpriced. There is a cheap restaurant and occasional 'cultural' entertainment.

Batian Grand Hotel (☎ 30743; Gakere Rd; singles/doubles KSh700/1000), formerly the Crested Eagle Hotel, has been rebranded but apparently not refurbished. It's a well-appointed place with good facilities (when the boilers aren't leaking), and rooms at the front face Mt Kenya, hence the new name. There's guarded parking, a coffee shop, restaurant and the Zebra Pub downstairs.

Green Hills Hotel (☎ 30604; singles/doubles KSh1350/2300), some distance out of town, is a more expensive place popular with conferences. The grounds are extensive and surprisingly nice, although most rooms are in modern concrete blocks; there are also seven cottages, which are better looking but smaller. There's a swimming pool, bar and restaurant (set meals KSh550).

Places to Stay – Top End

Outspan Hotel (☎ 2424, in Nairobi ☎ 02-540780; singles/doubles half-board US$104/130 in low season, US$130/160 in high season), about 1km out of town on the road to Kiandongoro Gate in the Aberdares, belongs to Block Hotels and is the check-in for Treetops

Lodge in the national park. Sited in beautifully landscaped gardens, the whole complex resembles an immaculate little village, and has all the facilities you would expect from a top-end country resort. Wildlife drives into the Aberdares and nature walks can be arranged.

Aberdare Country Club *(☎ 55620; in Nairobi ☎ 02-216940; e ark@form-net.com; singles/doubles full board US$98/154 in low season, US$148/195 in high season)*, southeast of Mweiga about 17km north of Nyeri, is part of the Lonrho Hotels group and acts as reception for the Ark in the Aberdares. The views here are superb, and the club is surrounded by its own 500-hectare wildlife sanctuary. Activities available include swimming, tennis, golf, horse riding, walking safaris and trout fishing, as well as wildlife drives into the Aberdares or to the nearby Solio Game Ranch. Temporary membership costs KSh500 per day.

Peter and Petra run Allmendinger's **guesthouse** *(☎ 55261; per person full board US$50)*, just north of the Aberdare Country Club, comes highly recommended, although the road to it can be difficult in the rainy season. Horse riding, wildlife drives and excursions to Lake Nakuru can be arranged here.

Places to Eat

Nyeri seems to be a good place for cheap chicken. **Kenchic Inn** *(Gakere Rd)* does the usual greased fowl, but for something a bit more imaginative try **Bahati Bar & Restaurant** or the relaxed **Markab Restaurant**, both on Kimathi Way.

Green Oak Restaurant *(Gakere Rd; mains KSh120-150)* is a local favourite – the food is good, there's a lively bar and the balcony is a great place to watch the action in town.

Raybells *(Kimathi Way; mains KSh120-200)*, an excellent Western-style 'family' restaurant, does a wide range of dishes, including pizza, and also has a takeaway section. If it served alcohol, it might be the best place in town!

The restaurants in the **Ibis**, **Central** and **Batian Grand** hotels are all quite popular and worth trying. The Batian Grand is the priciest: meals will cost you around KSh300 or KSh450 for the buffet.

The area around the upper matatu stand on Kimathi Way is good for breakfast, with

mandazi (semi-sweet doughnuts) going for as little as KSh5; try **Starlight Cafe** first.

You can get coffee and snacks at **Nyeri Town View Cafe**, overlooking the Agip petrol station. Brits may also like to scoff at **Tayiri Fish & Chips**, one way or another.

Entertainment

Nyeri is a good town for drinkers, if you don't mind rough-and-ready dives and pool halls (**Drips Bar** is a good example). Less hardened souls should head for the hotel bars, such as **White Rhino Hotel**, which also has a lively disco every weekend; reggae nights here are particularly popular. More upmarket choices include **Zebra Pub** at the Batian Grand, while the **Impala Place Pub**, behind Central Hotel, also looks a more civilised than some.

Green Hills Hotel has a club on site, although it's a bit of a dark walk at night. In town, **Seven Stars Nightclub**, next to Green Oak restaurant, is suitably loud and messy.

Getting There & Away

Generally speaking the upper bus stand deals with big buses, while the lower stand takes care of the matatus and local buses; local matatus can also be found on Kimathi Way.

Matatus run to Nairobi (KSh200, two hours), Nanyuki (KSh80, 45 minutes), Thika (KSh150, 1½ hours), Nakuru (KSh200, two

---

Naming of Places

Unintentionally amusing names have long been a source of entertainment for travellers, and despite being an English-speaking country Kenya has more than its fair share of businesses seemingly named with scant regard for the actual meaning of words.

One prime example is Dream Makers Hog and Drink Store (a great place to pig out?). You can also ponder the practicalities of the Internet Butchery, the workings of a Posho Mill or the gender status of Mama John, indulge in some Bible Zipping, go down Go-Down Road, shop for perfume and textiles at the Isiolo Book Centre, find a Suitable Bar & Restaurant, or even book your camel in for a service at the Camel Improvement Group Butchery. And if none of that has ruffled your feathers, you could try having your hair done by Professional Nancys.

hours) and Nyahururu (KSh130, one hour), as well as further afield to western destinations such as Kisumu (KSh450, four hours) and Eldoret (KSh400, four hours). Buses duplicate most of these lines; you may occasionally have to change at Karatina for Nairobi.

To get to the Aberdare National Park headquarters, catch a matatu to Mweiga (KSh30, 20 minutes).

ABERDARE NATIONAL PARK

Created in 1950, this park *(nonresident adult/ child per day US$30/10, residents KSh500/ 200, trekkers US$10; smartcard required)* essentially encloses two different environments: the Kinangop Plateau in the west is a 60km stretch of moorland, peaks and forest, while the Salient is an outcrop of dense rainforest to the east. As on Mt Kenya, rain can be expected at any time and when it does arrive, it's heavy.

The park has a variety of fauna, flora and scenery that you won't find elsewhere, except perhaps on Mt Kenya. Elephants and buffaloes are the dominant animals, but rarer species are to be found here including black rhinos, bongo antelopes, bush pigs, giant forest hogs, black servals and rare black leopards. Hundreds of bird species can be seen (look out for the giant kingfishers) and it's worth looking out for the small lion population when at the viewing platforms next to the dramatic **Chania Falls** and **Karura Falls**. **Gura Falls**, which drops a full 300m down into thick forest, is more difficult to get to.

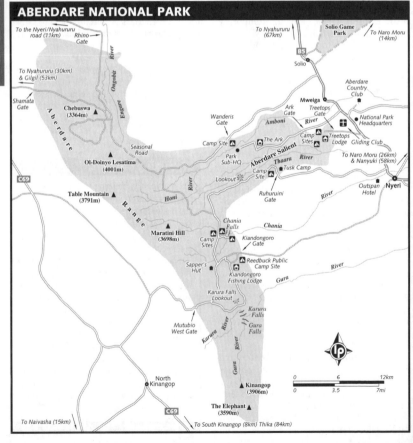

ABERDARE NATIONAL PARK

Viewing wildlife here is not like on the open savanna of Amboseli and Masai Mara. The dense rainforest of the Salient provides excellent cover for the animals, so it's best to take your time and stay a few nights. There is a selection of excellent banda accommodation and camp sites (although facilities are minimal), plus two renowned and very expensive lodges, the Ark and Treetops.

The park is rarely included in safari itineraries and is even less visited by independent travellers. The main reason for this is that vehicle entry is restricted to 4WD. KWS is currently grading the roads up to Wanderis Gate; at the moment the main roads are well-constructed *murram* (dirt) and passable in most weather, but when it rains the lesser trails become dangerously muddy. However, if you are prepared to hire a vehicle, join the tours operated by a couple of lodges in the area, or trek through the beautiful park, your rewards will easily justify the effort.

If you want to enter the park through the Treetops or Ark gates you must get permission from the park headquarters. This is readily granted. If you intend to move through the Salient to the Kinangop Plateau by vehicle you must also arrange for the road barrier below Tusk Camp to be unlocked.

For the past few years the Rhino Ark organisation has been constructing an electric fence around the park perimeter. Once finished, the 278km fence will keep animals within the park, and it will stop the encroachment on the forest by local villagers whose crops are then protected from marauding wildlife. So far good progress has been made, but unfortunate incidents do still occur: in summer 2002 a herd of 500 elephants unexpectedly arrived in the south of the park, disrupting local crops and actually killing a farmer who had slept on his land to protect it.

Information

Aberdare National Park is one of the parks piloting the new KWS Smartcard; you can get a card and pay entry fees at the **park headquarters** (☎ 0171-55024; PO Box 22, Nyeri) at Mweiga.

To help fund Rhino Ark, the excellent new 1:25,000 *Map of the Aberdare Salient and the Aberdare National Park* has been produced. It's available for KSh250 only from the park headquarters. The 1:150,000 *The Aberdares National Park and Environs* produced by Tourist Maps is not a bad general guide to the area (KSh250).

Trekking

KWS currently advises against trekking in the Salient, as the dense cover for animals makes walking dangerous for visitors, but the high moorland and the four main peaks (all about 3500m to 4000m) are accessible. You must be prepared for bad weather and obtain advance permission from the warden at the Mweiga park headquarters, who will provide an armed ranger (KSh500 per day) to guide and protect you against inquisitive wildlife. Lonely Planet's *Trekking in East Africa* has full details of the walks. See also the Mt Kenya National Park section later in this chapter for general details on trekking or contact the Mountain Club of Kenya (see Things to See & Do in the Nairobi chapter), which is a good source of information.

Fishing

Trout fishing in the park is very popular, especially high up on the moors. Kiandongoro Fishing Lodge makes a good base, but you'll need a licence from the park headquarters (KSh400). The Chania River is especially good for brown trout, but watch your back – there are tales of fishermen being stalked by lions! It's a good idea to get an armed ranger to escort you.

Places to Stay – Budget & Mid-Range

There are seven **public camp sites** (adult/child US$8/2) and three **special camp sites**; ask at the headquarters which sites are open. Reservations must be made at the park headquarters.

Excellent **Tusk Camp** (exclusive use per night KSh5000), close to the Ruhuruini Gate, and **Sapper Hut** (per night KSh2000), overlooking a waterfall on the Upper Magura River, can be booked through KWS Headquarters (☎ 02-550224) or Let's Go Travel (☎ 02-340331; e info@letsgosafari.com) in Nairobi. Tusk Camp's two wooden huts sleep eight, and there are cooking facilities and hot water. The views of Mt Kenya are fantastic and rhinos have been seen grazing in front of the huts. Sapper Hut is a simple banda with an open fire, two beds and a hot-water boiler.

The **Kiandongoro Fishing Lodge** (cottages US$200 in low season, US$250 in high season), booked through the park headquarters, is an excellent spot up on the high moor by the Gura River. The two large stone cottages each sleep seven people and have bathrooms, gas-powered kitchens, dining rooms and fireplaces.

Places to Stay – Top End

Both of the lodges in this park are built beside waterholes, and attract animals – especially elephants and buffaloes – by the dubious practice of spreading salt below the viewing platforms each day. While this ensures a stream of sightings for the mostly sedentary punters, the impact on the immediate environment is highly detrimental: the constant trampling from the heavier animals reduces the waterline to something resembling a matatu stand, which then makes more timid animals reluctant to approach because of the lack of cover.

You are not permitted to drive your own vehicle to either of these lodges. Transfers are included in the price, so you just have to present yourself to the lodge receptions at Outspan Hotel in Nyeri (for Treetops) or the Aberdare Country Club near Mweiga (for the Ark) on the right day. Park fees are not included for either lodge, and children under seven are prohibited. Both places have animal alert buzzers in all the rooms, for guests who can't be bothered to spot their own wildlife.

Treetops (book through Block Hotels ☎ 02-540780; singles/doubles full board US$144/180 in low season, US$224/280 in high season) looks to be in a bit of a state, with peeling outsides and creaking floors. For this price, you'd really expect more than shared bathrooms and benches in the dining room! It's long been a favourite haunt of the British royals, among others, although it's anyone's guess why; the original building was burned down by Mau Mau guerrillas, and you can't really blame them for trying.

The Ark (book through Lonrho Hotels ☎ 02-216940; singles/doubles full board US$163/189 in low season, US$299/352 in high season) does at least have en suite facilities, but they've gone a bit overboard (sorry) with the theme – rooms really do resemble poky ships' cabins, which at this price is frankly criminal. The public areas here are a bit nicer

than at Treetops, but if it's luxury you want you're much better off visiting Lake Nakuru or the Masai Mara.

Getting There & Away

There are regular matatus from Nyeri to Mweiga (KSh30, 20 minutes) that pass KWS headquarters and the main park gates.

However, as trekking in the Salient is inadvisable, it's best to start at one of the other gates or have some form of transport arranged.

Outspan Hotel in Nyeri offers wildlife drives into the lower Salient area of the park for KSh1500 per person (minimum two people). Drives organised by the Aberdare Country Club cost US$169 per vehicle; both rates exclude park entry fees.

Peter and Petra Allmendinger also run wildlife drives from their guesthouse near Mweiga (see Places to Stay under Nyeri for contact details).

NYAHURURU (THOMSON'S FALLS)
☎ 0365

At 2360m, Nyahururu is one of the highest towns in Kenya but, despite the cool and invigorating climate, there's little going on here. One of the last white settlements to be established in the colonial era, the town didn't really take off until the arrival of the railway spur from Gilgil in 1929; the trains here now only carry freight, and the town is once again becoming an agricultural backwater. The surrounding plateau is intensively cultivated with maize, beans and sweet potatoes all well represented in Nyahururu's lively markets.

The best approach to town is the excellent and very scenic road from Nakuru, which snakes up and down through undulating farmlands and dense forests with spectacular views over the Aberdares.

Information

Internet access is available at **Stanrod Internet**, which charges KSh5 per minute, in the Mimi Centre at the north end of town. There are cardphones around town and in front of the post office; Barclays Bank has an ATM.

The Falls

Located on the outskirts of town, the falls are named after Joseph Thomson, the first

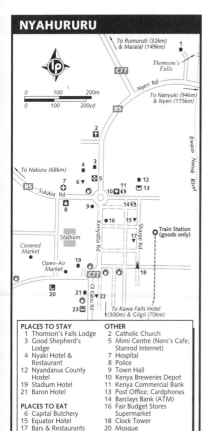

NYAHURURU

PLACES TO STAY
1 Thomson's Falls Lodge
3 Good Shepherd's Lodge
4 Nyaki Hotel & Restaurant
12 Nyandarua County Hostel
19 Stadium Hotel
21 Baron Hotel

PLACES TO EAT
6 Capital Butchery
15 Equator Hotel
17 Bars & Restaurants
22 Connection Cafe

OTHER
2 Catholic Church
5 Mimi Centre (Noni's Cafe; Stanrod Internet)
7 Hospital
8 Police
9 Town Hall
10 Kenya Breweries Depot
11 Kenya Commercial Bank
13 Post Office; Cardphones
14 Barclays Bank (ATM)
16 Fair Budget Stores Supermarket
18 Clock Tower
20 Mosque
23 Bus & Matatu Station

European to walk from Mombasa to Lake Victoria in the early 1880s. They're a popular stopover for safari companies en route to Maralal and the north, and are well worth a visit.

Formed by the waters of the Ewaso Narok River, the falls plummet over 72m into a ravine and the resulting spray bathes the dense forest below in a perpetual mist. A series of stone steps leads down to the bottom of the ravine and this is the only safe access – don't attempt to go down any other way as the rocks on the side of the ravine are often very loose.

There are some fantastic walks downstream through the forested valley of the Ewaso Narok River and upstream a couple of kilometres to one of the highest hippo

pools in Kenya. Take time to explore a little. Guides are fairly easy to find, especially around the souvenir shacks overlooking the falls, but you'll have to bargain hard.

Places to Stay

There are a couple of places around town where you can get single rooms for KSh150, but they're really scraping the barrel. The exception is **Nyandarua County Hostel**, behind the post office and the provincial headquarters; it has quiet self-contained rooms within this price bracket, but only offers singles (the beds may be big enough for couples to share).

Good Shepherd's Lodge (Nyeri Rd) is also worth a look, although it was temporarily closed at the time of research.

Stadium Hotel (☎ 32773; singles/doubles with bathroom KSh300/500) is more expensive but offers decent value, with light rooms and good security.

Nyaki Hotel & Restaurant (☎ 22313; singles/doubles with bathroom KSh350/750) is a relatively modern five-storey building just off Nyeri Rd. The doubles are essentially suites, although hardly in the top-end sense! There's secure parking and a popular bar/restaurant.

Baron Hotel (☎ 22262; Ol Kalou Rd; singles/doubles with bathroom KSh300/400, suites KSh800), a large and slightly tatty modern place, has pretty variable prices, especially out of season. In season, when it's properly up and running, the bar and restaurant are good, suites have phones and rates include breakfast.

Kawa Falls Hotel (Ol Kalou Rd; singles/doubles with bathroom KSh350/600) has similar rooms, but is a bit more consistent and has electric showers. Some overpriced suites may also be available.

Thomson's Falls Lodge (☎ 22006, fax 32170; camping per person KSh300, singles/doubles KSh1900/2400), overlooking the falls, is about the only place with any character in town. The white planters are long gone and even the nostalgia is looking slightly worn, but it's a cosy spot with some great views. Accommodation is available in the main building or in cottages scattered around the grounds; rooms have fireplaces and decent facilities with probably the only power showers in Kenya! Rates include breakfast, and there's a bar, lounge and a dining room. Picnicking here costs KSh50.

THE CENTRAL HIGHLANDS

This is also the best place to camp if you have your own gear. Firewood and hot showers are included in the price.

Places to Eat

Most of the budget hotels and many of the bars along Sharpe Rd have restaurants where you can get standard African food. **Kawa Falls Hotel**, **Baron Hotel** and **Nyaki Hotel & Restaurant** are probably the best value, with prices around KSh130 to KSh150 for a main course.

Capital Butchery, next to Nyaki Hotel, is also good for *nyama choma* (barbecued meat).

Connection Cafe, opposite the matatu stand, and **Noni's Cafe**, in the Mimi Centre, are pretty good for breakfast or a cheap lunch.

Equator Hotel *(Sharpe Rd; mains from KSh50)* is another cheap joint that turns into a pretty rowdy bar in the evenings. Rooms are also available if you really need them.

The restaurant at **Thomson's Falls Lodge** *(breakfast KSh200, lunch/dinner KSh500)* is the best (and only) place to go for a minor splurge.

Advance notice is necessary if you intend to take your meal in the main dining room; guests can also arrange packed lunches (KSh300), or there's an open-air grill (meat dishes KSh250) at lunch times.

For those who want to prepare their own meals, there's an excellent choice of fruit, vegetables and meat available in the **covered market**, and at the **Fair Budget Stores** supermarket.

Entertainment

The lodge has the most interesting bars in town, with comfortable armchairs and blazing log fires. If you stay in town, there are plenty of noisy drinking holes on Sharpe Rd.

When it's fully open there's a **disco** every Saturday night at Baron Hotel (where the usual Kenyan diet of reggae and Congolese music applies). Another possibility is **Kenya Breweries Depot** *(Subukia Rd)*; events here are usually flyered all over town. The **Equator Hotel** also runs discos.

Getting There & Away

There are plenty of matatus during the day until late afternoon between Nyahururu and Nakuru (KSh100, 45 minutes) and also Nyeri (KSh130, 1½ hours). Other destinations served include Nairobi (KSh250, 2½ hours), Nanyuki (KSh160, two hours) and Naivasha (KSh120, 1½ hours). There is only one daily bus to Nairobi (KSh220, three hours), leaving around dawn.

A number of matatus head up to Maralal (KSh250 to KSh300, three hours), but departures dry up after about 1pm. Advance booking is a good idea for the irregular morning bus route. For the rest of the day, hitching is feasible but not easy.

The road to the north is surfaced as far as Rumuruti (KSh70), after which it's *murram* and sharp stones. While it's by no means impassable, parts of this road are in bad shape, and punctures are common.

RUMURUTI & AROUND
☎ 0176

This tiny town is little more than a pit stop for vehicles heading to Maralal, with a petrol station and a handful of basic *dukas* (shops) and cafés.

Eighteen kilometres north of town, on top of a smallish hill, is **Bobong Camp Site** *(☎ 32718; e olmaisor@africaonline.co.ke; PO Box 5, Rumuruti; camping KSh250, bandas per person KSh300, full board KSh2400)*. It's a friendly little place in the middle of nowhere, with good basic facilities, a swimming pool, simple mud bandas and a cheetah called Claudia! Some basic supplies are available and self-catering equipment can be hired. Various activities can also be arranged here, including cultural visits to the Turkana and Samburu communities (KSh5000) and one of the cheapest camel safaris in Kenya – KSh750 per day for basic hire of one camel and a handler (see Camel Safaris in the Safaris chapter for more details).

Further north, about 77km from Maralal, is **Mugie Ranch** *(☎ 31045; w www.mugieranch .com; PO Box 30)*, a private farm that has branched out into tourism and offers exclusive top-end accommodation in **Mutamaiyu House** *(book through Richard Bonham Safaris ☎ 02-884475; e bonham.luke@swift kenya .com; per person full board from US$425)*. As it is still a fully functioning ranch, there is far more to the site than most lodges; you can drive anywhere on the 19,600-hectare farm (guides US$50 per day) and get involved in the tracking of six radio-collared lions, part of a predator research project. Full board in-

The jagged peaks of Mt Kenya, Central Highlands

Giant tortoise, near Naro Moru

Aerial shot of elephants and buffaloes, Aberdare National Park

Distant rain passing over Masai Mara National Reserve, western Kenya

Moving with a herd of elephants, Masai Mara National Reserve

A fishing dhow, Lake Victoria

cludes almost everything except champagne and clay-pigeon shooting!

Maralal–Nyahururu matatus will drop you at the signs for either of these places, but may try and charge you the full fare (KSh200); local transport from the town to the signs starts around KSh50 for Bobong, but goes up the later it is and the more desperate you look! Leaving the camp, hitching is usually the only option. If you can afford a private charter, transfers to and from Mugie airstrip are included in the room rates.

Mt Kenya National Park

If you're not an early riser it's quite possible never to see Mt Kenya clearly until you get into the national park; once you do, you'll understand why the Kikuyu deified it. At 5199m, it's Africa's second-highest mountain. It's also the seat of Ngai, the Kikuyu god; fortunately for the many travellers who try the ascent every year, Ngai does not concern himself much with the normal lives of individuals, although it's worth remembering that he should not be needlessly bothered!

Mt Kenya's highest peaks, Batian and Nelion, can only be reached by mountaineers with technical skills. However, Point Lenana, the third-highest peak, can be reached by trekkers and is the usual goal for most people, offering a fantastic experience without the risks of real climbing. As you might imagine, there are superb views over the surrounding country from Point Lenana and other high points around the main peaks, although the summit is often cloaked in mist from late morning until late afternoon. The glaciers on the mountain are something of a geographical marvel, being just 16km south of the equator. Above 3000m is mountain moorland, characterised by some remarkable flora (see the boxed text 'Mt Kenya's Flora', later).

As marvellous as the summit is, a common complaint from trekkers is that they didn't allow enough time to enjoy the whole of the mountain. Walks through the foothills, particularly those to the east and northeast of the main peaks, and the circular traverse around Batian and Nelion are dramatic and tremendously rewarding. You won't regret

setting aside a week or 10 days rather than just four days for a summit rush.

If time is short or you don't want to do all the planning yourself, see Organised Treks, later.

INFORMATION

Entry fees to the national park are US$15 per day (US$8 for children and students). If you take a guide and/or porters you'll have to pay their entry fees too. Camping fees are an additional US$2 per person.

Before you leave Nairobi buy a copy of *Mt Kenya 1:50,000 Map & Guide* (1993) by Mark Savage & Andrew Wielochowski. It has a detailed topographical map and a full description of the routes, mountain medicine, flora and fauna, and accommodation. It's stocked by the main bookshops in Nairobi and Stanford's in London.

Lonely Planet's *Trekking in East Africa* by David Else has more information, details on wilder routes and some of the more esoteric variations that are possible on Mt Kenya.

Those who intend to do some technical climbing or mountaineering should get a copy of the **Mountain Club of Kenya's** (MCK; in Nairobi ☎ 02-501747; ⓦ www.mck.or.ke) *Guide to Mt Kenya & Kilimanjaro*, edited by Iain Allan. This is a substantial and comprehensive guide and is available in bookshops or from the MCK offices (see Things to See & Do in the Nairobi chapter). MCK also has reasonably up-to-date mountain information posted on its website.

THE ROUTES

There are at least seven different routes up the mountain. The routes covered here are Naro Moru (which starts from the village of the same name), the easiest and most popular, and Sirimon (which starts close to Nanyuki) and Chogoria (starts from the village of the same name), which are excellent alternatives.

You can also mix and match ascending and returning routes by tackling the exciting but demanding Summit Circuit path.

The Burguret and Timau routes are less well known and described in Lonely Planet's *Trekking in East Africa*.

The normal weather pattern on the mountain is clear mornings with the mist closing in from 10am, although this sometimes clears again in the early evening. This means that if you want to make the most of the trek you

THE CENTRAL HIGHLANDS

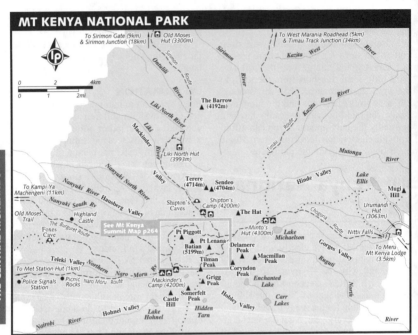

MT KENYA NATIONAL PARK

To Sirimon Gate (9km) & Sirimon Junction (18km)
Old Moses Hut (3300m)
To West Marania Roadhead (5km) & Timau Track Junction (34km)
Kazita West River
Ontulili River
Sirimon Route
Sirimon River
The Barrow (4192m)
Liki North River
Liki River
Mackinder River
Liki North Hut (3993m)
Nanyuki Valley
Kazita East River
Timau Route
Mutonga River
Terere (4714m)
Sendeo (4704m)
Hinde Valley
Lake Ellis
Nanyuki River
Nanyuki North River
Hausberg Valley
Nanyuki South Rv
To Kampi Ya Machengeni (11km)
Shipton's Caves
Shipton's Camp (4200m)
The Hat
Mugi Hill
Urumandi Hut (3063m)
Old Moses Trail
Highland Castle
The Burguret Route
Foxes Cave
See Mt Kenya Summit Map p264
Pt Piggott
Pt Lenana
Batian (5199m)
Minto's Hut (4300m)
Lake Michaelson
Chogoria Route
Nittii Falls
To Meru & Mt Kenya Lodge (3.5km)
Teleki Valley
Northern Naro Moru Rv
Delamere Peak
Macmillan Peak
Gorges Valley
To Met Station Hut (1km)
Police Signals Station
Picnic Rocks
Naro Moru Route
Mackinder's Camp (4200m)
Tilman Peak
Grigg Peak
Coryndon Peak
Enchanted Lake
Ruguti River
Castle Hill
Somerfelt Peak
Hobley Valley
Carr Lakes
Hohnel Valley
Lake Hohnel
Hidden Tarn
Nairobi River
River

THE CENTRAL HIGHLANDS

should set off early every morning; for the final assault on Point Lenana, you need to make a very early start if you want to see the sunrise and the views from the top, which (if you're lucky) can include Mt Kilimanjaro.

SAFETY

Mt Kenya's accessibility and the technical ease with which Point Lenana is reached create their own problems for enthusiastic trekkers. Many people ascend much too quickly and end up suffering from headaches, nausea and other (sometimes more serious) effects of altitude sickness (see Health in the Facts for the Visitor chapter). By spending at least three nights on the ascent you'll enjoy yourself much more; with proper clothes and equipment, you stand a much better chance of making it back down as well.

Another problem can be unpredictable harsh, cold, wet and windy weather. The trek to Point Lenana (just under 5000m) is not an easy hike and people die on the mountain every year. The best time to go is from mid-January to late February or from late August to September.

If you're not a regular mountain walker and don't know how to use a map and compass, trekking anything other than the Naro Moru or Sirimon routes without a competent companion or a local guide is simply asking for trouble. A guide is not compulsory, but it's a very good idea, especially for the Summit Circuit path.

CLOTHING & EQUIPMENT

The summits of Mt Kenya are surrounded by glaciers and often covered by snow. The temperature at night often drops to below -10°C (it feels like it in Mackinder's hut), so you need a good sleeping bag. A closed-cell foam mat is also advisable for extra insulation if you are going to sleep on the ground. A good set of warm clothes is equally important and that should include quality headgear and gloves. As it can rain at any time of year – and heavily – you will also need waterproof clothing. A decent pair of boots is an advantage but not strictly necessary; a pair of joggers is quite adequate most of the time, although it's good to have a pair of sandals or canvas tennis shoes to wear in the evening if your main shoes get wet. The one thing you will be very glad you brought is a pair of sunglasses. When the sun hits those snow-beds and glaciers on the summits, your eyes will hurt unless they're protected.

It's not a good idea to sleep in clothes you have worn during the day because the sweat your day clothes absorb from your skin keep them moist at night, reducing their heat-retention capabilities.

If you don't intend to stay in the huts along the way, you'll need a tent and any associated equipment.

You'll also need a stove, basic cooking equipment, eating utensils, a water container with a capacity of at least 2L per person per day, and water-purifying tablets. Stove fuel in the form of petrol and kerosene (paraffin) is fairly easily found in towns, and methylated spirits is available in Nairobi, as are gas cartridges, although the supply of these is not guaranteed. Fires are prohibited in the open except in an emergency; in any case, there's no wood available once you get beyond about 3300m. If you intend to engage porters you'll have to supply each of them with a backpack to carry your gear and theirs.

If you have a functioning mobile phone it may be worth taking it along, suitably protected of course; reception in the higher reaches of the mountain is actually very good, and a link to the outside world could be invaluable in an emergency.

Equipment Hire

Rental gear is available at the **Naro Moru River Lodge** (☎ *0176-62212; PO Box 18, Naro Moru*) and from **Mountain Rock Lodge** (☎ *0176-62625; PO Box 333, Nanyuki*). The gear is mostly in good condition and well maintained, although it can not be booked in advance and tends to be relatively expensive. Most guiding companies will have some equipment for hire, although you'll have less choice and lower standards.

GUIDES, COOKS & PORTERS

Taking on a guide and porter will improve your chances of getting to the top and avoiding altitude sickness. Having someone carry your heavy gear up this mountain is like the difference between travelling in a matatu and a Mercedes, and your guide will help set a sustainable pace.

Both will enhance your appreciation of this mountain a hundred-fold and, for the price, it's a bargain.

Considerable effort has been made in recent years to regulate guides and porters operating on the mountain. The KWS now issues vouchers to all registered guides and porters, who should also hold identity cards; they won't be allowed into the park without them. In addition, reputable trekking companies, guiding organisations and hotels will be members of the **Association of Mount Kenya Operators** (*AMKO;* ☎ *0166-22096*), which is backed by KWS and MCK. AMKO also organises the Mt Kenya Challenge in August, a fundraising event for conservation projects in which trekkers are sponsored by companies and individuals on their way to Point Lenana.

THE CENTRAL HIGHLANDS

Mt Kenya's Flora

The volcanic soil and the many rivers that radiate from the central cone of Mt Kenya have created a fertile environment, especially on the southern and eastern slopes, which receive the most rain. Despite encroaching farms on the mountain up to 1900m altitude, the lower slopes are well wooded. Above this zone, apart from where logging occurs, is the untouched rainforest. Among the abundant species of plants here are the giant camphors, along with vines, ferns, orchids and other epiphytes. On the drier northern and western slopes, the predominant trees are conifers.

On the southern and western slopes, as altitude increases, the forest gradually merges into a belt of dense bamboo. This eventually gives way to more open woodland consisting of hagena and hypericum trees, along with an undergrowth of flowering shrubs and herbs. Further up still is a belt of giant heather that forms dense clumps of up to 4m high, interspersed with tall grasses.

Open moorland forms the next zone and this is often very colourful with a profusion of small flowering plants. Here you'll find the amazing groundsel tree with its enormous cabbage-like flowers and the bizarre giant lobelias and senecios. This moorland zone extends up to the snow line at around 4600m. Beyond the snow line, the only plants you will find are mosses and lichens.

Female guides are becoming more common and technical guides for climbing Batian and Nelion are widely available.

Costs

The charges for guides, porters and cooks vary according to the route and the organisation. For the Naro Moru Route, the basic pay rates for guides and cooks are KSh450 per person per day and KSh350 for porters; on the Sirimon and Chogoria routes you'll pay around US$15 for guides and US$10 for porters. These fees will go up if you hire guides from a hotel, and do not include park entry fees and tips (budget around a day's wages per person as a tip, but make it clear it's only for good service).

If you ascend the mountain along one route and descend along a different one, you will be responsible for arranging and paying the transport costs for your porter and guide back to where they started from. It would be a good idea to sort this out before you set off and agree on a price for return transport plus any additional wages (a day spent travelling home counts as a working day), food and hotel costs along the way.

Porters will carry up to 18kg for a three-day trip or 16kg for a longer trip, excluding the weight of their own food and equipment. If you want them to carry more, you'll have to negotiate a price for the extra weight. A normal day's work is regarded as one stage of the journey; if you want to go further than this you'll have to pay two days wages, even if they don't do anything the following day.

ACCOMMODATION

There are a lot of huts on the mountain but not all are available to the general public. Several are owned by the MCK. A few of these huts are reserved exclusively for use by members and others can be used by the public, although these are all small, basic and most are in very bad condition.

MCK huts can be booked and paid for at the **MCK Clubhouse** (☎ 02-501747) or **Let's Go Travel** (☎ 02-340331; ℮ info@letsgosafari.com) in Nairobi, or at the Naro Moru River Lodge. They cost around US$3 per person per night, but they're in such bad condition that very few trekkers use them – it's much better to camp.

Apart from these huts, there are also some larger bunkhouses with more facilities.

These places are owned by lodges outside the park, but can also be used by independent trekkers for a fee. They must be booked and paid for in advance.

Officially, you can camp anywhere on the mountain, but it is usual to camp near one of the huts or bunkhouses as there is often a water supply and toilet nearby.

For information about accommodation before and after your trek, see the Around Mt Kenya section later in this chapter.

FOOD

In an attempt to reduce luggage, many trekkers forgo taking a stove and cooking equipment and exist entirely on canned and dried foods. You can certainly do this as long as you keep up your fluid intake, but it's not a good idea. That cup of hot soup in the evening and pot of tea or coffee in the morning can make all the difference between enjoying the trek and hating it or, at least, feeling irritable.

There are, however, a few things to bear in mind about cooking at high altitudes. The major consideration is that the boiling point of water is considerably reduced. At 4500m, for example, water boils at 85°C. This is too low to sufficiently cook rice or lentils (pasta is better) and you won't be able to brew a good cup of tea from it either (instant coffee is the answer). Cooking times are also considerably increased as a result, with consequent increased use of fuel.

The best range of suitable foods for the mountain is to be found in the supermarkets of Nairobi, especially Nakumatt and Uchumi. Elsewhere, there's a good range in the towns around the mountain (Nyeri, Nanyuki, Embu and Meru), but precious little at Naro Moru.

When you're buying dehydrated foods, get the pre-cooked variety to cut down on cooking time – two-minute noodles are a solution. It's a good idea to bring these from home.

Take plenty of citrus fruits and/or citrus drinks as well as chocolate, sweets or dried fruit to keep your blood sugar-level high. Fresh fruit and vegetables are available in all reasonably sized towns and villages.

To avoid severe headaches caused by dehydration or altitude sickness, drink at least 3L of fluid per day. Bringing rehydration sachets is an excellent idea.

ORGANISED TREKS

If your time is limited or you'd prefer someone else to make all the arrangements for a trek on Mt Kenya, there are plenty of possibilities, and it's hard to go anywhere in this region without being approached by several prospective guides. All-inclusive packages can be a good deal, particularly if you don't have any of your own equipment, and these can start from as little as US$40 per day.

As always, you need to watch out for the sharks; picking the right company is even more important here than on a normal wildlife safari, as an unqualified or inexperienced guide could put you in real danger as well as spoiling your trip.

Mountain Rock Hotels & Safaris (☎ 02-242133; Wabera St; PO Box 50484, Nairobi; e reservations@mountainrockkenya.com), in Jubilee Insurance House in Nairobi, is a real specialist in Mt Kenya climbs and runs the **Mountain Rock Lodge** (☎ 0176-62625) near Naro Moru. It offers budget packages for trekkers with their own transport and 'executive' packages for those wanting a little more luxury; costs are on a sliding scale based on group size – with twelve people it's cheap, but twice as expensive if you're on your own.

Day rates for budget/executive trips start at US$115/140 for the Naro Moru Route, US$110/135 for the Sirimon Route and US$135/170 for a trek up Sirimon and down the Chogoria Route. These prices are a good benchmark and include park entry and camping fees, food, huts, a guide, cook and porters, and transfers to the lodge before and after a climb. Other packages also include accommodation and transfers to and from Nairobi.

Naro Moru River Lodge (☎ 0176-62212; PO Box 18, Naro Moru; e mt.kenya@africaonline.co.ke) also runs a range of trips, all including a guide/cook, porters, all meals, park entry fees, camping fees, and transport to and from the road heads. Its prices are more expensive than most, and the normal route is up and down Naro Moru. If you take one of its treks, you're entitled to a special half-board deal at the hotel.

There are several safari companies in Nairobi that offer Mt Kenya treks, but many just sell the treks operated by Naro Moru and Mountain Rock Lodges, charging you an extra commission on top. Companies that do run their own treks include the following.

Bike Treks (☎ 02-446371, fax 243439; w www.angelfire.com/sk/biketreks) Kabete Gardens (PO Box 14237), Westlands, Nairobi. Bike Treks offers a range of possibilities from three-day Naro Moru route to four-day Sirimon/Naro Moru routes for US$400, and seven-day Sirimon/Chogoria routes for US$720. Prices include transfers, park entry and camping fees, guide, cook and porters, food and tents, but exclude backpacks, clothing and boots, and tips.

IntoAfrica (☎/fax 0114-255 5610; e enquiry@intoafrica.com; w www.intoafrica.co.uk) 59 Langdon St, Sheffield, UK, S11 8BH. This environmentally and culturally sensitive company places an emphasis on fair trade and offers a variety of routes (taking seven days), including the challenging Burguret/Chogoria route. Treks usually work out at around US$128 per person per day, based on a minimum of two.

KG Mountain Expeditions (☎ 0176-62403; e kgexpd@arcc.or.ke, w www.kgmountainexpd.com) PO Box 199, Naro Moru. This company, run by a highly experienced mountaineer, offers all-inclusive packages from US$265 per day (depending on group size), as well as no-frills budget options for around US$70.

Mountain View Tours & Trekking Safaris (☎ 0176-62088) PO Box 48, Naro Moru. It is recommended by a number of readers as being cheap and reliable. Prices are negotiable, but expect to pay around US$60 to US$70 per day.

Sana Highlands Trekking Expeditions (☎ 02-227 820; e info@sanatrekkingkenya.com; w www.sanatrekkingkenya.com) Arrow House, Koinange St (PO Box 39439), Nairobi. Sana operate five-day treks on the Sirimon or Naro Moru routes that start at US$300 for five people, including transfers.

RESPONSIBLE TREKKING

The popularity of trekking on Mt Kenya is placing great pressure on the natural environment. You can help preserve the ecology and beauty of the area by taking note of the following information.

- Carry out all your rubbish. Never ever bury it.
- Minimise the waste you must carry out by taking minimal packaging and taking no more food than you will need.
- Where there is no toilet, bury your waste at least 100m from any watercourse. Consider carrying a lightweight trowel for this purpose. Burn the waste before burying it.
- Don't use detergents or toothpaste within 50m of watercourses, even if they are biodegradable.
- Stick to existing tracks and avoid short cuts that bypass a switchback. If you blaze a new trail straight down a slope, it will erode the hillside with the next heavy rainfall.

THE CENTRAL HIGHLANDS

- Avoid removing the plant life that keeps topsoils in place.
- Open fires are not permitted. Cook on a light-weight kerosene, alcohol or Shellite (white gas) stove. Butane gas canisters are not widely available in Kenya.
- Do not feed the wildlife as this can lead to ani-mals becoming dependent on hand-outs and provide them with an unbalanced diet.

NARO MORU ROUTE

This is the most straightforward and popular of the Mt Kenya routes. It's also the least scenic, although it's still a spectacular and very enjoyable trail. You should allow a min-imum of four days for the trek; it can be done in three if you arrange transport between Naro Moru (see the Around Mt Kenya sec-tion later this chapter) and the Met Station, but doing it this quickly risks serious altitude sickness.

Accommodation & Bookings

An important thing to bear in mind is that the Naro Moru River Lodge has an exclu-sive franchise on the huts along this route, so you can only book here or through Let's Go Travel in Nairobi. It's all been carefully cal-culated to sew up the market; this shouldn't prevent you from climbing independently, as long as you're willing to camp and carry the appropriate equipment.

Guides & Porters

Apart from the **Naro Moru River Lodge** in Naro Moro itself, guides, porters and cooks can be booked through **Mount Kenya Guides & Porters Safari Club** (☎ 0176-62015; PO Box 128), a reliable AMKO-affiliated body. Its office is 5km along the road towards the Naro Moru gate, but its staff also pop up at the hotels in town scouting for business.

Mountain Rock Lodge (☎ 0176-62625; e base@mountainrockkenya.com) specialises in the Burguret Route north of Naro Moru, but can also provide guides/porters for this route at US$17/10 per day. However, like most places it 'encourages' you to take an expensive all-inclusive package.

The Trek

Starting in Naro Moru town, the first part of the route takes you along a relatively good gravel road through farmlands for some 13km (all the junctions are signposted) to the start of the forest. Another 5km brings

you to the park entry gate (2400m), from where it's 8km to the road head and the **Met Station Hut** (3000m; US$9 per person), where you stay for the night.

You can get up to the park gate (18km from Naro Moro) in 2WD in dry weather, although you won't make it to the Met Sta-tion in anything other than a 4WD. Both roads are getting worse and often become impassable in wet weather. You can get a matatu from the post office in Naro Moru to Kiambuthi (KSh50), 3km short of the park gate. This takes you past Blue Line Hotel, Mt Kenya Guides & Porters Safari Club and Mt Kenya Hostel & Camp Site. Transport to the gate costs US$140 per vehicle from Naro Moru River Lodge, US$170 per ve-hicle from Mountain Rock Lodge and almost anywhere else in town; Mt Kenya Hostel is probably the cheapest option. Hitching is possible but much easier on the way out.

On the second day you set off up the Teleki Valley to the edge of the forest at about 3200m. From here you scale the so-called **Vertical Bog** onto a ridge, where the route divides into two. You can either take the higher path, which gives better views but is often wet, or the lower path, which crosses the Naro Moru River and continues gently up to **Mackinder's Camp** (4160m; US$12 per person). This part of the trek should take about 4½ hours. Here you can stay in the dormitories or camp. There are toilets, and drinking water is available. The caretaker checks your bunkhouse booking receipts.

On the third day you can either rest at Mackinder's Camp to acclimatise or aim for Point Lenana. This stretch takes four to five hours, so it's common to leave around 2am (you'll need a torch or flashlight) to reach the summit in time for sunrise. From the bunkhouse, continue up past the ranger sta-tion to a fork in the path. Keep right, and go across a swampy area, followed by a moraine and then up a very long scree slope – this is a long, hard slog. MCK's **Austrian Hut** (4790m; KSh1000 per person) is three to four hours from Mackinder's and about one hour below the summit of Lenana, so it's a good place to rest before the final push. Alterna-tively, you could arrive here on the third day, then go for the summit on the morning of the fourth. Facilities are very basic, although the hut itself has been refurbished.

The section of the trek from Austrian Hut up to **Point Lenana** (4895m) takes you up a narrow rocky path that traverses the southwest ridge parallel to the Lewis glacier, which has shrunk more than 100m since the 1960s. A final climb or scramble brings you up onto the peak. In good weather it's fairly straightforward, but in bad weather you should not attempt to reach the summit unless you are experienced in mountain conditions or have a guide. Plenty of inexperienced trekkers have come to grief on this section, falling off icy cliffs or even disappearing into crevasses.

From Point Lenana most people return along the same route; assuming you summit early, you can reach the Met Station on the same day. Alternatively, you can return to Austrian Hut, then take the Summit Circuit path around the base of the main peaks to reach the top of one of the other routes before descending.

SIRIMON ROUTE
A popular alternative to Naro Moru, this route has more spectacular scenery, greater flexibility and a gentler rate of ascent, although it's still easy to climb too fast. Allow at least five days for a trek here; it's also well worth considering combining it with the Chogoria route for a six- to seven-day traverse that will really bring out the best of the mountain.

Nanyuki (see the Around Mt Kenya section later this chapter) is the best launching point for this route.

Accommodation & Bookings
The huts on this route are owned by Mountain Rock Hotels & Safaris and should be booked through **Mountain Rock Lodge** (☎ 0176-62625; ⓔ base@mountainrockkenya .com), near Naro Moru.

Guides & Porters
In Nanyuki, guides operating out of **Mt Kenya Mountaineering Information Office** (☎ 0176-31710) at Nanyuki Riverside Hotel are generally quite reliable; ask for Josphat. The people at **Montana Trek & Information Centre** (☎ 0176-31894) in Jambo House Hotel also seem to know their stuff but are a bit more pushy. Treks from Naro Moru's Mountain Rock Lodge can be booked at **Mountain Rock Cafe** (☎ 0176-23094).

The Trek
It's 15km from Nanyuki to the Sirimon Gate, and if you've booked a package transport will be included; otherwise you can take a matatu towards Timau or Meru or arrange a lift from town. From the gate it's about 9km through the forest to **Old Moses Hut** (3300m; US$10 per person), where you can spend the first night.

On the second day you could head straight through the moorland for Shipton's Camp, but it's worth taking an extra day to go via **Liki North Hut** (3993m), a tiny place on the floor of a classic glacial valley. The actual hut here is a complete wreck and is only meant for porters, but it's a good camp site, with a toilet and a stream nearby. You can also walk further up the valley to help acclimatise.

On the third day, head straight up the western side of the Liki North Valley and over the ridge into Mackinder's Valley, joining the direct route about 1½ hours in. After crossing the river, follow the path for another 30 minutes to reach the bunkhouse at **Shipton's Camp** (4200m; US$12 per person), set in a fantastic location right below Batian and Nelion and within sight of two glaciers, which can often be heard cracking.

From Shipton's you can push straight for Point Lenana, a tough three- to four-hour slog via Harris Tarn and the tricky north face approach, or take the Summit Circuit path in either direction around the peaks to reach **Austrian Hut** (4790m; KSh1000 per person), about one hour below the summit. The left-hand (east) route past Simba Col is shorter but steeper, while the right-hand (west) option takes you on the Harris Tarn trail nearer the main peaks.

From Austrian Hut take the standard southwest traverse up to **Point Lenana** (4895m) – see Naro Moru Route, earlier for details. If you're spending the night here, it's worth having a wander around to catch the views up to Batian and down the Lewis Glacier into Teleki Valley, as well as the spectacular ice cave by the Curling Pond.

CHOGORIA ROUTE
This route is justly famous for crossing some of the most spectacular and varied scenery on Mt Kenya, and is often combined with the Sirimon route (usually as the descent). The only disadvantage is the long distance between Chogoria village (see the

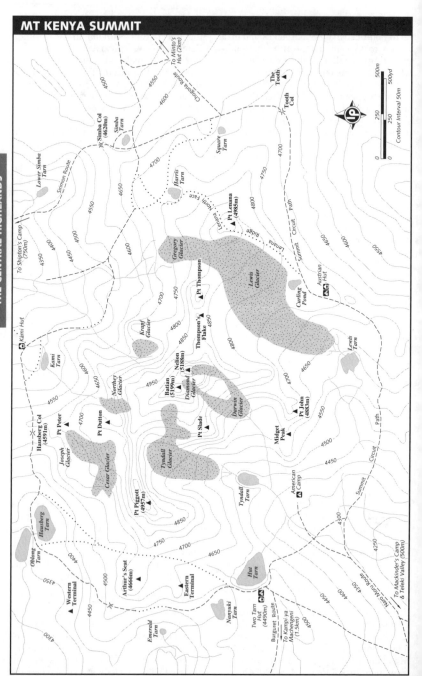

MT KENYA SUMMIT

Around Mt Kenya section later in this chapter) and the park gate. Allow at least five days for a trek here.

Guides & Porters

The best place to organise guides and porters is the **Mount Kenya Chogoria Guides & Porters Association** (☎ 0733-550606) at Transit Motel. Guides and porters are not available beyond Chogoria Forest Station.

If you want porters to walk the whole stretch between Chogoria and the park gate, you may be charged two extra days' wages – make sure you negotiate everything before you leave.

The Trek

The main reason this route is more popular as a descent is the first stage: it's 29km from Chogoria to the park gate, passing through farmland, rainforest and bamboo zones, and while it's not overly steep the rain here can make things very slippy. You can camp near the Forest Station 6km out of town, but you'll still have 23km to walk the next day. Transport is available from the village, but it'll cost you, and even a Land Rover may struggle in the wet.

Camping is possible at the gate, or you can stay nearby in **Meru Mt Kenya Lodge** (3000m; US$22 per person), a group of almost luxury huts administered by Meru County Council – with transport to town available and a small shop selling beer, this is also a favourite with people coming down!

On the second day head up through the forest to the trailhead (camping is possible here), from where it's another 7km over the rolling foothills to the Hall Tarns area and **Minto's Hut** (4300m). Like Liki North, this hut is only intended for porters and conditions are pretty nasty (the long-drop toilet has no door!), but there's plenty of space for camping and a stream for water. Don't use the tarns here to wash anything, as they have already been polluted by careless trekkers.

From here you follow the trail up alongside the stunning Gorges Valley (another possible descent route for the adventurous) and scramble up some steep ridges to meet the Summit Circuit path, which can take you in either direction. It is possible to go straight for the north face or southwest ridge of Point Lenana, but stopping at Austrian Hut or detouring to Shipton's Camp is probably a

better idea and gives you more time to enjoy the scenery – see Sirimon and Naro Moru routes, earlier, for details of all these options.

Around Mt Kenya

Mt Kenya is the only landmark that counts in this area. Circled by an excellent sealed road along which the main towns are found, its vast bulk looms over the entire region, and the snow-covered peaks can be seen for miles until the late-morning clouds obscure the view. While it's a distinctly separate massif from the Aberdares, the mountain is part of the Central Highlands, and like the Aberdares is intensively cultivated on its lower slopes, supporting the local populations of Kikuyu and the closely related Embu and Meru people.

Unfortunately this cultivation has had severe environmental repercussions for the area, as the forests here constitute one of Kenya's most important water catchment areas; the additional pressures of illegal logging, excessive water use and the large-scale clearance of rainforest to plant *miraa* (a leafy shoot with amphetamine-like effects) and marijuana have all taken their toll on the delicate ecosystem, and environmentalists are warning of a severe water crisis in near future.

NARO MORU
☎ 0176

The village of Naro Moru, on the western side of the mountain, is little more than a dusty string of shops and houses, with a couple of very basic hotels, a market and the famous Naro Moru River Lodge, but it's the most popular starting point for treks up Mt Kenya. There's a post office here, but no banks (the nearest are at Nanyuki and Nyeri).

Trekking

Apart from climbing Mt Kenya, there are other opportunities for trekking in this area. Mt Kenya Hostel & Campsite, east of Naro Moru, organises a number of excursions, including nature walks and day trips to the mountain.

Mountain Rock Lodge also runs a wide range of trips, from four-hour guided walks to a Mau Mau cave (KSh350), village visits (US$20) and nature walks (US$5) to two-day local treks. All prices are quoted for groups of twelve or more. Horse riding (US$10 per hour) and fishing (KSh450 including rod and licence) are also available.

Places to Stay – Budget & Mid-Range

There are a number of basic hotels in Naro Moru, but very few travellers stay there. Most options are out of town.

If you do want to stay here, **Mountain View Hotel** (☎ 62088; singles with bathroom KSh520) on the main road is the best option, but it's quite pricey for what you get and there are no doubles. Treks can be arranged here. **Joruna Lodge** (singles/doubles KSh250/ 300) is cheaper but nastier, and only the singles have bathrooms.

Mt Kenya Hostel & Camp Site (☎ 62412; camping KSh250, dorm beds KSh400) is 12km from Naro Moru but only 6km from the park gate. The original hostel burnt down years ago but has since been rebuilt and offers simple accommodation, a large camp site, meals (lunch/dinner KSh200/300), kitchen facilities and a bar. It's a simple but good place to crash and is very friendly. The hostel has some mountain gear and a 4WD vehicle for hire, and runs nature walks nearby as well as treks on the mountain (check that all of the guides are registered with KWS, though).

You can also camp at **Mt Kenya Guides & Porters Safari Club** (☎ 62015; camping KSh300), which can provide tents. The site has water and toilets, but it doesn't look very comfortable.

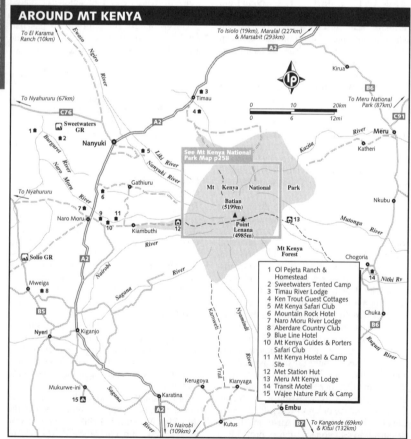

AROUND MT KENYA

1 Ol Pejeta Ranch & Homestead
2 Sweetwaters Tented Camp
3 Timau River Lodge
4 Ken Trout Guest Cottages
5 Mt Kenya Safari Club
6 Mountain Rock Hotel
7 Naro Moru River Lodge
8 Aberdare Country Club
9 Blue Line Hotel
10 Mt Kenya Guides & Porters Safari Club
11 Mt Kenya Hostel & Camp Site
12 Met Station Hut
13 Meru Mt Kenya Lodge
14 Transit Motel
15 Wajee Nature Park & Camp

Blue Line Hotel (☎ 62217; singles/doubles with bathroom KSh350/700), the nicer sister hotel to Mountain View, is 3km from Naro Moru and 2km from the Mt Kenya Guides & Porters office (convenient for organising guides the day before), but is 13km short of the park gate. The hotel is generally pleasant and quiet, and has a bar and restaurant (mains KSh200 to KSh300). Rooms are clean and there's safe parking.

Places to Stay – Top End
Naro Moru River Lodge (☎ 62212, in Nairobi 02-448000; ℮ mt.kenya@africaonline.co.ke; camping US$5, dorm beds US$7, standard singles/doubles half board US$52/78 in low season, US$86/115 in high season, cottages US$63-150 in low season, US$81-190 in high season) is about 1.5km north of Naro Moru village, set in pleasant landscaped gardens down a gravel track off the main road. This is the place for those seeking a bit of comfort before or after the mountain climb. You have the option of half board in standard or pricier 'superior' rooms, or self-catering in the luxury cottages; there is also a well-equipped camp site and dormitory block with hot showers, toilets and firewood. Campers can use all the hotel facilities, which include a swimming pool, two bars, a restaurant (breakfast/dinner KSh500/750) and secure parking.

The lodge can arrange various excursions, fishing and horse riding as well as equipment hire, transport to the mountain, hut bookings and excess-baggage store (KSh20 per piece per day). Nonguests can also use these services.

Mountain Rock Lodge (☎ 62625, in Nairobi ☎/fax 02-210051; ℮ base@mountainrock kenya.com; camping US$5, standard singles/doubles US$43/68, budget triples/quads US$78/92), formerly Bantu Lodge, is 7km north of Naro Moru, tucked away in the woods less than 1km from the Nanyuki road. The standard rooms are reasonable, but the budget quads are quite cramped; you can pay a bit more for the pleasant concrete cottages or a bit less for fixed tents. It's a friendly and reliable place with a spacious dining room, two bars, a lounge and a beer garden, and rates include breakfast. The camp site here has hot water, toilets, cooking facilities, electricity and ample firewood.

The hotel organises a large number of activities including guided walks, horse riding, traditional dances and walks to search for rare animals. The main reason for coming here, however, is to take one of the hotel's specialist Mt Kenya treks (see Organised Treks in the Mt Kenya National Park section, earlier).

Places to Eat
There are no restaurants worth a mention at Naro Moru, so you'll either have to cook your own food or eat at Naro Moru River Lodge. There's very little choice of food available at the shops in Naro Moru so bring your own or, if you have transport, go to Nanyuki to buy it.

Getting There & Away
Plenty of buses, matatus and Peugeots (shared taxis) from Nairobi and Nyeri to Nanyuki or Isiolo stop off in Naro Moru. The matatu fare from Nairobi to Naro Moru is about KSh200 and the journey takes about 2½ hours. From Nyeri to Naro Moru the fare is KSh50 (30 minutes).

Naro Moru River Lodge operates transfers between the lodge and Nairobi (US$75) or Nanyuki airstrip (US$17), but you must book 24 hours in advance. In Nairobi, book in the mall in Westlands through **Alliance Hotels** (☎ 02-448000; PO Box 49839; ℮ alliance@africaonline.co.ke).

NANYUKI
☎ 0176
Founded by white settlers in 1907, Nanyuki is a small but very lively country town. Its popularity as a base for the Burguret and Sirimon trekking routes means there are plenty of guides, touts and hawkers around, while the annual invasion of British army units on joint manoeuvres has spawned a whole posse of street boys spouting rhyming slang ('Lee Marvin' – starvin' – is a particular favourite).

If you can escape the initial hassle, however, Nanyuki is a fairly pleasant place to stay; most people are friendly and there's a good range of facilities here.

Information
There are a couple of cardphones next to the post office. Barclays and Standard Chartered Banks have ATMs.

Several places around town offer Internet access, but prices vary wildly; **Mt Kenya Cyberworld** (*Kenyatta Ave; which charges KSh2 per minute*), is the cheapest. Connections everywhere are much slower at weekends.

Trekking

There's no shortage of options for potential trekkers in Nanyuki. The speciality here is the Sirimon Route (see the Mt Kenya National Park section earlier in this chapter).

For a shorter walk you could visit the **Equator**, 3km south of town. There's a cluster of souvenir shacks flogging sarongs to bored minibus tourists around the standard yellow sign, and for KSh100 someone will demonstrate how water 'rotates' here.

Places to Stay – Budget

The only camping place here is the fabulous **Nanyuki River Camel Camp** (☎ 32327; *Laikipia Rd;* e *camellot@wananchi.com; camping KSh300, huts half board US$22*), 2km out of town. Only recently opened to the public after years catering for the British Army, it's an unique site modelled on a traditional Somali nomadic village; the huts are highly

authentic, the food is excellent and the 200 camels are available for hire. In 2002 a camel triathlon was held here to replace the cancelled Maralal Derby!

In town, **Nanyuki Youth Hostel** (☎ 0722-377146; *off Kimathi Rd; dorm beds KSh70*) is the cheapest place, but it's predictably basic.

There are also some simple lodges. **Silent Lodge** (*singles KSh150*), behind the Youth Hostel, is basic but friendly; **Nyahururu Horizon Hostel** (☎ 31004; *singles/doubles KSh200/350*), next to Jambo House Hotel, has simple rooms with bathroom.

Jambo House Hotel (☎ 31894; *singles/doubles with bathroom KSh250/400*) is similar in price and is not a bad option, but some rooms are better than others. The hotel has a bar and restaurant.

Joskaki Hotel (☎ 22820; *singles/doubles with bathroom KSh400/600*) is more expensive but a popular place to stay, with a lively bar and restaurant on the 1st floor and secure parking.

Nanyuki Riverside Hotel (☎ 31685; *singles/doubles with bathroom KSh400/600*) has a lovely site next to the river and is the best place to meet other travellers. Rooms are

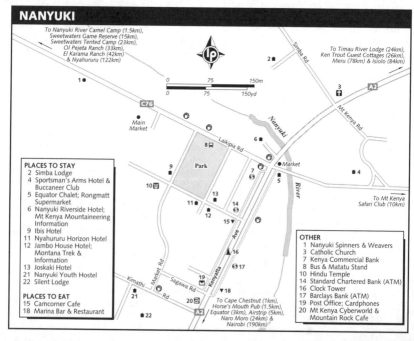

NANYUKI

PLACES TO STAY
2 Simba Lodge
4 Sportsman's Arms Hotel & Buccaneer Club
5 Equator Chalet; Rongmatt Supermarket
6 Nanyuki Riverside Hotel; Mt Kenya Mountaineering Information
9 Ibis Hotel
11 Nyahururu Horizon Hotel
12 Jambo House Hotel; Montana Trek & Information
13 Joskaki Hotel
21 Nanyuki Youth Hostel
22 Silent Lodge

PLACES TO EAT
15 Camcorner Cafe
18 Marina Bar & Restaurant

OTHER
1 Nanyuki Spinners & Weavers
3 Catholic Church
7 Kenya Commercial Bank
8 Bus & Matatu Stand
10 Hindu Temple
14 Standard Chartered Bank (ATM)
16 Clock Tower
17 Barclays Bank (ATM)
19 Post Office; Cardphones
20 Mt Kenya Cyberworld & Mountain Rock Cafe

spacious and fairly comfortable; however, the souvenir sellers around the entrance can be a pain, and don't expect much sleep when the disco is on.

Ibis Hotel (☎ 31536; singles/doubles with bathroom KSh400/700), one of three associated hotels in the region, is excellent value. Rooms have decent showers, mosquito nets and phones; there is a pleasant bar/restaurant in the covered courtyard, and secure parking is available.

Places to Stay – Mid-Range

Simba Lodge (☎ 22556; off Simba Rd; singles/doubles KSh700/1400), five minutes' walk from town, is a comfortable, quiet place in its own complex with nyama choma bar, restaurant, bar and secure parking. The rooms are slightly overpriced for what you get.

Equator Chalet (☎ 31480; Kenyatta Ave; singles/doubles KSh800/1200), a brand new place in the centre of town, is much nicer, with an internal courtyard opening onto two balcony areas and a roof terrace. Rooms are good looking and very comfortable, and rates include breakfast.

Sportsman's Arms Hotel (☎ 32347/8; e sarms@nanyukiafricaonline.com; singles/doubles/twins KSh3000/4000/4600, cottages KSh7000), set in landscaped gardens along the road east of town, was once the white settlers' main rendezvous, and is still popular with tourists and soldiers. The rooms have a touch of style, but the cottages are better: there is a choice of older thatched huts and stunning new modern ones dripping with facilities. Rates include breakfast. The complex boasts a swimming pool, sauna, gym, Jacuzzi, tennis, squash, three bars (with table football!), a restaurant and the Buccaneer Club.

Places to Eat

There are few restaurants in Nanyuki that are not attached to hotels. Of the hotels, the restaurant at the **Sportsman's Arms** serves the best food in town; **Ibis Hotel** and **Equator Chalet** are also good and a bit cheaper.

Marina Bar & Restaurant (Kenyatta Ave) is a popular expats' watering hole, and also offers pricey Internet access in the upstairs terrace bar.

Camcorner Cafe (Kenyatta Ave) is a delightful oddity serving up the usual stews and steaks, as well as fiery curries and a selection of camel products (including biltong – camel jerky).

Cape Chestnut (☎ 32526; open Mon-Sat), off the main road 1km south of town, is an excellent coffee garden and snack place catering mostly for white farmers, expats and tourists. The smoked trout (KSh250) is recommended and it's a good place to pick up information about the local area.

Horse's Mouth Pub (Haile Selassie Rd), nearby, caters for a similar clientele.

Entertainment

Discos are held at **Buccaneer Club** in the Sportsman's Arms every night and at **Simba Lodge** and **Nanyuki Riverside Hotel** on weekends (admission KSh100). Prostitutes are common at all these places, especially when the army is in town.

Shopping

There's a number of souvenir stalls and shops around town, catering mostly to the British army – if you have gear to swap, this is the place to do it! For something less tacky, try **Nanyuki Spinners & Weavers** (Laikipia Rd), a women's craft cooperative that specialises in woven woollen goods. The product and pattern design is high quality and is cheaper than the same work in Nairobi.

Getting There & Away

Air Kenya (☎ 02-605745; e info@airkenya .com) flies daily from Wilson Airport in Nairobi to Nanyuki, also serving Lewa Downs (on request) and Samburu National Reserve. It departs Nairobi at 9.15am, Nanyuki at 10.10am, Samburu at 10.50am, Nanyuki at 11.30am and arrives back in Nairobi at 12.15pm. Fares from Nanyuki are US$84 (Nairobi) and US$60 (Lewa Downs/Samburu) one way. There is also a daily service to the Masai Mara (US$173, 1½ hours) leaving at 10am.

There are daily buses from Nairobi to Nanyuki (KSh200, three hours) as well as matatus/shared taxis (KSh250/320, 2½ hours). Both buses and matatus run to Meru (KSh80/100, one hour), Isiolo (KSh100, one hour) and Nyeri (KSh70/80, 1½ hours).

AROUND NANYUKI

The area around Nanyuki is not frequently visited but does have its attractions, particularly if you're into outdoor activities such as fishing, trekking and wildlife viewing. There are several private wildlife parks and ranches open to the public here, including Sweetwaters Game Reserve, and you'll find a few places to stay that are definitely a bit out of the ordinary.

North of Nanyuki, on the road to Isiolo, is the town of **Timau**, which has a couple of interesting options. **Timau River Lodge** (☎ 0177-41230; camping per person KSh300, cottages KSh1250) is a wonderfully offbeat place, consisting of several lovely thatched cottages of varying sizes and a well-equipped camp site with a large covered cooking area. There is a good restaurant, and rates include breakfast; most of the power comes from solar panels and a water wheel powered by a nearby stream. It's convenient for treks up the rarely used Timau Route or through the local forests, and there are plenty of activities on offer, including fishing, cultural visits, safaris to Sweetwaters Game Reserve and camel trekking. There's a good chance of seeing elephants and other wildlife nearby.

Ken Trout Guest Cottages (☎ 0177-41016, book through Let's Go Travel in Nairobi ☎ 02-340331; e info@letsgosafari .com; camping KSh331, cottages half board per person KSh2650), 3km off the main road through Timau, is a more mainstream establishment with an excellent restaurant (if you like trout) and swish cottages. There is some very good fishing here, although you pay for everything you catch.

East of Nanyuki, almost exactly on the equator, is **Mt Kenya Safari Club** (☎ 0176-30000, in Nairobi ☎ 02-216940; e mksc@form-net.com; singles/doubles full board US$290/376), part of the Lonrho Group and one of the flashiest top-class resorts in Kenya. Originally the homestead of a white settler family, it was founded in the 1950s by a group including the late actor William Holden. The views up to Mt Kenya are excellent, and facilities include golf, tennis, croquet, snooker, swimming pool, fishing, bowls, an art gallery and a private wildlife sanctuary with a herd of rare bongo antelopes. Standard rooms are perhaps a little disappointing, but there's a presidential suite and some even more expensive cottages and villas.

Nonguests pay KSh420 entry; it's a good idea to phone in advance. Access is either from west of Nanyuki past the Sportsman's

Arms Hotel (a distance of about 10km, paved almost all the way) or from a turn-off about 2km south of Nanyuki, from where it's 9km along a dirt road.

About 42km to the northwest of Nanyuki, **El Karama Ranch** (☎ 0722-256753, book through Let's Go Travel in Nairobi ☎ 02-340331; e info@letsgosafari.com; bandas per person KSh1000), on the Ewaso Ngiro River, is more remote but infinitely more affordable. Billed as a 'self-service camp,' it is an old family run settlers' ranch with a number of basic but comfortable riverside bandas. Seated long-drop toilets and showers are close by. You should bring everything you need, including food, although you can rent various types of practical equipment for KSh200 per set. Activities here include wildlife walks (KSh400 per person) and horse riding (KSh2000 per person); longer horse and camel safaris can also be arranged (see **w** www.horsebackinkenya.com for details).

Let's Go Travel in Nairobi provides a map with directions. During the rainy seasons you'll need a 4WD to get here; however, as driving around the ranch is discouraged and there's little public transport, it's usually better to phone and arrange to be picked up, generally from Nanyuki.

Sweetwaters Game Reserve

About 15km west of Nanyuki, this 9000-hectare private reserve (admission KSh1500, residents KSh1000), run by Ol Pejeta Ranch, is home to a wide variety of plains wildlife. There is an important chimpanzee sanctuary here, operated by the Jane Goodall Institute, and the site is also a dedicated black rhino breeding area.

There are two top-end accommodation options in the reserve. **Sweetwaters Tented Camp** (in Nairobi ☎ 02-216940; e lonhotsm@ form-net.com; singles/doubles full board US$112/187 in low season, US$226/293 in high season), managed by Lonrho, consists of 40 luxury permanent tents beside a floodlit waterhole, with restaurant, bar and reception inside the quaint original farmhouse. Activities available here include wildlife drives (US$39), bird walks (free) and horse/camel rides (US$19/13 per hour). Lunch here is particularly popular with day visitors, and you can get it included with your entrance fee for KSh2000.

Ol Pejeta Homestead (*☎ 0176-32408, book through Let's Go Travel in Nairobi ☎ 02-340331; e info@letsgosafari.com; singles/ doubles full board US$340/560*), on Ol Pejeta Ranch, was once home to Lord Delamere and subsequently became the holiday get-away of the now bankrupt international arms dealer Adnan Kashoggi. As he was not one to spare any expense, the hotel is lavishly decorated and still features the gunrunner's massive 4m-wide bed! Rates include food, drinks and wildlife drives.

The reserve can be visited independently if you have your own vehicle. Access is off the C76 Laikipia road out of Nanyuki. Mt Kenya Safari Club runs half-day wildlife drives here for US$385 per vehicle; guests staying two or more nights at the club are entitled to free entry to the park and lunch at Sweetwaters Tented Camp.

MERU
☎ 0164

Stretched out along the eastern side of the Mt Kenya ring road, Meru is a bit of a rough and ready place. Few tourists stay here so there's not much in the way of hassle, but equally there's little to do here apart from stock up on various commodities. It's certainly too far away from any trekking routes to be a suitable base.

One local 'attraction' is the *miraa* market, (see the boxed text 'Miraa'). Any unforested land in the area around Meru is heavily cultivated, and the *miraa* plant is a popular (and profitable) alternative to the usual cash crops.

It's quite a climb up to Meru from either Isiolo or Embu, and in the rainy season you'll find yourself in the clouds up here along with the dense forest that frequently reaches right down to the roadside. When the weather is clear there are superb views for miles over the surrounding lowlands, and you may catch glimpses of Mt Kenya through the tree cover.

The town is a focal point for the Meru people (see the special section 'Tribes of Kenya').

Information
Internet access is expensive in Meru. **Mekha Communications** (*Kenyatta Hwy*), which charges KSh15 per minute, has the best connections, although **Snowline Com-**

puters in the River Side Trade Centre is cheaper. Cardphones can be found outside the post office; Barclays Bank has an ATM.

The market here is large and chaotic; the local market a dozen kilometres down the road at **Nkubu** is more fun. A huge new branch of **Uchumi** has also opened in town recently, with more armed guards than the three banks here!

Meru National Museum
This small **museum** (*☎ 20482; admission KSh200; open 9.30am-6pm Mon-Sat, 11am-6pm Sun, 1pm-6pm public holidays*), just off Kenyatta Hwy, is worth visiting. The usual displays are present, with an explanation of evolution and copious stuffed and mounted wildlife, but there's also a small and informative section concerning the clothing, weapons, and agricultural and initiation practices of the Meru people.

Places to Stay
There are a few basic budget places in the centre of town, but they tend to be a bit nasty – the cheapies further up around Angaine Rd are slightly better.

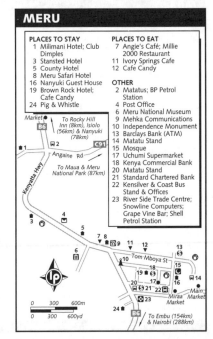

MERU

PLACES TO STAY	PLACES TO EAT
1 Milimani Hotel; Club Dimples	7 Angie's Café; Millie 2000 Restaurant
3 Stansted Hotel	11 Ivory Springs Cafe
5 County Hotel	12 Cafe Candy
8 Meru Safari Hotel	
16 Nanyuki Guest House	OTHER
19 Brown Rock Hotel; Cafe Candy	2 Matatus; BP Petrol Station
24 Pig & Whistle	4 Post Office
	6 Meru National Museum
	9 Mehka Communications
	10 Independence Monument
	13 Barclays Bank (ATM)
	14 Matatu Stand
	15 Mosque
	17 Uchumi Supermarket
	18 Kenya Commercial Bank
	20 Matatu Stand
	21 Standard Chartered Bank
	22 Kensilver & Coast Bus Stand & Offices
	23 River Side Trade Centre; Snowline Computers; Grape Vine Bar; Shell Petrol Station

THE CENTRAL HIGHLANDS

Brown Rock Hotel (*Njiru Ncheke St; singles/ doubles with bathroom KSh250/350*), near the worryingly Soviet-style independence monument, is the best cheap place in town. It is nicely laid out, with a restaurant, a small TV lounge and fairly clean rooms (some with balconies); hot water is only intermittent.

Nanyuki Guest House (☎ 30670; *Mosque Hill Rd; singles/doubles KSh250/500*) is central but a bit more basic, although rooms are a good size and come with bathroom.

Stansted Hotel (☎ 31119; *Kenyatta Hwy; singles/doubles KSh250/500*) is another reasonable option. It is clean, quiet and rooms have bathroom (with steamy shower). The hotel has a bar and restaurant.

Milimani Hotel (☎ 20224; *Stadium Rd; singles/doubles KSh500/700*), further up the hill, has large but slightly shabby rooms with some shocking bathrooms. There's almost always a crowd of 'idlers' around this place – the bar, restaurant and terrace are all popular and there's a disco at weekends.

Meru Safari Hotel (☎ 31500; *Kenyatta Hwy; singles/doubles/twins KSh800/1150/ 1200*) is a touch overpriced, although breakfast is included and the (more expensive) superior rooms have good views. The terrace bar is the best thing here.

Pig & Whistle (☎ 31411; *off Kenyatta Hwy; singles/doubles KSh1000/1200*) has a distinctly ramshackle charm to it, with nice quiet grounds, and a colonial-style bar/ restaurant and lounge. Rates include breakfast. The cottages are uninspiring concrete blocks, but TV, phone and a dining area go some way towards compensating.

County Hotel (☎ 20432; *Kenyatta Hwy; singles/doubles KSh1000/1500*) is the other main contender in town, with a bit less style but a few more facilities, including a restaurant, an excellent *nyama choma* terrace and a lively bar. Breakfast is included. The standard rooms are OK, but 'studio suites' are worth the extra KSh100.

Places to Eat & Drink

Cafe Candy (*Tom Mboya St; meals around KSh120*) is a good place for cheap meals during the day. It's a welcoming place and has a second branch behind Brown Rock Hotel.

Miraa

The small twigs and leaves you'll see people chewing on the coast and around Mt Kenya are *miraa*, the product of an evergreen tree native to East and Southern Africa, Afghanistan and Yemen. Known as *coas*, *khat* and over 40 other different names around the world, chewing *miraa* is an increasingly popular pastime in Kenya, but it's not nearly as important as in Somalia, where the drug is ingrained in the culture: in 1983 consumption reached such epidemic proportions that the government tried to ban it!

Some of the best *miraa* in the world is grown around Meru and exported directly to Somalia. After 48 hours its potency is diminished, so soon after picking, massively overladen pick-up trucks race to Wilson Airport in Nairobi for the morning flight to Mogadishu.

A mild stimulant, chewing *miraa* predates coffee and is deep-rooted in the cultural traditions of some societies, especially in Muslim countries. It's usually chewed in company to encourage confidence, contentment and a flow of ideas, and also to increase alertness for everyday purposes such as driving a matatu. The active ingredient, *cathinone*, is closely related to amphetamine, and the euphoric effects can last for up to 24 hours.

Chewing too much can be habit-forming and has serious consequences, known medically as '*khat* syndrome.' Aggressive behaviour, nightmares and hallucinations are common mental side effects, while reduced appetite and malnourishment, constipation and brown teeth are common physical consequences. Even less pleasant are recent claims that *miraa* can cause hypothermia and spermatorrhoea (abnormal leakage of sperm – just delightful), leading to infertility.

Miraa is illegal in the USA but is legally imported into several European countries, including the UK, where it can be ordered over the Internet. In Kenya it's sold in handfuls known as *kilos* or *gizas* for between KSh100 and KSh300, depending on size. Meru is a good place for curious travellers to give it a go, but most people can't get past the bitter taste and unpleasant texture – funnily enough, it's just like chewing twigs.

Angie's Café and **Millie 2000**, both on Kenyatta Hwy, are also worth checking out.

It's surprisingly hard to find anywhere to eat in Meru in the evening, especially on Sunday. Once **Ivory Springs Cafe** *(Tom Mboya St; mains around KSh120)* starts to run out of things, the hotel restaurants may be your only option; **County Hotel** *(mains from KSh200, set meals KSh450)* is probably the best of these.

Weekend discos at **Club Dimples** in Mili-mani Hotel are lively affairs, while the **Pig & Whistle** is probably the best place for a beer. **Grape Vine Bar** in the River Side Trace Centre is also fun: it's an open, weirdly piratical structure, which sometimes hosts live bands.

Getting There & Away
Kensilver has 13 daily departures from 6.45am onwards, covering Nairobi (KSh260, 4½ hours), Embu (KSh200, two hours) and Thika (KSh240, 2½ hours). Coast buses also go to Isiolo (KSh100, one hour), Nanyuki (KSh200, two hours) and Mombasa (KSh700, ten hours). Both services leave from outside offices on Mosque Hill Rd

There are regular matatu/Peugeot depar-tures to all these destinations from the matatu stand by the main market and from opposite the Shell petrol station.

MERU NATIONAL PARK
This national park *(adult/child & student US$23/10)* is the cornerstone of the Meru Conservation Area, a 4000-sq-km expanse that also includes the adjacent Kora Na-tional Park, and Bisanadi, Mwingi and North Kitui National Reserves (which are closed), covering the lowland plains east of Meru town.

KWS has big plans for this park. In the 1970s the populations of rhinos and ele-phants could pull in up to 40,000 visitors a year, but banditry and poaching during the 1980s effectively put paid to tourism here, wiping out the white rhinos and leaving the area almost abandoned until the late 1990s. Today substantial foreign investment, no-tably from French development agencies and the International Fund for Animal Welfare (IFAW), has enabled a flurry of re-habilitation projects: a new sealed access road is planned, all the park roads are being upgraded, and there's now a bridge across the Tana River at Adamson's Falls (worth a visit) into Kora National Park, which was recently reopened.

So far there's not a great deal to show for all these improvements, but with the major concern of security in the park settled, visitor numbers have been gradually climbing, and were just short of 10,000 in 2001 (double the 1999 figure and almost ten times as many as in 1997). With two new luxury lodges and good budget options, Meru's fortunes should soon be on the up again.

This resurgence is definitely a good thing, as the park is a complete contrast to the nearby savanna reserves of Samburu, Buf-falo Springs and Shaba. Abundant rainfall and numerous permanent watercourses flow-ing down from the Mt Kenya massif support a luxuriant jungle of forest, bush, swamp and tall grasses, which, in turn, provide fodder and shelter to a wide variety of herbivores and their predators. This is one of the most geographically diverse parks in Kenya and a favourite with the safari cognoscenti; you need to spend a few days here to fully appreciate what the park has to offer.

Due to sustained poaching, the wildlife is not as abundant here as in other parks. The large reduction in elephant numbers has led to an increase in vegetation cover, making it difficult to spot the animals. However, numbers are increasing, and with a little pa-tience you can see elephants (often found in the marshy Bisanadi Plains at the north of the park), lions and cheetahs along with lesser kudus, elands, waterbucks, gazelles and oryxes. Buffaloes, reticulated giraffes, and Grevy's zebras are common, while monkeys, crocodiles and a plethora of bird species, including the palm nut vulture and Marshal eagle, can be found in the dense vegetation along the watercourses.

The major advantage of Meru is that you're unlikely to come across another sa-fari vehicle anywhere in the park, except perhaps at the lodges. At present you need a 4WD or be on a tour to visit; most road junctions are numbered, so a matching copy of the Survey of Kenya's *Meru National Park* map (KSh600) is very useful if you want to find your way around. You can theoretically buy it at the park headquarters.

Maua is the nearest town to the park and has a good selection of facilities, including a Barclays Bank.

THE CENTRAL HIGHLANDS

Places to Stay

There are several special camp sites but **Bwatherongi Camp Site** *(camping per person KSh150, bandas per person US$15)* is the only public site in the park. It is very well equipped with showers, toilets, fireplaces and an *askari* in attendance. Also at this site are four excellent bandas with mattresses, sofas and mosquito nets. Two have en suites.

Kiringo Hill Lodge *(☎ 0167-21081; singles/doubles with bathroom KSh700/1200)*, outside the park, at the turn-off to Murera Gate, can make a convenient base. Rates include breakfast, and while it's probably overpriced it's cheaper than anything in the park itself. The rooms are small but clean and tidy, and it's a nice site; the *nyama choma* restaurant gets quite busy at weekends.

Murera Education Centre *(bandas per person US$15)*, by the main gate, has a hostel and some bandas that may be available for visitors. Ask at the gate.

Leopard Rock Lodge *(in Nairobi ☎ 02-246982, fax 212389)* was being thoroughly renovated at time of research, and was due to reopen in late 2002. Prices for full-board singles/doubles will be probably be around US$175/320 in the low season and US$250/420 in high season.

Elsa's Kopje *(in Nairobi ☎ 02-603090; e saf aris@chelipeacock.co.ke; singles/doubles full board US$266/496 in low season, US$374/636 in high season)* is the definition of sensitively designed luxury, with open-fronted thatched cottages nestled discreetly among rocks and bushes. The site, Mughwango

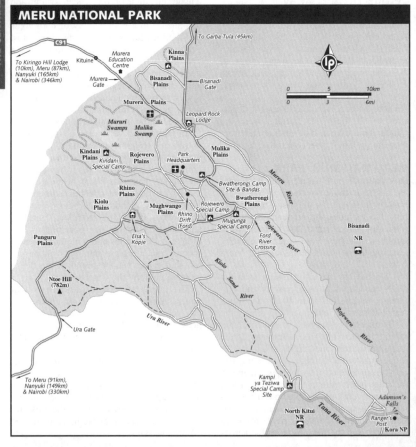

MERU NATIONAL PARK

Hill, was George Adamson's first camp in Meru, and the panoramic views are stunning. Night drives, walking safaris, fishing and rafting trips can be arranged here.

Getting There & Away

Frequent matatus run between Meru town and Maua (around KSh80, one hour), and a Coast bus also passes through (KSh100, 1½ hours); there are some fantastic views across the plains from this road as it climbs into the Nyambeni Hills.

Some trucks and matatus do come down the road towards the park gate, but most stop at Kiutine, about 3km away. You really need to arrange your own transport or come with a tour operator to visit the park; safaris to Meru are still few and far between (see the Safaris chapter for details), but things may change after access is improved.

On Wednesday, Friday and Sunday the Nairobi-Samburu **Air Kenya** (☎ 02-605745; *ℯ info@airkenya.com*) service stops here on the way north. The fare from Nairobi is US$150; singles to Samburu from there (US$190) also allow for a stopover in Meru. Arrange to be picked up by one of the top-end lodges if staying there.

CHOGORIA
☎ 0166

The only reason to come to this small town on the lower eastern slopes of Mt Kenya is because it is the access point to one of the most scenic routes up the mountain – the Chogoria route (see the Mt Kenya National Park section earlier in this chapter).

There is a lively Sunday market and a couple of half-decent cafés in the village, but Chogoria has quite a reputation for hassle, with every man and his dog offering to take you up the mountain. On arrival, it's much better to bypass the village altogether, get yourself sorted at the Transit Motel, then head back if you need basic supplies.

Information

Transit Motel (*☎/fax 22096; PO Box 190, Chogoria; singles/doubles KSh700/1000*) is your best bet for accommodation here and is well signposted. It can be reached by alighting from the bus on the main road just south of the village and walking about 1.5km down a dirt road. Alternatively, it's about half an hour's walk from the centre of Chogoria.

Rooms are clean but a bit overpriced; there's a restaurant (lunch/dinner KSh250/300), a lounge area and a bar. Camping may also be possible. Don't believe rival mountain touts claiming the motel has burnt down!

As with Meru, the best transport options are the Kensilver buses to and from Nairobi (KSh220, 3½ hours). There are also regular matatus to Embu (KSh120, one hour) and Meru (KSh40, 30 minutes).

EMBU
☎ 0161

Spread out along the B6 highway on the edge of Mt Kenya's southeastern slopes, Embu is an unlikely but important provincial centre, set in a very hilly area that is intensively cultivated. It's also the administrative headquarters of Eastern Province, although it's on the extreme eastern edge of this area and can only have been chosen because of its agreeable climate.

Despite its local significance, there's not a whole lot to detain travellers here, and it's a long way from the mountain. However, the town can make a good stopover on the way to Thika or Nairobi, and those with their own transport can use it as a base for exploring Mwea National Reserve (see later in this chapter) or stop off at one of the numerous coffee nurseries signposted off the B6 and A2 highways.

Information

Embu has a post office, several banks (Barclays Bank has an ATM) and plenty of cardphones. Internet access here is much cheaper than in Meru; **Beatnet Cybercafe**, opposite the library, is probably the best place in town and charges from KSh3 per minute.

Places to Stay

Kenya Scouts Training Centre (*☎ 20623; Kenyatta Hwy; camping per person KSh100, dorm beds KSh250*) is the nearest camping place to town, and also has small basic dorms. Campers can use the facilities in the main building, which include hot showers, a shop and a café. Judging from all the anti-drug posters, it's not a good idea to saunter in here with your mouth full of *miraa*!

There are quite a few cheap hotels spread out along Kenyatta Hwy in town but most of them are very basic and cannot be recommended.

EMBU

To Kenya Scouts
Training Centre (500m),
Izaak Walton Inn (1.5km)
& Meru (154km)

1	Post Office
2	Eagles Nest Bar
3	Town Hall
4	Library
5	Meals on Wheels Café; Kobil Petrol Station
6	Beatnet Cybercafe
7	Kenchic Inn
8	Morning Glory Hotel
9	Highway Court Hotel
10	Buses; BP Petrol Station
11	Sunbird/Coast Bus Office; Roska Café
12	Mario's Cafe
13	Eden Guesthouse
14	Morning Glory Plaza
15	Barclays Bank (ATM)
16	Prime Lodge
17	Bars
18	Classic Cafe
19	Bus & Matatu Stand
20	Kubu-Kubu Lodge; Royal Club

Kenyatta Hwy

Mama Ngina St

To Embu Motel (150m)

To Thika (94km) & Nairobi (134km)

To Mwea National Reserve (45km) & Kitui (142km)

0   75   150m
0   75   150yd

Down the hill next to Morning Glory Plaza is **Eden Guesthouse** (☎ 30021; singles KSh200), which is a decent cheap option. It's all pretty basic, but the rooms are clean and quiet.

Kubu-Kubu Lodge (☎ 20334; singles/doubles with bathroom KSh250/400), further down the road, is also good value, although the rooms are quite small.

Prime Lodge (☎ 30692; singles/doubles with bathroom KSh400/650), just off Kenyatta Hwy south of town, is slightly erratic – some rooms have baths instead of showers, unreliable hot water and useless nets. That said, the bar and restaurant are good and it's generally quiet.

Highway Court Hotel (☎ 20046; singles/doubles with bathroom KSh500/800), in the centre of town, is more expensive than it was, although there are some small singles for KSh350 (not mentioned at reception!). Security is excellent; the only drawback is noise from the lively bar and restaurant.

Although the back-alley location leaves something to be desired, the brand new **Embu Motel** (☎ 0722-462277; singles/doubles with bathroom KSh500/600) is easily the best deal in town. There's secure parking, a TV lounge, two dining rooms and proper boilers. Rates, which include breakfast, will doubtless rise dramatically once it's 'discovered.'

Izaak Walton Inn (☎ 20128, in Nairobi ☎ 02-746527; Kenyatta Hwy; singles/doubles KSh2600/3600), about 1.5km north of town, is a well-known top-end place set in fantastic old colonial grounds. Accommodation is in small cottages, and expensive executive rooms are also available. Rates include breakfast; there's a good restaurant and a cosy bar, both with fireplaces.

Places to Eat & Drink
Classic Cafe is a good-looking but cheap locals' place opposite the Kobil petrol station south of town. **Mario's Cafe**, off Mama Ngina St, is also worth a look.

Morning Glory Hotel (Kenyatta Hwy; meals around KSh150) is a popular place with a large back room and a takeaway section. It also does good breakfasts. Next door, **Kenchic Inn** does its usual thing, although the 'end products' are often seen sleeping outside!

Meals on Wheels Café in the northern Kobil petrol station is open 24 hours.

If you want the full treatment, head for the restaurant at **Izaak Walton Inn**, where mains cost around KSh300.

For a drink, try **Eagles Nest Bar** near the post office or one of the lively joints south of Prime Lodge. **Royal Club**, next to the Kubu-Kubu Lodge, is the best disco in town.

Getting There & Away
Kensilver buses between Meru and Nairobi pass through Embu, stopping at the BP petrol station in the centre of town. The first departure out of Nairobi is at 7.30am (KSh240, two hours) and the first from Meru is at 6.45am (KSh200, two hours).

Sunbird and Mombasa Liners go to Meru (KSh150, two hours) and Mombasa (KSh600, eight hours) via Nairobi (KSh150, two hours) daily. The booking office is in Roska Cafe, next to the BP petrol station.

Matatus and Peugeots offer the same service as buses, but the usual perils apply doubly here: the B6 road between Nairobi and Meru is one of the quickest in the country and accidents are common. The fare to Nairobi is KSh150 and KSh180, respectively.

Matatus also run to most highlands destinations, including Meru (KSh180, 1½ hours), Nyeri (KSh130, one hour) and Nanyuki (KSh180, 1½ hours). They're not quite the same hair-raising prospect as there

THE CENTRAL HIGHLANDS

are fewer pressures on the drivers, but taking a bus or a Peugeot would still be safer.

MWEA NATIONAL RESERVE

The Kamburu Dam at the meeting point of the Tana and Thiba Rivers forms the focus for this 48-sq-km park. Enclosed by an electric fence, elephants, hippos, buffaloes, lesser kudus and myriad birdlife are present here; evenings at Hippo Point, when the animals amble down to the water's edge, are a particular highlight.

A 4WD is just about essential to get to Mwea and around the park. Entry is US$15; a sketch map and bird list is available at the gate.

There's a **camp site** *(camping US$2)* with basic facilities (no water) close to the park headquarters and another site with no facilities whatsoever, close to Hippo Point.

The nearest formal accommodation is **Masinga Dam Lodge** *(in Nairobi ☎ 02-535834;* 🖃 *tardal@nbnet.co.ke; camping KSh500, standard singles/doubles KSh650/800)*, some 14km southwest of the park gate (signposted from Kangonde). Run by the Tana & Athi Rivers Development Authority, it's a nice site, with two restaurants, a TV lounge and a swimming pool. The standard rooms are unfancy but reasonable, and there are slightly more expensive VIP/executive rooms with views over Masinga Dam and the plains. Guided walks and boat trips on the dam can be arranged here.

To access Mwea turn off the B7 1km north of Kangonde (via Masinga) or 14km south of Embu (the route is signposted). You can also go via Karaba, off the B6 Thika–Embu road.

OL DONYO SABUK NATIONAL PARK

This tiny park *(adult/child & student US$15/ 5)* was gazetted in 1967 and covers an area of just 20.7 sq km. The focus of the park is the summit of **Ol Donyo Sabuk** (2146m), surrounded by an oasis of dense primeval forest that supports a huge variety of birds and numerous primates, including black and white colobus and blue monkeys. The Kikuyu call the mountain Kilimambongo (buffalo mountain) and buffaloes are indisputably the dominant animals here. Below the picnic site on the summit is a salt lick that attracts regular herds.

The park is about 27km east of Thika and can be reached by public transport with a little effort; you can explore on foot if you're accompanied by a ranger. Guides can be arranged at the main gate and cost KSh500 for a full day or KSh300 for a half day. It takes three or four hours to get to the summit.

There's a **camp site** *(camping per person US$2)* just before the main gate, but facilities are minimal: one long-drop toilet and a rusty tap. The small *duka* before the gate sells some basics, but you'll need to bring most supplies.

Getting There & Away

Take a matatu heading to Kitui from Thika and ask to be dropped off at the Kilimambongo stop (KSh50, 45 minutes). From here you need to get another matatu or pick-up to take you the 6km to the village of Ol Donyo Sabuk; once in the village the main gate (signposted) is a 2km walk along a straight dirt road.

THE CENTRAL HIGHLANDS

Western Kenya

Despite this region's many attractions and friendly people, it has been criminally overlooked by travellers in the past, and you still won't find many safari minibuses out this way except in the Masai Mara. For this reason alone it's worth spending a bit of time exploring here. There is plenty to see and do if you're prepared to make the effort, and it's one of the best areas in Kenya to get to know the locals.

You will find plenty of tourists in the world-famous Masai Mara National Reserve, along the Tanzanian border. While its vast vistas of grassland are a familiar and thoroughly African sight, they are entirely atypical of this area as a whole. Elsewhere, the countryside is for the most part green and well watered, with beautiful rolling hills. It is also often cultivated, with frequent bright-green tea plantations.

In the far west, on the shore of Lake Victoria, is the regional capital of Kisumu, from which there are plenty of possibilities to pursue. To the southwest are the accessible islands of Rusinga and Mfangano, as well as the little-known but unique Ruma National Park. A short distance to the north lies the Kakamega Forest Reserve, with its lush vegetation and abundant wildlife. Further north still, close to the town of Kitale, are the national parks of Mt Elgon (well worth exploring) and Saiwa Swamp, where the only way of getting around is on foot and the main attraction is the rare sitatunga antelope. From there, trekking in the Cherangani Hills, which drops away into the wonderful Kerio Valley, is a great option.

This western part of the country is home to Kenya's Luo people. Numbering around two million, they make up the third-largest tribal group in the country, but have been consistently marginalised politically; nevertheless, they are a friendly people, and more than willing to chew the fat with visitors (see the boxed text 'Question Time'). This area is also home to the Luyha, the second-largest tribal group here, as well as the Gusii and the renowned distance runners of the Kalenjin (see the special section 'Tribes of Kenya').

So, especially if you're passing this region on the way to Uganda, or going to Tanzania via Isebania, stay awhile.

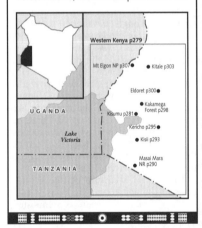

Getting Around

This region is the most densely populated part of the country, so the road system is good and there are hundreds of matatus of varying shapes and sizes plying the routes. Accidents are unerringly common, but they usually seem to involve the small Nissan matatus, which are often dangerously overloaded. The larger truck matatus are a lot safer, as they generally travel more slowly and can carry loads with greater ease (although given the state of them, it's all relative). Peugeots (shared taxis) are more popular in the west than anywhere else in Kenya.

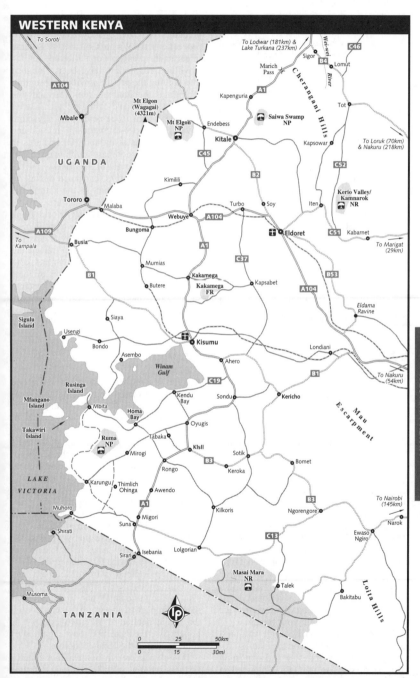

WESTERN KENYA

Question Time

When you speak to locals in this part of Kenya, they will invariably have a lot of questions for you, usually about life in your country. It will quickly becomes clear that there are some pretty strange ideas floating around; British and American citizens in particular may be asked some or all of the questions below.

• Does the West have a cure for AIDS? (If not, why do some tourists behave so badly in Kenya?)
• Does the law limit the number of children parents can have? Can children be taken away if you have too many?
• Can you be jailed if you're caught with pornographic magazines?
• Is Britain bigger than Kenya?
• Can you be made to change sex in America?
• Are over 40% of the adult British population homosexual?

Remember, your answers to such posers may well shape the way your country is perceived by entire communities of Kenyans!

Lake Victoria

With an area approaching 70,000 sq km, Lake Victoria is the major geographical feature in this part of the continent. Unlike the lakes further west, Victoria is not part of the Rift Valley system, and is wide and shallow: it's only 80m deep, compared with Lake Tanganyika's 1500m.

Bilharzia is prevalent in Lake Victoria, so don't swim in the water or walk in the grass along its shores – this is the hide-out of the snails that host the parasites that invade your body. However, you are at far greater risk of contracting malaria here than bilharzia (see Health in the Facts for the Visitor chapter).

The lake has shores in Uganda, Tanzania and Kenya but, at present, the only boat traffic between the countries is made up of large freighters and small dhow-like vessels that are often smuggling (fruit is serious contraband!). There is some talk of a ferry service restarting, but don't hold your breath.

The ornamental water hyacinth was, until recently, a major problem on the lake, 'suffocating' the fishing industry and confining many large ships to port. First reported in 1986, this 'exotic' pond plant had no natural predators here and quickly reached plague proportions; the Winam Gulf area by Kisumu in particular, was the worst affected.

Millions of dollars have been ploughed into solving the problem, with programmes including mechanical removal and the introduction of weed-eating weevils. The investment seems to be paying off. Hyacinth coverage dropped dramatically in 2000 and currently stands at around 100 hectares in Kenyan waters, compared with over 15,000 hectares at the height of the crisis.

However, scientists fear much of this reduction may just be part of the natural life cycle of the plant, and levels are already creeping up again. Ongoing World Bank funding has also brought its own problems – local concerns highlight the lack of environmental impact assessments and transparent procedures for hiring consultants and contractors, as well as the exclusion of local communities from projects. So, the hyacinth saga is not over yet.

Local ferry transport is slowly returning to the lake, but is still very far from becoming useful for travellers again.

KISUMU
☎ 035

Kisumu is Kenya's third-largest town, and was finally declared a city during its centenary celebrations in 2001. It has a much more relaxed atmosphere than either Nairobi or Mombasa; it also attracts far fewer tourists.

Until 1977 the port was one of Kenya's busiest, but decline set in with the demise of the East African Community (made up of Kenya, Tanzania and Uganda). Increasing co-operation between these, now Comesa, countries looks like restoring the town's fortunes, as it is becoming a major international shipment point for petroleum products.

Surprisingly, the lake that supported the town's original growth has so far had no part to play in its revival. Even the raw fuel for processing is piped in from Mombasa, and the end products are shipped out by truck! This is due in no small part to the environmental impact of the water hyacinth. With the recent decline of weed coverage, it is hoped that the lake will once again start contributing to the local economy.

If you've arrived from the higher country further east, it won't take you long to notice

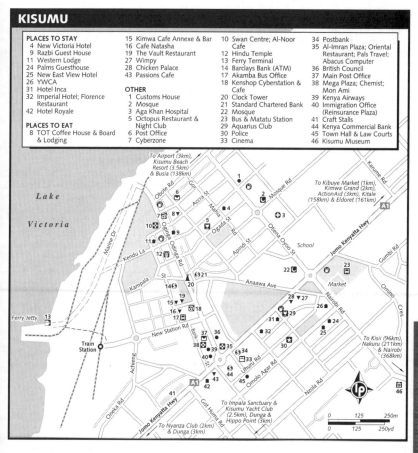

KISUMU

PLACES TO STAY
4 New Victoria Hotel
9 Razbi Guest House
11 Western Lodge
24 Palms Guesthouse
25 New East View Hotel
26 YWCA
31 Hotel Inca
32 Imperial Hotel; Florence Restaurant
42 Hotel Royale

PLACES TO EAT
8 TOT Coffee House & Board & Lodging

15 Kimwa Cafe Annexe & Bar
16 Cafe Natasha
19 The Vault Restaurant
27 Wimpy
28 Chicken Palace
43 Passions Cafe

OTHER
1 Customs House
2 Mosque
3 Aga Khan Hospital
5 Octopus Restaurant & Night Club
6 Post Office
7 Cyberzone

10 Swan Centre; Al-Noor Cafe
12 Hindu Temple
13 Ferry Terminal
14 Barclays Bank (ATM)
17 Akamba Bus Office
18 Kenshop Cyberstation & Cafe
20 Clock Tower
21 Standard Chartered Bank
22 Mosque
23 Bus & Matatu Station
29 Aquarius Club
30 Police
33 Cinema

34 Postbank
35 Al-Imran Plaza; Oriental Restaurant; Pals Travel; Abacus Computer
36 British Council
37 Main Post Office
38 Mega Plaza; Chemist; Mon Ami
39 Kenya Airways
40 Immigration Office (Reinsurance Plaza)
41 Craft Stalls
44 Kenya Commercial Bank
45 Town Hall & Law Courts
46 Kisumu Museum

the humidity here. Kisumu is always a few degrees hotter than the highland cities, and the steamy conditions add to the generally languid air.

Despite its relative isolation, Kisumu has excellent travel connections to the east of Kenya. There's also enough to do to make it an interesting place to stop for a few days.

Orientation
Kisumu is a fairly sprawling town, but everything you'll need is within walking distance. Most shops, banks and other facilities such as the post office can be found on Oginga Odinga Rd.

The train station and ferry jetty are about a five-minute walk from the end of Oginga Odinga Rd, while the noisy bus and matatu

station is behind the market on Jomo Kenyatta Hwy, a 10-minute walk from the centre.

Most of the cheap hotels are in the area between Oginga Odinga Rd and Otiena Oyoo St. The mid-range and top-end hotels are mostly found around Jomo Kenyatta Hwy. The best access to the lake itself is at Dunga, a small village about 3km south of town along Nzola Rd.

Information
Barclays Bank (with ATM), **Kenya Commercial Bank** and **Standard Chartered Bank** have branches in or near the centre of town.

Pel Travels has a foreign-exchange bureau and is probably the best travel agent in town (see Getting Around later). **Kenya Airways** (☎ 41620; Oginga Odinga Rd) has an office here and also deals with Flamingo Airlines bookings.

The **main post office** *(Oginga Odinga Rd; open 8am-5pm Mon-Fri, 9am-noon Sat)* is in the centre of town. There are a number of cardphones on the opposite side of the road and a second **post office** off Obote Rd.

Fast Internet services can be found at **Cyberzone** *(Oginga Odinga Rd)*, which charges KSh2 per minute, **Kenshop Cyberstation** *(Oginga Odinga Rd)* for KSh4 per minute and **Abacus Computer** *(Al-Imran Plaza)*, which charges KSh2 per minute; all open on Sunday. You can also browse over at the British Council (see Places to Stay following) and Hotel Royale (see Places to Stay later).

For visa extensions, **immigration** *(1st floor Reinsurance Plaza, cnr Oginga Odinga Rd & Jomo Kenyatta Hwy)* is next to the Mega Plaza shopping centre.

The **British Council** *(☎ 45004; Oginga Odinga Rd; open 10am-6pm Tues-Fri, 9.30am-1pm Sat)* has newspapers, magazines and a decent library. Day membership is KSh250 or you can join for a year for KSh3000, entitling you to an hour's free Internet access daily (usually KSh154 per half hour).

In case of an emergency head to the **Aga Khan Hospital** *(☎ 43516; Otiena Oyoo St)*, which also has a **satellite laboratory** for malaria blood testing in Mega Plaza. There's a good **chemist** a couple of doors down.

While Kisumu is not notoriously dangerous, travellers may prefer not to walk around too much at night.

Markets
Kisumu's **main market**, off Jomo Kenyatta Hwy, is one of the most animated in the country, and certainly one of the largest. Whether you're after a bag of potatoes or are just curious, it's worth a stroll around.

The **Kibuye Market**, held every Sunday, is a huge outdoor affair that draws people from all around the district. Everything from second-hand clothes to furniture and food can be found spread out along Jomo Kenyatta Hwy, about 1km north of the intersection with Nairobi Rd. Peugeots from the intersection cost KSh15.

The various **pavement stalls** near Hotel Royale are some of the best places in Kenya for soapstone carvings. Quality varies, as ever, but if you take your time you should be able to get a good deal.

Hippo Point
Hippo Point at Dunga, about 3km south of town, is a nice place to head for, though you are not guaranteed to see any hippos.

If you want to get out on the lake, there are a number of young boys hanging around who will help, though the best place to organise trips is Dunga fish market, where you're sure to find someone to take you out. The usual asking price is around KSh800, but negotiate.

Impala Sanctuary
About 500m before Kisumu Yacht Club, on the road to Dunga, is the Kenya Wildlife Service (KWS) Impala Sanctuary *(adult/child US$5/2)*. This 1-sq-km sanctuary is home to a small herd of impala, but also provides important open grazing for the local hippo population. There's an animal orphanage here, but it's pretty grim.

Kisumu Bird Sanctuary
About 8km southeast of town, on the way to Ahero, this reserve covers a large area of swampland and is an important breeding ground for herons, storks, cormorants and egrets. The best time to visit is between April and May. Transport is easy along the A1, but you'll have a 3km walk once you reach the turn-off.

Kisumu Museum
Unlike many local museums, Kisumu Museum *(Nairobi Rd; admission KSh200; open 8.30am-6pm daily)* is an interesting and often informative place, and must rank among the best in Kenya.

The displays are well presented and wide ranging. There's a very good collection of everyday items used by the various peoples of the area, including agricultural implements, bird and insect traps, food utensils, clothing, furniture, weapons and musical instruments. There's also a fairly motley collection of stuffed birds and animals, including an amazing centrepiece of a lion riding on a wildebeest.

Outside, a traditional Luo homestead has been constructed, consisting of the husband's mud and thatch house and separate houses for each wife.

There are also the usual crocodile and tortoise enclosures, which are small and a bit depressing.

Ndere Island National Park

Only gazetted as a national park in 1986, tourism to this small 4.2-sq-km island has never really taken off. The island, which is forested and very beautiful, is home to a variety of bird species, plus hippos, a few impalas (introduced) and a population of the spotted crocodile, which is not as well known as its big cousin the Nile crocodile. Tsetse flies are a big problem after the rains.

There is no accommodation on the island and just about your only way of getting there is with a boat trip from the Kisumu Beach Resort (see Places to Stay following). Boat trips cost around KSh500 per person, and there's a good chance of seeing hippos in the surrounding waters.

Places to Stay – Budget

Kisumu Beach Resort (☎ 44006; camping per person KSh200, cottages KSh1250-1500), on the opposite side of the bay from the town, is the best spot for campers, set in a large open area on the lakeshore. There's a bar and restaurant (meals around KSh500) with a disco here at weekends; reasonable thatched cottages with fans are available, and boat trips can be arranged.

It's 3km from the main road to the resort, so take a taxi (KSh300) or 'Pipeline' matatu from the main matatu station (KSh20). Transport is laid on for the disco on Friday and Saturday (KSh50), leaving from behind the Nakumatt supermarket in town.

Another option is **ActionAid** (☎ 62016; camping per person KSh100, singles KSh550, full board KSh1500), a residential study centre about 3km out of town on Kenyatta Hwy. It's mainly used by Kenyans taking development courses and the like, but visitors are welcome and there's a good range of facilities.

Budget hotels in Kisumu are not that easy to find, and the cheapest places tend to be complete dives.

YWCA (☎ 43192; cnr Nairobi & Omolo Agar Rds; dorm beds KSh250, singles/doubles KSh300/600) is one of the more reasonable options. It's a bit smelly but could be worse; there are three- and four-bed dorms and some rooms with bathroom. Basic meals are available from the cafeteria (lunch or dinner costs KSh150).

Razbi Guest House (☎ 22408; cnr Oginga Odinga Rd & Kendu Lane; singles/doubles KSh300/500) is another secure budget place.

Places to Stay – Mid-Range

Western Lodge (☎ 42586; Kendu Lane; singles KSh500) has a number of simple singles with bathroom. It's an OK place, but they won't let you see the rooms first.

New Victoria Hotel (☎ 21067; cnr Gor Mahia Rd & Kendu Lane; singles/doubles KSh850/1050) is a touch overpriced, but rates do include breakfast and there are some cheaper singles with shared facilities. Front rooms have balconies and some great views of Lake Victoria; there's also a good café and a TV lounge.

Hotel Inca (☎ 40158; singles/doubles KSh500/950), just off Jomo Kenyatta Hwy, is also reasonable value. The rooms are spacious and have small TVs, for whatever that's worth; hot water runs all day (although the bathrooms could be nicer) and there's a good bar and café area.

New East View Hotel (☎ 41871; Omolo Agar Rd; singles/doubles KSh1000/1300) and **Palms Guesthouse** (☎ 0722-221593; Omolo Agar Rd; singles with bathroom KSh1000) are a bit more expensive, but generally good. Prices include breakfast, and most rooms have fans. Both places have restaurants and Palms has a comfortable TV lounge.

There are two options out at Dunga if you don't want to be in town. **Joy Guest House** (☎ 0733-794898; singles/doubles KSh600/800), at the turn-off to Hippo Point, is excellent. Rooms have fans and rugs, some have balconies; there are kitchen facilities and one luxury double with TV.

Sunset Beach (☎ 43676; camping KSh500, singles/doubles KSh600/1200) is more of a resort-type place on the lakeshore, and is the only real option for campers here. The rooms are fairly basic but the café/bar area is good.

Places to Stay – Top End

Hotel Royale (☎ 40924; Jomo Kenyatta Hwy; singles/doubles KSh1000/1500), an old colonial hotel with a popular terrace bar overlooking the lake, lacks the top-end polish of Imperial Hotel but retains a fair bit of character. Unfortunately, some of the wooden interior is fading badly; rooms on the 1st floor are best. In addition to the bar, there is a restaurant, a disco at weekends and a small Internet bureau (KSh4 per minute).

Imperial Hotel (☎ 20002, fax 40345; e im perial@africaonline.co.ke; Jomo Kenyatta Hwy;

standard singles/doubles KSh3500/4750) is the best hotel in town. The cheaper rooms are a bit underwhelming but still very pleasant, and there are some rather more luxurious rooms and suites.

Facilities include a rooftop bar and two restaurants (lunch/dinner KSh650/750), a coffee shop, a business centre with Internet services, a picture gallery and also a small swimming pool.

Nyanza Club *(☎ 42703; singles/doubles KSh2250/2750)*, off Jomo Kenyatta Hwy, is the poshest option, with a plethora of facilities and well-equipped rooms. It's strictly members only, but you can take out temporary membership for KSh100. It's a good idea to phone in advance, otherwise you may not get through the gate.

Places to Eat

TOT Coffee House & Board & Lodging is a good little place away from the main streets. The Indian food here is not bad and there is a bar with a pool table and dart board.

Off Oginga Odinga Rd, **Cafe Natasha**, part of the hotel of the same name, has a wide range of good, cheap meals and is a popular spot for breakfast. Across the street **Kimwa Cafe Annexe & Bar** is also pretty well frequented, serving cheap local dishes such as *matoke* (mashed plantains) and stew. **Passions Cafe**, next to the Hotel Royale, is similar but smaller and more central.

The café at the **New Victoria Hotel** does excellent breakfasts and some decent standard dishes, although the chapatis aren't great and there have been some bad reports about the eggs. As the hotel is Muslim-run, alcohol isn't served.

For fast food, both **Chicken Palace** and **Wimpy** on Jomo Kenyatta Hwy offer the usual greasy delights, while the terrace of **Hotel Royale** is rather more civilised.

Mon Ami, in Mega Plaza, is a favourite expat pit-stop, with Western standards such as hamburgers for about KSh350. It's a lively bar with a pool table. The overloud satellite TV can get a bit wearing, unless you're a big fan of European sports and/or American soap operas.

The Vault Restaurant *(mains from KSh350)*, off Oginga Odinga Rd, is also good for home comforts (pizzas with real cheese!), plus the added 'bonus' of a casino and a bar that stays open until 3am. It's

housed in a former bank and still has the massive vault door inside.

Indian cuisine is well represented in Kisumu, particularly towards the lake end of Oginga Odinga Rd. **Al-Noor Café** *(mains around KSh200)*, in the new Swan Centre, has a good varied menu, although the service is not always up to much.

If you want Chinese food, head to **Oriental Restaurant** *(☎ 41388; Al-Imran Plaza; mains KSh400)*. The food is so-so, but there's free Internet access for customers and it's very relaxed.

The restaurants in the **Nyanza Club** and **Kisumu Yacht Club** *(☎ 22050; Dunga)* are fine places to drink and eat; temporary membership applies (at KSh100 and KSh200, respectively) and you may need to make a reservation. However, the **Florence Restaurant**, at Imperial Hotel, is generally agreed to be the best in town, and will cost about KSh750 per person.

Entertainment

Kisumu's nightlife has a reputation for being even livelier than Nairobi's, but it's harder to find if you don't know the scene; check flyers and ask around for the best parties.

Octopus Restaurant & Night Club *(Ogada St)* is a frisky place with a popular bar and its own disco (admission KSh90). It's definitely on the dodgy side, but fun if you can handle it! **Aquarius Club**, opposite Hotel Inca, is much the same.

Hotel Royale has regular discos on Friday, Saturday and Wednesday, and **Kisumu Beach Resort** has parties most weekends. **Kimwa Grand**, apparently relocated a couple of kilometres down Kenyatta Hwy after the original building burnt down, was also quite 'in' at the time of writing. Take a taxi if you want to check it out.

There is a small **cinema** *(☎ 44091; stalls/ balcony KSh100/150)*, near the town hall off Kenyatta Hwy, showing mostly mainstream Western and Hindi films.

Getting There & Away

Air There are four daily services (three on Sunday) to and from Nairobi with **Flamingo Airlines**. The trip takes one hour and costs KSh4300 one way.

Bus & Matatu Most buses, matatus and Peugeots to destinations within Kenya leave from the large bus and matatu station just north of the market off Jomo Kenyatta Hwy.

Akamba has its own depot in the centre of town. Departures for Nairobi are at 7am, 9am and 1pm (KSh490, 5½ hours). There's also the deluxe Akamba Royal service to Nairobi at 11am daily (KSh750). **Stagecoach** and various other companies charge around KSh300 to Nairobi.

There are plenty of Nissans/Peugeots to Nairobi (KSh400/600, five hours), Nakuru (KSh250/350, 2½ hours), Busia (KSh150/250, 1½ hours), Eldoret (KSh180/250, two hours) and Kakamega (KSh80/100, 45 minutes). Only matatus go to Kericho (KSh150, 1½ hours), Kisii (KSh150, 1½ hours) and Homa Bay (KSh150, 1½ hours). There are very few direct services to Kitale; it's best to take a vehicle to Kakamega or Eldoret and change there.

There are also daily bus and matatu services to Malaba in Uganda as well as the Tanzanian border at Isebania/Sirari.

Boat Some ferries have now started operating out of Kisumu again, but no-one seems very clear on exact timetables or prices! It should be possible to get a Sunday service to Homa Bay (KSh150, four hours) and Mbita (five hours) or Asembo Bay, but check at the port booking office first.

Getting Around
To/From the Airport A taxi is probably the easiest way to get into town from the airport, and will cost about KSh500. The Pipeline matatu (KSh20) also comes past here, but you'll have to follow the locals to find the pick-up point.

Matatu There are a couple of circular routes that may be useful. The first heads down Jomo Kenyatta Rd, turns right into Oginga Odinga Rd, up Anaawa Ave and then cuts back onto Jomo Kenyatta Hwy heading out of town towards Kimwa (useful for Kibuye market on Sunday). You can get one outside Imperial Hotel or from the junction of Jomo Kenyatta Hwy and Nairobi Rd.

The second 'service' starts from outside Hotel Royale and heads south to the ring road. It continues to Dunga Junction before turning around and heading back into town via Got Huma Rd. Vehicles on these routes are usually old Peugeots, but if passengers

are few, they may turn into a taxi and charge 20 times as much.

Any journey on these routes should cost around KSh20.

Car For car rental try **Pel Travels** (☎ 41525; @ peltrvls@africaonline.co.ke; Al-Imran Plaza), which has a number of 2WD vehicles and a couple of 4WDs. Standing charges per 2WD/4WD are KSh2000/3000 and KSh500/1000 insurance per day, plus KSh20/30 per kilometre. Excess is set at KSh35,000.

There are no small (and cheap) Suzuki 4WDs available for rental in Kisumu.

Taxi A taxi around town costs between KSh100 and KSh200.

LAKE VICTORIA'S SOUTH SHORE
Kendu Bay
This small lakeside village has little to offer apart from the strange volcanic **Simbi Lake** a couple of kilometres from town. The circular lake, sunk into the earth like a bomb crater, has a footpath around it and is quite popular with bird-watchers.

There is some basic accommodation in town, such as the **Big Five Hotel & Bar** (☎ 0385-22416), on the road to Homa Bay, but there's no real reason to stay unless you have to.

Homa Bay
☎ 0385
Further down the terrible road from Kisumu, Homa Bay is a highly unlikely growth town on a small bay on Lake Victoria. There are a surprising number of facilities, and while many existing businesses seem to think adding the current year to their name constitutes modernisation, a lot of new building work is actually going on. Who this will benefit is not entirely clear.

Barclays Bank has an ATM, and there are cardphones by the **post office**. Internet access is available at **Homa Bay Computer Services**, near Bay Lodge, and **Ramoria Computer**, on the main road, but connections are slow and fairly expensive and the power supply is unreliable.

Near the town is the intriguing volcano-shaped Mt Homa.

Places to Stay & Eat There are a number of budget hotels around the main road in

Homa Bay, but the best is probably **Summer Bay Hotel** *(singles/doubles KSh300/500)*, just off the main road on the lane to the post office. It's all squat and bucket facilities, but the triples (KSh800) are pretty sizable and breakfast is included.

Up the hill behind the new bus station and not far from the post office, is **Bay Lodge** *(☎ 21436; singles/doubles KSh300/450)*, which is clean, tidy and quiet.

Hippo Buck Hotel *(☎/fax 22032; singles/doubles with bathroom KSh950/1250)*, about 1.5km out of town towards Mbita, is the nearest thing to an upmarket place here. The rooms are a shade overpriced, but rates include breakfast and the restaurant is pleasant (although it's not recommended for vegetarians).

Homa Bay Women's Centre, on top of the hill overlooking the town, has a good restaurant and café. You could also try **Plaza Cafeteria**, near Barclays Bank, or **Holy Cafe**, by the harbour. For nightlife, you have the enviable task of choosing between **Club Asego View**, **Club Mega 2002** and **Cave Inn Club**.

Getting There & Away A new bus station has just been completed, so it's likely all departures will soon leave from there.

Akamba departures to Nairobi (KSh450, ten hours) leave at 7am and 7.30pm, and go via Kericho (KSh250, four hours), Nakuru (KSh350, six hours) and Naivasha (KSh400, nine hours); the company also serves Kisii (KSh70, 1½ hours). Numerous other companies and matatus ply these routes, and there are also matatus to Kisumu (KSh150, three hours) and Mbita (KSh100, one hour).

RUSINGA & MFANGANO ISLANDS
Rusinga Island & Mbita

The island is connected to the small town of Mbita by a short causeway. Mbita is the place with all the transport connections (including boats to Mfangano and Takawiri Islands), petrol stations, accommodation of sorts and cheap eateries, while Rusinga has been left green and rugged, a beautiful and pleasant place to wander around – the hill in its centre makes an attractive viewpoint.

The main feature on Rusinga is the **mausoleum of Tom Mboya** on the north side of the island (see the boxed text 'Tom Mboya').

Tom Mboya

A former sanitary inspector in Nairobi, Tom Mboya was one of the few Luos ever to achieve any kind of political success in a Kenyan government. As Jomo Kenyatta's right-hand man, he held a huge amount of influence up until his assassination in 1969, and is still well remembered today.

Despite his cherubic appearance, Mboya was a serious political heavyweight. An outspoken unionist and Pan-Africanist, he effectively controlled KANU while Kenyatta was in prison before independence, and was widely tipped to succeed him as president. Official investigations into his death petered out a little suspiciously, and many people believe it was tribally motivated, orchestrated by his Kikuyu political rivals.

Places to Stay & Eat There's not much in the way of decent accommodation in Mbita, though you can probably find a bed if you don't set your standards too high. You can stay at the **ICIPE Research Station** *(singles KSh500)* some distance out of town, but it's pricey and unimpressive.

New Foxton Hotel, close to Mbita's tiny post office, is probably the best cheap eating house. **New Capital Town Hotel Suba** is also OK. For a drink, try **Green Garden Hotel**, a lively bar with some good music.

Rusinga Island Club *(book through Let's Go Travel ☎ 02-340331; e info@letsgosafari .com; singles/doubles all-inclusive US$410/700)* is an exclusive place on the northern side of Rusinga Island itself. Fishing is the dominant activity, but if you're not a keen worm-dangler there are various water sports available and the birdlife nearby is prolific. Accommodation here is in flash individual thatched huts, each with a fine lake view. It is possible to come here on a flying safari from the Masai Mara – a trip with Mara Intrepids costs US$425 per day.

Mfangano Island

There's very little in the way of facilities on this imposing little island. The main activity for visitors is to climb **Mt Kwitutu** (1694m) in the centre of the island – the views are stunning. It's about a 1½- to two-hour climb. What should not be ignored is the set of **rock** paintings a short distance from the summit and high in the hills above the northern shore. You'll need to take a guide to find them, though.

The chief's camp (if you need anything sorted out) and **post office** is at Sena village, where the main jetty still stands. Also on the island is **St Linus' Church** (check out the mural inside) and **St Luke's Clinic**, which is handy in an area where malaria is common.

Places to Stay & Eat There are no hotels on Mfangano, but it may be possible to arrange **home stays** with the local residents. Campers may also be able to stay in the grounds of St Linus' Church.

Failing that, the only possibility on the island is the upmarket **Mfangano Island Camp** (book through Governor's Camps ☎ 02-331871; e reservations@governorscamp.com; singles/doubles full board US$150/300 in low season, US$340/500 in high season) on the northern side. Built in traditional Luo style (albeit with a few more-modern amenities), this is primarily a fishing resort, and fishing trips are available at US$120 per day.

On the nearby Takawiri Island, **Takawiri Island Resort** (☎ 035-43141, Nairobi ☎ 02-577490; e info@dreamtravel.co.ke; singles/doubles full board US$120/180 in low season, US$160/220 in high season) is a similar place run by the ecofriendly Dream Travel company. Transfers from Mbita Point cost KSh8000 per boat, but it should be possible to pick up a taxi-boat to the island.

Getting There & Away

There are usually three daily buses going each way between Mbita and Kisumu (KSh200, 2½ hours), but they leave Mbita first thing in the morning (the last one at about 8am). Matatus to Homa Bay are far more frequent (KSh100, one hour).

Until the ferries get their act together, 10m canoes are the only transport between the islands. These leave from the causeway at Mbita. There are usually three boats per day to Mfangano and Takawiri islands, and more on Thursday (market day in Mbita). Fares should be around KSh100 to KSh200 for Mfangano and KSh50 for Takawiri, but you may be charged KSh4000 for the whole boat instead! The first boat for Mbita (via Takawiri) leaves the pier at Mfangano at around 6.30am.

RUMA NATIONAL PARK

This hot and wet park (adult nonresidents/residents US$15/KSh500) is one of the least visited in Kenya, although for no good reason. Established in 1966 originally as the Lambwe Valley Nature Reserve, Ruma National Park covers 120 sq km of riverine woodland and savanna grassland in the Lambwe Valley, with the (seasonal) Lambwe River running through it. Some magnificent cliffs can be found on the park's borders, including the dramatic **Kanyamaa Escarpment**, and some of this rock may have climbing potential. Trekking and fishing are also possibilities, but both activities would need considerable planning and prior permission. Contact the **warden** (☎ 0385-22656; PO Box 420, Homa Bay) in advance. A guide costs KSh500 per day and KSh300 per half day.

Ruma is the only place in Kenya where the roan antelope is found, while Bohor's reedbuck, Rothschild's giraffe, Jackson's hartebeest and the tiny oribi antelope are other rarities. You can also see 145 different bird species, including the fish eagle and white egret. Tsetse flies can be a problem after the rains.

There are **camp sites** (camping US$2) with basic facilities at each of the entrance gates.

Getting There & Away The main park entrance is 23km from Homa Bay. Head south out of town for a couple of kilometres and turn right onto the Homa Bay–Mbita road. About 12km towards Mbita is the main access road and it's another 11km from here.

There's public transport to the turn-off, but it's pointless to get to the park without your own transport unless you've made arrangements with the warden. All the roads within the park have been upgraded with World Bank money, but a 4WD is still essential in the rainy season.

THIMLICH OHINGA

East of Ruma National Park is possibly one of the most important archaeological discoveries in East Africa. The remains of a dry-stone enclosure, 150m in diameter and containing another five smaller enclosures, were discovered here. Stylistically, the structure is similar to traditional Luo buildings, but may date back as far as the Late Iron Age of the 15th century. The name is essentially a description of the site, which means 'stone enclosure in frightening dense forest'!

Getting to Thimlich is a problem without your own transport, although as always in Kenya, not completely impossible with patience. Head down the Homa Bay–Rongo road for 12km, then turn right at Rod Kopany village, heading southwest through Mirogi to the village of Miranga. The site is signposted from there.

The Mara

The Mara, as the Masai Mara National Reserve is often called by residents and blasé travellers, is more than just the most popular wildlife park in the country; in many cases it is the reason why people come to Kenya in the first place. One look at the region is enough to explain its popularity: this is the classic savanna you see in just about every African film and nature programme ever made, and the sheer density of wildlife is amazing. This is also traditionally the land of the Maasai, but they have largely been displaced in favour of the more profitable animals, and many now rely on tourism for their primary income (see the boxed text 'The Hard Sell').

Cheaper lodges on the edge of the Masai Mara National Reserve run an increasing number of activities outside of the reserve itself, where there's an abundance of wildlife (the animals don't recognise park boundaries!)

NAROK
☎ 0305

This small provincial town a couple of hours west of Nairobi is the main access point for the Mara, and most safari vehicles stop to refuel here (it's the last place to do so before the park) or spend the night before heading to the park. There are branches of **Barclays Bank** (with an ATM) and **Kenya Commercial Bank**, a **post office** (with a cardphone) and a selection of budget and mid-range hotels. **Internet access** will cost you at least KSh25 per minute.

Narok is not a great place for independent travellers, as prices reflect the heavy tourist traffic and the town is also rife with souvenir sellers, transport touts and rip-off merchants.

Places to Stay & Eat
Spear Hotel *(singles/doubles KSh300/600)* is the most popular of the limited accommodation options. It has reasonable rooms. Videos play in the bar every evening (usually to a crowd of Maasai!), but it's better to eat elsewhere.

Chambai Hotel *(☎ 22660, fax 22591; standard/super rooms KSh650/1000)* is the only vaguely tourist-class place in town, and is actually surprisingly good. All rooms are singles with bathroom; super rooms come with TV and slightly better facilities. The bar and restaurant here (mains around KSh250) are civilised and well worth trying.

Kim's Dishes and **Transit Hotel** are reasonably popular options for food, but don't

---

The Hard Sell

A common complaint among travellers in this region, particularly in the Mara, is that the Maasai can be incredibly hard-nosed when it comes to business, and 'cultural' visits to villages can turn into high-pressure sales ventures the moment your minibus arrives.

While it would be unfair to generalise, it is certainly true that some Maasai, especially in high-density tourist areas, will treat you purely as a cash cow. Favourite techniques include: dropping wares in your lap and refusing to take them back; coming into camp sites to offer dances at non-negotiable rates; demanding extra fees for services you've already paid for; and charging for absolutely everything, from camping to walking across their land. Of course, this kind of behaviour is not limited to the Maasai, but their aggressive and utterly unapologetic attitude seems to upset more travellers than the day-to-day hassle elsewhere!

If you do feel you're being taken for a ride by anyone, Maasai or otherwise, you shouldn't let them get away with it. At the same time just think. If your people had been consistently displaced and dispossessed for the last 100 years and you yourself were subjected to constant streams of gawping foreigners with seemingly bottomless pockets, wouldn't you do the same?

Hot-air balloon, the Mara

Tropical rainforest, Kakemega Forest Reserve, western Kenya

The annual wildebeest migration

A cheetah surveys its territory

El-Molo village on the shore, Lake Turkana, northern Kenya

Remarkable hanging birds' nests

Cottage at Il Ngwesi Group Ranch

Gerenuks utilising their unique talent of feeding upright

expect too much. There are also several basic but busy bars on the main street.

Getting There & Away

There are frequent matatus/Peugeots between Narok and Nairobi (KSh200/250, two hours) and less-frequent matatu departures to Naivasha (KSh200, 2½ hours), Nakuru (KSh300, three hours) and Kisii (KSh300, three hours). Matatus leave from near Spear Hotel. There is usually daily transport to Sekenani Gate and a long-suffering matatu runs to Talek Gate for about KSh200; ask by the BP petrol station.

MASAI MARA NATIONAL RESERVE

☎ 0305

The Masai Mara is the northern extension of the Serengeti Plains, watered by the Mara River and its tributary the Talek. The reserve comprises 1510 sq km of open grassland tucked away in the southwestern corner of the country. Concentrations of wildlife are highest on the western edge of the reserve, in the swampy area around the spectacular Esoit Oloololo (Siria) Escarpment. However, driving can be tricky after the rains, and the eastern side sees the greatest numbers of tourists, as the Oloolaimutiek and Talek gates are easily accessible from Nairobi.

All over the Mara, you'll see an astonishing amount of wildlife, often in one place at one time. Of the big cats, lions are found in large prides everywhere and it's not uncommon to see them hunting. Cheetahs and leopards are harder to spot, but are still fairly common. Elephants, buffaloes, zebras and hippos also exist in large numbers.

Of the antelopes, the black-striped Thomson's gazelle and larger Grant's gazelle are found in huge numbers, while impalas, topis, Coke's hartebeests and wildebeests are also profuse. About 37 black rhinos live in the park but are rarely seen. Other common animals include Maasai giraffes, baboons (especially around the lodges), warthogs, grey (or side-striped) jackals, bat-eared foxes and matriarchal clans of spotted hyenas.

The ultimate attraction is without doubt the annual wildebeest migration in July and August, when literally millions of these ungainly beasts move north from the Serengeti in search of lusher grass before turning south again around October. While you're more likely to see the endless columns grazing or trudging along than you are to witness dramatic TV-style river fordings, it is still a staggering experience to be in the reserve at these times.

In the high season you get almost as many people as animals here, and minibuses have a tendency to take off and make new tracks wherever they feel fit. This should not be encouraged.

Information

Entry to the reserve is US$30 per person per day (US$10 for children and students), and you pay KSh200 for a car. Park officials do not seem to be entirely adverse to sharp practices, especially in the more remote gates. It's not unknown to be offered half-price entry if you decline a receipt (ie, your ticket), and we've had unconfirmed reports of park fees being demanded from tourists camping outside the gates or even travelling on local matatus!

Driving around is not allowed after dark, and nonguests must be out of the park by 6.30pm. The best places to buy fuel are probably Mara Sarova Lodge, Mara Serena Lodge and Keekorok Lodge, though prices are higher than in Narok or Nairobi.

There is a **post office** located next to the Warden's Headquarters.

Wildlife Drives & Walks

If you're not on an organised safari and you've arrived by matatu and/or hitching, you can organise drives with almost any of the lodges here. Dream Camp, Fig Tree Camp, Kichwa Tembo Camp and Simba Lodge are good starting points. Fig Tree and Dream Camp are just inside, and fairly easily reachable from, Talek Gate. They're relatively accessible and friendly towards independent travellers. Expect to pay around US$35 plus park fees for a two-hour wildlife drive. Doing a safari this way isn't recommended, though, as outlined in Getting There & Away, later. Most top-end places also offer a wide range of guided walks and other activities such as horse riding and dinners in the bush.

Alternatively you can walk with a Maasai *moran* (warrior) outside the park, where there is still a large amount of wildlife. This can be a wonderful experience, but be aware that on top of guiding fees, local Maasai

MASAI MARA NATIONAL RESERVE

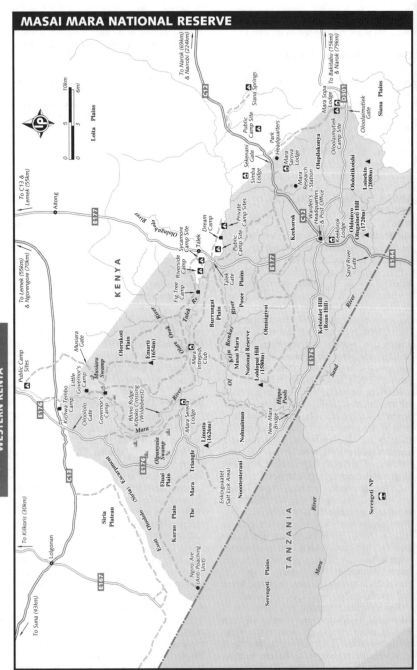

groups will probably charge you for crossing their land. **Talek** is a good base for walking.

Ballooning
If you can afford the US$350 price tag, a balloon safari is definitely the way to go. It's a superb experience and a world away from the standard minibus circuit. The Mara is definitely the best place in Kenya to do it; trips can be arranged through Keekorok Lodge, Mara Sopa Lodge, Governor's Camp, Mara Intrepids Club and Fig Tree Camp.

Maasai Village
The Maasai village just outside Oloolaimutiek Gate is open to tourists. Once you've paid the entry fee you can walk around and take as many pictures as you like. But negotiating admission can be a fraught process, especially if you're with a large group – prices can start as high as US$10 per person!

Unsurprisingly, it's not much of a cultural experience with a dozen snap-happy tourists poking around. If you can visit when there's no-one else it's not too bad, but at other times you'll be hassled continuously.

Places to Stay – Budget & Mid-Range
Camping is really the only option for budget travellers here; the top-end lodges have got the market pretty much sewn up for other accommodation. You can camp just outside any of the gates for KSh150. There are no facilities but you can usually get water from the rangers.

Oloolaimutiek Camp Site (camping KSh250), near the gate of the same name, and **Riverside Camp** (☎ 22128; camping KSh300, tents per person KSh1000, bandas per person KSh1250), near Talek Gate in the northeast, are both run by local Maasai. They're good sites but you will have to pay extra for everything from firewood to night watchmen! Riverside is better equipped, with kitchen facilities, hot water and electric lighting (run off car batteries).

There are several **public camp sites** along the Talek River not far from Riverside Camp, as well as a number of private camps belonging to safari companies. **Sycamore** (camping KSh300) is a site that only has long-drop toilets.

Some similar **camp sites** can be found on the banks of the Mara River, outside the

Olooolo Gate, but these are not secure – baboons and thieves both thrive here – and charge as much as US$15 per person.

Places to Stay – Top End
The whole area around the reserve is absolutely heaving with top-end lodges, safari clubs and tented camps, most of which are chain-run and advertised extensively in Nairobi. Quality does vary, but on the whole standards are high, and you won't get this much choice anywhere else in the country.

Oloolaimutiek & Sekanani Gates Surprisingly unobtrusive, **Mara Sopa Lodge** (☎ 22196, in Nairobi ☎ 02-750235; e sopa lodges@nbi.ispkenya.com; singles/doubles full board US$78/120 in low season, US$162/302 in high season) resembles a Maasai boma, with a cluster of thatched huts tucked away on a hillside just outside Oloolaimutiek Gate. Inside, of course, it's 24-carat luxury, with all the expensive extras you could ask for.

Keekorok Lodge (book through Block Hotels ☎ 02-540780; singles/doubles full board US$104/130 in low season, US$160/200 in high season) is one of the top options, with bungalows, cabins and cottages to choose from. It has all the usual facilities, with the added attraction of a hippo pool, and is the closest lodge to the Tanzanian border.

Mara Sarova Lodge (in Nairobi ☎ 02-713333, fax 715566; e reservations@sarova.co.ke; singles/doubles full board US$60/120 in low season, US$150/200 in high season) is not far from the Sekenani Gate. It has the works, including a swimming pool.

Siana Springs (in Nairobi ☎ 02-750780, fax 746826; e conscorp@conscorp.co.ke; singles/doubles full board US$95/189 in low season, US$210/294 in high season) is a tented lodge about 15km outside Sekenani Gate. The cottages are dotted around a beautiful green clearing with an open-air bar and dining room. There's a lot of wildlife around the camp and a full range of activities is available, including dawn walks, spotlit night drives, and bush dinners with mock Maasai attacks!

Talek Gate Three of the better tented camps can be found along the Talek River. **Fig Tree Camp** (☎ 22163, book through Mada Hotels ☎ 02-221439; e sales@madahotels.com; singles/doubles full board US$55/110

in low season, US$147/200 in high season), reached via a wooden bridge from the car park on the opposite bank, is an agreeable site with a swimming pool. The permanent tents overlook the river; there are similarly equipped cabins and a luxury chalet.

Mara Intrepids Club *(☎ 22321, book through Heritage Hotels ☎ 02-446651; e mara intrepids@heritagehotels.co.ke; singles/doubles full board US$234/315 in low season, US$390/525 in high season)* is jaw-droppingly expensive, although rates do include three wildlife drives. It's a pleasant site with a wide range of activities, from Swedish massage to ethically dubious leopard baiting, but it's still distinctly overpriced.

Dream Camp *(☎ 57239, book through Dream Travel ☎ 02-577490; e kristofer@ dreamtravel.co.ke; per person full board US$80)* is the only ecolodge in the Mara, and must be one of the friendliest places in the park. It's definitely not your average tourist complex: solar panels provide power, organic waste is composted and dirty water is reused to water the grounds. The 18 permanent tents are individually designed and have excellent views. There's also a superb observation tower with a small exhibition space, and local conservationists often give informal lectures. Walking safaris with the local Maasai can be arranged here.

Musiara & Oloololo Gates Sitting on a superb site overlooking the Mara River, **Mara Serena Lodge** *(☎ 22059, in Nairobi ☎ 02-711077; e cro@serena.co.ke; singles/ doubles full board US$75/150 in low season, US$200/250 in high season)* was built to resemble a modern Maasai village. It blends in beautifully with its surroundings and is very popular.

Governor's Camp and **Little Governor's Camp** *(in Nairobi ☎ 02-331871, fax 726427; e govscamp@africaonline.co.ke; per person full board US$150 in low season, US$250 in high season)* are excellent tented camps with personal service, great riverside locations and plenty of activities; as at Intrepids, the hefty rates include three wildlife drives. You are requested not to feed the warthogs.

Kichwa Tembo Camp *(in Nairobi ☎ 02-750298; e conscorp@conscorp.co.ke; singles/ doubles full board US$95/189 in low season, US$210/294 in high season)*, run by the same people as Siana Springs, is just outside the

northern boundary, with traditional-style huts and spectacular savanna views. The food here has an excellent reputation.

Places to Eat & Drink

If you can't afford to stay in the expensive lodges or camps, it's worth dropping in for a drink or a snack. Most are relaxed and highly civilised places, although the prices are predictably high.

Otherwise, the staff canteens of **Mara Sopa Lodge** and **Keekorok Lodge** are worth a try; you may feel a bit out of place, but people are usually friendly.

There are a number of small *dukas* (small shops) and eating places in the tiny village of Talek, as well as a lively Maasai market.

Getting There & Away

Air There are two flights daily between Nairobi's Wilson Airport and the Masai Mara with **Air Kenya Aviation** *(in Nairobi ☎ 02-605745; e info@airkenya.com)*. Flights leave Nairobi at 10am and 3pm and the Mara at 11am and 4pm. The fares are US$107/188 one way/return, not including airstrip transfers. There are also flights from Nanyuki (US$173) and Samburu (US$220).

If you're being picked up from one of the many airstrips in the Mara, the aeroplane does not wait around even when it arrives early, so you could be left alone waiting for a lift.

Matatu, Car & 4WD There's very little point coming to the Mara without transport. Most lodges can arrange wildlife drives for independent travellers (see earlier), but you still have to get there somehow, and the whole process will seldom work out cheaper than an organised safari. Public transport of sorts runs from Narok to the Sekenani and Talek Gates but won't take you into the park (matatus are hardly all-terrain vehicles!), and your chances of getting a free lift with a safari vehicle are minimal.

From Kisii you can get as far as Kilkoris or Suna on the main A1 route with public transport, but you'll have problems after this.

For those with their own vehicle, there is about 52km of good road after Narok until the bitumen runs out and the road becomes bad for the next 40km. It's also possible to approach the reserve from the west via Lolgorian, but the roads are very rough and rocky in places and there's very little signposting in this end of the park.

Western Highlands

Benefiting from reliable rainfall and fertile soil, the western highlands make up the agricultural heartland of Kenya, separating Kisumu and Lake Victoria from the rest of the country. The south is cash crop country, with vast tea plantations covering the region around Kisii and Kericho, while further north, near Kitale and Eldoret, some denser farmland takes over.

The settlements here are predominantly agricultural service towns, with very little of interest unless you need a chainsaw or a water barrel. For visitors, the real attractions lie outside these places – the tea plantations around Kericho, the tropical beauty of Kakamega Forest, walking in Mt Elgon and Saiwa Swamp national parks, and exploring the dramatic Cherangani Hills northeast of Kitale and Eldoret.

KISII
☎ 0381

Kisii is basically just a transport hub for the surrounding area, and has very little to offer the traveller apart from a being convenient stopover. The town centre is compact and has some reasonable facilities. For a relatively small town, it has an unusual number of modern office blocks and construction projects; speculation about money laundering here probably won't win you any friends!

The town is the main centre of the region known as the Gusii highlands, home of the Gusii people.

The Gusii, numbering around one million, are a Bantu-speaking people in the middle of a non-Bantu area; the Maasai to the south, Luo to the west and north and Kipsigis to the east all speak unrelated languages (see the special section 'Tribes of Kenya').

While Kisii soapstone does obviously come from this area, it's not actually on sale here at all. Quarrying and carving still go on in the small village of **Tabaka**, and you can usually visit the workshops there. However, as most of the carvings made here are sold on to dealers and shops in Nairobi at rock-bottom prices, many local people feel exploited, and you may not get a particularly warm welcome.

Information
There are a number of cardphones outside the **post office**; Internet access is available at **Westernet Computer** for KSh3 per minute in the New Sansora Complex by the local matatu stand. **Barclays Bank** and **Kenya Commercial Bank** have ATMs.

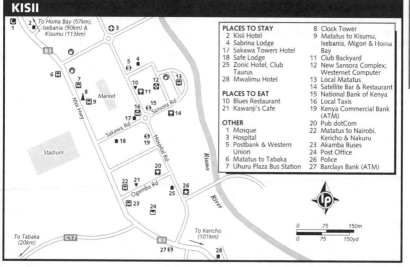

KISII

To Homa Bay (57km), Isebania (90km) & Kisumu (113km)

Mor Hwy

Market

Sakawa Rd

Sansora Rd

Hospital Rd

Ogemba Rd

Stadium

Riana

River

To Tabaka (20km)

To Kericho (101km)

PLACES TO STAY
2 Kisii Hotel
4 Sabrina Lodge
17 Sakawa Towers Hotel
18 Safe Lodge
25 Zonic Hotel; Club Taurus
28 Mwalimu Hotel

PLACES TO EAT
10 Blues Restaurant
21 Kawanji's Cafe

OTHER
1 Mosque
3 Hospital
5 Postbank & Western Union
6 Matatus to Tabaka
7 Uhuru Plaza Bus Station

8 Clock Tower
9 Matatus to Kisumu, Isebania, Migori & Homa Bay
11 Club Backyard
12 New Sansora Complex; Westernet Computer
13 Local Matatus
14 Satellite Bar & Restaurant
15 National Bank of Kenya
16 Local Taxis
19 Kenya Commercial Bank (ATM)
20 Pub dotCom
22 Matatus to Nairobi, Kericho & Nakuru
23 Akamba Buses
24 Post Office
26 Police
27 Barclays Bank (ATM)

0   75   150m
0   75   150yd

Places to Stay

There is very little in the way of decent accommodation in Kisii, and the budget places are particularly poor. There is generally a lot of noise at night wherever you stay, but especially if you're near the market or the transport stands.

Sabrina Lodge *(singles/doubles KSh250/ 500)*, just around the corner from the local matatu stand, is friendly with slightly musty rooms and shared facilities (bucket showers). Security is good, and the hotel has a bar and restaurant.

Safe Lodge *(Sakawa Rd; singles/doubles 250/450)*, tucked away in a shopping passage, has rooms with bathrooms, but it's still just squat 'n' bucket here. The pool bar can get quite lively.

Mwalimu Hotel *(☎ 31636; Moi Hwy; singles/doubles KSh320/520, suites KSh1020)*, set in its own compound at the southeastern end of town, has a selection of good-sized rooms and two-room suites. The rooms are OK, but there are no nets and some pretty big bugs! The hotel has a popular bar, terrace, beer garden and restaurant. There's also guarded parking.

Sakawa Towers Hotel *(☎ 21218; Sakawa Rd; singles/doubles KSh500/700)*, a modern high-rise building next to the market, has also seen better days. Rooms have balconies (some with good views, all with copious litter), nets and slightly scabby bathrooms with dubious water supply. There's a big bar and restaurant and rates include breakfast.

Kisii Hotel *(☎ 20715; Moi Hwy; singles/ doubles KSh650/850)* is a relaxed place with large gardens. Rates include breakfast and all rooms have bathrooms. The restaurant and bar are still deservedly popular, but the performing turkey and ducks seem to have disappeared.

Built in a bizarre half-modernish, half-plywood style, **Zonic Hotel** *(☎ 30298; Hospital Rd; singles/doubles US$25/40, suites from US$65)* is new and the nearest you'll get to top-end accommodation here. The rooms are actually pretty good, especially the suites with TV and balcony, but the prices are slightly off-putting.

Places to Eat & Drink

There's not a lot of choice when it comes to eating. The tiny restaurant inside **Sabrina Lodge** does local standards at sensible prices. **Kawanji's Cafe** *(Ogemba Rd)* is also generally reliable.

For something a bit more sophisticated, **Blues Restaurant** *(Hospital Rd; mains around KSh250)* is a great modern place with a balcony overlooking the market and proper cable TV. Cartoon Network is popular in the afternoons!

The restaurants in **Kisii Hotel** and **Mwalimu Hotel** are also popular, and the food at the **Zonic Hotel** is much more reasonably priced than the rooms.

Entertainment

To compensate for its other shortcomings, Kisii has some of the cheapest beer around (KSh55 for a large Tusker), and there is a moderate amount of nightlife.

Pub dotCom is a rowdy locals' drinking place and usually packed. **Klub Taurus** underneath the Zonic Hotel gets in pro DJs from as far afield as Mombasa. **Club Backyard** and **Satellite Bar & Restaurant** head up the more established local competition.

Getting There & Away

Most matatus leave from in front of the market on the main drag. There are regular departures to Kisumu (KSh160, 1½ hours), Kericho (KSh150, 1½ hours), Homa Bay (KSh80, one hour) and Isebania (KSh120, 1½ hours) on the Tanzanian border.

Matatus for local destinations leave from the stand at the end of Sansora Rd.

Akamba has two direct buses daily to Nairobi (KSh450, eight hours) via Nakuru (KSh290, 4½ hours) at 4.40am and 7.50pm. Tickets should be booked one day in advance.

Various other companies have offices in Uhuru Plaza on Moi Hwy. International bus departures for Mwanza in Tanzania also leave from here (see the introductory Getting There & Away chapter for further information).

KERICHO
☎ 0361

There's not a great deal to Kericho, but it's a pleasant enough place to stop for the night, especially if you're fond of a brew – this is the tea capital of western Kenya, surrounded by hectares of rolling green plantations (see the boxed text 'Picking Tea'). The climate is perfect for it, mainly because of the afternoon showers that fall almost every day of the year.

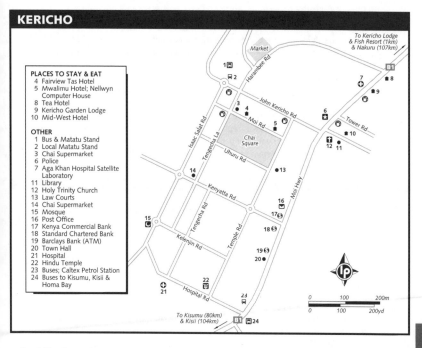

KERICHO

To Kericho Lodge
& Fish Resort (1km)
& Nakuru (107km)

Market

Harambee Rd

John Kericho Rd

Tower Rd

Chai Square

Moi Rd

Isaac Salat Rd

Tengecha La

Uhuru Rd

Kenyatta Rd

Moi Hwy

Tengecha Rd

Temple Rd

Kelenjin Rd

Hospital Rd

To Kisumu (80km)
& Kisii (104km)

0   100   200m
0   100   200yd

PLACES TO STAY & EAT
4 Fairview Tas Hotel
5 Mwalimu Hotel; Nellwyn
   Computer House
8 Tea Hotel
9 Kericho Garden Lodge
10 Mid-West Hotel

OTHER
1 Bus & Matatu Stand
2 Local Matatu Stand
3 Chai Supermarket
6 Police
7 Aga Khan Hospital Satellite
   Laboratory
11 Library
12 Holy Trinity Church
13 Law Courts
14 Chai Supermarket
15 Mosque
16 Post Office
17 Kenya Commercial Bank
18 Standard Chartered Bank
19 Barclays Bank (ATM)
20 Town Hall
21 Hospital
22 Hindu Temple
23 Buses; Caltex Petrol Station
24 Buses to Kisumu, Kisii &
   Homa Bay

Luckily these downpours are generally too brief to be a nuisance, and the atmosphere is cool enough to keep it fresh instead of humid.

The town takes its name from the Maasai chief Ole Kericho, who was killed by the Gusii in the 18th century in a territorial battle. The Maasai had been in the area for years and didn't appreciate the Gusii moving in, though the Gusii themselves were being pressured for land by the advancing Luo. Both groups have since moved on and the area is now the home of the Kipsigis people, part of the greater Kalenjin group of Nandi-speaking tribes which also includes the Pokot, the Nandi and the Marakwet (see the special section 'Tribes of Kenya' for details).

Information
The **post office** (with cardphones) and the three main **banks** *(open 8am-1pm Mon-Fri, 8.30am-11am Sat)* are all on Moi Hwy. Barclays Bank has an ATM.

Cheap but variable Internet access is available at **Nellwyn Computer House**, in the same building as Mwalimu Hotel. **Tea Hotel** has faster connections but higher

prices (KSh20 per minute at peak times, KSh10 per minute off-peak).

North of town on Moi Hwy is a **satellite laboratory** of the Aga Khan Hospital in Kisumu, which can do blood tests.

Things to See & Do
The closest **tea plantation** to town is behind Tea Hotel. If you walk through the hotel grounds and out of the back gate, the path leads through the tea bushes to the hotel workers' huts. If you're lucky, there may be picking in progress. Organised tours of the tea plantations are surprisingly uncommon in Kericho, but it's worth asking at the hotel.

You can arrange guided river walks, fishing trips and hikes through tea estates at Kericho Lodge & Fish Resort.

Places to Stay & Eat
Campers have a couple of options. **Kericho Garden Lodge** *(☎ 0722-753050; camping per tent KSh250, singles/doubles KSh500/780)* has pleasant grounds with plenty of room for tents. The lodge has a homely bar and lounge; the rooms are a bit pricey, although

Picking Tea

Kenya is the world's third-largest tea exporter, with tea accounting for between 20% and 30% of the country's export income. Tea picking is a great source of employment around Kericho: the bushes are picked every 17 days, and the same worker picks the same patches each time. A good picker can collect 100kg of tea each day.

The Kenyan tea industry is unique in that its small landholders produce the bulk (66%) of the country's tea. All the leaves used to be sold to the Kenya Tea Development Authority (KTDA), which did the processing and supposedly guaranteed farmers 70% of the sale price.

Corrupt and inefficient, the KTDA was replaced in 2000 by the Kenya Tea Development Agency (spot the difference!), run as a private company. However, smallholders are gradually taking a bigger role in the management of Kenya's most important cash crop, and the problems which have beset the coffee industry are not quite so prevalent in this area.

rates include breakfast, and cheaper basic singles are available.

Kericho Lodge & Fish Resort *(☎ 20035; camping per person KSh150, single/double bandas KSh1000/1350)* is on the bank of the Kimugi River, which runs behind the Tea Hotel. It's a great location with a good bar and restaurant. However, the bandas are unreasonably expensive. You can organise a number of activities are possible from here.

Fairview Tas Hotel *(☎ 21507; Moi Rd; singles/doubles KSh300/600)* is a tatty and shambolic place but about as good as cheap accommodation gets around here. Prices seem to vary for tourists and are probably negotiable. The 1st-floor balcony restaurant is a reasonable option for cheap meals and can knock up a good breakfast.

Nearby, **Mwalimu Hotel** *(☎ 30351; Moi Rd; singles/doubles KSh500/650)* is a slightly better option, although it houses a large collection of junk. The bar and restaurant are quite amenable and there's a pool table.

Mid-West Hotel *(☎ 20611, fax 206615; standard singles/doubles KSh1500/2000, suites KSh2950/3550)*, off Moi Hwy on the way into town, is the cheaper of the two big hotels but is still hardly worth the price. Even the suites are unimpressive, and the bathrooms leave something to be desired. The hotel has its own bar and restaurant, which goes some way towards redeeming it. The set dinner is good value at KSh350.

Tea Hotel *(☎ 30004, fax 20576;* e *Teaho tel@chemtech.africaonline.com; camping per person KSh200, singles/doubles US$60/84)* is a grand, old place built in the 1950s by the Brooke Bond company. The extensive grounds seem to be somewhat better tended

than the hotel itself: the rooms are nice but well worn, with bathrooms erring on the grimy side. Standard rooms are overpriced, but the same rate applies to cottages and superior rooms, which are a bit better.

There are two bars and a lounge area with a pleasant terrace. The **buffets** *(lunch/dinner US$11/12)* are rather expensive but offer a wide selection, and there is a grand piano which you may be allowed to play if you're feeling musical.

Getting There & Away

The bus and matatu station is fairly well organised, with matatus on the upper level and minibuses and buses on the lower level. However, it's often easiest to catch buses to Nairobi (KSh300, 4½ hours) from the Caltex petrol station on the main road; similarly, buses and matatus to Kisumu and Kisii can be picked up from just south of here. Ask around in town first, wherever you're heading.

As is the case throughout western Kenya, there is plenty of transport in any direction. Matatus/Peugeots leave regularly for Kisumu (KSh100/120, 1½ hours), Kisii (KSh120/140, 1½ hours), Eldoret (KSh200/250, 2½ hours), Nakuru (KSh140/200, two hours) and Nairobi (KSh300/450, four hours).

If you are hitching, the turn-off to Kisumu is about 2km south of town along the Kisii road.

KAKAMEGA
☎ 0331
This small but busy town is spread out along the A1 Hwy north of Kisumu. There's no real reason to stay here, but if you arrive late in the day it can be convenient to sleep

over and stock up with supplies before heading to the Kakamega Forest Reserve, the area's main attraction.

The town has the usual facilities – with a couple of **banks** (Barclays has an ATM), a **post office**, an **Internet café**, a **market**, some cheap cafés, a few board and lodgings and an overpriced hotel.

For entertainment there's also an outdoor police training ground, where you can watch Kenya's finest practice their riot control! Just behind it is the **KWS Area Headquarters** where you can get some information about the forest.

The Luyha people are centred around Kakamega (see the special section 'Tribes of Kenya'), although they're quite Westernised and unobtrusive as a community. This is also part of the traditional Bungoma district (see the boxed text 'The Kindest Cut').

Off the road south of town is the **Crying Stone of Ilesi**, a local curiosity that has become a regional emblem. The formation consists of a large round boulder balanced on top of an 8m column of rock, with water somehow flowing constantly down a groove in the middle. It's worth a look; locals will show you the way from the road for a small tip, and may be able to tell you some of the legends associated with it.

Places to Stay

There are a number of reasonable cheap hotels here, but if you arrive early enough the places in the forest itself are generally more pleasant. **Salama Hotel** has very basic rooms for around KSh200; **Bendera Hotel** (*doubles with bathroom KSh350*) is nicer and fairly popular with travellers.

At the top of the range is **Golf Hotel** (☎ 20125; singles/doubles US$60/75), which is shockingly overpriced but has some good views of Mt Elgon.

Cheap food is also readily available in town, although the various cafés have little to distinguish them.

Getting There & Around

Akamba and **Coast** buses have offices just off Kenyatta Rd. Fares to Nairobi are between KSh470 and KSh550 and departures are mostly in the afternoon and evening.

The main matatu station, behind the Total petrol station on the northern edge of town, has services to Kisumu (KSh100, 45 minutes), Kitale (KSh160, two hours), Eldoret (KSh160, 2½ hours) and Nakuru (KSh250, four hours), from where you can change for Nairobi. Hitching is not too difficult.

For one reason *poda-podas* (bicycle taxis) are very popular here, and you can get across town for about KSh20.

KAKAMEGA FOREST RESERVE
☎ 0331

This superb small slab of virgin tropical rainforest is home to a huge variety of birds and animals, and is becoming particularly popular with independent travellers.

The wildlife is a major attraction. Only here and at Mt Elgon can you find the rare De Brazza's monkey. Other primates here

WESTERN KENYA

The Kindest Cut

The Bungoma/Trans-Nzoia district goes wild in August with the sights and sounds of the Bukusu Circumcision Festival, an annual jamboree dedicated to the initiation of young boys into manhood.

The tradition was apparently passed to the Bukusu by the Sabaot tribe in the 1800s, when a young hunter cut the head off a troublesome serpent to earn the coveted operation (too symbolic to be true?). The evening before the ceremony is devoted to substance abuse and sex; in the morning the fortunate youngsters are trimmed with a traditional knife in front of their entire village.

Unsurprisingly, this practice has attracted a certain amount of controversy in recent years. Health concerns are prevalent, as the same knife can be used for up to 10 boys, posing a risk of AIDS and other infections. The associated debauchery also brings a seasonal rush of underage pregnancies and family rifts that seriously affect local communities.

Education and experience now mean that fewer boys undergo the old method, preferring to take the safe option at local hospitals. However, those wielding the knife are less likely to let go of their heritage. To quote one prominent circumciser: 'Every year at this time it's like a fever grips me, and I can't rest until I've cut a boy'. It seems that in Bukusuland, some traditions die hard.

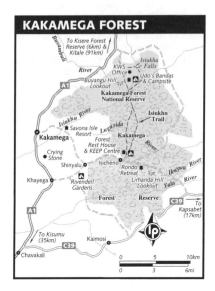

KAKAMEGA FOREST

To Kisere Forest
Reserve (6km) &
Kitale (91km)

Busembuli

River

KWS
Office

Isiukhu
Falls

Buyangu Hill
Lookout

Udo's Bandas
& Campsite

A1

Kakamega Forest
National Reserve

Isiukhu
Trail

Isiukhu River

Lugusida

Savona Isle
Resort

Kakamega

Kakamega

Forest
Rest House
& KEEP Centre

Crying
Stone

Shinyalu

Isicheno

River

Rondo
Retreat

Ikuywa River

Khayega

Rivendell
Gardens

Lirhanda Hill
Lookout

Yala River

Forest

Reserve

C39

To
Kapsabet
(17km)

A1

To Kisumu
(35km)

Kaimosi

Chavakali

C39

0   5   10km
0   3   6mi

include the red-tailed monkey, black and
white colobus and blue monkey. At night
the hammer-headed fruit bat and flying
squirrel can also be seen.

However, the birdlife is the biggest draw.
More than 330 species have been recorded,
and casqued hornbill, Ross's turaco and
great blue turaco are all common. The best
viewing months are June, August and October, when many migrant species arrive. The
wildflowers are also wonderful in October,
supporting around 400 species of butterfly.

The forest is divided into two sections: the
southern **Kakamega Forest Reserve**, centred
around Isecheno and maintained by the Forest Department; and the more accessible
Kakamega Forest National Reserve in the
northern Buyangu area, which is looked after
by KWS. Basic accommodation is available
in both areas. There is also the small **Kisere
Forest Reserve**, a couple of kilometres north
of the main park.

The northern section of the forest has a
variety of habitats but is generally very
dense, with considerable areas of primary
forest and regenerating secondary forest;
there is a total ban on grazing, wood collection and cultivation in this zone. The
southern section is predominantly forested,
but supports several communities and is
under considerable pressure from farming
and illegal logging.

Other tribal practices in the forest persist:
mugumu trees are considered sacred, circumcisions are sometimes performed in the
forest, and bullfights are still held on Sunday in Khayega and Shinyalu. Intervillage
wrestling also used to be common, but was
eventually banned, as the prize (the victor's
pick of the young women present) tended to
provoke more fights than the match itself!

Information
This is not a national park, and entry fees of
US$10/KSh500 for nonresidents/residents
have only recently been introduced. In 1994
the Kenya Indigenous Forest Conservation
Programme (Kifcon) published an excellent
guide to the forest, which is still available
from the KWS office (KSh300) and Rondo
Retreat (KSh500!).

Walking Trails
The best way to appreciate the forest is to
walk, and trails radiate out from the two accommodation centres in the north and
south. It is possible to drive, but the roads
are pretty tough going, and the engine noise
will scare off any wildlife nearby as well as
annoying everyone else in the area.

A guide is just about essential when exploring the forest, as you'll probably get lost
without one (many of the trail signs are missing) and certainly won't get much out of it.
The Kakamega Biodiversity Conservation
and Tour Operators Association (Kabicotoa)
trains official guides, who are available from
any of the offices and accommodation places.
The standard charge is KSh200 for a short
walk, but you should tip generously: not only
will they show you around, but the majority
are excellent naturalists who can recognise
birds by call alone and provide information
about numerous animals.

The trails vary in length from 1km to 7km,
the longest being the **Isiukhu Trail** up to
Isiukhu Falls in the north. Short walks to
Buyanga Hill in the north or **Lirhanda Hill** in
the south for sunrise or sunset are highly recommended. River walks are also rewarding.
As ever, the early morning and late afternoon
are the best times to view birds, but night
walks can also be a fantastic experience.

Places to Stay & Eat
Buyangu Area Named after Udo Savalli, a
well-known ornithologist, **Udo's Bandas &**

Campsite (☎ 20425; PO Box 879, Kakamega; camping US$2, bandas per person US$10) is run by the KWS. It's a tidy, well-maintained camp site with seven simple thatched bandas; nets are provided but you'll need your own sleeping bag and other supplies. There's a communal cooking and dining shelter, long-drop toilets and bucket showers.

Isecheno Area Really suffering from its location, **Savona Isle Resort** (☎ 30250, in Kisumu 035-42377; e kasamani@net2000ke .com; singles/doubles KSh1300/1800) is too far from town to get drive-through customers but too far from the forest to make an easy walking base (guides are not available here). However, it's a lovely quiet site on a tiny island, with good, thatched accommodation and plentiful facilities, and is definitely worth considering if you have your own transport.

Forest Rest House (camping per person KSh150, doubles KSh500) is much more convenient, located in the reserve itself. There are four double rooms with rudimentary bathrooms (no hot water) and toilets in a rickety wooden building on stilts, looking directly out over the forest. You'll need your own sleeping bag, food and preferably something to cook on, although fires are allowed and the small canteen here can cook for you. You can get basic supplies from the *dukas* about 2km back towards Shinyalu.

Also on site is the **Kakamega Environmental Education Programme** (KEEP; ☎ 072-619150; e keeporg@yahoo.com) resource centre and library. You can book accommodation here or through the **Forest Ranger** (PO Box 88, Kakamega).

Rondo Retreat (☎ 30268; e tf-rondo@mul titech.web; per person half board KSh4400), 3km further along the road from Isecheno, was built in the 1920s as a sawmiller's residence and is now owned by a church group. The six cottages have bathrooms and house up to 34 people, with striking traditional-style fittings and large verandas; the gardens are beautiful and there's plenty of wildlife around. The meals are excellent, although the kitchen prefers advance warning. Transfers from Kakamega, guides and forest tours can be arranged here.

Getting There & Away
Buyangu Area Local matatus heading north on the Kakamega–Kitale road pass the access road about 18km north of Kakamega town. You'll have a 2km walk from where the matatus drop you off. The route to the park office and Udo's is well signposted.

Isecheno Area Matatus linking Isecheno with Kakamega leave in both directions at 6.30am. There are matatus from Kakamega to Shinyalu, and even the occasional one from Khayega to Shinyalu during the day. Numerous *poda-podas* also serve most of the route (Khayega to Shinyalu KSh50, Shinyalu to Isecheno KSh30).

The roads become extremely treacherous after rain and you may prefer to walk once you've seen the trouble vehicles have! It's about 7km from Khayega to Shinyalu, or about 10km from Kakamega to Shinyalu, then 5km to Isecheno and 8km to Rondo.

The dirt road from the rest house continues on to Kapsabet, but it's a long walk in either direction if you can't get a lift.

ELDORET
☎ 0321

There's always a certain amount of hustle and bustle around Eldoret; the town doesn't have much in the way of attractions but it's not a bad place to spend a couple of days, particularly if you are heading north to the Cherangani Hills or the national parks.

Critics of former President Moi, who just happens to come from this area, have often questioned Eldoret's favoured status as a site for new developments. The town has certainly benefited hugely from the new Moi University, and the construction of the international airport here caused particular controversy – a munitions factory was also built nearby, prompting questions about exactly what exports were intended! It will be interesting to see if Moi is still sighted here as frequently now he has retired.

Information
The **post office** (open 8am-5pm Mon-Fri, 9am-noon Sat) and most of the **banks**, including Barclays Bank (with an ATM) are on Uganda Rd.

There are plenty of cardphones around town. Eldoret is also the best place for Internet access in the western highlands; there are dozens of places with fast connections from as little as KSh1.50 per minute. Try **D2D Cyber Village** (Dharma Rd) or **Klique**

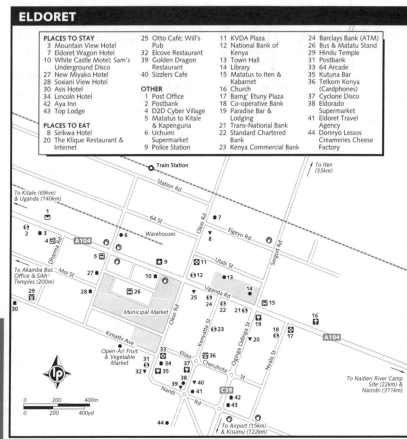

ELDORET

PLACES TO STAY
3 Mountain View Hotel
7 Eldoret Wagon Hotel
10 White Castle Motel; Sam's Underground Disco
27 New Miyako Hotel
28 Sosiani View Hotel
30 Asis Hotel
34 Lincoln Hotel
42 Aya Inn
43 Top Lodge

PLACES TO EAT
8 Sirikwa Hotel
20 The Klique Restaurant & Internet

25 Otto Café; Will's Pub
32 Elcove Restaurant
39 Golden Dragon Restaurant
40 Sizzlers Cafe

OTHER
1 Post Office
2 Postbank
4 D2D Cyber Village
5 Matatus to Kitale & Kapenguria
6 Uchumi Supermarket
9 Police Station

11 KVDA Plaza
12 National Bank of Kenya
13 Town Hall
14 Library
15 Matatus to Iten & Kabarnet
16 Church
17 Barng' Etuny Plaza
18 Co-operative Bank
19 Paradise Bar & Lodging
21 Trans-National Bank
22 Standard Chartered Bank
23 Kenya Commercial Bank

24 Barclays Bank (ATM)
26 Bus & Matatu Stand
29 Hindu Temple
31 Postbank
33 64 Arcade
35 Kutuna Bar
36 Telkom Kenya (Cardphones)
37 Cyclone Disco
38 Eldorado Supermarket
41 Eldoret Travel Agency
44 Dorinyo Lessos Creameries Cheese Factory

Internet (Oginga Odinga St; KSh4 per min) or the Internet cafés in the new **64 Arcade** and **KVDA Plaza** buildings.

There is a large branch of **Uchumi supermarket**, off Uganda Rd, with all the usual stock.

Dorinyo Lessos Creameries Cheese Factory

One slightly unusual attraction is the cheese factory (☎ 63308; Kenyatta St), which doesn't look like much but produces over 30 different types of cheese, from Stilton to Gruyere and Cheddar. You can taste as many as you like; the average price is KSh500 per kg, with a minimum purchase of 250g. The company also makes yogurt and ice cream (KSh30 for 100ml).

Places to Stay – Budget

Naiberi River Camp Site (☎ 61195; e camp site@africaonline.co.ke; camping per person KSh200, dorm beds KSh500, cabins with bathroom KSh1500), 22km southeast of town on the C54 to Kaptagat, is your best option for camping, although it's very popular with overland companies. The site is a bit of a maze, with passages connecting a dormitory, a few cabins and two bars, where Moi's picture scowls disapprovingly amid homemade overland banners. Meals, laundry, Internet access and nature walks can all be arranged here.

Getting here by local transport is tricky, but the owner, Raj Shah, runs the Ken-Knit factory in Eldoret during the week, so you can call him (☎ 32644) before 5pm for a lift.

Top Lodge (☎ 61564; Oginga Odinga St; singles/doubles KSh200/300) and **Aya Inn** (singles/doubles KSh350/600), next door, are among the cheaper options. Aya Inn has a restaurant upstairs, a bar downstairs and small but clean rooms out the back.

Sosiani View Hotel (☎ 33215; singles/doubles KSh350/500), opposite the market and matatu stand, is a bit grotty but handy if you're leaving early.

New Miyako Hotel (☎ 22002; singles/doubles KSh400/500), just up the road, is very similar. There are hot-water showers and the hotel has an upstairs bar.

Mountain View Hotel (☎ 32179; Uganda Rd; singles/doubles KSh400/550) is distinctly prison-like (you have to be let out as well as in!), but has a decent terrace bar and a restaurant. Rooms are small but OK; some have balconies.

Places to Stay – Mid-Range & Top End

All rates at the following places include breakfast.

Lincoln Hotel (☎ 22093; Oloo Rd; singles/doubles KSh600/800) is an excellent, cheap hotel with guarded parking, a bar, restaurant and pool bar. Rooms are good value and have water heaters, although the fixtures are slightly disfigured. Watch out for security guards 'trying it on'.

Asis Hotel (☎ 61807; Kimathi Ave; singles/doubles KSh750/1250) is a relatively new conference-class place with small but comfortable rooms and reasonable facilities.

White Castle Motel (☎ 62773; Uganda Rd; singles/doubles KSh850/1700) has rather bigger rooms with some decent views, as well as a café, bar, sauna, pool bar and disco on the premises.

Eldoret Wagon Hotel (☎ 62270; Oloo Rd; singles/doubles KSh1550/2250) is another good option, approaching the upper end of the scale with a certain amount of colonial charm. It's overpriced, but retains some suitably eccentric memorabilia, and there's a casino to make you feel like a high roller.

Sirikwa Hotel (☎ 63433, fax 61018; singles/doubles KSh4000/5000) is the only proper top-end hotel here and boasts the only swimming pool in town (KSh100 for nonguests). The suites are best, but standard rooms still come with TV and phone and are quite reasonable, if a little worn.

Places to Eat

Otto Cafe (Uganda Rd) and **Sizzlers Cafe** (Kenyatta St) are popular snack joints serving good, cheap Western meals for about KSh100 to KSh200.

The Klique Restaurant (Oginga Odinga St) is a smart new place pitched halfway between a sports bar and a restaurant, with good pizzas for about KSh200 to KSh300, and all the big matches on satellite.

Golden Dragon Restaurant (Kenyatta St; mains KSh300-400) is the only Chinese restaurant in town, and is worth a look.

The restaurant of the **Sirikwa Hotel** (lunch/dinner KSh500/600) is a good posh option. However, **Elcove Restaurant** (Oloo Rd) is probably the best restaurant in town, despite its somewhat erratic opening hours. Indian, Chinese and Western dishes are all available; expect to spend around KSh750.

Entertainment

Will's Pub (Uganda Rd) and **Paradise Bar & Lodging** (Oginga Odinga St) are good spots for a beer in the evening.

Sam's Underground Disco, in the White Castle Motel, and **Cyclone** (Kenyatta St) are among the livelier discos, while **Kutuna Bar** (Oloo Rd) often has live music. For something a little more sophisticated try the lounge-like **Places** on Uganda Rd.

Getting There & Away

Air There are twice daily flights (one at weekends) between Eldoret and Nairobi (KSh4300, one hour) with **Flamingo Airlines**. Bookings are handled by **Eldoret Travel Agency** (☎ 33351; Kenyatta St).

Bus & Matatu The bus and matatu stand is in the centre of town, by the market.

Matatus/Peugeots depart throughout the day for Nairobi (KSh350/500, 4½ hours), Kisumu (KSh180/250, two hours), Kericho (KSh220/250, 2½ hours), Nakuru (KSh180/220, two hours) and Kitale (KSh100/130, one hour). Buses duplicate all these routes.

Akamba buses leave from the company's depot on Moi St.

There are two executive buses to Nairobi (KSh400, five hours) via Nakuru (KSh200, two hours), as well as a daily run to Kampala in Uganda (KSh750, six hours) and occasional services to Dar es Salaam in Tanzania (KSh1900, 12 hours).

Getting Around

A matatu to or from the airport costs KSh30, and a taxi will cost around KSh800.

Parking is tricky in the town centre, and most streets have a KSh30 charge, collected by yellow-jacketed wardens.

KABARNET

☎ 0328

With a spectacular location on the eastern edge of the Kerio Valley, Kabarnet is one of many little towns nestled in the Tugen Hills. The road here is excellent, and the journey from Marigat is absolutely stunning, with views right across the arid but tree-covered ridges and valleys of the region. The town is also the best launching point for treks into the Kerio Valley.

As chief town of the Baringo district, Kabarnet boasts better facilities than most, including a **post office** (with an Internet bureau), a couple of **banks**, some cardphones and a decent supermarket.

Places to Stay & Eat

Mwananchi Hotel (singles/doubles KSh150/250) is the cheap and basic option here. The attached **Kasoiyo Women's Group Restaurant** is good for local food (and there's a video theatre (KSh10) on the 1st floor).

Sinkoro Hotel (singles/doubles KSh300/500), next to the matatu stand, is a step up and seems to have dropped its prices considerably. The modern rooms have some great views, and there's a pool room, restaurant and bar.

Food at the **Sportsline Hotel** is generally good.

Getting There & Away

Matatus/Peugeots leave for numerous locations including Eldoret (KSh180/200, 1½ hours), Nakuru (KSh180/200, two hours) and Marigat (KSh100, one hour).

LAKE KAMNAROK & KERIO VALLEY NATIONAL RESERVES

These two little-visited national reserves lie in the heart of the beautiful Kerio Valley, sandwiched between the **Cherangani Hills** and **Tugen Hills** and divided by the Kerio River. Prolific birdlife, crocodiles, elephants, wonderful landscapes and also the chance to get totally off the beaten track are the main attractions.

Lake Kamnarok (☎ 0328-22169; PO Box 53, Kabarnet), on the eastern side of the river, is probably the most accessible of the two reserves, although you'll need to be totally self-sufficient while you're there. There's a **camp site** beside the lake. At present you can walk anywhere on foot, but it is best to contact the warden in advance and let him know you're coming, especially as there has been an increase in wild dog attacks in this area recently.

It's possible to cross into Kerio Valley National Reserve from Kamnarok in the dry season, but you'll have to wade across the river north of the lake. To the south of the reserve is the beautiful **Cheplooch Gorge**.

The rest of the Kerio Valley begs to be explored and there's been talk of two other national reserves being created: one around Kapkut (2799m), a beautiful mountain close to Eldama Ravine, and another in the Tugen Hills. The best person to contact for up-to-date information is William, the dynamic and friendly warden at **Lake Bogoria National Reserve** (☎ 037-40746; PO Box 64, Marigat).

You can get close to the reserve by public transport. A matatu leaves Kabarnet for Barwesa every morning and passes through Muchukwo (about 25km from the main Kabarnet–Iten road), from where you'll have a 5km walk to the park gate.

CHERANGANI HILLS

Part of the Rift Valley, this dramatic range of hills extends for about 60km from the northeast of Eldoret, forming the western wall of the spectacular **Elgeyo Escarpment**. You could easily spend weeks exploring here and never come across a single tourist. For details of the northern reaches of the hills, see Marich Pass in the Northern Kenya chapter.

The area is best explored on foot as the roads are rough and some that scale the Elgeyo Escarpment are incredibly steep. In wet conditions roads become treacherous. The town of Kapsowar is a good place to begin a trek but for serious exploration you would need copies of the relevant Survey of Kenya maps, which are almost impossible to get (see Maps in the Facts for the Visitor chapter). Lonely Planet's *Trekking in East Africa* is also a handy reference.

The area is the home of the Marakwet or Markweta people (part of the greater Kalenjin grouping), who migrated here from the north. The area was secure, and the streams were ideal for agriculture as the rainfall was relatively high; little has changed since then, and you will still see countless small *shambas* (plots of land) in the hills.

Sirikwa Safaris in Kitale can organise ornithological tours in this area (see Places to Stay under Kitale following).

Getting There & Away
From Eldoret it should be possible to hitch or take a matatu as far as Kapsowar, 70km northeast in the Kerio Valley. Coming from the north, there is a challenging road from Sigor to Kapsowar via Tot and the impossibly steep escarpment road. Streams crossing the road swell up considerably during the rains and there's little transport available.

KITALE & AROUND
☎ 0325

Kitale is considerably smaller than its nearest neighbour Eldoret, and has more of an agricultural feel to it, although there are more street kids than in most normal service towns. It does have an interesting museum, but its main function for travellers is as a base for explorations further afield – Mt Elgon and Saiwa Swamp national parks – and a take-off point for the trip up to the western side of Lake Turkana. As such, Kitale is a pleasant enough town and can be an enjoyable place to pass through.

Information
The **post office** is, logically, on Post Office Rd and is open the usual hours. It's possible to make international calls here, or there are plenty of cardphones in front of the Telkom building next door. **Star Computer** (*Askari Rd*) in the new Vision Gate House complex is the best place for Internet access, charging KSh5 per minute.

Kitale has the usual **banks** (Barclays has an ATM), some well-stocked shops and a busy market.

Kitale Museum
The museum (*admission KSh200; open 8am–6pm daily*) was founded on the collection of butterflies, birds and ethnographic memorabilia left to the nation in 1967 by the late Lieutenant Colonel Stoneham. The more recent ethnographic displays of the Pokot, Akamba, Marakwet and Turkana peoples

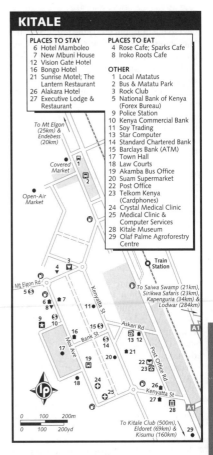

KITALE

PLACES TO STAY
6 Hotel Mamboleo
7 New Mbuni House
12 Vision Gate Hotel
16 Bongo Hotel
21 Sunrise Motel; The
   Lantern Restaurant
26 Alakara Hotel
27 Executive Lodge &
   Restaurant

PLACES TO EAT
4 Rose Cafe; Sparks Cafe
8 Iroko Roots Cafe

OTHER
1 Local Matatus
2 Bus & Matatu Park
3 Rock Club
5 National Bank of Kenya
   (Forex Bureau)
9 Police Station
10 Kenya Commercial Bank
11 Soy Trading
13 Star Computer
14 Standard Chartered Bank
15 Barclays Bank (ATM)
17 Town Hall
18 Law Courts
19 Akamba Bus Office
20 Suam Supermarket
22 Post Office
23 Telkom Kenya
   (Cardphones)
24 Crystal Medical Clinic
25 Medical Clinic &
   Computer Services
28 Kitale Museum
29 Olaf Palme Agroforestry
   Centre

WESTERN KENYA

are a bit more interesting than the rows of dead things (although the hilariously badly stuffed cheetah is a must-see). The outdoor exhibits include some traditional tribal homesteads as well as the inevitable snakes, crocodiles and tortoises, plus an interesting 'Hutchinson Biogas Unit'.

Probably the best thing here is the small **nature trail** that leads through some virgin rainforest at the back of the museum and links with the arboretum of the Olaf Palme Agroforestry Centre. There are numbered points along the way, and the forest is teeming with birdlife, but the small guidebook to accompany the trail is out of print.

The craft shop here is worth a look, stocking some nice stuff at good, nominally fixed prices.

Olaf Palme Agroforestry Centre

Next to the museum along the highway is the Olaf Palme Agroforestry Centre *(admission free; open 9am-5pm daily)*. It's a Swedish-funded programme aimed at educating local people about protection and rehabilitation of the environment by integrating trees into farming systems. The project includes a small demonstration farm and agroforestry plot, an information centre and an arboretum containing 46 rare species of indigenous trees; it's well worth a visit.

Places to Stay – Budget

Sirikwa Safaris *(☎ 0733-793524; camping KSh360, single/double tent KSh1080/1440, indoors singles/doubles KSh2400/3360)*, 23km north of Kitale on the Kapenguria road, is the only camping place in the area. Run by Jane and Julia Barnley at their family farmhouse, it's a friendly and very homey place to stay.

As well camping in the garden, you can stay in furnished tents or in two lovely rooms in the farmhouse itself; 10% service charge is added for these options. Meals can be taken outside (KSh480) or in the main house (KSh720) and should be ordered in advance.

Various excursions can be arranged from here, including ornithological tours of the Cherangani Hills and Saiwa Swamp (bird guides KSh1200 per day). The owners also have an informal arrangement with staff at **Soy Trading** *(☎ 20061; PO Box 332)* in Kitale, who will take messages and are generally helpful. From Kitale matatus to Kapenguria pass Sirikwa's entrance (KSh60) 1km after Kasogon.

New Mbuni House *(Moi Ave; singles KSh200)* and **Hotel Mamboleo** *(☎ 20172; Moi Ave; singles/doubles KSh200/300)* are among the cheapest places in town, but their standards are not very high.

Executive Lodge *(☎ 0722-56089; Kenyatta St; singles/doubles KSh600/700)* is a bit better but overpriced, although rates do include breakfast. Rooms vary in quality (the courtyard ones aren't terribly nice), and you'll pay KSh900 for en suite.

Places to Stay – Mid-Range & Top End

Bongo Hotel *(☎ 20593; Moi Ave; singles/doubles KSh600/800)* is a popular place with a nice courtyard area; rates include breakfast and hot water is provided.

Alakara Hotel *(☎ 20395; Kenyatta St; singles/doubles KSh600/900)* is about the best value in town. The comfortable rooms have phones, the staff are friendly and prices include breakfast. There is a good bar and restaurant, secure parking and a TV room.

Sunrise Motel *(☎ 31138; Kenyatta St; singles/doubles with bathroom KSh750/900)* is also worth a look. Prices include breakfast in the Lantern restaurant. There are some larger, more expensive 'executive' rooms with balconies.

Vision Gate Hotel *(Askari Rd; rooms KSh1500-2000)*, in Vision Gate House, should be open by the time you read this. The facade looked quite promising at the time of writing, but the other side of the building wasn't quite finished!

Kitale Club *(☎ 31330; singles KSh1050-2555, doubles KSh1825-3400)*, about a kilometre out of town on the Eldoret road, is a classic colonial watering hole with a golf course, swimming pool, sauna, tennis and squash courts, darts and snooker rooms. The accommodation is seriously overpriced; 'new' rooms are better than 'old', but the pricey luxury cottages are easily the best. Temporary membership (KSh500) gives you use of all the facilities, but you'll need your own sports kit.

Places to Eat & Drink

Rose Cafe and **Sparks Cafe** on Mt Elgon Rd are good cheap places doing the usual basics.

Executive Restaurant is a popular lunch spot, and is slightly better value than the attached lodge. The restaurant in the **Vision Gate Hotel** building is also well frequented and has a great balcony.

The **Bongo** and **Alakara** hotels are both good for evening meals. They have takeaway food sections and lively bars.

By far the best place to eat in town, though, is **The Lantern** *(Kenyatta St; mains KSh250-300)*, part of the Sunrise Motel and sister to the Elcove in Eldoret. It's fantastically atmospheric, especially the cocktail bar, and conveniently also stocks aspirin!

The restaurant at the **Kitale Club** *(set menu KSh390)* is similarly priced. It's also a lovely place to have a drink (the Sports Bar is excellent) and spend a few hours hanging around.

There is not much other nightlife in Kitale. **Iroko Roots Cafe** *(Moi Ave)* is a good popular bar and does some food; **Rock Club** *(Mt Elgon Rd)* seems to be the only disco worthy of the name.

Getting There & Away
The bus and matatu park is fairly chaotic – it's just a matter of wandering around and finding a vehicle going your way. Competition for passengers is usually keen and you'll soon be pointed in the right direction.

Two **Kenya Witness** buses leave for Lodwar every morning (KSh400, six hours). The Nissan matatus (KSh600) are more reliable and leave about five times daily.

On the Nairobi route there is a variety of transport – bus, matatu, Peugeot – so it's a matter of finding which suits you. Most bus companies have offices around the bus station, apart from **Akamba** *(Moi Ave)*, which runs daily buses to Nairobi at 9am (KSh470, six hours) and 9pm (KSh500, seven hours).

Matatus/Peugeots also run to Nairobi (KSh400/640, six hours), Eldoret (KSh80/120, 30 minutes), Kabarnet (KSh150/200, one hour), Nakuru (KSh200/300, two hours) and Kisumu (KSh180/230, three hours). For Kericho change at Eldoret.

For Mt Elgon National Park, catch a matatu to Endebess (KSh70, 45 minutes).

SAIWA SWAMP NATIONAL PARK
This small park *(adult/child & student US$15/5)* north of Kitale is a real delight. Originally set up to preserve the habitat of the *nzohe* or sitatunga antelope, the 3-sq-km reserve is also home to blue, vervet and De Brazza's monkeys and some 370 species of birds. The fluffy black and white colobus and the impressive crowned crane are both present, and you may see the Cape clawless and spot-throated otter.

Despite its size, the park is under pressure. Hardwood trees have been known to disappear overnight, and fertiliser from the surrounding fields has encouraged the growth of tall grasses that suffocate the wild sage, the sitatunga's typical food. However, education programmes are encouraging local people to get involved in the protection of the park, with some success.

What makes this park unique is that it is only accessible on foot. There are marked walking trails that skirt the swamp, duckboards go right across it, and there are some extremely rickety observation towers (number four is the best placed).

Places to Stay
There is a beautiful **camp site** *(camping US$2)* by the river here. Facilities include flush toilets, showers and two covered cooking bandas with barbecues and picnic tables.

About 5km north of the Saiwa turn-off along the Kapenguria road, **Sirikwa Safaris** (see Places to Stay under Kitale earlier) can arrange transport to the park entrance as well as an excellent guide.

Getting There & Away
The park is 18km northeast of Kitale; take a matatu towards Kapenguria (KSh60, 30 minutes) and get out at the signposted turn-off, from where it's a 5km walk.

MT ELGON NATIONAL PARK
Mt Elgon sits astride the Kenya/Uganda border and while it offers similar trekking possibilities to Mt Kenya, its location makes it a far less popular goal. The main advantage of Mt Elgon is that the lower altitude means conditions are not as extreme, though rain is more frequent.

The mountain is an extinct volcano with a distinctive shape – the Maasai name means 'mountain shaped like human breast'! The highest peak on the Kenyan side is Koitoboss (4187m); the actual summit is Wagagai (4321m), on the far side of the crater in Uganda. There are hot springs in the crater itself, the floor of which is around 3500m above sea level. The national park boundaries extend from the lower slopes right up to the border.

The mountain's biggest attractions are the elephants, renowned the world over for their predilection for digging salt out of the caves on the lower eastern slopes. The elephants are such keen excavators that some people have been fooled into believing they are totally responsible for the caves! Sadly, the numbers of these saline-loving creatures has declined over the years, mainly due to incursions by poachers from Uganda.

Four main caves are open to visitors: **Kitum**, **Chepnyalil**, **Mackingeny** and **Rongai**. Kitum is where you are most likely to see elephants (especially if you're there

WESTERN KENYA

before dawn) while Mackingeny, with a waterfall cascading across the entrance, is the most spectacular. A good torch (flashlight) is essential if you want to explore the caves, and you should be wary of rock falls – the bones of at least one crushed elephant can be seen in the cave.

The mountain's fauna and flora are also great attractions. Starting with rainforest at the base, the vegetation changes as you ascend to bamboo jungle and finally alpine moorland with the bizarre giant groundsel and giant lobelia plants. Commonly sighted animals include buffalos, bushbucks, olive baboons, giant forest hogs and duikers; Defassa waterbucks are also present. The lower forests are the habitat of the black and white colobus, blue and De Brazza's monkeys (most likely seen near waterways).

There are more than 240 species of birds on the mountain, including red-fronted parrots, Ross's turacos and casqued hornbills. On the peaks you may even see a lammergeyer raptor gliding through the thin air. The **Elephant Platform** and **Endebess Bluff** viewpoints are good places to survey the scene on the way up.

Elgon can be a wet place at any time of the year, but the driest period seems to be between December and February. As well as bringing waterproof gear, you'll need warm clothes as it gets cold up here at night. Altitude may also be a problem for some people (for details see Health in the Facts for the Visitor chapter).

Information

Access to the 169-sq-km national park is now permitted without a vehicle. Entry costs US$10 for hikers or US$15 if arriving by vehicle, and residents pay KSh500; a printed leaflet is available at the gate for KSh20.

It's worth considering walking in the park even if you have your own transport, as you'll need a good 4WD to tackle many of the tracks here, and the frequent rain makes the going even more treacherous.

A ranger must escort you to the camp site (1km inside the park) and on any walks on the lower forested slopes (such as to the caves; a small fee may be payable. For any trekking on the higher slopes you'll need a tent and all your own camping gear. A guide is also essential and will cost KSh600 per

day. See Clothing & Equipment, Safety and Responsible Trekking in the Mt Kenya section of the Central Highlands chapter for general advice.

Lonely Planet's *Trekking in East Africa* has more details on the various trekking and walking routes, and Andy Wielochowski's *Mt Elgon Map & Guide* is an essential purchase, available in Nairobi for around US$5 or from Stanford's in London for UK£6.95. *Kitum Cave Guide Book* is also a good buy.

The streams that run off the mountain are filled with trout; fishing permits are available from the park headquarters for KSh400.

Trekking

Trekkers are encouraged to stay within the park boundaries, as security here has been a problem in the past. Check the situation with **KWS headquarters** (☎ 02-506169; e kws@kws.org) in Nairobi or **Mt Elgon National Park** (☎ 0325-31456; PO Box 753, Kitale) before you plan anything. Crossing into Uganda is only possible with prior arrangement (ie, a *lot* of hassle) in Nairobi.

Allow at least four days for any round trip and two or three days for any direct ascent of **Koitoboss** if you're walking from the Chorlim Gate. It's best to arrange any guiding requirements at the park headquarters in advance.

The **Park Route** offers some interesting possibilities and there is a well-worn route from Chorlim Gate up to Koitoboss Peak which requires one or two overnight camps. If you have a vehicle you can drive up to 3500m, but the current state of the roads means the 32km drive can take half a day, and then it's a two- to three-hour walk up to the peak.

Descending, you have a number of options. Firstly, you can descend northwest into the crater to the **Suam Hot Springs**. Alternatively, if the security situation improves, you could go east around the crater rim and descend via the **Masara Route**, which leads to the small village of Masara on the eastern slopes of the mountain (a trek of about 25km) and then returns to Endebess. Lastly, you can head southwest around the rim of the crater (some very hard walking) to **Lower Elgon Tarn**, where you can camp before ascending **Lower Elgon Peak** (4301m).

MT ELGON NATIONAL PARK

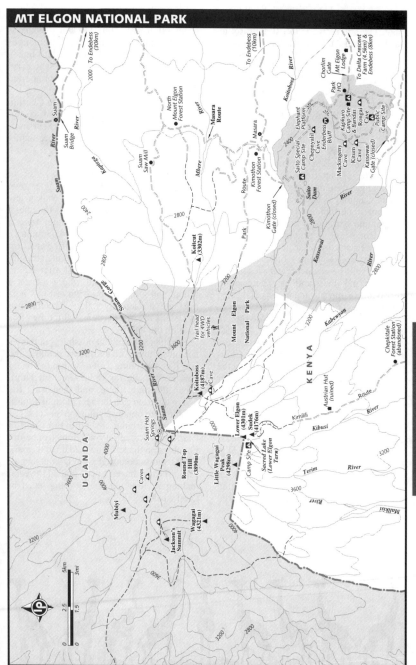

WESTERN KENYA

To return you can head back the way you came. The alternative is the **Kimilili Route**, via the ruined Austrian Hut and the abandoned Chepkitale Forest Station, which leads down to the KWS post at Kaberua Forest Station. From here it's a 5km walk down to **Kapsakwany**, where there's basic accommodation and matatus to Kimilili. However, this route should only be attempted if it is declared safe.

Places to Stay

There are no lodges in the park, but **Kapkuro Camp Site** just up from Chorlim Gate is great and has running water, toilets and barbecues. Camping is US$2, and there are two excellent stone **bandas** *(US$10 per person)* with simple bathrooms and small kitchen areas. Hot water is provided by a wood stove, electricity by solar panels. Bring all your own food as there's only one small shop that sells beer and a few basics for the park staff and their families. There is another public camp site and one special camp site in the lower section of the park.

Mt Elgon Lodge *(☎ 0722-866480, in Nairobi ☎ 02-330820; camping KSh250, singles/doubles US$20/40 in low season, US$25/46 in high season)*, outside the Chorlim Gate, belongs to Msafiri Inns, but the owners don't seem too worried about their investment. The place has pretty much gone to seed, and how it makes enough to survive is anyone's guess. Camping is the only worthwhile option here.

Delta Crescent Farm *(☎ 0722-261022; camping KSh200, bandas KSh1500)*, 5.5km from Chorlim Gate, makes a great stopover before heading into the park. Behind the farmhouse are three round bandas nestling in a secluded camp site, as well as fixed tents sleeping between two and 10 people (KSh600 to KSh1500). Organic produce is available and the owners keep a number of horses and camels (KSh300 per half hour); there is even a small 'wildlife sanctuary' (KSh100) with giraffes and zebras imported from other national parks.

The owners can drive you up to Chorlim Gate for KSh1500 per vehicle, and also offer 4WD tours of the park and other excursions. Decide where you want to go before setting off and they will work out a price.

Getting There & Away

The park is accessible without your own transport if you're prepared to walk a few kilometres. The nearest village is Endebess, about 9km from Chorlim Gate; take a matatu from Kitale (KSh70, 45 minutes), then walk down to the post office and turn left onto a dirt road. Keep walking straight, ignore the first crossroad and after 3.5km turn right at the second where there's a school and a misleading signpost to Chorlim Gate (it's actually 5.5km). The entrance to Delta Crescent Farm is 200m down this road on the left.

Hitching is just about possible, but there's not much transport into the park itself and you'll end up doing a lot of waiting. A better idea is to make for Delta Crescent Farm, spend the night there, and then walk the 5.5km up to the gate the next morning (you'll need time to organise guides in any case).

If you're driving, a short cut to Chorlim Gate is signposted several kilometres before Endebess on the left. The road up to the park is OK, but once inside a 4WD is essential. The dirt roads haven't been graded in years, making it slow and heavy going, even in good weather.

Northern Kenya

Sparsely populated, wild and often desolate, the vast area of northern Kenya covers thousands of square kilometres up to the little-used borders with Sudan, Ethiopia and Somalia. Setting foot in these parts is, often as not, like leaving the 21st century entirely; it's an explorer's paradise, and the tribes that live here are some of the most fascinating people in the world.

The prevalent groups are the Samburu, Turkana and Rendille, while smaller communities of Boran, Gabra and El-Molo are also present; most of them have little contact with the modern world, preferring centuries-old traditional lifestyles that bind members of a tribe together and ensure that each individual has a part to play.

Despite their isolation, modernity is slowly invading the lives of these people as a result of missionary activity, employment in national parks and reserves, the construction of dams and roads, and the tourist trade. However, tribespeople here seem unlikely to lose their pride in their customs and heritage. It's not uncommon to see young men dressed smartly in Western-style clothing doing business in a small town and then, later on the same day, meet them in the bush decked out in traditional regalia (see the special section 'Tribes of Kenya' for more information on tribal practices).

Unfortunately, the strong warrior traditions of these nomadic peoples are in part responsible for the security problems that have plagued the region for years (see the boxed text 'Warning'). The main cause, however, is the massive influx of cheap guns from the many conflict zones just outside Kenya. This has dramatically altered the traditional balance of power. Minor conflicts stemming from grazing rights and cattle rustling, formerly settled by compensation rather than violence, can now quickly escalate into full-blown wars, and the authorities may have trouble restoring order. After a period of intense drought in 1996, the army was forced to intervene in a serious clash between the Samburu and the Turkana over grazing land. Hundreds died and as if to prove how things had changed, the *Ng'oroko* (Turkana bandits), who were hiding out in the Suguta Valley, shot down an army heli-

Highlights

- Catching your first glimpse of the 'Jade Sea' on the road to Loyangalani
- Leaving civilisation behind to explore the Matthews Range
- Trekking through tribal lands into the dramatic Suguta Valley
- Raising hell at the Maralal International Camel Derby
- Visiting the classic savanna of Samburu National Reserve and the rocky plains of Shaba National Reserve
- Meeting the living heritage of Kenya's most traditional tribes

Major National Parks & Reserves

Samburu National Reserve, Buffalo Springs National Reserve, Shaba National Reserve, Maralal National Reserve, Sibiloi National Park, Central Island National Park, Marsabit National Park & Reserve

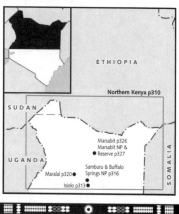

copter, killing the district commissioner and a number of army officers.

Not only are the people here a world away from Nairobi and the more developed areas of the country, but the environments in this part of Kenya are tremendous and diverse. Samburu, Buffalo Springs and Shaba National Reserves showcase a wonderful range of wildlife, including regional specialities such as Grevy's zebra and the reticulated

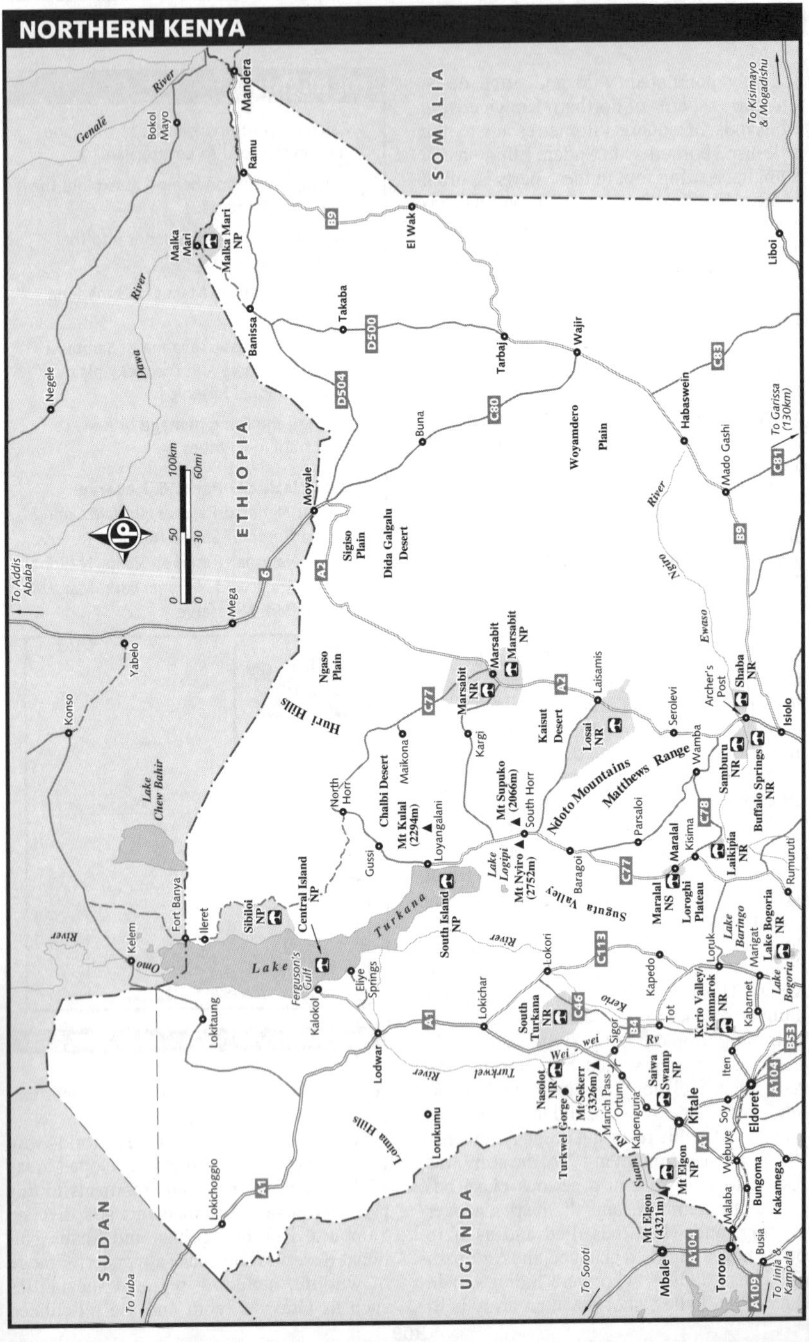
NORTHERN KENYA
SUDAN
ETHIOPIA
SOMALIA
UGANDA
To Juba
To Addis Ababa
To Kisimayo & Mogadishu
To Garissa (130km)
To Soroti
To Jinja & Kampala
0
50
100km
0
30
60mi
Genalē River
Dawa River
Omo River
Kerio River
Turkwel River
Ewaso Ngiro River
Suam Rv
Wei wei Rv
Mandera
Bokol Mayo
Ramu
Malka Mari
Malka Mari NP
El Wak
Takaba
Banissa
Tarbaj
Wajir
Negele
Buna
Moyale
Habaswein
Mado Gashi
Liboi
Woyamdero Plain
Sigiso Plain
Dida Galgalu Desert
Mega
Yabelo
Konso
Ngaso Plain
Huri Hills
Marsabit
Marsabit NR
Marsabit NP
Maikona
Kargi
Laisamis
Kaisut Desert
Losai NR
Serolevi
Archer's Post
Shaba NR
Isiolo
Wamba
Samburu NR
Buffalo Springs NR
Lake Chew Bahir
Fort Banya
Ileret
Kelem
Sibiloi NP
Central Island NP
North Horr
Chalbi Desert
Mt Kulal (2294m)
Loyangalani
Gussi
Mt Supuko (2066m)
South Horr
Ndoto Mountains
Matthews Range
Parsaloi
Baragoi
Lake Logipi
Mt Nyiro (2752m)
Suguta Valley
Maralal
Maralal NS
Kisima
Loroghi Plateau
Laikipia NR
Rumuruti
Lake Turkana
South Island NP
Ferguson's Gulf
Eliye Springs
Kalokol
Lokitaung
Lodwar
Lokichar
Lokori
Kapedo
Loruk
Lake Baringo
Marigat
Lake Bogoria NR
Lake Bogoria
Kabarnet
Kerio Valley/Kamnarok NR
Tot
South Turkana NR
Sigor
Iten
Eldoret
Nasolot NR
Mt Sekerr (3326m)
Marich Pass
Ortum
Saiwa Swamp NP
Kitale
Soy
Turkwel Gorge
Kapenguria
Lorukumu
Loima Hills
Lokichoggio
Mt Elgon NP
Mt Elgon (4321m)
Webuye
Bungoma
Kakamega
Malaba
Busia
Tororo
Mbale
A1
A2
A104
A109
B4
B9
B53
C46
C77
C78
C80
C81
C83
C113
D500
D504
6

Warning

The north of Kenya has always been wild and unpredictable. Competition for grazing land and cattle rustling inevitably leads to intertribal conflicts, though the passing traveller will rarely see evidence of them. However, the increase in a more general form of banditry does pose a significant threat in this area, and the UN and most foreign governments still advise against travelling here. Total avoidance is probably unnecessary, but if you do intend to travel here make sure you are well informed about the current situation in the areas you propose to visit.

The whole region around Garsen, Garissa, Wajir and Mandera can be *shifta* (bandit) country and you should not travel here. Buses heading to Lamu and between Garissa and Thika have also been attacked. Flamingo Airlines now offer two daily flights to Lokichoggio, near the Sudanese border. The town is more or less safe in itself, but the road between it and Lodwar is one of the most dangerous routes in the country and should be avoided. Unless you're an aid worker there's not much reason to come along this route anyway.

Early in 1999 the conflict between the Ethiopian government and Oromo Liberation Front, which is fighting for an independent homeland in southern Ethiopia, spilled over into Kenya around Moyale. Land mines have been found in the area; the border remains open and is still used by trucks supported by convoys and armed guards, but few independent travellers venture through.

Lesser danger zones include the Marsabit–Isiolo road and the Marich Pass–Lodwar road, which can be travelled with certain precautions.

Intrepid trekkers heading up the Suguta Valley should be aware that armed gangs roam these lands. During the conflicts of 1996 the *Ng'oroko* (Turkana bandits) attacked at least one party of trekkers. While we have heard reports of travellers getting away after losing only a couple of packets of cigarettes upon meeting large groups of armed men, you may not be so lucky.

On the other hand, no trucks heading up to Lake Turkana have been held up so far. As a general rule of thumb, seek local advice before you travel and don't take any unnecessary risks.

giraffe. On the eastern shore of Lake Turkana (which contains the largest population of Nile crocodiles in Kenya) is the fantastic Sibiloi National Park. The beaten track definitely stops here.

Geography

The diversity of the landscape in northern Kenya is truly amazing. Huge tracts of scrub and desert are dissected by *luggas* (dry river beds that burst into violent life whenever it rains) and peppered with acacia trees. Extinct and dormant volcanoes border barren, shattered lava beds, while deep canyons with cool, clear streams and waterfalls feed oases of lush vegetation nestling between the cruel ridges of the region's many mountains. Even the desert can be strangely attractive, with its endless plains of dust and sand broken by startling peaks and yawning gullies.

The big draw in the region, however, has always been Lake Turkana, the 'Jade Sea'. Kenya's largest lake, Turkana stretches south from the Ethiopian border for some 250km, yet is never more than 50km wide. The area around it is home to the very traditional Turkana and El-Molo tribes. While it looks fairly placid most of the time, the lake is notorious for vicious squalls that can whip up out of nowhere, wreaking havoc on nearby settlements and often causing casualties.

Originally known as Anam, 'Great Water', the lake was first reached by Europeans in the late 19th century, when the explorers von Hehnel and Teleki arrived there and renamed it Lake Rudolf, after the Austrian Crown Prince at the time (an obvious choice!). It wasn't until the early 1970s that the Swahili name Turkana was adopted.

Thanks to years of archaeological digs, the area is regarded by many as the birthplace of humanity (see History in the Facts about Kenya chapter for details). It is believed that 2½ million years ago the lake was far more extensive than it is today, and supported a richer plant and animal life. Even 10,000 years ago the water level was high enough for the lake to be one of the sources of the Nile, which accounts for the huge Nile perch still found here.

Climate

The climate of northern Kenya reflects the incredible contrasts of the landscape. Temperatures on the plains can reach 50°C, without a breath of wind, only for the dead calm of the desert to be shattered by sudden violent thunderstorms which drench everything and disappear as quickly as they came. What you'll notice most of the time is the overwhelming heat and the strong winds around Lake Turkana. However, it's not uncommon to go through several weather systems in the course of a day and still sleep under clear, star-studded skies.

Getting There & Around

There is regular public transport as far north as Kalokol on the west side of Lake Turkana. On the east side there are only three regular routes: Nyahururu (Thomson's Falls) to Baragoi via Maralal, Isiolo to Marsabit, and Isiolo to Maralal. Anywhere else you're pretty much on your own and, if you don't have your own vehicle, you'll have to organise lifts in trucks (see Getting There & Away under Isiolo for more details).

The easiest way to see this region is by organised safari (see Safaris later), but this does limit your flexibility.

Hiring a vehicle is definitely the best and most flexible way to explore, but comes with its own set of problems. You'll need to bring a high-rise jack, sand ladders, a shovel, a long and strong rope or chain (to hitch up to camels or other vehicles) plus enough fuel and water.

The only regular petrol pumps are at Lodwar, Isiolo, Maralal, Marsabit and Moyale. Elsewhere your options are limited to local *dukas* (shops) – Baragoi usually has fuel – and as a last resort, begging from Christian missions. A 4WD vehicle is obligatory and, with the exception of visits to Samburu and Buffalo Springs National Reserves, you'd be extremely foolhardy to attempt such a journey in anything else.

Hitching Away from the public transport routes mentioned previously you are going to have to hitch, and the only reliable possibilities are the routes already serviced by public transport. There is *very* little traffic on other routes. However, travellers report that hitching to Loyangalani is possible, although it does take time.

If you are intending to hitch you must have no deadlines to meet and you must be the sort of person who is quite happy to wait around for days for a ride. In some ways, this could be a very interesting way of travelling and you'd certainly meet a lot of local people, but in light of the general security situation it's not something that can be recommended unreservedly.

You could, of course, buy a camel and strike out on your own. This isn't something to approach lightly, but it's far from impossible, especially if you are part of a small group. You'd certainly have the adventure of your life!

Safaris A few organised safaris and overland trucks now go to the west of Lake Turkana, but the majority still only visit the east side of the lake. An average trip lasts from seven to 10 days (though there are other 14-day trips) and they all seem to follow much the same route.

Other options include camel and donkey safaris, although treks down into the Suguta Valley should be approached with caution for environmental and security reasons. See Lake Turkana Safaris in the Safaris chapter for a full rundown.

South of Turkana

The main routes to the lake from southern Kenya pass through this region. There is public transport between Isiolo, Marsabit and Maralal. North of Maralal, the only public transport is a 4WD matatu between Maralal and Baragoi that leaves once daily if there's enough demand. You're better off negotiating a ride on a truck.

Car & 4WD

None of the roads in this region are surfaced and the main A2 Hwy is compacted, corrugated *murram* (dirt road), which will shake the guts out of both you and your vehicle. Expect punctures – one spare tyre is seldom enough!

The road connecting Isiolo with Maralal (which branches off the A2 north of Archer's Post) is similarly rough, but otherwise in good shape. The El Nino rains have taken their toll on all the roads in the north and the trip between Loyangalani to Maralal takes at least a day. There is a diabolical section of several kilometres from the plateau down to Lake Turkana.

There's also a minor cross route from Isiolo that bypasses Maralal and joins the Loyangalani road about 15km south of Baragoi. Though a minor route, this road is relatively smooth most of the way; its main drawback is the many steep-sided *luggas* (dry river beds) along it. In the dry season you won't have any problems as long as you're in a 4WD, but you can forget about it in the wet season.

ISIOLO
☎ 0165

Isiolo marks the frontier of northeastern Kenya – a vast area of both forested and barren mountains, deserts and scrub, and home to the Samburu, Rendille, Boran and Turkana peoples. However, the town itself has largely outgrown its outpost days, with numerous new developments reflecting the increasing amount of business in the area.

The resident population is largely Somali in origin as a result of the resettlement of Somali ex-soldiers following WWI. There is also a large military presence, with no fewer than four army-training grounds nearby! Isiolo's reputation as a frontier town has persisted, particularly among the foreign embassies who frequently warn against travel here, but for the most part the people seem friendly and helpful, and there's less hassle than in Maralal or Nanyuki. If you're driving, beware of the numerous speed bumps in and around town.

Information
Isiolo is a vital pit stop for those heading up north, as it's the last place with any decent facilities until you get to either Maralal or Marsabit. Stock up on everything you'll need here. There is a branch of the **Consolidated Bank of Kenya** but no ATMs (and none further north). And, if you bypass Maralal, there are no banks at all on the way to or at Lake Turkana, so it's worth planning carefully if you're travelling over a weekend. Likewise, there are no petrol stations except in Samburu National Reserve and then at Marsabit and Moyale. Some Christian mission stations elsewhere may be persuaded to sell you a tank-full, but you will pay through the nose for it.

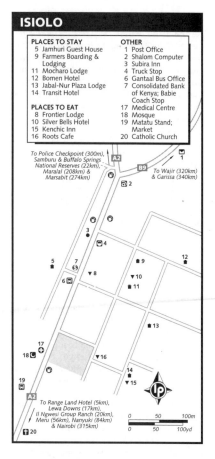

ISIOLO

PLACES TO STAY
5 Jamhuri Guest House
9 Farmers Boarding & Lodging
11 Mocharo Lodge
12 Bomen Hotel
13 Jabal-Nur Plaza Lodge
14 Transit Hotel

PLACES TO EAT
8 Frontier Lodge
10 Silver Bells Hotel
15 Kenchic Inn
16 Roots Cafe

OTHER
1 Post Office
2 Shalom Computer
3 Subira Inn
4 Truck Stop
6 Gantaal Bus Office
7 Consolidated Bank of Kenya; Babie Coach Stop
17 Medical Centre
18 Mosque
19 Matatu Stand; Market
20 Catholic Church

To Police Checkpoint (300m), Samburu & Buffalo Springs National Reserves (22km), Maralal (208km) & Marsabit (274km)

To Wajir (320km) & Garissa (340km)

To Range Land Hotel (5km), Lewa Downs (17km), Il Ngwesi Group Ranch (20km), Meru (56km), Nanyuki (84km) & Nairobi (315km)

0   50   100m
0   50   100yd

Self-catering travellers should load up with food and drink in Isiolo as there's very little available beyond here. The sprawling market next to the mosque is good and the general stores are generally well stocked.

The town has a large **medical centre**, **post office** and many shops selling mobile-phone cards (Kencell recently put up a transmitter here). Internet access is available at **Shalom Computer** and a couple of other little places for around KSh15 a minute – if you're heading south it's cheaper to wait until Nanyuki or Meru, but if you're going north this is your last chance to get online.

Due to the Muslim influence, alcohol is prohibited in some hotels, and women wearing shorts or short skirts may attract a lot of unwanted attention.

Places to Stay

Range Land Hotel *(☎ 2340; camping per person KSh200, cottages per person KSh1000)*, 5km south of town, is about the only camp site around here; the current tent space is a bit stony but it's being extended. The stone cottages are well equipped, if slightly pricey, and there's a decent restaurant and bar for meals. Use of the children's playground is 'at owner's risk'!

Isiolo is not short on cheap, basic accommodation, especially on the roads behind the main street, although basic is usually the operative word. **Farmers Boarding & Lodging** *(☎ 2325; singles/doubles KSh130/300)* is about the cheapest, but is neither overly friendly nor particularly pleasant. **Jabal-Nur Plaza Lodge** *(☎ 2460)* costs about the same and has some rooms with bathrooms.

Jamhuri Guest House *(☎ 2065; singles/ doubles KSh150/200)*, west of the main road, is a Muslim place that's been popular with travellers in the past. It's still pretty good value, and has now opened an annexe next door with secure parking and singles with bathroom for KSh250.

Mocharo Lodge *(☎ 2385; singles/doubles KSh300/350)* is certainly the best deal in Isiolo, if not in the whole of Kenya! The rooms look to have been recently renovated (again) and are clean and comfortable with excellent facilities. Rooms with shared bathroom are available for KSh200. There is secure parking and a TV room, but, sadly, no restaurant.

In comparison, **Bomen Hotel** *(☎ 2389; singles/doubles KSh900/1400)* is laughably overpriced, its only real advantages being the tiny TV sets in some of the rooms (for which you apparently sacrifice luxuries such as toilet seats) and a tourist-class restaurant.

The mid-range newcomer **Transit Hotel** *(☎ 2207; singles/doubles KSh1200/1500)* does a bit more to justify its inflated price tag, but again it's far better just to eat here and stay in the Mocharo instead.

Places to Eat

Most of the boarding houses in Isiolo also have restaurants where you can eat typical African-style meals for less than KSh100. **Silver Bells Hotel** does the usual standards pretty well and there are two branches of the ubiquitous **Kenchic Inn**.

The most popular place in town is the **Roots** café/bar, which is usually packed with locals in the evening. A decent stew or chicken curry should cost you around KSh150, if you can find anywhere to sit.

Frontier Lodge is a bit more unusual, sporting a delightful Day-Glo paint job and UV lighting. It's the principal disco in town on Wednesday and Friday to Sunday (admission KSh80 for men and KSh50 for women), with occasional live bands playing, and although it has the feel of a 24-hour bar, it does some reasonable food.

For a minor splurge, the restaurants in the **Bomen** or **Transit** hotels can be good value.

Shopping

Hawkers abound in Isiolo, mostly selling brass, copper and aluminium or steel bracelets at knock-down prices. The craft here can be quite fine, so it's worth the time you'll have to spend haggling – it's possible to get three bracelets for less than KSh100! The same people also sell daggers in leather scabbards but the craftwork in these is generally unremarkable.

If you're walking around Isiolo you're likely to be approached by these sellers now and again. If you're driving, however, you can expect considerably more hassle, especially when stopping at the roadblock north of town (where the safari vehicles to Samburu have to pass) or at any of the petrol stations. Wares will be thrust in front of your face from all sides and you'll be hard pressed to drive away.

Getting There & Away

The Akamba office here has closed, so their only regular scheduled bus is the daily Gantaal service to Nairobi (KSh350, four hours) via Nanyuki (KSh150, two hours).

A Babie Coach usually leaves for Maralal (KSh500, five to eight hours) every other day at around 1pm from outside the bank.

Miraj Express buses run to Marsabit (KSh350, six hours) on Tuesday, Thursday and Saturday.

Matatus leave from a chaotic stand around the market. The fare to Nairobi is KSh330; regular matatus also head to Nanyuki (KSh150), taking about the same time as the bus, and Meru (KSh100, one hour).

Trucks to Marsabit (KSh300 to KSh500, seven hours) leave from the northern end of the main street. Services become irregular when the security situation deteriorates; for information try the cheap hotels and cafés on the main road (the Subira Inn may be helpful), petrol stations or the police checkpoint.

Getting a lift on a truck is the only way to get to Moyale, Garissa, Wajir or Mandera. Check the security situation thoroughly before heading to Moyale; the other routes are currently considered unsafe for travellers. If you get a lift, you'll have to pay (about KSh1000) and bring your own supplies. If going to Ethiopia, consider breaking the journey in Marsabit as it's a long, hard haul. For more details of taking a truck in this direction, see Getting There & Away under Marsabit later in this chapter.

AROUND ISIOLO
Lewa Downs

Lewa Downs (☎ 0164-31405; ⓔ lewa@swift kenya.com; adult/child US$35/17; open 16 May-30 Oct, 16 Dec-31 Mar), 12km south of Isiolo, is a privately owned ranch of 16,000 hectares that has been turned into a 'wildlife conservancy', although ranching activities are still maintained. The entire area is enclosed by a solar-powered electric fence to keep out stock from neighbouring properties. Wildlife drives in private vehicles are not permitted, and Lewa is officially closed to tourism during the rainy seasons.

Black rhino from other parts of the country have been relocated here and are now breeding. The ranch also has a small group of the more placid white rhino, a big attraction since those in Meru National Park were slaughtered years ago. Other wildlife abounds and visitors can expect to see all the usual suspects, as well as some more elusive creatures such as leopards and sitatungas.

Vehicles are not allowed into the reserve unless accommodation has been booked. Options include **Wilderness Trails** (book through Bush Homes of East Africa ☎ 02-571661; ⓔ Bushhomes@africaonline.co.ke; singles/doubles full board US$460/750), a small, superbly sited stone and makuti (thatched roof of palm leaves) set-up with stunning views across to Isiolo and the northern plains. The standard of service is excellent. Bookings can also be made through Let's Go Travel (☎ 02-340331, fax 336890; ⓔ info@letsgosafari.com).

Lewa Safari Lodge (in Nairobi ☎ 02-571661; ⓔ Bushhomes@africaonline.co.ke; singles/doubles US$260/520), also handled by

Bush Homes of East Africa, and **Lerai Tented Camp** (in Nairobi ☎ 02-331684; ⓔ eaos@africa online.co.ke; singles/doubles US$270/440), run by East African Ornithological Safaris, both offer luxury tented accommodation with a good level of service.

Air Kenya Aviation (in Nairobi ☎ 02-605745; ⓔ info@airkenya.com) flies daily from Wilson Airport in Nairobi to Samburu National Reserve, stopping at Lewa Downs on request. Services leave Nairobi at 9.15am and arrive at 10.20am; returning flights leave Lewa at 11am. The return fare is US$210. It is also possible to charter a plane, though this can cost at least twice as much.

Il Ngwesi

Il Ngwesi Group Ranch (book through Let's Go Travel in Nairobi ☎ 02-340331; ⓔ info@ letsgosafari.com; lodge per night US$385) is a 6400-hectare property 20km west of Isiolo, right next to Lewa Downs (which has given considerable support to the project). The ranch is now divided equally between cattle ranching and tourism, with profits going to the local Samburu people.

Refurbished in 2001, the lodge in the ranch is made up of six open-fronted cottages that are constructed almost entirely from local materials, but still provide considerable luxury and all the trappings of a top-end lodge, including a swimming pool. They look out across the bush from a small hill at the base of a dramatic escarpment. Green technologies are used throughout and the emphasis is on relaxation and bird and nature walks in the local area.

Be warned: the lodge is usually booked up months in advance; it's always rented out exclusively by one group (up to 12 people) on either a self-catering or a full-board basis. The only snag, and this is a big snag, is that you need a 4WD or a plane to get there (a Suzuki just wouldn't cut it). However, if you can get there, you'll be at one of *the* places to stay in Kenya.

SAMBURU, BUFFALO SPRINGS & SHABA NATIONAL RESERVES

Just north of Isiolo, these three national reserves along the banks of the **Ewaso Ngiro River** cover an area of some 300 sq km, and are becoming an increasingly popular stop on the tourist trail as security concerns in the region lessen. The landscape is a mixture

NORTHERN KENYA

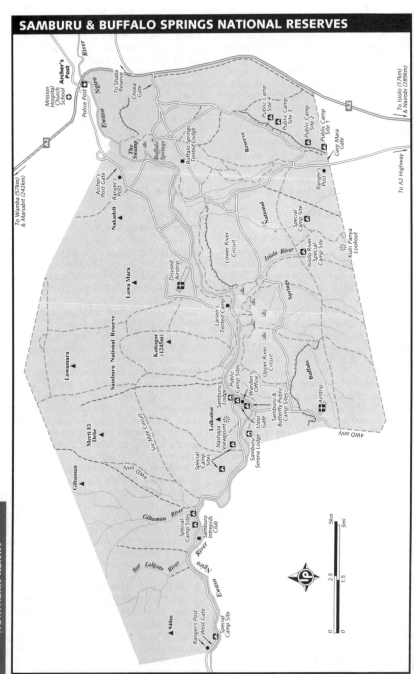

of plains and peaks, scrub desert and savanna; Shaba is more hilly and spectacular, with springs and great rocky kopjes (isolated hills).

The green swathe around the river, which is permanent, is the lifeline for all three parks and supports a wide variety of wildlife, including Grevy's zebras, Somali ostriches, gerenuks and reticulated giraffes. You are almost guaranteed close-up sightings of elephants, reticulated giraffes and various species of gazelle in both Samburu and Buffalo Springs. Wildlife in Shaba is not as prolific, but there is still plenty to see. Many of the lodges along the river have crocodile-feeding sessions, and some huge beasts can be seen when the water is high.

After a number of brazen lodge-hold-ups in Samburu a few years ago, security in all the parks has been considerably improved, with ranger and Kenya Wildlife Service (KWS) lookouts posted on most of the vantage points within the park. However, this was apparently not enough to stop poachers killing 25 elephants in early 2002, even after one of their number was shot dead by wardens.

Admission *(nonresident adult/child or student US$30/10, resident KSh500/200)* for Buffalo Springs and Samburu are interchangeable, but if you want to enter Shaba you pay the same fee again.

If you're driving, the Survey of Kenya map *Samburu & Buffalo Springs Game Reserves* (SK 85) is still your best bet, if you can find it. It's not difficult to get around, but roads away from the main routes are not well maintained (some are 4WD only) and the maze of tracks formed by wayward minibuses can get you lost.

Signage in the parks has improved, but you'll still need to keep your eyes open.

Places to Stay

Buffalo Springs There are four **public camp sites** *(camping KSh440)* in Buffalo Springs, close to the Gare Mara entrance gate (the nearest to Isiolo and accessible from the main Isiolo–Marsabit road). However, security is not that good, and it's worth paying someone to look after your stuff while you're out in the park.

There are also a number of **special camp sites** *(camping KSh825)* along the Isiolo and Maji ya Chumvi Rivers further west.

Buffalo Springs Tented Lodge *(Box 71, Isiolo; cottages per person KSh1000)* is still struggling to recover from the years when it was run by the hilariously slack and now defunct African Tours & Hotels Ltd. The rooms are OK and certainly a bargain compared to the other lodges here, but you have to bring your own food and there's not even a phone on the premises, so booking is tricky. Emergency buttons are provided in all the rooms, which is novel, but it's hard to imagine the long-suffering staff running to your aid (or anywhere else, for that matter).

Samburu Serena Lodge *(☎ 0164-30800, in Nairobi ☎ 02-711077, fax 718102; e sam buru@serena.co.ke; full board singles/doubles US$75/150 in low season, US$200/250 in high season)* is actually in Buffalo Springs. The main building burnt down in 1998, but has since been completely rebuilt in the usual, luxury-lodge style, complete with native decor and water features in reception. The cottages themselves are very pleasant, and there is a full range of activities available, including camel rides and, sadly, leopard baiting.

Samburu In Samburu National Reserve, the most convenient places to stay are the **public camp sites** *(camping KSh440)* between Samburu Lodge and the wooden bridge that connects the western extremity of Buffalo Springs to Samburu across the Ewaso Ngiro River. The sites are fairly pleasant and adjacent to the river; **Butterfly Camp Site** is probably the best, but all facilities are minimal and the 'toilets' are disgusting. If you don't want to cook for yourself, the sites are conveniently close to the lodge with its bar and restaurant.

There are also two **special camp sites** *(camping KSh825)* further west, but finding them is no easy feat.

For those with money, there's a choice of three top-range lodges and tented camps. **Samburu Lodge** *(☎ 0164-30778, in Nairobi ☎ 02-535412, fax 545954; e blockreserva tions@net2000ke.com; singles/doubles half board US$104/130 in low season, US$160/200 in high season)*, part of the Block Hotels chain, is perhaps the most popular. It's built right alongside the river and consists of several thatched, longhouse-type buildings strung out along the bank. Prices are the same for simple rooms and cottages (which are far

NORTHERN KENYA

more pleasant). Wildlife drives through the park can be organised for US$125 per vehicle and bird walks cost KSh450. The lodge is the only place in the two parks where you can buy petrol.

Larsens Tented Camp (☎ 0164-31373, in Nairobi 02-535412, fax 545954; e blockreser vations@net2000ke.com; singles/doubles full board US$144/180 in low season, US$224/280 in high season), also owned by Block Hotels, is further east and also alongside the river. The slightly shabby permanent tents and safari memorabilia give the game away: you're paying through the nose for nostalgia, and 80s nostalgia at that.

Samburu Intrepids Club (☎ 0164-30453, Nairobi ☎ 02-446651, fax 446600; e sambu ruintrepids@kenyaweb.com; singles/doubles full board US$133/180 in low season, US$222/ 300 in high season), further upstream on the northern side of the river, is another luxury tented lodge. The setting is one of the nicest in the parks and the wooden walkways are a nice touch. This is possibly the friendliest and best of the three places.

Shaba There are only **special camp sites** (KSh825) in Shaba, which have no facilities. **Funan Camp Site**, in the heart of the park on the way out to Shaba Gate, is probably the best of these, shaded by acacia trees with a semipermanent spring providing clean water for visitors and wildlife alike. An *askari* (security guard) must accompany you to these camp sites; the cost is included in the fee but a tip would be appropriate.

Shaba Sarova Lodge (in Nairobi ☎ 02-713333, fax 715566; e reservations@sarova.co .ke; singles/doubles full-board US$55/110 in low season, US$130/165 in high season) is a spectacular, almost-over-the-top place sitting on the Ewaso Ngiro River. It has a good pool, great service and excellent rooms.

Getting There & Away

Air Kenya operates daily flights from Nairobi to Samburu, direct (US$100) or via Nanyuki (US$120), but it's difficult to see much if you come here independently. You really need to organise your own vehicle or book a safari.

MATTHEWS RANGE

North of the small town of Wamba, off the link road to Baragoi, is the Matthews Range. Much of this area is thickly forested and supports rhinos, elephants, lions and buffaloes, as well as many other animal species. The highest peak here rises to 2285m.

The area, which is populated by Samburu people, is largely undeveloped and there are plans to turn the area into a wildlife sanctuary protecting the rhino, as the mountains contain the largest remaining free-ranging herd in Kenya. The major initiative here has come from the private sector, with the foundation of the Namunyak Wildlife Conservation Trust and the creation of a 30,375-hectare **wildlife sanctuary** in the heart of the mountains. Like Il Ngwesi near Isiolo, the profits from tourism here flow back to the local Samburu community.

If you really want to get off the beaten track the Matthews Range is the place to do it. Camping is probably your best option here, as the nearest accommodation is in Wamba and is very basic, unless you can bag a bed at the local mission (which incidentally has the best hospital in northern Kenya, a fact that's worth remembering when you're in the bush). However, if you're not short of a bob or two there are a couple of fantastic top-end lodges in the area.

Kitich Camp (book through Let's Go Travel ☎ 02-340331, fax 336890; e info@letsgosa fari.com; singles/doubles US$480/750) sits on the banks of the Ngeng River about 40km north of Wamba. Children aged under 12 are not allowed to stay here, and there's a conservation-area fee of US$30 per person. It's mainly set up as a luxury tented camp with full facilities, but there's also a basic **camp site** nearby, which really offers the genuine African bush experience.

You are kilometres from the nearest village and the local wildlife tends to wander through your camp in the middle of the night!

During the day, traditionally dressed Samburu warriors will probably visit you to ask if you need a guide (which you will if you want to see wildlife or climb to the top of the range). Agree on a reasonable price beforehand, and remember that you'll have to pay someone to stay behind and guard your vehicle. Also, don't forget that the rules of hospitality oblige you to provide your guides with drinks, a few cigarettes and perhaps a snack when you get back to camp. They're extremely friendly people. One or two will be able to speak English (the nearest school is in

Wamba) but most can converse in Swahili as well as Samburu.

Sarara Camp *(book through Let's Go Travel* ☎ *02-340331, fax 336890;* e *info@letsgosafari .com; camp hire per night US$385)* is a more flash option if you've got access to a serious 4WD or are prepared to charter a plane. The five luxury tents sleep 10, and rates include the exclusive use of camp facilities, camp staff (cooks, waiters, tent attendants and bush guide) and camel rides. The emphasis is on getting out and experiencing the bush at first hand. Guests are also required to pay a daily conservation fee of US$20 per person to the Namunyak Wildlife Conservation Trust.

Getting There & Away

Getting to Kitich or (especially) Sarara independently is not easy, even with a 4WD; it's probably best to arrange a transfer or at least get detailed directions when booking.

For Kitich, the best approach is from the Wamba–Parsaloi road. Just before Wamba you reach a T-junction; instead of going into the town, continue north and take the first obvious main track off to the right, several kilometres after the junction. If there are tyre tracks in the sand, follow them. There are two missions down this track (one of them next to a large fordable river) and both have vehicles. You will be able to ask the way at either one of them.

If you get lost, ask a local tribesman to come along and guide you, but you will have to drive him back to his *manyatta* (livestock camp) after you have found the place. No-one in their right mind walks around in the bush after dark unless they're in large groups – the

buffalo and elephant make it too dangerous. It might sound like a *tour de force* getting to these places, but it's well worth it!

MARALAL
☎ **0368**

High in the hills above the Loroghi Plateau, Maralal seems to enjoy its slightly renegade reputation, despite being more of a provincial centre than a frontier town these days. The wide streets and shabby verandas encourage comparisons with the classic Wild West image (there's currently a wooden structure on the main street that distinctly resembles a gallows!) and the rough 'n' ready atmosphere is decidedly different from anywhere further south.

In recent years the population has swelled considerably due to insecurity in the surrounding areas but now that order has largely been restored people are starting to leave.

Maralal is the preferred route and overnight centre for safari companies taking people up to Lake Turkana. If you are travelling independently you're likely to find yourself spending at least a couple of days here waiting for one thing or another; it may take some getting used to, but there are definitely worse places to get stuck. The best time to come here is the week of the Maralal International Camel Derby (see the boxed text), when the whole town goes crazy.

People here are generally friendly, but you'll quickly encounter the so-called Plastic Boys, Maralal's own professional tout posse. You'll be offered everything from bangles to guiding services, friendly 'advice' to Samburu weddings, and their persistence

---

Maralal International Camel Derby

Inaugurated by Yare Safaris in 1990, the annual Maralal International Camel Derby is one of the biggest events in Kenya, attracting riders and spectators from the four corners of the earth. The races are open to anyone and the extended after-parties at Yare camp site are notorious – you're likely to bump into some real characters here!

The races usually take place between July and October, but in 2002 the whole derby was cancelled, with catastrophic results on the local economy. Apparently, rumours of insecurity in the region caused a number of visitors to cancel their bookings, which in turn led to the sponsors (major companies such as Coca Cola and Kenya Breweries) withdrawing the prize money and thus killing the event.

The predicted dangers appear not to have materialised, and it is hoped that the derby will be held as usual from 2003. For further information contact **Maralal International Camel Derby** *(MICD; Secretariat, PO Box 281, Maralal)* or **Yare Safaris** *(PO Box 63006, Nairobi)*.

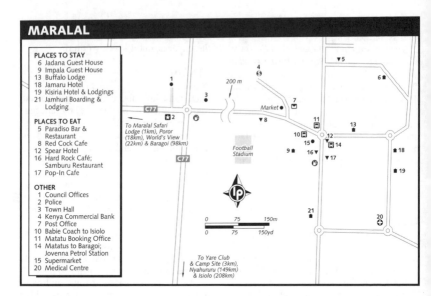

MARALAL

PLACES TO STAY
6 Jadana Guest House
9 Impala Guest House
13 Buffalo Lodge
18 Jamaru Hotel
19 Kisiria Hotel & Lodgings
21 Jamhuri Boarding &
    Lodging

PLACES TO EAT
5 Paradiso Bar &
   Restaurant
8 Red Cock Cafe
12 Spear Hotel
16 Hard Rock Café;
    Samburu Restaurant
17 Pop-In Cafe

OTHER
1 Council Offices
2 Police
3 Town Hall
4 Kenya Commercial Bank
7 Post Office
10 Babie Coach to Isiolo
11 Matatu Booking Office
14 Matatus to Baragoi;
    Jovenna Petrol Station
15 Supermarket
20 Medical Centre

To Maralal Safari
Lodge (1km), Poror
(18km), World's View
(22km) & Baragoi (98km)

Market

Football
Stadium

200 m

0   75   150m
0   75   150yd

To Yare Club
& Camp Site (3km),
Nyahururu (149km)
& Isiolo (208km)

can be truly astounding. No-one's sure where the name comes from; cynics suggest that it's because given a chance, they'll happily take your credit cards! That may be a bit harsh, but it's certainly advisable not to let them 'translate' prices for you in hotels or shops.

Surrounding the town is the **Maralal National Sanctuary**, home to a variety of plains wildlife, which you can see for free from the road leading into Maralal from the south. In the colonial era, white settlers coveted this attractive area of undulating grassland and coniferous forests.

However, their designs for taking it over were scotched by the colonial authorities due to anticipated violent opposition from the Samburu, for whom it holds a special significance.

Information
The **Kenya Commercial Bank** is open during normal banking hours. This is the last bank going north, apart from those in Marsabit, so stock up on cash. Outside banking hours, you can try Maralal Safari Lodge or Yare Club & Camp, but neither have great rates and they may have not change travellers cheques at weekends.

The **post office** keeps the usual opening hours and the staff are very helpful if you want to make national or international calls. Mobile phones and Internet connections have

yet to reach Maralal or anywhere north of here.

There are three **petrol stations** in town (the BP is the most reliable) and you'll usually have no problem getting what you need at regular prices. However, further north you will only find an irregular supply of petrol at Baragoi and Loyangalani, and then out of barrels at a much higher price.

Other facilities in town include a medical centre, mechanics, some well-stocked shops and an alarming number of butcheries.

Safaris & Treks
The hills and plains around Maralal make excellent walking country; Lonely Planet's *Trekking in East Africa* has full details.

Regular camel safaris depart from the Yare Club & Camp, where you can hire guides and camels for more independent treks. **Bobong Camp Site**, near Rumuruti, also arranges budget camel safaris (see the Safaris chapter for full details).

Places to Stay
Advance booking is absolutely essential for any sort of accommodation here when the camel derby is on.

Yare Club & Camp (*☎/fax 2295, in Nairobi ☎/fax 02-214099; e yare@africaonline.co.ke; camping KSh200, single/double bandas with bathroom US$15/23)* is the best place to stay, and is very popular with travellers. It's 3km south of town on the Isiolo–Nyahururu road. You can camp here or stay in the wooden bandas; soap and towels are provided and a free bucket of hot water is available in the morning.

Thoughtfully constructed, Yare's facilities include a well-stocked bar and lounge, a self-service restaurant, *nyama choma* (barbecued meat) on Wednesdays and Saturdays, a games room, camel hire and guiding services. There's also guarded parking. The camp site has its own (cold) showers and toilets.

There are a number of decent places to stay in the town itself. **Buffalo Lodge** *(☎ 2080; singles/doubles KSh150/300)* offers rooms with clean sheets, towels and hot water in the morning, but suffers slightly from having two lively bars below the rooms.

Impala Guest House *(singles/doubles KSh150/300)*, close to the football stadium, has some good-sized rooms, but it's a bit of a dark walk there at night. There are hot showers and secure parking is available.

Other options for basic, cheap accommodation (around KSh100 for a single) include **Jamhuri Boarding & Lodging** and **Kisiria Hotel & Lodgings**, both clean and tidy places with acceptable standards of comfort.

Jadana Guest House *(☎ 2033; singles/doubles KSh250/400)* has simple rooms with bathroom and secure parking. It seems to have dropped its prices recently, making it an even better deal. There is a noisy bar and butchery, reputedly one of the best places in Maralal for *nyama choma*.

Jamaru Hotel *(☎ 2093; singles/doubles KSh300/600)* offers good rooms with interesting but functional plumbing, as well as cheaper rooms with less-pleasant shared facilities. All rooms have mosquito nets, there's hot water, and the restaurant, hidden behind a large bush out front, is worth a try.

Maralal Safari Lodge *(☎ 2220, in Nairobi 02-211124; singles/doubles full-board US$80/160 in low season, US$140/195 in high season)*, about 3km along the road to Baragoi, is the only top-end resort in town. However, it's not tremendously impressive and the half-board rates (high season only) net you all of US$5 off the full price.

The best feature is the watering hole in front of the bar, which nearly justifies paying KSh110 for a beer there. Other facilities include a golf course and swimming pool – certainly the only ones for some distance in any direction.

Places to Eat
There is a cluster of small eating places around the Jovenna petrol station, just off the main roundabout in town. The Somali-run **Hard Rock Café** (no relation to the chain) is still probably the best of them; the food is good and cheap and the staff are friendly. **Pop-In Cafe** and the new plywood-fronted **Spear Hotel** are OK for the usual basics, while the **Samburu Restaurant** is about as upmarket as you'll get here. **Red Cock Cafe**, back past the matatu stand, is a good place for breakfast and *mandazi* (semisweet doughnuts).

Entertainment
Some years ago, the District Commissioner ordered the closure of Maralal's discos due to the insecurity of the region. Apparently no-one here has thought of fighting for their right to party, as this order is yet to be repealed.

Buffalo Lodge is probably the most popular boozer in town, with two good bars (the one at the back, although the best, is essentially a pool hall). **Paradiso Bar & Restaurant** is another contender with a pool table. The bars at **Yare Club & Camp** and **Maralal Safari Lodge** are much nicer, but if you're staying in town transport back may pose a problem!

Getting There & Away
Matatus ply the route between Maralal and Nyahururu (KSh250 to KSh300, three hours) via Rumuruti (KSh200, 2½ hours) on a daily basis, usually in the mornings and early afternoon. There is also a fairly regular bus to Nairobi (KSh400, eight hours).

The Babie Coach to Isiolo (KSh500, five to eight hours) leaves every other day.

The only other public transport out of Maralal is north to Baragoi by 4WD matatu. There's usually one each day or two, depending on demand, but no-one ever seems to know when it's leaving. The cost and journey time varies (KSh250 on average, about three hours). You need to make inquiries about this service in advance and, preferably, meet the driver.

If you're intending to head further north to Lake Turkana, lifts on trucks are just about your only option (unless you are very lucky and hitch a ride with some 4WD tourists).

NORTHERN KENYA

Maralal is the best place to sort this out, because if you try hitching from Baragoi or South Horr you may find the trucks are already full. It's far, far better to be stuck here for a couple of days than it is to get stranded further north. The trip to Lake Turkana from Maralal is around KSh800, but you'll have to negotiate. It takes one and a half days and you'll probably spend the night in South Horr.

All the buses and matatus leave from the dirt patch opposite the Shell petrol station. Trucks are usually parked nearby or in the petrol stations, with the drivers in the bars.

AROUND MARALAL

Eighteen kilometres from Maralal, at the end of a long plateau, is the small village of **Poror**, unspectacular in itself but only a short drive from **World's View**. Set in the middle of a sweeping escarpment, on a good day this viewpoint offers some of the best panoramas in Kenya, looking across the Rift Valley to the Cherangani Hills.

There are a number of trails down the escarpment to the valley floor and you're bound to find a few willing guides. The local people now levy a tourist tax on people entering World's View (KSh100) and trips down the escarpment incur further costs, payable either to the local chief or women's group. Prices vary, but expect to pay around KSh300 per person per day. You can camp just behind the viewpoint, though there are no facilities other than a spring a short distance away.

Getting There & Away

Poror is on the main road up to Baragoi and Lake Turkana, 5km before the viewpoint. It's about 18km from Maralal and at the end of a long plateau. There's little transport heading this way, and what there is can often be full, but if you ask around in Maralal it's possible to get a ride for a few shillings or, if that fails, hire a vehicle from one of the various enterprising drivers around. Early morning and late afternoon seem to be the best times for lifts. Once at the T-junction in Poror turn left (west) and follow the rolling dirt track to the viewpoint.

If you end up having to walk, head west out of town past the BP petrol station, ignore the turn-off on the left up to Yare and keep on this road as it climbs up onto the Loroghi Plateau. A couple of kilometres before Poror

the road turns left off the flat and drops down to a stream, then continues past a dam up to the T-junction in the middle of town.

East of Turkana

From southern Kenya there are two main routes to the eastern side of the lake. The first is the A2 Hwy from Nairobi to Marsabit via Isiolo; the other is from Nairobi to Maralal via Nyahururu and Rumuruti, or via Nakuru and Lake Baringo, and north from there to Loyangalani on Lake Turkana via Maralal, Baragoi and South Horr. From Loyangalani you can make a loop through the Chalbi Desert to Marsabit via Gusii and Kargi or North Horr and Maikona.

BARAGOI

On the road between Maralal and Loyangalani is Baragoi, a slightly more substantial market town with a couple of very basic lodges and a few shops. Petrol can usually be bought from a barrel here – the locals will show you where to find it. Quite a few people speak English, and the town has its own official (!) Plastic Boys self-help group, so you can expect to get a lot of attention as soon as you arrive, especially if you have your own vehicle. Prices here can be suspiciously high for new arrivals.

Treks through the Suguta Valley up to Lake Turkana are possible from Baragoi, but you should get a good appraisal of the security situation before heading down into the valley.

Be careful not to take photographs in the town as it's supposedly forbidden and the police are keen to enforce the rule.

Places to Stay & Eat

Unless you are planning on trekking in this area with a local guide, there's not much reason to stay in Baragoi. If you ask at any of the restaurants in town they'll usually come up with accommodation, but it will be very basic.

If you have the equipment, some places will allow you to camp in their back yards, or you can try the **water-pumping station** (camping KSh200), about 4km north of town off the road towards South Horr.

Bowmen Hotel (singles/doubles KSh350/650) by the post office is about the only decent place in town. Rooms are clean and have shared baths. It's the first building you come to when arriving from the south.

The main eating options in town are **Hotel Al-Mukhram** and **Wid-Wid Inn**.

Entertainment

There are a number of bars around; **Bosnia Bar**, set up by a soldier who served with the UN in former Yugoslavia, and **Joy Bar** are worth are look.

SOUTH HORR & AROUND

The next village north is South Horr, set in a beautiful lush canyon between the craggy peaks of **Mt Ngiro** (2752m), **Mt Porale** (1990m) and **Mt Supuko** (2066m). It's a lively little place with a huge Catholic mission (note that the missionaries won't sell you petrol).

For campers, the **camp site** *(camping KSh100)* at the forestry headquarters (signposted off to the left as you enter from the south) is a bit rough. There's a river running past the site but only minimal facilities.

Kurungu Camp Site *(camping KSh200)*, on the right 15km north of South Horr, is run by Safari Camp Services in Nairobi and is a much better site with reasonable facilities and plenty of firewood, although it seems to be a little more neglected than it was. Guards can be arranged to watch your tent if you want to eat in town.

In town, there are a couple of small and very basic hotels on the main street, where you can find accommodation of sorts as well as reasonably tasty meals. A good one to try is **Good Tourist Hotel**; prices are entirely negotiable.

For a drink, **Serima Bar** on the main road heading north seems to get pretty lively in the evenings, despite the tepid beer.

APPROACHING THE LAKE

As the spectacular rocky hills along the Maralal–Loyangalani road (the C77) flatten out and the lushness of the Horr Valley starts to give way to reddish dust and sand, you finally reach the shattered lava beds at the southern end of Lake Turkana (make sure you take a left turn after South Horr rather than ploughing straight on into the desert!). Climb the ridge here and there it is in front of you – the Jade Sea. This breathtaking sight is vast and yet apparently totally barren, with only a few stunted thorn trees struggling to grow in the highly saline environment. The northern end of the lake isn't anywhere near as salty because it's fed by the freshwater Omo River from Ethiopia. Swimming is possible if you don't mind the taste, but watch out for crocodiles: while their usual diet is Nile perch, they're unlikely to turn down a bit of red meat.

LOYANGALANI

A little further up the lake shore, surrounded by the stick and doum-palm dwellings of the Turkana tribespeople, Turkana 'city' boasts an airstrip, a post office, a fishing station, a Catholic mission and very little else. Taking photographs of tribespeople or their houses will attract 'fees'.

If you're an independent traveller and want to visit the village where the El-Molo tribe lives, ask the safari-truck drivers at the camp sites if they have room for you and agree on a price. The El-Molo is one of the smallest tribes in Africa and is quite different from the Turkana, though it seems its days are numbered as a distinct tribe (see the special section 'Tribes of Kenya'). As with the Maasai, tourism has wrought inevitable changes in the El-Molo peoples' lifestyle and many travellers feel that the tribal issue has been overly commercialised. You'll certainly pay handsomely for taking any photographs.

Trips to **Mt Kulal** forest and **Mt Porr**, a well-known gold-panning site, can be arranged at the Oasis Lodge (see Places to Stay & Eat following), but they're expensive. If you can find him, it may be better to get in touch with Francis Langachar, a very friendly young Turkana man, and ask him to organise something similar for you. If you do this trip by yourself in your own 4WD, allow two days and stay overnight. You cannot do it in one day there and back from Loyangalani.

South Island National Park

Opened as a public reserve in 1983, this tiny 39-sq-km island is similar to Central Island, and is uninhabited apart from large populations of crocodiles, poisonous snakes and feral goats. There is a run-down airstrip here if you can afford a private charter, or you can hire boats from Loyangalani. A couple of basic **camp sites** can be found on the island, but no-one usually stays here.

Places to Stay & Eat

El-Molo Camp *(camping KSh200)* is nothing more than a nice shaded camp site with a swimming pool fed from a hot spring. Use of the pool costs KSh200. There is a big open banda providing shade and some basic toilets and showers. You may be able to get a beer at Oasis Lodge next door.

Sunset Strip Camp *(camping KSh200)* is another site run by Safari Camp Services in Nairobi. Facilities include showers, toilets and covered dining areas, but you cannot buy food or drinks here and there's no electricity. It's also dusty when the wind blows, which is most of the time. You may not be able to stay if a full truck is already here.

Neither site has firewood so you'll have to bring your own from further south. Be aware that in the early evening the wind picks up tremendously and can be blowing at 60km/h by 8pm. Tie down your tent and beware of the sudden storms that can descend from Mt Kulal.

Oasis Lodge *(book through Will Travel* ☎ 02-503267; **e** *willtravel@swiftkenya.com; singles/doubles US$150/200)* has 15 luxury bungalows with private bathroom and electricity (own generator). It's a beautiful place with two spring-fed swimming pools, ice-cold beer and a good view across the lake. Nonguests can use the facilities for KSh300, but there are times when you won't be allowed in. You can hire boats here for trips to South Island National Park at KSh2500 per hour.

Mosaretu Women's Group Camp Site *(huts KSh200)* is outside the gates of the Oasis Lodge. You can pitch your tent here or take one of the traditional Turkana grass huts that come with beds and mattresses. The only drawback is the noise from the lodge's generator.

Hilton Hotel and **Cold Drink Hotel** on the main street offer meals. If you ask around you'll meet villagers who will cook up a meal of Nile perch for you in their homes.

Getting There & Away

There is no scheduled transport of any sort in or out of Loyangalani, so you need to be completely independent. For the rich and/or famous, Oasis Lodge can arrange a light plane to the local airstrip.

Going north or northeast from here involves crossing the Chalbi Desert towards North Horr. It's OK in the dry season but can be treacherous after rain. Make sure you're carrying adequate supplies when you set out, in case of minor emergencies.

You also need to stop and ask for directions every chance you get, otherwise it's very easy to go off on the wrong track and not realise until hours later. Don't assume tyre tracks in the sand will lead you in the right direction.

SIBILOI & CENTRAL ISLAND NATIONAL PARKS

Sibiloi *(adult/child & student US$15/5)* is probably Kenya's most remote national park, located far up the eastern shore of Lake Turkana and covering an area of 1570 sq km. Despite the area's fascinating prehistory, fossil sites and wonderful arid ecosystem, the difficulties involved in getting this far north tend to discourage visitors, which is a real shame. It seems slightly ironic that the so-called 'Cradle of Mankind' is now almost entirely unpopulated.

The nickname comes from the hundreds of archaeological finds relating to early hominids in the area; the park itself was established after Dr Richard Leakey discovered the skull of a *Homo habilis* (see the boxed text 'Skull 1470') believed to be 2½ million years old. Evidence of *Homo erectus* has also been unearthed here.

All the human fossils have long since been removed and taken to Nairobi, but the National Museums of Kenya have enclosed and protected three other fascinating fossil sites in the park. Fossils of a giant tortoise some three million years old, an ancient species of crocodile (*Euthecodon brumti*) that grew up to 15m long, and a big-tusked behemoth (*Elephas recki*), an ancestor of today's elephant, can all be seen. The petrified forest south of these sites is evidence that the area was lush and densely forested seven million years ago. Every year the rains and the wind expose other fossils, so many that the most impressive are simply ringed with stones. However, do not remove any fossils as future research may be compromised.

The National Museums of Kenya maintain a research base at **Koobi Fora**, a small point jutting out into the lake. It's often home to permanent researchers, visiting scientists and students. There is a small museum 2km south of the base explaining the most important finds and the surrounding environment.

Skull 1470

In the early 1970s, palaeontologist Richard Leakey made a significant find on the shores of Lake Turkana. This was the discovery of a fossilised skull, which came to be known somewhat prosaically by its Kenya Museum index number, 1470.

The almost complete but fragmented skull was thought to be from an early hominid. It was hoped that it would support earlier fossil discoveries made by the Leakey family in the Olduvai Gorge in Tanzania, suggesting that the direct human ancestral line went back further than the 1½ million years that most people thought at the time.

The pieces of the skull were painstakingly fitted together – a demanding task that kept two people fully occupied for over six weeks. The completed jigsaw confirmed what they had suspected: here was an evolutionarily sophisticated hominid, named *Homo habilis*, which was a direct ancestor of *Homo sapiens*. It was 2½ million years old.

Since Leakey's discovery, other hominid fossils have been found to push that date back even further, but for a while 1470 was a head of his time!

Central Island, a separate national park out in the lake, is a unique place, consisting of three large volcanic craters (which eventually formed two lakes) and a dust bowl, all of which are now visible.

The island is famous for its crocodiles, 12,000 by some estimates, and there are some real monsters here! April to May is the best time to see hatchlings breaking out of their shells. The birdlife is also prolific at any time of year.

Information

It's ferociously hot this far north for most of the year (especially December to March), but June and July are the coolest months. From May to September very strong winds blow from the southeast both morning and evening.

Contact the **National Museums of Kenya office** (☎ 02-742131, fax 741424; PO Box 40658, Nairobi; w www.museums.or.ke) for information on booking transport and accommodation.

Places to Stay

A basic **camp site** is close to the museum and there is another one at the KWS headquarters at Allia Bay 20km further south. When you arrive in Koobi Fora, you will also need to pay admission for the museum (KSh500) and park fees.

Some simple thatched **bandas** (*per person KSh1000*) consisting at Koobi Fora can be arranged through the National Museums of Kenya (you must pay in advance). There is a communal eating area, showers and flush toilets.

Getting There & Away

The best way to get to Sibiloi is to fly, which means chartering a plane. It's expensive, but not *that* expensive if you are in a big enough group. There are airstrips at the KWS headquarters and Koobi Fora.

Alternatively, if you have your own vehicle you can drive, but it's a three-day trip from Nairobi and the last petrol stations and banks are in Maralal.

The best option for budget travellers is to get to Lodwar, Kalokol or Ferguson's Gulf on the western shore of the lake and charter a boat to Koobi Fora. KWS (☎ 02-501081; e kws@users.africaonline.co.ke) has a boat that runs two to three times weekly (price negotiable); hiring a local boat will cost you around KSh8000 to KSh10,000.

Trips to Central Island can also be arranged with locals, but make sure the boat is sound (see Ferguson's Gulf later in this chapter).

MARSABIT
☎ 0183

To the east of the Chalbi Desert, Marsabit is a bit of a tribal frontier town. The mixture of tribal peoples, Ethiopian and Somali immigrants can be volatile at times (see the boxed text 'Marsabit Tribespeople'), although tourists are unlikely to encounter any problems.

The thickly forested hills around here stand in stark contrast to the desert plains on all sides, making it an excellent area for walking. The main attraction is the Marsabit National Park & Reserve, centred around Mt Marsabit (1702m), but the views from the communications tower on the summit above town are also magnificent in all directions.

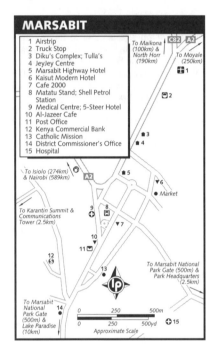

MARSABIT

1 Airstrip
2 Truck Stop
3 Diku's Complex; Tulla's
4 JeyJey Centre
5 Marsabit Highway Hotel
6 Kaisut Modern Hotel
7 Cafe 2000
8 Matatu Stand; Shell Petrol Station
9 Medical Centre; 5-Steer Hotel
10 Al-Jazeer Cafe
11 Post Office
12 Kenya Commercial Bank
13 Catholic Mission
14 District Commissioner's Office
15 Hospital

To Maikona (100km) & North Horr (190km)
To Moyale (250km)
To Isiolo (274km) & Nairobi (589km)
To Karantin Summit & Communications Tower (2.5km)
Market
To Marsabit National Park Gate (500m) & Park Headquarters (2.5km)
To Marsabit National Park Gate (500m) & Lake Paradise (10km)
0   250   500m
0   250   500yd
Approximate Scale

The whole area is peppered with extinct volcanoes and *gofs* (volcanic craters), some of which have a lake on the floor of the crater. There is no shortage of people offering to guide you to these, local villages and the 'singing wells' just outside town.

Facilities in Marsabit include two petrol stations, a **medical centre**, a **Kenya Commercial Bank,** a **post office** and a shiny new Catholic mission, plus good transport connections and an airstrip.

Places to Stay & Eat

There is a surprising amount of half-decent accommodation in Marsabit, including a growing number of reliable Muslim-run places. Most have secure parking, but no nets or toilet seats.

Marsabit Highway Hotel (☎ 110; singles KSh150) has about the cheapest basic singles in town. Rooms with bathroom are also available, but as there is no water in the bathrooms they're hardly worth the price!

JeyJey Centre (singles/doubles KSh200/ 300) is probably the best lodge in town, with rare singles with bathroom for KSh400. It's the biggest building along the road towards Moyale.

Just along from the JeyJey are a couple of new Muslim-run places tucked away behind wholesale stores. **Diku's Complex** (☎ 2465; singles/doubles KSh250/400) is a good choice, although it can get noisy on a TV night. **Tulla's** next door is virtually identical.

Kaisut Modern Hotel (☎ 2212; singles/ doubles KSh200/300) is another Muslim place above some shops in the centre of town, with a delightful purple exterior. There is a good restaurant but the rooms are basic and a bit drab.

Cafe 2000 seems popular for cooked snacks, while **Al-Jazeer Cafe** and **5-Steer Hotel** are worth a try for meals. They're all found around the Shell petrol station.

Getting There & Away

Miraj Express buses run from Marsabit to Isiolo (KSh350, six hours) on Wednesday, Friday and Sunday. There are also frequent trucks down this road, costing between KSh300 and KSh500.

Marsabit Tribespeople

As one of the safer northern frontier towns, Marsabit has acquired a considerable population of immigrants from Kenya's less-stable neighbours. On top of the increasing number of Ethiopians, there is a large and well-established Somali population whose influence on business and customs here is immediately perceptible.

Most noticeable of the local tribes are the nomadic Rendille, dressed in skins and sporting elaborate braided hairstyles and beaded accessories. Like the Samburu and Maasai, they have shown little interest in adopting a more sedentary lifestyle, and remain defiantly non-Muslim people in what is otherwise a largely Muslim area.

Unsurprisingly, these religious and cultural differences can cause friction between the communities, and outbreaks of violence are not unheard of. As recently as August 2002 a woman was shot dead in Marsabit, apparently by her rival in a cross-cultural love triangle.

NORTHERN KENYA

If you have your own vehicle, you should report to the police station and inquire about joining a convoy (if they are operating) or taking your own armed escort to Isiolo (around US$30). At the time of writing there was a bandit problem, but check the latest situation locally. As a rule, if the buses and trucks have a soldier on board you should take one too!

A lift on a truck to Moyale on the Ethiopian border should cost you around KSh500, but it's a long, uncomfortable ride. At various times, this route is not safe; otherwise trucks head off in convoys or take their own armed guards.

Fuel is available in Moyale, but taking a car across the border could involve a lot of hassle, including extra paperwork and customs checks.

It is possible to get to or from Loyangalani by driving through the Chalbi Desert via North Horr or Gusii. However, this can be a tough route, especially in the rainy season, and it's all too easy to get lost and/or stuck in the middle of nowhere; make sure you're well prepared with spare tyres, fuel and food.

There are rumours that you will soon be able to get direct flights to and from Nairobi; ask around or check the bank notice board for the latest news.

MARSABIT NATIONAL PARK & RESERVE

This relatively small park *(adult/child or student US$15/5, resident KSh100; open 6am-7.15pm)* lies just outside the town, nestled in the much wider area that constitutes the national reserve.

The terrain is thickly forested and is home to a wide variety of wildlife, including large mammals such as lions, leopards, elephants, rhinos, and giraffes.

You won't see much on a quick drive-through of the park; it's better to stick around for a while and camp at **Lake Paradise**. This small lake, which occupies much of the crater floor of Gof Sokorte Guda, is a very pleasant spot right out in the bush. Like the rest of the park, it looks to be suffering slightly from recent dry spells, but the next long rains should remedy the situation.

The Survey of Kenya map *Marsabit National Park & Reserve* (SK 84) is worth buying if you are touring this park, *if* you can find it in Nairobi.

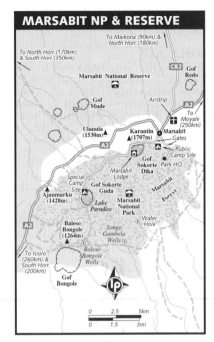

Places to Stay & Eat

The **special camp site** *(camping US$15, set-up fee KSh5000)* at Lake Paradise is easily the best place to stay here. There are no facilities except lake water and firewood. A ranger must be present when you camp here, but it's well worth the effort.

There's a **public camp site** *(camping US$8)* next to the main entrance gate, with water and plenty of firewood, but the facilities, especially the showers, are in severe need of an overhaul.

Marsabit Lodge *(☎ 2411, fax 2416; singles/doubles US$60/70 in low season, US$80/90 in high season)* is the only luxury lodge anywhere around here. The site overlooks the crater lake in Gof Sokorte Dika, and you can camp for KSh500; buffaloes and elephants are frequent visitors (mainly due to the salt that's spread around daily).

It's not a bad place to stay, but it's looking a bit faded in parts, and transfers will cost you a packet.

Getting There & Away

Use the access road from Marsabit to get to the park gate. You'll find it very hard to get into or around the park without your own transport.

MOYALE
Straddling the Kenyan–Ethiopian border, Moyale lies some 250km north of Marsabit across the Dida Galgalu Desert. It's a small town of sandy streets and traditional houses with bars, a post office, police station, bank, several shops selling a reasonable selection of commodities and a small market area. Houses here have sturdy pole frames supporting mud and stick roofs that can be up to half a metre thick, thus ensuring the interiors stay cool even when the outside temperature is 30°C and more.

The Ethiopian side of the town is somewhat larger and the facilities are much better, with sealed roads, electricity, a number of bars and small restaurants, hotels and a lively market. It's possible to cross freely into the Ethiopian side of town.

Security incidents have led to heightened tension in the area in recent years. The border may close during these times. Seek local advice before travelling up to the border.

Places to Stay & Eat
The few places to stay on the Kenyan side of the border are very basic. **Barissah Hotel** and **Bismillahi Boarding & Lodging** both offer passable accommodation for around KSh150. The Barissah also has a bar and does some reasonable food.

Options on the Ethiopian side are generally better and cost roughly the same; **Hotel Awasha** and **Bekele Molla Hotel** are worth a look.

Getting There & Away
The truck trip between Isiolo and Moyale takes at least two days and costs up to KSh1000 (see Getting There & Away under Isiolo earlier in this chapter for more details).

Buses going north from the Ethiopian side of Moyale leave at around the break of dawn.

West of Turkana

The only road north on this side of the lake is the A1 Hwy, which winds through the fertile highlands outside Kitale before reaching **Kapenguria**. This small town is most famous for being the place where Jomo Kenyatta and

five associates were held and tried in 1953 for their alleged part in the Mau Mau rebellion; the prison now houses a small museum illustrating the struggle for independence.

The change in scenery after Kapenguria is dramatic, as the road snakes its way along a forested ridge to pass through the stark rocky gorges of the Cherangani Hills, eventually emerging through the steep-sided **Marich Pass**. The only town in this part of the hills is **Ortum**, just off the road, which saw some unaccustomed excitement in 2002 when a leading bandit was captured and held there! If you want to stop and explore the area, there is basic accommodation in the town, but the Marich Pass Field Studies Centre is a better option (see Marich Pass Area following).

Once you leave Marich there is little to see. After rattling over kilometres of endless plains and dry creek beds, you'll eventually reach the town of **Lokichar**, little more than a collection of dismal roadside *dukas* and the last stopping point before Lodwar. The heat here is oppressive and the settlement seems to be gripped by a permanent torpor. However, it is possible to buy basketware and other Turkana trinkets at cheaper prices than you'll find further north.

MARICH PASS AREA
While few tourists seem to visit this area, it is a fascinating stretch of country offering countless possibilities for excursions, particularly if you are a keen walker.

If you do intend to do any walking in the vicinity you need to be adequately prepared for a variety of weather conditions. Those with their own vehicles should also bring sufficient supplies of petrol, as there is only one small service station (at Sigor, some 7km east of Marich Pass) between Kapenguria and Lodwar.

A few kilometres to the northwest, **Mt Sekerr** (3326m) can be climbed comfortably in a three-day round trip via the agricultural plots of the Pokot tribe, passing through forest and open moors. The views from the top are magnificent in clear weather.

To the south are the **Cherangani Hills**, which offer some of the best hill walks anywhere in Kenya, ranging from half-day excursions to week-long safaris by vehicle and on foot. Possibilities include: a half-day walk along the old road perched high on the eastern side of the Marich Pass; a hard day's slog up the dome of **Koh**, which soars some 1524m above the adjacent plains; and a safari of several days' duration along the verdant **Wei-Wei Valley** to **Tamkal** and then up to **Lenan Forest** and the main peaks of the **Cherangani**. See the Western Kenya chapter for more details about the Cherangani Hills.

There are numerous small **caves** dotted around the hills and most have special significance for the local Pokot. The Marich Pass Field Studies Centre sells a small guidebook to many of them, though you'll need to take a guide.

Elgeyo Escarpment rises above the Kerio Valley to more than 1830m in places and offers spectacular views and waterfalls. It's only 1½ hours away from the field studies centre along a road that passes through several local market centres and intensively farmed garden plots.

Lomut, at the foot of the escarpment (and accessible by matatu), holds a fascinating market every Saturday, bringing together the pastoral Pokot from the northern plains and the farming Pokot from the hills to the south. Much of the Pokot culture remains intact and tourists are pretty much ignored.

Nasolot and **South Turkana National Reserves**, in the dry and rugged hills north of the field studies centre, are largely the domain of Turkana herders and rarely visited by outsiders. There is no entrance fee at present; the KWS is currently upgrading roads within the reserves (4WD only) and there is a beautiful natural camp site by some hot springs on the eastern side of South Turkana. The area has a large elephant population and herds of up to 150 have been seen. The 40km drive to get there traverses grazing lands of the pastoral Pokot.

Turkwel Gorge hydroelectric station is 40km from the study centre along a fine tarmac road. Much of the gorge, with its towering rock walls, has not been affected by the construction, while the dam itself (the highest of its type in Africa) is spectacular. KWS levies fees on visitors, and, in theory, you need prior permission from the Kerio Valley Development Authority in Eldoret to visit the site.

Places to Stay & Eat
Marich Pass Field Studies Centre (PO Box 564, Kapenguria; W www.marich-pass.org; camping KSh250, dorm beds KSh300, cottages singles/doubles KSh750/950, bandas with bathroom 1100/1500) is the best place to stay in this area. It's essentially a residential facility for visiting student groups, but is also open to independent travellers who want to spend some time in a little-known corner of Kenya.

The centre occupies a beautiful site alongside the Maruni River and is surrounded by dense bush and woodland. The birdlife here is prolific, monkey and baboon have the run of the place, and warthog, buffalo, antelope and elephant are all regular visitors. Facilities include a secure camp site with drinking water, toilets, showers and firewood, as well as dorm beds and simple but comfortable bandas.

English-speaking Pokot and Turkana guides are available on request for half-day (KSh300), full-day (KSh450) and overnight (KSh900) excursions, while three-hour bird walks are KSh600 for a group of five people. There's a restaurant where you can buy meals for around KSh300; vegetarian food is available and all meals should be ordered in advance. You can also bring your own food and cook it at the centre. There's little to buy in the villages of this area.

Amolem Elephant Camp Site has, unfortunately, been closed due to insecurity in the region, as quarrels between the local Pokot and Turkana communities have intensified in recent years.

Getting There & Away
To reach the field studies centre, take the main Kitale–Lodwar road and watch out for the centre's signpost 2km north of the Sigor–Tot road junction. The centre is about 1km down a clearly marked track.

There are three approaches to Marich Pass. The first and easiest is through Kitale and Kapenguria and then a further 67km down a tarmac road (often described as 'Kenya's most spectacular tarmac road'). There are daily bus services from Nairobi to Kapenguria, and matatus (KSh80) from Kitale to Kapenguria. There are also a few daily matatus covering the stretch from Kitale to Lokichar via Marich Pass.

The second approach is through Iten, either from Eldoret or via Kabarnet, using the scenic road across the upper Kerio Valley. The all-weather Cherangani Hwy can be picked up from Iten to cross the main pass of the Cherangani Hills, joining up with the Kitale–Lodwar road near Kapenguria.

The roughest of the three approaches is the road from Lake Baringo through the Kito Pass and across the Kerio Valley to Tot; it's tough going with little in the way of signs, but allows you to visit the hot waterfalls at **Kapedo**. From Tot, the track skirts the northern face of the Cherangani Hills and may be impassable after heavy rain.

LODWAR
☎ 0393

The only town of any size in the northwest (although that's not saying much), Lodwar makes up for what it lacks in facilities with a dusty kind of outback charm. It is no longer just an isolated administrative outpost of the Northern Frontier District, however, and is becoming increasingly popular with overland companies and independent travellers.

As Lodwar is the only feasible base for excursions to Lake Turkana from the western side, you will probably find it convenient to stay here for at least one night. There's little to do in the town itself, but the atmosphere is not altogether unpleasant if you can stand the heat, and just listening to the garrulous locals is entertainment in itself. The small market is a good place to watch women weaving baskets, and there is an endless stream of Turkana hawkers who wander around town selling the usual souvenirs.

If you're around for a while it's worth walking into the stark volcanic hills before dawn and watching the sunrise. You are bound to be approached by a group of sharp young businessmen calling themselves the Lodwar Tour Guides Association and offering to escort you to the lake, into the hills and local communities, or further afield to Sibiloi and Central Island National Parks. They try hard to please and are a useful source of information, although their prices are a bit steep for the services provided – KSh1500 just for a guide to the lake!

The town has a **Kenya Commercial Bank**, a **post office** and several **petrol stations**.

Places to Stay

Unless you're both cold-blooded and thick-skinned, it's worth spending a bit more on accommodation in Lodwar: the cheaper places are hellishly hot and the mosquitoes can be fierce, so the extra money you pay for a fan and a net is almost invariably well spent.

New Surburb Tourist Lodge (☎ 2067; singles/doubles KSh300/450), east of the crossroads in the centre of town, is probably the best of the cheapies. Most rooms have fans and nets; upstairs rooms may catch some breeze, but can also attract an extra charge. The management seem to have improved, but don't let them get away with anything.

Africana Silent Lodge (☎ 21270; singles/doubles KSh250/400) is another reasonable place, and now has an annexe building offering much the same kind of accommodation. The rooms have fans and nets, but can be a bit dusty.

Nawoitorong Guest House (☎ 21208; camping KSh100, dorm beds KSh400/600, bandas KSh1200/1500) is an excellent option, and the only one in Lodwar for campers. The turn-off is signposted 1km south of Lodwar on the main road. This place was built entirely out of local materials and is run by a local women's group, which operates a conference centre and runs extensive training and education programmes. All the accommodation is thatched, making it cooler; there are no fans, but nets are provided. Meals are available in a very pleasant open banda, and dormitory prices include breakfast.

Turkwel Hotel (☎ 21218; singles/doubles KSh350/500, cottages KSh800/1050) is probably the best option in town, despite the '70s curtains and stolen pillowcases! All the rooms have fans and most now have at least one net, while the cottages at the rear are quiet and spacious.

Places to Eat

For cheap basic Kenyan fare, **Africana Silent Lodge** and **Lucky Star Hotel** are worth a try, while **Hotel Salama** does excellent Somali dishes in the evening. They can all be found east of the main crossroads. On the other side of town, the **Turkwel Hotel** restaurant does a good line in slightly more sophisticated Western fare starting at about KSh150. The **Nature Hotel**, just opposite, offers you a choice of fried, stewed or roasted meat, and also has good-value curries at KSh100.

If you're self-catering, the **Stop in Rose Grocery**, on the main street, is good, or there is a well-stocked **Naipa supermarket** next to the Kobil petrol station.

Harambee

The women's group hostel in Lodwar is just one example of the very Kenyan concept of *harambee*, a cornerstone of independence ideology drummed into the national consciousness by the first president, Jomo Kenyatta. Essentially it encapsulates the idea of a common goal, encouraging community self-help, and today few towns in Kenya are without their own local initiatives.

In practice, this can take on many forms. Numerous highly respected enterprises have sprung up around the country, from the Green Towns Partnership to the Youth Awareness and Resource Initiative (YARI), founding projects promoting everything from women's rights and community health to street kids and drug awareness with considerable success. However, there are also plenty of organisations whose fund-raising activities are limited to fleecing tourists, and probably an equal number whose profits somehow never quite make it back to the community.

In politics, too, *harambee* has proved to be a double-edged sword. The idea of togetherness pre-occupied Kenyatta to such an extent that any opposition came to resemble a dangerous strain of dissent, renewing his determination to run a one-party state. Despite increasing democratisation, this situation largely prevailed under Moi, and the rallying cry of 'national unity' can still overrule any number of objections. It remains to be seen whether the December 2002 elections have finally put the darker side of *harambee* to rest.

Entertainment

The main forms of entertainment for the locals are the many **video booths** scattered around town, where a third-rate action movie or kung fu flick will cost you about KSh10. Be warned, the volume controls in all these places go up to 11.

The large outdoor bar at the **Nature Hotel** is probably the best place in town to have a drink, although the **Turkwel Hotel** seems to be more popular.

Every Friday and Saturday **Vibrations Disco** kicks off, close to Turkwel Hotel. Also try the **Lodwar Club** past the airstrip.

Getting There & Away

Two converted trucks run by the Kenya Witness company travel from Kitale to Lodwar daily (KSh400, six hours), usually leaving around 9am. The five daily Nissan matatus are more reliable (KSh600, five hours); there is sometimes a midnight departure in either direction, but this needs to be booked before 6pm.

There's a matatu to Lokichoggio (KSh400, 1½ hours) but use of this road is currently strongly inadvisable – see the 'Warning' boxed text at the beginning of this chapter.

The tarmac road from Kitale deteriorates badly north of Marich Pass, due in part to constant use by heavy vehicles carrying aid and refugees; it improves slightly after Lokichar but it's still a rough ride. You may be required to travel in convoy to or from

Kainuk, about 10km north of Marich Pass, although in practice this can just mean waiting for a couple more cars to turn up. Usual departure times from Lodwar are 6am, 10am and 2pm.

Matatus going from Lodwar to Kalokol (KSh100, one hour) leave when full from the centre of town. To hitch to Kalokol, wait with the locals wait under the tree about 200m north of the Kobil petrol station.

KALOKOL

Most visitors to the area head on from Lodwar to Kalokol, a fairly dismal little town a few kilometres from the lake shore. The main building in this one-street town is the disused fish-processing factory, which was built with Scandinavian money and expertise but closed down some years ago. Kalokol is also the starting point for boat trips to Lake Turkana (see Sibiloi & Central Island National Parks earlier in this chapter).

There is very little in the way of accommodation. On the whole it's probably better to stay in Lodwar and make the trip to the lake from there, unless you are particularly keen to stay around here.

The **Lobolo camp site** is apparently quite good, but you need a 4WD or boat to get there, and at KSh1000 per person for camping it's hardly a budget option.

Kalokol Tourist Lodge is probably the best place for a cheap feed, and you can get a beer at the **Green Bar**.

NORTHERN KENYA

Irregular matatus do the run to Lodwar (KSh100) and there may even be a service to Kitale.

It's a hot, sandy 1½-hour walk to the lakeshore from here. Locals will point you in the right direction or offer to be your guide.

FERGUSON'S GULF

This is the most accessible part of the lakeshore, but there's really not a lot to see apart from a few fishing boats. After receding for years, the lake has been filled by the El Niño rains and a boat is now required to reach the thin strip on which Lake Turkana Fishing Lodge is located. The birdlife along the shore is prolific, particularly in March and April, when thousands of European migratory birds stop here on their way back north. There are also hippos and crocodiles (and bilharzia), so seek local advice before diving in.

There's an expanding settlement of grass huts leading up to the Lake Turkana Fishing Lodge where you can get a drink.

In the middle of the lake is the **Central Island National Park**, a barren, yet scenic, volcanic island. The best way to get here is to hire a boat from Lodwar or from Lake Turkana Fishing Lodge. It's good value if you are in a group, but will take some planning.

Talk to the fishermen and they *might* take you out, but make sure their craft is sound – the danger posed by the lake's squalls is not to be taken lightly.

Places to Stay

If you don't mind roughing it, local villagers may put you up for a small fee or you could pitch your tent on the shore.

Lake Turkana Lodge *(book through Hill Barrett Travel* ☎ *02-760226;* e *turkana@hill barrett.com; camping US$10, singles/doubles US$25/40)* is the only formal accommodation option, although it is currently run on a 'basic services' level with a skeleton staff, limited lighting and untreated lake water pumped direct to the rooms. Simple meals are available or you can bring your own food. The bar has cold drinks and is an excellent place to watch the wildlife on the lake. Boat hire is usually available at around KSh6000 to Central Island and KSh800 for a short round trip.

If you follow the road straight you'll arrive at a jetty from where transport can easily be arranged across the channel (try not pay an inflated 'taxi fare'). You can cut through the scrub to the ferry stage almost opposite Lake Turkana Fishing Lodge, but this involves paddling through a maze of dead acacia bushes; taking a guide is a good idea, as it's easy to get lost.

ELIYE SPRINGS

Also called Ille Springs, this is a far more attractive place than Ferguson's Gulf, but inaccessible without a 4WD. The small village here consists of little more than an army post and a couple of dozen grass huts, but the lakeside location is fantastic. Bizarrely, the springs provide enough moisture to allow a large number of doum palms to grow, giving the usually barren lakeshore a somewhat incongruous tropical feel. The trees are spread by elephants, who love the fruit but cannot digest the rock-hard seeds.

On arrival you'll encounter an instant small crowd of people wanting lifts, as well as various Turkana women selling trinkets at absurdly cheap prices. It's worth having a look if you're planning on buying souvenirs at all, as chances are half the stuff sold in Lodwar was made here! As only a few vehicles visit each week, it's a real buyer's market. Some of the more unusual items you might find include fossilised hippo teeth and fish backbones threaded into necklaces.

Places to Stay

The **camp site** *(camping KSh200)* and **lodge** have long since ceased to function as an upmarket establishment and are now run on an informal basis by the locals. However, the dilapidated **bandas** *(KSh800)* are gradually being rethatched, and the palm trees, the great views of the lake and the hot-spring swimming pool make this a wonderful location at which to stay.

Getting There & Away

The turn-off for Eliye Springs is signposted about halfway along the Lodwar–Kalokol road. There are a few patches of heavy sand, some awkwardly 'paved' with palm leaves, which makes a 4WD just about essential. As there are so few vehicles, hitching is not an option and it's a hot, sandy 35km trek.

You may be able to arrange transport in Lodwar, but it will cost around KSh3000.

Language

WHO SPEAKS WHAT?

English and Swahili (called *Kiswahili* in the language itself) are the official languages of Kenya and are taught in schools throughout the country. There are also many major indigenous languages (including Kikuyu, Luo, Kikamba, Maasai and Samburu) and a plethora of minor tribal languages. Hindi and Urdu are still spoken by residents of Indian subcontinent origin.

Most urban Kenyans and even tribal people who deal with tourists speak English, so you shouldn't experience too many problems making yourself understood. Italian is almost the second language on the coast, and Kenyans working in the tourist industry may also speak German. Most tourists to the coast also visit the national parks, so safaris operators almost always speak some Italian and German.

Swahili is widely spoken in Kenya, but the language becomes more basic the further you get away from the coast, with a lot more English words creeping in. You'll also find that there are more books and newspapers available in English than there are in Swahili. Nonetheless, a working knowledge of Swahili, especially outside urban areas is useful, since this will open doors and often enable you to communicate with people who don't speak English, particularly speakers of different tribal languages.

Another language you may come across in Kenya is Sheng, which is spoken almost exclusively by the young people. Essentially a patois, it's a mixture of Swahili and English, with a fair sprinkling of Hindi, Gujarati, Kikuyu and other tribal languages. Unless you can speak reasonable Swahili, you probably won't realise Sheng is being spoken – listen out for the distinctive greeting between friends – *Sassa!*. The response can be, *Besht*, *Mambo* or *Fit* (pronounced almost like 'feet').

SWAHILI

The Swahili language has a long and complicated history. It is a member of the Bantu language family found in Africa's midriff. The Bantu languages have been spoken on the Indian Ocean coast from at least as early as the 1st millenium AD.

Swahili has developed over many centuries of trade along the East African coast, with the influx of many early linguistic influences from Arabic. By the time Portuguese ships began calling at East African ports in 1498, a version of Swahili was spoken by the coastal inhabitants, the Wa-Swahili, and over time a few Portuguese elements slipped into the language. Numerous words have also been borrowed from English. Generally, the Swahili people have retained the foreign words for the objects foreigners brought with them, such as *kitabu* from the Arabic *kitab* for 'book', *mvinyo* from the Portuguese *vino* for 'wine', and *baisikeli* for 'bicycle'.

For a more in-depth guide to the language, get a copy of Lonely Planet's compact and comprehensive *Swahili phrasebook*.

Pronunciation

Vowels

a	as in 'father'
e	between the 'e' in 'better' and the 'a' in 'may'
i	as in 'marine'
o	as in 'old'
u	as the 'oo' in 'too'

Any two vowels occurring together are pronounced as two separate syllables. Thus *saa* (time/hour) is pronounced 'sa-a', and *yai* (egg) is pronounced 'ya-ee'.

Consonants

dh	as the 'th' in 'this'
ky	as the 'ch' in 'chat'
th	as in 'thing'
ny	as the 'ñ' in Spanish *señora*
ng'	as the 'ng' in 'sing'
gh	like a 'g', but more of a gargle
r	in English closer to a 'd', but 'r' will also be understood

Word Stress

In words with more than two syllables, the stress generally falls on the second to last syllable.

Greetings & Civilities

It's considered rude to speak to someone without first greeting them, so even if you only want directions, greet the person first. *Jambo* and *Salama* can be used as the Swahili equivalents of 'excuse me'.

Hello.	*Jambo* or *Salama*.

Shikamoo is also a respectful greeting used for elders: the reply is *marahaba*.

Welcome.	*Karibu.*
Goodbye.	*Kwa heri.*
(Until) tomorrow.	*Kesho.*
Goodnight.	*Lala salama.*
See you later.	*Tutaonana.*
Please. (if asking a big favour)	*Tafadhali.*
Thank you.	*Asante.*
Thanks very much.	*Asante sana.*
You're welcome.	*Karibu.*
How are you?	*Habari?*
I'm fine, thanks.	*Nzuri.*
What's your name?	*Unaitwa nani?*
My name is ...	*Jina langu ni ...*
Where are you from?	*Unatoka wapi?*
I'm from ...	*Mimi ninatoka ...*
Where do you live?	*Unakaa wapi?*
I live in ...	*Ninakaa ...*
May I take a picture?	*Naomba kupiga picha.*

Useful Words & Phrases

Yes.	*Ndiyo.*
No.	*Hapana.*
Sorry.	*Pole sana.*
No problem.	*Hakuna matata/ Hamna shida.*
No hurry.	*Hakuna haraka.*
Easy! Piece of cake!	*Muteremko!*
I don't understand.	*Nisamehe sifahamu.*
I'm going to the toilet.	*Nina enda choo.*
cigarette	*sigara*

Getting Around

I want to go to ...	*Mimi nataka kwenda ...*
Is this the way to ...?	*Hii njia ya ...?*
How much to go to ...?	*Shillingi ngapi kwenda ...?*

When does the ... leave?	*... inakwenda saa ngapi?*
bus	*basi*
train	*treni*
truck/car	*gari*
boat	*boti*
shared taxi	*gari ndogo*

Drive slowly.	*Endesha pole pole.*
Wait a minute.	*Ngoja kidogo.*
Stop here.	*Simama hapa.*

ticket	*tikiti*
airport	*kiwanja cha ndege*
bus station	*stesheni ya basi*
train station	*stesheni ya treni*
taxi	*teksi*
left	*kwa kushoto*
right	*kwa kulia*

Accommodation

Where is a ...?	*Wapi ...?*
hotel	*hoteli ya kulala*
very good hotel	*hoteli mzuri sana*
guesthouse	*nyumba ya wageni*
Do you have a room for ...?	*Kuna rumu ya ...?*
one person	*mtu moja*
two people	*watu wahili*
How much is the room?	*Rumu ni shillingi ngapi?*
I'd like to see the room, please.	*Nataka kuona rumu tafadhali.*
Is there hot water?	*Kuna maji ya moto?*

for one day	*kwa siku moja*
for a week	*kwa wiki mzima*
shower	*shawa*
bath	*bafu*
fan	*feni*
sheet	*shiti*
towel	*tauli*
key	*ufunguo*
noisy	*kelele*

Around Town

Where is a/the ...?	*Wapi ...?*
bank	*benki*
hotel	*hoteli ya kulala*
hospital	*hospitali*
police station	*stesheni ya polisi*
post office	*posta*
restaurant	*hoteli ya chakula*
toilet	*choo*

Shopping

Where is a/the ...?	*Wapi ...?*
bookshop	*duka la vitabu*
chemist/pharmacy	*duka la dawa*
grocery	*duka*
market	*sokoni*

I want to buy ...	*Mimi nataka kununua ...*
Do you have ...?	*Kuna ...?*
There is.	*Kuna*
There isn't.	*Hakuna*
How much?	*Ngapi?*
This is very expensive.	*Hii ni bei ghali sana.*

clothing	*nguo*
insect repellent	*dawa ya mdudu*
laundry detergent	*omo*
medicine	*dawa*
mosquito coil	*dawa ya mbu ya kuwashia*
soap	*sabuni*
toilet paper	*karatasi ya choo*
toothpaste	*dawa ya meno*
too big	*kubwa*
too small	*kidogo*
more	*zaidi*

On Safari

Look there.	*Tazama pale.*
What is there?	*Iko nini pale?*
What animal is that?	*huyo mnyama gani?*
electric fence	*usiguse sengeni*
Watch out!	*Angalia!/Chunga!*
Danger (on signs)	*Hatari*

African buffalo	*mbogo*
antelope	*pofu/kulungu*
baboon	*nyani*
bird	*ndege*
bushbaby	*komba*
cheetah	*duma*
crocodile	*mamba*
elephant	*ndovu/tembo*
gazelle	*swala/swara/paa*
giraffe	*twiga*
hippopotamus	*kiboko*
impala	*swala pala*
jackal	*mbweha*
leopard	*chui*
lion	*simba*
mongoose	*nguchiro*

Health & Emergencies

Help!	*Nisaidie!/Njoo!*
I'm ill.	*Mimi mgonjwa.*
Please call a . doctor	*Tafadhali wewe umwite daktari.*
It hurts here.	*Ninaumwa hapa.*
I'm pregnant.	*Nina mimba.*
Leave me alone!	*Niache!*
I'm lost.	*Nimepotea.*
I've been robbed.	*Nimeibiwa.*

rhinoceros	*kifaru*
snake	*nyoka*
spotted hyena	*fisi*
water buffalo	*nyati*
zebra	*punda milia*

Time & Days

Bear in mind that Swahili time and Western time differ by six hours, although unless you get right out into the small towns this should be no cause for confusion.

What's the time?	*Saa ngapi?*
It's 8 o'clock.	*Saa nane.*
When?	*Saa ngapi?*
today	*leo*
tomorrow	*kesho*
yesterday	*jana*
hour	*saa*
week	*wiki*
month	*mwezi*
year	*mwaka*

Monday	*Jumatatu*
Tuesday	*Jumanne*
Wednesday	*Jumatano*
Thursday	*Alhamisi*
Friday	*Ijumaa*
Saturday	*Jumamosi*
Sunday	*Jumapili*

Numbers

1	*moja*
2	*mbili*
3	*tatu*
4	*nne*
5	*tano*
6	*sita*
7	*saba*
8	*nane*
9	*tisa*
10	*kumi*

The 'teens' are *kumi na ...* (10 plus ...), the 20s *ishrini na ...* (20 plus ...) and so on. The hundreds are *mia*, and the thousands *elfu*.

11	*kumi na moja*
12	*kumi na mbili*
20	*ishrini*
30	*thelathini*
40	*arobaini*
50	*hamsini*
60	*sitini*
70	*sabini*
80	*themanini*
90	*tisini*
100	*mia*
200	*mia mbili*
1000	*elfu*
2126	*elfu mbili mia moja ishrini na sita*

Food
Useful Words

boiled	*chemka*
bread	*mkate*
butter	*siagi*
cup	*kikombe*
curry	*mchuzi*
egg(s)	*yai (mayai)*
food	*chakula*
fork	*uma*
fried	*kaanga*
glass	*glasi*
hot/cold	*moto/baridi*
hot (spicy)	*hoho*
Indian bread	*chapati*
knife	*kisu*
napkin	*kitambaa*
pepper	*pilipili*
plate	*sahani*
raw	*mbichi*
ripe	*mbivu*
roast	*choma*
table	*mesa*
teaspoon	*kijiko*
salt	*chumvi*
sauce	*mchuzi*
soup	*supu*
sugar	*sukari*
sweet	*tamu*
yogurt	*maziwalala*

Vegetables & Grains

aubergine	*biringani*
cabbage	*kabichi*
capsicum	*pilipili baridi*
carrots	*karoti*
cassava	*muhogo*
corn/maize	*mahindi*
garlic	*vitunguu saumu*
kidney beans	*maharagwe*
lettuce	*salad*
maize porridge	*ugali*
mashed plantains	*matoke*
mashed beans, potatoes, maize and greens	*mataha*
onions	*vitunguu*
plantains	*ndizi*
potatoes	*viazi*
rice	*wali*
spinach	*sukuma wiki*
boiled spinach	*sukuma wiki*
tomatoes	*nyana*
vegetables	*mboga*
vegetable stew	*mboga*

Meat & Fish

barbecued meat	*nyama choma*
beef	*nyama (ya) ng'ombe*
crab	*kaa*
fish	*samaki*
kebabs	*mushkaki*
lobster	*kamba*
meat	*nyama*
meat stew	*karanga*
goat meat	*nyama (ya) mbuzi*
pork	*nyama (ya) nguruwe*
squid	*ngisi*
steak	*steki*

Fruit

bananas	*ndizi*
coconut (green)	*dafu*
coconut (ripe)	*nazi*
custard apples	*stafeli*
dates	*tende*
fruit	*matunda*
grapefruits	*madanzi*
guava	*pera*
limes	*ndimu*
mangoes	*maembe*
oranges	*machungwa*
papayas	*paipai*
passionfruit	*pasheni*
pineapples	*mananasi*
sugar cane	*miwa*
watermelon	*tikiti*

Glossary

The following are words you are likely to come across when in Kenya. For a more complete glossary of food terms see the Language chapter.

askari – security guard, watchman

banda – thatched-roof hut with wooden or earthen walls or simple wooden and stone-built accommodation
bao – traditional African board game
boda-boda – see *poda-poda*
boma – village
bui-bui – black cover-all garment worn by Islamic women outside the home

chai – tea, but also a bribe
chai masala – sweet tea with spices
chakula – food
chang'a – dangerous home-made alcoholic brew containing methyl alcohol
choo – toilet; pronounced as 'cho'
Cites – UN Convention on International Trade in Endangered Species

dhow – traditional Arabic sailing vessel
dudu – a small insect or bug; a creepy crawly
duka – small shop or kiosk selling household basics

fundi – repair man or woman who fixes clothing, cars or is in the building trades; also an expert

gofs – volcanic craters

hakuna matata – no problem; watch out – there often is!
harambee – the concept of community self-help – voluntary fundraising; a cornerstone of Kenyatta's ideology
hatari – danger
hoteli – basic local eatery

idli – south Indian rice dumpling
ito – wooden 'eyes' to allow a dhow to see obstacles in the water

jinga! – crazy!; also used as an adjective
jua kali – literally 'fierce sun'; usually an outdoor vehicle-repair shop or market

kali – fierce or ferocious; eg *hatari mbwa kali* – 'danger fierce dog'
kanga – printed cotton wraparound incorporating a Swahili proverb; worn by many women both inside and outside the home
KANU – Kenya African National Union
kikoi – striped cotton sarong traditionally worn by men
kiondos – woven baskets
kitu kidogo – 'a little something'; a bribe
kofia – cap worn by Muslim men
KWS – Kenya Wildlife Service

Laibon – chief or spiritual leader of the Maasai; known as Olonana earlier, and Lenana today
lugga – dry river bed, mainly in northern Kenya

makonde – woodcarving style, originally from southern Tanzania
makuti – thatch made with palm leaves used for roofing buildings, mainly on the coast
malaya – prostitute
manamba – matatu tout, often a veritable style guru and all-round dude
mandazi – semisweet, flat doughnut
manyatta – Maasai or Samburu livestock camp often surrounded by a circle of thorn bushes
mataha – mashed beans, potatoes, maize and green vegetables
matatu – minibus with mega-decibel sound system, seemingly unlimited carrying capacity and two speeds – stationary and flat out
matoke – mashed plantains (ie, green bananas)
mboga – vegetables
miraa – bundles of leafy twigs and shoots that are chewed as a stimulant and appetite-suppressant
mkate mayai – fried, wheat pancake filled with minced meat and raw egg; literally bread eggs
moran – Maasai or Samburu warrior (plural *morani*)
murram – dirt or part-gravel road
mwananchi – worker of any kind but usually agricultural (plural *wananchi*, which is also used to refer to 'the people')

mwizi – a thief
mzee – an old person or respected elder
mzee kipara – bald man, literally means 'mosquito airport'
mzungu – white person (plural *wazungu)*

Narc – National Rainbow Coalition
Ng'oroko – Turkana bandits
nyama choma – barbecued meat, often goat
Nyayo – a cornerstone of Moi's political ideology, literally meaning 'footsteps'; to follow in the footsteps of Jomo Kenyatta

panga – machete, carried by most people in the countryside and often by thieves in the cities
parking boys – unemployed youths or young men who will help park a vehicle and guard it while the owner is absent
pesa – money
Peugeot – shared taxi
poda-poda – bicycle taxi
pombe – Kenyan beer, usually made with millet and sugar

rondavel – Circular hut, usually a thatched building with a conical roof

safari – 'journey' in Swahili
sambusa – deep-fried pastry triangles stuffed with spiced mince meat; similar to Indian samosa
shamba – small farm or plot of land
shifta – bandit
shilingi – money
sigana – traditional African performance form containing narration, song, music, dance, chant, ritual, mask, movement, banter and poetry
siwa – ornately carved ivory wind instrument unique to the coastal region and often used as a fanfare at weddings

taka taka – rubbish
Tusker – Kenyan beer

ugali – maize meal set hard and served in brick-shaped pieces
uhuru – freedom or independence

wa benzi – someone driving a Mercedes-Benz car bought with, it's implied, the proceeds of corruption
wananchi – workers or 'the people' (singular *mwanchi*)
wazungu – white people (singular *mzungu*)

Thanks

Many thanks to the traveller who used the last edition and wrote to us with helpful hints, useful advice and interesting anecdotes.

Alison Allgaier, Ann Alton, Helen J Altshul, Karen Ambrose Hickey, Rik Arnoudt, Ruth Ash, Inna & Daniel Baichtok, Tony Banks, Cary Barbor, Gabi Barkay, Anke & Pino Barnbrock, Phil Barnett, Jane Bauer, Kate Belton, Gali Ben, Jo Bennett, Rose Bernfried, Sebastiaan Biehl, Jan Bolt, Lisa Bonnell, Alex Bornstein, Claire Bosch, Magnus & Liselott Karlsson Bostrom, Kate Botham, Will Bourne, Matthew Bowell, Chad Bramble, Pamela Bregman, Zella Bridle, Eric Brown, Ben Buston, Zoe Cahill, Jo Campion, Julie Carter, Tamara Cassels, Jennifer Cassone, Hedvig Castberg Tresselt, Linda Cawley, Paul Chamberlain, Cathy Chesson, Hannah Clayton, Charlie Collman, Wazza Coulston, Mavis Coxon, Benedict Croell, Ron Czajkowski, Laura Danforth, Brian Davies, Ruth Davies, Nicky & Jim Davis, Jan de Roo, Carine de Wit, Robert Deane, Hilary Dean-Hughes, Marieke Dekker, Philippe Delesalle, Martha Denny, Andre DeSimone, Kari Detwiler, Stefano Di Marino, Brian Dixson, Marjan Dixson, Rudolf Doppler, Simon Dowse, Ken Driese, Dr R A Duncan, Jake Easton, Peter & Tanja Eberhard, Heidi Engbring, Peter Enrhardt, Steve Ernest, Norbert Ernst, Oliver Evans, Rebecca Evans, Paul Fairbanks, Raelene Farrell, Ornella Ferrari, Eric Fisher, Gordon Fisher, Julie Fisher, Bente Fisker Sorensen, Jason Francis, William Franklin, Alastair Fraser, Emma Fraser, Andrea French, Flynn & Jo Ellen Fuller, Garrett Fulton, Go Funai, Carolina Galt, Robert Gathu, Patricia Gelman, Christine Gemon, Francesca Gettelman, Bruno Gilissen, Michael & Noa Glaun, Clare Goldwater, Tom Graham, David Grant, Hamish Grant, Sian Green, Michael Griffiths, Emerson Grossmith, Peder Gustafsson, Angela Hale, Mitch Hale, Linfang Han, Charlotte Hanratty, Inge Hanson, Steven Harlow, Brian & Jane Harvey, Rassin Saleh Hassan, Erica Hastings, Klara Henderson, Consuela & Vincent Hendriks, Hartmut Heppe, Ruediger Herrmann, Sarah Hilding, Edward Hillman, J Y Hinxman, Nina Hjellegjerde, Gavin Hogg, Wei-Hsiang Huang, Michael Hurst, Zirker-Lee Hyunjoo, Ingo Inberland, Kaye Ireson, Alene Ivey, Tone Jacobsen, Asa Johansson, Kirsten Jones, Thomas Jungbluth, Kerry Just, Oscar Kafati, Andrew Kariuki, Edwina Kearney, Nicolien Kegels, Chris Kennedy, Jonathan Kern, A & A Kershaw, Nils-Einar Kjendlie, Lara Knudsen, Olka Kolker, Walter Kondik, Rudolf Konecny, Arnout Kroezen, Nitesh Kumar, Diane Kunz, Chrissy Labenz, Sharon Lagan, James Laight, Sandy Lam, James Lane, Moti Lang, Thomas Latein, Jurgen Lerche, Matthew Lerner, Carolien Libbrecht, Dr Peter Liu, Peter Liu, William & Gisela Loader, Jesse Long, Harro Lotsy, Alanna MacDougall, A A J Mackinnon, John K Magerer, Mike Mannion, Andrew Margolin, Noela Marr, David Marshall, Melissa Matheny, Lois Mativo, Claire Mawdsley, David Mayer, LaSalle McDaniel, Narelle McFadden, Chris McLaren, Emma McLoughlin, David McNeill, Paul D McNeill, Karin Meeussen, Catharina Meinen, Arne Meissner, Judith Mitchel, Sarah Moore, Chris Morris, Doug Moseley, Patricia Mulkeen, Margo Muurling, Alf Nathoo, Nannette Nayyar, Nigel Vere Nicoll, Brad Nilson, Terry O'Callaghan, Shauna O'Connell, John & Eveleen O'Keeffe, David & Ailne O'Malley, Nick Pace, Iris Palmer, John Parkinson, Seth Parks, Sanjeev Parmar, Matthew Philbrook, Anja & Thomas Platen, Helen Poole, Vicky & Martin Pringle, R Ramesh, Kevin Ramsey, Wayne Rasmus, Goolzaar Rattanshi, L H Rees, Gill & Tony Reeves, Adir Regev, A J Rieks, Morgan Riley, Neil Robinson, Anna Rockert, Leif Roise, Paul Roos, William Rowden, Synnove Roysland, Marc Rudin, Malin Sanden, A Sanderson, Maya Sapone, Mark Savage, Achim Schaffert, Roger Schmidgall, Ehsan Shariati, Tara Short, Karolina Simmons, Katherine Sims, Cheryl Singer, Barun Sinha, Siri Sitton, Jonas Sjoblom, Kathryn Smith, Jennifer Solomon, Andrea Soutschek, Ken Sparkes, Henk Staal, Christine Steiner, Nan Stevens, Garry & Marita Stout, Eileen Sutherland, Ricardo Taboada, Heidi Tavakoli, Liz Taylor, Charlot Teng, Abam Thompson, Jesper Thomsen, Mel Tilkicioglu, Sandra Timmermans, Ivar Tjernberg, Julie Trayner, Bex Tyrer, Fabio Umehara, Maria Valeria Urbani, Henk van Asselt, Kaspar van den Berg, Sandra van der Graaf, Hans van der Kwast, Jan van Kooten, Tamara van Vliet, Marian Venema, Carna Von Hove, Charlie Wade, Robert Wagner, Gary Walder, Malcolm Wallace, Ian Ward, Jeremy Ward, Guy Westoby, Frances Wiig, Ollie Wilkins, Merlin Williams, Ruth Wiltshire, Julie Woffingon, Karin Wohlgemuth, Ross Wold, Arielle Wolfe, Theresa Wolters, Pablo Yee, Jim Ying, Lisa Young, Bianca Zegers.

LONELY PLANET

You already know that Lonely Planet produces more than this one guidebook, but you might not be aware of the other products we have on this region. Here is a selection of titles that you may want to check out as well:

Africa on a Shoestring
ISBN 0 86442 663 1
US$29.99 • UK£17.99

Swahili Phrasebook
ISBN 0 86442 509 0
US$5.95 • UK£3.99

East Africa
ISBN 1 74059 131 3
US$27.99 • UK£15.99

Tanzania
ISBN 1 74059 046 5
US$19.99 • UK£12.99

Watching Wildlife East Africa
ISBN 1 86450 033 6
US$19.99 • UK£12.99

Trekking in East Africa
ISBN 1 86450 289 4
US$19.99 • UK£12.99

Ethiopia Eritrea & Djibouti
ISBN 0 86442 292 X
US$21.99 • UK£13.99

Available wherever books are sold

LONELY PLANET

Guides by Region

Lonely Planet is known worldwide for publishing practical, reliable and no-nonsense travel information in our guides and on our Web site. The Lonely Planet list covers just about every accessible part of the world. Currently there are 16 series: Travel guides, Shoestring guides, Condensed guides, Phrasebooks, Read This First, Healthy Travel, Walking guides, Cycling guides, Watching Wildlife guides, Pisces Diving & Snorkeling guides, City Maps, Road Atlases, Out to Eat, World Food, Journeys travel literature and Pictorials.

AFRICA Africa on a shoestring • Botswana • Cairo • Cairo City Map • Cape Town • Cape Town City Map • East Africa • Egypt • Egyptian Arabic phrasebook • Ethiopia, Eritrea & Djibouti • Ethiopian Amharic phrasebook • The Gambia & Senegal • Healthy Travel Africa • Kenya • Malawi • Morocco • Moroccan Arabic phrasebook • Mozambique • Namibia • Read This First: Africa • South Africa, Lesotho & Swaziland • Southern Africa • Southern Africa Road Atlas • Swahili phrasebook • Tanzania, Zanzibar & Pemba • Trekking in East Africa • Tunisia • Watching Wildlife East Africa • Watching Wildlife Southern Africa • West Africa • World Food Morocco • Zambia • Zimbabwe, Botswana & Namibia
Travel Literature: Mali Blues: Traveling to an African Beat • The Rainbird: A Central African Journey • Songs to an African Sunset: A Zimbabwean Story

AUSTRALIA & THE PACIFIC Aboriginal Australia & the Torres Strait Islands •Auckland • Australia • Australian phrasebook • Australia Road Atlas • Cycling Australia • Cycling New Zealand • Fiji • Fijian phrasebook • Healthy Travel Australia, NZ & the Pacific • Islands of Australia's Great Barrier Reef • Melbourne • Melbourne City Map • Micronesia • New Caledonia • New South Wales • New Zealand • Northern Territory • Outback Australia • Out to Eat – Melbourne • Out to Eat – Sydney • Papua New Guinea • Pidgin phrasebook • Queensland • Rarotonga & the Cook Islands • Samoa • Solomon Islands • South Australia • South Pacific • South Pacific phrasebook • Sydney • Sydney City Map • Sydney Condensed • Tahiti & French Polynesia • Tasmania • Tonga • Tramping in New Zealand • Vanuatu • Victoria • Walking in Australia • Watching Wildlife Australia • Western Australia
Travel Literature: Islands in the Clouds: Travels in the Highlands of New Guinea • Kiwi Tracks: A New Zealand Journey • Sean & David's Long Drive

CENTRAL AMERICA & THE CARIBBEAN Bahamas, Turks & Caicos • Baja California • Belize, Guatemala & Yucatán • Bermuda • Central America on a shoestring • Costa Rica • Costa Rica Spanish phrasebook • Cuba • Cycling Cuba • Dominican Republic & Haiti • Eastern Caribbean • Guatemala • Havana • Healthy Travel Central & South America • Jamaica • Mexico • Mexico City • Panama • Puerto Rico • Read This First: Central & South America • Virgin Islands • World Food Caribbean • World Food Mexico • Yucatán
Travel Literature: Green Dreams: Travels in Central America

EUROPE Amsterdam • Amsterdam City Map • Amsterdam Condensed • Andalucía • Athens • Austria • Baltic States phrasebook • Barcelona • Barcelona City Map • Belgium & Luxembourg • Berlin • Berlin City Map • Britain • British phrasebook • Brussels, Bruges & Antwerp • Brussels City Map • Budapest • Budapest City Map • Canary Islands • Catalunya & the Costa Brava • Central Europe • Central Europe phrasebook • Copenhagen • Corfu & the Ionians • Corsica • Crete • Crete Condensed • Croatia • Cycling Britain • Cycling France • Cyprus • Czech & Slovak Republics • Czech phrasebook • Denmark • Dublin • Dublin City Map • Dublin Condensed • Eastern Europe • Eastern Europe phrasebook • Edinburgh • Edinburgh City Map • England • Estonia, Latvia & Lithuania • Europe on a shoestring • Europe phrasebook • Finland • Florence • Florence City Map • France • Frankfurt City Map • Frankfurt Condensed • French phrasebook • Georgia, Armenia & Azerbaijan • Germany • German phrasebook • Greece • Greek Islands • Greek phrasebook • Hungary • Iceland, Greenland & the Faroe Islands • Ireland • Italian phrasebook • Italy • Kraków • Lisbon • The Loire • London • London City Map • London Condensed • Madrid • Madrid City Map • Malta • Mediterranean Europe • Milan, Turin & Genoa • Moscow • Munich • Netherlands • Normandy • Norway • Out to Eat – London • Out to Eat – Paris • Paris • Paris City Map • Paris Condensed • Poland • Polish phrasebook • Portugal • Portuguese phrasebook • Prague • Prague City Map • Provence & the Côte d'Azur • Read This First: Europe • Rhodes & the Dodecanese • Romania & Moldova • Rome • Rome City Map • Rome Condensed • Russia, Ukraine & Belarus • Russian phrasebook • Scandinavian & Baltic Europe • Scandinavian phrasebook • Scotland • Sicily • Slovenia • South-West France • Spain • Spanish phrasebook • Stockholm • St Petersburg • St Petersburg City Map • Sweden • Switzerland • Tuscany • Ukrainian phrasebook • Venice • Vienna • Wales • Walking in Britain • Walking in France • Walking in Ireland • Walking in Italy • Walking in Scotland • Walking in Spain • Walking in Switzerland • Western Europe • World Food France • World Food Greece • World Food Ireland • World Food Italy • World Food Spain **Travel Literature:** After Yugoslavia • Love and War in the Apennines • The Olive Grove: Travels in Greece • On the Shores of the Mediterranean • Round Ireland in Low Gear • A Small Place in Italy

LONELY PLANET

Mail Order

Lonely Planet products are distributed worldwide. They are also available by mail order from Lonely Planet, so if you have difficulty finding a title please write to us. North and South American residents should write to 150 Linden St, Oakland, CA 94607, USA; European and African residents should write to 10a Spring Place, London NW5 3BH, UK; and residents of other countries to Locked Bag 1, Footscray, Victoria 3011, Australia.

INDIAN SUBCONTINENT & THE INDIAN OCEAN Bangladesh • Bengali phrasebook • Bhutan • Delhi • Goa • Healthy Travel Asia & India • Hindi & Urdu phrasebook • India • India & Bangladesh City Map • Indian Himalaya • Karakoram Highway • Kathmandu City Map • Kerala • Madagascar • Maldives • Mauritius, Réunion & Seychelles • Mumbai (Bombay) • Nepal • Nepali phrasebook • North India • Pakistan • Rajasthan • Read This First: Asia & India • South India • Sri Lanka • Sri Lanka phrasebook • Tibet • Tibetan phrasebook • Trekking in the Indian Himalaya • Trekking in the Karakoram & Hindukush • Trekking in the Nepal Himalaya • World Food India **Travel Literature**: The Age of Kali: Indian Travels and Encounters • Hello Goodnight: A Life of Goa • In Rajasthan • Maverick in Madagascar • A Season in Heaven: True Tales from the Road to Kathmandu • Shopping for Buddhas • A Short Walk in the Hindu Kush • Slowly Down the Ganges

MIDDLE EAST & CENTRAL ASIA Bahrain, Kuwait & Qatar • Central Asia • Central Asia phrasebook • Dubai • Farsi (Persian) phrasebook • Hebrew phrasebook • Iran • Israel & the Palestinian Territories • Istanbul • Istanbul City Map • Istanbul to Cairo • Istanbul to Kathmandu • Jerusalem • Jerusalem City Map • Jordan • Lebanon • Middle East • Oman & the United Arab Emirates • Syria • Turkey • Turkish phrasebook • World Food Turkey • Yemen **Travel Literature**: Black on Black: Iran Revisited • Breaking Ranks: Turbulent Travels in the Promised Land • The Gates of Damascus • Kingdom of the Film Stars: Journey into Jordan

NORTH AMERICA Alaska • Boston • Boston City Map • Boston Condensed • British Columbia • California & Nevada • California Condensed • Canada • Chicago • Chicago City Map • Chicago Condensed • Florida • Georgia & the Carolinas • Great Lakes • Hawaii • Hiking in Alaska • Hiking in the USA • Honolulu & Oahu City Map • Las Vegas • Los Angeles • Los Angeles City Map • Louisiana & the Deep South • Miami • Miami City Map • Montreal • New England • New Orleans • New Orleans City Map • New York City • New York City City Map • New York City Condensed • New York, New Jersey & Pennsylvania • Oahu • Out to Eat – San Francisco • Pacific Northwest • Rocky Mountains • San Diego & Tijuana • San Francisco • San Francisco City Map • Seattle • Seattle City Map • Southwest • Texas • Toronto • USA • USA phrasebook • Vancouver • Vancouver City Map • Virginia & the Capital Region • Washington, DC • Washington, DC City Map • World Food New Orleans **Travel Literature**: Caught Inside: A Surfer's Year on the California Coast • Drive Thru America

NORTH-EAST ASIA Beijing • Beijing City Map • Cantonese phrasebook • China • Hiking in Japan • Hong Kong & Macau • Hong Kong City Map • Hong Kong Condensed • Japan • Japanese phrasebook • Korea • Korean phrasebook • Kyoto • Mandarin phrasebook • Mongolia • Mongolian phrasebook • Seoul • Shanghai • South-West China • Taiwan • Tokyo • Tokyo Condensed • World Food Hong Kong • World Food Japan **Travel Literature**: In Xanadu: A Quest • Lost Japan

SOUTH AMERICA Argentina, Uruguay & Paraguay • Bolivia • Brazil • Brazilian phrasebook • Buenos Aires • Buenos Aires City Map • Chile & Easter Island • Colombia • Ecuador & the Galapagos Islands • Healthy Travel Central & South America • Latin American Spanish phrasebook • Peru • Quechua phrasebook • Read This First: Central & South America • Rio de Janeiro • Rio de Janeiro City Map • Santiago de Chile • South America on a shoestring • Trekking in the Patagonian Andes • Venezuela **Travel Literature**: Full Circle: A South American Journey

SOUTH-EAST ASIA Bali & Lombok • Bangkok • Bangkok City Map • Burmese phrasebook • Cambodia • Cycling Vietnam, Laos & Cambodia • East Timor phrasebook • Hanoi • Healthy Travel Asia & India • Hill Tribes phrasebook • Ho Chi Minh City (Saigon) • Indonesia • Indonesian phrasebook • Indonesia's Eastern Islands • Java • Lao phrasebook • Laos • Malay phrasebook • Malaysia, Singapore & Brunei • Myanmar (Burma) • Philippines • Pilipino (Tagalog) phrasebook • Read This First: Asia & India • Singapore • Singapore City Map • South-East Asia on a shoestring • South-East Asia phrasebook • Thailand • Thailand's Islands & Beaches • Thailand, Vietnam, Laos & Cambodia Road Atlas • Thai phrasebook • Vietnam • Vietnamese phrasebook • World Food Indonesia • World Food Thailand • World Food Vietnam

ALSO AVAILABLE: Antarctica • The Arctic • The Blue Man: Tales of Travel, Love and Coffee • Brief Encounters: Stories of Love, Sex & Travel • Buddhist Stupas in Asia: The Shape of Perfection • Chasing Rickshaws • The Last Grain Race • Lonely Planet ... On the Edge: Adventurous Escapades from Around the World • Lonely Planet Unpacked • Lonely Planet Unpacked Again • Not the Only Planet: Science Fiction Travel Stories • Ports of Call: A Journey by Sea • Sacred India • Travel Photography: A Guide to Taking Better Pictures • Travel with Children • Tuvalu: Portrait of an Island Nation

Index

Abbreviations

Text

Bold indicates maps.

Boxed Text

MAP LEGEND

CITY ROUTES

Freeway........Freeway	= = = =........Unsealed Road
Highway........Primary Road	——————........One Way Street
Road........Secondary Road	██████........Pedestrian Street
Street........Street	⊓⊓⊓⊓⊓........Stepped Street
Lane........Lane	)= = =........Tunnel
————........On/Off Ramp	————........Footbridge

TRANSPORT ROUTES & STATIONS

——●——........Train	– – – · · ·........Walking Trail

REGIONAL ROUTES

——————........Tollway, Freeway
——————........Primary Road
——————........Secondary Road
··········........Minor Road

BOUNDARIES

—·—··—·—........International
—··—··—··........State
— — —........Disputed
◼—◼—........Fortified Wall

HYDROGRAPHY

～～........River, Creek	▓▓▓........Dry Lake
～＜～........Dry River, Dry Creek	▒▒ ▒▒........Swamp
▓▓▓........Lake	ⓦ ＋⧸◀........Waterfalls

AREA FEATURES

▓▓▓........Building	▒▒▒........Market	⋰❀⋰........Beach	▓▓▓........Glacier
▓❀▓........Park, Gardens	⬭........Sports Ground	＋ ＋........Cemetery	⎽⊓⎽........Plaza

POPULATION SYMBOLS

✪ CAPITAL........National Capital	● City........City	● Village........Village
◉ CAPITAL........State Capital	● Town........Town	▓▓........Urban Area

MAP SYMBOLS

▪........Place to Stay	▼........Place to Eat	●........Point of Interest
✈ ✚........Airport, Airfield	❷........Golf Course	℗........Parking	⊙........Spring
⚓........Anchorage	♨........Hindu Temple	)(........Pass	▥........Stately Home
⑨........Bank	✚........Hospital	◉........Petrol or Gas Station	▣........Swimming Pool
▣........Bus/Matatu Station	▣........Internet Café	☻........Picnic Area	▣........Taxi
▭........Bus/Matatu Stop	▣........Jain Temple	✚........Police Station	▣........Telephone
▲........Camping	☼........Lookout	✉........Post Office	▣........Theatre
⌂........Cave	♟........Monument	▣........Pub or Bar	▣........Tomb
▣........Chalet/Lodge	☾........Mosque	▣........Ruins	❶........Tourist Information
▰ ✝........Church	▲........Mountain	▣........Shopping Centre	�☓........Trailhead
▣........Cinema	▥........Museum	▣........Sikh Temple	▣........Transport
▣........Embassy	▣........National Park	＋........Spot Height	▣........Wildlife Sanctuary

Note: not all symbols displayed above appear in this book

LONELY PLANET OFFICES

Australia
Locked Bag 1, Footscray, Victoria 3011
☎ 03 8379 8000 fax 03 8379 8111
email: talk2us@lonelyplanet.com.au

UK
10a Spring Place, London NW5 3BH
☎ 020 7428 4800 fax 020 7428 4828
email: go@lonelyplanet.co.uk

USA
150 Linden St, Oakland, CA 94607
☎ 510 893 8555 TOLL FREE: 800 275 8555
fax 510 893 8572
email: info@lonelyplanet.com

France
1 rue du Dahomey, 75011 Paris
☎ 01 55 25 33 00 fax 01 55 25 33 01
email: bip@lonelyplanet.fr
www.lonelyplanet.fr

World Wide Web: www.lonelyplanet.com *or* AOL keyword: lp
Lonely Planet Images: www.lonelyplanetimages.com